Inside the
Judicial Process

Inside the Judicial Process

A Contemporary Reader in Law, Politics, and the Courts

Jennifer Segal Diascro
American University

Gregg Ivers
American University

Houghton Mifflin Company   **Boston**   **New York**

For Matthew
—JSD

For Janet, Max, and Claire
—GI

Publisher: Charles Hartford
Associate Editor: Christina Lembo
Editorial Assistant: Kristen Craib
Senior Project Editor: Kathryn Dinovo
Senior Manufacturing Buyer: Renee Ostrowski
Executive Marketing Manager: Nicola Poser
Marketing Associate: Kathleen Mellon

Cover image: C Squared Studios/Getty Images

Printed in the U.S.A.

Library of Congress Control Number: 2003110137

ISBN: 0-618-39182-7

123456789-MP-09 08 07 06 05

Contents

11   Judicial Impact   437

Preface

Like most political scientists who teach undergraduate courses in judicial politics, we face difficult choices from the array of outstanding textbooks currently available. And, like most teachers, our choice often comes down to personal preferences rooted in what we believe is important and timely for our students. As positive as our experience has been with the textbooks we have chosen for our courses, however, we often find ourselves adding an additional reading here and there to "bring alive" major themes. After years of selecting these supplemental readings, we created a reader that includes much of the material we have found to be successful in our courses, and more.

Inside the Judicial Process offers an approach not currently found on the market. Our primary purpose, while teaching students about various topics related to judicial process and politics, is to make the material accessible. To facilitate this goal, our collection contains a wide variety of readings, including social science and law review articles, interviews and journal entries, and court cases and other legal and historical documents. Some teachers may argue reasonably that students should be exposed to more scientific research than we include here; after all, one of our goals as political science professors is to encourage our students to think scientifically about politics. We agree, yet our classroom experience tells us that undergraduates respond best to information that they understand most readily. In order to reach our students, then, we feel compelled to include other academic and nonacademic accounts of judicial politics from journalists and the "insider views" of lawyers, judges, and other legal and political participants. Our hope is that students will be intrigued by the topics discussed in these pieces and encouraged to pursue the scientific inquiry into these issues. To facilitate this pursuit, each chapter includes a list of suggested readings, most of which are political science approaches to the topics addressed therein.

Our selection of readings reflects another purpose as well. There are several ways to teach a course on judicial process and politics; indeed, we approach these topics differently in our own classes. As a result, the collection in this reader is designed to accommodate the needs of different professors as they design their courses. We have organized the chapters of this reader such that they follow closely the tables of contents found in the major textbooks used in most judicial process and politics courses.

Outline of the Book

Chapters 1 and 2 emphasize the political nature of the United States Constitution and the social and political forces that shape judicial decision making. These chapters cover such topics as the Framers' intent for the Constitution, and whether such intent is knowable and applicable in contemporary society; the generational evolution in the way that lawyers, judges, and other legal actors interpret the Constitution; the role of the courts in mediating the social and political disputes that lie at the root of most legal disputes; and whether legal norms or personal policy preferences account for the way judges make decisions.

Chapters 3, 4, and 5 cover the organization and structure of the federal courts, how judges are selected for the bench, and the role of lawyers in the judicial process. Issues covered in these chapters include the institutional role of the courts in the American political system, the political dimension of the judicial nomination and confirmation process, and how the adversarial nature of the American trial system shapes the advocacy strategies of lawyers.

Chapters 6, 7, and 8 examine different dimensions of the litigation process, including the resolution of civil and criminal disputes, some of which have important constitutional questions attached to them. These chapters focus on such issues as the role of organized interests in shaping and driving the litigation process, the influence that such groups have over the decision making of judges, the processing of civil claims by the courts, the importance of class-action lawsuits in civil cases, the evolution of sentencing guidelines and how these changes have affected the work of judges, and the impact that such new evidentiary techniques as DNA testing have had on the outcome of criminal cases.

Chapter 9 examines the work of appellate courts, with an emphasis on intermediate appellate courts. So much scholarly, journalistic, and public attention focuses on the work of the U.S. Supreme Court that we often forget that only a tiny fraction—less than 1 percent—of all appeals are decided by the nation's highest tribunal. While this chapter includes selections that describe the work of the Supreme Court and the individual justices, we also include readings that offer a window into the workings of the lower appeals courts, the judges who preside over them, and the lawyers who appear before them.

Chapters 10 and 11 conclude our reader by examining the relationship between public opinion and judicial decision making and the impact that judicial decisions have on public policy. The distinctiveness of the federal judiciary in the American political scheme makes questions about its role in a democracy compelling. We have included a number of pieces in these chapters that address some of these questions, including those about the legitimacy of the Supreme Court, the conflict between a free press and an independent judiciary, public knowledge and attitudes about the law and courts, and whether courts create or react to social and political change.

Features of the Book

Within each chapter, the readings are organized around four major themes:

Foundations and History

In this section we draw from a broad range of materials, ranging from the *Federalist Papers* and landmark Supreme Court decisions to classic readings from the disciplines of law and social science. These readings share the common purpose of demonstrating the origin and major ideas around the theme of each chapter and how those ideas continue to shape scholarly inquiry. Some of our selections will look familiar, as they are fundamental to the discussion of each chapter's topic. Most readings, though, are unique contributions to the discussion and distinguish this collection of readings from others.

Contemporary Judicial Politics

Most textbooks have room for only brief attention to contemporary policies and controversies as examples of more general concepts and processes. It is these topics, though, that give shape to the more mundane details of the judiciary, and so we have included a section in each chapter that provides a more thorough discussion of many of the hot judicial and legal topics of the day. A variety of sources are included to provide different perspectives on these topics.

A View from the Inside

Perhaps the most enjoyable way to learn about processes is to hear from practitioners. This section highlights the perspectives of lawyers, political activists, judges, and others of the American legal system as they are expressed in interviews, court opinions and briefs, law review articles, news articles, and features. These selections are a particularly novel element of our collection as they present information that is especially interesting to students, many of whom are looking forward to participating in the legal system themselves.

A Comparative Perspective

The overarching focus of this collection is the American federal judiciary. But in order to fully understand the judicial processes and politics, it is important to know about other American courts and legal systems as well as judicial institutions in other countries. The selections in this section reflect the efforts by many scholars to study state courts in the United States and the legal systems of other nations.

In the final analysis, the readings we have included in this collection highlight elements of law and the judiciary that we find most compelling and timely. We expect that they will stimulate critical thinking and thoughtful discussion. We hope that they are a source of pleasant surprise for students who believe there is nothing interesting or relevant in the study of judicial politics.

Acknowledgments

First and foremost, our gratitude goes to the hundreds of students whom we have had in our courses who have critiqued—sometimes in brutal fashion—our choice of textbooks, readers, and supplemental readings. This volume reflects our attention to their desires and needs.

We are extremely thankful for the help we had collecting and selecting the readings included in this volume. Our research assistants, Rebecca Kane and Kate Hudson, were tireless in their search for relevant articles, book chapters, speeches, and court cases. Their contribution to our effort is immeasurable and greatly appreciated. Several reviewers made critical comments and insightful suggestions that helped shape this text. Our sincere thanks to Larry Baas, Valparaiso University; Roger Handberg, University of Central Florida; Valerie Hoekstra, Arizona State University; Timothy R. Johnson, University of Minnesota, Twin Cities; Shannon Ishiyama Smithey, Westminster College; Arthur G. Svenson, University of Redlands; Garry Young, The George Washington University; and Jeanne Zaino, Iona College.

Several people at Houghton Mifflin have been instrumental in bringing this volume to press. We are grateful to Katherine Meisenheimer for being receptive to our ideas, to Christina Lembo for getting the manuscript off the ground, and to Kellie Cardone for keeping it airborne. Additionally, we must acknowledge the patience, precision, and care that Nancy Benjamin of Books By Design and her team of book designers, proofreaders, and copyeditors paid to this volume. Their work behind the scenes cannot be overestimated.

Finally, but certainly not least, we are indebted to our families, who have provided unwavering support and encouragement. Jennifer would like to thank her husband, Matthew, for enduring countless hours of weekend work and endless chatter about things judicial with characteristic ease and humor, and her son, Roman, for the pure joy of first smiles, first steps, and first words. Gregg would like to thank his wife, Janet, for her support and patience, and his children, Max and Claire, for keeping their Dad delightfully distracted with hockey, baseball, soccer, ballet, and music.

Jennifer Segal Diascro
Gregg Ivers

Chapter 1

The Political Constitution

Introduction

The notion that the Constitution, and thus the meaning of constitutional law, has a fixed and precise meaning has always been very attractive to legal scholars. Indeed, the idea that the Constitution is neutral and representative of consensus values is certainly a familiar one to students of American politics, especially to those who pay close attention to the relationship between law, the courts, and politics. The courts should remain "impartial" in dealing with the cases brought before them. In particular, the courts—and individual justices—should not seek to impose a particular political theory or policy preference on constitutional questions. Courts are to discover the meaning of law, not create it. A key principle underlying judicial independence is that such insulation protects the courts from political pressure, leaving them free to make decisions solely on the basis of law.

But is this so? Remember that the Constitution was ratified in 1789 only after an intense debate throughout the thirteen states. Far from reflecting a consensus over the distribution and exercise of political power and the relationship between majority rule and individual rights, the ratification process exposed deep philosophical differences throughout the Republic over the Constitution. Whatever one believes the Constitution means, it is hard to dispute that it cannot be understood without careful attention to the political and philosophical ideas underpinning it.

It should come as no surprise that the courts, and especially the Supreme Court, have had plenty to say about what the Constitution means. And it should also come as no surprise that judges often disagree on how the Constitution applies to legal and political disputes. This disagreement stems not from dishonesty or sleight of hand in interpreting the Constitution, but from very real and deeply held political and philosophical beliefs. Because of the position of the courts in the separation of powers, judges often have the last word on constitutional controversies. When judges resolve a constitutional question, they also establish new rules and boundaries for the formation of public policy. In the end, the act of judging is a political act. Or, as Chief Justice Charles Evans Hughes once said, "We are under a Constitution, but the Constitution is what the judges say it is."

Foundations and History

Few essays from *The Federalist Papers* are more celebrated than the first selection of this chapter. In *Federalist* No. 78 (1788), Alexander Hamilton described the role that judicial review would have in relation to the other branches of government. Hamilton argued that an independent federal judiciary was necessary to "guard the Constitution and the rights of individuals" from the ill-designed wishes of the majority. At no point, wrote Hamilton, would the "courts, on the pretense of a repugnancy . . . substitute their own pleasure to the constitutional intentions of the legislature." Hamilton's explanation and defense of judicial review are often discussed in conjunction with the Supreme Court's first and most well-known decision upholding the judicial exercise of this power, *Marbury v. Madison* (1803). In *Marbury,* Chief Justice John Marshall wrote that it was "emphatically the province and duty of the Judicial Department to say what the law is," and that the exercise of such power was "the very essence of judicial duty." Marshall's defense of the Court's power to strike down federal as well as state laws has been a source of continuous debate since the day *Marbury* was decided. Despite the fact that the Judiciary Act of 1789 explicitly authorized the federal courts to strike down state laws that violated the Constitution, and that judicial review was understood, as far back as the Constitutional Convention, to be an integral part of judicial power, some scholars contend that Hamilton never intended the courts to wield such power over what they believed were political disputes over public policy choices. Can Hamilton's defense of judicial review be squared with the language of the Constitution? Is it reasonable to conclude that judicial review and an independent judiciary are bound together?

In 1881, Oliver Wendell Holmes Jr. published *The Common Law,* which to this day may well be the most influential commentary in the history of Anglo-American law. Holmes explicitly rejected the natural law tradition, and argued instead, in the clearest and most comprehensive terms to date, that law reflected the deliberate choices made by people in response to perceived social and political needs. His central thesis, that law embodied policy preferences and that such preferences should be allowed to stand in the absence of a clear constitutional mistake on the part of the legislature, had little influence on the Court during the late nineteenth and early twentieth centuries. By the time of the New Deal's arrival in the 1930s, however, Holmes's approach to law and constitutional interpretation had become much more widely accepted. The vast degree of legislative experimentation to address widespread poverty and social dislocation was justified by the belief that law determined the social order and did not reflect a natural or predetermined state of affairs.

The "myth of neutrality" as a underlying principle of the Constitution is at the heart of the selection drawn from Cass Sunstein's book *The Partial Constitution* (1993). Sunstein argues that the Constitution does not justify any and all government action simply because a political majority is in the position to exert power. Rather, Sunstein argues that government policy must bear some reasonable relationship to political principle. The Constitution is flexible enough not to mandate any particular political outcome. Law does indeed reflect social, economic, and political preferences, says Sunstein, and the enactment of such preferences forms the heart of democratic government. But majorities must be able to explain how their action is consistent with a political theory permitted by the Constitution.

Contemporary Judicial Politics

The courts have never been strangers to the American electoral process. From questions involving access to the ballot to fairness in legislative apportionment to issues of racial discrimination in constituent representation, the courts, and especially the Supreme Court, have handed down important decisions that have dramatically affected elections and voting in the United States. Not until *Bush v. Gore* (2000), however, was the Court ever asked to intervene directly in the outcome of a presidential election. In "Judicial Independence Through the Lens of *Bush v. Gore*: Four Lessons from Political Science" (2002), Howard Gillman examines several traditional assumptions behind the idea of judicial independence. Rather than adhere to the traditional notion that judicial independence permits the courts to make decisions challenging the political status quo, Gillman, using the *Bush v. Gore* case, suggests that such independence allows judges to promote a particular political agenda because they are insulated from electoral pressure.

Included here as well are excerpts from the Court's decision in *Bush v. Gore.* The Court's decision to stop the recount of ballots cast by Florida voters in the 2000 presidential election awarded Republican presidential nominee George W. Bush the electoral votes he needed to defeat Democratic candidate Al Gore. The Court's decision came five weeks after the November 7 election and ended an extraordinarily contentious sequence of litigation that moved from the Florida state courts into the federal courts at an unprecedented pace. Note the very different approaches to the case taken, on the one hand, by the *Bush v. Gore* majority and Chief Justice William Rehnquist in his concurring opinion and, on the other hand, the dissenting justices.

A View from the Inside

Supreme Court opinions are not the only forum for individual justices to express their views on matters of American constitutional law and development. We include two selections here that feature justices offering their views on the Constitution outside the judicial forum. In "The Notion of a Living Constitution" (1976), Justice William Rehnquist addresses the question of whether judges should interpret the Constitution in light of social, economic, and political change in American society. While acknowledging that the Framers left certain clauses and phrases of the Constitution written in rather general terms to allow their application to issues and problems encountered by subsequent generations, Justice Rehnquist also cautions against allowing judges to address social problems that, in their view, the other institutions of government have not. Justice Rehnquist believes that the Constitution places authority to solve societal problems in the hands of the elected branches, and it is there, not the courts, from which policy innovation should originate. In contrast,

Justice Thurgood Marshall, in a speech delivered in conjunction with the two hundredth anniversary celebration of the Constitution, offers a far less laudatory view of the Framers' Constitution. The same men who designed the American system of representative government, comments Marshall, also crafted a document that permitted slavery and was later interpreted to exclude African Americans from equal standing in American life. Rather than celebrate the original Constitution, Americans should spend more time on a "sensitive understanding of the Constitution's inherent defects." In Marshall's view, judges are under no obligation to adhere to original positions that were flawed from their very outset.

For our final selection in this section, we turn to one of the Court's most recent and notable decisions in the realm of civil liberties, *Lawrence v. Texas* (2003). In *Lawrence,* the Court struck down a state law banning consensual sodomy between persons of the same sex on the grounds that it violated the right to privacy protected by the due process clause of the Fourteenth Amendment. Of particular note in *Lawrence* was the Court's decision to use the challenge to the Texas statute to overturn *Bowers v. Hardwick* (2003), where a sharply divided 5–4 majority *upheld* a Georgia law banning consensual sodomy. Although the Georgia law did not specify sexual orientation, the *Bowers* majority treated it as if it did, concluding that the Constitution did not secure "a fundamental right to engage in homosexual sodomy." Seventeen years later, Justice Anthony Kennedy, writing for a 6–3 majority, emphatically rejected that approach to sexual intimacy and privacy rights and overruled *Bowers.* Kennedy was not on the Court for the *Bowers* decision, nor was Justice Antonin Scalia, whose dissent is also excerpted here. They have very different views of the Texas law and the role of the Court in settling disputes previously left to the political process. Is Kennedy's opinion an example of Oliver Wendell Holmes Jr.'s observation that "the life of the law has not been logic; it has been experience"? Is Scalia's dissent persuasive in arguing that the Court should leave "political disputes" to the political branches of government?

A Comparative Perspective

How does judicial independence in the United States compare with that of other countries? Does partisanship finds its way into the relationship between the courts of other democratic nations and the elected branches of governments? In the final selection of this chapter, "Judicial Independence in Comparative Perspective" (2001), Peter H. Russell addresses these questions and offers some very interesting perspectives on how different nations view judicial independence from the political process and what role judges see for themselves in engaging hot-button political and policy questions.

Foundations and History

1.1   *Federalist* No. 78 (1788)

Alexander Hamilton

To the People of the State of New York:
We proceed now to an examination of the judiciary department of the proposed government.

In unfolding the defects of the existing Confederation, the utility and necessity of a federal judicature have been clearly pointed out. It is the less necessary to recapitulate the considerations there urged, as the propriety of the institution in the abstract is not disputed; the only questions which have been raised being relative to the manner of constituting it, and to its extent. To these points, therefore, our observations shall be confined. . . .

Whoever attentively considers the different departments of power must perceive, that, in a government in which they are separated from each other, the judiciary, from the nature of its functions, will always be the least dangerous to the political rights of the Constitution; because it will be least in a capacity to annoy or injure them. The Executive not only dispenses the honors, but holds the sword of the community. The legislature not only commands the purse, but prescribes the rules by which the duties and rights of every citizen are to be regulated. The judiciary, on the contrary, has no influence over either the sword or the purse; no direction either of the strength or of the wealth of the society; and can take no active resolution whatever. It may truly be said to have neither *force* nor *will*, but merely judgment; and must ultimately depend upon the aid of the executive arm even for the efficacy of its judgments.

This simple view of the matter suggests several important consequences. It proves incontestably, that the judiciary is beyond comparison the weakest of the three departments of power; that it can never attack with success either of the other two; and that all possible care is requisite to enable it to defend itself against their attacks. It equally proves, that though individual oppression may now and then proceed from the courts of justice, the general

liberty of the people can never be endangered from that quarter; I mean so long as the judiciary remains truly distinct from both the legislature and the Executive. For I agree, that "there is no liberty, if the power of judging be not separated from the legislative and executive powers." And it proves, in the last place, that as liberty can have nothing to fear from the judiciary alone, but would have every thing to fear from its union with either of the other departments; that as all the effects of such a union must ensue from a dependence of the former on the latter, notwithstanding a nominal and apparent separation; that as, from the natural feebleness of the judiciary, it is in continual jeopardy of being overpowered, awed, or influenced by its coordinate branches; and that as nothing can contribute so much to its firmness and independence as permanency in office, this quality may therefore be justly regarded as an indispensable ingredient in its constitution, and, in a great measure, as the citadel of the public justice and the public security.

The complete independence of the courts of justice is peculiarly essential in a limited Constitution. By a limited Constitution, I understand one which contains certain specified exceptions to the legislative authority; such, for instance, as that it shall pass no bills of attainder, no ex-post-facto laws, and the like. Limitations of this kind can be preserved in practice no other way than through the medium of courts of justice, whose duty it must be to declare all acts contrary to the manifest tenor of the Constitution void. Without this, all the reservations of particular rights or privileges would amount to nothing.

Some perplexity respecting the rights of the courts to pronounce legislative acts void, because contrary to the Constitution, has arisen from an imagination that the doctrine would imply a superiority of the judiciary to the legislative power. It is urged that the authority which can declare the acts of another void, must necessarily be superior to the one whose acts may be declared void. As this doctrine is of great importance in all the American constitutions, a brief discussion of the ground on which it rests cannot be unacceptable.

There is no position which depends on clearer principles, than that every act of a delegated authority, contrary to the tenor of the commission under which it is exercised, is void. No legislative act, therefore, contrary to the Constitution, can be valid. To deny this, would be to affirm, that the deputy is greater than his principal; that the servant is above his master; that the representatives of the people are superior to the people themselves; that men acting by virtue of powers, may do not only what their powers do not authorize, but what they forbid.

If it be said that the legislative body are themselves the constitutional judges of their own powers, and that the construction they put upon them is conclusive upon the other departments, it may be answered, that this cannot be the natural presumption, where it is not to be collected from any particular provisions in the Constitution. It is not otherwise to be supposed, that the Constitution could intend to enable the representatives of the people to substitute their *will* to that of their constituents. It is far more rational to suppose, that the courts were designed to be an intermediate body between the people and the legislature, in order, among other things, to keep the latter within the limits assigned to their authority. The interpretation of the laws is the proper and peculiar province of the courts. A constitution is, in fact, and must be regarded by the judges, as a fundamental law. It therefore belongs to them to ascertain its meaning, as well as the meaning of any particular act proceeding from the legislative body. If there should happen to be an irreconcilable variance between the two, that which has the superior obligation and validity ought, of course, to be preferred; or, in other words, the Constitution ought to be preferred to the statute, the intention of the people to the intention of their agents.

Nor does this conclusion by any means suppose a superiority of the judicial to the legislative power. It only supposes that the power of the people is superior to both; and that where the will of the legislature, declared in its statutes, stands in opposition to that of the people, declared in the Constitution,

the judges ought to be governed by the latter rather than the former. They ought to regulate their decisions by the fundamental laws, rather than by those which are not fundamental.

This exercise of judicial discretion, in determining between two contradictory laws, is exemplified in a familiar instance. It not uncommonly happens, that there are two statutes existing at one time, clashing in whole or in part with each other, and neither of them containing any repealing clause or expression. In such a case, it is the province of the courts to liquidate and fix their meaning and operation. So far as they can, by any fair construction, be reconciled to each other, reason and law conspire to dictate that this should be done; where this is impracticable, it becomes a matter of necessity to give effect to one, in exclusion of the other. The rule which has obtained in the courts for determining their relative validity is, that the last in order of time shall be preferred to the first. But this is a mere rule of construction, not derived from any positive law, but from the nature and reason of the thing. It is a rule not enjoined upon the courts by legislative provision, but adopted by themselves, as consonant to truth and propriety, for the direction of their conduct as interpreters of the law. They thought it reasonable, that between the interfering acts of an *equal* authority, that which was the last indication of its will should have the preference.

But in regard to the interfering acts of a superior and subordinate authority, of an original and derivative power, the nature and reason of the thing indicate the converse of that rule as proper to be followed. They teach us that the prior act of a superior ought to be preferred to the subsequent act of an inferior and subordinate authority; and that accordingly, whenever a particular statute contravenes the Constitution, it will be the duty of the judicial tribunals to adhere to the latter and disregard the former.

It can be of no weight to say that the courts, on the pretense of a repugnancy, may substitute their own pleasure to the constitutional intentions of the legislature. This might as well happen in the case of two contradictory statutes; or it might as well happen in every adjudication upon any single statute. The courts must declare the sense of the law; and if they should be disposed to exercise *will* instead of *judgment*, the consequence would equally be the substitution of their pleasure to that of the legislative body. The observation, if it prove any thing, would prove that there ought to be no judges distinct from that body.

If, then, the courts of justice are to be considered as the bulwarks of a limited Constitution against legislative encroachments, this consideration will afford a strong argument for the permanent tenure of judicial offices, since nothing will contribute so much as this to that independent spirit in the judges which must be essential to the faithful performance of so arduous a duty.

This independence of the judges is equally requisite to guard the Constitution and the rights of individuals from the effects of those ill humors, which the arts of designing men, or the influence of particular conjunctures, sometimes disseminate among the people themselves, and which, though they speedily give place to better information, and more deliberate reflection, have a tendency, in the meantime, to occasion dangerous innovations in the government, and serious oppressions of the minor party in the community. Though I trust the friends of the proposed Constitution will never concur with its enemies, in questioning that fundamental principle of republican government, which

admits the right of the people to alter or abolish the established Constitution, whenever they find it inconsistent with their happiness, yet it is not to be inferred from this principle, that the representatives of the people, whenever a momentary inclination happens to lay hold of a majority of their constituents, incompatible with the provisions in the existing Constitution, would, on that account, be justifiable in a violation of those provisions; or that the courts would be under a greater obligation to connive at infractions in this shape, than when they had proceeded wholly from the cabals of the representative body. Until the people have, by some solemn and authoritative act, annulled or changed the established form, it is binding upon themselves collectively, as well as individually; and no presumption, or even knowledge, of their sentiments, can warrant their representatives in a departure from it, prior to such an act. But it is easy to see, that it would require an uncommon portion of fortitude in the judges to do their duty as faithful guardians of the Constitution, where legislative invasions of it had been instigated by the major voice of the community. . . .

1.2   From *The Common Law* (1881)

Oliver Wendell Holmes Jr.

The object of this book is to present a general view of the Common Law. To accomplish the task, other tools are needed besides logic. It is something to show that the consistency of a system requires a particular result, but it is not all. The life of the law has not been logic; it has been experience. The felt necessities of the time, the prevalent moral and political theories, intuitions of public policy, avowed or unconscious, even the prejudices which judges share with their fellow-men, have had a good deal more to do than the syllogism in determining the rules by which men should be governed. The law embodies the story of a nation's development through many centuries, and it cannot be dealt with as if it contained only the axioms and corollaries of a book of mathematics. In order to know what it is, we must know what it has been, and what it tends to become. We must alternately con-

sult history and existing theories of legislation. But the most difficult labor will be to understand the combination of the two into new products at every stage. The substance of the law at any given time pretty nearly corresponds, so far as it goes, with what is then understood to be convenient; but its form and machinery, and the degree to which it is able to work out desired results, depend very much upon its past.

In Massachusetts to-day, while, on the one hand, there are a great many rules which are quite sufficiently accounted for by their manifest good sense, on the other, there are some which can only be understood by reference to the infancy of procedure among the German tribes, or to the social condition of Rome under the Decemvirs.

I shall use the history of our law so far as it is necessary to explain a conception or to interpret a rule, but no further. In doing so there are two errors equally to be avoided both by writer and reader. One is that of supposing, because an idea seems very familiar and natural to us, that it has always been so. Many things which we take for granted have had to be laboriously fought out or thought out in past times. The other mistake is the opposite one of asking too much of history. We start with man full grown. It may be assumed that the earliest barbarian whose practices are to be considered, had a good many of the same feelings and passions as ourselves. . . .

1.3   From *The Partial Constitution* (1993)

Cass Sunstein

In American constitutional law, government must always have a reason for what it does. If it is distributing something to one group rather than to another, or depriving someone of some good or benefit, it must explain itself. The required reason must count as a public-regarding one. Government cannot appeal to private interest alone.

We will encounter several conceptions of neutrality. . . . To distinguish this principle from others, I will describe it as one of impartiality. As I understand it, the principle forbids government from acting on the basis of pure self-interest, or power, or whim. In this light, status quo neutrality is quite different from, even at an opposite pole from, the impartiality principle. From the viewpoint of impartiality, the problem with status quo neutrality is that it takes existing practices as given, and does not require government to bring reasons forward on their behalf. Status quo neutrality refuses to treat the impartiality principle with the seriousness and depth that it demands. It treats existing practices and distributions as a kind of inexorable brute fact. It does not subject them to legal or democratic scrutiny, or to deliberation at all.

For the moment, however, the relationship between the impartiality principle and status quo neutrality must remain a bit obscure. My focus here is on founding aspirations, and on how impartiality is a minimal condition for democratic deliberation.

The framers of the American Constitution sought to create a system of government that would simul-taneously counteract three related dangers: the legacy of monarchy; self-interested representation by government officials; and the power of faction, or "majority tyranny." The impartiality principle was part of the attempt to respond to all these problems.

Any description of the framing period should note that the period involved a diverse array of influential people and an extraordinarily wide range of sometimes conflicting ideas. In influential writings from the period, we can find, among other things, a belief in a form of aristocratic rule; an enthusiasm for agrarian populism; a willingness to accept interest-group warfare; a belief in the need for radical centralization of politics in the national government; acceptance of slavery in particular and of racial and sexual hierarchy in general; Calvinism; a commitment to natural rights; hostility to commerce; enthusiasm for commerce; and insistence on the need for decentralization as an indispensable part of democratic government. In light of the sheer diversity of influential ideas, any description of the framing commitments will have to be selective. It will inevitably downplay certain elements and emphasize others. . . .

The impartiality principle is conspicuously connected with the desire, traceable to the early period of the founding, to limit the potential arbitrariness of the king and indeed of everything entailed by the institutions of monarchy. The Constitution should be understood against the backdrop set by prerevolutionary America, which had been pervaded by monarchical characteristics, including well-entrenched patterns of deference and hierarchy. In the prerevolutionary period, many of these patterns were attributed to nature itself. These included not merely the institution of slavery but also existing family structures, relations between employers and employees, occupational categories, education, the crucial concept of the gentleman, and of course the structures of government. Indeed, those very structures were thought to be modeled on the family and to grow out of the same natural sources.

A large element in the American Revolution consisted of a radical rebellion against the monarchical legacy. The rebellion operated with special force against the traditional belief in a "natural order of things." Thus the Americans insisted, in direct opposition to their English inheritance, that "culture" was "man-made." In America, social outcomes had to be justified not by reference to nature or to traditional practices, but instead on the basis of reasons.

The American framers were alert not only to the legacy of monarchy, but also to the general risk that public officials would act on behalf of their own self-interest rather than the interests of the public as a whole. Actual corruption in government was the most dramatic illustration of this danger. But self-interested representation could be found in many places in which officials seek to aggrandize their own powers and interests at the expense of the people as a whole. The responsibility of the public official was to put personal interest entirely to one side. The impartiality principle, requiring public officials to invoke public-regarding reasons on behalf of their actions, was a check on self-interested representation.

Finally, the framers sought to limit the power of self-interested private groups, or "factions," over governmental processes. For Madison, this was the greatest risk in America: "[I]n our Governments the real power lies in the majority of the Community, and the invasion of private rights is chiefly to be apprehended, not from acts of Government contrary to the sense of its constituents, but from acts in which the Government is the mere instrument of the major number of the constituents." Hence majority rule was, for the framers, a highly ambiguous good. On their view, even an insistent majority should not have its way, if power was the only thing to be invoked on its behalf.

It is relevant here that the framers operated in the light of their experiences under the Articles of Confederation. Under the Articles, powerful private groups appeared to dominate state and local gov-

ernment, obtaining measures that favored them but no one else, and that could be explained only by reference of private self-interest. The new Constitution was intended to limit this risk.

Above all, the American Constitution was designed to create a deliberative democracy. Under that system, public representatives were to be ultimately accountable to the people; but they would also be able to engage in a form of deliberation without domination through the influence of factions. A law based solely on the self-interest of private groups is the core violation of the deliberative ideal.

The minimal condition of deliberative democracy is a requirement of reasons for governmental action. We may thus understand the American Constitution as having established, for the first time, a republic of reasons. A republic of this sort is opposed equally to outcomes grounded on self-interest and to those based solely on "nature" or authority. Where the monarchical system saw government as an outgrowth of a given or natural order, the founding generation regarded it as "merely a legal man-made contrivance having little if any natural relationship to the family or to society.". . .

The basic institutions of the . . . Constitution were intended to encourage and to profit from deliberation, thus understood. The system of checks and balances—the cornerstone of the system—was designed to encourage discussion among different governmental entities. So too with the requirement of bicameralism, which would bring different perspectives to bear on lawmaking. The same goals accounted for the notion that laws should be presented to the President for his signature or veto; this mechanism would provide an additional perspective. The federal system would ensure a supplemental form of dialogue, here between states and the national government.

Judicial review was intended to create a further check. Its basic purpose was to protect the considered judgments of the people, as represented in the extraordinary law of the Constitution, against the ill-considered or short-term considerations introduced by the people's mere agents in the course of enacting ordinary law. As we will see, many of the original individual rights can be understood as part of the idea of deliberative democracy. Indeed, the goals of protecting rights and of promoting deliberation were understood to march hand in hand. The special status of property rights was an effort to ensure against precipitous, short-sighted, or ill-considered intrusions into the private sphere. Deliberative government and limited government were, in the framers' view, one and the same. . . .

Drawing on the classical tradition, the antifederalist "Brutus," complaining of the theory behind the proposed nationalist Constitution, wrote, "In a republic, the manners, sentiments, and interests of the people should be similar. If this be not the case, there will be a constant clashing of opinions; and the representatives of one part will be continually striving against those of the other." Hamilton, by contrast, thought that heterogeneity, as part of the deliberative process, could be a creative and productive force. Thus he suggested that the "differences of opinion, and the jarrings of parties in [the legislative] department . . . often promote deliberation. . . . As the framers saw it, the exchange of reasons in the public sphere was a condition for this process.

Read against this background, the principle of impartiality requires government to provide reasons that can be intelligible to different people operating from different premises. The requirement might be understood in this respect as a check on government by fiat, helping to bar authoritarianism generally. Drawing from our founding aspirations, we might even define authoritarian systems as all those that justify government outcomes by reference to power or will rather than by reference to reasons. At the heart of the liberal tradition and its opposition to authoritarianism lies a requirement of justification by reference to public-regarding explanations that are intelligible to all citizens. The principle of impartiality is the concrete manifestation of this commitment in American constitutional law. . . .

Whether pluralist ideas accurately describe current American politics is a subject of much dispute. There can be little doubt that the American framers were not pluralists. Some people also think that contemporary real-world government outcomes actually reflect reasons and justifications, and that those outcomes diverge from legislative and constituent self-interest (unless the concept of self-interest is understood so broadly as to be trivialized—as in the idea that altruism reflects self-interest, because altruists are interested in altruism). As we will see, interest-group pluralism is not

an attractive political ideal. But if interest-group pluralism does describe contemporary politics, a requirement of impartiality, understood as a call for public-regarding justifications for government outcomes, is inconsistent with the very nature of government. It imposes on politics a requirement that simply cannot be met. . . .

Judicial interpretation of many of the most important clauses of the Constitution reveals a remarkably common theme. Although the clauses have different historical roots and were originally directed at different problems, they appear to be united by a concern with a single underlying evil: the distribution of resources or opportunities to one group rather than to another solely on the ground that those favored have exercised the raw political power to obtain what they want. I will call this underlying evil—a violation of the impartiality requirement—a *naked preference*. . . .

The prohibition of naked preferences therefore underlies a wide range of constitutional provisions. The prohibition is connected with the original idea that government must be responsive to something other than private pressure, and with the associated notion that politics is not the reconciling of given interests but instead the product of some form of deliberation about the public good. As it operates in current constitutional law, the prohibition of naked preferences—like Madison's approach to the problem of factionalism—focuses on the motivations of legislators, not of their constituents. The prohibition therefore embodies a particular conception of representation. Under that conception, the task of legislators is not to respond to private pressure but instead to select values through deliberation and debate.

The notion that governmental action must be grounded in something other than political power is of course at odds with pluralism. Naked preferences are common fare in the pluralist conception; interest-group politics invites them. The prohibition of naked preferences stands as a repudiation of theories claiming that the judicial role is only to police the processes of representation to ensure that all affected interest groups may participate. In this respect, the prohibition of naked preferences reflects a distinctly substantive value and cannot easily be captured in procedural terms. Above all, it presupposes that constitutional courts will serve as critics of the pluralist vision, not as adherents striving only to "clear the channels" for political struggle. And if a judicial role seems odd here, we should recall that the founding generation itself regarded courts as an important repository for representation and preservation of republican virtue, standing above the play of interests. . . .

. . . Many provisions of the Constitution are thus aimed at a single evil: the distribution of resources to one person or group rather than to another on the sole ground that those benefited have exercised political power in order to obtain government assistance.

Contemporary Judical Politics

1.4   # Judicial Independence Through the Lens of *Bush v. Gore:* Four Lessons from Political Science (2002)

Howard Gillman

The experiences with the 2000 election litigation, particularly the United States Supreme Court's decision in *Bush v. Gore,* illustrate aspects of judicial independence that may be overlooked if too much focus is placed on linking the concept to the simple virtue of pressure-free, good-faith judging. This article explores the advantages of discussing judicial independence as if it was a subset of the more general practice of insulating policy-making institutions—like central banks or regulatory commissions—from conventional political pressures or mechanisms of political accountability. Unfettered, neutral, professional decision-making may be one outcome that is desired whenever such independence is considered. However, these are not the only relevant political considerations or the only likely political consequences.

This article adopts a "regime politics" or "dominant coalition" view of institutional independence. This approach examines institutional structures, including the organization of judicial power, in terms of the political advantages for power-holders who are interested in promoting substantive political agendas. . . .

Bush v. Gore is a useful starting point for thinking about judicial independence in terms of regime politics rather than the neutral application of law. Few scholars have been willing to defend the deci-

sion as an exemplar of impartial decision-making or as a stoic defense of the rule of law in the face of enormous political pressure, although some do make this argument. It is already common to treat the case as an example of the sort of political agendas that might be pursued from within an institution that enjoys insulation from conventional mechanisms of political accountability. Perhaps even those with a different view might find value in some of this article's more general points about judicial independence.

. . . [T]he analysis of *Bush v. Gore* reveals four major lessons about judicial independence and the Supreme Court that are sometimes overlooked in conventional discussions.

Lesson One

The Decision to Grant Independence to a Policy-Making Institution Has as Much to Do with Insulating Preferred Political Agendas from Electoral Pressure as with Ensuring Impartiality

It is a basic assumption of political science that the United States Supreme Court is designed to be a national policy-making institution, not a forum for the routine and neutral resolution of everyday disputes. Conventional ideological and political considerations dominate staffing decisions. Justices

From *Ohio State Law Review* (2002). Reprinted by permission of the author.

may not always act in a way that is preferred by the appointing president, but political explanations usually exist for these relatively rare circumstances, and they do not undermine the basic point. As Terri Peretti stated, ideological voting by justices "is not merely the arbitrary expression of a justice's idiosyncratic views [but] [r]ather . . . is the expression and vindication of those political views deliberately 'planted' on the Court" by policy-conscious presidents and senators.

Because dominant coalitions are largely successful at planting trustworthy agents on the Supreme Court, the justices almost never engage in policy-making that challenges those power-holders who are in a position to assault their nominal independence. It is extremely rare, although not unheard of, for the Court to void an act of a current or "live" national majority. It is more common for the justices to go after national legislation passed by a previous governing coalition or to impose a national policy consensus on local or regional "outliers." In other words, judicial independence, defined as decision-making autonomy, is largely a function of political alignment with potential adversaries rather than the maintenance of political neutrality. . . .

Thinking about judicial independence simply in terms of neutral, rule-of-law values, it may be a mystery why a narrow majority of Supreme Court justices took the remarkable step of involving themselves in the 2000 election controversy. It is possible to construct a story about how the justices were merely seeking to ensure that all those involved played by the rules. However, if it is accepted that the justices have personal and institutional interests in the configuration of power in the rest of the federal government, then the involvement of the *Bush v. Gore* majority can be seen as an effort to create a more favorable political climate for its (emergent but still vulnerable) constitutional agenda—that is, a political climate that would be less likely to trigger a negative response to conservative decisions and more likely to result in the appointment of justices who would maintain or solidify this agenda.

On this view, the Court's involvement in the 2000 election was not extraordinary simply because it revealed a rare instance of political bias. Political bias (or, more generously, political per-

spective) is revealed routinely in the ideological patterns of the justices' decision-making. Rather, the Court's involvement was extraordinary because it demonstrated the Court's fortuitous ability to shape which candidates and parties would control the White House and the Senate, and thus make it less likely that political opponents would be able to interfere with its policy-making. Stated another way, this case is extraordinary because the policy alignment between the Court and the political system, which normally is established by the legislative and executive branches, was established by the Court.

Lesson Two

Independent Courts Are Often Supported by Other Power-Holders Because They Can Act as a Forum Within Which Contentious Political Questions May Be Channeled

The desire of power-holders to insulate preferred political agendas is not the only reason that they may have an interest in establishing or deferring to the authority of relatively autonomous policy-making institutions such as agencies, commissions, central banks, or judicial bodies. Delegation is sometimes also a mechanism by which elected office-holders attempt to achieve political benefits by channeling contentious and potentially unpopular issues into the hands of "expert" decision-makers. . . .

The justices in the *Bush v. Gore* majority may have revealed their own attachment to a political agenda when they decided to intervene in the presidential election dispute. However, the unwillingness of other power-holders to defend their own decision-making prerogatives suggests that they believed that there were perceived political advantages to having the Supreme Court take control of this dispute. Republican legislators in Florida were being pressured by legislative leaders to take the controversial step of challenging the Florida courts by appointing a new slate of Bush electors, but there was some grumbling about the need to take this course of action, and there was a public expression of hope that the Washington justices would make it unnecessary for them to go on record with that vote. Similarly, Republican congressional leaders had been preparing for some weeks to take control of the outcome in the event that Florida courts were able to complete a recount that resulted in a Gore victory, but there was not a lot of enthusiasm for this outcome, and a number of Republicans publicly expressed the view that they would prefer it if the Supreme Court resolved the issue first. It is reasonable to assume that the justices were quite aware that those other power-holders who might claim the prerogative to resolve the dispute nevertheless were in support of channeling the process into the federal courts, and it is no surprise that many of these legislators expressed relief rather than indignation after the justices decided the outcome.

A related version of this interpretation is offered by those who characterize the Supreme Court's intervention as necessary and appropriate to avoid a constitutional crisis, or at least to end a prolonged political crisis that had tried the patience of the country and was not likely to result in a different outcome if it continued through the process of counting (and challenging) electoral votes in the Congress. This version is different because it characterizes the political benefits for elected officials in a more bipartisan way. Rather than assume that Republican officials were supportive of the Court because it prevented them from having to face the possibility of handing the election to Bush after a Gore recount victory, the argument suggests that both Democrats and Republicans may have been relieved that the dispute was channeled into the Supreme Court rather than remain in the legislative branches. This interpretation probably overstates the extent to which congressional Democrats actually supported the Court's intervention, although it might capture the sentiments of some Democrats— particularly more moderate or conservative Senate Democrats from states that supported Bush in the election—who had little enthusiasm for a Gore presidency and little interest in challenging House Republicans in a way that threatened a deadlock. Still, the argument offers another perspective on how the judiciary's independence can provide political benefits that would lead potentially competing power-holders to defer to judges when they address sensitive or controversial disputes.

Lesson Three

Because Institutional Independence Is Never Complete—and Is Easily Overcome by Determined Power-Holders—Nominally Independent Decision-Makers Still Need to Assess Their Political Context Before Choosing Politically Risky Courses of Action

Supreme Court justices are privileged to have an institutional setting that insulates them from direct political supervision or manipulation. "Good behavior" tenure, combined with having the last word on the interpretation of law in a given case cycle and the difficulties of mustering a consensus to retaliate against the Court, mean that the justices have enormous freedom to decide cases as they see fit. In fact, it is precisely these structural features that make it reasonable to assume that justices normally decide cases based mostly on their personal policy preferences (or views of the law) rather than other political motivations or influences, such as direct constituency pressures or the demands of party leaders.

However, all structural protections for political independence can be overcome by sufficiently determined power-holders. Those who might threaten judicial autonomy are usually not tempted to interfere, both because judges typically decide cases that are of little interest to other power-holders (and thus benefit from the same considerations that protect low-level bureaucrats) and because judges typically decide more politically-sensitive issues in a way that is broadly consistent with the preferences of other power-holders. Nonetheless, on occasion, judges find themselves in situations that threaten to disturb the hornet's nest of politics. In such situations, the normal practice of deciding cases as a judge sees fit may give way to a more complicated set of strategic calculations. This is why, despite their nominal structural independence, Supreme Court justices are demonstrably attentive to the political environment within which they operate. . . .

In light of . . . this, it might be tempting to interpret the Court's involvement as an example of how structural mechanisms for political independence make it unnecessary for judges to take into account political considerations when deciding a course of conduct. In fact, though, the strategic political environment was actually quite hospitable to the course of conduct that the conservative majority set in motion around Thanksgiving when they voted to grant certiorari in the first Bush appeal of the Florida Supreme Court's decision to extend the deadline for hand recounts. Assuming that the conservatives were interested in preventing any hand recounts that might overturn the initially reported results in favor of a Bush victory—an assumption that is consistent with the three anti-recount positions taken by these five justices across three separate legal issues—then what they needed to assess was whether they had enough support in the political system to avoid retaliation for a set of decisions that either blocked recounts or rolled back the results of recounts. While the political environment might not have been conducive to any imaginable course of conduct the Court might have adopted (such as one to require recounts), it was conducive to an anti-recount effort. The conservatives knew that they had a fully mobilized Republican constituency that would vehemently support such an intervention. More importantly, Republicans were in control of virtually all of the potential competing political institutions, including the state legislature and executive branch of Florida and the U.S. House of Representatives. They also knew that the U.S. Senate and, of course, the presidency would be in Republican hands if they were successful in ensuring a Bush victory. Given this configuration of power, the conservatives could be confident that their decisions would not be met by any institutional resistance or short-term acts of retribution.

There were other strategic advantages as well. Immediately prior to the final decision, public opinion polls showed that 73% of respondents said they would consider any Supreme Court decision to be legitimate. . . .

In considering the lessons for judicial independence presented by *Bush v. Gore,* it is too simple to assert that the formal, constitutional sources of the justices' independence were sufficient to give the conservative majority the political insulation it needed to intervene in the 2000 election controversy. Counterfactuals can only reach so far, but if the Court had been faced with a fully mobilized and determined Democratic Party in control of the U.S. Congress as well as Florida's legislative and

executive branches, the *Bush v. Gore* majority would have had a lot more to consider before inserting themselves into this process. The main point is that Supreme Court independence is a function, not merely of formal structural protections, but also of historically contingent political alignments and the tendency of the justices to assess the strategic context within which they are operating. Without attention to these contextual and strategic variables, a lack of pressure, interference, or retribution might be explained as a function of well-functioning institutional barriers rather than the relation between these structural features and the constraints or opportunities generated by the background political climate.

Lesson Four

Greater Degrees of Structural Insulation from Electoral Accountability Do Not Necessarily Make Good Faith Decision-Making More Likely

It is tempting to assume that greater degrees of structural independence will reduce the likelihood that political considerations will shape decision-making. In other words, if independence is considered a good thing, then perhaps appointive methods are better than elective methods; non-competitive retention elections are better than competitive elections; and longer terms of office are better than shorter terms. On this analysis, the federal structure of political appointment and life tenure might seem like a better way to reduce the corrupting effects of politics on judicial decision-making than state models that typically include some sort of electoral accountability.

It is a truism that when judges are insulated from elections, some of the dynamics of electoral politics are eliminated from their decision-making calculus. Judges who do not have to run for election or reelection will not have to raise money to run campaigns and may worry less about how their decisions might be used by electoral opponents in political advertising. However, it would be a mistake to assume that insulating judges from elections (or from easy removal by competing power-holders) will eliminate political motivations, pressures, or calculations from judicial decision-making. It would be more accurate to say that different structures of judicial selection and removal will produce slightly different political dynamics. Appointive systems marginally increase the influence of chief executives over the ideological make-up of the judiciary, although governors tend to dominate even elective and merit-based systems. Partisan election systems provide voters with one very salient cue that they would not be officially provided in non-partisan systems, although even in non-partisan systems parties may exert influence over the process by supporting particular candidates. Judges who enjoy life tenure have to worry less about whether voting their preferences will cause a political firestorm, although even life-tenured judges must pay attention to political opposition to their decisions. It may be that there are good reasons to prefer the political dynamics associated with some of these structures and to oppose those created by others, especially in light of the increasing importance of money in some judicial elections. However, in making these comparisons, we should debate the relative advantages and disadvantages associated with different political dynamics and try to avoid too much reliance on misleading, simplistic sloganeering about the elimination of political influence. . . .

Of all the judges who were involved in the 2000 election dispute, the ones whose behavior appeared the most partisan, and the least motivated by good faith understandings of the law, were the ones who enjoyed the most extreme insulation from conventional political pressure. The five conservatives in the *Bush v. Gore* majority were the only judges involved in this election dispute whose decisions across a variety of legal issues were consistent with their political preferences and arguably inconsistent with their pre-election views on issues

such as the meaning of the equal protection clause and the appropriateness of having federal courts second-guess state court interpretations of state law. Whether these judges are viewed as loyal partisans, ideological policy-makers protecting their fragile constitutional agenda, or, most benignly, interested decision-makers exhibiting the influence of "motivated reasoning," it is hard to resist the conclusion that their actions were tainted by political considerations or motivations. This is just another way of pointing out that, while judicial independence may sometimes free a judge from unwanted political pressure, those structures do nothing to prevent an insulated judge from indulging her or his own political preferences or private agendas. To guard against those unwanted influences, one has to focus more on the character of the decision-maker than the characteristics of the office.

None of this is to deny the importance of debating the practical consequences of adopting one set of institutional structures over another. All power-holders are affected in some way, whether positively or negatively, by the political architecture of the institutions within which they operate. Moreover, as these issues are analyzed and debated, it is essential to consider the relationship between these structural questions and the promotion of rule-of-law norms. However, it also is useful to keep in mind the full range of motivations and consequences that are related to the question of whether judge-politicians should be given more or less decision-making autonomy. After all, "the choice of judicial selection and retention mechanisms is inherently a political choice with political implications," including unintended implications, such as the use of that independence to choose a president.

Bush v. Gore
531 U.S. 98 (2000)

PER CURIAM.

The petition presents the following questions: whether the Florida Supreme Court established new standards for resolving Presidential election contests, thereby violating Art. II, § 1, cl. 2, of the United States Constitution . . . and whether the use of standardless manual recounts violates the Equal Protection and Due Process Clauses. With respect to the equal protection question, we find a violation of the Equal Protection Clause.

The closeness of this election, and the multitude of legal challenges which have followed in its wake, have brought into sharp focus a common, if heretofore unnoticed, phenomenon. Nationwide statistics reveal that an estimated 2% of ballots cast do not register a vote for President for whatever reason, including deliberately choosing no candidate at all or some voter error, such as voting for two candidates or insufficiently marking a ballot. In certifying election results, the votes eligible for inclusion in the certification are the votes meeting the properly established legal requirements.

This case has shown that punch card balloting machines can produce an unfortunate number of ballots which are not punched in a clean, complete way by the voter. After the current counting, it is likely legislative bodies nationwide will examine ways to improve the mechanisms and machinery for voting. . . .

The right to vote is protected in more than the initial allocation of the franchise. Equal protection applies as well to the manner of its exercise. Having once granted the right to vote on equal terms, the State may not, by later arbitrary and disparate treatment, value one person's vote over that of another. It must be remembered that, "the right of suffrage can be denied by a debasement or dilution of the weight of a citizen's vote just as effectively as by wholly prohibiting the free exercise of the franchise," *Reynolds v. Sims* (1964).

There is no difference between the two sides of the present controversy on these basic propositions. Respondents say that the very purpose of vindicating the right to vote justifies the recount procedures now at issue. The question before us, however, is whether the recount procedures the Florida Supreme Court has adopted are consistent with its obligation to avoid arbitrary and disparate treatment of the members of its electorate. . . .

For purposes of resolving the equal protection challenge, it is not necessary to decide whether the Florida Supreme Court had the authority under the legislative scheme for resolving election disputes to define what a legal vote is and to mandate a manual recount implementing that definition. The recount mechanisms implemented in response to the decisions of the Florida Supreme Court do not satisfy the minimum requirement for non-arbitrary treatment of voters necessary to secure the fundamental right. Florida's basic command for the count of legally cast votes is to consider the "intent of the voter." This is unobjectionable as an abstract proposition and a starting principle. The problem inheres in the absence of specific standards to ensure its equal application. The formulation of uniform rules to determine intent based on these recurring circumstances is practicable and, we conclude, necessary. . . .

The want of those rules here has led to unequal evaluation of ballots in various respects. As seems to have been acknowledged at oral argument, the standards for accepting or rejecting contested ballots might vary not only from county to county but indeed within a single county from one recount team to another. . . .

An early case in our one person, one vote jurisprudence arose when a State accorded arbitrary and disparate treatment to voters in its different counties, *Gray v. Sanders* (1963). The Court found a constitutional violation. We relied on these principles in the context of the Presidential selection process in *Moore v. Ogilvie* (1969), where we invalidated a county-based procedure that diluted the influence of citizens in larger counties in the nominating process. There we observed that "[t]he idea that one group can be granted greater voting strength than another is hostile to the one man, one vote basis of our representative government." . . .

The State Supreme Court ratified this uneven treatment. It mandated that the recount totals from two counties, Miami-Dade and Palm Beach, be included in the certified total. The court also appeared to hold sub silentio that the recount totals from Broward County, which were not completed until after the original November 14 certification by the Secretary of State, were to be considered part of the new certified vote totals even though the county certification was not contested by Vice President Gore. Yet each of the counties used varying standards to determine what was a legal vote. Broward County used a more forgiving standard than Palm Beach County, and uncovered almost three times as many new votes, a result markedly disproportionate to the difference in population between the counties.

In addition, the recounts in . . . [Miami-Dade, Palm Beach, and Broward Counties] were not limited to so-called undervotes but extended to all of the ballots. The distinction has real consequences. A manual recount of all ballots identifies not only those ballots which show no vote but also those which contain more than one, the so-called overvotes. Neither category will be counted by the machine. This is not a trivial concern. At oral argument, respondents estimated there are as many as 110,000 overvotes statewide. As a result, the citizen whose ballot was not read by a machine because he failed to vote for a candidate in a way readable by a machine may still have his vote counted in a manual recount; on the other hand, the citizen who marks two candidates in a way discernable by the machine will not have the same opportunity to have his vote count, even if a manual examination of the ballot would reveal the requisite indicia of intent. Furthermore, the citizen who marks two candidates, only one of which is discernable by the machine, will have his vote counted even though it should have been read as an invalid ballot. The State Supreme Court's inclusion of vote counts based on these variant standards exemplifies concerns with the remedial processes that were under way.

That brings the analysis to yet a further equal protection problem. The votes certified by the court included a partial total from one county, Miami-Dade. The Florida Supreme Court's decision thus gives no assurance that the recounts included in a final certification must be complete. Indeed, it is respondent's submission that it would be consistent with the rules of the recount procedures to include whatever partial counts are done by the time of final certification, and we interpret the Florida

Supreme Court's decision to permit this. This accommodation no doubt results from the truncated contest period established by the Florida Supreme Court in *Bush* [v. Gore] I, at respondents' own urging. The press of time does not diminish the constitutional concern. A desire for speed is not a general excuse for ignoring equal protection guarantees.

In addition to these difficulties the actual process by which the votes were to be counted under the Florida Supreme Court's decision raises further concerns. That order did not specify who would recount the ballots. The county canvassing boards were forced to pull together ad hoc teams comprised of judges from various Circuits who had no previous training in handling and interpreting ballots. Furthermore, while others were permitted to observe, they were prohibited from objecting during the recount. . . .

The question before the Court is not whether local entities, in the exercise of their expertise, may develop different systems for implementing elections. Instead, we are presented with a situation where a state court with the power to assure uniformity has ordered a statewide recount with minimal procedural safeguards. When a court orders a statewide remedy, there must be at least some assurance that the rudimentary requirements of equal treatment and fundamental fairness are satisfied.

Given the Court's assessment that the recount process underway was probably being conducted in an unconstitutional manner, the Court stayed the order directing the recount so it could hear this case and render an expedited decision. The contest provision, as it was mandated by the State Supreme Court, is not well calculated to sustain the confidence that all citizens must have in the outcome of elections. The State has not shown that its procedures include the necessary safeguards. The problem, for instance, of the estimated 110,000 overvotes has not been addressed, although Chief Justice Wells called attention to the concern in his dissenting opinion.

Upon due consideration of the difficulties identified to this point, it is obvious that the recount cannot be conducted in compliance with the requirements of equal protection and due process without substantial additional work. It would require not only the adoption (after opportunity for argument) of adequate statewide standards for determining what is a legal vote, and practicable procedures to implement them, but also orderly judicial review of any disputed matters that might arise. In addition, the Secretary of State has advised that the recount of only a portion of the ballots requires that the vote tabulation equipment be used to screen out undervotes, a function for which the machines were not designed. If a recount of overvotes were also required, perhaps even a second screening would be necessary. Use of the equipment for this purpose, and any new software developed for it, would have to be evaluated for accuracy by the Secretary of State. . . .

. . . [Florida law] . . . requires that any controversy or contest that is designed to lead to a conclusive selection of electors be completed by December 12. That date is upon us, and there is no recount procedure in place under the State Supreme Court's order that comports with minimal constitutional standards. Because it is evident that any recount seeking to meet the December 12 date will be unconstitutional for the reasons we have discussed, we reverse the judgment of the Supreme Court of Florida ordering a recount to proceed.

Seven Justices of the Court agree that there are constitutional problems with the recount ordered by the Florida Supreme Court that demand a remedy. (SOUTER, J., dissenting); (BREYER, J., dissenting). The only disagreement is as to the remedy. . . .

None are more conscious of the vital limits on judicial authority than are the members of this Court, and none stand more in admiration of the Constitution's design to leave the selection of the President to the people, through their legislatures, and to the political sphere. When contending parties invoke the process of the courts, however, it becomes our unsought responsibility to resolve the federal and constitutional issues the judicial system has been forced to confront.

The judgment of the Supreme Court of Florida is reversed, and the case is remanded for further proceedings not inconsistent with this opinion. . . .

It is so ordered.

CHIEF JUSTICE REHNQUIST, with whom JUSTICE SCALIA and JUSTICE THOMAS join, concurring.

In most cases, . . . respect for federalism compels us to defer to the decisions of state courts on issues of state law. That practice reflects our understanding that the decisions of state courts are definitive pronouncements of the will of the States as sovereigns. Of course, in ordinary cases, the distribution of powers among the branches of a State's government raises no questions of federal constitutional law, subject to the requirement that the government be republican in character. But there are a few exceptional cases in which the Constitution imposes a duty or confers a power on a particular branch of a State's government. This is one of them. Article II, § 1, cl. 2, provides that "[e]ach State shall appoint, in such Manner as the Legislature thereof may direct," electors for President and Vice President. Thus, the text of the election law itself, and not just its interpretation by the courts of the States, takes on independent significance. . . .

In Florida, the legislature has chosen to hold statewide elections to appoint the State's 25 electors. Importantly, the legislature has delegated the authority to run the elections and to oversee election disputes to the Secretary of State (Secretary), Fla. Isolated sections of the code may well admit of more than one interpretation, but the general coherence of the legislative scheme may not be altered by judicial interpretation so as to wholly change the statutorily provided apportionment of responsibility among these various bodies. In any election but a Presidential election, the Florida Supreme Court can give as little or as much deference to Florida's executives as it chooses, so far as Article II is concerned, and this Court will have no cause to question the court's actions. But, with respect to a Presidential election, the court must be both mindful of the legislature's role under Article II in choosing the manner of appointing electors and deferential to those bodies expressly empowered by the legislature to carry out its constitutional mandate.

JUSTICE STEVENS, with whom JUSTICE GINSBURG and JUSTICE BREYER join, dissenting.

The Constitution assigns to the States the primary responsibility for determining the manner of selecting the Presidential electors. When questions arise about the meaning of state laws, including election laws, it is our settled practice to accept the opinions of the highest courts of the States as providing the final answers. On rare occasions, however, either federal statutes or the Federal Constitution may require federal judicial intervention in state elections. This is not such an occasion.

The federal questions that ultimately emerged in this case are not substantial. Article II provides that "[e]ach State shall appoint, in such Manner as the Legislature thereof may direct, a Number of Electors." It does not create state legislatures out of whole cloth, but rather takes them as they come — as creatures born of, and constrained by, their state constitutions. Lest there be any doubt, we stated over 100 years ago in *McPherson v. Blacker* (1892), that "[w]hat is forbidden or required to be done by a State" in the Article II context "is forbidden or required of the legislative power under state constitutions as they exist." In the same vein, we also observed that "[t]he [State's] legislative power is the supreme authority except as limited by the constitution of the State." The legislative power in Florida is subject to judicial review pursuant to Article V of the Florida Constitution, and nothing in Article II of the Federal Constitution frees the state legislature from the constraints in the state constitution that created it. Moreover, the Florida Legislature's own decision to employ a unitary code for all elections indicates that it intended the Florida Supreme Court to play the same role in Presidential elections that it has historically played in resolving electoral disputes. The Florida Supreme Court's exercise of appellate jurisdiction therefore was wholly consistent with, and indeed contemplated by, the grant of authority in Article II.

It hardly needs stating that Congress, pursuant to 3 U. S. C. § 5, did not impose any affirmative duties upon the States that their governmental branches could "violate." Rather, § 5 provides a safe harbor for States to select electors in contested elections "by judicial or other methods" established by laws prior to the election day. Section 5, like Article II, assumes the involvement of the state judiciary in interpreting state election laws and resolving election disputes under those laws. Neither § 5 nor Article II grants federal judges any special authority to substitute their views for those of the state judiciary on matters of state law. . . .

Admittedly, the use of differing substandards for determining voter intent in different counties employing similar voting systems may raise serious concerns. Those concerns are alleviated—if not eliminated—by the fact that a single impartial magistrate will ultimately adjudicate all objections arising from the recount process. Of course, as a general matter, "[t]he interpretation of constitu-

tional principles must not be too literal. We must remember that the machinery of government would not work if it were not allowed a little play in its joints." If it were otherwise, Florida's decision to leave to each county the determination of what balloting system to employ—despite enormous differences in accuracy—might run afoul of equal protection. So, too, might the similar decisions of the vast majority of state legislatures to delegate to local authorities certain decisions with respect to voting systems and ballot design. . . .

What must underlie petitioners' entire federal assault on the Florida election procedures is an unstated lack of confidence in the impartiality and capacity of the state judges who would make the critical decisions if the vote count were to proceed. Otherwise, their position is wholly without merit. The endorsement of that position by the majority of this Court can only lend credence to the most cynical appraisal of the work of judges throughout the land. It is confidence in the men and women who administer the judicial system that is the true backbone of the rule of law. Time will one day heal the wound to that confidence that will be inflicted by today's decision. One thing, however, is certain. Although we may never know with complete certainty the identity of the winner of this year's Presidential election, the identity of the loser is perfectly clear. It is the Nation's confidence in the judge as an impartial guardian of the rule of law.

I respectfully dissent.

JUSTICE SOUTER, with whom JUSTICE BREYER joins and with whom JUSTICE STEVENS and JUSTICE GINSBURG join with regard to all but Part C, dissenting.

The Court should not have reviewed either *Bush v. Palm Beach County Canvassing Bd.* or this case, and should not have stopped Florida's attempt to recount all undervote ballots, by issuing a stay of the Florida Supreme Court's orders during the period of this review. If this Court had allowed the State to follow the course indicated by the opinions of its own Supreme Court, it is entirely possible that there would ultimately have been no issue requiring our review, and political tension could have worked itself out in the Congress following the procedure provided in 3 U. S. C. § 15. The case being before us, however, its resolution by the majority is another erroneous decision. . . .

In deciding what to do about this, we should take account of the fact that electoral votes are due to be cast in six days. I would therefore remand the case to the courts of Florida with instructions to establish uniform standards for evaluating the several types of ballots that have prompted differing treatments, to be applied within and among counties when passing on such identical ballots in any further recounting (or successive recounting) that the courts might order.

Unlike the majority, I see no warrant for this Court to assume that Florida could not possibly comply with this requirement before the date set for the meeting of electors, December 18. Although one of the dissenting justices of the State Supreme Court estimated that disparate standards potentially affected 170,000 votes, the number at issue is significantly smaller. The 170,000 figure apparently represents all uncounted votes, both undervotes (those for which no Presidential choice was recorded by a machine) and overvotes (those rejected because of votes for more than one candidate. But as JUSTICE BREYER has pointed out, no showing has been made of legal overvotes uncounted, and counsel for Gore made an uncontradicted representation to the Court that the statewide total of undervotes is about 60,000. To recount these manually would be a tall order, but before this Court stayed the effort to do that the courts of Florida were ready to do their best to get that job done. There is no justification for denying the State the opportunity to try to count all disputed ballots now.

I respectfully dissent.

JUSTICE GINSBURG, with whom JUSTICE STEVENS joins, and with whom JUSTICE SOUTER and JUSTICE BREYER join as to Part I, dissenting.

I

The CHIEF JUSTICE acknowledges that provisions of Florida's Election Code "may well admit of more than one interpretation." But instead of respecting the state high court's province to say what the State's Election Code means, THE CHIEF JUSTICE maintains that Florida's Supreme Court has veered so far from the ordinary practice of judicial review that what it did cannot properly be called judging. My col-

leagues have offered a reasonable construction of Florida's law. Their construction coincides with the view of one of Florida's seven Supreme Court justices. I might join THE CHIEF JUSTICE were it my commission to interpret Florida law. But disagreement with the Florida court's interpretation of its own State's law does not warrant the conclusion that the justices of that court have legislated. There is no cause here to believe that the members of Florida's high court have done less than "their mortal best to discharge their oath of office," and no cause to upset their reasoned interpretation of Florida law. . . .

In deferring to state courts on matters of state law, we appropriately recognize that this Court acts as an "'outside[r]' lacking the common exposure to local law which comes from sitting in the jurisdiction." That recognition has sometimes prompted us to resolve doubts about the meaning of state law by certifying issues to a State's highest court, even when federal rights are at stake. Notwithstanding our authority to decide issues of state law underlying federal claims, we have used the certification devise to afford state high courts an opportunity to inform us on matters of their own State's law because such restraint "helps build a cooperative judicial federalism." . . .

The extraordinary setting of this case has obscured the ordinary principle that dictates its proper resolution: Federal courts defer to state high courts' interpretations of their state's own law. This principle reflects the core of federalism, on which all agree. "The Framers split the atom of sovereignty. It was the genius of their idea that our citizens would have two political capacities, one state and one federal, each protected from incursion by the other." THE CHIEF JUSTICE's solicitude for the Florida Legislature comes at the expense of the more fundamental solicitude we owe to the legislature's sovereign. U.S. Const., Art. II, § 1, cl. 2. Were the other members of this Court as mindful as they generally are of our system of dual sovereignty, they would affirm the judgment of the Florida Supreme Court.

II

I agree with JUSTICE STEVENS that petitioners have not presented a substantial equal protection claim. Ideally, perfection would be the appropriate standard for judging the recount. But we live in an imperfect world, one in which thousands of votes have not been counted. I cannot agree that the recount adopted by the Florida court, flawed as it may be, would yield a result any less fair or precise than the certification that preceded that recount. Even if there were an equal protection violation, I would agree with JUSTICE STEVENS, JUSTICE SOUTER, and JUSTICE BREYER that the Court's concern about "the December 12 deadline," is misplaced. Time is short in part because of the Court's entry of a stay on December 9, several hours after an able circuit judge in Leon County had begun to superintend the recount process. More fundamentally, the Court's reluctance to let the recount go forward — despite its suggestion that "[t]he search for intent can be confined by specific rules designed to ensure uniform treatment," ultimately turns on its own judgment about the practical realities of implementing a recount, not the judgment of those much closer to the process. . . .

The Court assumes that time will not permit "orderly judicial review of any disputed matters that might arise." But no one has doubted the good faith and diligence with which Florida election officials, attorneys for all sides of this controversy, and the courts of law have performed their duties. Notably, the Florida Supreme Court has produced two substantial opinions within 29 hours of oral argument. In sum, the Court's conclusion that a constitutionally adequate recount is impractical is a prophecy the Court's own judgment will not allow to be tested. Such an untested prophecy should not decide the Presidency of the United States.

I dissent.

JUSTICE BREYER, with whom JUSTICE STEVENS, JUSTICE GINSBURG, and JUSTICE SOUTER join . . .

The Court was wrong to take this case. It was wrong to grant a stay. It should now vacate that stay and permit the Florida Supreme Court to decide whether the recount should resume.

The political implications of this case for the country are momentous. But the federal legal questions presented, with one exception, are insubstantial.

The majority raises three Equal Protection problems with the Florida Supreme Court's recount order: first, the failure to include overvotes in the manual recount; second, the fact that all ballots,

rather than simply the undervotes, were recounted in some, but not all, counties; and third, the absence of a uniform, specific standard to guide the recounts. As far as the first issue is concerned, petitioners presented no evidence, to this Court or to any Florida court, that a manual recount of overvotes would identify additional legal votes. The same is true of the second, and, in addition, the majority's reasoning would seem to invalidate any state provision for a manual recount of individual counties in a statewide election.

The majority's third concern does implicate principles of fundamental fairness. The majority concludes that the Equal Protection Clause requires that a manual recount be governed not only by the uniform general standard of the "clear intent of the voter," but also by uniform subsidiary standards (for example, a uniform determination whether indented, but not perforated, "undervotes" should count). The opinion points out that the Florida Supreme Court ordered the inclusion of Broward County's undercounted "legal votes" even though those votes included ballots that were not perforated but simply "dimpled," while newly recounted ballots from other counties will likely include only votes determined to be "legal" on the basis of a stricter standard. In light of our previous remand, the Florida Supreme Court may have been reluctant to adopt a more specific standard than that provided for by the legislature for fear of exceeding its authority under Article II. However, since the use of different standards could favor one or the other of the candidates, since time was, and is, too short to permit the lower courts to iron out significant differences through ordinary judicial review, and since the relevant distinction was embodied in the order of the State's highest court, I agree that, in these very special circumstances, basic principles of fairness may well have counseled the adoption of a uniform standard to address the problem. In light of the majority's disposition, I need not decide whether, or the extent to which, as a remedial matter, the Constitution would place limits upon the content of the uniform standard. . . .

Of course, the selection of the President is of fundamental national importance. But that importance is political, not legal. And this Court should resist the temptation unnecessarily to resolve tangential legal disputes, where doing so threatens to determine the outcome of the election.

The Constitution and federal statutes themselves make clear that restraint is appropriate. They set forth a road map of how to resolve disputes about electors, even after an election as close as this one. That road map foresees resolution of electoral disputes by state courts. But it nowhere provides for involvement by the United States Supreme Court.

To the contrary, the Twelfth Amendment commits to Congress the authority and responsibility to count electoral votes. A federal statute, the Electoral Count Act, enacted after the close 1876 Hayes-Tilden Presidential election, specifies that, after States have tried to resolve disputes (through "judicial" or other means), Congress is the body primarily authorized to resolve remaining disputes. . . .

The decision by both the Constitution's Framers and the 1886 Congress to minimize this Court's role in resolving close federal presidential elections is as wise as it is clear. However awkward or difficult it may be for Congress to resolve difficult electoral disputes, Congress, being a political body, expresses the people's will far more accurately than does an unelected Court. And the people's will is what elections are about. . . .

. . . [T]he Court is not acting to vindicate a fundamental constitutional principle, such as the need to protect a basic human liberty. No other strong reason to act is present. Congressional statutes tend to obviate the need. And, above all, in this highly politicized matter, the appearance of a split decision runs the risk of undermining the public's confidence in the Court itself. That confidence is a public treasure. It has been built slowly over many years, some of which were marked by a Civil War and the tragedy of segregation. It is a vitally necessary ingredient of any successful effort to protect basic liberty and, indeed, the rule of law itself. We run no risk of returning to the days when a President (responding to this Court's efforts to protect the Cherokee Indians) might have said, "John Marshall has made his decision; now let him enforce it!" But we do risk a self-inflicted wound—a wound that may harm not just the Court, but the Nation.

I fear that in order to bring this agonizingly long election process to a definitive conclusion, we have not adequately attended to that necessary "check upon our own exercise of power," "our own sense of self-restraint." Justice Brandeis once said of the Court, "What it does today, the Court should have left undone." I would repair the damage done as best we now can, by permitting the Florida recount to continue under uniform standards.

I respectfully dissent.

A View from the Inside

<table>
<tr><td>1.6</td><td>

The Notion of a Living Constitution (1976)
</td></tr>
</table>

William H. Rehnquist

. . . The first meaning [of a "living Constitution"] was expressed over a half-century ago by Justice Holmes in *Missouri v. Holland* with his customary felicity when he said:

. . . When we are dealing with words that also are a constituent act, like the Constitution of the United States, we must realize that they have

From *Texas Law Review* 54, no. 4 (May 1976): 673–706. Reprinted by permission of The Texas Law Review.

called into life a being the development of which could not have been foreseen completely by the most gifted of its begetters. It was enough for them to realize or to hope that they had created an organism; it has taken a century and has cost their successors much sweat and blood to prove that they created a nation.

I shall refer to this interpretation of the phrase "living Constitution," with which scarcely anyone would disagree, as the Holmes version.

The framers of the Constitution wisely spoke in general language and left to succeeding generations the task of applying that language to the unceasingly changing environment in which they would live. Those who framed, adopted, and ratified the Civil War amendments to the Constitution likewise used what have been aptly described as "majestic generalities" in composing the fourteenth amendment. Merely because a particular activity may not have existed when the Constitution was adopted, or because the framers could not have conceived of a particular method of transacting affairs, cannot mean that general language in the Constitution may not be applied to such a course of conduct. Where the framers of the Constitution have used general language, they have given latitude to those who would later interpret the instrument to make that language applicable to cases that the framers might not have foreseen.

In my reading and travels I have sensed a second connotation of the phrase "living Constitution," however, one quite different from what I have described as the Holmes version, but which certainly has gained acceptance among some parts of the legal profession. Embodied in its most naked form, it recently came to my attention in some language from a brief that had been filed in a United States District Court on behalf of state prisoners asserting that the conditions of their confinement offended the United States Constitution. The brief urged:

> We are asking a great deal of the Court because other branches of government have abdicated their responsibility. . . . Prisoners are like other discrete and insular minorities for whom the Court must spread its protective umbrella because no other branch of government will do so. . . . This Court, as the voice and conscience of contemporary society, as the measure of the modern conception of human dignity, must declare that the [named prison] and all it represents offends the Constitution of the United States and will not be tolerated.

Here we have a living Constitution with a vengeance. Although the substitution of some other set of values for those which may be derived from the language and intent of the framers is not urged in so many words, that is surely the thrust of the message. Under this brief writer's version of the living Constitution, nonelected members of the federal judiciary may address themselves to a social problem simply because other branches of government have failed or refused to do so. These same judges, responsible to no constituency whatever, are nonetheless acclaimed as "the voice and conscience of contemporary society."

If we were merely talking about a slogan that was being used to elect some candidate to office or to persuade the voters to ratify a constitutional amendment, elaborate dissection of a phrase such as "living Constitution" would probably not be warranted. What we are talking about, however, is a suggested philosophical approach to be used by the federal judiciary, and perhaps state judiciaries, in exercising the very delicate responsibility of judicial review. Under the familiar principle of judicial review, the courts in construing the Constitution are, of course, authorized to invalidate laws that have been enacted by Congress or by a state legislature but that those courts find to violate some provision of the Constitution. Nevertheless, those who have pondered the matter have always recognized that the ideal of judicial review has basically antidemocratic and antimajoritarian facets that require some justification in this Nation, which prides itself on being a self-governing representative democracy. . . .

. . . The brief writer's version seems . . . based upon the proposition that federal judges, perhaps judges as a whole, have a role of their own, quite independent of popular will, to play in solving society's problems. Once we have abandoned the idea that the authority of the courts to declare laws unconstitutional is somehow tied to the language of the Constitution that the people adopted, a judiciary exercising the power of judicial review appears in a quite different light. Judges then are no longer the keepers of the covenant; instead they are a small group of fortunately situated people with a roving commission to second-guess Congress, state legislatures, and state and federal administrative officers concerning what is best for the country. Surely there is no justification for a third legislative branch in the federal government, and there is even less justification for a federal legislative branch's reviewing on a policy basis the laws enacted by the legislatures of the fifty states. Even if one were to disagree with me on this point, the members of a third branch of the federal legislature at least ought to be elected by and responsible to constituencies, just as in the case of the other two branches of Congress. If there is going to be a council of revision, it ought to have at least some connection with popular feeling. Its members either ought to stand for reelection on occasion, or their terms should expire and they should be allowed to continue serving only if reappointed by a popularly elected Chief Executive and confirmed by a popularly elected Senate.

The brief writer's version of the living Constitution is seldom presented in its most naked form, but is instead usually dressed in more attractive garb. The argument in favor of this approach generally begins with a sophisticated wink—why pretend that there is any ascertainable content to the general phrases of the Constitution as they are written since, after all, judges constantly disagree about their meaning? We are all familiar with Chief Justice Hughes' famous aphorism that "We are under a Constitution, but the Constitution is what the judges say it is." We all know the basis of Marshall's justification for judicial review, the argument runs, but it is necessary only to keep the window dressing in place. Any sophisticated student of the subject knows that judges need not limit themselves to the intent of the framers, which is very difficult to determine in any event. Because of the general language used in the Constitution, judges should not hesitate to use their authority to make the Constitution relevant and useful in solving the problems of modern society. The brief writer's version of the living Constitution envisions all of the above conclusions.

At least three serious difficulties flaw the brief writer's version of the living Constitution. First, it misconceives the nature of the Constitution, which was designed to enable the popularly elected branches of government, not the judicial branch, to keep the country abreast of the times. Second, the brief writer's version ignores the Supreme Court's disastrous experiences when in the past it embraced contemporary, fashionable notions of what a living Constitution should contain. Third, however socially desirable the goals sought to be advanced by the brief writer's version, advancing them through a freewheeling, nonelected judiciary is quite unacceptable in a democratic society.

It seems to me that it is almost impossible, after reading the record of the Founding Fathers' debates in Philadelphia, to conclude that they intended the Constitution itself to suggest answers to the manifold problems that they knew would confront succeeding generations. The Constitution that they drafted was indeed intended to endure indefinitely, but the reason for this very well-founded hope was the general language by which national authority was granted to Congress and the Presidency. These two branches were to furnish the motive power within the federal system, which was in turn to coexist with the state governments; the elements of government having a popular constituency were looked to for the solution of the numerous and varied problems that the future would bring. Limitations were indeed placed upon both federal and state governments in the form of both a division of powers and express protection for individual rights. These limitations, however, were not themselves designed to solve the problems of the future, but were instead designed to make certain that the constituent branches, when *they* attempted to solve those problems, should not transgress these fundamental limitations.

Although the Civil War Amendments were designed more as broad limitations on the authority of state governments, they too were enacted in response to practices that the lately seceded states engaged in to discriminate against and mistreat the newly emancipated freed men. To the extent that the language of these amendments is general, the courts are of course warranted in giving them an application coextensive with their language. Nevertheless, I greatly doubt that even men like Thad Stevens and John Bingham, leaders of the radical Republicans in Congress, would have thought any portion of the Civil War Amendments, except section five of the fourteenth amendment, was designed to solve problems that society might confront a century later. I think they would have said that those amendments were designed to prevent from ever recurring abuses in which the states had engaged prior to that time.

The brief writer's version of the living Constitution, however, suggests that if the states' legislatures and governors, or Congress and the President, have not solved a particular social problem, then the federal court may act. I do not believe that this argument will withstand rational analysis. Even in the face of a conceded social evil, a reasonably competent and reasonably representative legislature may decide to do nothing. It may decide that the evil is not of sufficient magnitude to warrant any governmental intervention. It may decide that the financial cost of eliminating the evil is not worth the benefit which would result from its elimination. It may decide that the evils which might ensue from the proposed solution are worse than the evils which the solution would eliminate.

Surely the Constitution does not put either the legislative branch or the executive branch in the position of a television quiz show contestant so that when a given period of time has elapsed and a problem remains unsolved by them, the federal judiciary may press a buzzer and take its turn at fashioning a solution. . . .

Should a person fail to persuade the legislature, or should he feel that a legislative victory would be insufficient because of its potential for future reversal, he may seek to run the more difficult gauntlet of amending the Constitution to embody the view that he espouses. Success in amending the Constitution would, of course, preclude succeeding tran-

sient majorities in the legislature from tampering with the principle formerly added to the Constitution.

I know of no other method compatible with political theory basic to democratic society by which one's own conscientious belief may be translated into positive law and thereby obtain the only general moral imprimatur permissible in a pluralistic, democratic society. It is always time consuming, frequently difficult, and not infrequently impossible to run successfully the legislative gauntlet and have enacted some facet of one's own deeply felt value judgments. It is even more difficult for either a single individual or indeed for a large group of individuals to succeed in having such a value judgment embodied in the Constitution. All of these burdens and difficulties are entirely consistent with the notion of a democratic society. It should not be easy for any one individual or group of individuals to impose by law their value judgments upon fellow citizens who may disagree with those judgments. Indeed, it should not be easier just because the individual in question is a judge. We all have a propensity to want to do it, but there are very good reasons for making it difficult to do. . . .

1.7   **Reflections on the Bicentennial of the United States Constitution (1987)**

Thurgood Marshall

Nineteen eighty-seven marks the 200th anniversary of the United States Constitution. A Commission has been established to coordinate the celebration. The official meetings, essay contests, and festivities have begun.

The planned commemoration will span three years, and I am told 1987 is "dedicated to the memory of the Founders and the document they drafted in Philadelphia." We are to "recall the achievements of our Founders and the knowledge and experience that inspired them, the nature of the government they established, its origins, its character, and its

From *Harvard Law Review* (1987). Reprinted by permission of The Estate of Thurgood Marshall.

ends, and the rights and privileges of citizenship, as well as its attendant responsibilities."

Like many anniversary celebrations, the plan for 1987 takes particular events and holds them up as the source of all the very best that has followed. Patriotic feelings will surely swell, prompting proud proclamations of the wisdom, foresight, and sense of justice shared by the Framers and reflected in a written document now yellowed with age. This is unfortunate—not the patriotism itself, but the tendency for the celebration to oversimplify, and overlook the many other events that have been instrumental to our achievements as a nation. The focus of this celebration invites a complacent belief that the vision of those who debated and compromised in Philadelphia yielded the "more perfect Union" it is said we now enjoy.

I cannot accept this invitation, for I do not believe that the meaning of the Constitution was forever "fixed" at the Philadelphia Convention. Nor do I find the wisdom, foresight, and sense of justice exhibited by the Framers particularly profound. To the contrary, the government they devised was defective from the start, requiring several amendments, a civil war, and momentous social transformation to attain the system of constitutional government, and its respect for the individual freedoms and human rights, we hold as fundamental today. When contemporary Americans cite "The Constitution," they invoke a concept that is vastly different from what the Framers barely began to construct two centuries ago.

For a sense of the evolving nature of the Constitution we need look no further than the first three words of the document's preamble: "We the People." When the Founding Fathers used this phrase in 1787, they did not have in mind the majority of America's citizens. "We the People" included, in the words of the Framers, "the whole Number of free Persons." On a matter so basic as the right to vote, for example, Negro slaves were excluded, although they were counted for representational purposes at three-fifths each. Women did not gain the right to vote for over a hundred and thirty years.

These omissions were intentional. The record of the Framers' debates on the slave question is especially clear. The Southern States acceded to the demands of the New England States for giving Congress broad power to regulate commerce, in exchange for the right to continue the slave trade. The economic interests of the regions coalesced: New Englanders engaged in the "carrying trade" would profit from transporting slaves from Africa as well as goods produced in America by slave labor. The perpetuation of slavery ensured the primary source of wealth in the Southern States.

Despite this clear understanding of the role slavery would play in the new republic, use of the words "slaves" and "slavery" was carefully avoided in the original document. Political representation in the lower House of Congress was to be based on the population of "free Persons" in each State, plus three-fifths of all "other Persons." Moral principles against slavery, for those who had them, were compromised, with no explanation of the conflicting

principles for which the American Revolutionary War had ostensibly been fought: the self-evident truths "that all men are created equal, that they are endowed by their Creator with certain unalienable Rights, that among these are Life, Liberty and the pursuit of Happiness."

It was not the first such compromise. Even these ringing phrases from the Declaration of Independence are filled with irony, for an early draft of what became that Declaration assailed the King of England for suppressing legislative attempts to end the slave trade and for encouraging slave rebellions. The final draft adopted in 1776 did not contain this criticism. And so again at the Constitutional Convention eloquent objections to the institution of slavery went unheeded, and its opponents eventually consented to a document which laid a foundation for the tragic events that were to follow.

Pennsylvania's Gouverneur Morris provides an example. He opposed slavery and the counting of slaves in determining the basis for representation in Congress. At the Convention he objected that

> The inhabitant of Georgia [or] South Carolina who goes to the coast of Africa, and in defiance of the most sacred laws of humanity tears away his fellow creatures from their dearest connections and damns them to the most cruel bondages, shall have more votes in a Government instituted for protection of the rights of mankind, than the Citizen of Pennsylvania or New Jersey who views with a laudable horror, so nefarious a Practice.

And yet Gouverneur Morris eventually accepted the three-fifths accommodation. In fact, he wrote the final draft of the Constitution, the very document the bicentennial will commemorate.

As a result of compromise, the right of the southern States to continue importing slaves was extended, officially, at least until 1808. We know that it actually lasted a good deal longer, as the Framers possessed no monopoly on the ability to trade moral principles for self-interest. But they nevertheless set an unfortunate example. Slaves could be imported, if the commercial interests of the North were protected. To make the compromise even more palatable, customs duties would be imposed at up to ten dollars per slave as a means of raising public revenues.

No doubt it will be said, when the unpleasant truth of the history of slavery in America is mentioned during this bicentennial year, that the Constitution was a product of its times, and embodied a compromise which, under other circumstances, would not have been made. But the effects of the Framers' compromise have remained for generations. They arose from the contradiction between guaranteeing liberty and justice to all, and denying both to Negroes.

The original intent of the phrase, "We the People," was far too clear for any ameliorating construction. Writing for the Supreme Court in 1857, Chief Justice Taney penned the following passage in the Dred Scott case, on the issue whether, in the eyes of the Framers, slaves were "constituent members of the sovereignty," and were to be included among "We the People."

> We think they are not, and that they are not included, and were not intended to be included. . . . They had for more than a century before been regarded as beings of an inferior order, and altogether unfit to associate with the white race . . . ; and so far inferior, that they had no rights which the white man was bound to respect; and that the Negro might justly and lawfully be reduced to slavery for his benefit. . . . [A]ccordingly, a Negro of the African race was regarded . . . as an article of property, and held, and bought and sold as such. . . . [N]o one seems to have doubted the correctness of the prevailing opinion of the time.

And so, nearly seven decades after the Constitutional Convention, the Supreme Court reaffirmed the prevailing opinion of the Framers regarding the rights of Negroes in America. It took a bloody civil war before the 13th Amendment could be adopted to abolish slavery, though not the consequences slavery would have for future Americans.

While the Union survived the civil war, the Constitution did not. In its place arose a new, more promising basis for justice and equality, the 14th Amendment, ensuring protection of the life, liberty, and property of all persons against deprivations without due process, and guaranteeing equal protection of the laws. And yet almost another century

would pass before any significant recognition was obtained of the rights of black Americans to share equally even in such basic opportunities as education, housing, and employment, and to have their votes counted, and counted equally. In the meantime, blacks joined America's military to fight its wars and invested untold hours working in its factories and on its farms, contributing to the development of this country's magnificent wealth and waiting to share in its prosperity.

What is striking is the role legal principles have played throughout America's history in determining the condition of Negroes. They were enslaved by law, emancipated by law, disenfranchised and segregated by law; and, finally, they have begun to win equality by law. Along the way, new constitutional principles have emerged to meet the challenges of a changing society. The progress has been dramatic, and it will continue.

The men who gathered in Philadelphia in 1787 could not have envisioned these changes. They could not have imagined, nor would they have accepted, that the document they were drafting would one day be construed by a Supreme Court to which had been appointed a woman and the descendent of an African slave. "We the People" no longer enslave, but the credit does not belong to the Framers. It belongs to those who refused to acquiesce in outdated notions of "liberty," "justice," and "equality," and who strived to better them.

And so we must be careful, when focusing on the events which took place in Philadelphia two centuries ago, that we not overlook the momentous events which followed, and thereby lose our proper sense of perspective. Otherwise, the odds are that for many Americans the bicentennial celebration will be little more than a blind pilgrimage to the shrine of the original document now stored in a vault in the National Archives. If we seek, instead, a sensitive understanding of the Constitution's inherent defects, and its promising evolution through 200 years of history, the celebration of the "Miracle at Philadelphia" will, in my view, be a far more meaningful and humbling experience. We will see that the true miracle was not the birth of the Constitution, but its life, a life nurtured through two turbulent centuries of our own making, and a life embodying much good fortune that was not.

Thus, in this bicentennial year, we may not all participate in the festivities with flag-waving fervor.

Some may more quietly commemorate the suffering, struggle, and sacrifice that has triumphed over much of what was wrong with the original document, and observe the anniversary with hopes not realized and promises not fulfilled. I plan to celebrate the bicentennial of the Constitution as a living document, including the Bill of Rights and the other amendments protecting individual freedoms and human rights.

1.8   *Lawrence v. Texas*
539 U.S. 558 (2003)

JUSTICE KENNEDY delivered the opinion of the Court.

Liberty protects the person from unwarranted government intrusions into a dwelling or other private places. In our tradition the State is not omnipresent in the home. And there are other spheres of our lives and existence, outside the home, where the State should not be a dominant presence. Freedom extends beyond spatial bounds. Liberty presumes an autonomy of self that includes freedom of thought, belief, expression, and certain intimate conduct. The instant case involves liberty of the person both in its spatial and more transcendent dimensions. . . .

We conclude the case should be resolved by determining whether the petitioners were free as adults to engage in the private conduct in the exercise of their liberty under the Due Process Clause of the Fourteenth Amendment to the Constitution. For this inquiry we deem it necessary to reconsider the Court's holding in *Bowers*.

There are broad statements of the substantive reach of liberty under the Due Process Clause in earlier cases . . . but the most pertinent beginning point is our decision in *Griswold v. Connecticut* (1965).

In *Griswold* the Court invalidated a state law prohibiting the use of drugs or devices of contraception and counseling or aiding and abetting the use of contraceptives. The Court described the protected interest as a right to privacy and placed emphasis on the marriage relation and the protected space of the marital bedroom.

After *Griswold* it was established that the right to make certain decisions regarding sexual conduct extends beyond the marital relationship. In *Eisenstadt v. Baird* (1972), the Court invalidated a law prohibiting the distribution of contraceptives to unmarried persons. The case was decided under the Equal Protection Clause, but with respect to unmarried persons, the Court went on to state the fundamental proposition that the law impaired the exercise of their personal rights. . . .

The opinions in *Griswold* and *Eisenstadt* were part of the background for the decision in *Roe v. Wade* (1973). As is well known, the case involved a challenge to the Texas law prohibiting abortions, but the laws of other States were affected as well. Although the Court held the woman's rights were not absolute, her right to elect an abortion did have real and substantial protection as an exercise of her liberty under the Due Process Clause. The Court cited cases that protect spatial freedom and cases that go well beyond it. *Roe* recognized the right of a woman to make certain fundamental decisions affecting her destiny and confirmed once more that the protection of liberty under the Due Process Clause has a substantive dimension of fundamental significance in defining the rights of the person. . . .

The facts in *Bowers* had some similarities to the instant case. A police officer, whose right to enter seems not to have been in question, observed [Michael] Hardwick, in his own bedroom, engaging in intimate sexual conduct with another adult male. The conduct was in violation of a Georgia statute making it a criminal offense to engage in sodomy. One difference between the two cases is that the Georgia statute prohibited the conduct whether or not the participants were of the same sex, while the Texas statute, as we have seen, applies only to participants of the same sex. Hardwick was not prosecuted, but he brought an action in federal court to declare the state statute invalid. He alleged he was a practicing homosexual and that the criminal prohibition violated rights guaranteed to him by the Constitution. The Court, in an opinion by Justice White, sustained the Georgia law. Chief Justice Burger and Justice Powell joined the opinion of the Court and filed separate, concurring opinions. Four Justices dissented.

The Court began its substantive discussion in *Bowers* as follows: "The issue presented is whether the Federal Constitution confers a fundamental right upon homosexuals to engage in sodomy and hence invalidates the laws of the many States that still make such conduct illegal and have done so for a very long time." That statement, we now conclude, discloses the Court's own failure to appreciate the extent of the liberty at stake. To say that the issue in *Bowers* was simply the right to engage in certain sexual conduct demeans the claim the individual put forward, just as it would demean a married couple were it to be said marriage is simply about the right to have sexual intercourse. The laws involved in *Bowers* and here are, to be sure, statutes that purport to do no more than prohibit a particular sexual act. Their penalties and purposes, though, have more far-reaching consequences, touching upon the most private human conduct, sexual behavior, and in the most private of places, the home. The statutes do seek to control a personal relationship that, whether or not entitled to formal recognition in the law, is within the liberty of persons to choose without being punished as criminals.

This, as a general rule, should counsel against attempts by the State, or a court, to define the meaning of the relationship or to set its boundaries absent injury to a person or abuse of an institution the law protects. It suffices for us to acknowledge that adults may choose to enter upon this relationship in the confines of their homes and their own private lives and still retain their dignity as free persons. When sexuality finds overt expression in intimate conduct with another person, the conduct can be but one element in a personal bond that is more enduring. The liberty protected by the Constitution allows homosexual persons the right to make this choice.

Having misapprehended the claim of liberty there presented to it, and thus stating the claim to be whether there is a fundamental right to engage in consensual sodomy, the *Bowers* Court said: "Proscriptions against that conduct have ancient roots." In academic writings, and in many of the scholarly amicus briefs filed to assist the Court in this case, there are fundamental criticisms of the historical premises relied upon by the majority and

concurring opinions in *Bowers*. We need not enter this debate in the attempt to reach a definitive historical judgment, but the following considerations counsel against adopting the definitive conclusions upon which *Bowers* placed such reliance.

At the outset it should be noted that there is no longstanding history in this country of laws directed at homosexual conduct as a distinct matter. Beginning in colonial times there were prohibitions of sodomy derived from the English criminal laws passed in the first instance by the Reformation Parliament of 1533. The English prohibition was understood to include relations between men and women as well as relations between men and men. Nineteenth-century commentators similarly read American sodomy, buggery, and crime-against-nature statutes as criminalizing certain relations between men and women and between men and men. The absence of legal prohibitions focusing on homosexual conduct may be explained in part by noting that according to some scholars the concept of the homosexual as a distinct category of person did not emerge until the late 19th century. Thus early American sodomy laws were not directed at homosexuals as such but instead sought to prohibit non-procreative sexual activity more generally. This does not suggest approval of homosexual conduct. It does tend to show that this particular form of conduct was not thought of as a separate category from like conduct between heterosexual persons.

Laws prohibiting sodomy do not seem to have been enforced against consenting adults acting in private. A substantial number of sodomy prosecutions and convictions for which there are surviving records were for predatory acts against those who could not or did not consent, as in the case of a minor or the victim of an assault. . . . Instead of targeting relations between consenting adults in private, 19th-century sodomy prosecutions typically involved relations between men and minor girls or minor boys, relations between adults involving force, relations between adults implicating disparity in status, or relations between men and animals. . . .

The policy of punishing consenting adults for private acts was not much discussed in the early legal literature. We can infer that one reason for this was the very private nature of the conduct. Despite the absence of prosecutions, there may have been periods in which there was public criticism of homosexuals as such and an insistence that the criminal laws be enforced to discourage their practices. But far from possessing "ancient roots," American laws targeting same-sex couples did not develop until the last third of the 20th century. The reported decisions concerning the prosecution of consensual, homosexual sodomy between adults for the years 1880–1995 are not always clear in the details, but a significant number involved conduct in a public place.

It was not until the 1970s that any State singled out same-sex relations for criminal prosecution, and only nine States have done so. Post-*Bowers* even some of these States did not adhere to the policy of suppressing homosexual conduct. Over the course of the last decades, States with same-sex prohibitions have moved toward abolishing them.

In summary, the historical grounds relied upon in *Bowers* are more complex than the majority opinion and the concurring opinion by Chief Justice Burger indicate. Their historical premises are not without doubt and, at the very least, are overstated. . . .

The sweeping references by Chief Justice Burger to the history of Western civilization and to Judeo-Christian moral and ethical standards did not take account of other authorities pointing in an opposite direction. A committee advising the British Parliament recommended in 1957 repeal of laws punishing homosexual conduct. Parliament enacted the substance of those recommendations 10 years later.

Of even more importance, almost five years before *Bowers* was decided the European Court of Human Rights considered a case with parallels to *Bowers* and to today's case. An adult male resident in Northern Ireland alleged he was a practicing homosexual who desired to engage in consensual homosexual conduct. The laws of Northern Ireland forbade him that right. He alleged that he had been questioned, his home had been searched, and he feared criminal prosecution. The court held that the laws proscribing the conduct were invalid under the European Convention on Human Rights. Authoritative in all countries that are members of the Council of Europe (21 nations then, 45 nations now), the decision is at odds with the premise in *Bowers* that the claim put forward was insubstantial in our Western civilization.

In our own constitutional system the deficiencies in *Bowers* became even more apparent in the years following its announcement. The 25 States with laws prohibiting the relevant conduct referenced in the *Bowers* decision are reduced now to 13, of which 4 enforce their laws only against homosexual conduct. In those States where sodomy is still proscribed, whether for same-sex or heterosexual conduct, there is a pattern of non-enforcement with respect to consenting adults acting in private. The State of Texas admitted in 1994 that as of that date it had not prosecuted anyone under those circumstances.

Two principal cases decided after *Bowers* cast its holding into even more doubt. In *Planned Parenthood of Southeastern Pa. v. Casey* (1992), the Court reaffirmed the substantive force of the liberty protected by the Due Process Clause. The Casey decision again confirmed that our laws and tradition afford constitutional protection to personal decisions relating to marriage, procreation, contraception, family relationships, child rearing, and education. . . .

Persons in a homosexual relationship may seek autonomy for these purposes, just as heterosexual persons do. The decision in *Bowers* would deny them this right.

The second post-*Bowers* case of principal relevance is *Romer v. Evans* (1996). There the Court struck down class-based legislation directed at homosexuals as a violation of the Equal Protection Clause. *Romer* invalidated an amendment to Colorado's constitution which named as a solitary class persons who were homosexuals, lesbians, or bisexual either by "orientation, conduct, practices or relationships," and deprived them of protection under state antidiscrimination laws. We concluded that the provision was "born of animosity toward the class of persons affected" and further that it had no rational relation to a legitimate governmental purpose. . . .

Equality of treatment and the due process right to demand respect for conduct protected by the substantive guarantee of liberty are linked in important respects, and a decision on the latter point advances both interests. If protected conduct is made criminal and the law which does so remains unexamined for its substantive validity, its stigma might remain even if it were not enforceable as drawn for equal protection reasons. When homosexual conduct is made criminal by the law of the State, that declaration in and of itself is an invitation to subject homosexual persons to discrimination both in the public and in the private spheres. The central holding of *Bowers* has been brought in question by this case, and it should be addressed. Its continuance as precedent demeans the lives of homosexual persons. . . .

The foundations of *Bowers* have sustained serious erosion from our recent decisions in *Casey* and *Romer*. When our precedent has been thus weakened, criticism from other sources is of greater significance. In the United States criticism of *Bowers* has been substantial and continuing, disapproving of its reasoning in all respects, not just as to its historical assumptions. . . .

The doctrine of *stare decisis* is essential to the respect accorded to the judgments of the Court and to the stability of the law. It is not, however, an inexorable command. In *Casey* we noted that when a Court is asked to overrule a precedent recognizing a constitutional liberty interest, individual or societal reliance on the existence of that liberty cautions with particular strength against reversing course. The holding in *Bowers,* however, has not induced detrimental reliance comparable to some instances where recognized individual rights are involved. Indeed, there has been no individual or societal reliance on *Bowers* of the sort that could counsel against overturning its holding once there are compelling reasons to do so. *Bowers* itself causes uncertainty, for the precedents before and after its issuance contradict its central holding. . . .

Bowers was not correct when it was decided, and it is not correct today. It ought not to remain binding precedent. *Bowers v. Hardwick* should be and now is overruled. . . .

Had those who drew and ratified the Due Process Clauses of the Fifth Amendment or the Fourteenth Amendment known the components of liberty in its manifold possibilities, they might have been more specific. They did not presume to have this insight. They knew times can blind us to certain truths and later generations can see that laws once thought necessary and proper in fact serve only to oppress. As the Constitution endures, persons in every generation can invoke its principles in their own search for greater freedom.

The judgment of the Court of Appeals for the Texas Fourteenth District is reversed, and the case is remanded for further proceedings not inconsistent with this opinion.

It is so ordered.

JUSTICE SCALIA, with whom THE CHIEF JUSTICE and JUSTICE THOMAS join, dissenting.

Most of . . . today's opinion has no relevance to its actual holding—that the Texas statute "furthers no legitimate state interest which can justify" its application to petitioners under rational-basis review. Though there is discussion of "fundamental proposition[s]," and "fundamental decisions," nowhere does the Court's opinion declare that homosexual sodomy is a "fundamental right" under the Due Process Clause; nor does it subject the Texas law to the standard of review that would be appropriate (strict scrutiny) if homosexual sodomy were a "fundamental right." Thus, while overruling the outcome of *Bowers,* the Court leaves strangely untouched its central legal conclusion: "[R]espondent would have us announce . . . a fundamental right to engage in homosexual sodomy. This we are quite unwilling to do." Instead the Court simply describes petitioners' conduct as "an exercise of their liberty"—which it undoubtedly is—and proceeds to apply an unheard-of form of rational-basis review that will have far-reaching implications beyond this case.

I begin with the Court's surprising readiness to reconsider a decision rendered a mere 17 years ago in *Bowers v. Hardwick.* I do not myself believe in rigid adherence to *stare decisis* in constitutional cases; but I do believe that we should be consistent rather than manipulative in invoking the doctrine. . . .

Today's opinion is the product of a Court, which is the product of a law-profession culture, that has largely signed on to the so-called homosexual agenda, by which I mean the agenda promoted by some homosexual activists directed at eliminating the moral opprobrium that has traditionally attached to homosexual conduct. I noted in an earlier opinion the fact that the American Association of Law Schools (to which any reputable law school must seek to belong) excludes from membership any school that refuses to ban from its job-interview facilities a law firm (no matter how small) that does not wish to hire as a prospective partner a person who openly engages in homosexual conduct. . . .

Let me be clear that I have nothing against homosexuals, or any other group, promoting their agenda through normal democratic means. Social perceptions of sexual and other morality change over time, and every group has the right to persuade its fellow citizens that its view of such matters is the best. That homosexuals have achieved some success in that enterprise is attested to by the fact that Texas is one of the few remaining States that criminalize private, consensual homosexual acts. But persuading one's fellow citizens is one thing, and imposing one's views in absence of democratic majority will is something else. I would no more require a State to criminalize homosexual acts—or, for that matter, display any moral disapprobation of them—than I would forbid it to do so.

What Texas has chosen to do is well within the range of traditional democratic action, and its hand should not be stayed through the invention of a brand-new "constitutional right" by a Court that is impatient of democratic change. It is indeed true that "later generations can see that laws once thought necessary and proper in fact serve only to oppress," and when that happens, later generations can repeal those laws. But it is the premise of our system that those judgments are to be made by the people, and not imposed by a governing caste that knows best.

A Comparative Perspective

1.9 Judicial Independence in Comparative Perspective (2001)

Peter H. Russell

. . . In the more well-established liberal democracies, . . . the growth of judicial power . . . has triggered contemporary concerns about judicial independence. An interesting irony is at work here. As courts, especially the highest courts, become more activist and autonomous in their decision making by upholding challenges to the activities of the other branches of government and by dealing with hotly contested issues of public law, they attract much more political attention and criticism. Thus an increase in judicial autonomy and power means that the judiciary becomes more directly connected to a democratic society's politics. This has certainly been the case in . . . Canada. And . . . it is very much the case in the United States, the United Kingdom, Australia, Germany, and the Latin countries of Western Europe.

When the judicial power becomes more politically dominant in well-developed democracies, the pressure on judicial independence is felt not in

the form of interference with individual judges in their decision making but in concerns about the judiciary as a whole—in particular, at the structural level and with the appointing system. In this context, Martin Shapiro's phrase is apt: judicial independence is secure "at retail" but not "at wholesale.". . . [T]he European Court of Justice (ECJ) has played such a powerful role in shaping the constitution of the European Union. There is no evidence that member states have tried to counter the ECJ's activism by pressuring individual judges. But the political leaders of the states that make up the EU's new "pillar" on justice and home affairs have shown their apprehension of the ECJ's power by being very tentative about extending judicial review to this new pillar. The ECJ, in turn, has shown its sensitivity to this political concern by drawing back from its aggressive deregulatory stance.

. . . [In] the United States, a country in which the judicial power has historically been the strongest, again we can see that, while the individual judge's security of tenure is well protected by the impeachment process, there is constant pressure from political critics of the courts on judicial structures

Peter H. Russell, "Judicial Independence in Comparative Perspective," in *Age of Democracy: Critical Perspectives from Around the World,* Peter H. Russell and David O'Brien, eds. (Charlottesville: University of Virginia Press, 2001). Reprinted with permission of University of Virginia Press.

aimed at reining in judicial power. Never was this pressure greater than when President Franklin D. Roosevelt, in reaction to judicial vetoes of his New Deal legislation, threatened to enlarge the Supreme Court and pack it with judges sympathetic to his policies. When the court-packing bill came under vigorous political attack, this very popular president withdrew it. The episode demonstrated . . . that the American people would not stand for "any crass tampering with judicial independence." Conversely, we should note that this most powerful of supreme courts, without any change in its structure or membership, did adjust its jurisprudence in the direction desired by the political forces supporting the president.

. . . [T]he advent of a domestic bill of rights and the high-profile international case concerning the extradition of former Chilean dictator, Augusto Pinochet, have increased political interest in judicial restructuring in Britain. The direction of reform is interesting. Though England is the very cradle of the ideal of judicial independence at the level of the individual judge, up to now it has not treated the judiciary as a separate branch of government. Once the judiciary is cast more clearly in the role of a guarantor of rights and a check and balance on government, its close entanglement with the other branches becomes less acceptable. While . . . Britain will not suddenly embrace a full separation of powers, [one observer] anticipates adoption of a more representative and less executive-dominated appointing system.

In Australia, reaction to a more activist and politically prominent High Court also highlights the appointing process. A right-of-center national government has used its unfettered monopoly of power over federal judicial appointments to reverse High Court decisions recognizing the rights of Australia's indigenous peoples. Though this has increased public discussion of the kind of judicial appointments commission under consideration in the United Kingdom, no Australian government has shown any serious interest in such a reform. Indeed, senior Australian judges, in a country remarkably ill prepared for the age of judicial activism, by issuing their own declaration on the principles of judicial independence, give the sense of being a judiciary virtually under a state of siege.

Israel, too, has witnessed a remarkable increase in the judiciary's involvement in hot political issues, including matters of national security. Here too, this expansion of judicial power has made the judiciary a subject of political debate. . . . [T]he Supreme Court has responded by fine-tuning its relationship with the political branches. In so doing, it has had to tread a fine line between not withdrawing from areas vital to the protection of citizens' rights and yet not overstepping its involvement to the point of undermining the public's respect, which is the essential buttress of judicial power.

. . . [S]ince World War II, the civil law countries of Western Europe have been going through a remarkable ideological change with respect to the role and status of the judiciary in governance. The essence of the change is the transformation of highly bureaucratized judiciaries into judiciaries that come closer to performing and being recognized as independent and separate branches of government. This transformation in part stems from the democratic restructuring of former fascist dictatorships. But it has also been occurring in democratic France.

This judicial mutation has had two major dimensions, both of which have important implications for judicial independence. One is the adoption of judicial constitutional review by a special constitutional court or tribunal. The other is a reduction of the executive's and senior judges' domination of the regular judiciary and an injection of political pluralism into the appointing process.

In adopting "bifurcated" justice systems, France, Germany, Italy, Spain, and Portugal have balanced off the quantum leap in judicial power that comes from constitutional judicial review, with institutional designs increasing political accountability. The specialized constitutional courts that exercise the formidable power of nullifying proposed or enacted laws found to be unconstitutional are tied closely to the political system. Elected politicians (not just from the governing party) play a direct role in selecting the members of the constitutional courts, and the pool of candidates extends well beyond the professional judiciary. Holding members of these tribunals to limited-term appointments ensures a continuing political influence on their composition. . . .

Japan presents an interesting contrast with the post-fascist democracies of Western Europe. The postwar constitution provided for a strong and independent judiciary with the power of constitutional review based on the unitary American model. This was combined with a continental European-style professional judiciary. . . . [T]hese arrangements, rather than leading to the judicialization of politics that has occurred in Europe, have resulted in a relatively quiescent, nonactivist judiciary in Japan. [The] explanation is that the cadre of senior judges that control the judicial hierarchy has remained ideologically close to the Liberal Democratic Party, which has dominated Japanese politics since the war. In this setting, the chief threat to judicial independence comes not, as some have alleged, from politicians' attempts to manipulate the judiciary from the outside but from the conformity imposed internally on lower court judges by the judicial elite.

Post-Communist democratic regimes in Europe have kept much closer to the postwar civil law model of Western Europe, including constitutional courts with the power of judicial review. . . . [T]his has produced a relatively activist judiciary fairly well purged of known Communists and capable of acting independently of the government. When this activism has led to major collisions with the government, the judiciary, especially constitutional courts, have come under serious structural threat. . . . [However,] there may be a good deal of public support for the judiciary in these situations. A constitutional court that spends its "institutional capital" intelligently not only can survive these confrontations but also can come out of them with a stronger popular base for the judiciary's independence. . . .

A strong commitment to judicial independence has been built into South Africa's new democratic constitution. The constitution provides for a judicial system that combines a European-style Constitutional Court with the English common law system of magistrates and superior courts, the latter staffed by experienced barristers. . . . It must provide the stability and reassurance South Africa needs at a time of rapid social and political change. At the same time, as a powerful institution whose personnel will for some time come predominantly from the white minority, it must also show that it is responsive to the needs of the ordinary South African. The key institution for balancing judicial independence and accountability in the new

South Africa is the Judicial Service Commission (JSC). The JSC plays the lead role in judicial selection and other personnel matters. Its openness and pluralistic composition provide some assurance of independence and responsiveness in judicial administration. . . . The Judicial Service Commission appears to be the common law analogue of the national judicial councils in the civil law countries of Western Europe.

A Judicial Service Commission considerably weaker than South Africa's was one of the reforms introduced in Hong Kong to modify executive domination of the judiciary during the final period of British colonial rule. This institution and other features of Hong Kong's common law judicial system were carried over under the Basic Law governing Hong Kong's reunification with China. . . .

However, where the judiciary is subject to the final authority of an unreformed totalitarian dictatorship, there are clearly externally imposed limits on its power. . . . The Hong Kong judiciary's survival as an independent and effective branch of government will be a unique measure of how much an independent judiciary can do to secure the independence of a political community. . . .

This brief summary of the experience of judicial independence in the[se] parts . . . should make us aware of how dependent a variable judicial independence is. How judicial independence is understood and institutionally provided for depends very much on the status of law in a society's political culture and on its general political circumstances.

The one point common to all the countries we have looked at is a growth in the power of the judiciary. In constitutional democracies, both new and old, judiciaries have become visible centers of power not only providing a credible adjudicative service for increasingly litigious societies but also exercising considerable leverage on controversial issues of public policy. This development has required an ironic trade-off. A judiciary cannot be powerful unless it enjoys a high level of institutional independence and its individual members are free from internal as well as external direction of their decision making. But the price to be paid for such power is close and continuous public scrutiny and contentious debate of what judges do as well as increasing demands that their selection, promotion, education, and discipline be subject to more open and representative processes. This [selection] sends plenty of signals of the threats to judicial independence that can come from this more direct contact of the judiciary with politics.

We clearly still have much to learn about how to balance the independence and accountability of powerful judiciaries in a manner that enables our political communities to be both liberal and democratic.

For Further Reading

Fried, Charles. *Saying What the Law Is: The Constitution in the Supreme Court* (Cambridge, Mass.: Harvard University Press, 2004).

Posner, Richard A. *Law, Pragmatism and Democracy* (Cambridge, Mass.: Harvard University Press, 2003).

Sunstein, Cass R. *The Second Bill of Rights: FDR'S Unfinished Revolution and Why We Need It More Than Ever* (New York: Basic Books, 2004).

Tushnet, Mark. *Taking the Constitution Away from the Courts* (Princeton, N.J.: Princeton University Press, 1999).

Chapter 2

Judicial Decision Making

Introduction

What explains how and why judges make decisions as they do? Are judges guided solely by factors that we associate with the law—rules, principles of jurisprudence, and legal precedent—when they decide a case? Or do judicial decisions reflect personal biases and policy preferences couched in the authoritative language of the law? The essays, speeches, and articles excerpted in this chapter center on one question: Do judges follow the legal or attitudinal model when making judicial decisions?

Foundations and History

In Chapter 1, we discussed the influence of Oliver Wendell Holmes Jr.'s *The Common Law* on American law. There is not sufficient space here to give Holmes's contributions the attention they deserve. However, Holmes's belief that law is a dynamic and responsive instrument to changing social, economic, and political needs certainly ranks as among his most influential and lasting observations about the relationship of law, politics, and society. Among the first and most notable of American jurists to bring Holmes's ideas to the forefront of the judicial task was Benjamin N. Cardozo, whose classic exposition on the influence of external forces in judicial decision making, *The Nature of the Judicial Process* (1921), is excerpted here. Prior to his distinguished service on the Supreme Court, Cardozo served on the New York Court of Appeals. From this very visible platform, Cardozo wrote that law does not develop independent of social forces, but in tandem with them. He also dispelled the idea that judges approach the law in "coldly objective and impersonal" terms. In perhaps the most famous passage from his book, Cardozo wrote that "[t]he great tides and currents which engulf the rest of men, do not turn their course, and pass the judges by." Cardozo was an important figure in the *legal realist* movement, and helped frame future debates between scholars from law, political science, and sociology on the importance of attitudinal versus legal factors in judicial decision making.

By the late 1950s, a small group of political scientists studying law and the courts had begun to move away from the belief that case precedent, jurisprudential norms, and legal doctrine explained judicial decision making. In their view, the personal attitudes embodying the policy preferences of individual judges better explain judicial decision making. If judges are truly bound by traditional legal factors, then what explains their differences in voting behavior on identical legal questions? One early pioneer who transformed the way political scientists think about judicial decision making was Glendon Schubert, who was among the first to apply statistical analysis to the voting behavior of judges. In "Ideologies and Attitudes, Academic and Judicial" (1958), Schubert offers a clear description of what he calls the *traditional, conventional,* and *behavioral* approaches to judicial decision making. As you read this excerpt, consider the following questions: Does Schubert argue that one approach should dominate over the other, or does he suggest that each way of thinking about judicial decision making offers something useful?

Contemporary Judicial Politics

In this section, we offer three readings that provide three different yet interrelated approaches to thinking about judicial decision making. Lee Epstein and Tracey George, in their article "On the Nature of Supreme Court Decision Making" (1992), suggest that neither the "legal" nor the "extralegal" model provides a conclusive explanation of judicial behavior. Rather, they suggest that a codependent model incorporating legal and attitudinal variables can best explain, at least in this case, the Supreme Court's decision-making process. Moreover, this article serves as a fairly representative example of how behavioral scientists working in the field of judicial politics approach the study of judicial decision making. As a student, ask yourself if the assumptions of the attitudinal model hold up under scrutiny, and whether there is, in fact, such a thing as the legal model.

Howard Gillman's essay, "What's Law Got to Do with It? Judicial Behavioralists Test the 'Legal Model' of Judicial Decision Making" (2001), offers a marked contrast to as well as some pointed criticism of the behavioral approach to judicial decision making. Gillman is a political scientist who reflects a countermovement among some contemporary scholars to challenge many of the behavioralist assumptions about judicial decision making. He argues that legal factors, and, more generally, various aspects of the legal culture, should continue to inform the way that scholars think about judicial decision making. Far from considering legal factors obsolete, Gillman suggests that professional obligations and jurisprudential schools of thought continue to exercise influence in judicial decision making, and maintains that we can have a better-informed understanding of this process by keeping such considerations relevant in the way scholars approach the question.

Finally, we offer an excerpt from law professor Cass Sunstein's important book *One Case at a Time: Judicial Minimalism and the Supreme Court* (1999). Sunstein does not enter the debate over what motivates judges to decide cases in the way that they do. Rather, his concern is over *how* judges should decide cases. He eschews the stereotype that liberals like sweeping constitutional decisions whereas conservatives prefer deferring to the wishes of the elected branches. Sunstein argues that judges can best promote democratic deliberation in the elected branches by deciding constitutional questions according to certain moral and legal principles, but in the narrowest of terms. More interested in theories of jurisprudence than explanations of judicial decision making, Sunstein argues that leaving as much as possible to the democratic process while giving judges the authority to decide and, when necessary, correct matters of constitutional principle offers the best understanding of the judicial role.

A View from the Inside

Do the views of judges offered off the bench help explain how they approach the questions before them when hearing cases? To explore this question, we offer two excerpts from two contemporary Supreme Court justices, Justice John Paul Stevens and Justice Clarence Thomas, who occupy very different points on the ideological spectrum. Stevens, appointed to the Court in 1975 by President Gerald R. Ford, a Republican, has always held a reputation for being independent-minded in his approach to constitutional interpretation. Over the years, however, he has evolved from being a moderate without a clear ideological vision to becoming perhaps the Rehnquist Court's most consistently liberal justice. In his essay, "The Freedom of Speech" (1993), Justice Stevens argues that the First Amendment requires free societies to "tolerate intolerant speech," and maintains that constitutional protection for unpopular ideas serves democracies far better than does repression. Justice Stevens's views provide insight into how individual justices approach a particular constitutional problem outside the context of the Court's opinion-writing process.

Since his appointment to the Supreme Court in 1991, Clarence Thomas has earned a reputation as one of the Court's most conservative justices. Thomas's conservatism is reflected not just in his voting record, but in his willingness to revisit and, in many cases, overturn previous cases that he believes deviate from the intent of the Founders or the framers of subsequent constitutional amendments. In *Zelman v. Simmons-Harris* (2002), Justice Thomas, while agreeing with the Court's decision to uphold a state law that permitted religious schools to receive direct payments from a tuition voucher program, wrote separately to question whether the Establishment Clause of the First Amendment applied to the states through the Fourteenth Amendment. Justice Thomas suggested that the true purpose behind the Fourteenth Amendment was to require the states to establish equal rights for all persons, while the design of the Establishment Clause was to limit the national government on matters of religion, but not the states. Although Thomas's opinion did not carry the day, it does offer a clear statement of what many scholars refer to as the originalist approach to constitutional interpretation.

A Comparative Perspective

Judges serving on constitutional courts in the United States are not the only jurists who hold varying views on how to conduct their craft. In "Constitutional Interpretation and Original Intent—A Form of Ancestor Worship?" (1999), Australian jurist Michael Kirby offers a unique perspective on judicial decision making. He compares what he calls the American reliance on "ancestor worship" in constitutional interpretation with the less historically bound and more "creative" approach favored by judges such as himself. Are Justice Kirby's views more in line with the attitudinal or legalist approach to judicial decision making? Do you think that a comparative perspective offers insight into how American judges handle their responsibilities?

Foundations and History

2.1 ## From *The Nature of the Judicial Process* (1921)

Benjamin Cardozo

Lecture I. Introduction. The Method of Philosophy.

The work of deciding cases goes on every day in hundreds of courts throughout the land. Any judge, one might suppose, would find it easy to describe the process which he had followed a thousand times and more. Nothing could be farther from the truth. Let some intelligent layman ask him to explain: he will not go very far before taking refuge in the excuse that the language of craftsmen is unintelligible to those untutored in the craft. Such an excuse may cover with a semblance of respectability an otherwise ignominious retreat. It will hardly serve to still the pricks of curiosity and conscience. In moments of introspection, when there is no longer a necessity of putting off with a show of wisdom the uninitiated interlocutor, the troublesome problem will recur, and press for a solution. What is it that I do when I decide a case? To what sources of information do I appeal for guidance? In what proportions do I permit them to contribute to the result? In what proportions ought they to contribute? If a precedent is applicable, when do I refuse to follow it? If no precedent is applicable, how do I reach the rule that will make a precedent

for the future? If I am seeking logical consistency, the symmetry of the legal structure, how far shall I seek it? At what point shall the quest be halted by some discrepant custom, by some consideration of the social welfare, by my own or the common standards of justice and morals? Into that strange compound which is brewed daily in the caldron of the courts, all these ingredients enter in varying proportions. I am not concerned to inquire whether judges ought to be allowed to brew such a compound at all. I take judge-made law as one of the existing realities of life. There, before us, is the brew. Not a judge on the bench but has had a hand in the making. The elements have not come together by chance. *Some* principle, however unavowed and inarticulate and subconscious, has regulated the infusion. It may not have been the same principle for all judges at any time, nor the same principle for any judge at all times. But a choice there has been, not a submission to the decree of Fate; and the considerations and motives determining the choice, even if often obscure, do not utterly resist analysis. In such attempt at analysis as I shall make, there will be need to distinguish between the conscious and the subconscious. I do not mean that even those considerations and motives which I shall class under the first head are always in consciousness distinctly, so that they will be recognized and named at sight. Not infrequently they hover near the surface. They may, however, with comparative readiness be isolated and tagged, and when thus labeled, are quickly acknowledged as guiding principles of conduct. More subtle are the forces so far beneath the surface that they cannot reasonably be classified as other than subconscious. It is often through these subconscious forces that judges are kept consistent with themselves, and inconsistent with one another. We are reminded by William James in a telling page of his lectures on Pragmatism that every one of us has in truth an underlying philosophy of life, even those of us to whom the names and the notions of philosophy are unknown or anathema. There is in each of us a stream of tendency, whether you choose to call it philosophy or not, which gives coherence and direction to thought and action. Judges cannot escape that current any more than other mortals. All their lives, forces which they do not recognize and cannot name, have been tugging at them—inherited instincts, traditional beliefs, acquired convictions; and the resultant is an outlook on life, a conception of social needs, a sense in James's phrase of "the total push and pressure of the cosmos," which, when reasons are nicely balanced, must determine where choice shall fall. In this mental background every problem finds its setting. We may try to see things as objectively as we please. None the less, we can never see them with any eyes except our own. To that test they are all brought—a form of pleading or an act of parliament, the wrongs of paupers or the rights of princes, a village ordinance or a nation's charter. . . .

. . . The work of a judge in interpreting and developing [the law] has indeed its problems and its difficulties, but they are problems and difficulties not different in kind or measure from those besetting him in other fields. I think they can be better studied when those fields have been explored. Sometimes the rule of constitution or of statute is clear, and then the difficulties vanish. Even when they are present, they lack at times some of that element of mystery which accompanies creative energy. We reach the land of mystery when constitution and statute are silent, and the judge must look to the common law for the rule that fits the case. . . . [V]iewing his work in the dry light of realism, how does he set about his task?

The first thing he does is to compare the case before him with the precedents, whether stored in his mind or hidden in the books. I do not mean that precedents are ultimate sources of the law, supplying the sole equipment that is needed for the legal armory, the sole tools, to borrow Maitland's phrase, "in the legal smithy." Back of precedents are the basic juridical conceptions which are the postulates of judicial reasoning, and farther back are the habits of life, the institutions of society, in which those conceptions had their origin, and which, by a process of interaction, they have modified in turn. None the less, in a system so highly developed as our own, precedents have so covered the ground that they fix the point of departure from which the labor of the judge begins. Almost invariably, his first step is to examine and compare them. If they are plain and to the point, there may be need of nothing more. *Stare decisis* is at least the everyday working rule of our law. I shall have something to say later about the propriety of relaxing the rule in exceptional conditions. But unless those conditions are present, the work of deciding cases in accordance with precedents that plainly fit them is a process similar in its nature to that of deciding cases in accordance with a statute. It is a process of search, comparison, and little more. Some judges seldom get beyond that process in any case. Their notion of their duty is to match the colors of the case at hand against the colors of many sample cases spread out upon their desk. The sample nearest in shade supplies the applicable rule. But, of course, no system of living law can be evolved by such a process, and no judge of a high court, worthy of his office, views the function of his place so narrowly. If that were all there was to our calling, there would be little of intellectual interest about it. The man who had the best card index of the cases would also be the wisest judge. It is when the colors do not match, when the references in the index fail, when there is no decisive precedent, that the serious business of the judge begins. He must then fashion law for the litigants before him. In fashioning it for them, he will be fashioning it for others. The classic statement is Bacon's: "For many times, the things deduced to judgment may be meum and tuum, when the reason and consequence thereof may trench to point of estate." The sentence of today will make the right and wrong of tomorrow. If the judge is to pronounce it wisely, some principles of selection there must be to guide him among all the potential judgments that compete for recognition.

In the life of the mind as in life elsewhere, there is a tendency toward the reproduction of kind. Every judgment has a generative power. It begets in its own image. Every precedent, in the words of Redlich, has a "directive force for future cases of the same or similar nature." Until the sentence was pronounced, it was as yet in equilibrium. Its form and content were uncertain. Any one of many principles might lay hold of it and shape it. Once declared, it is a new stock of descent. It is charged with vital power. It is the source from which new principles or norms may spring to shape sentences thereafter. If we seek the psychological basis of this tendency, we shall find it, I suppose, in habit. Whatever its psychological basis, it is one of the living forces of our law. Not all the progeny of principles begotten of a judgment survive, however, to maturity. Those that cannot prove their worth and strength by the test of experience, are sacrificed mercilessly and thrown into the void. The common law does not work from pre-established truths of universal and inflexible validity to conclusions derived from them deductively. Its method is inductive, and it draws its generalizations from particulars. . . . The rules and principles of case law have never been treated as final truths, but as working hypotheses, continually retested in those great laboratories of the law, the courts of justice. Every new case is an experiment; and if the accepted rule which seems applicable yields a result which is felt to be unjust, the rule is reconsidered. It may not be modified at once, for the attempt to do absolute justice in every single case would make the development and maintenance of general rules impossible; but if a rule continues to work injustice, it will eventually be reformulated. The principles themselves are continually retested; for if the rules derived from a principle do not work well, the principle itself must ultimately be re-examined."

Lecture III. The Method of Sociology. The Judge as a Legislator

. . . But the truth is that there is no branch where the [sociological] method is not fruitful. Even when it does not seem to dominate, it is always in re-serve. It is the arbiter between other methods, determining in the last analysis the choice of each, weighing their competing claims, setting bounds to their pretensions, balancing and moderating and harmonizing them all. Few rules in our time are so well established that they may not be called upon any day to justify their existence as means adapted to an end. If they do not function, they are diseased. If they are diseased, they must not propagate their kind. Sometimes they are cut out and extirpated altogether. Sometimes they are left with the shadow of continued life, but sterilized, truncated, impotent for harm.

We get a striking illustration of the force of logical consistency, then of its gradual breaking down before the demands of practical convenience in isolated or exceptional instances, and finally of the generative force of the exceptions as a new stock, in the cases that deal with the right of a beneficiary to recover on a contract. England has been logically consistent and has refused the right of action altogether. New York and most states yielded to the demands of convenience and enforced the right of action, but at first only exceptionally and subject to many restrictions. Gradually the exceptions broadened till today they have left little of the rule. It survives chiefly in those cases where intention would be frustrated or convenience impaired by the extension of the right of action to others than the contracting parties. Rules derived by a process of logical deduction from pre-established conceptions of contract and obligation have broken down before the slow and steady erosive action of utility and justice. . . .

This conception of the end of the law as determining the direction of its growth . . . finds its organon, its instrument, in the method of sociology. Not the origin, but the goal, is the main thing. There can be no wisdom in the choice of a path unless we know where it will lead. The teleological conception of his function must be ever in the judge's mind. This means, of course, that the juristic philosophy of the common law is at bottom the philosophy of pragmatism. Its truth is relative, not absolute. The rule that functions well produces a title deed to recognition. Only in determining how it functions we must not view it too narrowly. We must not sacrifice the general to the particular. We must not throw to the winds the advantages of consistency and uniformity to do justice in the instance. We must keep within those interstitial limits which precedent and custom and the long and silent and almost indefinable practice of other judges through the centuries of the common law have set to judge-made innovations. But within the limits thus set, within the range over which choice moves, the final principle of selection for judges, as for legislators, is one of fitness to an end. "*Le but est la vie interne, l'âme cachée, mais génératrice, de tous les droits.*" We do not pick our rules of law full-blossomed from the trees. Every judge consulting his own experience must be conscious of times when a free exercise of will, directed of set purpose to the furtherance of the common good, determined the form and tendency of a rule which at that moment took its origin in one creative act. Savigny's conception of law as something realized without struggle or aim or purpose, a process of silent growth, the fruition in life and manners of a people's history and genius, gives a picture incomplete and partial. It is true if we understand it to mean that the judge in shaping the rules of law must heed the *mores* of his day. It is one-sided and therefore false in so far as it implies that the *mores* of the day automatically shape rules which, full grown and ready made, are handed to the judge. Legal norms are confused with legal principles. . . . Law is, indeed, an historical growth, for it is an expression of customary morality which develops silently and unconsciously from one age to another. That is the great truth in Savigny's theory of its origin. But law is also a conscious or purposed growth, for the expression of customary morality will be false unless the mind of the judge is directed to the attainment of the moral end and its embodiment in legal forms. Nothing less than conscious effort will be adequate if the end in view is to prevail. The standards or patterns of utility and morals will be found by the judge in the life of the community. They will be found in the same way by the legislator. That does not mean, however, that the work of the one any more than that of the other is a replica of nature's forms. . . .

My analysis of the judicial process comes then to this, and little more: logic, and history, and custom, and utility, and the accepted standards of right conduct, are the forces which singly or in combination shape the progress of the law. Which of these forces shall dominate in any case, must depend largely upon the comparative importance or value of the social interests that will be thereby promoted or impaired. One of the most fundamental social interests is that law shall be uniform and impartial. There must be nothing in its action that savors of prejudice or favor or even arbitrary whim or fitfulness. Therefore in the main there shall be adherence to precedent. There shall be symmetrical development, consistently with history or custom when history or custom has been the motive force, or the chief one, in giving shape to existing rules, and with logic or philosophy when the motive power has been theirs. But symmetrical development may be bought at too high a price. Uniformity ceases to be a good when it becomes uniformity of oppression. The social interest served by symmetry or certainty must then be balanced against the social interest served by equity and fairness or other elements of social welfare. These may enjoin upon the judge the duty of drawing the line at another angle, of staking the path along new courses, of marking a new point of departure from which others who come after him will set out upon their journey.

If you ask how he is to know when one interest outweighs another, I can only answer that he must get his knowledge just as the legislator gets it, from experience and study and reflection; in brief, from life itself. Here, indeed, is the point of contact between the legislator's work and his. The choice of methods, the appraisement of values, must in the end be guided by like considerations for the one as for the other. Each indeed is legislating within the limits of his competence. No doubt the limits for the judge are narrower. He legislates only between gaps. He fills the open spaces in the law. How far he may go without traveling beyond the walls of the interstices cannot be staked out for him upon a chart. He must learn it for himself as he gains the sense of fitness and proportion that comes with years of habitude in the practice of an art. Even within the gaps, restrictions not easy to define, but felt, however impalpable they may be, by every judge and lawyer, hedge and circumscribe his action. They are established by the traditions of the centuries, by the example of other judges, his predecessors and his colleagues, by the collective judgment of the profession, and by the duty of adherence to the pervading spirit of the law. . . .

There is in truth nothing revolutionary or even novel in this view of the judicial function. It is the way that courts have gone about their business for centuries in the development of the common law. The difference from age to age is not so much in the recognition of the need that law shall conform itself to an end. It is rather in the nature of the end to which there has been need to conform. There have been periods when uniformity, even rigidity, the elimination of the personal element, were felt to be the paramount needs. By a sort of paradox, the end was best served by disregarding it and thinking only of the means. Gradually the need of a more flexible system asserted itself. Often the gɔ between the old rule and the new was bridged by the pious fraud of a fiction. The thing which concerns us here is that it was bridged whenever the importance of the end was dominant. Today the use of fictions has declined; and the springs of action are disclosed where once they were concealed. . . .

Our survey of judicial methods teaches us, I think, the lesson that the whole subject-matter of jurisprudence is more plastic, more malleable, the moulds less definitively cast, the bounds of right and wrong less preordained and constant, than most of us, without the aid of some such analysis, have been accustomed to believe. We like to picture to ourselves the field of the law as accurately mapped and plotted. We draw our little lines, and they are hardly down before we blur them. As in time and space, so here. Divisions are working hypotheses, adopted for convenience. We are tending more and more toward an appreciation of the truth that, after all, there are few rules; there are chiefly standards and degrees. . . .

I have spoken of the forces of which judges avowedly avail to shape the form and content of their judgments. Even these forces are seldom fully in consciousness. They lie so near the surface, however, that their existence and influence are not likely to be disclaimed. But the subject is not exhausted with the recognition of their power. Deep below consciousness are other forces, the likes and the dislikes, the predilections and the prejudices, the complex of instincts and emotions and habits and convictions, which make the man, whether he be litigant or judge. I wish I might have found the time and opportunity to pursue this subject farther.

I shall be able, as it is, to do little more than remind you of its existence. There has been a certain lack of candor in much of the discussion of the theme, or rather perhaps in the refusal to discuss it, as if judges must lose respect and confidence by the reminder that they are subject to human limitations. I do not doubt the grandeur of the conception which lifts them into the realm of pure reason, above and beyond the sweep of perturbing and deflecting forces. None the less, if there is anything of reality in my analysis of the judicial process, they do not stand aloof on these chill and distant heights; and we shall not help the cause of truth by acting and speaking as if they do. The great tides and currents which engulf the rest of men, do not turn aside in their course, and pass the judges by. We like to figure to ourselves the processes of justice as coolly objective and impersonal. The law, conceived of as a real existence, dwelling apart and alone, speaks, through the voices of priests and ministers, the words which they have no choice except to utter. That is an ideal of objective truth toward which every system of jurisprudence tends. It is an ideal of which great publicists and judges have spoken as of something possible to attain. . . .

I have no quarrel . . . with the doctrine that judges ought to be in sympathy with the spirit of their times. Alas! assent to such a generality does not carry us far upon the road to truth. In every court there are likely to be as many estimates of the "Zeitgeist" as there are judges on its bench. Of the power of favor or prejudice in any sordid or vulgar or evil sense, I have found no trace, not even the faintest, among the judges whom I have known. But every day there is borne in on me a new conviction of the inescapable relation between the truth without us and the truth within. The spirit of the age, as it is revealed to each of us, is too often only the spirit of the group in which the accidents of birth or education or occupation or fellowship have given us a place. No effort or revolution of the mind will overthrow utterly and at all times the empire of these subconscious loyalties. . . .

2.2 | Ideologies and Attitudes, Academic and Judicial (1958)

Glendon Schubert

The Critical Function

Many of those academicians who are most vehement, in their disputation of the relevance of attitudinal analysis to political science argue from premises that are patently ideological in character. . . .

The range of the differences among us in the extent to which we seek to be either "political" or "scientific" in our own work makes it difficult for persons at the antipodes of these two continua to engage in effective communication with each other, let alone to find a level of discourse at which they profitably can debate each other's work. It may, therefore, be of greater benefit to the profession if we eschew logomachy—a game that both behavioralists and their critics can play without generating much light—in favor of an attempt to answer the question why political scientists do divide so sharply in their perceptions of others', as well as of their own, work. The major underlying cause, we might hypothesize, lies in these persons' divergent ideological orientations toward their professional work. A first step toward better common understanding may well consist of a clearer delineation of the relevant academic ideologies; and in an attempt to take that first step, I have suggested that among political scientists today, the three most important orientations toward study of law and courts are the *traditional,* the *conventional,* and the *behavioral.*

Academic Ideologies

The traditional approach among political scientists is that of the public lawyer, who is content to define his subject-matter as constitutional law. . . .

The conventional ideology is aptly so called because it corresponds to the modal, or political process, approach among political scientists today—when their subject matter is anything other than courts and law. The characteristic point of

From *American Political Science Review* 52 (1958): 1007–1025. Reprinted with the permission of Cambridge University Press.

view is that courts are political institutions and judges are political decision-makers, and therefore that political scientists ought to study them in the same way that they would seek to understand any other political phenomenon. . . .

Judicial behavioralism is an attempt to construct a systematic theory about human behavior, analyzing data about judges and adjudicatory processes of decision-making by using theories and methods from all of the behavioral sciences, according to their relevance to the particular inquiry at hand. . . .

The . . . ideologies can be viewed, alternatively, as the midpoints of segments which correspond to the humanities, the social sciences, and the behavioral sciences, respectively. The resulting sequence of academic disciplines (ranging from law through history, economics, political science, sociology, psychology, biology, anthropology, philosophy, and thus back to law) is of course schematic, but it may have some heuristic value in suggesting the ordinal relationship of the modal tendencies for the frequency distributions of ideological standpoints in these fields. Thus the humanities tend to be concerned with what we might call the letter of the law; the social sciences, with legal institutions and political groups; and the behavioral sciences, with the personality of legal decision-makers. Accordingly, the characteristic focus of attention of the three major ideological standpoints has been that traditionalists study law, conventionalists study courts, and behavioralists study judges. . . .

It is hardly surprising that behavioral research in the attitudes of judges has met with considerable skepticism, much discounting, and more than a little just plain disbelief. Given the value predispositions of most of the relevant professional audience, it could not have been otherwise.

Academic Attitudes

Academic ideologies tend to determine academic attitudes toward the study of judicial attitudes. Attitudinal differences imply differing choices among such core components of academic attitudes as modes of discourse, logic, statistical literacy, rationality, empiricism, methodology, and scientism. We shall now examine some of the differences in academic attitudes toward attitudinal research, in regard to each of these facets.

Concepts

From the traditionalist point of view, a judge's decisions are determined in part by an authoritative structure of norms (the law), in the manipulation of which he is skilled; and in part by what is called the judge's "philosophy." By judicial philosophy, public law scholars mean the judge's views on questions of public policy, which usually are related to a broadly defined linear continuum of liberalism and conservatism.

From the conventional point of view, judicial decision-making is the product of interaction among social groups; and the judge functions as a transmission belt for the articulation of group (social) interests. But group interests are equated to particular positions in regard to proposed dispositions of questions of public policy.

Hence concepts analogous to the behavioral concept of "attitude" are central to both the traditional approach and the conventional approach. This might suggest the facile conclusion that the problem of conflicting academic ideologies is primarily a matter of words, and that "philosophy," "group interests," and judicial "attitudes" are synonymous. There may be more truth in this observation than has been recognized, but there remain important differences in weighting. Behavioralists assign a predominant weight to judicial personality as a source of substantive decisional norms; traditionalists assign a subordinate weight, looking to the law as the more important and more usual source of norms; while conventionalists assign a minimal—usually zero—weight to the judge's personal values (as distinguished from his social role). It is not surprising, therefore, that most of the critique of so-called "attitudinal-statistical" analysis has come from conventionally-oriented rather than from traditionally-oriented scholars. Moreover, the conventional critique of scale analysis of judicial attitudes has been couched in what purports to be a dispassionate, and even a technical correction, of behavioralist blunders, by real experts in the theory and methods of social psychology. It seems appropriate, therefore, to examine the core arguments of

the critique of attitudinal analysis, since this offers some promise of constituting a subject upon which a more scientific debate might be possible. . . .

In order for rational decision-making to take place, it is not necessary that all justices be in precise agreement concerning the "facts of the case," as these might be inferred from the record. It *is* essential that they be in substantial agreement concerning what issue they are going to decide; and most of the time they are in such agreement. To the extent that agreement is lacking, clues usually are provided by separate opinions and by *jurisdictional* dissents. When their disagreement is sufficiently important (notwithstanding the milieu of consensus-pointing norms in which they work) to lead them to be willing to signify it in the articulate form of opinion-language or a minority vote, Supreme Court justices typically disagree about *how* the issue should be decided—not about what issue the case presents. Since those justices who join in it have agreed to accept the common opinion of the Court, in addition to voting the same way in the disposition of the case, it is reasonable to accept what they say there as evidence concerning the issue(s) to which their decision relates. Of course, not all justices are agreed upon consensual definitions of the issues in all cases; and to the extent that they are not in agreement, this is one (among several) of the sources of error variance. However, if this were a major difficulty, it ought to result in fewer and poorer, not more and better, acceptable cumulative scales. The procedure tests the hypothesis that all justices are responding to the same issue, in each set of votes (decision) of the scale. The only possible effect that can be produced by empirical deviations from the hypothesis is to *lower* the consistency apparent in the scale. We ought to expect that a set of judges, each responding individually to a different item in a miscellany of issues, will vote in random, not in consistent, patterns.

Statistical Literacy

(Un)critical references to "attitudinal-statistical" work tend to create the quite false impression that cumulative scaling is a statistical technique. A scalogram is an ordering of empirical data into a pattern, according to predetermined rules; it is neither a statistic nor the result of statistical analysis. Any claim to the contrary hardly rises above the vulgar linguistic practices whereby "statistics" are used as a substitute for "data," or the latter are used to refer to a single item. Once a scale—the ordering of empirical data in a particular pattern—has been constructed, the question then arises whether (and if so to what extent) the contrived pattern differs from a chance ordering of the same data, or from the least consistent pattern possible for these particular data, given such empirical parameters as the number of participants in each decision, and the number of decisions participated in by each respondent. The researcher can use his own judgment in this matter, just as one might examine a painting, by staring at the scale and thereby arriving at a subjective judgment concerning how consistently the justices voted in the cases that comprise the scale. Or the researcher might undertake to contrive some ad hoc index to help guide his judgment; this procedure would at least tend to assure greater consistency in the researcher's *own* judgments, concerning a set of different scales, than if he were to rely exclusively upon his intuitions and impressions. The difficulty with both of these procedures is that no two researchers are likely to come up with either the same subjective judgments or the same ad hoc indices; and even if they should happen to arrive at identical judgments, there is no precise way in which they can communicate this information to each other. . . .

Judicial Ideologies

In the study of judicial decision-making, policy attitudinal analysis is a necessary but by no means a sufficient condition for the development of comprehensive and systematic theory. Even a cursory knowledge of such earlier work as . . . Cardozo's lectures on "The Nature of the Judicial Process" suggests the probably critical relevance of sociometric analysis of intragroup relationships, and of biological parameters, to the task of constructing more general models. The study of judicial attitudes towards public policy issues focuses upon the sector of *cultural* parameters for judicial decision-making, since the belief systems of individual justices necessarily reflect the socialization effects of a lifetime of exposure both as a youth and as a professional, usually within the milieu of the same (at least, taking the nation as the universe) system

of values. . . . It is not necessary to assume that knowledge about judicial attitudes will explain everything about the decisions that (for example) the Supreme Court makes; it is enough to be warranted in assuming that a focus upon the attitudes of the justices toward policy issues will explain part of what we do not yet fully understand. Attempts to illuminate this one sector (among the several others) of our ignorance may also be of value in delineating the boundaries between cultural, social, psychological, and biological subsystems of the judicial decision-making process. . . .

The Function of Criticism

The foregoing analysis of the contemporary critique of judicial scaling should not be construed to imply that behavioral research is not subject to criticism. It is, and for mistakes at all levels and stages of research, from model-building to design to the details of empirical analysis of decisional content. And this is a kind of criticism which is much needed. No doubt some behavioralists have hesitated to publish technical criticism of each other's work, because of fears that to do so would give aid and comfort to traditionalist and conventionalist "enemies," who could be expected to seize upon any confessions of error and to exploit them as admissions of guilt. But surely, such a posture is appropriate—if at all—to the toddling stage; and it is out of place now that the question whether the behavioral approach is a passing fancy appears to be settled, and no longer necessary to debate. If behavioral research in adjudication is to improve its capacity to explain the past and to describe the present and to predict the future, it needs criticism from all points of view. Conversely, traditional research and conventional research might profit from behavioral critique.

To be effective, critics must make a much larger effort than has been apparent in the past, to carry on the discussion in the conceptual terms of the *subject* of their criticism—not necessarily those preferred by the critic. This implies that would-be critics must attempt to familiarize themselves with more than one language and level of discourse. Here is where a greater awareness and understanding of the respective points of view characteristic of the three academic ideologies becomes of crucial importance. Then, instead of traditionalists communicating almost exclusively with other traditionalists, conventionalists with conventionalists, and behavioralists with behavioralists, transideological discourse may become possible, and even common. And why not?

The field no longer is public law, but neither is it the judicial process, nor judicial behavior. It is all three of these, and is likely to remain such a combination for some time to come. Neither the tradi-

tionalist, the conventionalist, nor the behavioralist has a corner on the market of either wisdom or knowledge about adjudicatory processes; to the contrary, each is specialized in differing emphases upon what is important (or feasible) to study, and how to study it. The time has come when we all should give greater attention to how we can learn from each other, and less to the contemplation of our respective ideological umbilici.

Contemporary Judical Politics

2.3 What's Law Got to Do with It? Judicial Behavioralists Test the "Legal Model" of Judicial Decision Making (2001)

Howard Gillman

Does law influence judicial decision making? Many scholars, in law schools and elsewhere, spend a great deal of time reviewing, categorizing, and engaging legal texts. They assume that by knowing various rules, principles, or structures of argument we will be in a better position to understand a wide range of social relations and political practices, including why judges decide cases as they do. Advocates and analysts know that there is a personal element to judging, and they realize that a case often turns on who is making the decision. But it is also widely believed that the personal element is either checked, constrained, or filtered through distinctive professional obligations and jurisprudential schools of thought. It would be considered malpractice if a lawyer who was preparing a case asked only about a judge's partisan affiliation and spent no time reading past opinions and researching the state of the law. Judges reinforce this judgment by requiring lawyers to talk about precedents and doctrines and by writing opinions filled with arguments about precedents and doc-

trines. The entire structure of legal education and the nature of the judicial process in the United States is premised on the assumption that, one way or the other, law matters.

But not everyone agrees—at least not when talking about the U.S. Supreme Court. In other corners of the university, and increasingly even within the ranks of the law professorate, it is widely considered a settled social scientific fact that law has almost no influence on the justices. Most of these scholars are positivist-empiricists who insist, not unreasonably, that the impressions of "jurisprudentially inclined scholars" and the testimony of judges should not be taken at face value. From their point of view, decades of social science research designed to test these impressions has demonstrated instead that ideological and political considerations drive decision making. This research has been so completely internalized by many political scientists that it is considered the common sense of the discipline that Supreme Court justices (and, in the minds of many, appellate judges in general) should be viewed as promoters of their personal policy preferences rather than as interpreters of law. . . .

Judicial Behavioralism and the Law

The law professorate may think of critical legal scholars as the more modern heirs of the legal realist tradition, but it may be more accurate to say that among contemporary scholars none is more self-identified with that school of thought than judicial behavioralists. More than any other scholars over the past few decades, behavioralists embody the efforts of the realists to demonstrate that law is vague, internally inconsistent, revisable, or otherwise not amenable to a formal process of neutral application or logical deduction. They have taken to heart Holmes's famous aphorisms that "you can give any conclusion a logical form" but "behind the logical form lies a judgment as to the relative worth and importance of competing legislative grounds," and that "a legal duty so called is nothing but a prediction that if a man does or omits certain things he will be made to suffer in this or that way by judgment of the court." . . .

With rare exception, however, these early efforts to draw attention to the personal elements of judicial decision making had almost no sustained impact on the research agendas of law professors, for whom doctrinal analysis remained a preferred activity over improving empirical predictions about observable judicial behavior. It also took a while before behavioralism had an influence within political science. Political scientists such as Thomas Reed Powell, Charles Grove Haines, Edward S. Corwin, and Robert E. Cushman (among others) felt themselves in league with the law professorate in the interpretive-political analysis of public law. Even as the behavioral revolution started to unfold, scholars such as Alpheus Mason, C. Herman Pritchett, Robert G. McCloskey, Walter Murphy, and Martin Shapiro paved the way for vast numbers of political scientists who, to this day, adopt nonquantitative approaches to the study of law and courts.

But with the study of judicial behavior remaining unexplored in law schools an opportunity arose for some political scientists to distinguish their work from more jurisprudentially minded colleagues. [C. Herman] Pritchett took the first step in his [1948] study of the judicial voting blocs on "the Roosevelt Court," but he considered this work a modest supplement to more orthodox analyses of

legal doctrine, which he felt were still essential to an understanding of judicial decision making. It was not until Glendon Schubert's work [in the 1950s and 1960s] that some scholars in political science made the transformation (to borrow a title phrase from one of his essays) "From Public Law to Judicial Behavior."

As is suggested by this title, for a long time the focus on behavior meant that legal variables disappeared from the analysis. After all, the point of focusing on behavior was that one did not have to worry about the law. Some behavioralists claimed that this was actually a disciplinary advantage over traditional legal scholars, since legal reasoning was essentially "a low form of rational behavior," no more a science "than creative writing, necromancy, or finger painting." Because (at that time) it was generally believed that legal variables were not amenable to statistical analysis, scholars started with variables that could be easily coded, such as judges' party affiliation, background, or socialization and then increasingly turned their attention to the "attitudes," "values," or "personal policy preferences" of the judges. In the early years, this community of scholars diplomatically suggested that they "do not eschew the traditional methods of research in public law" and they were willing to acknowledge that "there is no substitute for substantive competence and insight." At the same time, they frequently delighted in demonstrating that these personal variables typically trumped the sort of legal norms that many jurisprudentially minded scholars spent much time analyzing, such as the norm of judicial restraint.

What is particularly noteworthy about the longstanding behavioralist aversion to legal variables is that it was premised on a fairly controversial conception of law as a set of clear, determinate rules. It was the same sort of formalist conception that had been the object of realist ridicule, and to some extent it found renewed expression around the time of the birth of behavioralism in H. L. A. Hart's reformulation of legal positivism. This conception of law allowed many behavioralists to discount the significance of legal influences whenever it could be demonstrated that different judges reached different decisions—and, since that could almost always be shown, it was an article of faith that no additional justification had to be given for focusing on other variables. . . . Behavioralists focus on non-legal variables precisely "because the constraints under which the Justices decide their cases do not inhibit them from expressing their preferences insofar as voting on the cases before them is concerned." Similarly, Gibson [has more recently] argued that the fact of variation in voting means that judges "have enormous discretion when they make their decisions. The text of constitutions, statutes, and precedents does not *command* the votes of the judges. Since there is no 'true' or 'objective' meaning to constitutional phrases like 'due process of law,' judges *cannot* merely follow the law." In this most extreme version of the realist position, if law's influence was not determinate, if it allowed for any free play of discretion or judgment, then it was assumed that it had no influence at all.

Despite these long-standing assumptions about the irrelevance of legal variables, by the 1980s there were some scholars interested in constructing more direct empirical tests of law. These scholars also conceptualized law as determinate rules or norms that should (if working) lead judges to behave in similar ways; after all, if this was not assumed there would be no way to set up behavioralist hypothesis tests that are designed to examine whether certain predicted behaviors are more likely to occur given the presence of particular variables or conditions. This methodological requirement of behavioral predictability does not strictly rest on a notion of mechanical jurisprudence (since some legal influences may be discerned even when judges do not exhibit perfect compliance), but it clearly presumes that law-influenced behavior conforms to a predetermined course of conduct. There is nothing unreasonable about this presumption, but it should be noted that it reflects only one contested conception of law. Unfortunately, behavioralist researchers were not always explicit about how their studies focused on certain (controversial) propositions made within certain jurisprudential schools of thought; instead, their results were often summarized in more general terms, about the presence or absence of any legal effects, and this led researchers to offer misleading or at least incautious conclusions about the extent to which law influenced judicial decision making. Still, this research did represent the first step toward constructing direct behavioralist tests of certain kinds of legalist claims. . . .

Is Law an External Constraint or a State of Mind Within a Practice?

Whatever else might be said about it, behavioralist work is at least fairly systematic about specifying how key concepts are defined and identifying what counts as evidence for and against certain contested claims. If legalists often disagree with these definitions and with behavioralist inferences about evidence, it is because behavioralists give them a basis for engaging their claims. . . .

To facilitate these clarifications it may be useful to distinguish two different kinds of claims made about the nature of legal influence. As we have seen, the legal positivist claim views law as an external constraint on judges, and this means that legal influence should result in at least a certain amount of judicial conformity to an identifiable rule or norm. This is the basis upon which it has been said that "the fundamental premise in the idea of impartial judges and rules of law is that certain kinds of decision-making, for example, by judges, can by institutional arrangements and role discipline be made to show less variance and less correlation to personal factors than other kinds of decision-making." This is also the version of the argument that we associate with legalist claims about how, on many multimember courts, the vast majority of cases are decided unanimously and with attitudinalist claims that when rules are less clear we should expect judges to base decisions on personal or extralegal factors. [Harold] Spaeth and [Jeffrey A.] Segal also have this understanding in mind when they explain that their attitudinal model is designed to apply specifically to the Supreme Court, precisely because the modern justices do not typically address cases considered routine or frivolous.

Not surprisingly, it is this positivist version of the legalist argument that positivist social scientists have considered the most amenable to behavioralist verification, and as noted earlier there has been some limited success in testing certain elements of these claims. Given the nature of contemporary legal positivism and formalism, it is unclear whether this version of legalism is sufficiently reductionist to accommodate behavioralist methods. (This is best worked out between the positivists and the behavioralists.). . .

In responding to behavioralist investigations of the legal model, many legalists today find themselves making arguments that are reminiscent of those made by Roscoe Pound, when he criticized realists' attempt to equate the failures of the model of mechanical jurisprudence with the less careful conclusion that law was insignificant:

> Radical neo-realism seems to deny that there are rules or principles or conceptions or doctrines at all, because all judicial action, or at times much judicial action, cannot be referred to them; because there is no definite determination whereby we may be absolutely assured that judicial action will proceed on the basis of one rather than another of two competing principles. . . . Such a view is not without its use as a protest against the assumption that law is nothing but a simple aggregate of rules. But nothing would be more unreal—in the sense of at variance with what is significant for a highly specialized form of social control through politically organized society—than to conceive of the administration of justice, or the legal adjustment of relations, or, for that matter, the working out of devices for the more efficient functioning of business in a legally ordered society, as a mere aggregate of single determinations.

Many legalists press these points because they believe that there is potentially a lot at stake in this academic debate. Some have argued that if we took seriously the behavioralists' findings that decision making is "a reflection of the justices' values" rather than a faithful "rendering of constitutional or statutory language" then "the inherent contradiction between policy making by nonelected, life-term justices and representative government is heightened." We might hope . . . that behavioralist claims that law does not matter are "mostly bluff" since legalist assumptions "are too deeply cemented into the structure of our political practices," but there is also every reason to think that unrefuted claims about law's irrelevance could lead to reforms of these practices.

For example, two law professors have recently used behavioralist findings as a basis for proposing that at least one Democratic or Republican be assigned to all three-judge panels of the U.S. Courts of Appeal. The researchers have evidence that when a panel is made up of judges from one political party there [is] a higher proportion of ideological decisions than when the panels have one member from another party. They argue that, from a behavioralist point of view, there is reason to think that more legalistic (transpartisan) outcomes will be produced with this structural change. This proposal provoked a strong response from Judge Patricia Wald. She acknowledged the behavioral differences (although also thought they were overstated), but more important she worried that this proposal would institutionalize an antilegalist sentiment on the court and would thus corrupt the legalist state of mind that the current structure is designed to nurture. "Most people, including judges, have a tendency to mold themselves into their assigned roles. Emphasize to a judge that she must act independently, and she will likely try to do that; tell her she is two-thirds or one-third of a bipartisan panel and has been selected to fill that role, it is far likelier that politics will bleed into her decision making."

This exchange not only further illustrates the difference between thinking of law as behavioral uniformity and thinking of it as good faith deliberation; it also captures some of the potential real world consequences of this debate, especially as it moves beyond the insulated borders of political science. We have perhaps reached a point where we need to be especially careful of what we mean by legal and political decision making, especially when faced with the possibility that reforms designed to promote one conception (e.g., greater panel uniformity) might undermine a competing conception (a good faith effort to avoid partisan decision making). . . . We might reflect on whether we really think that principles of legality would be better promoted if, somehow, we discouraged dissenting justices from resisting disagreeable precedents.

Like many legalists, [Ronald] Dworkin has suggested for quite some time that the picture of law advanced by positivists "has exercised a tenacious hold on our imagination, perhaps through its very simplicity," and he has expressed hope that "[i]f we shake ourselves loose from this model of rules, we may be able to build a model truer to the complexity and sophistication of our own practices." All researchers, behavioralists and interpretivists, attitudinalists and legalists, claim an interest in devising accurate portrayals. If scholars continue to view this debate as nontrivial then all sides should appreciate how progress on this question may have as much to do with the quality of our jurisprudence as with the rigor of our empirical methods.

2.4

On the Nature of Supreme Court Decision Making (1992)

Tracey E. George and Lee Epstein

The common law's . . . reverence for . . . *stare decisis* [means] that a policy made in a piecemeal manner would be better able to win support. . . . When the Court reverses itself or makes new law out of whole cloth . . . the holy rite of judges consulting a higher law loses some of its mysterious power.

—*Walter F. Murphy*

Judges are inevitably participants in the process of public policy formation; . . . they do in fact "make law"; [and] in making law they are necessarily guided in part by their personal conceptions of justice and public policy.

—*C. Herman Pritchett*

How does the U.S. Supreme Court reach decisions? The above statements answer that question quite differently. The first, grounded in positivist jurisprudence, suggests that the rule of law *stare decisis* is the key determinant. The second, reflecting political jurisprudence, posits the converse—that an array of sociological, psychological, and political factors having little to do with legal doctrine produce judicial outcomes. These perspectives represent the mainstream—albeit highly divergent—responses to the question we pose. That both have persisted, despite the obvious tension between them, is somewhat puzzling; that the subfield of law, courts, and judicial processes may be more polarized than ever is extraordinary. . . .

Can two highly divergent conceptualizations of judicial decision making coexist? Empirical evidence suggests that at minimum, each can account for variations in behavior. . . .

From *American Political Science Review* 86 (1992): 323–337. Reprinted with the permission of Cambridge University Press.

How legal and extralegal models of judicial decision making perform in head-to-head competition forms our central concern here. Using Court cases involving the imposition of the death penalty since 1972, we estimate and evaluate the ability of each to account for decisional outcomes. . . .

The Legal Model

Often termed *positivist,* or *analytical, jurisprudence,* the *legal model* was the primary modus operandi for political scientists through the 1940s and continues to dominate legal education in the United States. At its core, legalism centers around a rather simple assumption about judicial decision making, namely, that legal doctrine, generated by past cases, is the primary determinant of extant case outcomes. It views judges as constrained decision makers who "will base their opinions on precedent and will adhere to the doctrine of *stare decisis*." Some scholars label this *mechanical jurisprudence,* because the process by which judges reach decisions is highly structured. [Edward H.] Levi describes the basic pattern of legal reasoning, reasoning by example, as a process characterized by the doctrine of precedent and articulated in three steps: (1) observation of a similarity between cases, (2) announcement of the rule of law inherent in the first case, and (3) application of that rule to the second case.

Legal education and scholarship adopted this as a paradigm—the process by which judges and lawyers should proceed. Eschewing normative approaches, political scientists (from the 1920s through the 1950s) instead viewed "reasoning by example" as the way judges *do* proceed. [Robert E.] Cushman, [Edward S.] Corwin, and many others centered their work on the notion that previously announced legal doctrine provided the single best predictor and explainer of Court decisions.

How this model became so entrenched in the political science literature is readily discernible. Many scholars reasoned that judges (all schooled in legalism) would naturally gravitate to it upon ascension to the bench. After all, how else would they approach decision making? In addition, strong expectations exist within the legal community that judges will reason by example. As [Walter] Murphy suggests, following legal precedents is a well-entrenched norm of the deliberative process. Finally, the case studies of the day reinforced the model's value. Articles published in political science journals summarized the reasoning used and the precedents set by the justices, disregarding any other factors contributing to decisional outcomes. Cushman's analysis of constitutional law for 1936–37 (one of the most volatile terms in the Court's history) provides a wonderful example. After acknowledging "The 1936 term of the Supreme Court will probably be rated as notable," he enumerated some of the "facts . . . one should bear in mind"—that Roosevelt had won a landslide reelection and had submitted a plan to reorganize the Court. Rather than demonstrate how those "facts" might have affected Court decisions, however, Cushman noted simply that "no suggestion is made as to what inferences, if any, might be drawn from them" and proceeded to analyze the New Deal cases vis-à-vis existing precedent (a difficult task, indeed).

The Extralegal Model

While the legal model was predominating political science thinking about the Court, new perspectives emerged from the ranks of the nation's judiciary and law schools. In general, these thinkers denounced legalism as mechanical jurisprudence—sometimes subtly, sometimes loudly. Instead, they beckoned judges to consider more dynamic factors as bases for decisions. Many credit Holmes's *The Common Law* with initiating this plea. Students of this school often cite as exemplary his remark that "the life of the law has not been logic; it has been experience. . . . It cannot be dealt with as if it contained only the axioms and corollaries of a book of mathematics." Illustrative, too, is Louis Brandeis's famous brief in *Muller v. Oregon* (1908), containing 113 pages of sociological data but only 2 of legal

argument. It was Pound, however, who catalyzed the first strain of extrajudicialism, sometimes called *sociological jurisprudence.* In his seminal *Harvard Law Review* article [1931], Pound drew his now-famous distinction between "law in books" and "law in action," behooving judges to adopt the latter, without necessarily abandoning the former. Cardozo and many others followed suit.

Later adapters of sociological jurisprudence—the realists of the 1930s—though were far more radical in orientation, maintaining that rules based on precedents were nothing more than smokescreens or "myths, clung to by man out of a childish need for sureness and security. A mature jurisprudence recognizes that there is no certainty in law."

So began a long line of thinkers who harshly critiqued legal reasoning for its inadequacy as a basis for judicial decision making, an inadequacy stemming from various considerations. From a normative standpoint, many followed Brandeis's lead, arguing that extralegal factors should enter judicial deliberations. After all, if judges were constrained by precedent, law would remain static when it should reflect changing morals and values. Additionally, critics argued that justices, "like other human beings, are influenced by the values and attitudes learned in childhood." It would be extraordinary, they claimed, to think that judges, just because they don black robes, were any less susceptible to such influences. Indeed, justices may be even more vulnerable than other decision makers because the rules of law are "typically available to support either side." In making choices between competing precedents, then, other factors are bound to come into play.

Although legal realism gained a strong following within the nation's leading law schools during the 1930s, political scientists were reluctant adherents. It was not until the publication of [C. Herman] Pritchett's *Roosevelt Court* [1948] that students began to abandon a positivist approach and view Court decisions more critically and analytically. In essence, Pritchett brought legal realism to political science. He equipped scholars with the arsenal necessary to estimate and evaluate its propositions. And, as an important by-product, he provided the fodder for the development of political jurisprudence and behavioralism. . . . [These political scientists] viewed the Court's environment as one that provided the justices with "great freedom to base their decisions solely upon personal policy preferences." But unlike the realists, they proceeded operationally to define and systematically to test attitudinal models of judicial behavior.

Models: Current Status

The Extralegal Model

The underlying premise of *The Roosevelt Court*—that a host of internal, attitudinal factors other than "the law" contribute to case outcomes—continues to constitute a mainstay of research on Supreme Court decision making. Over the past decades, countless efforts have viewed court decisions as a function of personal attributes, attitudes, and role conceptions. In general, however, most of these depict a Court driven by single-minded seekers of legal policy, justices who wish to etch into law their personal views.

Though the basic tenets of behavioralism continue to shape our vision of the judicial process, we have made some attempts at refining that conceptualization. In general, we now know that Court decisions are a product of factors not only internal but also external to the Court. Research by myriad scholars reveals that litigants, attorneys, and parties can affect case outcomes. Although this body of literature is, conceptually speaking, quite murky, we acknowledge the validity of several of its basic premises. First, we recognize that attainment of "repeat player status" can translate into litigation success. How one becomes a "repeat player" is difficult to specify; but at least two factors contribute: association with a national litigating organization and regular appearance before the Court. Attorneys from the ranks of public interest law firms are ensured some level of financial and other support that many private counsel lack. Repeated and continuous use of legal recourse breeds familiarity, confidence, and expertise that one-shotters cannot possibly acquire. Second, and concomitantly, we acknowledge the extraordinary role played by one repeat player, the solicitor general of the United States. Whether participating as a direct party or as an amicus curiae, solicitors general seem to carry great weight with the justices. Their presumed legal expertise, their utility in preconference screening, and their embodiment of the interests of the nation are just some of the factors explaining the solicitors' general excellent record before the Court. Third, we accept the proposition that appellants are more likely to win their cases than appellees. This expectation is grounded both in fact and in theory. Thus, no extralegal model can afford to ignore it.

Political scientists also recognize that pressures emanating from outside the legal system can affect case outcomes. In particular, we believe that the Court is responsive to the larger political environment. Some suggest that its rulings reflect the wishes of the citizenry. But owing to difficult conceptual and analytical obstacles, scholars have yet to provide truly compelling support for this assertion. They have been more successful at establishing a link between the Court and the other branches of government. That is, even though the justices lack an electoral connection or mandate of responsiveness, we have several reasons to suspect that Congress and the president affect Supreme Court decision making and that the direction of their influence reflects their partisan composition. First, scholars assert that both Congress and the president possess a vast array of powers over matters important to the Court, which the justices can hardly afford to ignore. Some of these powers, such as presidential and senatorial roles in the appointment process, are obvious; some are not. As [Stephen A.] Wasby notes, Congress can restrict the Court's jurisdiction to hear cases; enact legislation, or even propose constitutional amendments, to recast Court decisions; and hold judicial salaries constant. In turn, "the Court's policies may be affected by a desire to deter Congress" from taking these steps. By the same token, [Walter] Murphy and [Robert] Scigliano point to the multifaceted relationship between the Court and the president, one that goes well beyond his power to nominate justices or even to send his solicitor general into the Marble Palace. It is no secret, for example, that many presidents have enjoyed special relationships with sitting justices and that presidential preferences have found their way into particular opinions. Nor can we ignore the role the president plays in shaping congressional responses to the Court.

Another set of literature focuses on the role of the Court within a democratic society, many scholars arguing that Court decisions do not significantly deviate from the preferences of the existing majoritarian regime. Though some argue that this is largely a result of the regularity with which presidents appoint justices, others suggest that it stems, at least in part, from the institutional nature of the Court. In short, because the justices lack any real mechanism to enforce their decisions, they depend on other political actors (and the public) for support of their positions. Without such support, the Court could lose its institutional legitimacy, a danger of which its members seem well aware. Accordingly, for the Court to have power within government it must "follow the election returns," or at the very least, consider them. Along similar lines, the Court, at least on occasion, takes cues from the political environment to guide its decisions. It has even gone so far as to build that dimension into some of its jurisprudential standards. In evaluating whether certain kinds of punishments violate the Eighth Amendment's cruel-and-unusual clause, for example, the Court proclaimed that it would look toward "evolving standards of decency" as defined by public morals.

Given this literature, then, we have sufficient reasons to suspect that the president and Congress can affect Supreme Court decision making or at least that Court rulings encapsulate the preferences of the other branches. What is more, we know something about the direction of this influence. The relationship between the Court and other branches of government, throughout history, has revolved around the ebb and flow of partisan politics. As [Stuart] Nagel observed, these patterns are "significantly shaped by such political considerations as the degree of party difference between Congress and the Court, the nature of the party in power in the national government and the party affiliations" of the individual justices. Put in more concrete terms, when the nation and its institutions move toward parties representing "have not" views (e.g., today's Democratic party), the Court tends to adopt more liberal policy postures, particularly on issues of rights and liberties. Conversely, as parties of "haves" (e.g., today's Republican party) come into power, the opposite effect will occur. In sum, while we continue to incorporate the premises of the attitudinal approach into our thinking about behavior, we also recognize that pressures external to the Court (be they from attorneys, parties, and litigants or from the larger political environment) supplement behavioral assumptions. . . .

The Legal Model

It is, of course, true that many of those engaged in the study of public law are less than content with this extralegal model, calling for a greater emphasis on doctrine as a valid explanation of case outcomes. [John] Brigham, [Charles] Johnson, and [Timothy] O'Neill have stressed that the language of law (precedents, etc.) channels and constrains judicial choices. Shapiro, too, suggests that "we have overemphasized extralegalism to the point [that] we somehow ignore the fact that appellate courts and the lawyers that serve them spend an overwhelming proportion of their energies communicating with one another, and that the judicial opinion itself conforming to the style of *stare decisis*, is the principal mode of communication." Two decades after publication of *The Roosevelt Court*, Pritchett even lamented that behavioralism may have gone too far: "Political scientists who have done so much to put the 'political' in 'political jurisprudence' need to emphasize that it is still 'jurisprudence'. It is judging in a political context, but it is still judging; and, judging is something different from legislating or administering."

Like behavioral models, legal perspectives have evolved over the years, not so much conceptually as analytically. In particular, work by [Fred] Kort and [Jeffrey A.] Segal demonstrated systematically—not contextually—that the law controls case outcomes. Rather than focus on a specific decision or strain of precedent, Kort and Segal isolated areas of law and used facts and legal doctrine, respectively, to predict judicial determinations. When they found that the Court responded to legal factors in a consistent manner, some social scientists began to question the sweeping generalizations of the behavioralist school.

Kort's work has been the subject of some criticism. [Louis] Fisher chastised his methods; others found his use of legally irrelevant facts puzzling. Segal's analyses overcame some of these shortcomings. He used probit (a multivariate analytic strategy), which allowed him to reach more precise conclusions about the relationship between doctrine and output. In addition, he limited his consideration to facts of legal significance. Virtually all his variables tap doctrine, rather than attributes of the sort incorporated by Kort. Indeed, he labels his analysis "a legal model."

Even so, Segal's model arguably failed to correct for some of the shortcomings of previous work. Scholars continue to construct legal models in a rather post hoc fashion. Segal, for example, included certain variables (e.g., warrantless searches made prior to arrest and consent searches) because the *Court* said they were important and not because he had a priori knowledge that they should be significant in search-and-seizure analysis. Another potential problem is more temporal in nature: most legal models incorporate doctrine that the Court enunciated *after* it decided some of the cases contemplated in a given analysis. Segal included a variable comprised of six "exceptions" to the warrant and probable cause requirements. Although the Court had not written any of these exceptions into law prior to 1967 (the balance came in the early 1970s), Segal incorporated them into a model developed to explain Court search-and-seizure decisions between 1962 and 1981.

Do these problems undermine the efforts of Segal and those following in his footsteps? We think not. On the contrary, they are endemic to legal models in general, rather than to specific scholarly efforts. Consider the temporal problem from the perspective of those who view the law as self-contained (as it is often presented to be in law school courses). Because, for them, the core notion is that all decisions are rooted in *stare decisis*, they would simply respond that the old doctrine anticipated the newer one, that the facts and questions varied, not the doctrine. They would bring much the same argument to bear on the post hoc nature of these models.

Seen in this light, the approach taken by Segal and others neatly parallels the conceptualization offered by legalists. What is more, by providing empirical verification for the legal model, they gave it greater status within the scientific community studying judicial decision making. Though their methods differed from those of the classicists and they often included attitudinal measures in their models, their conclusions lent support to traditional assumptions about the nature of legal deliberations. . . .

Explaining the Findings

Taken together, then, the legal and extralegal models seem to be working at cross purposes, produc-

ing opposing categorizations over time. Theoretically speaking, this is a puzzling phenomenon but one on which we can speculate. We first consider a traditional criticism of the legal model, namely, that it is too static to account for changes in the law. We found, however, that this was not necessarily the case for death penalty litigation. Rather, it does change over time, forecasting more liberal outcomes with each passing Natural Court era than actually happen.

Why this occurs is rather evident. Once the Court enunciates legal policies, attorneys will take a cue from those precedents, bringing better and better arguments within those doctrinal parameters. Quite exemplary are capital cases involving overly broad aggravating circumstances. In *Gregg v. Georgia* (1976) the defendant's attorney claimed that one of the state's aggravating circumstances, namely, that the offense was "outrageously or wantonly vile, horrible or inhuman in that it involved torture, depravity, or an aggravated battery to the victim," was overly broad and vague. The Court rejected this contention on the grounds that future courts need not construe it as such. This holding voided Gregg's particular claim but opened the doors to new challenges based on future interpretation of that circumstance. This is precisely what happened in *Godfrey v. Georgia* (1980) when an attorney challenged Georgia's construction of the very same aggravating circumstance. Based on *Gregg,* the justices agreed that the state courts had interpreted it in such a way as to make it overly broad and vague. Our legal model accurately classified the outcome of *Godfrey;* but it missed a 1989 case also involving aggravating circumstances, *Hildwin v. Florida.* In this instance, the Court ignored existing precedent and found for the state.

After this small deviation from *Gregg* and *Godfrey* in 1989, the justices moved more rapidly to distinguish existing precedent. For example, in the 1990 case of *Lewis v. Jeffers,* they held that the aggravating factor challenged in *Gregg* was not unconstitutionally vague as applied to the defendant even though a lower court, relying in part on *Godfrey,* held that it was. Once again, we used existing estimates to try to "postdict" *Lewis.* Not surprisingly, this effort failed. The legal model—built around earlier precedent—failed to categorize correctly the outcome of *Lewis v. Jeffers.*

This series of cases (and others) demonstrates that the legal model contains an inherent flaw. Because it only considers legally relevant facts, it will continue to forecast liberal outcomes as attorneys capitalize on existing precedent even though "the law" may not actually move in that direction. This is why our legal model accurately forecasted the Court's early "aggravating" cases but missed those decided in 1989 and 1990.

Does this mean that we should discount the legal model in favor of the extralegal one? We think not, because it, too, exhibits idiopathic behavior, prematurely predicting conservative outcomes. It accurately predicted *Hildwin* but missed several other cases in which the Court adhered to precedent and ruled in favor of the defendant. Particularly interesting is the one 1989 term ruling that it miscategorized, *McKoy v. North Carolina*. This case involved the constitutionality of a state sentencing scheme permitting juries to consider only those mitigating circumstances on which they unanimously agreed. Because so many pro-state "buttons" of our existing extralegal model were pushed (e.g., the defendant was not represented by a group, the high number of Nixon–Reagan appointees, etc.), it predicted that this case had virtually no chance of being decided in favor of the defendant. Yet, citing clear-cut doctrine suggesting the need for "flexibility" of mitigating circumstances, the Court held for the defendant.

Seen in this light, the extralegal model is too dynamic. It assumes that changes in the political environment will contemporaneously affect court decisions. Yet as the death penalty data suggest, this may be an incorrect assumption. Why does the model possess this flaw? Most importantly, as *McKoy* indicates, it fails to consider the doctrinal boundaries in which the Court works. If Brigham and others are right, *stare decisis* does constrain the array of available legal options. Accordingly, abrupt alternations in the political environment may not necessarily translate into concomitant, contemporaneous doctrinal change. . . .

Conclusion

We began with a relatively simple purpose—to determine how well legal and extralegal models performed in head-to-head competition. We thought this a significant enterprise because theories of judicial behavior are rarely subjected to this sort of examination. As it turned out, both models performed satisfactorily, evincing strong abilities to account for Court outcomes in capital punishment litigation.

Our analysis could have ended here, concluding that legal and extralegal models provide equally good frameworks by which to assess Court decision making. Such a conclusion, however, would have been premature, because, upon further evaluation, we found that both exhibited disturbing propensities. The legal one prematurely anticipated liberal outcomes, the extralegal model conservative ones. Given these results, we tested another proposition, namely, that extralegal and legal frameworks presented codependent, not mutually exclusive, explanations of decision making. Based on these results, we offered an integrated model of judicial decision making contemplating a range of legal and extralegal factors.

Taken as a whole, what does our model reveal about the nature of Supreme Court decision making? Can we now address our original research question, How does the Supreme Court reach decisions? On some level, its answer is obvious: the most complete explanation of judicial outcomes should incorporate legal and extralegal factors. Seen in this light, the views of neither the classical legal thinkers nor the behavioralists are incorrect; but they are incomplete. Both law and politics, as we would intuitively expect, play significant roles in the Supreme Court's decision-making process.

On another level, however, these roles may not necessarily be equivalent. Our analysis of capital cases reveals that legal factors have the greatest impact at the early stages of an issue's life; as it evolves, however, extralegal variables dominate. In a way, therefore, our results reinforce the legal paradigm set out by the pragmatic Benjamin Cardozo. When the law ceases to be consistent with the Court's "sense of justice," there occurs a greater willingness to abandon it. This, he wrote, *should* be the nature of the judicial process. Our analysis confirms that (at least for death penalty litigation) it *is*.

Where do we go from here? Surely our next research tasks must be to eliminate some of the shortcomings of this effort. In particular, our focus on a single area of the law hampers our ability to reach generalizable conclusions. Hence, future analyses ought to continue where we have left off by exploring other legal issues with an eye toward discerning whether the patterns we found are idiosyncratic or sufficiently universal.

Leaving Things Undecided (1999)

Cass Sunstein

The Constitution speaks broadly and abstractly and about some of our highest aspirations. Many of the great constitutional issues involve the meaning of the basic ideas of "equality" and "liberty." When, if ever, might the government discriminate on the basis of race or sex or sexual orientation? Does the government restrict free speech by, for example, regulating expenditures on campaigns, or controlling the Internet, or requiring educational programming for children or free air time for candidates?

These are large questions. Sometimes the Supreme Court answers them. We will have occasion to discuss the substance of those answers. For the moment let us notice something equally interesting: frequently judges decide very little. They leave things open. About both liberty and equality, they make deliberate decisions about what should be left unsaid. This is a pervasive practice: doing and saying as little as is necessary in order to justify an outcome. . . .

Let us describe the phenomenon of saying no more than necessary to justify an outcome, and leaving as much as possible undecided, as "decisional minimalism." Decisional minimalism has two attractive features. First, it is likely to reduce the burdens of judicial decision. It may be very hard, for example, to obtain a ruling on the circumstances under which single-sex education is legitimate. It may be especially hard to do this on a multimember court, consisting of diverse people who disagree on a great deal. A court that tries to agree on that question may find itself with no time for anything else. And a court that tries to agree on

that question may find itself in the position of having to obtain and use a great deal of information, information that may not be available to courts (and perhaps not to anyone else).

Second, and more fundamentally, minimalism is likely to make judicial errors less frequent and (above all) less damaging. A court that leaves things open will not foreclose options in a way that may do a great deal of harm. A court may well blunder if it tries, for example, to resolve the question of affirmative action once and for all, or to issue definitive rulings about the role of the First Amendment in an area of new communications technologies. A court that decides relatively little will also reduce the risks that come from intervening in complex systems, where a single-shot intervention can have a range of unanticipated bad consequences.

There is a relationship between judicial minimalism and democratic deliberation. Of course minimalist rulings increase the space for further reflection and debate at the local, state, and national levels, simply because they do not foreclose subsequent decisions. And if the Court wants to promote more democracy and more deliberation, certain forms of minimalism will help it to do so. If, for example, the Court says that any regulation of the Internet must be clear rather than vague, and that a ban on "indecent" speech is therefore unconstitutional simply because it is vague, the Court will, in a sense, promote democratic processes by requiring Congress to legislate with specificity. Or if the Court says that any discrimination against homosexuals must be justified in some way, it will promote political deliberation by ensuring that law is not simply a product of unthinking hatred or contempt.

An understanding of minimalism helps to illuminate a range of important and time-honored ideas in constitutional law: that courts should not decide issues unnecessary to the resolution of a case; that courts should refuse to hear cases that are not "ripe" for decision; that courts should avoid deciding constitutional questions; that courts should respect their own precedents; that courts should not issue advisory opinions; that courts should follow prior holdings but not necessarily prior dicta; that courts should exercise the "passive virtues" associated with maintaining silence on great issues of the day. All of these ideas involve the *constructive use of silence.* Judges often use silence for pragmatic, strategic, or democratic reasons. Of course it is important to study what judges say; but it is equally important to examine what judges do not say, and why they do not say it. As we shall see, the question whether to leave things undecided helps unite a series of otherwise disparate debates in constitutional law.

. . . My basic goal is to give a descriptive account of minimalism. In the process I offer two preliminary suggestions about a minimalist path. The first suggestion is that certain forms of minimalism can be democracy-promoting, not only in the sense that they leave issues open for democratic deliberation, but also and more fundamentally in the sense that they promote reason-giving and ensure that certain important decisions are made by democratically accountable actors. Sometimes courts say that Congress, rather than the executive branch, must make particular decisions; sometimes they are careful to ensure that good reasons actually underlie challenged enactments. In so doing, courts are minimalist in the sense that they leave open the most fundamental and difficult constitutional questions; they also attempt to promote democratic accountability and democratic deliberation. Judge-made doctrines are thus part of an effort to ensure that legitimate reasons actually underlie the exercise of public power.

My second suggestion is that a minimalist path usually—not always, but usually—makes a good deal of sense *when the Court is dealing with a constitutional issue of high complexity about which many people feel deeply and on which the nation is divided (on moral or other grounds).* The complexity may result from a lack of information, from changing circumstances, or from (legally relevant) moral uncertainty. Minimalism makes sense first because courts may resolve those issues incorrectly, and second because courts may create serious problems even if their answers are right. Courts thus try to economize on moral disagreement by refusing to take on other people's deeply held moral commitments when it is not necessary for them to do so in order to decide a case. For this reason courts should usually attempt to issue rulings that leave things undecided and that, if possible, are catalytic rather than preclusive. They should indulge a presumption in favor of minimalism.

We can link the two points with the suggestion that in such cases, courts should adopt forms of minimalism that can improve and fortify democratic processes. Many rules of constitutional law attempt to promote political accountability and political deliberation. Minimalism is not by any means democracy-promoting by its nature; but it is most interesting when it is democracy-promoting in this way.

Theories

What is the relationship among the Supreme Court, the Constitution, and those whose acts are subject to constitutional attack? We can easily identify some theoretically ambitious responses.

Perhaps the simplest one is *originalist.* On this view, the Court's role is to vindicate an actual historical judgment made by those who ratified the Constitution. Justices Antonin Scalia and Clarence Thomas have been prominent enthusiasts for originalism, at least most of the time. The infamous *Dred Scott* case, saying that the Constitution forbids efforts to eliminate slavery, is a vigorous early statement of the originalist approach. Originalists try to bracket questions of politics and morality and embark on a historical quest. . . . Originalism represents an effort to make constitutional law quite rule-like, and in that sense to settle a wide range of constitutional issues in advance. Indeed, that is a central part of the appeal of originalism.

The second response stems from the claim that majority rule is the basic presupposition of American democracy. This claim suggests that courts should uphold any plausible judgments from the democratic branches of government. On this view, courts should permit nonjudicial judgments unless those judgments are outlandish or clearly mistaken. James Bradley Thayer's famous law review article, advocating *a rule of clear mistake,* is the classic statement of this position. The position can be found as well in the writings of Justice Oliver Wendell Holmes, the first Justice Harlan, Justice Felix Frankfurter, and, most recently, Chief Justice William Rehnquist. Innumerable post–New Deal Supreme Court cases, upholding social and economic regulation, fall in this category. Here too there is an effort to resolve constitutional cases by rule and in advance, via a strong presumption in favor of whatever emerges from majoritarian politics.

The third response is based on a claim that the Supreme Court should make *independent interpretive judgments* about constitutional meaning, based not on historical understandings, but instead on the Court's own account of what understanding makes best sense of the relevant provision. When the Court struck down maximum-hour and minimum-wage legislation in the early part of the twentieth century, it spoke in these terms. When the Court created and vindicated a "right of privacy," it did the same thing. So too when the Court struck down bans on commercial advertising and restrictions on campaign spending. . . .

The fourth response characterizes one understanding of the Supreme Court under Chief Justice Earl Warren, a Court that continues to cast a long shadow over public debate. This response is represented by the most famous footnote in all of constitutional law: footnote 4 in the Carolene Products case. On this view, the Court acts to improve the democratic character of the political process itself. It does so by protecting rights that are preconditions for a well-functioning democracy, and also by protecting groups that are at special risk because the democratic process is not democratic enough. Insofar as it stressed the need to protect political outsiders from political insiders, *McCulloch v. Maryland* is probably the earliest statement of the basic position; there are many more recent examples in the area of voting, including *Baker v. Carr, Reynolds v. Sims,* and *Shaw v. Hunt.* This conception of the judicial role, defended most prominently by John Hart Ely, is based on the notion of *democracy-reinforcement.*

It is striking but true that as a whole, the current Supreme Court has not come close to making an official choice among these four approaches. The Court has not committed itself to a single theory. Even individual Supreme Court justices can be hard to classify. Justices Scalia and Thomas are out-

spokenly originalist, and certainly neither can fairly be accused of rampant inconsistency. But in opinions calling for broad protection of commercial advertising, Justice Thomas has interpreted the First Amendment with little reference to history, indeed his opinions look like a form of independent interpretive argument; and Justice Scalia's strong opposition to campaign finance regulation and affirmative action do not appear to result from extended historical inquiry. Chief Justice Rehnquist has often endorsed the rule of clear mistake, and he is probably the most consistent proponent of this view in recent decades. But in cases involving affirmative action, which he opposes on constitutional grounds, the Chief Justice speaks in quite different terms; here his method is more like a form of independent interpretive judgment.

We need not charge anyone with hypocrisy here. Perhaps different constitutional provisions are best treated differently. Thus we might say that the rule of clear mistake makes sense for the due process clause, whereas the idea of democracy-reinforcement is appropriate for the First Amendment and the equal protection clause. Indeed, the idea of democracy-reinforcement creates a great deal of space for the rule of clear mistake in those cases in which no democratic defect is at stake. Or we might think that independent judgment makes sense only for certain special cases, and that the rule of clear mistake, or originalism, is best elsewhere. Or we might adopt a presumption in favor of originalism but look elsewhere when history reveals gaps or ambiguities.

Against Theories, Against Rules

To come to terms with these abstract debates, it is necessary to take a position on some large-scale controversies about the legitimate role of the Supreme Court in the constitutional order. An endorsement of one or the other precommits the Court in a wide range of subsequent cases. To be sure, each of the theories has play in the joints. Thus, for example, the original understanding can be described in different ways and at various levels of generality; history leaves many gaps, and committed originalists disagree sharply on some issues. So too, the notion of representation-reinforcement is quite open-ended. People with diverse theoretical positions can accept that notion, and those who accept it are not committed to particular decisions in disputed cases. Perhaps the most underrepresented group is consumers, and perhaps aggressive judicial review of political regulation of the economy can be justified by notions of representation-reinforcement. But there can be no doubt that any of the four approaches constrains further inquiry. And perhaps it is both necessary and desirable for Supreme Court justices to stake out some position on the general question of constitutional method.

But let us notice a remarkable fact. Not only has the Court as a whole refused to choose among the four positions or to sort out their relations, but many of the current justices have refused to do so in their individual capacities. Consider Justices Ruth Bader Ginsburg, David Souter, Sandra Day O'Connor, Stephen Breyer, and Anthony Kennedy. These justices—the analytical heart of the current Court—have adopted no unitary "theory" of constitutional interpretation. Instead of adopting theories, they decide cases. It is not even clear that any of them has rejected any of the four approaches I have described. The most that can be said is that none of them is an originalist in the sense of Justices Scalia and Thomas, and that none of them believes that any of these approaches adequately captures the whole of constitutional law.

In their different ways, each of these justices tends to be minimalist. I understand this term to refer to judges who seek to avoid broad rules and abstract theories, and attempt to focus their attention only on what is necessary to resolve particular disputes. Minimalists do not like to work deductively; they do not see outcomes as reflecting rules or theories laid down in advance. They pay close attention to the particulars of individual cases. They also tend to think analogically and by close reference to actual and hypothetical problems. I believe that all of the justices named above understand themselves as minimalists in this sense, and that they have chosen to be minimalist for reasons that are, broadly speaking, of the sort I will be discussing here. In other words, these justices embrace minimalism—usually, not always—for reasons connected with their conception of the role of the Supreme Court in American government.

We might contrast minimalism with "maximalism." The term is far from perfect, for no one seeks to decide, in every case, everything that might be decided. Let us understand the term as a shorthand reference for those who seek to decide cases in a way that sets broad rules for the future and that also gives ambitious theoretical justifications for outcomes. At the opposite pole is reasonlessness, represented by a failure to give reasons at all. . . .

Narrowness and Width

As I am using the term here, the practice of minimalism involves two principal features, narrowness and shallowness. First, minimalists try to decide cases rather than to set down broad rules. In this way, minimalists ask that decisions be *narrow rather than wide*. They decide the case at hand; they do not decide other cases too, except to the extent that one decision necessarily bears on other cases, and unless they are pretty much forced to do so. . . .

It is important to say that narrowness is relative, not absolute. A decision that discrimination against the mentally retarded will face rational basis review, and ordinarily be upheld, is narrow compared to imaginable alternatives; it is much narrower than a decision that discrimination on all grounds other than race will face rational basis review, and ordinarily be upheld. But it is much broader than other imaginable decisions, such as a decision that holds for or against the mentally retarded in the particular case, without announcing a standard of review at all. The consistent minimalist seeks to render decisions that are no broader than necessary to support the outcome. Of course narrowness may run into difficulty if it means that similarly situated people are being treated differently; this very danger may press the Court in the direction of breadth. . . .

Shallow Rather Than Deep

The second point is that minimalists generally try to avoid issues of basic principle. They want to allow people who disagree on the deepest issues to converge. In this way they attempt to reach *incom-*

pletely theorized agreements. Such agreements come in two forms: agreements on concrete particulars amid disagreements or uncertainty about the basis for those concrete particulars, and agreements about abstractions amid disagreements or uncertainty about the particular meaning of those abstractions. Both forms are important to constitutional law. . . .

. . . Judges who disagree or who are unsure about the foundations of constitutional rights, or about appropriate constitutional method, might well be able to agree on how particular cases should be handled. They might think that whatever they think about the foundations of the free speech principle, the state cannot ban people from engaging in acts of political protest unless there is a clear and present danger. Judges who have different accounts of what the equal protection clause is all about, or who are unsure what the equality principle ultimately means, can agree on a wide range of specific cases. They might agree, for example, that government cannot segregate schools on the basis of race or exclude women from professions. Indeed, people with widely varying views on the most basic issues do agree that discrimination on the basis of race is generally banned (at least outside of the contested area of affirmative action). People who disagree on a great deal may agree that torture is unconstitutional, or that people deserve compensation for physical invasions of their property. Agreements on particulars and on unambitious opinions are the ordinary stuff of constitutional law; it is rare for judges to retreat to first principles.

Incompletely theorized agreements are by no means unaccompanied by reasons. On the contrary, judicial decisions infrequently take on foundational questions, and they are nonetheless exercises in reason-giving. There is a big difference between a refusal to give an ambitious argument for an outcome and a refusal to give any reasons at all. Sometimes ambition is simply unnecessary and low-level explanations, commanding agreement from diverse people, are entirely sufficient.

Incompletely theorized agreements on particular outcomes are an important means by which diverse citizens are able to constitute themselves as a society. Such agreements permit people to live together in a productive way; they also show a form of mutual respect. This is especially so when people hold fast or insistently to their more abstract beliefs (consider theological commitments, or commitments about freedom or equality). These beliefs operate as "fixed points," and sometimes they cannot be productively debated. Often debates become tractable only when they become more concrete. A kind of *conceptual descent* can produce agreement or in any case progress. Of course it is true that sometimes people hold more tenaciously to their commitments to particular cases than they hold to their theories; sometimes it is the particular judgments that operate as "fixed points" for analysis. All I am suggesting is that when theoretical disagreements are intense and hard to mediate, courts often make progress by trying to put those disagreements to one side, and by converging on an outcome and a relatively modest rationale on its behalf.

In this way minimalists try to make decisions *shallow rather than deep.* They avoid foundational issues if and to the extent that they can. By so doing the Supreme Court can use constitutional law both to model and promote a crucial goal of a liberal political system: to make it possible for people to agree when agreement is necessary, and to make it unnecessary for people to agree when agreement is impossible. Judicial minimalism is well suited to this goal. . . .

Conclusion: Minimalism and Democracy

In its procedural form, judicial minimalism consists of an effort to limit the width and depth of judicial decisions. Thus understood, minimalism has distinctive virtues, especially in a heterogeneous society in which reasonable people often disagree. When judges lack, and know they lack, relevant information, minimalism is an appropriate response. Sometimes judicial minimalism is a reasonable or even inevitable response to the sheer practical problem of obtaining consensus amid pluralism. Within the Supreme Court, as within other institutions, this problem produces incompletely specified abstractions and incompletely theorized, narrow rulings. And sometimes minimalism is a way for people who disagree to show one another mutual respect.

Minimalism also maintains flexibility for the future, an especially large virtue when facts and values are in flux. Minimalists refuse to freeze existing ideals and conceptions; in this way they retain a good deal of room for future deliberation and choice. This is especially important for judges who are not too sure that they are right. Like a sailor on an unfamiliar sea—or a government attempting to regulate a shifting labor market—a court may take small, reversible steps, allowing itself to accommodate unexpected developments. Certain forms of minimalism can promote democratic goals, not simply by leaving things undecided but also by allowing opinion to coalesce over time and by spurring processes of democratic deliberation. When the Court strikes down a statute as vague, for example, it effectively requires the legislature to make crucial judgments, rather than leaving those judgments to others.

With this idea we can see an especially important strand in constitutional doctrine and a distinctive form of minimalism: decisions that are not simply democracy-foreclosing or democracy-authorizing, but instead democracy-promoting. Such decisions promote both reason-giving and accountability. Democratic goals connect a wide range of seemingly disparate features of constitutional law: the void-for-vagueness and nondelegation doctrines, the requirement that Congress speak with clarity on certain issues, rationality review, the occasional concern with desuetude, and the requirement that certain forms of discrimination be justified by actual rather than by hypothetical purposes. . . .

The debate between minimalism and maximalism unsettles some of the categories through which judicial behavior has been understood and evaluated. A maximalist, for example, may be entirely devoted to the principle of judicial restraint; consider the idea that all congressional enactments should be upheld. Indeed, judicial restraint defines certain forms of maximalism. A minimalist may be quite willing to invalidate legislative outcomes, and also to maintain judicial flexibility for the future, as through a series of ad hoc decisions that Congress has gone too far in the particular case. Nor is there any simple connection between one's stand on minimalism and any particular set of substantive convictions. A "liberal" maximalist might want to uphold all affirmative action programs, and

to strike down all discrimination based on sexual orientation. A "conservative" minimalist might want to strike down certain affirmative action programs while leaving the general status of affirmative action undecided, and might seek to uphold (for example) the ban on same-sex marriages without saying much else about discrimination on the basis of sexual orientation. Originalism, as a guide to constitutional interpretation, is a form of maximalism; this is one reason that it is simultaneously attractive and repulsive. I have argued here that originalism should be rejected on the ground that it does not promote democracy, rightly understood. It is therefore an unacceptable form of maximalism— judicial hubris masquerading as judicial modesty.

The current Supreme Court is minimalist in character, and we can obtain a far better understanding of its distinctive character, and of continuing debates within the Court itself, if we keep this point in view. The Court's minimalist judges try to keep their judgments as narrow and as incompletely theorized as possible, consistent with the obligation to offer reasons. They are enthusiastic about avoiding constitutional questions. They like to use doctrines of justiciability and their authority over their docket to limit the occasions for judicial intervention into politically contentious areas. The ban on advisory opinions guides much of their work.

Maximalists might challenge a minimalist path along either of two dimensions. Some of minimalism's antagonists, most notably Justice Scalia, are enthusiastic about width, on the ground that rule-bound law has enormous virtues. On this view, particularistic law violates rule of law principles; it may not qualify as law at all. Other antagonists . . . are enthusiastic about depth, on the ground that shallow decisions are likely to produce both unfairness and inconsistency. Shallowness may well produce mistakes. Notably, it is possible to imagine decisions that are shallow and broad; consider the *Miranda* rules, creating a virtual code of police behavior without resolving the deepest issues about the meaning of "coercion." It is also possible to imagine decisions that are deep but narrow; the Supreme Court's invalidation of same-sex education at the Virginia Military Institute is a prime example.

These points show that no defense of minimalism should be unqualified. Sometimes minimalism is a blunder; sometimes it creates unfairness.

Whether minimalism makes sense cannot be decided in the abstract; everything depends on context, prominently including assessments of comparative institutional competence. The case for minimalism is strongest when courts lack information that would justify confidence in a comprehensive ruling; when the need for planning is not especially insistent; when the decision costs, for later courts, of a minimal approach do not seem high; and when minimalist judgments do not create a serious risk of unequal treatment. Thus minimalism tends to be the appropriate course when the Court is operating in the midst of reasonable pluralism or moral flux, when circumstances are changing rapidly, or when the Court is uncertain that a broad rule would make sense in future cases. If a court has reason for confidence about the theoretical foundations of some area of law, it has earned the right to depth; I have suggested that this is now true for the area of sex equality. When there is a great need for predictability, and good reason for confidence that an adequate rule can be devised, width is entirely appropriate and perhaps indispensable; consider property and contract law.

In some areas, broad rules make a good deal of sense, and in some cases diverse judges can and should converge on theoretically ambitious abstractions involving liberty or equality. These are the most glorious moments in any nation's legal culture. I have been stressing another point. When a democracy is in a state of ethical or political uncertainty, courts may not have the best or the final answers. Judicial answers may be wrong. They may be counterproductive even if they are right. On occasion courts do best by proceeding in a way that is catalytic rather than preclusive, and that is closely attuned to the fact that courts are participants in an elaborate system of democratic deliberation. Minimalism is not always the best way to proceed. But it has distinctive uses in constitutional law, where judges, well aware of their own limitations, know that sometimes the best decision is to leave things undecided.

A View From the Inside

2.6 *Zelman v. Simmons-Harris*
536 U.S. 639 (2002)

Justice Thomas, concurring.
Frederick Douglass once said that "[e]ducation . . . means emancipation. It means light and liberty. It means the uplifting of the soul of man into the glorious light of truth, the light by which men can only be made free." Today many of our inner-city public schools deny emancipation to urban minority students. Despite this Court's observation nearly 50 years ago in *Brown v. Board of Education,* that "it is doubtful that any child may reasonably be expected to succeed in life if he is denied the opportunity of an education," urban children have been forced into a system that continually fails them. These cases present an example of such failures. Besieged by escalating financial problems and declining academic achievement, the Cleveland City School District was in the midst of an academic emergency when Ohio enacted its scholarship program.

The dissents and respondents wish to invoke the Establishment Clause of the First Amendment, as incorporated through the Fourteenth, to constrain a State's neutral efforts to provide greater educational opportunity for underprivileged minority students. Today's decision properly upholds the program as constitutional, and I join it in full.

This Court has often considered whether efforts to provide children with the best educational resources conflict with constitutional limitations. Attempts to provide aid to religious schools or to allow some degree of religious involvement in public schools have generated significant controversy and litigation as States try to navigate the line between the secular and the religious in education. We have recently decided several cases challenging federal aid programs that include religious schools. To determine whether a federal program survives scrutiny under the Establishment Clause, we have considered whether it has a secular purpose and whether it has the primary effect of advancing or inhibiting religion. I agree with the Court that Ohio's program easily passes muster under our stringent test, but, as a matter of first principles, I question whether this test should be applied to the States.

The Establishment Clause of the First Amendment states that "Congress shall make no law respecting an establishment of religion." On its face, this provision places no limit on the States with regard to religion. The Establishment Clause originally protected States, and by extension their citizens, from the imposition of an established religion by the Federal Government. Whether and how this Clause should constrain state action under the Fourteenth Amendment is a more difficult question.

The Fourteenth Amendment fundamentally restructured the relationship between individuals and the States and ensured that States would not deprive citizens of liberty without due process of law. It guarantees citizenship to all individuals born or naturalized in the United States and provides that "[n]o State shall make or enforce any law which shall abridge the privileges or immunities of citizens of the United States; nor shall any State deprive any person of life, liberty, or property, without due process of law; nor deny to any person within its jurisdiction the equal protection of the laws." As Justice Harlan noted, the Fourteenth Amendment "added greatly to the dignity and glory of American citizenship, and to the security of personal liberty." When rights are incorporated against the States through the Fourteenth Amendment they should advance, not constrain, individual liberty.

Consequently, in the context of the Establishment Clause, it may well be that state action should be evaluated on different terms than similar action by the Federal Government. "States, while bound to observe strict neutrality, should be freer to experiment with involvement [in religion]—on a neutral basis—than the Federal Government." Thus, while the Federal Government may "make no law respecting an establishment of religion," the States may pass laws that include or touch on religious matters so long as these laws do not impede free exercise rights or any other individual religious liberty interest. By considering the particular religious liberty right alleged to be invaded by a State, federal courts can strike a proper balance between the demands of the Fourteenth Amendment on the one hand and the federalism prerogatives of States on the other.

Whatever the textual and historical merits of incorporating the Establishment Clause, I can accept that the Fourteenth Amendment protects religious liberty rights. But I cannot accept its use to oppose neutral programs of school choice through the incorporation of the Establishment Clause. There would be a tragic irony in converting the Fourteenth Amendment's guarantee of individual liberty into a prohibition on the exercise of educational choice.

The wisdom of allowing States greater latitude in dealing with matters of religion and education can be easily appreciated in this context. Respondents advocate using the Fourteenth Amendment to handcuff the State's ability to experiment with education. But without education one can hardly exercise the civic, political, and personal freedoms conferred by the Fourteenth Amendment. Faced with a severe educational crisis, the State of Ohio enacted wide-ranging educational reform that allows voluntary participation of private and religious schools in educating poor urban children otherwise condemned to failing public schools. The program does not force any individual to submit to religious indoctrination or education. It simply gives parents a greater choice as to where and in what manner to educate their children. This is a choice that those with greater means have routinely exercised.

Cleveland parents now have a variety of educational choices. There are traditional public schools, magnet schools, and privately run community schools, in addition to the scholarship program. Currently, 46 of the 56 private schools participating in the scholarship program are church affiliated (35 are Catholic), and 96 percent of students in the program attend religious schools. Thus, were the

Court to disallow the inclusion of religious schools, Cleveland children could use their scholarships at only 10 private schools.

In addition to expanding the reach of the scholarship program, the inclusion of religious schools makes sense given Ohio's purpose of increasing educational performance and opportunities. Religious schools, like other private schools, achieve far better educational results than their public counterparts. For example, the students at Cleveland's Catholic schools score significantly higher on Ohio proficiency tests than students at Cleveland public schools. Of Cleveland eighth graders taking the 1999 Ohio proficiency test, 95 percent in Catholic schools passed the reading test, whereas only 57 percent in public schools passed. And 75 percent of Catholic school students passed the math proficiency test, compared to only 22 percent of public school students. But the success of religious and private schools is in the end beside the point, because the State has a constitutional right to experiment with a variety of different programs to promote educational opportunity. That Ohio's program includes successful schools simply indicates that such reform can in fact provide improved education to underprivileged urban children.

Although one of the purposes of public schools was to promote democracy and a more egalitarian culture, failing urban public schools disproportionately affect minority children most in need of educational opportunity. At the time of Reconstruction, blacks considered public education "a matter of personal liberation and a necessary function of a free society." Today, however, the promise of public school education has failed poor inner-city blacks. While in theory providing education to everyone, the quality of public schools varies significantly across districts. Just as blacks supported public education during Reconstruction, many blacks and other minorities now support school choice programs because they provide the greatest educational opportunities for their children in struggling communities. Opponents of the program raise formalistic concerns about the Establishment Clause but ignore the core purposes of the Fourteenth Amendment.

While the romanticized ideal of universal public education resonates with the cognoscenti who oppose vouchers, poor urban families just want the best education for their children, who will certainly need it to function in our high-tech and advanced society. As Thomas Sowell noted 30 years ago: "Most black people have faced too many grim, concrete problems to be romantics. They want and need certain tangible results, which can be achieved only by developing certain specific abilities." The same is true today. An individual's life prospects increase dramatically with each successfully completed phase of education. For instance, a black high school dropout earns just over $13,500, but with a high school degree the average income is almost $21,000. Blacks with a bachelor's degree have an average annual income of about $37,500, and $75,500 with a professional degree. Staying in school and earning a degree generates real and tangible financial benefits, whereas failure to obtain even a high school degree essentially relegates students to a life of poverty and, all too often, of crime. The failure to provide education to poor urban children perpetuates a vicious cycle of poverty, dependence, criminality, and alienation that continues for the remainder of their lives. If society cannot end racial discrimination, at least it can arm minorities with the education to defend themselves from some of discrimination's effects.

Ten States have enacted some form of publicly funded private school choice as one means of raising the quality of education provided to underprivileged urban children. These programs address the root of the problem with failing urban public schools that disproportionately affect minority students. Society's other solution to these educational failures is often to provide racial preferences in higher education. Such preferences, however, run afoul of the Fourteenth Amendment's prohibition against distinctions based on race. By contrast, school choice programs that involve religious schools appear unconstitutional only to those who would twist the Fourteenth Amendment against itself by expansively incorporating the Establishment Clause. Converting the Fourteenth Amendment from a guarantee of opportunity to an obstacle against education reform distorts our constitutional values and disserves those in the greatest need.

As Frederick Douglass poignantly noted "no greater benefit can be bestowed upon a long benighted people, than giving to them, as we are here earnestly this day endeavoring to do, the means of an education."

The Freedom of Speech (1993)

John Paul Stevens

Throughout history the seeds of intolerance have produced injustice and conflict. In Rouen, France in 1431, a nineteen-year-old woman who wore men's clothes, who fought bravely in the French army, and who insisted that she communicated directly with God, was burned at the stake after she was found guilty of witchcraft and heresy. In Salem, Massachusetts in 1692, Samuel Sewall, a Harvard graduate, a devout man, and a duly elected judge, found nineteen persons, mostly women, guilty of witchcraft—a capital offense punishable by hanging. Today the weeds of intolerance poison the relations between neighbors in all parts of the globe—in Northern Ireland, in the Holy Land, in Bosnia, in Eastern Germany, in Azerbaijan, and in some parts of the United States. It seems appropriate, therefore, to ask why (or perhaps even whether) the First Amendment of our Constitution should afford extraordinary protection to the apostles of intolerance. . . .

The First Amendment contains a single sentence that reads as follows:

> Congress shall make no law respecting an establishment of religion, or prohibiting the free exercise thereof; or abridging the freedom of speech, or of the press; or the right of the people peaceably to assemble, and to petition the Government for a redress of grievances.

There are three dimensions to most, if not all, immunity rules. First, they provide protection against a specified category of potential harms. Judicial immunity, for instance, protects the judge from damages liability, while the statutory immunity granted to certain witnesses protects them from criminal prosecution. What the First Amendment protects all of us from is adverse lawmaking by the Congress. . . .

Second, a rule of immunity provides protection in a specified degree, either absolute or qualified.

Reprinted by permission of The Yale Law Journal Company and William S. Hein Company, from *The Yale Law Journal*, Vol. 102 (1993), pp. 1293–1313.

The judge's immunity from liability for damages is absolute; even malicious wrongdoing may be protected. Law enforcement officers, in contrast, have only qualified immunity; their knowledge of the law, or lack thereof, may determine their liability. As for the First Amendment, its text makes the uncompromising command that "Congress shall make no law . . . abridging the freedom of speech." The imperative tone of that command has an absolute ring; it is far stronger than one that is qualified by exceptions for time, place, and manner regulations or for speech that interferes with a compelling state interest (such as the interest in national security), or for speech that is harmful to children or offensive to captive audiences. The plain language of the First Amendment indicates that the Framers intended to establish a rule of absolute immunity.

The third dimension of an immunity rule identifies the category of behavior that it protects. Thus, judicial immunity protects a judge while he is performing judicial services within the scope of his jurisdiction, but not while he is out robbing banks or fighting with his neighbors. The particular category of protected human behavior that interests us this afternoon is that embraced within the term "*the* freedom of speech."

I emphasize the word "the" as used in the term "the freedom of speech" because the definite article suggests that the draftsmen intended to immunize a previously identified category or subset of speech. That category could not have been coextensive with the category of oral communications that are commonly described as "speech" in ordinary usage. For it is obvious that the Framers did not intend to provide constitutional protection for false testimony under oath, or for oral contracts that are against public policy, such as wagers or conspiracies among competitors to fix prices. The Amendment has never been understood to protect all oral communication, no matter how unlawful, threatening, or vulgar it may be. Thus, it seems doubtful that the word "speech" was used in its most ordinary sense. . . .

This understanding of the category of oral speech originally intended for absolute immunity by the

First Amendment would be consistent with the limited character of the writings that the Amendment also protects, at least by its plain terms. The word "press," though encompassing newspapers, periodicals, and political pamphlets, is by no means a synonym for "all written words." Moreover, the right to "petition the Government for a redress of grievances" recalls the formal petition of right by which English subjects sought a waiver of their Monarch's sovereign immunity. The plain language of the First Amendment can be read narrowly, as expressing the Framers' original intent to create an absolute immunity from federal interference with a limited category of freedoms.

This interpretation, though perhaps plausible as an historical matter, cannot fully capture the meaning of the First Amendment read as a whole. First, even assuming that the draftsmen of the Amendment focused their attention on a specific set of concerns, they used words that identify and express a faith in principles of tolerance and resistance to authority that bespeak a broader concept of liberty. Moreover, the several clauses that are juxtaposed in the text of the First Amendment illuminate one another and combine to form a whole larger than its parts. There is an obvious connection, for instance, between freedom of speech and freedom of the press, and of course, the exercise of the right to petition the government presupposes a right to speak freely in opposition to government policy. And that right, in turn, presupposes the same freedom of conscience that is protected by the Religion Clauses. Thus, when Justice Jackson referred to the "freedom to be intellectually and spiritually diverse" in [*West Virginia v. Barnette* (1943)] he was construing the central meaning of the entire Amendment. As he wrote, "If there is any fixed star in our constitutional constellation, it is that no official, high or petty, can prescribe what shall be orthodox in politics, nationalism, religion, or other matters of opinion or force citizens to confess by word or act their faith therein." . . .

The category of expression embraced by the term "*the* freedom of speech" has undergone parallel change and expansion as it has been tested in the crucible of litigation. Even if the concept originally embraced little more than matters that were appropriate subjects of debate at a New England town meeting, and even if the dictionary definition of the word "speech" has not changed since 1791,

it is now settled that constitutionally protected forms of communication include parades, dances, artistic expression, picketing, wearing arm bands, burning flags and crosses, commercial advertising, charitable solicitation, rock music, some libelous false statements, and perhaps even sleeping in a public park. . . .

My experience on the bench has convinced me that . . . categories [of speech] must be used with caution and viewed with skepticism. Too often, they neither account for the facts at issue nor illuminate the interests at stake. . . .

In sum, it seems to me that the attempt to craft black-letter or bright-line rules of First Amendment law often produces unworkable and unsatisfactory results, especially when an exclusive focus on rules of general application obfuscates the specific facts at issue and interests at stake in a given case. I offer this observation not only as a matter of academic interest, but also as a practical guide, for advocates, as well as scholars and judges, may emphasize legal abstractions at the expense of facts that could win a case. Indeed, a litigant's misplaced reliance on propositions of law instead of the special facts of the case may snatch defeat from the jaws of victory. . . .

In closing, I return to the question I posed at the beginning: whether, and why, our Constitution should be tolerant of intolerance. From what I have said so far, I suspect it is clear why I would suggest that the more relevant question is when, and under what circumstances, intolerant expressions merit protection. If the intolerance is expressed in the course of a public dialogue protected by the Speech and Debate Clause of the Constitution, or even in a public gathering where speech is not intermingled with actual or threatened harmful conduct, then the question is adequately answered by our commitment to open discussion as an antidote to plain error. Exposure to sunshine and fresh air can work wonderful changes in even the ugliest seeds.

The more difficult question arises when intolerant speech is associated with some form of expressive conduct. In those cases, we must forgo the appeal of the absolute or bright-line rule, and rely instead on attention to detail and sensitivity to context. As Professor [Mari] Matsuda explained in discussing the same problem, "This is not an easy legal or moral puzzle, but it is precisely in these places where we feel conflicting tugs at heart and mind that we have the most work to do and the most knowledge to gain."

A rule that mandates tolerance of offensive speech—that is to say, speech that conveys offensive messages—need not extend the same degree of tolerance to offensive conduct. It is nevertheless essential that any analysis of the difficult and close cases that arise in this area give full effect to the many dimensions of the idea of freedom. "The First Amendment presupposes that the freedom to speak one's mind is not only an aspect of individual liberty—and thus a good unto itself—but also is essential to the common quest for truth and the vitality of society as a whole." The arguments advanced by Justice Brandeis in his separate opinion in *Whitney v. California* merit repetition:

> Those who won our independence believed that the final end of the State was to make men free to develop their faculties; and that in its government the deliberative forces should prevail over the arbitrary. They valued liberty both as an end and as a means. They believed liberty to be the secret of happiness and courage to be the secret of liberty. They believed that freedom to think as you will and to speak as you think are means indispensable to the discovery and spread of political truth; that without free speech and assembly discussion would be futile; that with them, discussion affords ordinarily adequate protection against the dissemination of noxious doctrine; that the greatest menace to

freedom is an inert people; that public discussion is a political duty; and that this should be a fundamental principle of the American government. They recognized the risks to which all human institutions are subject. But they knew that order cannot be secured merely through fear of punishment for its infraction; that it is hazardous to discourage thought, hope and imagination; that fear breeds repression; that repression breeds hate; that hate menaces stable government; that the path of safety lies in the opportunity to discuss freely supposed grievances and proposed remedies; and that the fitting remedy for evil counsels is good ones. Believing in the power of reason as applied through public discussion, they eschewed silence coerced by law—the argument of force in its worst form. Recognizing the occasional tyrannies of governing majorities, they amended the Constitution so that free speech and assembly should be guaranteed.

> Fear of serious injury cannot alone justify suppression of free speech and assembly. Men feared witches and burnt women. It is the function of speech to free men from the bondage of irrational fears.

Let us hope that whenever we decide to tolerate intolerant speech, the speaker as well as the audience will understand that we do so to express our deep commitment to the value of tolerance—a value protected by every clause in the single sentence called the First Amendment.

A Comparative Perspective

2.8 Constitutional Interpretation and Original Intent: A Form of Ancestor Worship? (1999)

Michael Kirby

I want to pose some questions to open this lecture with a little provocation. Do United States judges,

unlike their Australian counterparts, when ascertaining the meaning of their Constitution, engage in a quaint ritual of ancestor worship? Are our American colleagues so mesmerised by the awe in which they hold the revolutionary founders of the republic who wrote their Constitution (Jefferson, Madison, Hamilton, etc.) that they feel obliged to construe the text, 220 years on, by ascertaining the intentions of those great men at the time they wrote it, however inapt those intentions might be to contemporary circumstances? In brief, when a problem arises under their Constitution, is the judicial duty to consult the historical records to find the original intentions of the founders? Is the task "rather like having a remote ancestor who came over on the *Mayflower*," (akin in our case, perhaps to the *Sirius*), and asking him or her the meaning of a political document that governs the affairs of the nation in the space age? Are there any risks that this quaint American ritual will travel to the Antipodes and capture the imagination of Australia's judges in the task of interpreting the Australian Constitution?

These were some of the controversies about constitutional interpretation which were debated recently in Auckland, New Zealand, at a conference on constitutionalism. Justice Scalia of the Supreme Court of the United States and Justice Binney of the Supreme Court of Canada gave different answers. The former is probably the "most eloquent expositor" of the modern theory of originalism. He believes that, of its nature, a written Constitution has a fixed meaning which does not change with time and that such meaning is the same as the words signified when the Constitution was first adopted. Justice Binney, recently appointed to the Supreme Court of Canada, was called upon to answer the criticisms implicitly directed by his United States colleague to the process of elaboration of the Canadian Constitution and its Charter of Fundamental Rights and Freedoms. It was in the context of defending the Canadian approach to that task, that Justice Binney let slip the opinion (which he suggested was held by some Canadian judges) that the approach of their counterparts in the United States could only be explained by appreciating that Americans were engaged in a ritual of ancestor worship.

The Constitutions of the United States of America (1776–1790), Canada (1867), and Australia (1901) are amongst the three most enduring of such documents in the world today. But what do they mean? The question of constitutional interpretation arises at the very threshold of every case in which the constitutional text must be elucidated. The text of the Australian Constitution—like that of the United States and Canada—is written in language which is brief, sometimes obscure and often ambiguous. As recent shifts in the Court's elaboration of the meaning of the Constitution demonstrate even an assertion that a particular construction of the text is "settled" by many past decisions does not necessarily bolt the door against re-examination of the Constitution if new scrutiny is considered necessary by the majority of the Justices of the High Court. This is why the approach to construction of the Constitution arises at the threshold of all the great constitutional disputes. It is one which has fascinated the Justices themselves. It has attracted a great deal of writing by scholars, both in Australia and overseas. It ought to concern all practitioners and students of the law in a federation, like Australia, with a written constitution adopted long ago. Citizens should know about it. . . .

Opposing Opinions on Original Intent

In the New Zealand conference, at which Justice Scalia was presented in intellectual combat with Justice Binney over this issue, each expressed, in eloquent language, the viewpoint he espoused. It was not difficult for Justice Scalia. He has been writing on this topic for many years, both as a member of the Supreme Court of the United States and extracurially. . . .

Justice Binney, for his part, appealed to developing notions about construing statutes generally so as to achieve and not frustrate their purposes; to the need for the courts to respond to cases before them which raise novel problems; to the frequent failures of the other branches of government to do so; and to the strongly supportive opinion of the Canadian people, as disclosed in successive opinion polls, concerning the work of the Supreme Court in the elaboration of the Canadian Constitution and Charter of Rights. In his paper, Justice Binney called in aid of his opinions the views expressed by another distinguished North American jurist, Chief Judge Richard Posner of the United States Court of Appeals in Chicago:

> Some constitutional and other legal issues cannot be resolved [on the facts or in terms of institutional competence] and then the judge has

two choices. One is to say that if public opinion is divided on a moral issue, judges should refuse to intervene, should leave resolution to the political process. The other is to say, with Holmes, that while this is ordinarily the right way to go, every once in a while, an issue on which public opinion is divided will so excite the judge's moral emotions that he simply will not be able to stomach the political resolution that has been challenged on constitutional grounds. I prefer the second route.

So there one has the competing views. The one that a Constitution is anti-evolutionary. The other that it must be evolutionary. . . .

Mason and Constitutional Interpretation

As might be expected, both in his judicial decisions and in his extra-curial writing, Sir Anthony Mason has addressed the issue of interpretation of the Constitution many times. Most recently he did so in an essay on "The Interpretation of the Constitution in a Modern Liberal Democracy." In that essay Sir Anthony classified various approaches to the interpretation of the Constitution: "originalism"; "intentionalism" . . . "literalism"; "progressivism" or "flexible interpretation," the last as favored by Chief Judge Posner; and various combinations of the others. Sir Anthony Mason does not expressly align himself with any of the doctrines. Perhaps at different times of his long judicial career, he has invoked different theories and applied different principles. But after recounting the opinions of leading United States and Australian scholars, he makes it fairly clear that the Australian High Court has, for a long time, turned its back upon originalism and pure intentionalism. . . .

Sir Anthony Mason concludes his survey of this subject with an emphasis which was certainly not present twenty or thirty years ago. He refers to the foundation of the Australian Constitution as resting in the sovereign rights of the people of Australia. Twenty or thirty years ago, especially in legal circles, the ultimate foundation of the legitimacy and binding force of the Australian Constitution was given, virtually without dissent, as the Act of the Imperial Parliament at Westminster. That Parliament

had enacted the Constitution. Its power therefore gave rise to the legal quality of the norms which it established. Nowadays, a different foundation for the Constitution must be found—one consistent with its origins, history, function and method of amendment. But that very fact illustrates, quite vividly, the evolutionary character of the Constitution—a fact which must affect approaches to the ascertainment of its meaning.

Sir Anthony Mason ends his essay on this subject by expressing the view that a constitutional court, such as the High Court of Australia, must interpret the constitutional charter in a way that will "reinforce and enhance the concept of a modern liberal democracy.". . .

There is no task performed by a Justice of the High Court which is more important than the task of interpreting the Australian Constitution. Each judge—and indeed every lawyer—who has ever embarked upon that task is obliged to do more than to stumble about looking for a solution to the particular case. Intuition and instinct about such matters are not enough. Sitting at a desk with the Constitution in one hand and a dictionary in the other, is also not enough. Following blindly judicial opinions written in earlier and very different times may not be enough. . . . That is why it is vital that each judge (indeed each reader of the Constitution) should have a theory of constitutional interpretation. Only such a theory will afford a consistent guide to a consistent approach to be taken to the task. In the absence of a theory, inconsistency will proliferate. The judge will be castigated, perhaps correctly, for saying incompatible things at different times and construing the same words at different times in incompatible ways. Guided by Sir Anthony Mason's introduction to this topic, I want to add a few words as to why history and original intent provide poor guides for the task and why it is incumbent on us to construe the Australian Constitution as a living document so that (as far as its words and structure permit) it serves effectively the governmental needs of contemporary Australians.

History in the High Court

To be a lawyer in Australia is, in a sense, to be a type of legal historian. It is an inescapable feature of the common law that judges and other lawyers live their lives in the presence of the great legal spirits of the past and the cases of those people. On our bookshelves, and now in electronic systems, are the tales of ancient conflicts and the attempts, mostly by rational people, to come to principled and just solutions to conflicts. Increasingly, in recent times, the solutions have been offered in the form of legislation. Yet for nearly seven centuries, five of them before modern Australia was founded, cases have been brought to the courts of our legal tradition. Their facts have been written down. The solutions to the problems which they presented have been expounded by judges. Those expositions have been duly recorded. They have been shared with colleagues at the time. They have been sent into the future for its instruction. The power of the judicial reasoning has been passed to new generations for their consideration and use. The principles emerging from a multitude of cases have gone together to make up the great body of the common law. To be a judge in our legal tradition, is thus to be a privileged participant in the making of this form of legal history. The contribution of no one, however brilliant and distinguished, is very great or enduring. Occasionally, a towering figure of the common law stands out only to see his or her reputation wither as history catches up and replaces that reputation with someone or something new. . . .

In the beginning the High Court was extremely cautious about the use of Australian legal history, at least in constitutional interpretation, so far as it arose from the debates at the Constitutional Conventions which, in the 1890s, had fashioned and finally settled the text of the Australian Constitution. In the earliest decisions of the Court, it rejected the idea that the Justices could seek enlightenment as to the meaning of the constitutional text from the contributions made in the debates at the Conventions in which all of the original Justices had themselves taken part. In part, this rejection derived from the then current view that language always had objectively discoverable meanings; that such meanings were to be found by careful study of the text and context; and that most external and historical materials would only be likely to confuse the task of interpretation. But in part, the attitude may also have derived from the sure conviction of the original Justices that they knew exactly what the Constitution meant from their own participation in the Conventions. They remembered. They did not need to be reminded, least of all of the words of

other delegates, some of whom they may have held in low regard. It is difficult as we look back on the generally high standard of the debates of the Australasian and Australian Constitutional Conventions of the 1890s to remember that the participants were human beings, much as ourselves: with foibles and vanities and weaknesses only too well known to their contemporaries. . . .

Original Intent or a Text Set Free?

To a superficial student of Australian legal history, it might appear that the abandonment of the prohibition on the use of the debates in the Constitutional Conventions amounted to the acceptance by the Australian High Court of techniques apt to the discovery of the original intentions of the drafters. Certainly, the study of their words in the debates of the 1890s would tend to show what they thought the text which they were adopting, amending or rejecting was supposed to mean. . . . Does it embrace original intent as the preeminent criterion for interpretation of the Constitution? Does it have implications for the construction of other lawmaking documents, such as statutes and subordinate legislation? Is this what the judicial search for meaning is now supposed to come up with whenever an ambiguity arises in a legal text? . . .

This doctrine of the Constitution as a "living force" is one which has proved influential over the years with several Justices of the High Court of Australia. When an old line of authority is overturned, this may sometimes be explained not by reference to an error in the perception of the Justices who propounded that authority at the time of its invention and first applications. But rather by reference to the fact that the eyes of new generations of Australians inevitably see the unchanged language in a different light. The words remain the same. The meaning and content of the words take color from the circumstances in which the words must be understood and to which they must be applied. . . .

So what is now needed in Australia is a consistent theory for the proper approach to the resolution of problems of this kind. The adoption in one case of a criterion of "the intention of the makers as evinced by the terms in which they expressed that intention" and the adoption in another case of something analogous to [the] "living force" doctrine, may suggest an element of ambivalence about the approach to constitutional interpretation which future cases will need to resolve. In my opinion, a consistent application of the view that the Constitution was set free from its founders in 1901 is the rule that we should apply. That our Constitution belongs to succeeding generations of the Australian people. That it is bound to be read in changing ways as time passes and circumstances change. That it should be read so as to achieve the purposes of good government which the Constitution was designed to promote and secure. The Australian Constitution belongs to the twenty-first century, not to the nineteenth.

Sir Anthony Mason was right to call this question to the notice of everyone concerned in the operation of the Australian Constitution. He continues to call to our attention the key issues for Australian constitutional life, and for the destiny of our nation as an independent state in a world of globalism and regionalism. It is that world, above all, that requires adaptability and imagination in the application of the text of 1901. This is not to defeat the intention of the Constitution and its framers. On the contrary. It is to achieve its high and enduring governmental purposes.

Sir Anthony Mason showed us the way. It is fitting that his leadership as a judge and scholar should be remembered and celebrated by the students of this Law School. It is important that we who follow, judge and student should learn from Sir Anthony Mason's example, and take strength from his practical creativity in the field of Australian constitutional law.

For Further Reading

Baum, Lawrence. *The Puzzle of Judicial Behavior.* Ann Arbor: University of Michigan Press, 1997.

Epstein, Lee and Jack Knight. *The Choices Justices Make.* Washington, D.C.: Congressional Quarterly, Inc., 1997.

Maltzman, Forrest, James F. Spriggs II, and Paul J. Wahlbeck. *Crafting Law on the Supreme Court: The Collegial Game.* New York: Cambridge University Press, 2000.

McGuire, Kevin T. *Understanding the U.S. Supreme Court.* New York: McGraw-Hill, 2002.

Segal, Jeffrey and Harold Spaeth. *The Supreme Court and the Attitudinal Model.* New York: Cambridge University Press, 1993.

Chapter 3

Politics of Judicial Structure and Organization

Introduction

The structure and organization of the judiciary is fundamentally the mechanics of the court system: the number, the type, and the function of courts, in addition to the kinds of cases they hear and whom they serve. As you will see, the structure and organization of courts and court systems are inherently political, extending from the process of creating courts to maintaining and changing courts. Of primary interest to political scientists is how the mechanics of the judiciary affects the operation of courts. In other words, how is the administration of justice influenced by the character of courts and the interactions among courts?

Foundations and History

Judicial federalism—the balance of power between federal and state judiciaries—has always been central to the politics of the judiciary. The early history of the Union demonstrates concerted efforts to establish and maintain a powerful federal judiciary relative to state courts. As *Federalist* No. 82 (1788) illustrates, Alexander Hamilton tried to appease concerns about the future of state court authority in the federal system by arguing that state courts would maintain much of their independent sphere of authority. However, he also acknowledged that there would be concurrent jurisdiction between the state and federal judiciaries. He described these parameters in this essay.

Several decades later, the Supreme Court made a significant contribution to judicial federalism in *Martin v. Hunter's Lessee* (1816) by asserting federal judicial supremacy. At issue was Section 25 of the Judiciary Act of 1789, passed by Congress to include in the Court's appellate jurisdiction appeals from the state courts of last resort. Justice Story delivered the Court's ruling upholding Section 25. In that ruling, he analyzed in detail the language of Article III granting appellate review to the Court and argued vehemently that the federal judiciary is superior to state judiciaries.

In so doing, Justice Story solidified the authority of the federal government over the states more generally.

Contemporary Judicial Politics

Justice Story's was not the last word on the nature of judicial federalism. Although the Supreme Court has the authority to overturn state court rulings, the Court is not required to exercise this power. In the past few decades, there has been frequent discussion about the Rehnquist Court's efforts to move power away from the federal judiciary (and the federal government, more generally) and give it to the states. Scholars have also been interested in the phenomenon of *new* judicial federalism, which is one focus of Michael E. Solimine's article, "Supreme Court Monitoring of State Courts in the Twenty-First Century" (2002). The contemporary interaction between the Supreme Court and state courts, he argues, has had an important influence on the administration of justice at both levels of the judiciary.

Most of us are aware of the common trial and appellate courts in the federal and state systems. In the federal system, we are most familiar with the district (trial) and circuit (intermediate appellate) courts and the Supreme Court. But there are lesser known, yet still powerful, courts in the federal system. In the wake of the attacks of September 11, 2001, you may have heard of the Foreign Intelligence Surveillance Court (FISC) and the Foreign Intelligence Surveillance Court of Review (FISCR). Both of these courts have been in existence for some time. They were established by the Foreign Intelligence Surveillance Act of 1978 (FISA), but until recently have not been the subject of public debate. Currently, there has been extensive discussion about FISA, the methods that it provides for collecting national security intelligence, and its modification by the USA Patriot Act of 2001 (short for Uniting and Strengthening America by Providing Appropriate Tools Required to Intercept and Obstruct Terrorism). The FISC and the FISCR have a very different mission and operate in a completely different manner from any other federal court. Among the many distinguishing features are their highly secretive and nonadversarial proceedings. The FISC has been quite active since its inception, issuing thousands of rulings permitting Democratic and Republican presidents to collect intelligence from foreigners as well as U.S. citizens for the purpose of national security. During its first twenty-four years, the FISC did not reject a single application for a warrant. That changed in May 2002, when the FISC rejected a motion by the Bush administration; but six months later, the FISCR overturned that decision. We have included edited versions of both rulings in this chapter.

A View from the Inside

The Ninth Circuit Court of Appeals is a perennial source of debate about judicial organization, and the best contemporary example of the politics inherent in the structure of the judiciary. For casual observers, this court is probably known for its ruling on the constitutionality of the Pledge of Allegiance (*Newdow v. U.S. Congress et al.,*

00-16423 [2002]). This ruling likely would have caused a furor regardless of which of the twelve circuit courts had decided it. However, that decision prompted particular condemnation because it came from the Ninth Circuit.

The Ninth Circuit is the largest circuit in the nation, serving nine rather distinctive states (and two territories) with diverse political interests. It is also known as the most liberal circuit, with its seat in San Francisco, and it has a relatively high reversal rate of its decisions at the Supreme Court. As a result of these and other characteristics, there has been a decades-long effort to divide the circuit led primarily by Republican politicians from states like Idaho, Nevada, and Montana who feel that the court does not serve their interests.

To illustrate the complexity of the debate about the Ninth Circuit, we present excerpts from a hearing about the division of that court conducted by the House Subcommittee on Courts, the Internet, and Intellectual Property. Several judges from the Ninth Circuit as well as interested elected officials from around the country shared their views on a House bill proposed in 2001. The views expressed in that hearing demonstrate the wide diversity of positions on the effort to divide the circuit. We have also included the March 2003 statement by Senator Lisa Murkowski (R-AK) introducing S. 562, the most recent attempt to restructure the circuit.

A Comparative Perspective

Significantly, the American form of judicial federalism is not the only one that exists among democratic nations. During the past several decades, the European Union has faced the dilemma of balancing authority between a centralized court of last resort (the European Court of Justice) and the individual state courts of its member nations. In "The European Preliminary Reference and U.S. Supreme Court Review of State Court Judgments: A Study in Comparative Judicial Federalism" (1996), Jeffrey Cohen discusses the power relationship that was established in Europe and suggests that the United States may have something to learn from the European experience.

Foundations and History

3.1   *Federalist* No. 82 (1788)

Alexander Hamilton

To the People of the State of New York:

The erection of a new government, whatever care or wisdom may distinguish the work, cannot fail to originate questions of intricacy and nicety; and these may, in a particular manner, be expected to flow from the establishment of a constitution founded upon the total or partial incorporation of a number of distinct sovereignties. It is time only that can mature and perfect so compound a system, can liquidate the meaning of all the parts, and can adjust them to each other in a harmonious and consistent *whole.*

Such questions, accordingly, have arisen upon the plan proposed by the convention, and particularly concerning the judiciary department. The principal of these respect the situation of the State courts in regard to those causes which are to be submitted to federal jurisdiction. Is this to be exclusive, or are those courts to possess a concurrent jurisdiction? If the latter, in what relation will they stand to the national tribunals? These are inquiries which we meet with in the mouths of men of sense, and which are certainly entitled to attention.

The principles established in a former paper [*Federalist* No. 31] teach us that the States will retain all *pre-existing* authorities which may not be exclusively delegated to the federal head; and that this exclusive delegation can only exist in one of three cases: where an exclusive authority is, in express terms, granted to the Union; or where a particular authority is granted to the Union, and the exercise of a like authority is prohibited to the States; or where an authority is granted to the Union, with which a similar authority in the States would be utterly incompatible. Though these principles may not apply with the same force to the judiciary as to the legislative power, yet I am inclined to think that they are, in the main, just with respect to the former, as well as the latter. And under this impression, I shall lay it down as a rule, that the State courts will *retain* the jurisdiction they now have, unless it appears to be taken away in one of the enumerated modes.

The only thing in the proposed Constitution, which wears the appearance of confining the causes of federal cognizance to the federal courts, is contained in this passage: "The *judicial power* of the United States *shall be vested* in one Supreme Court, and in *such* inferior courts as the Congress shall from time to time ordain and establish." This might either be construed to signify, that the supreme and subordinate courts of the Union should alone have the power of deciding those causes to which their authority is to extend; or simply to denote, that the organs of the national judiciary should be one Supreme Court, and as many subordinate courts as Congress should think proper to appoint; or in other words, that the United States

should exercise the judicial power with which they are to be invested, through one supreme tribunal, and a certain number of inferior ones, to be instituted by them. The first excludes, the last admits, the concurrent jurisdiction of the State tribunals; and as the first would amount to an alienation of State power by implication, the last appears to me the most natural and the most defensible construction.

But this doctrine of concurrent jurisdiction is only clearly applicable to those descriptions of causes of which the State courts have previous cognizance. It is not equally evident in relation to cases which may grow out of, and be *peculiar* to, the Constitution to be established; for not to allow the State courts a right of jurisdiction in such cases, can hardly be considered as the abridgment of a pre-existing authority. I mean not therefore to contend that the United States, in the course of legislation upon the objects intrusted to their direction, may not commit the decision of causes arising upon a particular regulation to the federal courts solely, if such a measure should be deemed expedient; but I hold that the State courts will be divested of no part of their primitive jurisdiction, further than may relate to an appeal; and I am even of opinion that in every case in which they were not expressly excluded by the future acts of the national legislature, they will of course take cognizance of the causes to which those acts may give birth. This I infer from the nature of judiciary power, and from the general genius of the system. The judiciary power of every government looks beyond its own local or municipal laws, and in civil cases lays hold of all subjects of litigation between parties within its jurisdiction, though the causes of dispute are relative to the laws of the most distant part of the globe. Those of Japan, not less than of New York, may furnish the objects of legal discussion to our courts. When in addition to this we consider the State governments and the national governments, as they truly are, in the light of kindred systems, and as parts of *one whole,* the inference seems to be conclusive, that the State courts would have a concurrent jurisdiction in all cases arising under the laws of the Union, where it was not expressly prohibited.

Here another question occurs: What relation would subsist between the national and State courts in these instances of concurrent jurisdiction?

I answer, that an appeal would certainly lie from the latter, to the Supreme Court of the United States. The Constitution in direct terms gives an appellate jurisdiction to the Supreme Court in all the enumerated cases of federal cognizance in which it is not to have an original one, without a single expression to confine its operation to the inferior federal courts. The objects of appeal, not the tribunals from which it is to be made, are alone contemplated. From this circumstance, and from the reason of the thing, it ought to be construed to extend to the State tribunals. Either this must be the case, or the local courts must be excluded from a concurrent jurisdiction in matters of national concern, else the judiciary authority of the Union may be eluded at the pleasure of every plaintiff or prosecutor. Neither of these consequences ought, without evident necessity, to be involved; the latter would be entirely inadmissible, as it would defeat some of the most important and avowed purposes of the proposed government, and would essentially embarrass its measures. Nor do I perceive any foundation for such a supposition. Agreeably to the remark already made, the national and State systems are to be regarded as *one whole*. The courts of the latter will of course be natural auxiliaries to the execution of the laws of the Union, and an appeal from them will as naturally lie to that tribunal which is destined to unite and assimilate the principles of national justice and the rules of national decisions. The evident aim of the plan of the convention is that all the causes of the specified classes shall, for weighty public reasons, receive their original or final determination in the courts of the Union. To confine, therefore, the general expressions giving appellate jurisdiction to the Supreme Court, to appeals from the subordinate federal courts, instead of allowing their extension to the State courts, would be to abridge the latitude of the terms, in subversion of the intent, contrary to every sound rule of interpretation.

But could an appeal be made to lie from the State courts to the subordinate federal judicatories? This is another of the questions which have been raised, and of greater difficulty than the former. The following considerations countenance the affirmative. The plan of the convention, in the first place, authorizes the national legislature "to constitute tribunals inferior to the Supreme Court." It declares, in the next place, that "the *judicial power* of the United States *shall be vested* in one Supreme Court, and in such inferior courts as Congress shall ordain and establish"; and it then proceeds to enumerate the cases to which this judicial power shall extend. It afterwards divides the jurisdiction of the Supreme Court into original and appellate, but gives no definition of that of the subordinate courts. The only outlines described for them are that they shall be "inferior to the Supreme Court," and that they shall not exceed the specified limits of the federal judiciary. Whether their authority shall be original or appellate, or both, is not declared. All this seems to be left to the discretion of the legislature. And this being the case, I perceive at present no impediment to the establishment of an appeal from the State courts to the subordinate national tribunals; and many advantages attending the power of doing it may be imagined. It would diminish the motives to the multiplication of federal courts, and would admit of arrangements calculated to contract the appellate jurisdiction of the Supreme Court. The State tribunals may then be left with a more entire charge of federal causes; and appeals, in most cases in which they may be deemed proper, instead of being carried to the Supreme Court, may be made to lie from the State courts to district courts of the Union.

3.2   *Martin v. Hunter's Lessee*
14 U.S. 304 (1816)

J. STORY delivered the opinion of the Court.

This is a writ of error from the court of appeals of Virginia, founded upon the refusal of that court to obey the mandate of this court, requiring the judgment rendered in this very cause, at February term, 1813, to be carried into due execution. The following is the judgment of the court of appeals rendered on the mandate: "The court is unanimously of opinion, that the appellate power of the supreme court of the United States does not extend to this court, under a sound construction of the constitution of the United States; that so much of the 25th section of the act of congress to establish the judicial courts of the United States, as extends the appellate jurisdiction of the supreme court to this court, is not in pursuance of the constitution of the United States; that the writ of error, in this cause, was improvidently allowed under the authority of that act; that the proceedings thereon in the supreme court were, *coram non judice*, in relation to this court, and that obedience to its mandate be declined by the court."

The questions involved in this judgment are of great importance and delicacy. Perhaps it is not too much to affirm, that, upon their right decision, rest some of the most solid principles which have hitherto been supposed to sustain and protect the constitution itself. The great respectability, too, of the court whose decisions we are called upon to review, and the entire deference which we entertain for the learning and ability of that court, add much to the difficulty of the task which has so unwelcomely fallen upon us. . . .

The constitution of the United States was ordained and established, not by the states in their sovereign capacities, but emphatically, as the preamble of the constitution declares, by "the people of the United States." There can be no doubt that it was competent to the people to invest the general government with all the powers which they might deem proper and necessary; to extend or restrain these powers according to their own good pleasure, and to give them a paramount and supreme authority. As little doubt can there be, that the people had a right to prohibit to the states the exercise of any powers which were, in their judgment, incompatible with the objects of the general compact; to make the powers of the state governments, in given cases, subordinate to those of the nation, or to reserve to themselves those sovereign authorities which they might not choose to delegate to either. The constitution was not, therefore, necessarily carved out of existing state sovereignties, nor a surrender of powers already existing in state institutions, for the powers of the states depend upon their own constitutions; and the people of every state had the right to modify and restrain them, according to their own views of policy or principle. On the other hand, it is perfectly clear

that the sovereign powers vested in the state governments, by their respective constitutions, remained unaltered and unimpaired, except so far as they were granted to the government of the United States.

These deductions do not rest upon general reasoning, plain and obvious as they seem to be. They have been positively recognized by one of the articles in amendment of the constitution, which declares, that "the powers not delegated to the United States by the constitution, nor prohibited by it to the states, are reserved to the states respectively, or to the people."

The government, then, of the United States, can claim no powers which are not granted to it by the constitution, and the powers actually granted, must be such as are expressly given, or given by necessary implication. On the other hand, this instrument, like every other grant, is to have a reasonable construction, according to the import of its terms; and where a power is expressly given in general terms, it is not to be restrained to particular cases, unless that construction grow out of the context expressly, or by necessary implication. The words are to be taken in their natural and obvious sense, and not in a sense unreasonably restricted or enlarged.

The constitution unavoidably deals in general language. It did not suit the purposes of the people, in framing this great charter of our liberties, to provide for minute specifications of its powers, or to declare the means by which those powers should be carried into execution. It was foreseen that this would be a perilous and difficult, if not an impracticable, task. The instrument was not intended to provide merely for the exigencies of a few years, but was to endure through a long lapse of ages, the events of which were locked up in the inscrutable purposes of Providence. It could not be foreseen what new changes and modifications of power might be indispensable to effectuate the general objects of the charter; and restrictions and specifications, which, at the present, might seem salutary, might, in the end, prove the overthrow of the system itself. Hence its powers are expressed in general terms, leaving to the legislature, from time to time, to adopt its own means to effectuate legitimate objects, and to mould and model the exercise of its powers, as its own wisdom, and the public interests, should require. . . .

The third article of the constitution is that which must principally attract our attention. . . .

. . . The language of the article throughout is manifestly designed to be mandatory upon the legislature. Its obligatory force is so imperative, that congress could not, without a violation of its duty, have refused to carry it into operation. . . . The object of the constitution was to establish three great departments of government; the legislative, the executive, and the judicial departments. The first was to pass laws, the second to approve and execute them, and the third to expound and enforce them. Without the latter, it would be impossible to carry into effect some of the express provisions of the constitution. How, otherwise, could crimes against the United States be tried and punished? How could causes between two states be heard and determined? The judicial power must, therefore, be vested in some court, by congress; and to suppose that it was not an obligation binding on them, but might, at their pleasure, be omited or declined, is to suppose that, under the sanction of the constitution, they might defeat the constitution itself; a construction which would lead to such a result cannot be sound. . . .

The next consideration is as to the courts in which the judicial power shall be vested. It is manifest that a supreme court must be established; but whether it be equally obligatory to establish inferior courts, is a question of some difficulty. If congress may lawfully omit to establish inferior courts, it might follow, that in some of the enumerated cases the judicial power could nowhere exist. The supreme court can have original jurisdiction in two classes of cases only, viz. in cases affecting ambassadors, other public ministers and consuls, and in cases in which a state is a party. Congress cannot vest any portion of the judicial power of the United States, except in courts ordained and established by itself; and if in any of the cases enumerated in the constitution, the state courts did not then possess jurisdiction, the appellate jurisdiction of the supreme court (admitting that it could act on state courts) could not reach those cases. . . . It would seem, therefore, to follow, that congress are bound to create some inferior courts, in which to vest all that jurisdiction which, under the constitution, is exclusively vested in the United States, and of which the supreme court cannot take original cognizance. . . .

In what cases (if any) is this judicial power exclusive, or exclusive at the election of congress? It will be observed that there are two classes of cases enumerated in the constitution, between which a distinction seems to be drawn. The first class includes cases arising under the constitution, laws, and treaties of the United States; cases affecting ambassadors, other public ministers and consuls, and cases of admiralty and maritime jurisdiction. In this class the expression is, and that the judicial power shall extend to all cases; but in the subsequent part of the clause which embraces all the other cases of national cognizance, and forms the second class, the word "all" is dropped. . . . Here the judicial authority is to extend to controversies (not to all controversies) to which the United States shall be a party.

. . . as to cases arriving under the constitution, laws, and treaties of the United States. Here the state courts could not ordinarily possess a direct jurisdiction. The jurisdiction over such cases could not exist in the state courts previous to the adoption of the constitution, and it could not afterwards be directly conferred on them; for the constitution expressly requires the judicial power to be vested in courts ordained and established by the United States. This class of cases would embrace civil as well as criminal jurisdiction, and affect not only our internal policy, but our foreign relations. It would, therefore, be perilous to restrain it in any manner whatsoever, inasmuch as it might hazard the national safety. The same remarks may be urged as to cases affecting ambassadors, other public ministers, and consuls . . . and . . . to cases of admiralty and maritime jurisdiction. . . . All these cases, then, enter into the national policy, affect the national rights, and may compromise the national sovereignty. The original or appellate jurisdiction ought not, therefore, to be restrained, but should be commensurate with the mischiefs intended to be remedied, and, of course, should extend to all cases whatsoever.

A different policy might well be adopted in reference to the second class of cases; for although it might be fit that the judicial power should extend to all controversies to which the United States should be a party, yet this power might not have been imperatively given. . . . It might not have been deemed proper to submit the sovereignty of the

United States, against their own will, to judicial cognizance, either to enforce rights or to prevent wrongs; and as to the other cases of the second class, they might well be left to be exercised under the exceptions and regulations which congress might, in their wisdom, choose to apply. It is also worthy of remark, that congress seem . . . to have adopted this distinction. In the first class of cases, the jurisdiction is not limited except by the subject matter; in the second, it is made materially to depend upon the value in controversy.

. . . At all events, whether the one construction or the other prevail, it is manifest that the judicial power of the United States is unavoidably, in some cases, exclusive of all state authority, and in all others, may be made so at the election of congress. . . .

This leads us to the consideration of the great question as to the nature and extent of the appellate jurisdiction of the United States. We have already seen that appellate jurisdiction is given by the constitution to the supreme court in all cases where it has not original jurisdiction; subject, however, to such exceptions and regulations as congress may prescribe. It is, therefore, capable of embracing every case enumerated in the constitution, which is not exclusively to be decided by way of original jurisdiction. But the exercise of appellate jurisdiction is far from being limited by the terms of the constitution to the supreme court. There can be no doubt that congress may create a succession of inferior tribunals, in each of which it may vest appellate as well as original jurisdiction. . . .

If the constitution meant to limit the appellate jurisdiction to cases pending in the courts of the United States, it would necessarily follow that the jurisdiction of these courts would, in all the cases enumerated in the constitution, be exclusive of state tribunals. How otherwise could the jurisdiction extend to all cases arising under the constitution, laws, and treaties of the United States, or to all cases of admiralty and maritime jurisdiction? If some of these cases might be entertained by state tribunals, and no appellate jurisdiction as to them should exist, then the appellate power would not extend to all, but to some, cases. If state tribunals might exercise concurrent jurisdiction over all or some of the other classes of cases in the constitution without control, then the appellate jurisdiction of the United States might, as to such cases,

have no real existence, contrary to the manifest intent of the constitution. Under such circumstances, to give effect to the judicial power, it must be construed to be exclusive; and this not only when the *casus foederis* should arise directly, but when it should arise, incidentally, in cases pending in state courts. . . .

On the other hand, if, as has been contended, a discretion be vested in congress to establish, or not to establish, inferior courts at their own pleasure, and congress should not establish such courts, the appellate jurisdiction of the supreme court would have nothing to act upon, unless it could act upon cases pending in the state courts. Under such circumstances it must be held that the appellate power would extend to state courts. . . .

But it is plain that the framers of the constitution did contemplate that cases within the judicial cognizance of the United States not only might but would arise in the state courts, in the exercise of their ordinary jurisdiction. With this view the sixth article declares, that "this constitution, and the laws of the United States which shall be made in pursuance thereof, and all treaties made, or which shall be made, under the authority of the United States, shall be the supreme law of the land, and the judges in every state shall be bound thereby, any thing in the constitution or laws of any state to the contrary notwithstanding." It is obvious that this obligation is imperative upon the state judges in their official, and not merely in their private, capacities. . . . They were not to decide merely according to the laws or constitution of the state, but according to the constitution, laws and treaties of the United States—"the supreme law of the land." . . .

. . . It was foreseen that in the exercise of their ordinary jurisdiction, state courts would incidentally take cognizance of cases arising under the constitution, the laws, and treaties of the United States. Yet to all these cases the judicial power, by the very terms of the constitution, is to extend. It cannot extend by original jurisdiction if that was already rightfully and exclusively attached in the state courts. . . . [I]t must, therefore, extend by appellate jurisdiction, or not at all. It would seem to follow that the appellate power of the United States must, in such cases, extend to state tribunals. . . .

It has been argued that such an appellate jurisdiction over state courts is inconsistent with the genius of our governments, and the spirit of the constitution. That the latter was never designed to act upon state sovereignties, but only upon the people, and that if the power exists, it will materially impair the sovereignty of the states, and the independence of their courts. We cannot yield to the force of this reasoning; it assumes principles which we cannot admit, and draws conclusions to which we do not yield our assent.

It is a mistake that the constitution was not designed to operate upon states, in their corporate capacities. It is crowded with provisions which restrain or annul the sovereignty of the states in some of the highest branches of their prerogatives. . . . When, therefore, the states are stripped of some of the highest attributes of sovereignty, and the same are given to the United States; when the legislatures of the states are, in some respects, under the control of congress, and in every case are, under the constitution, bound by the paramount authority of the United States; it is certainly difficult to support the argument that the appellate power over the decisions of state courts is contrary to the genius of our institutions. . . .

Nor can such a [power] be deemed to impair the independence of state judges. . . . In respect to the powers granted to the United States, they are not independent; they are expressly bound to obedience by the letter of the constitution; and if they should unintentionally transcend their authority, or misconstrue the constitution, there is no more reason for giving their judgments an absolute and irresistible force, than for giving it to the acts of the other co-ordinate departments of state sovereignty. . . .

It is further argued, that no great public mischief can result from a construction which shall limit the appellate power of the United States to cases in their own courts: first, because state judges are bound by an oath to support the constitution of the United States, and must be presumed to be men of learning and integrity; and, secondly, because congress must have an unquestionable right to remove all cases within the scope of the judicial power from the state courts to the courts of the United States, at any time before final judgment, though not after final judgment. As to the first reason—admitting that the judges of the state courts are, and always will be, of as much learning, integrity, and wisdom, as those of the courts of the United

States, (which we very cheerfully admit,) it does not aid the argument. It is manifest that the constitution has proceeded upon a theory of its own, and given or withheld powers according to the judgment of the American people, by whom it was adopted. We can only construe its powers, and cannot inquire into the policy or principles which induced the grant of them. The constitution has presumed (whether rightly or wrongly we do not inquire) that state attachments, state prejudices, state jealousies, and state interests, might sometimes obstruct, or control, or be supposed to obstruct or control, the regular administration of justice. Hence, in controversies between states; between citizens of different states; between citizens claiming grants under different states; between a state and its citizens, or foreigners, and between citizens and foreigners, it enables the parties, under the authority of congress, to have the controversies heard, tried, and determined before the national tribunals. . . .

This is not all. A motive of another kind, perfectly compatible with the most sincere respect for state tribunals, might induce the grant of appellate power over their decisions. That motive is the importance, and even necessity of uniformity of decisions throughout the whole United States, upon all subjects within the purview of the constitution. Judges of equal learning and integrity, in different states, might differently interpret a statute, or a treaty of the United States, or even the constitution itself: If there were no revising authority to control these jarring and discordant judgments, and harmonize them into uniformity, the laws, the treaties, and the constitution of the United States would be different in different states, and might, perhaps, never have precisely the same construction, obligation, or efficacy, in any two states. The public mischiefs that would attend such a state of things would be truly deplorable; and it cannot be believed that they could have escaped the enlightened convention which formed the constitution. What, indeed, might then have been only prophecy, has now become fact; and the appellate jurisdiction must continue to be the only adequate remedy for such evils.

There is an additional consideration, which is entitled to great weight. The constitution of the United States was designed for the common and equal benefit of all the people of the United States.

The judicial power was granted for the same benign and salutary purposes. It was not to be exercised exclusively for the benefit of parties who might be plaintiffs, and would elect the national forum, but also for the protection of defendants who might be entitled to try their rights, or assert their privileges, before the same forum. Yet, if the construction contended for be correct, it will follow, that as the plaintiff may always elect the state court, the defendant may be deprived of all the security which the constitution intended in aid of his rights. Such a state of things can, in no respect, be considered as giving equal rights. To obviate this difficulty, we are referred to the power which it is admitted congress possess to remove suits from state courts to the national courts. . . .

On the whole, the court are of opinion, that the appellate power of the United States does extend to cases pending in the state courts; and that the 25th section of the judiciary act, which authorizes the exercise of this jurisdiction in the specified cases, by a writ of error, is supported by the letter and spirit of the constitution. We find no clause in that instrument which limits this power; and we dare not interpose a limitation where the people have not been disposed to create one. . . .

The next question which has been argued, is, whether the case at bar be within the purview of the 25th section of the judiciary act, so that this court may rightfully sustain the present writ of error. This section . . . enacts, in substance, that a final judgment or decree in any suit in the highest court of law or equity of a state, where is drawn in question the validity of a treaty or statute of, or an authority excised under, the United States, and the decision is against their validity; or where is drawn in question the validity of a statute of, or an authority exercised under, any state, on the ground of their being repugnant to the constitution, treaties, or laws, of the United States, and the decision is in favor of such their validity; or of the constitution, or of a treaty or statute of, or commission held under, the United States, and the decision is against the title, right, privilege, or exemption, specially set up or claimed by either party under such clause of the

said constitution, treaty, statute, or commission, may be re-examined and reversed or affirmed in the supreme court of the United States, upon a writ of error. . . .

That the present writ of error is founded upon a judgment of the court below, which drew in question and denied the validity of a statute of the United States, is incontrovertible. . . . That this judgment is final upon the rights of the parties is equally true; for if well founded, the former judgment of that court was of conclusive authority, and the former judgment of this court utterly void. The decision was, therefore, equivalent to a perpetual stay of proceedings upon the mandate, and a perpetual denial of all the rights acquired under it. The case, then, falls directly within the terms of the act. It is a final judgment in a suit in a state court, denying the validity of a statute of the United States. . . .

In causes remanded to the circuit courts, if the mandate be not correctly executed, a writ of error or appeal has always been supposed to be a proper remedy, and has been recognized as such in the former decisions of this court. The statute gives the same effect to writs of error from the judgments of state courts as of the circuit courts; and in its terms provides for proceedings where the same cause may be a second time brought up on writ of error before the supreme court. There is no limitation or description of the cases to which the second writ of error may be applied; and it ought, therefore, to be coextensive with the cases which fall within the mischiefs of the statute. It will hardly be denied that this cause stands in that predicament; and if so, then the appellate jurisdiction of this court has rightfully attached. . . .

We have thus gone over all the principal questions in the cause, and we deliver our judgment with entire confidence, that it is consistent with the constitution and laws of the land. . . .

It is the opinion of the whole court, that the judgment of the court of appeals of Virginia, rendered on the mandate in this cause, be reversed, and the judgment of the district court, held at Winchester be, and the same is hereby affirmed.

Contemporary Judicial Politics

3-3 Supreme Court Monitoring of State Courts in the Twenty-First Century (2002)

Michael E. Solimine

Introduction

Over two centuries ago, the Framers of the Constitution contemplated that the United States Supreme Court would, in certain circumstances, review decisions of state courts. Fulfilling that vision, the Supreme Court has periodically reviewed cases from state courts—at least those dealing in some way with federal law. As a result, there is nothing particularly novel about the Supreme Court hearing cases on appeal from state court, along with those from the lower federal courts. . . .

. . . [J]udicial federalism relates to the interaction of federal and state courts. Examples here include the impact of jurisdictional and other procedural requirements in federal court by past, concurrent, or future litigation in state court; how state courts adjudicate issues of federal law; how the Supreme Court reviews such adjudication; and how state courts have interpreted their own constitutions to protect rights to an extent not found in federal constitutional law. The latter development of the past three decades is often referred to as the "new judicial federalism."

In this article, I will address . . . the role of Supreme Court review of decisions of state courts and its impact on the judicial system. In that regard, I will consider two apparent shocks to the system of review, one recent and well known, the other one long-standing, not so well known, and less the subject of comment. The first is *Bush v. Gore,* in which the Supreme Court reversed a decision of the Florida Supreme Court, thus resolving the post-presidential

Excerpt from Michael E. Solimine, "Supreme Court Monitoring of State Courts in the Twenty-First Century," in *Indiana Law Review* 335 (2002). Copyright 2002, The Trustees of Indiana University. Reproduced with permission from The Indiana Law Review.

election controversy in favor of then Texas Governor George W. Bush. The Florida court's decision, ordering manual recounts of votes, was ostensibly based on state law, yet the Supreme Court majority (or at least three Justices thereof), in effect, disagreed with the interpretation of state law to enable it to reach the federal issues. The question is whether the majority's aggressive review portends a new role for the Court in other state court cases.

The second, less noticeable but potentially as profound a shock to the understood system of Supreme Court review, is the Court's decreasing caseload. Through most of the Twentieth Century the Court was deciding well over 100 cases per Term on the merits. As late as the mid-1980s, the number was almost 150. But starting in about 1990, the number has spiraled sharply downward, and for much of the 1990s, the Court was only deciding seventy to eighty cases per Term. Meanwhile, caseloads in the lower federal courts, and state courts, are either increasing or, at least, static. So the likelihood of review of any given decision, not high to begin with, is even lower today. What might account for the Supreme Court's shrunken caseload, and what are its implications for state court decision-making?. . .

Michigan v. Long, Bush v. Gore, and the Development of State Constitutional Law

Setting the Stage: Supreme Court Review and the New Judicial Federalism

As already stated, the Supreme Court has been reviewing decisions from state courts for two centuries. It is beyond dispute that the Supreme Court is, and should be, the final expositor of federal law (within the court system, at least), as derived from the text and history of Article III of the Constitution. To perform that role and to ensure uniformity of federal law, the Supreme Court has from the beginning been statutorily empowered by Congress to review decisions of state courts. The somewhat complicated history of those provisions and the cases interpreting them need not concern us here. The principal statute as it stands now, enacted in 1914, has been interpreted to limit Supreme Court review to state court decisions based on federal law, not those based on state law grounds.

State courts have long been deciding issues of federal constitutional and statutory law, and have, for equally long, been rendering decisions interpreting their own state constitutions as well. But only in the last three decades has state constitutional law, particularly regarding individual rights and liberties, been the special focus of attention by judges, litigants, and commentators. In the new judicial federalism, some state courts (particularly the highest courts of a state) have interpreted their own constitutions to protect liberty interests above the floor of rights found in the U.S. Constitution, as interpreted by the Supreme Court. *State Constitutions and the Protection of Individual Rights* was an influential law review article by U.S. Supreme Court Justice William Brennan, who urged state judges to interpret expansively the rights-granting provisions of their own constitutions in response to the restrictive decisions of his own Court. As a result, for several decades state courts have issued hundreds of decisions expanding rights based on state law, beyond that found in the federal constitution. . . .

. . . [S]ystematic studies demonstrate that most state courts, when presented with the opportunity, have chosen not to depart from federal precedents when interpreting the rights-granting provisions of state constitutions. In other words, the majority of state courts, on most issues, engage in an analysis in lockstep with their federal counterparts. This trend was first documented by Barry Latzer and James Gardner in the early 1990s and has been confirmed by numerous subsequent studies. Some of these studies either covered limited time periods or studied only one or two specific issue areas. More recent and comprehensive empirical studies essentially have confirmed the dominance of lock-step analysis, but also present a more nuanced picture than previous studies. For example, one recent study examined 627 state supreme court decisions, from twenty-five randomly chosen states, covering states' bills of rights in nineteen issue areas. The study confirmed the dominance of the lockstep for most issue areas, but found at least three areas (free exercise of religion, right to jury trial, and certain search and seizure issues) in which over half of the cases departed from the lockstep and granted more protection to the right involved. . . .

The Impact of *Michigan v. Long*

United States Supreme Court decisions have played some role in the development of the new judicial federalism. Recent developments in state constitutional law can be attributed, in part, to explicit or implicit reaction to Supreme Court decisions refusing to uphold or expand a particular right. It might seem, however, that potential Supreme Court review of state court decisions would not play a role. Since those decisions are based on state law, normally the Supreme Court should not be reviewing them at all.

The review function comes into play when the state court decision explicitly relies on both federal and state law, or is ambiguous on the issue of what source(s) of law is relied upon. In the former situation, the Supreme Court has held that review is normally unavailing if the state law component of the reasoning is adequate to resolve the case and is independent of federal law grounds. That principle, or something like it, has been the rule for years. In the latter situation, to determine if the independence prong has been met, the Court used various approaches, but settled in 1983 on a clear statement approach in the oft-discussed case, *Michigan v. Long*. . . . The Michigan Supreme Court held a police search to be unlawful, and in doing so relied exclusively on federal case law, but for brief citations to the provisions of the Michigan Constitution analogous to the Fourth Amendment. The majority opinion by Justice O'Connor adopted as an interpretative rule that the adequacy and independence of a state ground must be "clear from the face of the opinion." This default rule was necessary, the Court explained, to avoid advisory opinions, refrain from the "intrusive practice of requiring state courts to clarify" their opinions, and to maintain the uniformity of federal law. Under the newly clarified test, the Court found no plain statement of reliance on state law in the Michigan Supreme Court opinion and thus proceeded to reach the merits of the case. The Court has adhered to and applied the "plain statement rule" in subsequent cases. . . .

Coming as it did, just as the idea of increased state court reliance on their own constitutions began to flower, it was no shock that *Michigan v. Long* generated considerable academic commentary. . . .

In my view, *Michigan v. Long* has had relatively little effect on state court decision-making, and to the extent that it has, it has been more positive than negative. Start with the proposition of some critics that the Supreme Court should not at all be reviewing state court decisions that overenforce federal rights. The proposition is not persuasive. In our hierarchical system of courts, it has long been the norm that appellate courts will review the actions of lower courts. The norm has a long pedigree for Supreme Court review of state courts. Since state courts are, after all, staffed by state personnel, it is no insult to state judges that their exposition of federal law will be subject to review by the final expositor of federal law for all fifty states. Indeed, such review heightens the probability that state judges are correctly following federal law, no small matter given the vast numbers of state court cases and the limited caseload capabilities of the Supreme Court.

To the extent *Michigan v. Long* in theory permits more review of state court decisions bearing on federal law, it will in theory lead to greater uniformity of federal law. This seems unobjectionable enough, but in a federal system of government, a "fetish should not be made out of uniformity." Even with regard to federal law, uniformity is impossible. The Supreme Court cannot review even a significant percentage of cases raising federal issues decided in the lower federal courts, much less those from state courts, and as a result federal law will always be marked by some lack of uniformity. However, we should not go out of our way to institutionalize a lack of uniformity in federal law either.

Difficulty in compliance with the plain statement rule likewise cannot be seriously contended. More intriguing is, given that ease, why it appears that many state courts do not make plain statements of reliance on state law when given the opportunity, or simply remain ambiguous on the issue. One possible reason, of course, is that state judges may find it inappropriate to depart from federal precedent, and thus reject developing a different state constitutional rule. In many instances, however, they do not clearly articulate that in their opinions. Another possible reason is that attorneys out of design or ignorance may ignore the issue and rely exclusively on federal law in their briefing.

The relatively low rate of making plain statements has also been linked to the alleged electoral effects of *Michigan v. Long.* Some supporters and critics of the decision appear to argue, to varying degrees, that the plain statement rule encourages strategic behavior by judges. State judges, many of whom are elected, may take more or less political heat from interested people for decisions, depending on the reasoning they supply for the decision. Thus, for example, Ann Althouse has suggested that the plain statement rule "forces state judges to endure one form of scrutiny or the other and deprives them of the ability to immunize themselves with ambiguity." . . .

. . . [T]he asserted electoral connection is overstated. It is well documented that the vast majority of state judicial elections, whether in contested races or for retention elections, are low-profile affairs. Many voters do not vote in judicial races at all. Those who do often base their vote on name recognition or partisan affiliation rather than on the "issues" in any meaningful sense of the term. There is a very high rate of reelection for incumbent judges under any electoral scheme, and many judges, especially on lower courts, run unopposed.

To be sure, there is evidence that elections for state judges, particularly on supreme courts, have become more contentious and contested. Some of this is due, at least in part, to controversial rulings based on state constitutional law. But there seems to be little systemic evidence that the increasing attention given to some judicial races is driven by the parsing of court decisions to see if reliance has been made on federal or state law. If anything, data from a broad range of cases seems to suggest the lack of a connection between the judicial electoral structure of a state and its propensity to develop state constitutional law. For example, one of the systemic studies of the new judicial federalism, referenced earlier, found that states whose supreme court justices were appointed or selected by merit with retention elections were less likely to provide protections above the federal floor than states that used contested elections. Studies of state supreme court decision-making on more specific issues, such as school-financing litigation or the legality of confessions to police, found no correlation between the method of judicial selection and the level of activism (or lack thereof) on these issues.

These studies, then, seem to undermine the notion that the plain statement rule, for good or ill, impacts the propensity of judges to rely on state constitutional law. If it did, we would expect state judges less subject to popular accountability to be more likely to develop state constitutional law. Over the broad range of cases and issues, the evidence does not support that view.

The Impact of *Bush v. Gore*

We now come to the two Supreme Court decisions handed down in December 2000, *Bush v. Palm Beach County Canvassing Board* (*Bush I*), and *Bush v. Gore* (*Bush II*). The two cases vacated decisions from the Florida Supreme Court, upheld the certification of Florida's electoral votes for then-Governor George W. Bush, and effectively determined the winner of the presidential election. Some critics, arguing that the decisions were result-oriented, contended that the Supreme Court had unnecessarily and inappropriately reviewed state court decisions based exclusively on state law. Much can and should be said about the cases. But in my view, the Supreme Court reviewing these purportedly state-law-based decisions was unremarkable, given precedent, and it is unlikely to be an omen for more aggressive Supreme Court review in the future.

To see why, we need to review briefly *Bush I* and *Bush II*. . . . In *Bush I*, the Florida Supreme Court ordered the Florida Secretary of State to permit certain manual recounts of votes in the presidential election to go forward. The Supreme Court granted certiorari on whether the Florida court's order effectively changed state electoral law after the vote in a way that violated federal statutory and constitutional provisions that seemingly limit such changes after election day; and lodge exclusive authority in state legislatures to designate presidential electors. The Florida Supreme Court had only briefly referred

to the federal statutes in a footnote, and the Supreme Court thought the opinion was unclear on the Florida court's construction and application of state law in light of the federal provisions. In a unanimous per curiam decision, the Supreme Court vacated and remanded for further proceedings, given the "considerable uncertainty as to the precise grounds for the [Florida court's] decision."

Several days later, in parallel litigation, the Florida Supreme Court again ordered that certain manual recounts of votes for President go forward. Review was again sought and obtained, and this time the Supreme Court in *Bush II* reversed on the merits. The five-member majority, in a per curiam opinion, held that the Equal Protection Clause was violated by the Florida court ordering that manual recounts could proceed by different standards in different counties.

Chief Justice Rehnquist, in a concurring opinion joined by Justices Scalia and Thomas, further found that the Florida Supreme Court's interpretation and application of the state election statute so departed from the original legislative scheme that it violated Article II. To reach that conclusion, the concurring opinion extensively reexamined the state law basis of the opinion. As a preface to doing that, the opinion provided several pages justifying the Court's review of the state law basis of the decision below. "In most cases," the concurring members of the Court conceded, "comity and respect for federalism compel us to defer to the decisions of state courts on issues of state law." But the opinion cited two examples where "the Constitution requires this Court to undertake an independent, if still deferential, analysis of state law."

One example cited was the 1958 decision of *NAACP v. Alabama ex rel. Patterson*, in which the Supreme Court refused to defer to the Alabama Supreme Court's asserted reason for not permitting a federal issue to be raised, specifically that the correct appellate remedy had not been sought. That was not an adequate ground of state law, the Court held, because the novelty of the rationale could not be squared with Alabama precedent. Similarly, in the 1964 decision of *Bouie v. City of Columbia*, the Court concluded that the South Carolina Supreme Court had violated due process by improperly broadening the scope of a state criminal statute, as that reading was not supported by state precedent. The concurrence in *Bush II* stated that what it was doing "in the present case [was] precisely parallel."

All four dissenting Justices submitted separate opinions, but for present purposes the most relevant is Justice Ginsburg's dissent because she was the only one who directly confronted the concurring opinion's treatment of precedent on the review issue. Justice Ginsburg, like the Chief Justice, began with the customary reminder that the Court should only reexamine state law to protect federal rights in rare occasions, with deference to a state court's interpretations of its own law. "Rarely," she wrote, "has this Court rejected outright an interpretation of state law by a state high court." The cases cited by the Chief Justice, she acknowledged, were "such rare instances," but she argued that "those cases are embedded in historical contexts hardly comparable to the situation here." She noted that *NAACP* was decided "in the face of Southern resistance to the civil rights movement," as was *Bouie* and that "this case involves nothing close to the kind of recalcitrance by a state high court that warrants extraordinary action by this Court." She concluded that the Florida Supreme Court's construction of election statutes was reasonable and did not violate the Federal Constitution.

Despite the obvious high importance and drama of these decisions, to the extent they frame the Supreme Court's relationship with state courts, they are for the most part unexceptional applications of settled doctrine. First, consider *Bush I*. When it was vacated and remanded for further clarification by the Florida Supreme Court, it relied on precedent permitting that disposition in deference to the state court. Invoking the *Michigan v. Long* plain statement rule would have been inappropriate, because "the ambiguity of the state court opinion was not about whether it rested on a state or a federal ground, but rather (at least with regard to the question of the import of the state constitution) about what the state ground of decision was." It is unlikely that *Bush I* makes any change to *Michigan v. Long* and its progeny.

Bush II is something else but, properly understood, works no change in existing doctrine. For present purposes the most significant part of that opinion is the debate between Chief Justice Rehnquist and Justice Ginsburg on the propriety of the Supreme Court reexamining state law on its own terms, even when expounded by the state's highest court. At the outset, this debate did not implicate the core of the adequate and independent state ground doctrine. The typical case is one where the state court does not reach an asserted federal ground because the party pressing that issue has waived the issue for failure to comply with a state procedural rule. Here, in contrast, the lower court did not purport to fail to reach a federal issue for that reason. Rather, it was the very state-law-based nature of the decision below that itself was alleged to violate the Federal Constitution. Ample precedent permits the Supreme Court to review such a case. In any event, despite Justice Ginsburg's efforts to undermine the precedential value of the cases where the Court reexamined state law, those cases have an impressive pedigree. For example, the two modern cases relied upon by the Chief Justice, *NAACP* and *Bouie*, were written by Justices Harlan (for a unanimous Court) and Brennan, respectively. Those cases, and others, have been routinely discussed by scholars as unexceptional and almost uncontroversial precedent permitting the Court to reexamine state law.

Justice Ginsburg also suggested that the generative force of those cases was lessened by their being rendered to vindicate federal rights undermined by state courts during the civil rights movement. The Florida Supreme Court in *Bush II,* she said, "surely should not be bracketed with state high courts of the Jim Crow South." Her forthright description of the political context of the decisions, then and now, is refreshingly candid and to my knowledge not matched in other opinions involving the adequate and independent grounds doctrine.

Considerable evidence also supports her view of the recalcitrance of at least some of the state courts in the deep South during the Civil Rights Era, and of subsequent changes. Nor is Justice Ginsburg the first to suggest that the Court may have bent jurisdictional rules during the Civil Rights Era to enable it to reach the merits of cases where, for example, review would otherwise have been barred by the adequate and independent state ground doctrine. But it is hard to take seriously her apparent argument that cases like *NAACP* and *Bouie* are contextual, situational, and entitled to little or no precedential value, depending on the "real" motives of the court below. Such an inquiry on that basis alone would open other precedent to similar attack. For example, a number of modern authorities assert that many path-breaking criminal procedure decisions of the Warren Court were driven, at least in part, by the treatment of black suspects in deep South courts. Now that conditions in southern courts have presumably and hopefully changed, would Justice Ginsburg urge that those precedents be discarded as well?

A more persuasive component of Justice Ginsburg's opinion was her argument that the Florida Supreme Court's construction of its own election law was due greater deference. She observed that simply disagreeing with another tribunal's construction of its own law does not make it unreasonable. While both she and the Chief Justice called for some level of deference, neither were entirely clear on the level of deference. From the standpoint of using precedent, this is perhaps the most problematic aspect of the jurisdictional basis of *Bush II*. Even on these narrow points, only opinions joined by four Justices were fully engaged on the issue, and only the concurring opinion undertook arguably undeferential reexamination of state law. Add to that the highly unusual facts presented, and it is fair to conclude that "*Bush v. Gore* seems unlikely to become a leading precedent for the scope of review [by the Supreme Court] of state law questions that implicate federal protections."

The Supreme Court's Shrunken Docket and the Development of Federal Law in State Courts

The Shrunken Docket

The adequate and independent state ground doctrine, whatever its formulation, in theory permits the Supreme Court to review and, if necessary, correct state court holdings that were based on federal law. Whether the Supreme Court has the institutional resources or desire to seriously undertake this function is another matter. The Court's own docket is the starting point for studying this issue.

For virtually all of the Twentieth Century, the Supreme Court decided an average of 150 cases per Term. As of the late 1980s, that number was almost 130 per Term. Starting in 1990, the numbers began rapidly falling below 100, until by the late 1990s the Court was only deciding seventy or eighty cases per Term. . . .

The Supreme Court's Monitoring of Federal Law in State Court

Similarly [i]n the 1990s both the absolute and proportional number of cases from state courts reviewed on the merits by the Supreme Court has declined. What has been the effect of this decline on the adjudication of federal issues in state courts? The same question can be posed with regard to the development of federal law in the lower federal courts. [Arthur] Hellman has suggested that over the long run, a limited docket will create "the risk that the paucity of decisions will leave wide gaps in the doctrines governing important areas of law." Those gaps may make it difficult for federal and state lower court judges to resolve correctly or uniformly issues of federal law. Likewise, under a reduced docket, "[l]ower-court judges will no longer feel the spirit of goodwill and cooperation that comes from participation in a shared enterprise. Without that spirit, it is hard to see how a hierarchical judiciary can function effectively."

Beyond these abstractions it is difficult to test in more detail how, if at all, the shrunken docket has affected adjudications in state courts. Indeed, it is too soon to tell, because the smaller docket is a relatively recent phenomenon, albeit one that has been consistent over the last decade. However, several sources of data can suggest some tentative conclusions on the effect of the recent docket.

One source of data could be the rate of reversal of state court decisions. If the rate of reversal of such decisions by the Supreme Court were relatively high, it might suggest that state courts were not doing a noteworthy job of adjudicating federal law. Over the past half-century, the average reversal rate by the Court for all cases has been about sixty percent. During the same time period, the Supreme Court reversed and/or remanded state supreme court decisions at a higher rate, about seventy percent. Perhaps not surprisingly, the rate of reversal was particularly high during the Warren Court and was closer to the overall average during the Burger and Rehnquist Courts.

The data available for the 1990s is for the last three Terms. . . . For those Terms, the overall reversal/vacate rate for all cases was about sixty-five percent. In the same time period, the same rate for state court cases was again higher, about seventy-three percent. This data might suggest that state courts have not been correctly applying federal law, as compared to their federal court counterparts. But any conclusion like this must be drawn with great caution, not only because of the small number of cases involved, but because reversal could be based on a variety of factors. The Supreme Court does not sit merely to correct errors—its primary function is law development. If that were not the case, we might expect all cases accepted for review to be reversed.

The disposition of cases decided on the merits by the Supreme Court tells us something, but formally it is only the top rung of the appellate ladder. To get a better sense of the effect of the Court's docket, ideally, we should examine all cases decided by lower courts. Only that examination would enable us to determine how well the Court supervises lower courts. A useful metaphor to frame our thinking here is to envision the Supreme Court as a manager. The metaphor has both normative and empirical force. Regarding the former, rather than accepting cases in a largely ad hoc way, the managerial Court would usually only accept a case for review if the issues raised have been thoroughly addressed in one or more cases below, and it would give more substantive content to the "importance" criterion. This managerial model also suggests ways in which to gauge empirically its workability. If we conceive the Supreme Court and the lower courts as having a principal-agent relationship, then we would be concerned with how the principal monitors its agents. Among other things, this suggests that we should examine the vast majority of lower court cases where Supreme Court review is either denied or not sought at all, to see whether those courts are nevertheless following Court precedent.

One way to test these models is to examine the concept of parity, meaning whether and to what extent state courts can and do fully and fairly adjudicate federal constitutional rights. . . .

. . . Several studies have compared the adjudication of specific federal constitutional rights in federal and state courts. While studies are ongoing and do not all point in one direction, in my view, it is fair to say that most of these studies show that, overall, state courts as compared to federal courts are not systematically under-enforcing federal rights.

This is not to say that in contemporary America all federal rights enjoy the fullest protection in state courts; consider the administration of the death penalty by state courts. Recent studies by James Liebman and others demonstrate that well over one-half of capital sentences handed down in state courts are initially overturned in some manner by a later reviewing court. Because denial of federal constitutional rights is often the source of error, the high rate of reversal undermines notions of parity. To some, it is evident that elected state judges, beholden to voters in favor of the death penalty, improperly deny the federal rights of capital defendants. There is evidence supporting this concern, but it must be tempered by the realization that many state actors (e.g., prosecutors, defense counsel), not just judges, are also potential sources of error. Moreover, it is worth noting that the high error rate is due in significant part to state appellate courts identifying and reversing error in trial courts.

Some recent studies of state court decision-making, in part, examined the Supreme Court's monitoring ability. One study examined a sample of search and seizure cases from state supreme courts from 1961–1990. Compliance with Supreme Court doctrine over the same period was tested by, among other things, coding the results and fact patterns in both Supreme Court and state high court cases. The study found substantial compliance with Supreme Court doctrine, indeed as much compliance as in similar cases between the Supreme Court and the U.S. Court of Appeals. A methodologically similar study has been done of cases in state supreme courts concerning the legality of confessions to the police. It, too, concluded that the results of the cases substantially mirrored the results of similar cases in the Supreme Court over the same time period.

Supreme Court Monitoring in the Twenty-First Century

More empirical work needs to be done to examine the development of federal law in state courts. Nonetheless, the studies discussed above do suggest that, by and large, state courts (or at least state high courts) comply with Supreme Court precedent. Does this necessarily mean that the Supreme Court is acting as an effective monitor of state courts? It is difficult to say. The vast majority of these state court decisions, of course, are not reviewed by the Court. While the possibility of any given state court decision being reviewed is quite low, it would seem that the threat of review and possible reversal by the Supreme Court nonetheless plays a role. Still, those possibilities are so remote, it would seem that the simple norm of following Supreme Court precedent is the principal compelling force.

To what extent does a shrunken or expanded docket of the Supreme Court affect its monitoring role? This, too, is difficult to say. With regard to reviewing decisions of state courts, in my view, it does not make a quantum difference whether the docket is shrunken or not. Even in the heyday of the expanded docket, only a small percentage of state court decisions susceptible to review were reviewed. To be sure, severely downsizing the docket at some point will limit the ability of the Court to monitor state courts. Perhaps the Court's current docket approaches that limit. Future Courts in this century may well re-expand the docket, but even if they do, it seems doubtful that the docket will go beyond the 150 case average of most Terms in the past century.

Whether under an expanded or shrunken docket, available evidence seems to indicate that the Supreme Court has been able, to a tolerable degree, to carry out the monitoring function. Data from the Terms before the shrunken docket indicates (not surprisingly) that cases from more densely populated states were more likely to appear on the docket, as did decisions from state supreme courts in the deep South during the Civil Rights Era. Even during the current diminished docket, Hellman concludes that, as compared to earlier Terms, the Court has continued to accept certiorari petitions from litigants asserting federal rights in state court cases. Hellman optimistically concludes that:

> In this respect, however, the Court is simply going back to its roots. From the earliest days of the nation's history, no function of the Court has ranked higher than the protection of federal rights from hostility or misunderstanding on the part of state courts. We would not expect the Court to break with that tradition, and it has not. . . .

3.4   Memorandum Opinion (As corrected and amended)
May 17, 2002

United States Foreign Intelligence Surveillance Court

I

The Department of Justice has moved this Court to vacate the minimization and "wall" procedures in all cases now or ever before the Court, including this Court's adoption of the Attorney General's July 1995 intelligence sharing procedures, which are not consistent with new intelligence sharing procedures submitted for approval with this motion. The Court has considered the Government's motion, the revised intelligence sharing procedures, and the supporting memorandum of law as required by the Foreign Intelligence Surveillance Act (hereafter the FISA or the Act) . . . to determine whether the proposed minimization procedures submitted with the Government's motion comport with the definition of minimization procedures. . . . The Government's motion will be GRANTED, EXCEPT THAT THE PROCEDURES MUST BE MODIFIED IN PART.

The Court's analysis and findings are as follows: . . .

. . . Prior to May of 1979, when the FISA became operational, it was not uncommon for courts to defer to the expertise of the Executive Branch in matters of foreign intelligence collection. Since May 1979, this Court has often recognized the expertise of the government in foreign intelligence collection and counterintelligence investigations of espionage and international terrorism, and accorded great weight to the government's interpretation of FISA's standards. However, this Court, or on appeal the Foreign Intelligence Surveillance Court of Review having jurisdiction "to review the *denial* of any application," is the arbiter of the FISA's terms and requirements. The present seven members of the Court have reviewed and approved several thousand FISA applications, including many hundreds of surveillances and searches of U.S. persons. The members bring their specialized knowledge to the issue at hand, mindful of the FISA's preeminent role in preserving our national security, not only in the present national emergency, but for the long term as a constitutional democracy under the rule of law.

II

We turn now to the government's proposed minimization procedures which are to be followed in all electronic surveillances and physical searches past, present, and future. In addition to the Standard Minimization Procedures for a U.S. Person Agent of a Foreign Power that are filed with the Court, which we continue to approve, the government has submitted new supplementary minimization procedures adopted by the Attorney General and promulgated in the form of a memorandum addressed to the Director of the FBI and other senior Justice Department executives and dated March 6, 2002. . . .

The focus of this decision is . . . the acquisition, retention, and dissemination of information obtained through electronic surveillances and physical searches of U.S. persons to be approved as part of the government's applications and incorporated in the orders of this Court.

Our duty regarding approval of these minimization procedures is inscribed in the Act, as is the standard we must follow in our decision making. . . . We cannot add to, subtract from, or modify the words used by Congress, but must apply the FISA's provisions with fidelity to their plain meaning and in conformity with the overall statutory scheme. The FISA is a statute of unique character, intended to authorize electronic surveillances and physical searches of foreign powers and their agents, including U.S. persons. . . .

The Attorney General's new minimization procedures are designed to regulate the acquisition, retention, and dissemination of information involving the FISA (i.e., disseminating information, consulting, and providing advice) between FBI counterintelligence and counterterrorism officials on the one hand, and FBI criminal investigators, trial attorneys in the Justice Department's Criminal Division, and U.S. Attorney's Offices on the other hand. These new minimization procedures supersede similar

procedures issued by the Attorney General in July 1995 which were augmented in January 2000, and then in August 2001 by the current Deputy Attorney General. . . .

The 2002 procedures have been submitted to the Court . . . to supplement the Standard Minimization Procedures for U.S. Person Agents of Foreign Powers. Both sets of procedures are to be applied in past and future electronic surveillances and physical searches subject to the approval of this Court. . . .

. . . The operative language of each section [of the act] to be applied by the Court provides that minimization procedures must be reasonably designed in light of their purpose and technique. . . .

Thus in approving minimization procedures the Court is to ensure that the intrusiveness of foreign intelligence surveillances and searches on the privacy of U.S. persons is "consistent" with the need of the United States to collect foreign intelligence information from foreign powers and their agents.

Our deliberations begin with an examination of the . . . acquisition, retention and dissemination of U.S. person information. Most of the rules and procedures for minimization are set forth in the Standard Minimization Procedures which will continue to be applied along with the 2002 procedures, and permit exceptionally thorough acquisition and collection through a broad array of contemporaneous electronic surveillance techniques. Thus, in many U.S. person electronic surveillances the FBI will be authorized to conduct, simultaneously, telephone, microphone, cell phone, e-mail and computer surveillance of the U.S. person target's home, workplace and vehicles. Similar breadth is accorded the FBI in physical searches of the target's residence, office, vehicles, computer, safe deposit box and U.S. mails where supported by probable cause. The breadth of acquisition is premised on the fact that clandestine intelligence activities and activities in preparation for international terrorism are undertaken with considerable direction and support from sophisticated intelligence services of nation states and well-financed groups engaged in international terrorism.

The intrusiveness of the FBI's electronic surveillances and sophisticated searches and seizures is sanctioned by the following practices and provisions in the FISA:

- a foreign intelligence standard of probable cause instead of the more traditional criminal standard of probable cause;
- having to show only that the place or facility to be surveilled or searched is being used or about to be used without the need of showing that it is being used in furtherance of the espionage or terrorist activities;
- surveillances and searches are conducted surreptitiously without notice to the target unless they are prosecuted;
- surveillances and now searches are authorized for 90 days, and may continue for as long as one year or more in certain cases;
- large amounts of information are collected by automatic recording to be minimized after the fact;
- most information intercepted or seized has a dual character as both foreign intelligence information and evidence of crime (e.g., the identity of a spy's handler, his/her communication signals and deaddrop locations; the fact that a terrorist is taking flying lessons, or purchasing explosive chemicals) differentiated primarily by the persons using the information;
- when facing criminal prosecution, a target cannot obtain discovery of the FISA applications and affidavits supporting the Court's orders in order to challenge them because the FISA mandates in camera, ex parte review by the district court "if the Attorney General files an affidavit under oath that disclosure or an adversary hearing would harm the national security."

It is self evident that the technical and surreptitious means available for acquisition of information by electronic surveillances and physical searches, coupled with the scope and duration of such intrusions and other practices under the FISA, give the government a powerful engine for the collection of foreign intelligence information targeting U.S. persons.

Retention under the standard minimization procedures is also heavily weighted toward the government's need for foreign intelligence information. Virtually all information seized, whether by electronic surveillance or physical search, is minimized hours, days, or weeks after collection. The principal steps in the minimization process are the same for electronic surveillances and physical searches:

- information is reduced to an intelligible form: if recorded it is transcribed, if in a foreign language it is translated, if in electronic or computer storage it is accessed and printed, if in code it is decrypted and if on film or similar media it is developed and printed;
- once the information is understandable, a reviewing official, usually an FBI case agent, makes an informed judgment as to whether the information seized is or might be foreign intelligence information related to clandestine intelligence activities or international terrorism;
- if the information is determined to be, or might be, foreign intelligence, it is logged into the FBI's records and filed in a variety of storage systems from which it can be retrieved for analysis, for counterintelligence investigations or operations, or for use at criminal trial;
- if found not to be foreign intelligence information, it must be minimized, which can be done in a variety of ways depending upon the format of the information: if recorded the information would not be indexed, and thus become nonretrievable, if in hard copy from facsimile intercept or computer print-out it should be discarded, if on re-recordable media it could be erased, or if too bulky or too sensitive, it might be destroyed.

These same principles of minimization are applied to all information collected, whether by electronic surveillance or physical search. The most critical step in retention is the analysis in which an informed judgment is made as to whether or not the communications or other data seized is foreign intelligence information. . . . Minimization is required only if the information "*could not be*" foreign intelligence. Thus, it is obvious that the standard for retention of FISA-acquired information is weighted heavily in favor of the government.

This brings us to the third and perhaps most complex part of minimization practice, the dissemination and use of FISA-acquired information. Recognizing the broad sweep of acquisition allowed under FISA's definition of electronic surveillance (and, subsequently, physical searches), coupled with the low threshold for retention in the "could not be foreign intelligence" standard, Congress has provided guidance for the Court in the FISA's legislative history:

. . . [T]he committee believes it is imperative that with respect to information concerning U.S. persons which is retained as necessary for counterintelligence or counterterrorism purposes, *rigorous and strict controls* be placed on the retrieval of such identifiable information and its dissemination or use *for purposes other than counterintelligence or counterterrorism.* (emphasis added)

The judge has the *discretionary power to modify* the order sought, such as with regard to the period of authorization . . . or the *minimization procedures* to be followed. (emphasis added) The Committee contemplates that the court would give these procedures most careful consideration. If it is *not* of the opinion that they will be *effective,* the procedures *should be modified.* (emphasis added)

Between 1979 when the FISA became operational and 1995, the government relied on the standard minimization procedures described herein to regulate all electronic surveillances. In 1995, following amendment of the FISA to permit physical searches, comparable minimization procedures were adopted for foreign intelligence searches. . . . In January 2000, the Attorney General augmented the 1995 procedures to permit more information sharing from FISA cases with the Criminal Division, and the current Deputy Attorney General expanded the procedures in August 2001. Taken together, the 1995 procedures, as augmented, permit substantial consultation and coordination. . . .

The Court came to rely on these supplementary procedures, and approved their broad information sharing and coordination with the Criminal Division in thousands of applications. In addition, because of the FISA's requirement (since amended) that the FBI Director certify that "the purpose" of each surveillance and search was to collect foreign intelligence information, the Court was routinely apprised of consultations and discussions between the FBI, the Criminal Division, and U.S. Attorney's offices in cases where there were overlapping intelligence and criminal investigations or interests. This process increased dramatically in numerous FISA applications concerning the September 11th attack on the World Trade Center and the Pentagon.

In order to preserve both the appearance and the fact that FISA surveillances and searches were not being used *sub rosa* for criminal investigations, the Court routinely approved the use of information screening "walls" proposed by the government in its applications. Under the normal "wall" procedures, where there were separate intelligence and criminal *investigations,* or a single counterespionage investigation with overlapping intelligence and criminal *interests,* FBI criminal investigators and Department prosecutors were not allowed to review all of the raw FISA intercepts or seized materials lest they become defacto partners in the FISA surveillances and searches. Instead, a screening mechanism, or person . . . would review all of the raw intercepts and seized materials and pass on only that information which might be relevant evidence. . . . In significant cases, involving major complex investigations such as the bombings of the U.S. Embassies in Africa, and the millennium investigations, where criminal investigations of FISA targets were being conducted concurrently, and prosecution was likely, this Court became the "wall" so that FISA information could not be disseminated to criminal prosecutors without the Court's approval. In some cases where this Court was the "wall," the procedures seemed to have functioned as provided in the Court's orders; however, in an alarming number of instances, there have been troubling results.

Beginning in March 2000, the government notified the Court that there had been disseminations of FISA information to criminal squads in the FBI's New York field office, and to the U.S. Attorney's Office for the Southern District of New York, without the required authorization of the Court as the "wall" in four or five FISA cases. . . .

In September 2000, the government came forward to confess error in some 75 FISA applications related to major terrorist attacks directed against the United States. The errors related to misstatements and omissions of material facts. . . .

In November of 2000, the Court held a special meeting to consider the troubling number of inaccurate FBI affidavits in so many FISA applications. After receiving a more detailed explanation from the Department of Justice about what went wrong, *but not why,* the Court decided not to accept inaccurate affidavits from FBI agents whether or not intentionally false. . . .

In March of 2001, the government reported similar misstatements in another series of FISA applications in which there was supposedly a "wall" between separate intelligence and criminal squads in FBI field offices to screen FISA intercepts, when in fact all of the FBI agents were on the same squad and all of the screening was done by the one supervisor overseeing both investigations.

To come to grips with this problem, in April of 2001, the FBI promulgated detailed procedures governing the submission of requests to conduct FISA surveillances and searches, and to review draft affidavits in FISA applications, to ensure their accuracy. These procedures are currently in use and require careful review of draft affidavits by the FBI agents in the field offices. . . .

In virtually every instance, the government's misstatements and omissions in FISA applications and violations of the Court's orders involved information sharing and unauthorized disseminations to criminal investigators and prosecutors. These incidents have been under investigation by the FBI's and the Justice Department's Offices of Professional Responsibility for more than one year to determine how the violations occurred in the field offices, and how the misinformation found its way into the FISA applications and remained uncorrected for more than one year despite procedures to verify the accuracy of FISA pleadings. As of this date, no report has been published, and how these misrepresentations occurred remains unexplained to the Court. . . .

Given this history in FISA information sharing, the Court now turns to the revised 2002 minimization procedures. We recite this history to make clear that the Court has long approved, under controlled circumstances, the sharing of FISA information with criminal prosecutors, as well as consultations between intelligence and criminal investigations where FISA surveillances and searches are being conducted. However, the proposed 2002 minimization procedures eliminate the bright line in the 1995 procedures prohibiting direction and control by prosecutors on which the Court has relied to moderate the broad acquisition, retention, and dissemination of FISA information in overlapping intelligence and criminal investigations. . . .

As we conclude the first part of our statutory task, we have determined that the extensive acquisition of information concerning U.S. persons through secretive surveillances and searches authorized under FISA, coupled with broad powers of retention and information sharing with criminal prosecutors, weigh heavily on one side of the scale which we must balance to ensure that the proposed minimization procedures are "consistent" with the need of the United States to obtain, produce, and disseminate *foreign intelligence information.*

III

The 2002 minimization rules . . . continue the existing practice approved by this Court of in-depth dissemination of FISA information to Criminal Division trial attorneys and U.S. Attorney's Offices (*hereafter criminal prosecutors*). These new procedures apply in two kinds of counterintelligence cases in which *FISA is the only effective tool available* to both counterintelligence and criminal investigators:

1. those cases in which separate intelligence and criminal investigations of the same U.S. person FISA target are conducted by different FBI agents (*overlapping investigations*), usually involving international terrorism, and in which separation can easily be maintained, and
2. those cases in which one investigation having a U.S. person FISA target is conducted by a team of FBI agents which has both intelligence and criminal interests (*overlapping interests*) usually involving espionage and similar crimes in which separation is impractical.

In both kinds of counterintelligence investigations where FISA is being used, the proposed 2002 minimization procedures authorize extensive consultations between the FBI and criminal prosecutors. . . .

. . . [M]ost relevant to this Court's finding, criminal prosecutors are empowered to advise *FBI intelligence officials* concerning "*the initiation, operation, continuation, or expansion of FISA searches or surveillance.*" (emphasis added) This provision is designed to use this Court's orders to enhance criminal investigation and prosecution, consistent with the government's interpretation of the recent amendments that FISA may now be "used *primarily* for a law enforcement purpose." . . .

A fair reading of these provisions leaves only one conclusion—under . . . the 2002 minimization procedures, criminal prosecutors are to have a significant role *directing* FISA surveillances and searches from start to finish in counterintelligence cases having overlapping intelligence and criminal investigations or interests, guiding them to criminal prosecution. The government makes no secret of this policy, asserting its interpretation of the Act's new amendments which "allows FISA to be used *primarily* for a law enforcement purpose."

Given our experience in FISA surveillances and searches, we find that these provisions . . . particularly those which authorize criminal prosecutors to advise FBI intelligence officials on the initiation, operation, continuation or expansion of FISA's intrusive seizures, are designed to enhance the acquisition, retention and dissemination of *evidence for law enforcement purposes, instead* of being consistent with the need of the United States to "obtain, produce, and disseminate *foreign intelligence information*" (emphasis added). . . . The 2002 procedures appear to be designed to amend the law. . . . This may be because the government is unable to meet the substantive requirements of these law enforcement tools, or because their administrative burdens are too onerous. In either case, the FISA's definition of minimization procedures has not changed, and these procedures cannot be used by the government to amend the Act in ways Congress has not. We also find the provisions . . . wanting because the prohibition in the 1995 procedures of criminal prosecutors "*directing or controlling*" FISA cases has been revoked by the proposed 2002 procedures. The government's memorandum of law expends considerable effort justifying deletion of that bright line, but the Court is not persuaded.

The Court has long accepted and approved minimization procedures authorizing in-depth information sharing and coordination with criminal prosecutors as described in detail above. In the Court's view, the plain meaning of consultations and coordination now specifically authorized in the Act is based on the need to adjust or bring into alignment two different but complementary interests—intelligence gathering and law enforcement. In FISA cases this presupposes separate intelligence and criminal investigations, or a single investiga-

tion with intertwined interests, which need to be brought into harmony to avoid dysfunction and frustration of either interest. If criminal prosecutors direct both the intelligence and criminal investigations, or a single investigation having combined interests, *coordination becomes subordination* of both investigations or interests to law enforcement objectives. The proposed 2002 minimization procedures require the Court to balance the government's use of FISA surveillances and searches against the government's need to obtain and use evidence for criminal prosecution, *instead of* determining the "need of the United States to obtain, produce, and disseminate foreign intelligence information." . . .

Advising FBI intelligence officials on the initiation, operation, continuation or expansion of FISA surveillances and searches of U.S. persons means that criminal prosecutors will tell the FBI when to use FISA (perhaps when they lack probable cause . . .), what techniques to use, what information to look for, what information to keep as evidence and when use of FISA can cease because there is enough evidence to arrest and prosecute. The 2002 minimization procedures give the Department's criminal prosecutors every legal advantage conceived by Congress to be used by U.S. intelligence agencies to collect foreign intelligence information . . . based on a standard that the U.S. person is only using or about to use the places to be surveilled and searched, without any notice to the target unless arrested and prosecuted, and, if prosecuted, no adversarial discovery of the FISA applications and warrants. All of this may be done by use of procedures intended to minimize collection of U.S. person information, consistent with the need of the United States to obtain and produce foreign intelligence information. If direction of counterintelligence cases involving the use of highly intrusive FISA surveillances and searches by criminal prosecutors is necessary to obtain and produce foreign intelligence information, it is yet to be explained to the Court.

THEREFORE, . . . [t]he Court *FINDS* that parts . . . of the minimization procedures submitted with the Government's motion are NOT reasonably designed, in light of their purpose and technique, "consistent with the need of the United States to obtain, produce, or disseminate foreign intelligence information." . . .

THEREFORE, pursuant to this Court's authority . . . to issue *ex parte* orders for electronic surveillances and physical searches "*as requested or as modified,*" the Court herewith grants the Government's motion BUT MODIFIES the pertinent provisions. . . .

These modifications are intended to bring the minimization procedures into accord with the language used in the FISA, and reinstate the bright line used in the 1995 procedures, on which the Court has relied. The purpose of minimization proce-

dures as defined in the Act, is not to amend the statute, but to protect the privacy of Americans in these highly intrusive surveillances and searches, "consistent with the need of the United States to obtain, produce, and disseminate foreign intelligence information."

A separate order shall issue this date.

All seven judges of the Court concur in the Corrected and Amended Memorandum Opinion.

3.5 On Motions for Review of Orders of the United States Foreign Intelligence Surveillance Court
Argued September 9, 2002; Decided November 18, 2002

United States Foreign Intelligence Surveillance Court of Review

In re: Sealed Case No. 02-001

Theodore B. Olson, Solicitor General, argued the cause for appellant the United States, with whom *John Ashcroft,* Attorney General, *Larry D. Thompson,* Deputy Attorney General, *David S. Kris,* Associate Deputy Attorney General, *James A. Baker,* Counsel for Intelligence Policy, and *Jonathan L. Marcus,* Attorney Advisor, were on the briefs.

Ann Beeson, Jameel Jaffer, Steven R. Shapiro, for *amicus curiae* American Civil Liberties Union, with whom *James X. Dempsey* for Center for Democracy and Technology, *Kate Martin* for Center for National Security Studies, *David L. Sobel* for Electronic Privacy Information Center, and *Lee Tien* for Electronic Frontier Foundation, were on the brief.

John D. Cline, Zachary A. Ives, and *Joshua Dratel,* for *amicus curiae* National Association of Criminal Defense Lawyers.

Before: GUY, *Senior Circuit Judge, Presiding;* SILBERMAN and LEAVY, *Senior Circuit Judges.*

Opinion for the Court Filed *Per Curiam.*

Per Curiam. This is the first appeal from the Foreign Intelligence Surveillance Court to the Court of Review since the passage of the Foreign Intelligence Surveillance Act (FISA) in 1978. This appeal is brought by the United States from a FISA court surveillance order which imposed certain restric-

tions on the government. Since the government is the only party to FISA proceedings, we have accepted briefs filed by the American Civil Liberties Union (ACLU) and the National Association of Criminal Defense Lawyers (NACDL) as *amici curiae.*

Not surprisingly this case raises important questions of statutory interpretation, and constitutionality. After a careful review of the briefs filed by the government and *amici,* we conclude that FISA, as amended by the Patriot Act, supports the government's position, and that the restrictions imposed by the FISA court are not required by FISA or the Constitution. We therefore remand for further proceedings in accordance with this opinion. . . .

We think it fair to say . . . that the May 17 opinion of the FISA court does not clearly set forth the basis for its decision. It appears to proceed from the assumption that FISA constructed a barrier between counterintelligence/intelligence officials and law enforcement officers in the Executive Branch—indeed, it uses the word "wall" popularized by certain commentators (and journalists) to describe that supposed barrier. Yet the opinion does not support that assumption with any relevant language from the statute.

The "wall" emerges from the court's implicit interpretation of FISA. The court apparently believes it can approve applications for electronic surveillance only if the government's objective is *not* primarily directed toward criminal prosecution of the foreign agents for their foreign intelligence activity. But the court neither refers to any FISA language supporting that view, nor does it reference the Patriot Act amendments, which the government contends specifically altered FISA to make clear that an application could be obtained even if criminal prosecution is the primary counter mechanism.

Instead the court relied for its imposition of the disputed restrictions on its statutory authority to approve "minimization procedures" designed to prevent the acquisition, retention, and dissemination within the government of material gathered in an electronic surveillance that is unnecessary to the government's need for foreign intelligence information. . . .

Essentially, the FISA court took portions of the Attorney General's augmented 1995 Procedures—adopted to deal with the primary purpose standard—and imposed them generically as minimization procedures. In doing so, the FISA court erred. It did not provide any constitutional basis for its action—we think there is none—and misconstrued the main statutory provision on which it relied. The court mistakenly categorized the augmented 1995 Procedures as FISA minimization procedures and then compelled the government to utilize a modified version of those procedures in a way that is clearly inconsistent with the statutory purpose. . . .

. . . [M]inimization procedures are designed to protect, as far as reasonable, against the acquisition, retention, and dissemination of nonpublic information which is not foreign intelligence information. If the data is not foreign intelligence information as defined by the statute, the procedures are to ensure that the government does not use the information to identify the target or third party, unless such identification is necessary to properly understand or assess the foreign intelligence information that is collected. . . .

The minimization procedures allow, however, the retention and dissemination of non-foreign intelligence information which is evidence of *ordinary crimes* for preventative or prosecutorial purposes. Therefore, if through interceptions or searches, evidence of "a serious crime totally unrelated to intelligence matters" is incidentally acquired, the evidence is *"not* . . . required to be

destroyed." . . . In light of these purposes of the minimization procedures, there is simply no basis for the FISA court . . . to limit criminal prosecutors' ability to advise FBI intelligence officials on the initiation, operation, continuation, or expansion of FISA surveillances to obtain foreign intelligence information, even if such information includes evidence of a foreign intelligence crime.

The FISA court's decision and order not only misinterpreted and misapplied minimization procedures it was entitled to impose, but as the government argues persuasively, the FISA court may well have exceeded the constitutional bounds that restrict an Article III court. The FISA court asserted authority to govern the internal organization and investigative procedures of the Department of Justice which are the province of the Executive Branch (Article II) and the Congress (Article I). Subject to statutes dealing with the organization of the Justice Department, however, the Attorney General has the responsibility to determine how to deploy personnel resources. . . .

We also think the refusal by the FISA court to consider the legal significance of the Patriot Act's crucial amendments was error. The government, in order to avoid the [FISA] requirement of meeting the "primary purpose" test, specifically sought an amendment to [FISA] which had required a certification "that the purpose of the surveillance is to obtain foreign intelligence information" so as to delete the article "the" before "purpose" and replace it with "a." The government made perfectly clear to Congress why it sought the legislative change. Congress, although accepting the government's explanation for the need for the amendment, adopted language which it perceived as not giving the government quite the degree of modification it wanted. Accordingly, [the] wording became "that *a significant* purpose of the surveillance is to obtain foreign intelligence information" (emphasis added). There is simply no question, however, that Congress was keenly aware that this amendment relaxed a requirement that the government show that its primary purpose was other than criminal prosecution. . . .

To be sure, some Senate Judiciary Committee members including the Chairman were concerned that the amendment might grant too much authority to the Justice Department—and the FISA court.

Senator Leahy indicated that the change to signifi-cant purpose was "very problematic" since it would "make it easier for the FBI to use a FISA wiretap to obtain information where the Govern-ment's most important motivation for the wiretap is for use in a criminal prosecution." Therefore he suggested that "it will be up to the courts to deter-mine how far law enforcement agencies may use FISA for criminal investigation and prosecution *beyond* the scope of the statutory definition of 'foreign intelligence information.'" But the only dissenting vote against the act was cast by Senator Feingold. Senator Feingold recognized that the change to "significant purpose" meant that the gov-ernment could obtain a FISA warrant "even if the primary purpose is a criminal investigation," and was concerned that this development would not respect the protections of the Fourth Amendment.

In sum, there can be no doubt as to Congress' in-tent in amending [FISA]. . . .

Neither *amicus* brief defends the reasoning of the FISA court. NACDL's brief makes no attempt to interpret FISA or the Patriot Act amendments but rather argues the primary purpose test is constitu-tionally compelled. The ACLU relies on Title III of the Omnibus Crime Control and Safe Streets Act of 1968 to interpret FISA, passed 10 years later. That technique, to put it gently, is hardly an orthodox method of statutory interpretation. FISA was passed to deal specifically with the subject of foreign intel-ligence surveillance. The ACLU does argue that Congress' intent to preclude law enforcement offi-cials initiating or controlling foreign intelligence investigations is revealed by FISA's exclusion of the Attorney General—a law enforcement official—from the officers who can certify the foreign intelli-gence purpose of an application under section 1804. The difficulty with that argument is that the Attorney General supervises the Director of the FBI who is both a law enforcement and counterintelli-gence officer. The Attorney General or the Deputy Attorney General, moreover, must approve *all* ap-plications no matter who certifies that the informa-tion sought is foreign intelligence information.

The ACLU insists that the significant purpose amendment only "clarified" the law permitting FISA surveillance orders "even if foreign intelli-gence is not its *exclusive* purpose" (emphasis added). In support of this rather strained interpreta-

tion, which ignores the legislative history of the Pa-triot Act, the ACLU relies on a *September 10, 2002* hearing of the Judiciary Committee (the day after the government's oral presentation to this court) at which certain senators made statements—some-what at odds with their floor statements prior to the passage of the Patriot Act—as to what they had in-tended the year before. The D.C. Circuit has de-scribed such post-enactment legislative statements as "legislative future" rather than legislative history, not entitled to authoritative weight. *See General In-strument Corp. v. FCC* (2000).

Accordingly, the Patriot Act amendments clearly disapprove the primary purpose test. And as a mat-ter of straightforward logic, if a FISA application can be granted even if "foreign intelligence" is only a significant—not a primary—purpose, another purpose can be primary. One other legitimate pur-pose that could exist is to prosecute a target for a foreign intelligence crime. . . .

The important point is . . . the Patriot Act amend-ment, by using the word "significant," eliminated any justification for the FISA court to balance the relative weight the government places on criminal prosecution as compared to other counterintelli-gence responses. . . .

The government claims that even prosecutions of *non*-foreign intelligence crimes are consistent with a purpose of gaining foreign intelligence informa-tion so long as the government's objective is to stop espionage or terrorism by putting an agent of a for-eign power in prison. That interpretation trans-gresses the original FISA. . . . [T]he FISA process cannot be used as a device to investigate wholly unrelated ordinary crimes.

Having determined that FISA, as amended, does not oblige the government to demonstrate to the FISA court that its primary purpose in conducting electronic surveillance is *not* criminal prosecution, we are obliged to consider whether the statue as amended is consistent with the Fourth Amend-ment. . . .

Although the FISA court did not explicitly rely on the Fourth Amendment, it at least suggested that this provision was the animating principle driving its statutory analysis. . . . The government, recog-nizing the Fourth Amendment's shadow effect on the FISA court's opinion, has affirmatively argued that FISA is constitutional. And some of the very senators who fashioned the Patriot Act amendments expected that the federal courts, including presumably the FISA court, would carefully consider that question. . . .

We are, therefore, grateful to the ACLU and NACDL for their briefs that vigorously contest the government's argument. Both NACDL . . . and the ACLU rely on two propositions. The first is not actually argued; it is really an assumption—that a FISA order does not qualify as a warrant within the meaning of the Fourth Amendment. The second is that any government surveillance whose *primary purpose* is criminal prosecution *of whatever kind* is *per se* unreasonable if not based on a warrant.

The FISA court expressed concern that unless FISA were "construed" in the fashion that it did, the government could use a FISA order as an improper substitute for an ordinary criminal warrant under Title III [Refers to 18 USC 2510 (1968), Omnibus Crime Control and Safe Streets Act (regarding wiretapping)]. . . . [I]n asking whether FISA procedures can be regarded as reasonable under the Fourth Amendment, we think it is instructive to compare those procedures and requirements with their Title III counterparts. Obviously, the closer those FISA procedures are to Title III procedures, the lesser are our constitutional concerns. . . .

. . . [T]o the extent the two statutes diverge in constitutionally relevant areas—in particular, in their probable cause and particularity showings—a FISA order may not be a "warrant" contemplated by the Fourth Amendment. The government itself does not actually claim that it is, instead noting only that there is authority for the proposition that a FISA order is a warrant in the constitutional sense. . . . We do not decide the issue but note that to the extent a FISA order comes close to meeting Title III, that certainly bears on its reasonableness under the Fourth Amendment. . . .

FISA's general programmatic purpose, to protect the nation against terrorists and espionage threats directed by foreign powers, has from its outset been distinguishable from "ordinary crime control." After the events of September 11, 2001, though, it is hard to imagine greater emergencies facing Americans than those experienced on that date.

We acknowledge, however, that the constitutional question presented by this case—whether Congress's disapproval of the primary purpose test is consistent with the Fourth Amendment—has no definitive jurisprudential answer. The Supreme Court's special needs cases involve random stops (seizures) not electronic searches. In one sense, they can be thought of as a greater encroachment into personal privacy because they are not based on any particular suspicion. On the other hand, wiretapping is a good deal more intrusive than an automobile stop accompanied by questioning.

Although the Court in *City of Indianapolis* cautioned that the threat to society is not dispositive in determining whether a search or seizure is reasonable, it certainly remains a crucial factor. Our case may well involve the most serious threat our country faces. Even without taking into account the President's inherent constitutional authority to conduct warrantless foreign intelligence surveillance, we think the procedures and government showings required under FISA, if they do not meet the minimum Fourth Amendment warrant standards, certainly come close. We, therefore, believe firmly . . . that FISA as amended is constitutional because the surveillances it authorizes are reasonable.

Accordingly, we reverse the FISA court's orders in this case to the extent they imposed conditions on the grant of the government's applications . . . and remand with instructions to grant the applications as submitted and proceed henceforth in accordance with this opinion.

A View from the Inside

3.6 Ninth Circuit Court of Appeals Reorganization Act of 2002
107th Congress, Second Session (July 23, 2002)

House Subcommittee on Courts, the Internet, and Intellectual Property

The Subcommittee met, pursuant to call, at 3:04 p.m., in Room 2141, Rayburn House Office Building, Hon. Howard Coble [Chairman of the Subcommittee] presiding.

Mr. Coble: [R–North Carolina, 6th]: Good afternoon, ladies and gentlemen. The Subcommittee will come to order. Good to have a distinguished panel before us. . . .

Today we will evaluate the merits of H.R. 1203, the Ninth Circuit Court of Appeals Reorganization Act of 2001, which was introduced by our colleague, Representative Mike Simpson of Idaho.

This is the latest installment of a long-running saga involving the Ninth and its operations. I can recall at least 5 or 6 years ago, we went through a similar exercise.

I'm hopeful that we will review the legislation and history of the Ninth in a sober and thoughtful way by adhering to the facts. We need to explore whether the Ninth has become so big or so cumbersome, if you're in favor of splitting it, in geographic size, in workload, in number of active and senior judges, that it can no longer appropriately discharge its civic functions on behalf of the American people.

My own opinion is that judicial temperament as it is reflected in a given case or by a trend in case law is not an adequate reason by itself to split a circuit.

I guess, to sum up, will the reconfiguring of the Ninth Circuit, or the establishment or creation of a new twelfth circuit, result in more detriment or more benefit? Or will there be subtle shades of gray between the white and black extremes of the equation?

We'll hear from both sides in this matter, and I'm looking forward to a good discussion. I think it will be paired off, two versus two, in favor of the split or retaining its present boundary lines.

I'm now pleased to recognize the distinguished gentleman from California, my friend Mr. Berman, the Ranking Member, for his opening statement. . . .

Mr. Berman: [D–California, 28th] Thank you very much, Mr. Chairman.

Unfortunately, today I can't express my appreciation to you for convening our Subcommittee on this subject. As you know, I don't fault you at all for the holding of this hearing, as I understand that the Chairman of the full Committee insisted on it. And I certainly don't blame our colleague for doing everything he can to try and get a hearing on a bill that he believes in, has introduced, and cares about.

But the fact that my respect and affection for you remain as strong as ever doesn't mean that I'm happy to be here.

For several years now, I've had the honor of being your Ranking Member, and you've graciously shared with me a schedule of Subcommittee activities for the upcoming months. With your typical grace, you have conferred with me about the scheduling of hearings and, on many occasions, have accommodated requests for scheduling changes. Unfortunately, this hearing is a deviation from the norm.

This hearing was nowhere to be found on our Subcommittee schedule for May, June, and July. And we only learned of it in the middle of last week. Despite entirely reasonable concerns about the short notice and inconvenience to our witnesses, who have had to shuffle very busy hearing dockets and travel across the country, the full Committee Chairman refused to reschedule this hearing for September.

And frankly, one could take these very unique circumstances on a subject which we've had a number of hearings on already, and look at the very short timeframe for the calling of this hearing, and one could perhaps reasonably come to a conclusion that it is an attempt to punish or embarrass the Ninth Circuit for a Ninth Circuit panel's decision involving the Pledge of Allegiance. Most troubling, these circumstances lend credence to those who believe proposals to split the Ninth Circuit are more about politics than judicial efficiency.

And I don't have to just rely on speculation, because the majority's memo starts out: "Proposals to split the Ninth Circuit have percolated with varying intensity for nearly 30 years. The issue is currently topical in light of a recently issued Ninth Circuit decision." Which one? "A three-judge panel ruled on June 26 that the Pledge of Allegiance violates the first amendment's prohibition against the establishment of a State religion. This decision spotlights the reputation of the Ninth for being metaphorically 'isolated' from the rest of the country, based on its size."

I don't quite understand how one follows from the other, but perhaps the proponents of the legislation can explain that. . . .

Well-meaning minds can differ regarding which judicial structures will best promote judicial efficiency and consistency in circuit decisions. But it's equally true that those with political motives may adopt such proposals to advance their agendas. For my part, I don't intend to mask my opinion on the merits of this issue by questioning the process. By the way, no one has ever accused me of always being devoid of political motives.

In any event, I am unequivocally opposed to splitting the Ninth Circuit. However, I believe it is a serious issue worthy of discussion by our Subcommittee. I would just have preferred that we had been given a little more notice and an opportunity to identify a more convenient hearing date, not simply for me but more importantly, I think, for at least some of the witnesses.

We have studied this issue extensively through Subcommittee hearings. I find merit in arguments on both sides. Each time, I eventually come around to the same conclusion: The Ninth Circuit isn't broken, so why try to fix it? And can we be sure that the cure won't be worse than the supposed disease?

For each reason offered as a justification to split the Ninth Circuit, there is an equally reasonable response. . . .

Similarly, many statistics can be cited to support the arguments of both sides in this debate. . . .

. . . Without clear evidence that the current situation is detrimental and understanding that a dramatic restructuring could end up a costly failure, I don't believe it's appropriate or prudent for Congress to legislate a split of the Ninth Circuit.

That's not to say that the Ninth Circuit is incapable of improvement. Even Chief Judge Schroeder and Judge Thomas, who appear today to oppose a split, are advocates of further improvements to the efficiency and operations of their circuit.

Frankly, the best way for Congress to participate constructively in the effort to improve the Ninth Circuit would be to create additional judgeships at both the district and circuit court level. There is an absolute crisis in the Southern District of California—that's the San Diego area—due to the insufficient number of judges, and the Central District is only marginally better off. The Ninth Circuit has four vacancies and, according to the Judicial Conference, needs Congress to create several new judgeships.

While my colleagues in the Senate may not appreciate the added aggravation, I believe Congress should move to create and approve new judges in the Ninth Circuit and its district courts.

And aside from that, Mr. Chairman, I'm totally open on the issue. [Laughter.]. . .

Mr. Coble: I thank the gentleman. Thank you, Mr. Berman. . . . I'm now pleased to recognize the gentleman on my right-hand side, Mr. Issa, the distinguished gentleman from California, for his opening statement.

Mr. Issa: [R–California, 49th]: Thank you, Mr. Chairman. . . .

It may not come as a surprise to you that I start off interested in hearing what you have to say, but with a slightly different bent than Mr. Berman. I do find that those of my friends who say that the Ninth Circuit is too large and those who say that it's too liberal, I'm with both of them, because there is no question that this is a circuit that has a long history of being overturned; this is a Court of Appeals that has more on its plate than its fair share.

If I do the simple business arithmetic, if there are 11 circuits, that means about one out of every nine Americans should be represented by a circuit.

California alone is about one out of every nine Americans. So on its face, breaking up the circuit, in order to get a closer to equality size of the circuit, seems to make sense.

In San Diego, where we are short and are working desperately to get five more judges, I'm acutely aware . . . of the growth in the Federal judiciary, and the likelihood that your caseloads are only going to grow.

To that extent, what I'm hoping to hear from this panel is not do we or don't we, but if we did, what would be the benefits? If we did, how would we do it in a way that did not simply say we are punishing the Ninth Circuit for being too liberal, because that alone would not be enough of a justification?

I need to know why the Ninth, Tenth, Eleventh and Twelfth would all be better for the particular proposals. And my colleague will hopefully lead the charge, but to each of the judges and the attorney general, that's my big concern. It's not, "Do we do it?" I believe that eventually we will do it. But are the potential plans that are being proposed of sufficient merit that we should begin the dialogue on the Committee of either the existing proposals or follow-up proposals, because I believe sooner or later, the load and the size and the growth in the West is going to mandate this.

. . . I start off with an assumption that we will have this discussion again and again until eventually we break it up. I would hope that we are not citing one isolated panel in order to have this hearing, but rather the ongoing growth of the West and the likelihood that eventually you cannot have a circuit that is twice the size of other circuits and then call it, if you will, equal in the justice that it hands out.

Mr. Berman: Would the gentleman yield?

Mr. Issa: I certainly would yield to my colleague from California.

Mr. Berman: Thank you for yielding.

Actually, the new judgeships in the Southern District have not yet been authorized.

Mr. Issa: They're in the process. We have a deal.

Mr. Berman: A lot of things are in the process.

Mr. Issa: We're going to get them, Howard.

Mr. Berman: All right.

Mr. Issa: Trust me, as a San Diegan, we're going to get them.

Mr. Berman: That's good to know.

Mr. Issa: Thank you, Mr. Chairman. I yield back.

Mr. Coble: I thank the gentlemen for their opening statements. And before we begin with the formal witness introduction, I would like to recognize our friend and colleague, Representative Mike Simpson of the Second District of Idaho. He is the co-sponsor of H.R. 1203 and would like to introduce his attorney general, Attorney General Lance, also of Idaho. . . .

Our first witness today is the Honorable Mary M. Schroeder, the Chief Judge for the United States Court of Appeals for the Ninth Circuit. Prior to her service on the Federal bench, Judge Schroeder worked as a trial attorney at the Department of Justice, clerked for the Arizona Supreme Court, and practiced law with the firm of Lewis & Roca. She also served as a judge for the Arizona Court of Appeals. President Carter appointed her to the Ninth Circuit in 1979. Judge Schroeder earned her B.A. in 1962 from Swarthmore College and her J.D. in 1965 from the University of Chicago School of Law.

Our second witness is the attorney general for the State of Idaho, and I will permit Representative Simpson to introduce his attorney general.

Mr. Simpson: Thank you, Mr. Chairman. . . . When I was in the State legislature, he was in the State legislature with me. And when I became Speaker, he became the caucus chairman or the conference chairman. So we have served together many years. Then he went on to much greater things and was elected attorney general of the State of Idaho and is completing his second term. . . .

Since Al has become the attorney general in the State of Idaho, he has been an advocate for splitting the court for efficiency reasons. Whatever reason brings us here today—Mr. Berman suggests maybe it's politics—I want to tell you that we've been dealing with this for a number of years, and we've been advocates for a number years. And he's correct; reasonable people can disagree on that. . . .

Mr. Coble: I thank you, Mike. . . .

Our next witness is the Honorable Judge Diarmuid F. O'Scannlain, who was appointed to the Ninth Circuit by President Reagan in 1986. Judge O'Scannlain has also practiced law and worked for the State of Oregon in various public capacities. He retired from the U.S. Army Reserve in 1978, having obtained the rank of major. Judge O'Scannlain earned his J.D. in 1963 from the Harvard Law School and his B.A. in 1957 from St. John's University. He also earned the LL.M. degree at the University of Virginia School of Law in 1992 and was awarded the LL.D. degree by the University of Notre Dame in 2002.

Our final witness today is also a Ninth Circuit judge, the Honorable Sidney R. Thomas, who was nominated by President Clinton in 1995. Judge Thomas has worked on educational pursuits in the Montana State Government, practiced law, and taught. He has received numerous awards and authored publications on the law and other topics. Judge Thomas received his B.A. in 1975 at the Montana State University and his J.D. in 1978 from the Montana School of Law.

It's good to have each of you panelists with us. . . . Judge Schroeder, why don't we begin with you?

Judge Schroeder [Chief Judge, U.S. Court of Appeals, Ninth Circuit]: Thank you, Mr. Chairman. And I thank you for the opportunity to be here this afternoon. . . .

The Ninth Circuit Court of Appeals since 1984 has had a total of 28 authorized active judgeships. Because of vacancies and last week's welcome confirmation, we now have 24 active judges and 22 senior judges. The Judicial Conference U.S. has approved our requests for additional judgeships as part of its own proposals, but no legislation is currently pending for any national judgeships.

As chief judge, I chair our circuit's governing body, the Ninth Circuit Judicial Council, which has consistently opposed our circuit's division. I want to make it clear, however, that I do not speak for the Judicial Conference U.S., which has never taken any position with respect to Ninth Circuit division or realignment.

I appear in opposition to H.R. 1203 that deals only with the Ninth Circuit and which proposes to divide the circuit into two circuits but does not address the growing need for additional judgeships or any other resources to handle greater numbers of increasingly complex cases.

I begin by observing that my opposition to legislation to divide the circuit is the same as the position of my predecessors as chief and of the overwhelming majority of our judges since this subject was first broached between 30 and 40 years ago. We have had a lot of exhaustive studies of circuit realignment, the most recent by the congressionally created Commission on Structural Alternatives for the Federal Courts of Appeals, chaired by former Justice Byron White and known as the White Commission.

It reached a number of conclusions that are relevant, but I quote one that may be especially pertinent today. The commission report concluded that "there is one principle that we regard as undebatable: It is wrong to realign circuits and to restructure courts because of particular judicial decisions or particular judges. This rule must be faithfully honored, for the independence of the judiciary is of constitutional dimension and requires no less."

The White Commission also observed that there are many advantages to our circuit remaining intact. These include the ability of a large circuit to make temporary assignments of judges from one area of the circuit to other areas that are experiencing heavy demands on limited resources. And in this time, we are today experiencing those demands in our border districts.

The commission also recognized that our circuit is a Pacific jurisdiction with ports and airports that look toward Asia and Australia. And the report concluded that to split the Ninth Circuit would deprive the courts now in the Ninth Circuit of the administrative advantages afforded by the present circuit configuration and deprive the West and the Pacific seaboard of a means of maintaining uniform Federal law in that area. . . .

Let me turn briefly to the practical matter of costs. Circuit division is expensive. The cost of a new courthouse and administrative headquarters for a new circuit would begin at $100 to $120 million. Our Court of Appeals' administrative staff includes a Clerk's Office, staff attorneys to provide assistance to judges, an office of mediation that was a pioneer in the area and remains a model to the country, and libraries and satellite libraries. We have growing computer resources. Replicating all of these would cost $10 million annually.

A new circuit will have administrative needs, including assessing budgetary requirements and meeting the now heightened security requirements to protect our judges, our staff, and our public buildings. The Circuit Executive's Office now provides these services for the Circuit and would have to be replicated for a new circuit at an annual cost of over $4 million.

In any new circuit, there would be large distances and multiple large population centers. Substantial travel costs will remain. It's a long way from Seattle to Honolulu, no matter what circuit they're located in. And any circuit with Alaska would be the largest circuit in terms of area and any circuit with California would be the largest circuit in terms of population and caseload. . . .

And finally, since the White Commission report, we have seen undiminished acceleration in technology advances around the world. Our Federal courts face increasing numbers of international and global issues. Fracturing the Federal courts does not contribute to the solution of these looming issues.

So I return, in closing, to our greatest need, which is additional judgeships. We have had no additional judgeships since 1984. Our caseload since that time has doubled. It is that need I urge the Committee to address. . . .

Mr. Coble: Thank you, Your Honor. . . .

If you will give your testimony, Mr. Lance. . . .

Mr. Lance [Attorney General, Idaho]: Thank you very much, Mr. Chairman.

Mr. Chairman, I have submitted to the clerk some supplement to my written testimony, which is a letter signed by 48 attorneys general, joining with the State of California petitioning the Ninth Circuit Court of Appeals to take another look at the Pledge of Allegiance case. Let me point out that that's signed by 32 Democrats and 16 Republicans.

The Ninth Circuit issue has been an ongoing concern since I became attorney general of the State of Idaho in 1995. In 1995, five northwestern attorneys general, three Democrats and two Republicans, urged Congress to split the Ninth Circuit Court of Appeals and create a new twelfth circuit.

H.R. 1203 would accomplish just that. It's good government. It's good legislation, which would improve efficiency, service, predictability, and justice.

The Ninth Circuit has certainly received considerable attention recently, and I hope this attention is channeled into constructive problem-solving. The problem is not the Pledge of Allegiance. The problem is the Ninth Circuit Court of Appeals.

The Ninth Circuit issue is the most important law and justice issue in the West. Thirty years ago, the Hruska Commission recommended to Congress that both the Fifth and Ninth circuits be split. Congress split the Fifth Circuit in 1980, and we're still waiting for ours.

The reason underlying the Ninth Circuit's problems are quite simple: size. The Ninth Circuit's population is two and one half times greater than the average of the other circuits. All Ninth Circuit States are in the top 20 projected growth States. By 2025, over 75 million people will live in the Ninth Circuit. The Ninth Circuit covers 40 percent of the United States. That is more that 1.3 million square miles. The other circuits average about 200,000 square miles. The Ninth Circuit consists of nine States and two territories. The other circuits average about three and one half. The Ninth Circuit has 28 authorized circuit judges. The other circuits average about 12 and one half.

This is quite significant. As the commission chaired by former U.S. Supreme Court Justice Byron White advised Congress 3 years ago, and I quote, "The maximum number of judges for an effective appellate court functioning as a single decisional unit is somewhere between 11 and 17." None of the other circuits have more than 17 judges.

These structural facts certainly distinguish the Ninth Circuit from the other Federal circuits. They also lead directly to some very serious problems.

Almost 25 percent of the Nation's entire backlog of appeals is in the Ninth Circuit. The Nation's appeals backlog has increased by 1 percent since 1997; in the Ninth Circuit, the backlog has increased 20 percent. Last year, appeals increased nationally by 5 percent; the Ninth Circuit appeals increased by 13 percent. Also last year, the Ninth Circuit accounted for almost one-third of all requests filed for Supreme Court review.

The U.S. Supreme Court has struck down a large number and a very high percentage of Ninth Circuit cases. From 1990 to 1996 the Supreme Court struck down 73 percent of the Ninth Circuit decisions it reviewed. The other circuits averaged about 46 percent.

In 1997, 27 out of 28 Ninth Circuit decisions were reversed. Since 1998, the Supreme Court has granted review in 103 Ninth Circuit cases, affirming only 13 decisions. Also since 1998, the Supreme Court has unanimously reversed or vacated 26 Ninth Circuit decisions.

In addition to the backlog and reliability problems, citizens in the Ninth Circuit have to wait longer to receive justice. Last year, the Ninth Circuit was in last place and 53 percent slower than the other circuits in resolving its appeals. . . .

Justice delayed is justice denied. All Americans are entitled to equal justice and equal protection under the law, and we in the West are not getting it.

Idahoans have lost confidence in our Federal circuit court. It's too big, too slow, and too unreliable. We want out of this unmanageable judicial bureaucracy.

Attorneys general must be able to advise their Governors, their legislators, and citizens as to the status of the law. In the Ninth Circuit Court of Appeals at the present time, that can be best facilitated with a Ouija board and not a law library. We urge you to give favorable consideration to H.R. 1203. Thank you, sir. . . .

Mr. Coble: . . . Your Honor, Judge O'Scannlain.

Judge O'Scannlain [U.S. Court of Appeals, Ninth Circuit]: Thank you, Chairman Coble and Members of the Subcommittee. . . .

Perhaps the heightened profile that our court has received may have a fortunate development in that it has sparked a renewed interest in how the Ninth Circuit conducts its business.

Nevertheless, I wish to emphasize that I have supported a fundamental restructure of the Ninth Circuit for many years, and I do support a bill like H.R. 1203, but based solely on judicial administration grounds, not premised on reaction to unpopular decisions or Supreme Court batting averages.

Of course, I speak only for myself and eight colleagues of my court, specifically Judges Sneed, Hall, and Fernandez from California; Judges Trott and Nelson from Idaho; Judges Beezer and Tallman from Washington; and Judge Kleinfeld from Alaska. I do not speak for the court, of course, nor, I should add, for the American Bar Association, where I happen to be the national Chair of its Judicial Division.

When the circuit courts of appeal were created over 100 years ago by the Everts Act of 1891, there were only nine regional circuits, and now there are 12. For the longest time, there were only three judges on each circuit, including the time when I was at law school, when there were only three on the First Circuit.

As circuits became unwieldy because of size, they were restructured. The District of Columbia Circuit goes back to a few years after the Everts Act was passed. The Tenth was split out of the Eighth in 1929. The Eleventh was split off from the Fifth in 1981. And in due course, I have absolutely no doubt that a new twelfth circuit will be created out of Ninth, hopefully through legislation like the one we are considering today.

Mr. Chairman, there is nothing sinister, immoral, fattening, politically incorrect, or unconstitutional about the reconstructing of judicial circuits. This is simply the natural evolution of the Federal appellate court structure responding to population changes. As courts grow too big, they evolve into smaller, more manageable judicial circuits. No circuit, not even mine, has a God-given right to an exemption from the natural order of evolution. And there is nothing sacred about the Ninth Circuit keeping essentially the same boundaries for over 100 years. The only legitimate consideration is the optimal size and structure for judges to perform their duties.

The problem with our court and the circuit can be stated quite simply: We are too big now, and we are getting bigger every day. And this is so whether you measure size in terms of number of judges, caseload, or population. Even though we're officially allocated 28 judges, we currently have 24 and 22 seniors. In other words, regardless of our allocation, there are 46 judges on our court today. And when the four existing vacancies are filled, there will be 50 judges. . . .

To put the figure of 50 in perspective, consider the fact that this is almost double the number of total judges of the next-largest circuit, more than quadruple that of the smallest circuit. . . . [I]t's a remarkable array of judge power—more judges on one court than the entire Federal judiciary when the circuit courts of appeal were created.

With every additional judge that takes senior status, we grow even larger. Indeed, if we get the seven new judgeships that we have asked for, there will be 57 judges on the circuit, while the average size of all other circuits is only 19.

. . . Looking at the population, which ranges from the Rocky Mountains to the Sea of Japan, and from the Mexican border to the Arctic Circle, we have 56 million people. We have double the average number of judgeships handling double the average number of appeals and double the average population of all other circuits. And in essence, this means that the Ninth Circuit is already two circuits in one.

Mr. Chairman, . . . I do want to state that a common argument made again today by my chief judge is that we need to stay together to keep a consistent law for the West and for the Pacific seaboard. Mr. Chairman, you live on the Atlantic Coast, where there are five separate circuits. Have you noticed whether freighters are colliding more frequently off Cape Hatteras than they are Long Island or along the Pacific Coast? I tend to doubt it. I simply think that the idea of a single circuit because of a single seacoast is simply, if I may say so, with respect, an absurd argument.

Mr. Chairman, I'm going to conclude by saying that, unfortunately, the problems of size and growth are irrepressible. They will only get worse. We've been engaged in guerrilla warfare on this circuit split now for much too long. What we need to do is get back to judging, and I ask that you do indeed force us to restructure now one way or another, so that we can concentrate on our sworn duties and end the distractions caused by this never-ending controversy.

Thank you very much, Mr. Chairman. . . .

Mr. Coble: Thank you, Judge O'Scannlain. . . . Judge Thomas, good to have you with us, sir.

Judge Thomas: [U.S. Court of Appeals, Ninth Circuit]: Thank you, sir. . . .

Chief Judge Schroeder requested that I testify because of my familiarity with our case management and en banc procedures. . . .

First, allow me to address the question of delay. At the present time, the Ninth Circuit is resolving appeals at a faster rate than they are being filed. That means that we are keeping up with current filings. Further, we have not been consistently the circuit with the longest delay in total case processing. That's varied from year to year. In recent years, circuits such as the Sixth, Second, and Eleventh have

had the longest periods of total case delay. Our circuit remains among the fastest circuits in resolving cases after a presentation to a panel of judges.

When all of our judgeships were filled, our circuit was current with the caseload. Our present total processing delay is due primarily to the backlog of cases that developed from a period of time in which approximately one-third of our judgeships remained unfilled. To address this backlog, our court has initiated a program, which should significantly reduce and perhaps eliminate the backlog within the next few years.

This program, implemented by the court last January, is in its very initial stages. However, we have already diverted nearly 600 appeals to expedited screening panels and have already noticed a 2-month reduction in overall case processing time. If no complications occur, we should be able to significantly reduce or eliminate the backlog of cases within the next several years.

Over the years, the Ninth Circuit has developed a number of other innovative programs that have reduced delay and allowed us to remain current with filings. These have included a judicial screening program that resolved nearly 1,300 appeals last year, a mediation program that resolved 750 appeals, a pro se unit dedicated to handling the 40 percent of appeals filed by litigants who do not have an attorney, an appellate commissioner who issued orders on 2,500 routine administrative motions last year, and a bankruptcy appellate panel that resolved over 700 appeals last year.

In my personal opinion, circuit division would not reduce delay; it would create more delay.

Every scholarly analysis of the issue, including the White Commission, has concluded that size alone is not the primary cause of delay and that circuit division would not reduce delay. The real question is how best to meet the challenge of expanding caseloads with the entire Federal judiciary.

The Ninth Circuit is not unique in having a large caseload. For example, although we had 10,000 appeals filed in our court last year, there were nearly 9,000 new appeals filed in the Fifth Circuit.

The best method, in my opinion, for delay reduction is aggressive and innovative case management and use of administrative efficiencies that economies of scale permit. . . .

Second, let me address briefly the question of consistency and the ability of our judges to monitor opinions. Our circuit is not alone in issuing a large number of opinions. Several other circuits publish nearly as many opinions as we do. Every study to date has indicated that the consistency of Ninth Circuit decisions does not vary from that of other circuits.

Even so, we have implemented measures to improve our system of case monitoring, including a database of issues, tracking of issues by staff attorneys, grouping cases for presentation to oral argument panels, a pre-publication report identifying cases, and an experimental program allowing parties to cite unpublished dispositions that they believe are inconsistent.

We also have a very good system of en banc review, during which disappointed parties present petitions for rehearing and judges and law clerks review cases independently. The shear number of judges and law clerks examining our opinions makes it unlikely that any opinion will evade scrutiny for consistency or for legal soundness.

During the last several years, Supreme Court reversal rates of Ninth Circuit decisions have been consistent with that of other circuits. For example, during this past term, on a percentage basis, there were seven other circuits whose reversal rates exceeded ours. Perhaps more importantly, the number of petitions for certiorari granted by the Supreme Court arising out of decisions of the Ninth Circuit has declined significantly in recent years.

Even in the year most frequently cited by critics, 1996, our circuit was not the most reversed circuit on a percentage basis. That year, five circuits had all of their decisions reversed: the First, Second, Seventh, D.C., and Federal circuits. And since that time, we've had 14 new members added to our court. . . .

. . . We must continue to develop better means of case management and staying in touch with the needs of our constituents. . . . [I]n my opinion, circuit division would not assist us in that effort. It would seriously complicate it and impede it.

I thank the Subcommittee for the opportunity to testify. Thank you very much, Mr. Chairman. . . .

Mr. Coble: Thank you, Judge Thomas. . . .

[L]et me put a question, Judge O'Scannlain, to you and Attorney General Lance, since you two are the advocates for the change.

How should the Ninth be split? Now, Mr. Simpson proposes what appears to be a compact pro-posal, and he would place California Nevada, and Arizona in a reconfigured Eleventh. And then the remaining eight entities would be elsewhere, a newly created circuit.

Do you all like that proposal, or would you like to see a split that would differ from that?

Mr. Lance: Mr. Chairman and Members of the Committee, the proposal dealing with Montana, Idaho, Washington, Oregon, and Alaska I think holds a certain amount of merit. First of all, we are, with the exception of Alaska, all part of the Columbia River basin, and in that drainage, we have Endangered Species Act lawsuits filed quite frequently. We have commonalities relative to Native American tribal cases that are litigated quite frequently. And we think there's a commonality of interests. Alaska, by virtue of geography, would be joined there.

Mr. Chairman, as you are aware, we have the issue of Guam, the Northern Mariana Islands, and Hawaii. I suspect that those issues are somewhat unique to those insular holdings. And they should be in the same circuit, in my opinion, regardless of whether it's the Ninth or the twelfth, however you all decide to do something like that.

But keeping in mind that the Ninth Circuit has two major river basins, the Columbia that we're part of, and the Colorado, which is the Southwest, and issues that are common frequently arise, sir.

Mr. Coble: . . .

Judge O'Scannlain, do you want to weigh in on that?

Judge O'Scannlain: Well, Mr. Chairman, the fundamental problem is, what do you do about California? California is 60 percent of our caseload. It's about 62 percent of our population. And even at that, you will observe that that one State is larger than the average population of all other circuits. It's larger in caseload than the average for all other circuits.

So what are your choices? One choice would be . . . [to] create two circuits by putting the northern half of California in a northern circuit and the southern half of California in a southern circuit. But as I understand it, there are some sensitivities from the standpoint of the State of California. And I have had a chance to talk with Senator Feinstein about this, and she seems to be quite determined that it would be inappropriate to put the State of California into two circuits. I think it could be done, and the scholars have all indicated how it can be done. But let's assume that that's out of the picture.

Then what do you have left? You could have California by itself. That's certainly a reasonable option. There are four districts there. But then if you want to have more than one State attached, then, sure, Nevada makes the most sense, because that's the next-door State, and there's a very strong sense, particularly from Senator Reid's point of view, that Nevada and California have to stay together.

Once you go beyond that, it's almost any kind of structure would work. You could conceivably have Arizona assigned to the Tenth Circuit. Or you could even have California by itself surrounded by all the other—I mean, there are lots of options. . . .

Mr. Coble: I thank you, sir. . . .

Now, Chief Judge Schroeder, I like the idea of making it smaller geographically. I also am bothered by the costs that you mentioned.

Now, surely there would not have to be new Federal courthouses constructed in each of these entities that would be assigned to the new circuit. Am I correct about that, as far as construction costs are concerned?

Judge Schroeder: There would have to be a new circuit headquarters constructed, because the circuit headquarters in San Francisco would be adequate for one circuit, but there's nothing in the other circuit that is designed to handle a circuit headquarters with all the staff involved. . . .

Mr. Berman: . . . This notion of consistency of decisions, which I guess—is there a difference between the issue of consistency and the issue of predictability? For those who favor the change, they want to enhance consistency and they want to enhance predictability. . . .

Judge O'Scannlain: The problem is that there are nine conceivable panels that could be hearing cases on the very same day, if they were organized that way, with the 28 judges that we have. In fact, you could even have more than that. And the chance that one panel would see something one way and another panel on a similar issue might see it another is a risk, notwithstanding the efforts that we have taken to identify possible similar cases and be sure to get them all to the same panel.

So we've been receiving criticism that you don't know what the law of the circuit is going to be because it may depend on the panel you get.

Now, in answer to your question, I suppose it is the same. The predictability issue is the same as the consistency issue.

Mr. Berman: I don't understand this for several reasons. One, as I understand it, on an issue of precedential value, what the first panel within a circuit decides binds the entire circuit. Is that an accurate statement?

Judge O'Scannlain: That's the way it's supposed to work. That's correct.

Mr. Berman: Surely, I can't believe more than very, very rarely has there been a problem of two panels meeting on a similar issue for which there is no precedent, a new, novel question of law, and deciding on the same day, each unaware of the other's decision. Has this been a problem that's occurred in the Ninth Circuit?

Judge O'Scannlain: Well, my colleagues can answer with me, but, yes, it has occurred. Now, we have mechanisms to try to clean that up. Typically, the best reason to go en banc is because there is a conflict. . . .

Mr. Berman: Well, that's because the earlier precedent decision wasn't followed by the subsequent decision. That's a different issue than two panels coming down on the same day with different—

Judge O'Scannlain: I'm assuming that all the panels are made up of men and women of good faith, and the second panel may not have seen things the same way as the first panel, at least in terms of the underlying rule, and may have reached a different conclusion. And that's why, among other reasons, you have re-hearings en banc.

Mr. Berman: While your motivations are not political, and we've talked about this in my office several years ago— . . . And you have testified, and I believe you and accept that you think this is helpful to the administration of justice. There clearly is, among the advocates of this split, a bit of a political agenda, just as there may very well be from the opponents of the split.

And that makes me think that it is the consistency of the Ninth Circuit decisions that bothers some people, and that they prefer a different circuit, with the hope of getting different decisions, and that that is why they seek this split. I'm just wondering if you have any reaction to that.

In other words, you have a situation now where you have a precedent decision that binds the Ninth Circuit until either the Supreme Court decides, based on conflict with another circuit, or for some other reason, to reverse. You now have a new circuit—by the way, what are the precedent decisions binding that new circuit? I am curious how that works.

Judge O'Scannlain: Well, I would assume that the precedents of the old circuit survive in both places. That would be at least from the starting point.

Mr. Berman: Judge Schroeder? . . .

Judge Schroeder: There have, in fact, only been two divisions of circuits since the circuits were established over 100 years ago. And the last division was about 30 years ago, of the Fifth Circuit. And their first decision was that the law of the old Fifth Circuit will govern both the Fifth and the Eleventh until there's a change.

Judge O'Scannlain: I would assume that would be the same for any division that would come out of this bill.

Mr. Berman: So at least initially, the importance of following what all the different panels have decided up to that time is not eased by virtue of a split, right?

Judge O'Scannlain: I'm not sure I follow the last part of the point.

Mr. Berman: It seems like part of what you're saying is, a reason for the split is so that—there are too many panels in the Ninth Circuit, too many decisions for a new panel to have to be aware of, and

we want to cut that down. And I'm saying, based on what's been said, that a split will not cut that down. You'll still have to review the panel decisions of the old Ninth Circuit, as well as the new decisions within your new circuit.

Judge O'Scannlain: Presumably, they would be smaller circuits. Both of them would be smaller than what we have today.

Mr. Berman: But there's a lot of precedent there.

Judge O'Scannlain: Sure. But the focus should be on the decision-making process. I had a chance, when I was teaching at NYU Law School earlier this year, to visit with Chief Judge Walker of the Second Circuit. They have, I believe, 13 or so judges. They pre-screen, pre-circulate every opinion, published opinion, that comes out of that court. In other words, before it gets published, every judge of that circuit, certainly the First, certainly the Third, and I believe several other circuits, [will] have seen that case, that decision, before it is released to the public. We do not do that in our court, for, among other reasons, there are just so many panels meeting all the time, it would be very, very difficult to do that.

Mr. Berman: My time has expired. I don't know if, Judge Schroeder, if you had anything to add to this? Or Judge Thomas?

Judge Thomas: Just briefly, on the question of consistency—

Mr. Coble: Judge Thomas, if you would, could you hold your thought?

Judge Thomas: Sure.

Mr. Coble: We've been joined by two other Members from California. Let me recognize them. Hold your thought, and we'll get back to you the next round.

Ms. Waters appeared first, so we'll now recognize the gentlelady from California, Ms. Waters, for 5 minutes.

Ms. Waters: Thank you very much, Mr. Chairman.

I'm sorry that I'm late for this meeting. I think that I'm simply going to give my statement, because I think that explains what I feel about this bill.

Mr. Coble: That'd be fine.

Ms. Waters: I am dismayed at the timing of this hearing. Here we have a bill that was introduced in March of 2001 and referred to this Subcommittee in April of that year, and yet no hearings were held or, frankly, even discussed, until a three-judge panel of the Ninth Circuit handed down its decision regarding the Pledge of Allegiance. It is impossible not to infer that this hearing is meant as a warning to all courts that Congress will interfere in your functioning and structure if you do not give us decisions that we like.

This is a blatant disregard for the separation of powers, for the idea of having an independent judiciary. One of the reasons the court of appeals judges are appointed for life is so that they will not be subjected to a politician's whim. Unfortunately, this hearing seems to demonstrate that politicians may choose to find other ways to interfere with the work being done by judges. . . .

Judges and courts often make rulings that we don't like. I've not always been thrilled with rulings in my State or circuit or in the Supreme Court. However, we simply cannot haul judges into Congress every time there's an unpleasant ruling and threaten to impose significant changes in the way they operate. . . .

I certainly appreciate the witnesses being here. And I do not look forward to hearing any more. Normally we say that, you know. But I don't want to have my Chair or the Members of this Committee believe that I really think that this is a serious discussion about whether or not we're concerned about the workload. I think it's political, and I think it's unfortunate. And I think we should not do it this way. But I would welcome, at another time, a discussion about how we increase the number of judges and judgeships. . . .

Mr. Coble: I thank the lady.

We've been joined again by the gentleman from California, Mr. Issa.

Mr. Issa: Thank you, Mr. Chairman.

Judge Schroeder, perhaps I could ask a rhetorical question, and I know those are always hard for panelists. But, if not today, and if the trends in the West and the Southwest continue, and at some point one out of every let's say five Americans live in the Ninth Circuit, would the Ninth Circuit need to be split in order to maintain some—or would all the circuits need to be rebalanced? Or would you assume, rather, that size doesn't matter? . . .

Judge Schroeder: Congressman, it's hard to see into the future, and it is a rhetorical question. I would say that we have made so many strides in technology, in our ability to track cases, to instantly bring up research, that it's far easier for me to be a judge on the Ninth Circuit now than it was when I was a judge on the court of appeals in Arizona with only nine judges.

So I don't think that we can predict. But I do think that, when you have a stable structure that is working, that you should keep it.

Mr. Issa: Okay. Either of the other judges have a different opinion?

Judge O'Scannlain: Well, I certainly do, and it's laid out in my testimony, Congressman Issa. It just seems to me that there has to be a time—in my personal view, we've already passed that time. But there will be a time when it will be so obvious to everybody that we've grown so large, we can no longer function as a court. That's what it comes down to. . . .

Mr. Issa: And, Judge Schroeder, if I could do a second rhetorical because that is what we deal with a lot on these panels?. . . Then why wouldn't we have just five or four circuits for the entire United States? Wouldn't we then in fact have more consistency than we have with 11?

Judge Schroeder: Well, one of my predecessors, Chief Judge Browning of Montana, did advocate that circuits join rather than to divide them.

Much of this is history. The three circuits that are all growing are the Ninth, the Fifth, and the Eleventh, because that is where the population is growing. And as I think Judge Thomas' testimony brought out, the Fifth and the Eleventh are growing; their caseload is now much greater than it was when they originally divided.

And the East Coast reflects the shipping routes and the organization of the 13 colonies. That, too, is historic and geographic.

So while I have colleagues who would like to see circuits join and to have fewer circuits nationwide, because they believe that it would be more effective administratively, I don't see that happening.

Mr. Issa: So if I can paraphrase your testimony, you don't want to increase; you don't want to decrease; you think we're just right.

Judge Schroeder: I think the system is working well.

Mr. Issa: Yes, Judge Thomas?

Judge Thomas: I think one of the interesting things, if you look statistically, is that there is not a direct correlation between population increase and caseload increase. That certainly has been true for the Fifth, the Eleventh, and the Ninth. The population increase and caseload increase in the Fifth and Eleventh doesn't match that of the Ninth. Their caseload has grown faster than their population.

And within specific districts in the Ninth, that's been very true. For example, if you take the Northwest States, the caseload in the Northwest States, appellate caseload, has actually decreased over the last 10 years.

So what you have is a caseload that is based on other factors, and you're acutely aware of that in San Diego, because of the problems with the border.

The nice thing about a large circuit is that you can divert resources to deal with those temporary problems, and you cannot as easily in a small circuit. For example, in my home State of Montana, we recently had a judicial shortage. We only have three district judges, but we were down two. And judges flew in from Los Angeles, from Arizona, from Oregon, and helped us, because otherwise criminals would have walked free because of Speedy Trial Act violations. You lose that flexibility in a small circuit.

So I think that in the future what we ought to look at is how to best administer resources in a centralized way, because otherwise you're going to end up dividing circuits from now until the end of the century. . . .

Mr. Coble: Judge O'Scannlain, in your written testimony, you indicate that circuits function best with a reasonable, small body of judges, who have the opportunity to sit together frequently. Elaborate a little more on that. What are the advantages to be derived from that? Strike that. What are the advantages to be derived from that, and do you all enjoy that sort of opportunity in the Ninth?

Judge O'Scannlain: Well, the answer, of course, is we do not, because we're spread to far extremes from Phoenix, Arizona, on the southeast, all the way up to Fairbanks, Alaska, to Honolulu, to Billings, Montana. We only meet as a court four times a year, in terms of a regular court meeting. We also do have an event called the symposium, where we do try to do our best to overcome that obstacle.

But you look at courts like the First Circuit in Boston, which has all of its hearings in Boston. Judges are from neighboring States. They can drive to the headquarters and have their hearings there. The same thing is essentially true of New York, and in Pennsylvania, the Second or the Third. The D.C. Circuit, all the judges of that circuit are in one building, and they see each other every day.

Mr. Coble: Of course, Judge, if I may interrupt, we will never be able to emulate that sort of convenience back out where you all live.

Judge O'Scannlain: Well, that's true. But to the extent that you can reduce the amount of travel—and there are quite a few of my colleagues who express anxiety about the problem of travel not only because of the recent extra screening and so forth, but just simply the extent to which it cuts into personal time and that sort of thing, where people have to travel on the weekends and that kind of thing.

Mr. Coble: Chief Judge, do you or Judge Thomas want to weigh in on this in response to my question?

Judge Schroeder: Well, I believe that we have been quite successful at achieving collegiality. We think it's very important.

The court that is here in the District of Columbia has had a history at times of not being the most collegial of the intermediate appellate courts. And I personally think that many of our judges are very happy to see each other when we do see each other, and happy that we don't all live in the same building. [Laughter.]

Mr. Coble: Judge Thomas? . . .

Judge Thomas: When I joined the court, I was concerned about that issue. But I was pleasantly surprised that it's a very collegial court on the Ninth.

We keep in touch with each other electronically as well as in person, and other circuits do as well. So we communicate with each other constantly. We sit every month with each other in three-judge panels in various venues. . . .

Judge O'Scannlain: Mr. Chairman, could I be heard on the point of costs, just for a moment?

Mr. Coble: Yes, sir.

Judge O'Scannlain: I have to rather strongly disagree with my chief on this estimate of $100 to $110 or $120 million. The fact of the matter is, in Portland and in Seattle, there are empty courthouses.

The one in Portland is the Gus J. Solomon Courthouse, which is filled with commercial tenants. It was vacated to create the Hatfield Courthouse. And as far as I am aware, the GSA would make the courthouse available—it's still in the inventory as a Federal courthouse, but there are no Federal judges in it.

Whereas, up in Seattle, that building is not yet vacated. That's the Nakamura Courthouse. But there's going to be a major new district courthouse in Seattle, which will take all of the district judges and will create a huge vacancy in the Nakamura Courthouse.

So my estimate, in terms of new courthouse construction, is essentially zero. And as far as the staff costs are concerned, I would not replicate staff; I would allocate staff. If it takes 400 staff people to run the court in San Francisco, you'd split them up.

If it's going to be roughly one-third in the new circuit, two-thirds in the old, whatever the number is you just reassign people.

Mr. Coble: . . . Chief Judge?

Judge Schroeder: Yes, if I could respond briefly? My understanding is that the Gus Solomon Courthouse in Portland needs major seismic repair work and is not suitable for occupation as a courthouse now. And the Nakamura Courthouse in Seattle is currently being redesigned as a court of appeals courthouse, not as an administrative headquarters. It would have to start being redesigned all over again. And I do not believe that the space in that building is adequate, although we haven't looked at it from that standpoint, to hold an entire circuit headquarters.

Mr. Coble: Well, I'd like to get some current information about costs. I think it would be of interest to the entire Subcommittee and the entire full Committee, for that matter. . . .

Mr. Berman: . . . A new circuit would have the impact, perhaps, of increasing the Supreme Court workload, as I understand it, because now the Court would need to—it would be one more circuit dealing with intercircuit conflicts, which can only be settled by the Supreme Court. Is that an unfair assumption?

Judge O'Scannlain: Mr. Berman, there would be a very marginal increase, I suppose, only because it's an additional unit that the Supreme Court looks at. But in terms of the overall number of petitions for certiorari, I don't know that it would make the slightest difference, whether it's a single circuit or more than one circuit, because you're still dealing with a finite number of cases.

Mr. Berman: But the likelihood of more intercircuit conflicts has to go up, if there are more circuits.

Judge O'Scannlain: Well, presumably marginally, to the extent that you would have 13 circuits instead of 12. I'm including the D.C. Circuit, which is not a numbered circuit. . . .

. . . [I]f you'd be willing to add to this bill that we also get certiorari jurisdiction instead of having to require us to hear every single case that is filed, unlike the Supreme Court, that would be just marvelous. That's the secret about how nine Justices on the Supreme Court can sift out from about 10,000 filings a year. They only pick 85 cases to hear. I'd love to be in that position. I'm sure I speak for all three of us when I say that.

Mr. Berman: But there's a price, in terms of justice, for that.

Judge O'Scannlain: Sure. Sure. . . .

Mr. Coble: . . . I thank the witnesses again for their testimony. The Subcommittee very much appreciates their contribution and the attendance of those who very dutifully stayed in the audience throughout the hearing.

This concludes the oversight hearing on H.R. 1203, the Ninth Circuit Court of Appeals Reorganization Act of 2001. The record will remain open for 1 week. . . .

3.7 Statements Concerning Ninth Circuit Court of Appeals Reorganization Act of 2003
149th Congress, First Session (March 6, 2003)

Lisa Murkowski

Mr. President, earlier this week, the Senate, in a 94-0 vote, went on record expressing its unanimous opposition to last week's decision by the Ninth Circuit Court of Appeals refusing to review a three-judge panel ruling that bars children in public schools from voluntarily reciting the Pledge of Allegiance.

The Pledge decision rendered by the court is not an aberration. It is symptomatic of a court that has become dysfunctional and out-of-touch with American jurisprudence, common sense, and constitutional values. Unfortunately, citizens in the states that are within the Ninth Circuit's jurisdiction have had to contend with the court's idiosyncratic jurisprudence for decades.

One should not be surprised that the full Ninth Circuit refused to reconsider this ill-conceived decision. The recent history of the court suggests a judicial activism that is close to the fringe of legal reasoning. And it is for that reason that the Ninth Circuit has, by far, the highest reversal rate in the country. During the 1990s, almost 90 percent of cases from the Ninth Circuit reviewed by the Supreme Court were reversed. In 1997, a startling 27 of the 28 cases brought before the Supreme Court were reversed—two-thirds by a unanimous vote.

Over the last three years, one-third of all cases reversed by the Supreme Court came from the 9th Circuit. That's three times the number of reversals for the next nearest circuit. And 33 times higher than the reversal rate for the 10th Circuit

Last November, on a single day, the Supreme Court summarily and unanimously reversed three Ninth Circuit decisions. . . .

One of the reasons the Ninth Circuit is reversed so often is because the circuit has become too large and unwieldy. The Circuit serves a population of more than 54 million people, almost 60 percent more than are served by the next largest circuit. By 2010, the Census Bureau estimates that the Ninth Circuit's population will be more than 63 million.

According to the Administrative Office of the U.S. Courts, the Ninth Circuit alone accounts for more than 60 percent of all appeals pending for more than a year. And with its huge caseload, the judges on the Court just do not have the opportunity to keep up with decisions within the circuit, let alone decisions from other circuits

Another problem unique to the Ninth Circuit is that it never speaks with one voice. All other circuits sit as one entity to hear full-court, en banc, cases. The Ninth Circuit sits in panels of 11. Clearly, such a procedure injects unnecessary randomness into decisions. If an en banc case is decided 6 to 5, there is no reason to think it represents the views of the majority of the court's 24 active members.

In fact, some commentators believe a majority of the 24 members of the court may have disagreed with the Pledge decision, but were concerned that a random pick of 11 members of the Court to hear the case, en banc, might have resulted in the decision being affirmed.

It is inconceivable to me that a circuit court could render a decision based on its concern about the potential makeup of an en banc panel. What kind of jurisprudence is that? Citizens in no other circuit face that type of coin-flip justice. That is fundamentally unfair to every single one of the 54 million people who live within the jurisdiction of the Ninth Circuit and is reason alone to restructure the circuit.

It is time that Congress finally faces the fact that the Ninth Circuit is no longer a viable and functioning circuit. It is for that reason that I am today introducing the Ninth Circuit Court of Appeals Reorganization Act of 2003. I am pleased to be joined in this effort by Senators Stevens, Burns, Craig, Crapo, Inhofe, and Smith.

The bill we are introducing today would divide the Ninth Circuit into two independent circuits. The restructured Ninth Circuit would contain California and Nevada. A new Twelfth Circuit would be composed of Alaska, Hawaii, Arizona, Idaho, Montana, Oregon, Washington, Guam, and the Northern Mariana Islands.

Earlier I indicated a number of reasons why I believe the Circuit needs to be reorganized. Let us not forget the scope of this circuit and the 54 million people who live within it. The Ninth Circuit extends from the Arctic Circle to the Mexican border, spans the tropics of Hawaii and across the International Dateline to Guam and the Mariana Islands. Encompassing some 14 million square miles, the Ninth Circuit, by any means of measure, is the largest of all U.S. Circuit Courts of Appeal. It is larger than the First, Second, Third, Fourth, Fifth, Sixth, Seventh, and Eleventh Circuits combined!

Moreover, because of the sheer magnitude of cases brought before the Court, citizens within the court's jurisdiction face unprecedented delays in getting their cases heard. Whereas the national average time to get a final disposition of an appellate case is nearly 11 months, an appeal in the Ninth Circuit takes nearly 50 percent longer—almost one year and four months.

This is not the first time that Congress has recognized that the Ninth Circuit needs restructuring. Numerous proposals to divide the Ninth Circuit were debated in Congress even before World War II.

In 1973, the Congressional Commission on the Revision of the Federal Court of Appellate System Commission, commonly known as the Hruska Commission, recommended that the Ninth Circuit be divided. Also that year, the American Bar Association adopted a resolution in support of dividing the Ninth Circuit.

In 1995, a bill was reported from the Senate Judiciary Committee in which Chairman Orrin Hatch of Utah declared in his Committee's report that the time for a split had arrived: "The legislative history, in conjunction with available statistics and research concerning the Ninth Circuit, provides an ample record for an informed decision at this point as to whether to divide the Ninth Circuit . . . Upon careful consideration the time has indeed come."

In 1997, Congress commissioned a report on structural alternatives for the Federal courts of appeals. The Commission, chaired by former Supreme Court Justice Byron R. White, found numerous faults within the Ninth Circuit and recommended major reforms and a fundamental reorganization of the Circuit.

On the day my legislation is enacted into law, the concerns of the White Commission will be addressed. A more cohesive, efficient, and predictable judiciary will emerge.

Many who oppose legislation to reorganize the Ninth Circuit contend that all the Circuit needs is the appropriation of more Federal dollars for more Federal judges. However, I do not believe more money will solve the inherent problems that exist in a circuit of such magnitude. . . .

. . . The uniqueness of the Northwest, and in particular, Alaska, cannot be overstated. An effective appellate process demands mastery of State law and State issues relative to the geographic land mass, population and native cultures that are unique to the relevant region. Presently, California is responsible for almost 50 percent of the appellate court's filings, which means that California judges and California judicial philosophy dominate judicial decisions on issues that are fundamentally unique to the Pacific Northwest. This need for greater regional representation is demonstrated by the fact that the East Coast is comprised of five Federal circuits. A division of the Ninth Circuit will enable judges, lawyers, and parties to master a more manageable and predictable universe of relevant case law.

Further, a division of the Ninth Circuit would honor Congress' original intent in establishing appellate court boundaries that respect and reflect a regional identity. In spite of efforts to modernize the administration of the Ninth Circuit, its size works against the original purpose of its creation: the uniform, coherent and efficient development and application of Federal law in the region. Establishing a circuit comprised solely of States in the Northwest region would adhere to Congressional intent. And the State of Hawaii should rightfully be included in this circuit, for like Alaska, there are unique issues that are faced by the two States that are not part of the contiguous lower 48.

A new Twelfth Circuit, comprised of states of the Pacific Northwest, would respect the economic, historical, cultural, and legal ties which philosophically unite this region.

No single Court can effectively exercise its power in an area that extends from the Arctic Circle to the tropics. Legislation dividing the Ninth Circuit will create a regional commonality that will lead to greater uniformity and consistency in the development of federal law, and will ultimately strengthen the constitutional guarantee of equal justice for all.

It is my hope that this Congress will finally approve this necessary reorganization. It is long overdue.

I ask unanimous consent that the text of my bill be printed in the Record.

There being no objection, the bill was ordered to be printed in the Record. . . .

A Comparative Perspective

3.8 The European Preliminary Reference and U.S. Supreme Court Review of State Court Judgments: A Study in Comparative Judicial Federalism (1996)

Jeffrey C. Cohen

Article 177: European Certification

The Treaty of Rome provides for four main heads of jurisdiction under which the European Court of Justice may entertain cases: actions brought by the Commission of the European Communities against a Member State, actions brought by one Member State against another Member State, actions brought by a Member State, the Commission, the Council of the European Communities, or an affected private party against the Commission or Council, and preliminary references from Member State courts. The preliminary reference mechanism

From *American Journal of Comparative Law* 44 (Summer 1996). Reprinted by permission of *American Journal of Comparative Law.*

accounts for approximately 50% of the Court's caseload.

The importance of Article 177, however, is demonstrable by means other than case-counting. Of the four heads of jurisdiction, none enables a private party to bring an action in the Court of Justice against a Member State for failure to comply with Community law. . . . Thus, the setting most familiar to Americans as the forum for landmark constitutional rulings—litigation between an individual and a state—is possible in the Community, if at all, only by means of an Article 177 reference from a Member State court. . . .

Under Article 177, when a national court refers a question to the European Court of Justice for a preliminary ruling, the referring court does not pronounce on the European issue; it refers, or certifies, the question to the European Court of Justice. The

European Court hears argument and issues a Judgment which is binding on the referring court. After the European Court has issued its judgment, the proceedings in the referring court resume, and the referring court treats the judgment much as an American court would treat a judgment of remand. Although there is considerable controversy about this point . . . the preliminary ruling is in some limited sense binding erga omnes—i.e., on future cases raising the same issue, either before the referring court or before other courts. To the extent that this is so, it has precisely the same status vis-à-vis the Member States as do the holdings of a Supreme Court decision vis-à-vis American states.

If a Member State court were to defy the European Court and refuse to accept its interpretation of Community law, a constitutional crisis might ensue. . . . To date, no such crisis has occurred. It would be awkward, at the very least, for a court that has itself referred a question to refuse to comply with the answer it receives. Once a question has been referred, there is a momentum in favor of compliance, and so far this momentum has been sufficient to avoid conflict. The rule that has been accepted in principle by all Member States is that a preliminary ruling by the European Court is a supreme rule of decision for the courts of Member States, sufficiently authoritative to invalidate (more precisely, to empower a national court to disapply) national legislation.

Of the many issues surrounding Article 177, two are of especial interest to a comparative study of the type this paper is engaged in. The differences between the preliminary ruling, on the one hand, and review on certiorari of state supreme court decisions, on the other, may be . . . addressed under two rubrics, the distinction between interpretation and application, and the question of erga omnes effect.

Interpretation vs. Application

Article 177 confers authority on the Court of Justice to "interpret" the Treaty and Community legislation. The Court and commentators have, on occasion, made much of the distinction between interpretation and application. Some, indeed, have viewed the European Court's confinement to interpretation as one of the chief differences between its role in the Article 177 procedure and the role of the U.S. Supreme Court in its review of state-court judgments. If the European Court lacks authority to "apply" Community law, then it lacks authority to invalidate, or even blunt the effects of, Member State laws or actions that violate Community law.

The Court's confinement to the role of interpretation, however, is not as pure as its rhetoric suggests. To begin with, the national court, in referring a question to the European Court, forwards the entire record of the case, not just the question. When the Court responds to the question, the published report begins with a statement of the facts and often examines the consequences in the case at bar of alternative rules. It is clear that the facts of the case inform the Court's consideration of the question. Furthermore, the Court's preliminary rulings vary in the extent to which they "apply" the provision of the Treaty or of Community legislation that they are interpreting. In some cases, the Court coyly hints at what the result of its interpretation must be. In others, it is still bolder in proceeding to "application" of the provision in question.

The tension between application and interpretation is inevitable in a case where the Court is asked, in effect at least, whether a given national law violates either the Treaty or Community legislation. The Court has stressed time and again that it does not, in an Article 177 proceeding, have the power to strike down a national law, or even to "decide whether a national provision is compatible with Community law." This is so, not because Community law must give way before national law; the supremacy of Community law, though not provided for in the Treaty itself, is well-established. For the Court to declare a national law invalid would be, in the Court's view, to "apply" the Treaty, an activity in which it is not empowered to engage. Moreover, if the Court invalidated a national law under which a defendant was being prosecuted, it would be effectively deciding the case in favor of the defendant, a clear case of application rather than mere interpretation.

Yet the Court's deference to the application-interpretation dichotomy in its approach to national laws varies. As already noted, it has the facts of the case before it, as well as the national law being applied. If the Court intended to be absolutist about interpretation as against application, it might prohibit, or at least discourage, the referring court from forwarding the complete case file to it.

This it does not do. On the contrary, its tendency is to decide the case in such a way as to leave little doubt—and, given the principle that its ruling is binding on the referring court, little discretion—as to how the national court is to decide the case.

In a fairly typical case, a Monsieur Plaquevent had divided his working life between France and Germany. When he became disabled, he applied for disability benefits in both countries. After Germany awarded him benefits, the French administrators applied a complex formula to determine what benefits he was entitled to, and the result was unsatisfactory to Plaquevent. Plaquevent brought suit in France on the ground that the French formula violated a Community law. Plaquevent's argument was that the Community legislation "excludes a pro rata calculation" in certain situations, specifically the situation obtaining in his case. Plaquevent lost in the French appellate court, and appealed to the Cour de Cassation, France's highest court. The Cour de Cassation referred the question to the European Court, which rather clearly rejected Plaquevent's position, concluding that in situations such as that of Plaquevent, "the pro rata calculation must be made." The French Cour de Cassation duly affirmed the appellate court. To say that the Court merely interpreted but did not apply the relevant provision of Community law is to indulge in what can only be described as disingenuous formalism, or a formalist fiction. The Court left little for the French courts to do other than to enter judgment against the plaintiff. . . .

. . . The problems that emerge when the Court strives to confine itself to interpretation are illustrated by a recent series of cases concerning the effect of Sunday trading laws—i.e., of laws prohibiting shops from opening on Sunday. When an English chain of "do-it-yourself" stores was prosecuted by a local authority, the defendant argued that England's Sunday trading laws violated the Treaty. . . .

The defendant in Torfaen had opened his store on Sunday, in defiance of the English ban on Sunday trading. The effect of the preliminary ruling, translated into American terms, was to remand the case to the national (state) court for determination whether the restrictive effects on Community trade of the English ban on Sunday trading exceeded the effects intrinsic to rules of that kind. On its face, this sounds like a recipe for validation: If "rules of that kind" means Sunday trading rules, then the effects of such a rule are bound to be precisely—and hence not to exceed—the effects of rules of that kind. Yet if "rules of that kind" is understood more broadly, the relevant standard might be rules governing opening times; or, more broadly still, constraints on retailers.

The House of Lords, puzzled by this state of affairs, referred another case to the European Court, with precisely parallel facts. It asked whether it wasn't "immediately apparent, whether or not evidence is adduced, that the restrictive effects on intra-Community trade which result from national [Sunday trading] rules . . . do not exceed 'the effects intrinsic to rules of that kind,' as that phrase is used in [Torfaen]?" In response, the Court felt compelled to spell out its message in clearer terms: "the prohibition which [Article 30] lays down does not apply to national legislation prohibiting retailers from opening their premises on Sundays." The Court had sought to confine itself to "interpretation"; it had been forced, by the nature of things, to proceed to application. That the Court did not "uphold" or "reverse" a conviction is, from any perspective that is not slavishly formalist, immaterial. The British law had been found permissible, and the prosecution, given the facts transmitted to the Court, was bound to be successful.

However hazy may be the line between interpretation and application, though, the political value of the distinction should not be underestimated. There is a role for slavish formalism to play. For the European Court formally to invalidate a national law is to raise serious issues of sovereignty. Such an action results in confrontation between two institutions, the European Court on one side, and the national legislature and executive on the other. If, by contrast, the European Court can lead the national court to invalidate the national law, the confrontation is, or at least may be viewed as, far less intense, since it takes place (or may be viewed as taking place) within the sovereign state, between the state's courts and its legislature and executive. The Member State has a separation-of-powers issue to confront, and in Member States where a tradition of judicial review is lacking, this issue may ripen into crisis. But the "European" issue has been repressed and perhaps defused, so long as the national court is willing to assume responsibility vis-à-vis the political organs of its home state. . . .

Erga Omnes Effect

National courts have, with surprisingly little resistance, accepted the binding effect of a preliminary ruling on the case at bar, and there have been very few instances of defiance or even evasion (by means, for instance, of "applying" the Court's "interpretation" inventively). By contrast, the proposition that national courts are bound in future cases by interpretations provided by the Court remains a very controversial issue. At first blush, one might think that the interpretation-application dichotomy would be sufficient to dispel the issue. If the Court is to indulge the fiction that it merely interprets Treaty and legislative provisions, then efforts to confine the effect of a preliminary ruling to the case in which it takes place should be ill-fated. The interpretation, according to the myth, has nothing to do with the facts, so how can it be possible that an interpretation of a given article, for instance, would be different in one case from the interpretation provided in another case?. . .

Yet the Court has never declared that a national court confronted with a case strongly resembling a case in which the Court has issued a preliminary ruling is obligated to apply the prior preliminary ruling. Under Article 177(2), an inferior national court confronted with a Community issue may either interpret and apply Community law for itself or refer a question to the Court of Justice. If the inferior court believes that the case it is entertaining is "on all fours" with a case in which the European Court has issued a preliminary ruling, the inferior national court might choose to rely on that prior case in interpreting a provision of Community law. The prevailing view, however, is that nothing in the Treaty or the caselaw of the Court obliges it to do so. . . .

American Judicial Federalism

The authority of the U.S. Supreme Court to review on certiorari judgments of state courts may be thought to obviate any need for a certification procedure. The absence of similar authority in the European Court of Justice, coupled with the absence of any inferior European Community courts, is often cited as the justification for Article 177. Yet the benefits of Article 177 in the forms of comity, of an atmosphere of "cooperation rather than subor-dination," and of the "compliance pull" resulting from that atmosphere, are well-documented. These benefits are available to a system, such as that of the United States, where alternative means of accomplishing Article 177's broad purposes — uniformity of interpretation of Community/federal law, and ability of a private party to invoke Community/federal rights — are available. In the U.S., the federal court system and certiorari provide means of accomplishing these latter purposes. The former, comity-related objectives are often neglected.

The delicacy of the relationship between state courts and the U.S. Supreme Court was apparent from the outset. Hamilton addressed it in *The Federalist*, forthrightly defending the Court's authority to review state court judgments. Hamilton appears to have viewed the authority to exist even in the absence of congressional action. The First Congress provided for mandatory appellate review by the U.S. Supreme Court of state supreme court judgments in section 25 of the Judiciary Act of 1789, whenever a state supreme court either rebuffed a challenge to state law based on federal law or held invalid a federal law.

The early Court, however, has been characterized as "extremely cautious to avoid taking jurisdiction under this Act, wherever it could be avoided." In 1807, the Court, speaking through Justice Marshall, declared that the purpose of the Judiciary Act was to "give this Court the power of rendering uniform the construction of the laws of the United States, and the decisions upon the rights or titles claimed under those laws." In its first twenty-five years, the Court took jurisdiction under section 25 in sixteen cases without incident, and only in 1814 was the inflammatory nature of the jurisdiction put to the test.

The first great challenge to the Court's authority to review judgments of state courts came in *Martin v. Hunter's Lessee*. In *Fairfax's Devisee v. Hunter's Lessee,* the Court had relied on the Treaty of 1783 with Great Britain in reversing a judgment of the Virginia Supreme Court of Appeals. In addition to sending the Virginia court its opinion, the United States Supreme Court sent a mandate, addressed from the President of the United States to the judges of the Virginia court, and witnessed by John Marshall as Chief Justice (who had not participated in the case, having recused himself on the basis of his interests in the outcome). By means of this mandate, the Virginia court was notified that their judgment was "reversed and annulled," and the judgment of the trial court (which the Virginia Supreme Court of Appeals had reversed) was "affirmed.". . .

The Virginia court reacted with indignance:

> The court is unanimously of opinion, that the appellate power of the Supreme Court of the United States, does not extend to this court, under a sound construction of the constitution of the United States; that so much of the 25th section of the act of Congress . . . as extends the appellate jurisdiction of the Supreme Court to this court, is not in pursuance of the constitution of the United States; . . . and that obedience to its mandate be declined by the court.

Martin again appealed to the Supreme Court, and the Court again asserted jurisdiction under section 25. The resulting opinion, authored by Justice Story, is an eloquent and complex dissertation on federal jurisdiction, at the end of which Justice Story writes that "it is the opinion of the whole court, that the judgment of the court of appeals of Virginia, rendered on the mandate in this cause, be reversed, and the judgment of the [trial court] be, and the same is hereby affirmed.". . .

At present (indeed, since *Martin v. Hunter's Lessee*), American judicial federalism is unsparingly hierarchical and confrontational. With the increase in federal rights brought about by both Congress and the Warren and Burger courts, the hierarchy and confrontation were intensified. The broader the reach of federal law, both constitutional and statutory, the greater is the need for attentiveness to the relationship between the Supreme Court and state courts.

American Certification, Past and Present

In American legal culture, the practice of certification of questions of law has been regarded with something between ambivalence and hostility. The judicial culture of the nation has always been suspicious of a court's dodging responsibility by asking another court for guidance on a given issue. One might speculate that this suspicion is compensatory; a nation whose political system is notorious for diffusing responsibility and hence accountabil-

ity may be justified in seeking an institution that accepts, without evasion, the burden of decision-making.

Yet certification has a long history in the U.S. Although the Judiciary Act of 1789 did not provide for the practice, the Judiciary Act of 1802 provided for certification by circuit courts to the Supreme Court as a way of breaking deadlocks among circuit judges. The practice has fallen into desuetude; its original rationale was made irrelevant by restructuring of the federal judiciary, and the perception of "abuse" by circuit judges led the Supreme Court to resist certification altogether. Today certification from the federal courts of appeals to the Supreme Court is a rare occurrence, and calls for revival of the practice have been largely unheeded. Approximately half the state court systems of the United States provide for such intra-systemic vertical certification of questions of law from lower to higher courts.

In contrast to the intra-systemic certification from a federal court of appeals to the U.S. Supreme Court, inter-systemic certification—primarily from federal courts to state courts—has enjoyed some success in the U.S. An inferior federal court may, and in some cases must, certify a question to a state supreme court, not only when the federal court is exercising diversity jurisdiction, but also when a state action is challenged on federal grounds. A few state supreme courts may answer a question certified to them by the courts of another state—though the device appears never to have been used.

The U.S. Supreme Court itself may certify a question to a state supreme court, not only in diversity proceedings but under various other circumstances. In *Zant v. Stephens,* for instance, the Court was entertaining a habeas corpus petition that a District Court had denied. Having granted certiorari to the Fifth Circuit, which had reversed and remanded, the U.S. Supreme Court certified to the Georgia Supreme Court a question as to the "rationale" of the rule applied by the Georgia Supreme Court. The U.S. Supreme Court was in effect certifying a question to the very court whose decision it was reviewing. After the Georgia Supreme Court had responded, the U.S. Supreme Court reversed the Fifth Circuit's judgment, in effect affirming the Georgia Supreme Court's initial judgment. The process was a rare exchange among jurisdictions that facilitated a dialogue uncommon in state-federal court relations.

Like the dormant device of certification from a federal court of appeals to the U.S. Supreme Court, certification from a state supreme court to the U.S. Supreme Court would proceed along the same route that an appeal or petition for certiorari might proceed along. . . . [I]t would be inter-systemic. Thus certification to the U.S. Supreme Court by a state court would be unique in being both inter-systemic and an alternative to appeal or certiorari. The fact that inter-systemic certification has been received more favorably than intra-systemic certification suggests that the defect of certification from federal courts of appeals to the U.S. Supreme Court may have lain not in the fact that certification would be proceeding along the same route that appeal might proceed along, but the fact that intra-systemic certification was, as a general matter, inappropriate. If so, certification from state supreme courts to the U.S. Supreme Court would have all of the benefits of inter-systemic certification, and none of the drawbacks of intra-systemic certification.

A number of objections have been consistently interposed against certification as a general matter, and these objections have resulted in an American presumption against certification, a presumption that can be, and is, overcome in certain circumstances but that remains an obstacle to any expansion of the practice. First, it is argued that certification involves the court to which a question is certified in an enterprise that undermines its authority by forcing it to give advisory opinions that may or may not be followed by the certifying court. Second, courts to which questions are certified may be faced with overly abstract questions, divorced from the factual settings in which courts are by their nature best suited to resolving issues. . . . Third, the court to which a question is referred is arguably not entertaining either a case or a controversy, a problem that would be fatal with respect to federal courts on constitutional grounds. Fourth, the process of certification appears to some commentators to frustrate the discretionary power of the court to which a question is certified to limit its review to cases it deems worthy; it transfers control of the docket of the court to which questions are certified to the certifying courts. Fifth, the practical problems of delay and introduction of an addi-

tional venue, and the costs associated with these factors, have been noted by both the U.S. Supreme Court and commentators. Finally, a sixth criticism, not commonly made explicit but which one suspects informs much of the debate, is a suspicion of certification as a device for avoiding issues and "decision-ducking"; courts faced with difficult issues should not be permitted, much less encouraged, to avoid fulfilling their responsibilities to interpret and apply law. If they do so, the institutional authority of the court, and perhaps of courts generally, will be damaged. . . .

Unlike the first four objections, the fifth and sixth, noting the costs in time and money of certification and the problem of accountability, cannot be dispensed with by fiat. They are, indeed, costs that must be weighed against whatever benefits the device may offer.

Conclusion

The harshness and confrontation endemic to Supreme Court review of state-court judgments are obstacles to the comity among courts to which judicial federalism must aspire. Certification to state courts . . . may usefully be viewed as a partial mitigation of those characteristics. When used effectively, it fosters a dialogue between state and federal courts. *Zant v. Stephens,* discussed above, is an edifying example. . . . Certification provides a layer of varnish that is conspicuously absent in Supreme Court reversals of state court interpretations of federal law.

If certification fosters comity, and comity fosters consistency, uniformity, and fidelity, then certification merits more attention than it has received. Both the experience of the European Community and the experience of American inter-systemic certification suggest that those conditions are satisfied. And under current circumstances, comity, consistency, uniformity, and fidelity have more to offer than their intrinsic merits. If, as many observers believe, litigants invoking federal law should be more willing than they currently are to do so in a state court, then the virtues of comity, consistency, uniformity, and fidelity have very practical import. On the one hand, they will reduce the incentive for such litigants to get into federal court; and on the other hand, they will help ensure that, to the extent that the role of federal law in state courts does expand, state courts are effective agents of Supreme Court mandates.

The aim of this exercise in comparative judicial federalism has been to consider one of the questions that leap to the mind of an American student of European Community law. The European Court of Justice, like the U.S. Supreme Court, is confronted with the daunting task of ensuring uniformity of interpretation of federal law among disparate courts with diverse constituencies and traditions. The European Court has been given what appears to be a weaker tool with which to discharge this task, and yet it appears to have accomplished a great deal. It would be preposterous to maintain, and I have not maintained, that certification or referral is a superior device for ensuring uniformity of interpretation and application of federal law than review on appeal or certiorari. The only question I have sought to raise is whether cer-

tification of questions of law from state courts to the Supreme Court might not be an option to consider as a supplement to existing modes of interaction between state and federal judicial authorities. Certification of questions of law by federal courts to state courts is already one of those modes of interaction, and any proposal for new kinds of certification should build on the successes, and learn from the failures, of that practice and of the nearly-defunct practice of certification from federal courts of appeal to the U.S. Supreme Court.

Most of the traffic in political ideas between the U.S. and the European Community has flowed from west to east; any number of Community practices may be traced to American forebears. As the Community moves into its fourth decade of existence, the time may be ripe to seek re-payment. If Article 177 has played the seminal role in the development of the Community that many commentators have attributed to it, then it may have something to offer to its federal counterparts.

For Further Reading

Barrow, Deborah J. and Thomas G. Walker. *A Court Divided: The Fifth Circuit Court of Appeals and the Politics of Judicial Reform.* New Haven, Conn.: Yale University Press, 1988.

Brace, Paul and Melinda Gann Hall. "Studying Courts Comparatively: The View from the American States." *Political Research Quarterly* 48, no. 5 (1995).

Solimine, Michael E. and James L. Walker. *Respecting State Courts: The Inevitability of Judicial Federalism.* Westport, Conn.: Greenwood Press, 1999.

Songer, Donald R., Reginald S. Sheehan, and Susan B. Haire. *Continuity and Change on the United States Courts of Appeals.* Ann Arbor: University of Michigan Press, 2000.

Chapter 4

Politics of Judicial Selection

Introduction

The selection of judges at both the state and the federal level is based on at least two competing expectations. The first is that judges should be neutral and objective in their decision making, removed from the traditional politics associated with legislators and executives. As a result, all federal judges and many state judges are selected by executives and legislators rather than by the popular vote. This selection method distances them from the vagaries of popular opinion and shields them from the direct influence of political partisanship. However, in a democracy, judicial independence is not the only important principle. The second and conflicting expectation is that judges, as significant policymakers, should be accountable to the public they serve. Consequently, the vast majority of states subject their judges to some form of election.

Both selection systems are intrinsically political and at the heart of significant debate about the relative merits of each of these principles. Anyone who picks up a national newspaper these days cannot avoid reading about the struggle in Washington between Democrats and Republicans, senators and the president, over the selection of federal judges. The fierce nature of this conflict is not new, but has become particularly intense in the past ten years: Republican senators obstructed President Clinton's nominees to the federal bench in the 1990s, and Democratic senators are frustrating the progress of several of President Bush's nominees today. The process has become so contentious that it has prompted significant prescriptions for change. These include altering the methods by which the Senate and the president contribute to the nomination process and modifying the historic practice of filibustering in the Senate. How then can judicial independence be protected in light of the significant policymaking opportunities that seem to require at least some level of judicial accountability?

No less important, but less public, is the debate about state judicial selection. Of particular concern is the degree to which judicial elections have become typically electoral, involving campaign contributions and promises that rival those associated with traditional legislative and executive politics. How can judicial accountability be maintained while protecting the legitimacy of a fair and neutral justice system that requires at least some level of judicial independence?

Foundations and History

Significant to the discussion about federal judicial selection are the roles of the Senate and the president in the nomination and confirmation process. What did the Framers mean when they said that the president would nominate with the advice and consent of the Senate? What and whom does the process of nominating involve? Similarly, what does advising and consenting entail? In *Federalist* Nos. 66 and 76 (1788), Alexander Hamilton addresses several concerns about the relative power of the Senate and the president. In No. 66, he carefully distinguishes between the president's power to choose potential appointees, and the Senate's power to defeat those choices. In No. 76, Hamilton continues this discussion with more careful attention to appeasing the concerns that the president, a single individual, would have primary control over the selection process. He suggests that the power of the president to make appointments will be checked by the Senate, the Constitution, and, no less, the president himself.

Missing from Hamilton's discussions is the degree to which the Senate may or should advise the president in his choice, and to what extent the Senate may or should go to defeat the president's choice. According to Matthew D. Marcotte in "Advice and Consent: A Historical Argument for Substantive Senatorial Involvement in Judicial Nominations" (2001), American history demonstrates that the Senate has intervened quite extensively in the selection process, and that this intervention has been and should be based on political evaluations of judicial candidates.

Contemporary Judicial Politics

Sheldon Goldman's "Unpicking Pickering in 2002: Some Thoughts on the Politics of Lower Federal Court Selection and Confirmation" (2003) is a present-day analysis of the politics of judicial selection. Using President Bush's nomination of Charles Pickering as the basis of his analysis, Goldman explains the role of policy and judicial philosophy in the calculations of both the executive and the legislative branch in the selection process. He then examines empirically the claims of obstruction and delay in the Senate. In the end, he argues that the debates over Pickering, who was ultimately given a recess appointment by Bush to the Fifth Circuit Court of Appeals and then retired from the bench in December 2004, demonstrate the appropriate functioning of the selection process. It is worth considering whether Goldman's observations might be made in the context of several other Bush nominees, like Washington, D.C., lawyer Miguel Estrada, who finally removed himself from contention in September 2003 after two years of waiting for a vote in the Senate, and California Supreme Court Justice Janice Rogers Brown and Texas Supreme Court Justice Priscilla Owen, who were the subjects of successful Democratic filibusters, but then renominated by President Bush and eventually confirmed by the Senate.

The process of state judicial selection has been hotly contested as well, so much so that the Supreme Court recently addressed one of the fundamental issues involved in the debate concerning judicial elections. In *Republican Party v. White* (2002), the Court ruled that the portion of the Minnesota Code of Judicial Conduct that prohibited candidates for judicial office from expressing their views on legal and political issues was a violation of the First Amendment. Simply put, if Minnesota chose to administer nonpartisan elections for judicial office, which it does, then it could not prohibit judicial candidates from running for office. Running for office includes discussing issues and taking positions on them. Throughout the majority opinion, Justice Scalia addresses the concept of impartiality, its relevance to judges and judging, and the degree to which it is protected by the Minnesota Code of Judicial Conduct. Justice Stevens, in his dissent, contributes to this discussion of impartiality and independence by arguing that the code's provision is a legitimate way of protecting the distinctive nature of the judiciary while maintaining judicial accountability through elections.

A View from the Inside

The insider view on both federal and state judicial selection further demonstrates the divisiveness of these issues. Bill Moyers' 1999 PBS interview with Justices Kennedy and Breyer about the significance of the political independence of the judiciary speaks directly to the potential consequences to judicial neutrality and independence in financing state campaigns for judicial office. Justice Kennedy's concurrence in *Republican Party v. White* is particularly noteworthy in the context of this interview.

A look into the inner workings of federal selection is provided in an excerpt from Jan Mayer and Jill Abramson's *Strange Justice: The Selling of Clarence Thomas* (1994), which illustrates a portion of Justice Thomas's Supreme Court nomination hearings. The political nature of Thomas's nomination is matched by the confirmation hearings held by the Senate Judiciary Committee for the past decade. Here we present statements from Patrick Leahy (D-VT) and Orrin Hatch (R-UT) made between June 1999 and June 2003. During this time, President Bush replaced President Clinton in the White House and the majority party in the Senate switched from the Republicans to the Democrats and back to the Republicans. As these statements clearly demonstrate, the political tension between Senators Hatch and Leahy over judicial appointments was particularly heated.

A Comparative Perspective

Our last entry in this chapter brings us full circle in the complex discussion about judicial selection. In "Thoughts on Goldilocks and Judicial Independence" (2003), Frank B. Cross reminds us that the concept of judicial independence and the methods of judicial selection are intricately connected. Although many people think that independence is the most desirable characteristic of judges and the judiciary, Cross cautions us to consider the example of a truly independent judiciary in Iran and its consequences. He suggests that a balance between independence and accountability is not only appropriate in the American constitutional structure of checks and balances, but that the empirical evidence supports the argument that both accountability and independence influence the behavior of the federal and state judiciaries.

Foundations and History

4.1   *Federalist* **No. 66 (1788)**
Objections to the Power of the Senate to Set as a Court for Impeachments Further Considered

Alexander Hamilton

TO THE PEOPLE OF THE STATE OF NEW YORK:

. . . A *third* objection to the Senate as a court of impeachments is drawn from the agency they are to have in the appointments to office. It is imagined that they would be too indulgent judges of the conduct of men, in whose official creation they had participated. The principle of this objection would condemn a practice, which is to be seen in all the State governments, if not in all the governments with which we are acquainted: I mean that of rendering those who hold offices during pleasure, dependent on the pleasure of those who appoint them. With equal plausibility might it be alleged in this case, that the favoritism of the latter would always be an asylum for the misbehavior of the former. But that practice, in contradiction to this principle, proceeds upon the presumption, that the responsibility of those who appoint, for the fitness and competency of the persons on whom they bestow their choice, and the interest they will have in the respectable and prosperous administration of affairs, will inspire a sufficient disposition to dismiss from a share in it all such who, by their conduct, shall have proved themselves unworthy of the confidence reposed in them. Though facts may not always correspond with this presumption, yet if it be, in the main, just, it must destroy the supposition that the Senate, who will merely sanction the choice of the Executive, should feel a bias, towards the objects of that choice, strong enough to blind them to the evidences of guilt so extraordinary, as to have induced the representatives of the nation to become its accusers.

If any further arguments were necessary to evince the improbability of such a bias, it might be found in the nature of the agency of the Senate in the business of appointments.

It will be the office of the President to *nominate,* and, with the advice and consent of the Senate, to *appoint.* There will, of course, be no exertion of *choice* on the part of the Senate. They may defeat one choice of the Executive, and oblige him to make another; but they cannot themselves *choose,* they can only ratify or reject the choice of the President. They might even entertain a preference to some other person, at the very moment they were assenting to the one proposed, because there might be no positive ground of opposition to him; and they could not be sure, if they withheld their assent, that the subsequent nomination would fall upon their own favorite, or upon any other person in their estimation more meritorious than the one rejected. Thus it could hardly happen, that the majority of the Senate would feel any other complacency towards the object of an appointment than such as the appearances of merit might inspire, and the proofs of the want of it destroy. . . .

Federalist No. 76 (1788)
The Appointing Power of the Executive

Alexander Hamilton

TO THE PEOPLE OF THE STATE OF NEW YORK:

The President is "to *nominate* and, by and with the advice and consent of the Senate, to appoint ambassadors, other public ministers and consuls, judges of the Supreme Court, and all other officers of the United States whose appointments are not otherwise provided for in the Constitution. But the Congress may by law vest the appointment of such inferior officers as they think proper, in the President alone, or in the courts of law, or in the heads of departments. The President shall have power to fill up *all vacancies* which may happen *during the recess of the Senate,* by granting commissions which shall *expire* at the end of their next session."

It has been observed in a former paper, that "the true test of a good government is its aptitude and tendency to produce a good administration." If the justness of this observation be admitted, the mode of appointing the officers of the United States contained in the foregoing clauses, must, when examined, be allowed to be entitled to particular commendation. It is not easy to conceive a plan better calculated than this to promote a judicious choice of men for filling the offices of the Union; and it will not need proof, that on this point must essentially depend the character of its administration.

It will be agreed on all hands, that the power of appointment, in ordinary cases, ought to be modified in one of three ways. It ought either to be vested in a single man, or in a *select* assembly of a moderate number; or in a single man, with the concurrence of such an assembly. The exercise of it by the people at large will be readily admitted to be impracticable; as waiving every other consideration, it would leave them little time to do anything else. When, therefore, mention is made in the subsequent reasonings of an assembly or body of men, what is said must be understood to relate to a select body or assembly, of the description already given. The people collectively, from their number and from their dispersed situation, cannot be regulated in their movements by that systematic spirit of cabal and intrigue, which will be urged as the chief objections to reposing the power in question in a body of men.

Those who have themselves reflected upon the subject, or who have attended to the observations made in other parts of these papers, in relation to the appointment of the President, will, I presume, agree to the position, that there would always be great probability of having the place supplied by a man of abilities, at least respectable. Premising this, I proceed to lay it down as a rule, that one man of discernment is better fitted to analyze and estimate the peculiar qualities adapted to particular offices, than a body of men of equal or perhaps even of superior discernment.

The sole and undivided responsibility of one man will naturally beget a livelier sense of duty and a more exact regard to reputation. He will, on this account, feel himself under stronger obligations, and more interested to investigate with care the qualities requisite to the stations to be filled, and to prefer with impartiality the persons who may have the fairest pretensions to them. He will have *fewer* personal attachments to gratify, than a body of men who may each be supposed to have an equal number; and will be so much the less liable to be misled by the sentiments of friendship and of affection. A single well-directed man, by a single understanding, cannot be distracted and warped by that diversity of views, feelings, and interests, which frequently distract and warp the resolutions of a collective body. There is nothing so apt to agitate the passions of mankind as personal considerations whether they relate to ourselves or to others, who are to be the objects of our choice or preference. Hence, in every exercise of the power of appointing to offices, by an assembly of men, we must expect to see a full display of all the private and party likings and dislikes, partialities and antipathies, attachments and animosities, which are felt by those who compose the assembly. The choice which may at any time happen to be made under such circumstances, will of course be the result either of a victory gained by one party over the other, or of a compromise between the parties. In either case, the intrinsic merit of the candidate will be too often out of sight. In the first, the qualifications best adapted to uniting the suffrages of the party, will be more considered than those which fit the person for the station. In the last, the coalition will commonly turn upon some interested equivalent: "Give us the man we wish for this office, and you shall have the one you wish for that." This will be the usual condition of the bargain. And it will rarely happen that the advancement of the public service will be the primary object either of party victories or of party negotiations. . . .

The truth of the principles here advanced seems to have been felt by the most intelligent of those who have found fault with the provision made, in this respect, by the convention. They contend that the President ought solely to have been authorized to make the appointments under the federal government. But it is easy to show, that every advantage to be expected from such an arrangement would, in substance, be derived from the power of *nomination,* which is proposed to be conferred upon him; while several disadvantages which might attend the absolute power of appointment in the hands of that officer would be avoided. In the act of nomination, his judgment alone would be exercised; and as it would be his sole duty to point out the man who, with the approbation of the Senate, should fill an office, his responsibility would be as complete as if he were to make the final appointment. There can, in this view, be no difference between nominating and appointing. The same motives which would influence a proper discharge of his duty in one case, would exist in the other. And as no man could be appointed but on his previous nomination, every man who might be appointed would be, in fact, his choice.

But might not his nomination be overruled? I grant it might, yet this could only be to make place for another nomination by himself. The person ultimately appointed must be the object of his preference, though perhaps not in the first degree. It is also not very probable that his nomination would often be overruled. The Senate could not be tempted, by the preference they might feel to another, to reject the one proposed; because they could not assure themselves, that the person they might wish would be brought forward by a second or by any subsequent nomination. They could not even be certain, that a future nomination would present a candidate in any degree more acceptable to them; and as their dissent might cast a kind of stigma upon the individual rejected, and might have the appearance of a reflection upon the judgment of the chief magistrate, it is not likely that their sanction would often be refused, where there were not special and strong reasons for the refusal.

To what purpose then require the co-operation of the Senate? I answer, that the necessity of their concurrence would have a powerful, though, in general, a silent operation. It would be an excellent check upon a spirit of favoritism in the President, and would tend greatly to prevent the appointment of unfit characters from State prejudice, from family connection, from personal attachment, or from a view to popularity. In addition to this, it would be an efficacious source of stability in the administration.

It will readily be comprehended, that a man who had himself the sole disposition of offices, would be governed much more by his private inclinations and interests, than when he was bound to submit the propriety of his choice to the discussion and determination of a different and independent body, and that body an entire branch of the legislature. The possibility of rejection would be a strong motive to care in proposing. The danger to his own reputation, and, in the case of an elective magistrate, to his political existence, from betraying a spirit of favoritism, or an unbecoming pursuit of popularity, to the observation of a body whose opinion would have great weight in forming that of the public, could not fail to operate as a barrier to the one and to the other. He would be both ashamed and afraid to bring forward, for the most distinguished or lucrative stations, candidates who had no other merit than that of coming from the same State to which he particularly belonged, or of being in some way or other personally allied to him, or of possessing the necessary insignificance and pliancy to render them the obsequious instruments of his pleasure.

To this reasoning it has been objected that the President, by the influence of the power of nomination, may secure the complaisance of the Senate to his views. This supposition of universal venality in human nature is little less an error in political reasoning, than the supposition of universal rectitude. The institution of delegated power implies, that there is a portion of virtue and honor among mankind, which may be a reasonable foundation of confidence; and experience justifies the theory. It has been found to exist in the most corrupt periods of the most corrupt governments. The venality of the British House of Commons has been long a topic of accusation against that body, in the country to which they belong as well as in this; and it cannot be doubted that the charge is, to a considerable extent, well founded. But it is as little to be doubted, that there is always a large proportion of the body, which consists of independent and public-spirited men, who have an influential weight in the councils of the nation. Hence it is (the present reign not excepted) that the sense of that body is often seen to control the inclinations of the monarch, both with regard to men and to measures. Though it might therefore be allowable to

suppose that the Executive might occasionally influence some individuals in the Senate, yet the supposition, that he could in general purchase the integrity of the whole body, would be forced and improbable. A man disposed to view human nature as it is, without either flattering its virtues or exaggerating its vices, will see sufficient ground of confidence in the probity of the Senate, to rest satisfied, not only that it will be impracticable to the Executive to corrupt or seduce a majority of its members, but that the necessity of its co-operation, in the business of appointments, will be a considerable and salutary restraint upon the conduct of that magistrate. Nor is the integrity of the Senate the only reliance. The Constitution has provided some important guards against the danger of executive influence upon the legislative body: it declares that "No senator or representative shall during the time *for which he was elected,* be appointed to any civil office under the United States, which shall have been created, or the emoluments whereof shall have been increased, during such time; and no person, holding any office under the United States, shall be a member of either house during his continuance in office."

4.2   Advice and Consent: A Historical Argument for Substantive Senatorial Involvement in Judicial Nominations (2001)

Matthew D. Marcotte

Introduction

The events surrounding the 2000 presidential election gave rise to political outcry and heated debate. Crisis and controversy in elections, particularly presidential elections, strike at the heart of the American political system and call into question the legitimacy of elected leaders and the political process itself. Nonetheless, controversial presiden-

From *Journal of Legislation and Public Policy* 5 (2001). Reprinted by permission of the author.

tial elections are not new to American politics. The question is how American politics should respond to tumultuous presidential elections. The answer, far from requiring a radical response, can be determined through an examination of the foundations of the Constitution and the history of American political practices.

During the controversial struggle over the counting of votes in the 2000 presidential election and after the subsequent recognition that George W. Bush would become the forty-third President of the United States in January of 2001, Bush's critics raised questions about the potential impropriety of his executing certain functions of the presidency. In particular, Bush's critics pointed to Supreme Court nominations as one of the primary powers that Bush should have little or no right to exercise in light of the fact that it was the Supreme Court who ultimately resolved the question of how votes would be counted in the critical state of Florida. . . .

In contrast, supporters of President Bush have asserted that his nominations are due as much deference as any other president, and that the Senate should act on them with the usual speed. Additionally, some scholars have argued that political factors should play little or no role in the judicial confirmation process, and that the process should simply focus on whether or not an individual nominee is qualified to serve. . . .

. . . Both views are inconsistent with the history of how Supreme Court nominees have been scrutinized as part of the confirmation process. . . .

Supreme Court Confirmation and the Legislature

The Constitution provides that the President shall have the power to appoint "Judges of the supreme Court" and judges of lower federal courts "by and with the Advice and Consent of the Senate." However, the exact parameters of the Senate's duty to provide advice and consent have never been clear. Some have placed high emphasis on the "advice" portion of the duty, arguing for a strong congressional role in selecting judicial and other nominees. Other scholars envision a far more passive role for Congress in the process. How Congress carries out this duty has profound implications for the role of the Legislature in two major ways. First, the Supreme Court's composition directly affects public policy in a wide range of arenas, and appointments to the Court can have far-reaching, dramatic impacts on public policy. Second, the application of the Advice and Consent Clause in the context of the Supreme Court may have profound implications on the way the Senate deals with appointments to lower courts on the federal bench and all other appointments made by the President. This is an issue perpetually before the Legislature. . . .

How History Matters

What advice and consent means is a fundamental constitutional question about the balance of powers between Congress and the President. The Supreme Court has never examined, nor is it ever likely to have an opportunity to examine, what balance of power the language establishes between the President and Congress in judicial appointments. Therefore, this is a situation where the Legislature must determine the meaning of the Constitution for itself rather than having the judicial branch dictate the appropriate interpretation. . . .

. . . If Congress is to be charged with interpreting the Constitution, it must be allowed to use the same tools that courts and scholars have used in the past in their efforts to interpret the Constitution.

History provides two powerful tools that Congress may use in interpreting the Constitution. The first of these is original intent. . . . Under this inquiry, the goal is to determine either the original intent of the Framers or the original understanding of the Constitution by its first readers. . . . Under this philosophy, the sources to be relied upon primarily are records kept at the Constitutional Convention and documents from the era of ratification.

The second historical tool that can be used to interpret the Constitution is past political practice. Past political practice can be considered relevant in two major ways. First, early political practices are considered likely to be probative of original intent. . . . Second, a pattern of prior practice may be used as guidance to determine the appropriate balance of power. . . .

The history of the Advice and Consent Clause, both in its framing at the Constitutional Convention and as it has been practiced for much of the life of the Constitution, strongly suggests that not only should the Senate play a vital and important role in the confirmation process of Supreme Court and other nominees, but also that the Senate can and should be "political" in how it examines nominees. This means not merely looking at qualifications and personal qualities, but also determining whether political and judicial views are appropriate for a member of the Supreme Court. The strong (if somewhat discontinuous) historical pattern indicates that Congress should continue to engage in searching examination of nominees, especially with Supreme Court nominations.

The Founding

. . .

Judicial Appointments at the Constitutional Convention

The original fifteen resolutions proposed by Edmund Randolph on May 29, 1787, commonly known as the "Virginia Plan," only briefly mentioned a judicial branch for the new national government. The Virginia Plan called for the establishment of a judiciary "to consist of one or more supreme tribunals, and of inferior tribunals to be chosen by the National Legislature." The Convention gradually worked its way through the Virginia Plan, not reaching the question of judicial appointments again until June 5, when the Convention, in the form of the Committee of the Whole, debated whether the Legislature or the Executive should have the power of judicial appointment.

The members of the Convention were clearly divided on the question of whether Congress should hold the power to appoint judges, with John Rutledge of South Carolina the first to oppose giving a unilateral power of appointment to the Executive. Rutledge claimed that if a single person held the power to appoint judges, "the people will think we are leaning too much towards Monarchy." In contrast, James Wilson, a delegate from Pennsylvania, spoke in favor of centralizing the appointment process in the Executive because of his concern that "intrigue, partiality, and concealment were the necessary consequences" of appointment by a large group such as the National Legislature. James Madison and Benjamin Franklin both took a middle ground, as neither was satisfied with legislative appointment or with giving the whole power of appointments to the Executive. . . .

Madison . . . was clearly unhappy with having the appointment power rest solely in the legislative branch, saying that legislators "were not [good] judges of the requisite qualifications" that would be required of judges on the federal bench. However, Madison also substantially distrusted any powerful executive, and suggested that the appointment power could be properly divided between the Executive and the Senate, a group he viewed "as not so numerous as to be governed by the motives of

the other branch; and as being sufficiently stable and independent to follow their deliberate judgments." However, Madison's motion at the end of his comments was merely to strike the words "appointment by the Legislature. . . & and [sic] [replace it with] a blank left to be hereafter filled on maturer reflection." . . . The divisiveness of the issue was evident from Charles Pinckney's subsequent statement that he would move to restore the original language providing for legislative appointment when the clause next came before the Convention for debate.

After the Convention had debated the entirety of the Virginia Plan, Randolph resubmitted an amended version of it to the Convention on June 13. Under this revised proposal, Justices of the Supreme Court were to be appointed by the Senate, while lower court judges would be appointed by the entirety of the National Legislature. Pinckney, fulfilling the promise he had made after the first vote on the Virginia Plan's method for judicial appointments, along with Roger Sherman, the delegate from Connecticut, moved to amend the language in a way that would return the appointment power to both houses of the National Legislature. Madison then reiterated his objections to the appointment of judges by both houses of the Legislature, placing particular emphasis on the lower house's susceptibility to improper forms of influence. Apparently, Madison's argument was convincing, for after he spoke, Pinckney and Sherman withdrew their motion calling for the House to take a role in appointments, and the Convention then approved language that provided for senatorial appointment of Justices.

Despite agreeing to this language in the amended Virginia Plan, William Patterson went in a different direction in introducing the New Jersey Plan on June 15, giving the power to appoint federal judges to a different branch. The New Jersey Plan resolved that "a federal Judiciary [should] be established to consist of a supreme Tribunal the Judges of which to be appointed by the Executive." After the introduction of the New Jersey Plan, the Convention began to work its way through the clauses of Patterson's proposal, but never directly addressed its proposal for judicial appointments. The next mention of judicial appointment came in Alexander Hamilton's speech of June 18, where he proposed the system we have today—appointment of judges by the President, subject to confirmation by the Senate. Oddly, after Hamilton's comments on the matter, it seems as though the Convention put aside the question of what branch would hold the appointment power for an entire month, not returning to it until they began to vote on specific clauses of the proposed Constitution.

The first of these votes took place on July 18. The Convention unanimously passed portions of the proposed Constitution that created a national judiciary in a Supreme Court, but when the Convention reached the question of who should hold appointment power, divisions became evident. The debate on the appointment power was extensive, with members of the Convention split on the question of whether one branch of the Legislature, both branches of the Legislature, the Executive, or some combination thereof should hold the appointment power. A motion to vest appointment power solely in the Executive failed, with six delegations opposed and only two in favor. Then, Nathaniel Gorham of Massachusetts proposed an amendment that stated judges would "be (nominated and appointed) by the Executive, by & with the advice & consent" of the Legislature of the United States. Although this language is similar to the language that was eventually adopted by the Convention, the motion to accept it failed, as the Convention divided equally, with four delegations voting on each side of the motion to amend. After some further discussion on the subject, the Convention found that it was unable to come to any agreement about how judges should be appointed, and unanimously agreed to postpone further consideration of the appointment process for judges.

The Convention returned to its consideration of the appointment power three days later on July 21, when the Convention reconsidered James Madison's proposal that the Executive would hold the right of appointment of judges "unless [his appointments were] disagreed to by 2/3 of the 2d. branch of the Legislature." . . .

Lengthy debate followed, revealing the continued division of the Convention on this issue, and several proposals were made for different means of appointing judges. Yet again, the Convention rejected changing the method of appointment, this time by a margin of three votes in favor of Madison's motion and six votes opposed, and again gave its endorsement to appointment by the Senate, with six states favoring appointment by the Senate alone. The final language referred to the Convention's Committee of

Detail was "That a national Judiciary be established to consist of one Supreme Tribunal—the Judges of which shall be appointed by the second Branch of the national Legislature." The continuing presence of language giving the sole appointment power to the Senate, especially in conjunction with the often noisy opposition when motions were made to strip the Senate of that power, indicates that many Framers saw strong senatorial involvement in the judicial appointment and confirmation process as essential to the establishment of a proper form of government. . . .

Because of the clear division in the Convention about the appointment process, resolution of the issue was referred to a special committee, chaired by David Brearley from New Jersey. The committee substantially changed the clauses dealing with appointment power, creating new language that provided: "The President . . . shall nominate and by and with the advice and consent of the Senate shall appoint . . . Judges of the Supreme Court." Interestingly, despite all the prior debate on this subject, this new recommendation was adopted unanimously, with extremely minimal debate. The language adopted in this recommendation was again adopted by the Convention when the members signed the Constitution on September 17, 1787.

The final language of the Constitution represents a compromise—one that permitted a great deal of discretion on the part of the Executive in making the selection of judges and other officers while still allowing the Senate to maintain a substantial role in the selection and confirmation process. The Executive would have the power to appoint, allowing for many of the advantages of a unitary system of appointments, but the Senate would be there to check the Executive's actions through its advice and consent function. This system envisions both branches playing a critical role in the process of nominating and confirming judicial appointments, rather than one branch or the other having sole power.

The Ratification Debates on Judicial Nominations

For the most part, nominations to the judiciary provoked very little discussion during the debates over whether the new Constitution should be ratified by the states. However, there was some discussion of the issue by members of the Convention in private correspondence and in more public forums such as

The Federalist. These writings indicate that there was a diversity of opinion on the subject of how the process of judicial selection would function, with every writer having his own views on exactly what advice and consent would mean.

The Federalist, in particular, seems to have argued for a relatively small role for the Senate in the judicial selection process. In fact, Hamilton adopts this view directly when he states that "in the business of appointments the Executive will be the principal agent." However, Hamilton envisions at least some role for the Senate in the judicial appointment process when he says that "it could hardly happen that the majority of the senate would feel any other complacency towards the object of an appointment, than such, as the appearance of merit, might inspire, and the proofs of the want of it, destroy." Hamilton's writings suggest a role for the Senate that was limited to examining the qualifications of nominees. Others, even Hamilton's fellow *Federalist* authors, were less clear about their position on the subject.

James Madison implied his approval of an active role for the Senate when he argued in *The Federalist* that the Constitution's method of appointments was designed to strike a balance between giving the Executive absolute power and involving the Legislature at the early stages of the appointment process. In addition to Madison, several other important figures at the Constitutional Convention expressed deep concern during the ratification period about unchecked Executive power over appointments. Edmund Randolph, a delegate to the Convention from Virginia, stated in a letter to the Virginia House of Delegates that the President's involvement in judicial nominations was one of the reasons that he refused to sign the Constitution. Like Randolph, Luther Martin had refused to sign the Constitution, and he expressed the concern that without substantial involvement by the Senate in the appointment process, the President could have "an army of civil officers as well as Military." . . .

Although those who supported the adoption of the Constitution at least briefly discussed their views about the appropriateness of the constitutional scheme for judicial appointments, very little was said about the appointment power in the major writings of Anti-Federalist figures, who opposed the adoption of the Constitution. In the only major piece of Anti-Federalist writing that dealt ex-

plicitly with the appointment power, the author claimed that the Constitution would create a system in which the Senate "will not in practice be found to be a body to advise, but to order and dictate in fact." While the concern expressed by this Anti-Federalist does not necessarily indicate the meaning of the Constitution's appointment clause, it does reflect that at least some people held the view that the Senate would continue to take an extremely active role in the appointment of judges and other officers under the Constitution. . . .

. . . While the evidence from the ratification period is much more ambiguous on the question of which branch would hold more power, there is still substantial indication that the Senate was to play a major role. Events after the ratification of the Constitution indicate that this has continued to be the prevailing understanding of the Constitution throughout American history.

John Rutledge: Political Rejection in the Early Republic

Shortly after taking office, George Washington had the opportunity to shape the Supreme Court in a way that no President has since, with the opportunity to appoint every member of the Court at once. All six of Washington's initial nominees were swiftly confirmed by the Senate, as were his next three nominations for Associate Justices. However, in 1795, when Washington sought to appoint John Rutledge to replace John Jay as Chief Justice, one of the most contentious political battles of the early Republic erupted.

Given Rutledge's qualifications and his extensive experience in public service, it is rather surprising that politics became involved in the struggle over his confirmation. Prior to independence, Rutledge served with distinction in South Carolina's representative assembly, and was elected to and served in the Continental Congress of 1774 and on many of its committees. Between 1775 and 1782, Rutledge continued his political career in South Carolina, first as a member of the colonial assembly, and, from 1776 to 1782, as the Chief Executive of the state. Although Rutledge could no longer serve as governor after 1782 due to South Carolina's term limitations, he returned to representing South Carolina in the Continental Congress . . . prior to his retirement from Congress in June of 1783. In March of 1784, the South Carolina legislature appointed Rutledge to be Chief Judge of the newly created South Carolina Court of Chancery. In 1787, Rutledge served as one of four delegates from South Carolina to the Philadelphia Convention, and while he did object to portions of the Constitution, he signed it and recommended it for ratification. . . .

. . . Immediately after the passage of the Judiciary Act of 1789, Rutledge was named an Associate Justice of the Supreme Court, but served only until 1791, when he resigned to accept the position of Senior Judge of the Court of Common Pleas and Sessions of South Carolina. Rutledge served on the South Carolina court until July 29, 1795, when he agreed to accept Washington's nomination to return to the Supreme Court as Chief Justice after Jay's resignation. Given these extensive qualifications, it is at least superficially surprising that Washington's nomination of Rutledge failed. However, Rutledge's qualifications became irrelevant when he sharply criticized the terms of the much-debated Jay Treaty. The Jay Treaty was intended to serve as the final settlement of the Revolutionary War, restoring a normal relationship between Great Britain and the United States. Due to fears over the controversy that the text of the treaty would create, the text of the treaty was kept out of public view until after the Senate had (by the bare two-thirds majority required by the Constitution) ratified all but one of its articles. . . .

Rutledge's speech was fiery in its opposition to the Jay Treaty. . . . While no transcript of the speech is available, various newspapers and letter writers reported on it. The *Boston Independent Chronicle* claimed Rutledge's speech stated "that he had rather the President should die than sign that puerile instrument—and that he preferred war to an adoption of it." Rutledge also apparently took exception to the treaty's use of the word "will" rather than "shall" in certain areas, saying that the use of the word "will" implied that compliance with the treaty by the British was a favor rather than a duty. A letter written by a person in attendance at Rutledge's speech indicated that he even went so far as to claim that Jay had been bribed by "British gold" because the terms of the treaty were so favorable to the British. Finally, Rutledge's speech sharply criticized the Jay Treaty as being overly favorable to Britain at the expense of France. This criticism angered many of the High Federalists of the era, who strongly supported the Jay Treaty as a way of ensuring peaceful relations between the United States and Great Britain rather than a closer relationship with revolutionary France.

Almost immediately after the speech, Rutledge began his journey to Philadelphia, where he would begin to serve as Chief Justice. As he had been appointed during a recess of the Senate, Rutledge could serve on the Court for some time in the absence of Senate confirmation. However, his fiery speech ignited a great deal of concern among supporters of the Jay Treaty about whether Rutledge remained fit to serve as Chief Justice. . . . [Oliver] Wolcott [Jr.] and Timothy Pickering even expressed concerns that Rutledge's speech reflected that he had become insane. These accusations of insanity continued in private letters for some time until they were made public.

The first record of a public allegation that Rutledge was insane came on August 17, 1795, when a supporter of the Jay Treaty alleged that Rutledge's speech against the Treaty proved that he had lost his mind. These allegations became stronger, with those who supported the Treaty . . . suggesting that opponents of the Treaty were possessed by the Devil. Perhaps the most prominent political writer of the time, Alexander Hamilton, joined those saying that Rutledge was mad, claiming that Rutledge was in a "delirium of rage" when he delivered his remarks in opposition to the Jay Treaty, and that he was unfit to serve on the Supreme Court as a result of those remarks.

The allegations of madness were not the only ones levied against Rutledge in an effort to prevent him from being confirmed. Others attacked Rutledge's character, pointing to allegations that he owed substantial debts that he had never repaid. . . . It seems that these allegations of insanity and bad character served merely as a pretext for disagreement with Rutledge's strongly expressed political views.

In addition to the allegations of insanity and bad character, some explicitly cited political grounds for their opposition to Rutledge's nomination. For instance, Christopher Gore felt that Rutledge's confirmation would prevent the enforcement of the Jay Treaty by the Supreme Court, and he opposed confirmation on those grounds. . . .

In spite of calls for Rutledge's rejection, President Washington formally submitted Rutledge's nomination to the Senate on December 10, 1795, and there is no evidence of Washington asking Rutledge to withdraw his name. In fact, Rutledge and Washington dined together while Rutledge was in Philadelphia serving as Chief Justice during the recess period. . . . Some asserted that despite this conduct, Washington secretly wished that the Senate would defeat Rutledge's nomination. . . . Washington's lack of involvement likely reveals that he viewed the Senate as having a substantial and wholly independent role to play in the appointment process. Otherwise, he would have taken steps to ensure that Rutledge was either confirmed or rejected by the Senate, rather than simply standing aside during the contentious confirmation process.

Rutledge also drew public support from a number of people, many citing his opposition to the Jay Treaty as an excellent reason why he should be confirmed. . . .

Even before the Senate voted on confirmation, many speculated that the Senate would reject Rutledge's nomination. . . . Rutledge's supporters shared this fear. In one newspaper a supporter wrote: "I fear a cabal is forming to reject the appointment in Senate." These predictions came true when, on December 15, 1795, the Senate voted fourteen to ten to reject Rutledge's nomination.

That Rutledge's rejection was based on politics and ideology rather than his lack of qualifications or his personal behavior became clearer after the vote. After the rejection, Thomas Jefferson stated that he believed political grounds were the primary motivation for the Senate's action, writing that "the rejection of mr [sic] Rutledge by the Senate is a bold thing, because they cannot pretend any objection to him but his disapprobation of the treaty." . . .

The rejection of Rutledge's nomination provides a critical first step in understanding what advice and consent means for several reasons. First and foremost, a Senate that was made up largely of men involved in the creation of the Constitution acted upon Rutledge's nomination. Their action in refusing to confirm Rutledge indicates that they viewed the words "advice" and "consent" in the Constitution as requiring something more than acquiescence to presidential power. Second, this Senate sanctioned political involvement in the process of confirmation. With only one exception, whether a Senator supported or opposed Rutledge's confirmation was determined by the Senator's position on the Jay Treaty. This close tie between an external political issue and voting on a nomination reveals at least a tacit sanctioning of ideological voting, which has also been present in the voting on judicial nominations in recent years.

Finally, Rutledge's story demonstrates that the process is designed to involve more than just the nominee's academic ability to serve on the Court. No one seems to have doubted that Rutledge was qualified to serve on the Supreme Court from a purely legal standpoint, especially due to his experience as an Associate Justice. Those who opposed Rutledge, a group that included many Framers, attacked him on grounds other than his qualifications and were successful in their attempt to deny his confirmation. In addition, Rutledge's story reflects political activity and involvement not merely by those who opposed confirmation, but by those who supported it as well. Even in the early Republic, the propriety of Supreme Court nominations were the subject of violent public debate.

Stanley Matthews: Political Rejection in the Age of Hayes

The Senate continued to take an active role in the judicial confirmation process after its rejection of Rutledge. Seventeen nominations to the Supreme Court failed between 1810 and 1875. Then, in 1877, Congress was faced with an extraordinary situation. In the 1876 presidential election, the Democratic candidate, Samuel Tilden, had clearly won the popular vote, but the returns in three states—Florida, Louisiana, and South Carolina—were uncertain. If the Republican candidate, Rutherford B. Hayes, received the electoral votes of those states, he would have a one-vote majority in the electoral college. If Hayes lost even one of these states to Tilden, Tilden would win. In the end, a commission made up of members of the House, Senate, and Supreme Court voted eight to seven along party lines to certify Hayes as the winner in all three states, and Hayes assumed the Presidency in 1877. The ascension of Hayes to the Presidency has a number of obvious parallels to the 2000 election and the manner in which George W. Bush became President. Therefore, President Hayes's nominations to the Supreme Court are particularly worthy of examination in considering how the Senate should respond to President Bush's judicial nominations.

. . . [I]n the final days of the Hayes Presidency, Justice Noah H. Swayne resigned from the Supreme Court and Hayes nominated his old friend Stanley Matthews, who was then serving as a Senator from Ohio, to fill the vacancy. The nomination provoked a whirlwind of controversy for a wide variety of reasons—among them, his involvement in winning the election for Hayes, his close friendship with Hayes, his support of the coinage of silver, and his close ties to railroad interests.

The greatest surprise from an examination of documents about the Matthews nomination is what was not mentioned. The Matthews nomination was rarely criticized on the grounds that "lame duck" presidents should not be entitled to great deference in the making of appointments, and even more rarely was it mentioned that Matthews and Hayes had close personal ties. Instead, the opposition appears to have been almost purely political—based on concerns about the judicial philosophy Matthews was likely to invoke were he to be confirmed to the Supreme Court. During this era, the Senate was a closed body, and very few (if any) records of their discussions about the Matthews nomination exist. The nomination was never brought to the floor—discussed only in committees and informally amongst the Senators.

The only available sources of information regarding the basis of opposition to the Matthews nomination are newspapers from the era. Although newspapers of this era were no longer the partisan organs of the early Republic, they remained a reflection of political sentiment among the people and, frequently, their elected representatives as well. The *New York Times,* which opposed the Matthews confirmation, tacitly acknowledged that its grounds for opposition was political when it noted that Matthews had "abilities as high at least as the average of those now employed on the Supreme bench." Nonetheless, the *Times* still demanded that Matthews's "judicial character" be questioned and took a stand against his confirmation.

Later editorials further indicate that politics, rather than qualifications, were the reasons for op-

position to Matthews's confirmation. Editorials published in *The Sun,* a New York newspaper, repeatedly criticized Matthews's nomination by asserting that it was an attempt by Hayes to provide railroad magnate Jay Gould with greater influence over the government and that it would damage the protection of rights by the Court. In fact, *The Sun,* in a later editorial, went so far as to say that Matthews's nomination represented "an outrage on public decency" because of his political views.

At first, it appeared that Matthews would be confirmed. . . . However, the Senators began to examine Matthews's view that the power of Congress to regulate railroads was extremely limited. According to press coverage, because of Matthews's views on railroad regulation it was "generally believed that the nomination [would] be . . . either rejected by the Senate or suffered to lapse by expiration." An editorial in the *New York Times* stated that the nomination was supported by Democrats because "the views which Mr. Matthews holds on important constitutional questions are such as to be altogether pleasing to them." When arguing for careful scrutiny of the Matthews nomination, a piece in the *New York Times* made clear that the editors of the paper understood the Senate's duty of advice and consent as something "which should not be disposed of as a matter of courtesy or of personal favor." This statement makes clear that there were at least some members of the press and public who saw the Senate's responsibility as expansive rather than merely a perfunctory exercise. . . .

. . . [T]he Senate predictably declined to act on the nomination in the waning days of the Hayes administration. . . . By the time Hayes left office, neither the Judiciary Committee nor the entire Senate had acted upon the Matthews nomination.

Hayes's nomination of Matthews and the Senate's refusal to take action on it often go unnoticed by scholars because Matthews was re-nominated to the Supreme Court by President Garfield and the nomination was subsequently confirmed (by one vote) in a vote equally divided between the two major political parties of the time. However, it is clear that the Matthews controversy was rooted in a dispute over his political and judicial philosophies rather than his qualifications. . . . [T]he debate over Matthews focused on how he would decide particular cases that were likely to come before the Supreme Court in the near future. The

Senate's refusal to take action on the initial nomination, as well as its division in the second vote, reflects the perceived legitimacy of using judicial philosophy as grounds for rejection of a nomination to the Supreme Court. . . .

Political Involvement in the Modern Era

After Matthews's nomination, the Senate took a relatively inactive role in the confirmation process for the first time in American history. The Senate declined to confirm only three nominations to the Supreme Court between 1881 and 1968. Since 1968, the Senate has revived its active role in the confirmation process, with five nominations failing and only twelve passing muster. This reassertion of senatorial power reflects both a return to the historical roots of the confirmation process and the changes that modern society has forced upon the confirmation process due to increased media involvement and greater transparency in the American political and legal systems.

Haynsworth and Carswell: Political Rejection in the Nixon Years

The modern era for Supreme Court confirmations began when Richard Nixon became President in 1969. While Nixon's first nomination to the Court—Warren Burger as Chief Justice—passed with ease, his subsequent appointments met with far more difficulty. When Justice Fortas resigned from the Court under the specter of potential financial misdeeds and conflicts of interest, Nixon nominated Clement Haynsworth, a judge on the Fourth Circuit, to fill the vacancy as an Associate Justice. Haynsworth's nomination quickly provoked opposition from a number of groups, including civil rights groups, who portrayed him as a segregationist, and labor unions, who noted that Haynsworth had been reversed by the Supreme Court seven times on labor issues. However, political grounds alone did not lead to Haynsworth's defeat. It was subsequently discovered that Haynsworth owned stock in several companies that were parties to cases in his court and had refused to recuse himself. These allegations of conflicts of interest served

as a jumping-off point for later, more explicitly political, grounds for rejection.

The general understanding of advice and consent can be inferred from the manner in which political groups lobbied for and against the Haynsworth nomination. Groups opposed to Haynsworth lobbied the Senate directly in an effort to have the nomination rejected. Labor and civil rights organizations used political techniques like letter writing and telegram campaigns in an effort to make their opposition to Haynsworth known. This focus on the Senate indicates that these groups recognized a strong and independent role for the Senate in the confirmation process, as they otherwise would have lobbied the President to withdraw the nomination. This notion of a strong senatorial role was even accepted by supporters of Haynsworth, who involved themselves in grassroots politicking in support of the nomination. While this consensus supporting a strong senatorial role in the nominations process is not determinative of the Constitution's meaning, it indicates that there was little dispute over the meaning of advice and consent at the time.

That Haynsworth's nomination sparked a political controversy is relatively unexceptional. To begin with, the nomination was an essentially political act. Nixon sought to appoint a southerner to the Court in an effort to thank the South for its support of him in the 1968 election, and he sought a "law and order" conservative who he felt could curb the abuses he perceived as having occurred during the years of the Warren Court. Nixon's attempts to mobilize public support for Haynsworth through a media campaign made it clear that even he viewed public support for a Supreme Court nominee to be essential.

The Nixon administration used other traditional political tools to garner support for Haynsworth, including recruiting traditional party leaders in the House and Senate to "encourage" members to support the nomination, having state parties and officials pressure members of the Senate who were undecided, and even attempting to use campaign contributions. However, these efforts were clearly not successful, as Haynsworth's nomination failed by a forty-five to fifty-five vote on November 21, 1969. The Haynsworth nomination is notable not only because it marked the resurgence of the Senate as a major player in the confirmation process but also because it marked a general agreement among the political branches that the politics of the Senate had a substantial role to play in the judicial nomination process.

Much of the political firestorm surrounding the Haynsworth nomination carried over to Nixon's subsequent nomination of Harold Carswell of Florida to serve on the Court. In fact, the White House lobbying team became stronger and more entrenched during the Carswell battle than it had been in the battle over Haynsworth. Carswell was perhaps even more conservative than Haynsworth, and there were allegations that he was a racist. Despite the allegations, the American Bar Association's (ABA) Committee on the Federal Judiciary unanimously endorsed Carswell's confirmation. Given this endorsement by the ABA, it is difficult to believe claims such as those made by Senator Birch Bayh that "the President has confronted the Senate with a nominee who is incredibly undistinguished as an attorney and as a jurist." However, despite this claim, opposition to the Carswell nomination only truly began to rise after his opposition to desegregation became public.

With the ABA's endorsement and the realization that the revelation of Carswell's political views was what marked the expansion of opposition to his nomination, it seems likely that "qualification" served as little more than a veil for political attacks, as it did during the Rutledge confirmation. Carswell's nomination represents further legitimization of the involvement of politics in the modern confirmation process, with both sides of the confirmation process using increasingly sophisticated tools to influence public opinion and congressional action on the subject. Despite the claims that his nomination was rejected because of a lack of qualifications, it seems that the Senate reasserted its long-established (but recently neglected) power to make a searching inquiry into the politics of judicial nominees.

Ginsburg and Bork: Political Rejection in the Reagan Years

. . . In 1988, the Senate would again assert its advice and consent powers in the form of rejecting nominees when President Ronald Reagan nominated Robert Bork and Douglas Ginsburg to the Court.

Bork had perhaps the strongest credentials of any nominee to the Supreme Court in some time. A graduate of the University of Chicago Law School, Bork worked at several law firms before joining the faculty at Yale Law School. He also had experience in the government, having served as Nixon's Solicitor General between 1972 and 1977 before moving to the District of Columbia Circuit beginning in 1980. In addition, Bork had an extensive "paper trail," having written several books and articles on a variety of legal subjects, and having delivered numerous speeches and addresses throughout the country on legal issues. . . .

Because of Bork's well-documented record, he was unable to plausibly deny that he had formed views on a number of issues that Senators sought to question him. In particular, Bork's writings criticizing the right to privacy recognized by the Supreme Court in *Griswold v. Connecticut,* and its subsequent expansion to abortion rights in *Roe v. Wade,* led to harsh questions from many members of the Judiciary Committee. In the hearings, Bork was also questioned at great length on his positions on civil rights, church-state issues, and free speech, among other areas of the law.

The hearings were comprehensive, and, in the end, the Judiciary Committee voted nine to five to refer the nomination to the floor of the Senate with a recommendation that Bork not be confirmed. In its report, the majority of the Judiciary Committee was frank in spending less of its time on Bork's qualifications to serve as a Justice and far more time on Bork's political and legal views. The majority report begins with a lengthy section entitled: "Judge Bork's view of the Constitution disregards this country's tradition of human dignity, liberty and unenumerated rights." The report then moves forward, explaining that their grounds for recommending rejection included disagreement with Bork on many issues of legal doctrine, including the existence of a right to privacy, his understanding of civil rights for minorities and women, his understanding of the First Amendment, his expansive understanding of executive power, and his views on antitrust enforcement.

Senator Patrick Leahy, in a separate statement joining the majority report, stated even more explicitly that his grounds for opposing confirmation had nothing to do with Bork's qualifications, extensively praising Bork as an academic and a thinker, but making clear that "the central issue [of this confirmation] is [Bork's] judicial philosophy." Arlen Specter, one of the few Republicans to oppose the Bork nomination, also stated that his vote was "not a matter of questioning [Bork's] credibility or integrity . . . but [was] rather [based on] the doubts [that] persist as to his judicial disposition in applying principles of law which he has so long decried." . . .

The rejection of Bork on account of his political ideology did not go unchallenged. The minority report attacked the majority for the political considerations brought to bear on Bork's nomination, claiming that "the historical evidence reflects the Framers' expectations that the President would exercise great discretion in choosing nominees, while limiting the Senate's role to rejecting nonmeritorious candidates." However, this substantially misreads not only the Framers' intent in creating the shared power of appointment, but the historical record of Senate involvement in the confirmation process as well. The minority's report, rather than invoking the Senators' agreement with Bork's judicial philosophy as grounds for confirmation, focused its argument on two main points. First, the minority report spent numerous pages attempting to argue that the majority report mischaracterized Bork's testimony before the committee and that Bork's viewpoints on most issues were relatively moderate. Second, the minority continuously attacked the majority's view that politics should play a role in the confirmation process, saying that political involvement "will also see the judiciary have its independence threatened by activist special interest groups."

From a historical perspective, arguing that a nominee's views are actually within the mainstream is not unprecedented. This argument was used by the White House during the confirmation proceedings of John J. Parker in an attempt to explain his prior decisions on racial segregation and labor interests. However, the second idea is hardly supported by the historical record, as the record indicates that political factors played a role in the Supreme Court nomination and confirmation process for many years with little or no harm to the process. Perhaps the minority would have been more successful had they attempted to argue that Bork's views were correct interpretations of the Constitution, even if they did not square with precedent.

Despite the bitter minority report, Bork's nomination was rejected, with fifty-eight Senators voting against his confirmation and only forty-two supporting it. . . . After Bork's defeat by the Senate, Reagan nominated Douglas Ginsburg to the Court in 1987. Like Bork, Ginsburg had an extensive background in governmental service and academia, having taught at Harvard Law School and having served in several capacities in the Reagan Department of Justice prior to his appointment to the District of Columbia Circuit.

Almost as soon as he was nominated, Ginsburg began to draw many of the same political complaints that had plagued the Bork nomination. . . . Ginsburg withdrew his name from nomination only nine days after his nomination was submitted to the Senate amidst allegations (which Ginsburg admitted were true) that he had used marijuana while a professor at Harvard in the 1970s. While the marijuana revelations provided an excellent pretext for Ginsburg's withdrawal of his name from consideration, by that time it had already become clear that many Democratic Senators would oppose him on the same grounds they had opposed Bork. This clear political opposition, which included Senators from both parties, indicates the continuing powerful force of the Senate in the appointment and confirmation process.

Clarence Thomas: Political Near-Rejection Under Bush

George H. W. Bush had the opportunity to make two nominations to the Supreme Court during his four years in office. The first of his nominations, David Souter to replace William Brennan as Associate Justice, caused little difficulty in the Senate. Souter was confirmed by a substantial margin. When Thurgood Marshall resigned from the Court the following year, Bush nominated Clarence Thomas to fill the vacancy. Thomas had been an active political figure in the Reagan and Bush administrations, serving as Assistant Secretary for Civil Rights in the Education Department from 1981 until 1982, and then serving as Chairman of the Equal Employment Opportunity Commission until 1990, when he was elevated to the District of Columbia Circuit by President Bush. Bush nominated Thomas to the Supreme Court after Thomas had spent little more than a year on the District of Columbia Circuit.

Considering Thomas's relatively limited career as a jurist (and almost nonexistent career prior to that as a professor or active member of the bar), it is somewhat surprising that Thomas's qualifications were not the primary issue in his confirmation hearings. Instead, Thomas's confirmation hearings revolved around allegations that he sexually harassed Anita Hill, a former employee. However, the Congressional Record of the debates on the Thomas nomination reveals that political grounds played an extremely important role among those who opposed the nomination.

Several of the Senators who opposed the Thomas nomination asserted political grounds for their opposition. Herbert Kohl of Wisconsin criticized him for lacking a "comprehensive judicial philosophy," and for Thomas's unwillingness to express any views about the *Roe v. Wade* decision. Senator Claiborne Pell invoked political grounds for his opposition, stating that part of his reason for opposing the nomination was that Thomas had an "extremely conservative philosophy already well represented in the Court." Senator Riegle took an even stronger stance, claiming that since Thomas had "a record of a decade of bizarre and questionable legal theories and policy positions," he was unfit to serve on the Court. Several other Senators expressed similar concerns about Thomas's philosophy and intellectual ability in political terms.

A few of Justice Thomas's supporters also asserted political grounds for their support of his nomination. Senator Burns asserted that Thomas should be confirmed because "he understands the truest meaning of rights." While this does not signify direct support for Thomas's conservative philosophy, this statement does at least imply support for Thomas's philosophical point of view. Senator Connie Mack from Florida also implicitly invoked agreement with the nominee's judicial philosophy as reason for support when he stated that Thomas understood the "principles of self-reliance and personal freedom which must be at the core of the Supreme Court's reasoning."

The Senate confirmed Thomas by the extremely narrow margin of fifty-two votes in favor of confirmation to forty-eight votes opposed. Even though Thomas's nomination, unlike those of Carswell, Haynsworth, and Bork, was successful, the protracted struggle over his confirmation reveals that politics was as important as, if not more important than, the allegations of sexual misconduct. Yet again, both sides of a bitterly contested confirmation proceeding invoked political grounds in support of their stances on the confirmation. The battle over Thomas's confirmation shows that politics have come into play in the most recent nominations, even as the game has evolved with the advent of media involvement.

Moving Forward: Advice and Consent for President George W. Bush

During the Clinton years, the Senate confirmed both nominees to the Supreme Court with little struggle. However, both of Clinton's nominations to the Court took place while there was a clear Democratic majority in the Senate, and they were the product of careful political maneuvering on the part of the White House, which aimed to ensure quick confirmations for his nominees. Clinton's attempts to nominate judges became more problematic in 1994, when Republicans gained control of the Senate. His struggles to get district and circuit court judges confirmed by the Senate, especially in the later years of his Presidency, are well known. There is no question that politics continued to play a role in the judicial confirmation process, even under Clinton.

The Presidency of George W. Bush poses a number of unique questions about the degree to which politics should continue to be involved in the judicial confirmation process. The unusual circumstances under which Bush became President have led a number of scholars to examine the issue of how the Senate should respond to his nominees to the Supreme Court. Not only did Bush fail to win a plurality of the popular vote in the 2000 election, but the electoral votes in the state of Florida were disputed at great length, and in the end the dispute was settled by a decision of a closely divided Supreme Court. In addition, Bush may well have the opportunity to make an unusually high number of nominations to the Supreme Court because several of the Justices are nearing retirement age.

Many critics have demanded that Bush's nominees be treated with extreme scrutiny in the hopes of avoiding the confirmation of another "stealth candidate" like Justices Anthony Kennedy and Clarence Thomas. Those who expressed concern about the potential for Bush's nominees to hide their ideologies from the public became even more anxious when Bush announced that he would end the American Bar Association's role in the confirmation process. This announcement, coupled with the existing concerns about a conservative tilt on the Supreme Court, led many to assert that no nominees to the Supreme Court should be confirmed during the Bush presidency.

This argument fundamentally misunderstands the meaning of advice and consent in several respects. . . .

. . . Like George W. Bush, Rutherford B. Hayes became President only after a protracted post-election struggle over vote counting in Florida (as well as, in Hayes's case, several other southern states) that was resolved only by action of the Supreme Court. During his term, Hayes made three nominations to the Supreme Court, and only one of those nominations, Stanley Matthews, was rejected. That in the most direct historical parallel to Bush's presidency the Senate did not reject all Supreme Court nominees out of hand, but rather carefully scrutinized all nominees, indicates that out-of-hand rejection is not the appropriate remedy should President Bush have the opportunity to make a nomination to the Supreme Court. Rather, the Senate should follow the Matthews example and carefully examine both the qualifications and political views of Bush's nominees. . . .

The bases of the strong senatorial role in the nomination and confirmation process are only strengthened by three circumstances particular to the Bush administration. First, the Supreme Court is closely divided on several contentious issues at this time, with many opinions decided by five to four votes. The fact that laws relating to such a wide range of issues could easily be changed by only one appointment to the Supreme Court makes any appointment, regardless of who is President, worthy of careful scrutiny.

Second, it is likely that over the next few years, the Supreme Court and other federal courts will be dealing with new legislation passed in the wake of

the events of September 11, 2001, that may arguably intrude on civil liberties. Congress recently passed an anti-terrorism bill, quickly signed into effect by President Bush, that dramatically expands wiretapping authority, increases penalties for aiding terrorists, and lengthens the statute of limitations for prosecuting terrorist offenses. It is all but certain that these new governmental powers will be challenged in the federal courts, and constitutional issues are likely to reach the Supreme Court. . . .

Finally, greater scrutiny of Bush's nominees is justified because of the manner in which he assumed the presidency. Historically, those who have ascended to the Presidency as a result of a controversial election or after the death or resignation of a President have faced a considerably more difficult road in achieving confirmation of their Supreme Court nominees. Nine prior Presidents (including Hayes) have had the opportunity to make nominations to the Supreme Court without having been duly elected to the Presidency. Of their twenty-three nominations, ten (approximately forty-three percent) were not successfully confirmed. In contrast, duly elected Presidents have made 116 nominations to the Court, and only seventeen (or approximately fourteen percent) of their nominations have been rejected. This dramatically higher rejection rate for unelected Presidents reflects a clear historical trend—Presidents who were not duly elected are entitled to significantly less respect when making Supreme Court nominations than those who were. Given that Bush did not win a plurality of the popular vote in the 2000 election, the historical pattern of careful scrutiny should continue.

These factors all indicate that Bush's nominees are worthy of special scrutiny, although no more so than those of other Presidents not duly elected. Recall that even Hayes was able to achieve confirmation of the majority of his nominees to the Supreme Court, despite the highly unusual circumstances under which he came to office. President George W. Bush is entitled to the same deference as any other President who takes office under controversial circumstances. This means that his nominees to the Supreme Court should neither be rejected out of hand, nor confirmed without careful examination of their philosophies and qualifications to serve on the Supreme Court.

Conclusion

Understanding the Advice and Consent Clause requires a close look at its origins and its historical uses. The origins of the Clause indicate a division between those who wanted the appointment power to rest solely in the Executive and those who wanted the power to rest solely in the Legislature, with the final language proving to be a compromise designed to mollify both parties. Additionally, despite claims to the contrary, Congress has frequently used its advice and consent function to play an active role in the confirmation process. . . .

. . . The Senate owes the Constitution and America advice on whether particular nominations are proper and has a responsibility to consent only when the nominees are acceptable.

Contemporary Judicial Politics

4.3   ## Unpicking Pickering in 2002: Some Thoughts on the Politics of Lower Federal Court Selection and Confirmation (2003)

Sheldon Goldman

On March 14, 2002, the Committee on the Judiciary of the United States Senate voted down the nomination of Judge Charles W. Pickering Sr. for the United States Court of Appeals for the Fifth Circuit. The Committee voted not to approve nor send the nomination to the floor of the Senate. The vote was a straight party-line vote. It was the culmination of a swirl of advocacy group pressure, last minute politicking by the president, and some heated exchanges between Democratic and Republican senators. The bitterness continued to spill over onto the Senate floor up until the spring recess and beyond.

Editorial writers had a field day bemoaning what they saw as ideological and partisan bickering over judgeships. President Bush himself called the situation a "crisis." And depending upon their political orientation, editorialists apportioned the blame accordingly. Yet I think it behooves us to step back and more objectively consider both the federal judicial selection process and the confirmation process. This includes the role of ideology in the sense of a nominee's policy views and judicial philosophy. And I suggest that if we do so, the Pickering episode can be viewed as an altogether legitimate manifestation of the messy business of politics in a democracy. In some respects, Pickering provides a model of how confirmation ought to work. . . .

Policy Views and Judicial Philosophy in the Selection Process

The highly publicized battle over Pickering made transparent the high stakes involved in the selection of judges, and, in particular, appeals court judges. The United States Courts of Appeals are the nation's regional supreme courts, second in authority only to the United States Supreme Court. In more than 99 percent of the cases filed in the appeals courts, they are the end of the legal line. Thus, administrations have long recognized that it can make a difference who sits on the federal bench.

Indeed, the evidence is compelling that the Reagan administration thoroughly vetted the judicial

From *U.C. Davis Law Review* 36 (2003). Reprinted by permission of the author.

philosophy of potential nominees not only to the appeals courts but the district courts as well. Some examples from the Reagan presidential papers that have recently become available underscore this point as well as other facets of the selection process.

For example, a memorandum sent by Reagan's White House Counsel Fred F. Fielding to the members of the joint White House–Justice Department Judicial Selection Committee provided an analysis and recommendation for filling a vacancy on the district court bench of Montana. The memo reminded the Committee that earlier in the year the Committee had settled on a Montana state judge. Although the memo does not mention it, had that judge been confirmed, she would have been the first woman to sit on the Montana district court bench, a bench which as of 2002 continues to be all male. The recommendation was to reconsider her based on "certain concerns raised in the ABA review of her qualifications. . . . She is reported to have the highest reversal rate in the state and her temperament appears to be a major concern. . . . [She] is a 'clear case' of a candidate likely to receive a 'Not Qualified' ABA rating."

The memo went on to discuss three other candidates for the nomination. Charles C. Lovell was seen as a highly qualified lawyer who "has always been an active member of the Republican Party and has served since 1976 on the Montanans for Marlenee Committee; he has been strongly endorsed for this position by [U.S.] Rep. Ron Marlenee. . . . His views on crime issues and social policy appear consistent with those of this Administration."

The second candidate, Jack D. Shanstrom had previously been elected as a county attorney running on the Republican ticket. Shanstrom had received an interim appointment by Republican Governor Jim Babcock to a state judgeship at the age of 32. He was defeated for reelection some eighteen years later, and was subsequently appointed the first full-time United States Magistrate for the District of Montana. The memo noted:

> As a trial judge, Jack Shanstrom had a consistent reputation for being strong on law enforcement— he has upheld the death penalty, lobbied actively for a "good faith" amendment to the exclusionary rule, and was rated one of the state's

toughest judges in sentencing criminals. Though not regarded as a scholar, his service and experience on the bench are highly regarded by both the judiciary and the bar throughout Montana. . . . Although all three leading candidates are clearly conservative, [the Department of] Justice notes that Judge Shanstrom's long track record on the bench makes him the "safest" nomination in terms of the consistency of his judicial philosophy with that of this Administration.

The third candidate was Sam E. Haddon. The memo told that he graduated first in his law school class at the University of Montana and was "the most scholarly and articulate of the judicial candidates considered here. . . . [He is] one of the smartest and finest trial lawyers in the state. Haddon has been active in supporting Republican candidates, a very pro-law enforcement NRA member; and he is regarded by his colleagues as conservative."

Although the Reagan Justice Department recommended selecting Shanstrom, the Judicial Selection Committee recommended Lovell, who was nominated and confirmed in 1985. Shanstrom was later nominated to fill another vacancy on the federal district bench by President Bush in early 1990 and was confirmed later that year. President George W. Bush named Haddon in 2001 to the seat made vacant when Lovell assumed senior status. Haddon was confirmed later in the year.

Another example of the Reagan Administration's rigorous vetting of judicial nominees concerns the filling of a judgeship in Arizona. Senator Barry Goldwater recommended state Judge Robert C. Broomfield for one of two vacancies on the district court. The memo sent by Fielding to the Selection Committee observed that: "He is very well regarded by the legal community, and is praised by the [Justice] Department officials who know him." The memo also revealed that Supreme Court Justice Sandra Day O'Connor, a former colleague of Judge Broomfield on the Superior Court, "was especially enthusiastic in her endorsement. . . . She assured us that Judge Broomfield is " 'right on the button' philosophically." Broomfield was chosen and went on to the federal bench in 1985.

For the appeals courts there was even more consistent ideological vetting. For example, in scrutinizing candidates for a position on the Tenth Circuit, which was to be filled by a citizen of Colorado, a Fielding memo reported that Colorado Republican Senator Armstrong recommended elevating Federal District Judge John P. Moore. The memo further stated that four members of the House recommended the elevation of Chief U.S. District Judge Sherman G. Finesilver. In discussing Moore, the memo reported "[The] Justice [Department] states that a preliminary review of Judge Moore's reported decisions indicate his judicial philosophy is compatible with the President's." Not so with Judge Finesilver, who originally had been appointed by Richard Nixon. The memo stated:

> Justice's review of Judge Finesilver's articles and reported decisions showed that he is a "hardliner" on crime, but that he is relatively moderate on civil rights issues. . . . Justice has expressed particular concerns over Judge Finesilver's analysis of constitutional rights in *Foe v. Vanderhoof* (1975). In *Foe,* Judge Finesilver declared unconstitutional a Colorado statute which required parental consent before an unmarried minor could obtain an abortion, and stated that "the right to privacy as expounded in *Roe* and *Doe* to include a decision to terminate a pregnancy extends to minors." Additionally, the judge referred to parents in *Foe* as "third parties" who should not have "exclusive control over the activities of minors in this area." Based on an analysis of Judge Finesilver's writings, Justice has concluded that he is not a suitable candidate for the Tenth Circuit.

And that was the end of Finesilver's candidacy.

The evidence is equally compelling that the Bush, Sr. Administration scrutinized potential judicial nominees in terms of their ideology and judicial philosophy. Although the Bush, Sr. presidential papers have yet to be fully opened, there are examples from the already released papers that point up the vetting process. An example is the evaluation of then Federal District Court Judge Jose A. Cabranes's record as a potential Second Circuit nominee. The memo on Cabranes conceded that his "judicial writings are scholarly, reflecting a lucid style and careful attention to detail. He is seldom reversed. . . ." Nevertheless the memo asserted, "In general . . . Judge

Cabranes's academic writings and judicial opinions mark him as a judicial activist with deeply held views regarding the power of the courts to bring about social change." The evidence provided in the memo was a speech Cabranes made in a 1982 symposium, in which he defended the federal courts as a forum for protecting individual rights, particularly when state courts do not do the job. In addition, the memo opined, "Some of Judge Cabranes's criminal law decisions reflect a greater solicitude for the rights of criminal defendants than is found among conservative jurists." Finally, the memo concluded that "In construing the Constitution, Judge Cabranes is willing to look beyond the text and the intent of its Framers." Needless to say, Jose Cabranes was not promoted by the Bush administration. President Bill Clinton, however, did elevate Judge Cabranes to the Second Circuit in 1994.

Another example of ideological vetting for a circuit court post concerned the evaluation of an Idaho state judge, Duff McKee, who was one of four men recommended by Idaho Republican Senator McClure. The memo noted that the Justice Department had asked Judge McKee to submit "his ten favorite opinions." But the memo noted, "Three of these are quite problematic." One opinion concerned the counting of time spent on parole decided in favor of the convicted criminal. Another involved Judge McKee's refusal to apply a "good faith" exception to the exclusionary rule. The third was a finding that allowed a plaintiff to sue in a civil suit. The memo concluded: "These three opinions would likely be sufficient cause for rejecting Judge McKee even if they were part of a random sample of his work. That he selected them from his corpus as three of his favorites seems dispositive." McKee was not nominated. The evaluation of the candidacy of Federal District Judge Susan H. Black for a vacancy on the Eleventh Circuit had a more positive outcome. Judge Black, a Carter appointee to the district bench, was the subject of a detailed examination of her opinions. The examination revealed:

> [Judge Black's] extensive record of opinions generally demonstrates a commitment to strict interpretation of both substantive law and rules of procedure. . . . In the criminal law area— where she has handled large numbers of death row habeas petitions—Judge Black's decisions

are strict and unsentimental. . . . Judge Black's decisions on the civil side also demonstrate restrained interpretation of constitutional claims, strict application of procedural bars to recovery, and conscientious application of pertinent precedent. . . Judge Black's opinions do not reveal any discernible tendency towards overly expansive construction of asserted rights or judicial legislating.

Judge Black was elevated in 1992.

While campaigning for the presidency, President George W. Bush committed himself to naming judges like Justices Antonin Scalia and Clarence Thomas, two of the most conservative justices on the U.S. Supreme Court. As president, he has stated bluntly that he is looking to appoint "conservatives" to the courts. Judge Pickering's judicial record, no doubt, was thoroughly scrutinized by the Administration and found to be consistent with the Administration's policy agenda.

The judicial selection process is, of course, a political process with many facets. But the trend has been unmistakably to move away from primarily patronage concerns to concerns about furthering the president's policy agenda through judicial appointments.

Policy Views and Judicial Philosophy in the Confirmation Process

The President nominates but the Senate has the constitutional responsibility to advise and consent. And just as presidents have sought to further their policy agendas through their appointments, so too have senators made determinations about whether a nominee's views and philosophy are best for the country. Just as the Constitution gives the widest latitude to the President in making appointments to the judiciary, so too does the Constitution impose no restraints on the exercise of the confirmation power. This has meant, particularly since the 1980s, that senators feel free to oppose judicial nominees on policy and judicial philosophical grounds.

Given the important role that policy views and judicial philosophy play and have played in the selection process, . . . it is not surprising that they

also have played and continue to play a part in the confirmation process, as demonstrated by the events surrounding the defeat of Pickering in 2002.

By taking a stand against Pickering's nomination, Democratic senators suggested that they were acting out of concern that President George W. Bush, like his father and Ronald Reagan before him, was trying to pack the courts with conservative activists. Such judges, among other concerns, would undermine the rights of women in consultation with their physicians to make medical decisions concerning unwanted pregnancies, weaken the separation of church and state, dilute the rights guaranteed in the Bill of Rights to those accused of crimes, be unsympathetic to the rights of workers and organized labor, eviscerate the laws and regulations meant to protect the environment, and compromise gender and racial equality. Pickering's opponents argued that his record as a federal district judge suggested that he would be such a judge who would help push an already conservative Fifth Circuit even further to the right.

In support of Pickering, Republican senators argued that his record was being misrepresented and mischaracterized. Republicans argue that it is not the business of judges to create rights nor go beyond the intent of the framers. Further, they contend that liberal judicial activists conveniently overlook compelling competing values such as states rights and federalism, the right of a fetus to life, the guarantee of the free exercise of religion, the rights of crime victims, the rights of property owners, and the right to be treated fairly and not be discriminated against by ethnic and gender preference programs.

As for Pickering, his supporters argued that he was well trained in the law, having graduated first in his law school class at the University of Mississippi. They emphasized that he received the highest rating from the American Bar Association's Standing Committee on Federal Judiciary. They also portrayed him as a man of great personal courage, who in the 1960s openly opposed the Ku Klux Klan, and at great risk to himself and his family cooperated with the FBI by testifying against a Klan leader. Pickering's supporters noted that many in the local African American community in Mississippi supported his elevation to the Fifth Circuit despite opposition from the national civil rights leadership.

Pickering Compared to Other Bush Appeals Court Nominees

Pickering was in many respects a typical Bush nominee. During the 107th Congress, the President nominated thirty-one individuals to the appeals courts of general jurisdiction. Of the thirty-one:

- Eighteen (or 58%) were judges at the time of their nominations (including eleven federal district judges). Pickering was serving as U.S. District Judge for the Southern District of Mississippi;
- Twenty-three (or 74%) had judicial or prosecutorial experience or both in their professional background. Pickering had both types of experience;
- Twenty (or 65%) received the highest American Bar Association rating of "Well Qualified" (eleven received a unanimous committee rating of Well Qualified and nine received a Well Qualified rating by a majority of the ABA Committee). Pickering received a majority rating of Well Qualified with a minority voting for a Qualified rating;
- Twenty (or 65%) were white males. Of the remaining eleven, seven were white females, three were African American males, and one was a Hispanic male. Pickering is a white male. It should be noted that Bush has nominated proportionately more women and minorities to the appeals courts than any previous Republican administration;
- Eighteen (or 58%) had a net worth in excess of one million dollars. Pickering had a net worth in excess of one million. The figures for the Bush nominees set a new record of millionaires nominated to the appeals courts (the previous record was the Clinton appointees of whom 51% were millionaires). The net worth figures, however, indicate that relatively low judicial salaries all but guarantee that only those who can afford to serve on the bench will be candidates for judgeships.
- Twenty-seven of the thirty (or 90%) for whom there was political party information were Republicans. There were two Democrats and one Independent. Pickering is a Republican.

Pickering's age at the time of nomination was the only characteristic not typical of the Bush nominees. At 64 he was considerably older than the typical Bush nominee by almost fifteen years (the average age of the thirty-one Bush appeals court nominees at the time of nomination was 49.7 years of age). Pickering's powerful political backing—his friend, Trent Lott, the Senate Minority Leader (who was Majority Leader at the time of Pickering's nomination on May 25, 2001), and his son, a member of Congress (Republican Representative Charles W. Pickering, Jr.)—along with his philosophical and professional credentials no doubt secured his nomination in the first place.

The Problem of Obstruct and Delay

Charles Pickering was nominated on May 25, 2001. His first hearing was held the following October 18, some 146 days after his nomination was sent to the Senate. In the interim, partisan control of the Senate shifted from the Republican to the Democratic Party (after Vermont Senator Jim Jeffords left the Republican Party and voted with the Democrats to reorganize the Senate). Terrorists attacked the United States on September 11, and deadly anthrax was sent through the U.S. postal service to, among other targets, a Senate office building shutting it down. . . . [One hundred forty-six] days is below the average number of days for nominations to receive hearings during the 105th [230.9 days] and 106th [235.3 days] Congresses (coinciding with President Bill Clinton's second term) as well as the 107th [238.4 days] Congress but considerably above the average number of days from the ten previous Congresses [ranging from 14.8 days in the 98th Congress to 90.9 days in the 100th Congress]. However, the extraordinary events that intervened undoubtedly contributed to the delay. Democratic senators asked for a second hearing when they learned that there were a large number of unpublished decisions written by Pickering that had not been examined by the Committee. Pickering had this highly unusual second hearing on February 7, 2002. The Committee voted on his nomination on March 14, some 35 days after the second hearing.

The very public battle over Pickering was also unusual because most activity surrounding

nominees to the lower federal courts occurs behind
the scenes. Since the late 1980s, there has been a
tendency for a nominee, opposed on policy or ideological grounds by one or more senators of the
party controlling the Senate, to not even have a
hearing, leaving such nominations to wither. . . .
The proportion of Courts of Appeals nominees who
received hearings was at a high point during the
95th, 97th, and 99th Congresses at 100 percent
when the same party controlled the Senate and
White House. It was at a low point at about 47 percent during the 106th Congress (when Democrat
Bill Clinton was President and the Republicans
controlled the Senate). For the 107th Congress,
nineteen nominees to the appeals courts of general
jurisdiction (about 61%) had hearings.

The proportion of nominees confirmed has also
declined. It is true that Congresses that include a
presidential election year . . . have a lower proportion of confirmations than Congresses that do not.
Nevertheless, the evidence is suggestive of major
obstruct and delay tactics for judicial nominations
starting with the 100th Congress. Subsequent Congresses, on the whole, show increases in the average number of days from time of nomination to
hearing and from the date of the hearing to the
date the nomination was reported out of committee
and sent to the floor of the Senate and major de-
creases in the proportion of nominees who received hearings. . . . What was typically a routine
process once a nomination was favorably reported
and sent to the floor of the Senate (i.e. rapid floor
consideration with a substantial proportion of
nominees confirmed the same day reported or one
day after) is now a virtual obstacle course for some
nominees. The average number of days from the
date the nomination was reported to the date of
confirmation ranged from a low of 1.9 days for the
97th Congress to 68.5 days for the 106th. The proportion of nominees who were confirmed the same
day reported or one day after plummeted from a
high of almost 78 percent in the 101st Congress to
the single digits with the 104th through 106th Congresses. The proportion of nominees favorably reported who received confirmation floor votes
dipped below the 100 percent level for the first
time for two consecutive Congresses—the 104th
and 105th.

Judicial selection before the presidency of
Ronald Reagan was primarily patronage or partisan

as opposed to policy agenda driven. It was almost
inconceivable that a senator not of the President's
party would be able to prevent a nominee from
having a hearing. One dramatic exception occurred in 1948 when Republicans controlled the
Senate with Democrat Harry Truman in the White
House. Anticipating winning the presidency, Republicans simply took no action on almost all of
the Truman nominees. After Truman was reelected
and the Democrats regained control of Congress,
those Truman nominees as well as most others
breezed through the Senate with virtually no Republican opposition.

When the Senate Judiciary Committee holds no
hearings and takes no action on judicial nominations, it fails its constitutional responsibility to advise and consent. Similarly, when the Committee
and the Majority Leader slow down the confirmation process, that too represents a failure to advise
and consent. During Republican control of the
Senate during the Clinton presidency, some nominees waited years before finally being confirmed.
Many nominees to the appeals courts and district
courts never had hearings in the first place. At the
end of the Clinton presidency, nineteen nominations to the appeals courts (including two who had
hearings) were not acted upon by the Senate, and
those positions were vacant at the beginning of the
Bush presidency.

It is true that under Democratic Senate control
from 1987 through 1992, some Reagan and Bush
nominees to the appeals courts never had hearings. However, those who did . . . were for the
most part promptly given committee and confirmation votes. Not so with Republican control of
the Senate in the second half of the 1990s, where
obstruct and delay tactics were taken to much
greater levels.

. . . [An] Index of Obstruction and Delay is determined by the number of nominees for whom no
action was taken by the Senate added to the nominees for whom the confirmation process lasted
more than 180 days divided by the total number of
nominees. The Index thus ranges from 0.0000
which indicates an absence of obstruction and
delay to 1.0000 which indicates the maximum
level of obstruction and delay. There were low levels of obstruction and delay until the 100th Congress (Republican Ronald Reagan was president
with Democrats having regained control of the

Senate for the first time during his presidency). The Index dropped dramatically with the first Congress with President George H. Bush, although the Democrats still controlled the Senate. In the Congress that overlapped with the 1992 presidential election year, however, the Index rose, but not to the level of the 100th Congress. But starting with the 104th Congress, the Index climbed, setting new high levels through the 106th and 107th Congresses. Also, in every even numbered Congress, which always overlaps a presidential election year, the Index was higher than the previous non-presidential year Congress.

Beginning with the 104th Congress, the obstruct and delay phenomenon became so serious a problem that Chief Justice William H. Rehnquist publicly urged the Senate to act promptly on the Clinton nominees. The Republican leadership nevertheless continued the slow pace.

With the tables turned and Democrats controlling the Senate of the 107th Congress and a Republican in the White House, the Democrats appeared to be acting similar to the Republicans during the last six years of the Clinton presidency. Ideology or policy concerns on the part of one or more Democratic senators seemed to be responsible for a number of appeals court nominees not receiving hearings. Additionally, there was the special case of the Sixth Circuit nominees from Michigan who were being held up by the Democratic senators from Michigan. The senators were trying to force the Administration to name at least one of the Clinton nominees from Michigan, whom the Republicans had for years prevented from even having hearings.

To his credit, Senator Patrick Leahy, as chair of the Senate Judiciary Committee, moved rapidly on the less controversial nominees. He conducted hearings during the August 2001 recess, and soon after September 11, 2001, and during the anthrax scare that closed down a Senate office building. All thirty-six district court nominees nominated in 2001 had hearings. Of the sixty-two nominated in 2002, forty-seven had hearings (about 76%). Of the appeals court nominees to courts of general jurisdiction nominated in 2001, eighteen of twenty-eight (64%) had hearings. Of the three nominated in 2002, one had a hearing. Only a few of the controversial nominees, such as Pickering, had hearings. The figures for the 107th Congress show no

improvement over the two previous Congresses in the average number of days it took for courts of appeals nominees to have hearings. But there was an improvement from the 106th Congress in the average number of days to have the nomination reported. Once reported, the nominations took fewer days on average to be voted on by the full Senate than had been the case for the three previous Congresses. The Index of Obstruction and Delay for appeals court nominees was, however, higher for the 107th Congress than for the 106th. . . . However, the Index of Obstruction and Delay for the district courts for the 107th Congress was lower than that for the three previous Congresses under Republican control.

The Democratic and Republican leadership seem to have difficulty agreeing on a simple common-sense proposition: Regardless of the party controlling the Senate and presidency, all nominees should have hearings and votes by the Senate Judiciary Committee. Further, when reported out of Committee, all nominees should be placed promptly on the Senate calendar for full Senate debate and vote. Hearings allow opponents to state their case and supporters to offer rebuttals. Because the Senate works by the committee system, it is reasonable to argue that a vote by the Committee not to send a nomination to the floor of the Senate fulfills the advise and consent requirement of the Constitution. But by not holding hearings and votes in committee, or by delaying floor action when nominations are sent to the floor, the Senate has been engaged in obstruct and delay, not advise and consent. This was done in an unprecedented way by then Senate Majority Leader Trent Lott when he apparently honored holds placed on Clinton nominees by some Republican senators. Obstruct and delay is unfair to nominees who are in confirmation limbo. Most importantly, it is dysfunctional for the judicial branch of government, which requires a full complement of judges to do its work.

Unlike other Bush nominees to the appeals courts who waited for at least nine months to be scheduled for a hearing or who never received a hearing, Pickering had hearings on October 18, 2001 (about five months after his nomination) and then again on February 7, 2002. The highly unusual second hearing was held to consider unresolved questions concerning scores of Pickering's unpublished decisions as a U.S. District judge for the Southern District of Mississippi. Pickering has been serving on the district bench since his appointment by the first President Bush in 1990. Republicans could well have believed that the call for the second hearing was but a manifestation of the obstruct and delay phenomenon. The weeks between the hearings gave Pickering's opponents additional opportunity to mobilize their forces. This points up another facet of the changing selection and confirmation processes—the involvement of advocacy or interest groups.

Advocacy Group Involvement

Interest groups have long participated in the legislative process, but they were rarely involved in federal judgeship nominations and then primarily with nominations to the Supreme Court. But as American politics has become more ideological, and as federal judges have become recognized as important players in the field of public policy, interest groups have become regularly involved. Over the past two decades, advocacy groups have tried to influence judicial selection by the president and have monitored nominations, lobbying allies in the Senate to block objectionable nominees. They have even used such nominees as the subject of fund-raising appeals for the groups.

The politics involved in judicial nominations at times resembles the contest over contentious legislation in Congress. In effect, filling judgeships has become part of the democratic process, with all the strengths and weaknesses of democracy.

The advocacy groups feed press releases to the media. There is an unfortunate tendency to demonize or at least mischaracterize the qualities of the controversial nominees. Conservative groups and their allies in the Senate did this in the 1990s with Clinton judicial nominees. Similarly, liberals and their senatorial allies have done this with some Bush nominees. Some of the opposition to Pickering, for example, initially implied that he is racist, rather than simply criticizing his judicial record.

Conclusion

It has been said, I think correctly, that the contest over Pickering was but a dress rehearsal for the coming battle over a Bush Supreme Court nomination—if that nominee has a record similar to Pickering's. Civil rights and civil liberties groups, along with labor, environmental, and other liberal advocacy groups, have put President Bush on notice as to what to expect if he tries to name a conservative activist to the high court—and if he pushes such nominees to the lower courts.

As partisan and ideological debate as the Pickering episode generated during the 107th Congress, it was after all out in the open for the public to weigh the merits of the arguments and the weight of the evidence produced by both sides. This, I suggest, is healthy for a democracy even as the democratic process is contentious. Judicial nominations, particularly to the appellate bench, have tended to reflect the President's policy agenda. The debate over Pickering dramatized this. Just as the President took into account Pickering's judicial views and philosophy, so, too, did the Senate Judiciary Committee.

By holding hearings and advising the president that Pickering was considered too conservative by a majority of the Senate Judiciary Committee, the Senate, acting through the Committee, fulfilled its constitutional obligation. The President was now free to make another nomination. The system worked. When nominations are held up, the system is not working nearly as well. A wise President will aim for ideologically moderate nominees—a formula that surely is a prescription for success not only with the lower federal courts but the Supreme Court when the opportunity arises. This may be the most important lesson of the Pickering episode, but one which may not be heeded given the symbiotic relationship between advocacy groups and politicians and the results of the 2002 Congressional elections. That election returned control of the Senate to Republican hands and raised the possibility that stalled and even Committee-rejected nominees such as Pickering would be resubmitted, as indeed they were—thus ensuring major battles with uncertain results.

4.4   *Republican Party of Minnesota v. White* (2002)

JUSTICE SCALIA delivered the opinion of the Court.

The question presented in this case is whether the First Amendment permits the Minnesota Supreme Court to prohibit candidates for judicial election in that State from announcing their views on disputed legal and political issues.

I

Since Minnesota's admission to the Union in 1858, the State's Constitution has provided for the selection of all state judges by popular election. Since 1912, those elections have been nonpartisan. Since 1974, they have been subject to a legal restriction which states that a "candidate for a judicial office, including an incumbent judge," shall not "announce his or her views on disputed legal or political issues." This prohibition . . . is known as the "announce clause." Incumbent judges who violate it are subject to discipline, including removal, censure, civil penalties, and suspension without pay. Lawyers who run for judicial office also must comply with the announce clause. Those who violate it are subject to, *inter alia,* disbarment, suspension, and probation.

In 1996, one of the petitioners, Gregory Wersal, ran for associate justice of the Minnesota Supreme Court. In the course of the campaign, he distributed literature criticizing several Minnesota Supreme Court decisions on issues such as crime, welfare, and abortion. A complaint against Wersal challenging, among other things, the propriety of this literature was filed with the Office of Lawyers Professional Responsibility, the agency which, under the direction of the Minnesota Lawyers Professional Responsibility Board, investigates and prosecutes ethical violations of lawyer candidates for judicial office. The Lawyers Board dismissed the complaint; with regard to the charges that his campaign materials violated the announce clause, it expressed doubt whether the clause could constitutionally be enforced. Nonetheless, fearing that further ethical complaints would jeopardize his ability to practice law, Wersal withdrew from the election. In 1998, Wersal ran again for the same office. Early in that race, he sought an advisory opinion from the Lawyers Board with regard to whether it planned to enforce the announce clause. The Lawyers Board responded equivocally, stating that, although it had significant doubts about the constitutionality of the provision, it was unable to answer his question because he had not submitted a list of the announcements he wished to make.

Shortly thereafter, Wersal filed this lawsuit in Federal District Court against respondents, seeking, *inter alia,* a declaration that the announce clause violates the First Amendment and an injunction against its enforcement. Wersal alleged that he was forced to refrain from announcing his views on disputed issues during the 1998 campaign, to the point where he declined response to questions put to him by the press and public, out of concern that he might run afoul of the announce clause. Other plaintiffs in the suit, including the Minnesota Republican Party, alleged that, because the clause kept Wersal from announcing his views, they were unable to learn those views and support or oppose his candidacy accordingly. . . . [T]he District Court found in favor of respondents, holding that the announce clause did not violate the First Amendment. Over a dissent by Judge Beam, the United States Court of Appeals for the Eighth Circuit affirmed. We granted certiorari.

II

Before considering the constitutionality of the announce clause, we must be clear about its meaning. Its text says that a candidate for judicial office shall not "announce his or her views on disputed legal or political issues."

We know that "announc[ing]. . . views" on an issue covers much more than *promising* to decide an issue a particular way. The prohibition extends to the candidate's mere statement of his current position, even if he does not bind himself to maintain that position after election. All the parties agree this is the case. . . .

There are, however, some limitations that the Minnesota Supreme Court has placed upon the scope of the announce clause that are not (to put it politely) immediately apparent from its text. The statements that formed the basis of the complaint against Wersal in 1996 included criticism of past decisions of the Minnesota Supreme Court. One piece of campaign literature stated that "[t]he Minnesota Supreme Court has issued decisions which are marked by their disregard for the Legislature and a lack of common sense." It went on to criticize a decision excluding from evidence confessions by criminal defendants that were not tape-recorded, asking "[s]hould we conclude that because the Supreme Court does not trust police, it allows confessed criminals to go free?" It criticized a decision striking down a state law restricting welfare benefits, asserting that "[i]t's the Legislature which should set our spending policies." And it criticized a decision requiring public financing of abortions for poor women as "unprecedented" and a "pro-abortion stance." Although one would think that all of these statements touched on disputed legal or political issues, they did not (or at least do not now) fall within the scope of the announce clause. . . .

There are yet further limitations upon the apparent plain meaning of the announce clause: In light of the constitutional concerns, the District Court construed the clause to reach only disputed issues that are likely to come before the candidate if he is elected judge. The Eighth Circuit accepted this limiting interpretation by the District Court, and in addition construed the clause to allow general discussions of case law and judicial philosophy. The Supreme Court of Minnesota adopted these interpretations as well when it ordered enforcement of the announce clause in accordance with the Eighth Circuit's opinion.

It seems to us, however, that—like the text of the announce clause itself—these limitations upon the text of the announce clause are not all that they appear to be. First, respondents acknowledged at oral argument that statements critical of past judicial decisions are *not* permissible if the candidate also states that he is against *stare decisis*. Thus, candidates must choose between stating their views critical of past decisions and stating their views in opposition to *stare decisis*. Or, to look at it more concretely, they may state their view that prior decisions were erroneous only if they do not assert that they, if elected, have any power to eliminate erro-

neous decisions. Second, limiting the scope of the clause to issues likely to come before a court is not much of a limitation at all. One would hardly expect the "disputed legal or political issues" raised in the course of a state judicial election to include such matters as whether the Federal Government should end the embargo of Cuba. Quite obviously, they will be those legal or political disputes that are the proper (or by past decisions have been made the improper) business of the state courts. . . . Third, construing the clause to allow "general" discussions of case law and judicial philosophy turns out to be of little help in an election campaign. At oral argument, respondents gave, as an example of this exception, that a candidate is free to assert that he is a "'strict constructionist.'" But that, like most other philosophical generalities, has little meaningful content for the electorate unless it is exemplified by application to a particular issue of construction likely to come before a court—for example, whether a particular statute runs afoul of any provision of the Constitution. Respondents conceded that the announce clause would prohibit the candidate from exemplifying his philosophy in this fashion. Without such application to real-life issues, all candidates can claim to be "strict constructionists" with equal (and unhelpful) plausibility.

In any event, it is clear that the announce clause prohibits a judicial candidate from stating his views on any specific nonfanciful legal question within the province of the court for which he is running, except in the context of discussing past decisions—and in the latter context as well, if he expresses the view that he is not bound by *stare decisis*.

Respondents contend that this still leaves plenty of topics for discussion on the campaign trail. These include a candidate's "character," "education," "work habits," and "how [he] would handle administrative duties if elected." Indeed, the Judicial Board has printed a list of preapproved questions which judicial candidates are allowed to answer. These include how the candidate feels about cameras in the courtroom, how he would go about reducing the caseload, how the costs of judicial administration can be reduced, and how he proposes to ensure that minorities and women are treated more fairly by the court system. Whether this list of preapproved subjects, and other topics not prohibited by the announce clause, adequately fulfill the First Amendment's guarantee of freedom of speech is the question to which we now turn.

III

As the Court of Appeals recognized, the announce clause both prohibits speech on the basis of its content and burdens a category of speech that is "at the core of our First Amendment freedoms"—speech about the qualifications of candidates for public office. The Court of Appeals concluded that the proper test to be applied to determine the constitutionality of such a restriction is what our cases have called strict scrutiny. . . . Under the strict-scrutiny test, respondents have the burden to prove that the announce clause is (1) narrowly tailored, to serve (2) a compelling state interest. In order for respondents to show that the announce clause is narrowly tailored, they must demonstrate that it does not "unnecessarily circumscrib[e] protected expression."

The Court of Appeals concluded that respondents had established two interests as sufficiently compelling to justify the announce clause: preserving the impartiality of the state judiciary and preserving the appearance of the impartiality of the state judiciary. Respondents reassert these two interests before us, arguing that the first is compelling because it protects the due process rights of litigants, and that the second is compelling because it preserves public confidence in the judiciary. Respondents are rather vague, however, about what they mean by "impartiality." Indeed, although the term is used throughout the Eighth Circuit's opinion, the briefs, the Minnesota Code of Judicial Conduct, and the ABA Codes of Judicial Conduct, none of these sources bothers to define it. Clarity on this point is essential before we can decide whether impartiality is indeed a compelling state interest, and, if so, whether the announce clause is narrowly tailored to achieve it.

A

One meaning of "impartiality" in the judicial context—and of course its root meaning—is the lack of bias for or against either *party* to the proceeding. Impartiality in this sense assures equal application of the law. That is, it guarantees a party that the judge who hears his case will apply the law to him in the same way he applies it to any other party. This is the traditional sense in which the term is used. . . . It is also the sense in which it is used in the cases cited by respondents and *amici* for the proposition that an impartial judge is essential to due process. . . .

We think it plain that the announce clause is not narrowly tailored to serve impartiality (or the appearance of impartiality) in this sense. Indeed, the clause is barely tailored to serve that interest *at all,* inasmuch as it does not restrict speech for or against particular *parties,* but rather speech for or against particular *issues.* To be sure, when a case arises that turns on a legal issue on which the judge (as a candidate) had taken a particular stand, the party taking the opposite stand is likely to lose. But not because of any bias against that party, or favoritism toward the other party. *Any* party taking that position is just as likely to lose. The judge is applying the law (as he sees it) evenhandedly.

B

It is perhaps possible to use the term "impartiality" in the judicial context (though this is certainly not a common usage) to mean lack of preconception in favor of or against a particular *legal view.* This sort of impartiality would be concerned, not with guaranteeing litigants equal application of the law, but rather with guaranteeing them an equal chance to persuade the court on the legal points in their case. Impartiality in this sense may well be an interest served by the announce clause, but it is not a *compelling* state interest, as strict scrutiny requires. A judge's lack of predisposition regarding the relevant legal issues in a case has never been thought a necessary component of equal justice, and with good reason. For one thing, it is virtually impossible to find a judge who does not have preconceptions about the law. As then-JUSTICE REHNQUIST observed of our own Court: "Since most Justices come to this bench no earlier than their middle years, it would be unusual if they had not by that time formulated at least some tentative notions that would influence them in their interpretation of the sweeping clauses of the Constitution and their interaction with one another. It would be not merely unusual, but extraordinary, if they had not at least given opinions as to constitutional issues in their previous legal careers." Indeed, even if it were possible to select judges who did not have preconceived views on legal issues, it would hardly be desirable to do so. "Proof that a Justice's mind at the time he joined the Court was a complete *tabula rasa* in the area of constitutional adjudication would be evidence of lack of qualification, not lack of bias.". . . [S]ince avoiding judicial preconceptions on legal issues is neither possible nor desirable, pretending otherwise by attempting to preserve the "appearance" of that type of impartiality can hardly be a compelling state interest either.

C

A third possible meaning of "impartiality" (again not a common one) might be described as open-mindedness. This quality in a judge demands, not that he have no preconceptions on legal issues, but that he be willing to consider views that oppose his preconceptions, and remain open to persuasion, when the issues arise in a pending case. This sort of impartiality seeks to guarantee each litigant, not an *equal* chance to win the legal points in the case, but at least *some* chance of doing so. It may well be that impartiality in this sense, and the appearance of it, are desirable in the judiciary, but we need not pursue that inquiry, since we do not believe the Minnesota Supreme Court adopted the announce clause for that purpose.

Respondents argue that the announce clause serves the interest in open-mindedness, or at least in the appearance of open-mindedness, because it relieves a judge from pressure to rule a certain way in order to maintain consistency with statements the judge has previously made. The problem is, however, that statements in election campaigns are such an infinitesimal portion of the public commitments to legal positions that judges (or judges-to-be) undertake, that this object of the prohibition is implausible. . . .

The short of the matter is this: In Minnesota, a candidate for judicial office may not say "I think it is constitutional for the legislature to prohibit same-sex marriages." He may say the very same thing, however, up until the very day before he declares himself a candidate, and may say it repeatedly (until litigation is pending) after he is elected.

As a means of pursuing the objective of open-mindedness that respondents now articulate, the announce clause is so woefully underinclusive as to render belief in that purpose a challenge to the credulous. . . .

. . . [T]he notion that the special context of electioneering justifies an *abridgment* of the right to speak out on disputed issues sets our First Amendment jurisprudence on its head. "[D]ebate on the qualifications of candidates" is "at the core of our electoral process and of the First Amendment freedoms," not at the edges. . . . We have never allowed the government to prohibit candidates from communicating relevant information to voters during an election.

JUSTICE GINSBURG would do so—and much of her dissent confirms rather than refutes our conclusion that the purpose behind the announce clause is not open-mindedness in the judiciary, but the undermining of judicial elections. She contends that the announce clause must be constitutional because due process would be denied if an elected judge sat in a case involving an issue on which he had previously announced his view. . . . But elected judges—regardless of whether they have announced any views beforehand—*always* face the pressure of an electorate who might disagree with their rulings and therefore vote them off the bench. Surely the judge who frees Timothy McVeigh places his job much more at risk than the judge who (horror of horrors!) reconsiders his previously announced view on a disputed legal issue. So if, as JUSTICE GINSBURG claims, it violates due process for a judge to sit in a case in which ruling one way rather than another increases his prospects for re-election, then—quite simply—the practice of electing judges is itself a violation of due process. . . .

JUSTICE GINSBURG devotes the rest of her dissent to attacking arguments we do not make. For example, despite the number of pages she dedicates to disproving this proposition, we neither assert nor imply that the First Amendment requires campaigns for judicial office to sound the same as those for legislative office. What we do assert, and what JUSTICE GINSBURG ignores, is that, *even if* the First Amendment allows greater regulation of judicial election campaigns than legislative election campaigns, the announce clause still fails strict scrutiny because it is woefully underinclusive, prohibiting announcements by judges (and would-be judges) only at certain times and in certain forms. . . .

. . . [I]n any case, Justice Ginsburg greatly exaggerates the difference between judicial and legislative elections. She asserts that "the rationale underlying unconstrained speech in elections for political office—that representative government depends on the public's ability to choose agents who will act at its behest—does not carry over to campaigns for the bench." This complete separation of the judiciary from the enterprise of "representative government" might have some truth in those countries where judges neither make law themselves nor set aside the laws enacted by the legislature. It is not a true picture of the American system. Not only do state-court judges possess the power to "make" common law, but they have the immense power to shape the States' constitutions as well. Which is precisely why the election of state judges became popular. . . .

There is an obvious tension between the article of Minnesota's popularly approved Constitution which provides that judges shall be elected, and the Minnesota Supreme Court's announce clause which places most subjects of interest to the voters off limits. . . . The disparity is perhaps unsurprising, since the ABA, which originated the announce clause, has long been an opponent of judicial elections. . . . That opposition may be well taken (it certainly had the support of the Founders of the Federal Government), but the First Amendment does not permit it to achieve its goal by leaving the principle of elections in place while preventing candidates from discussing what the elections are about. . . .

The Minnesota Supreme Court's canon of judicial conduct prohibiting candidates for judicial election from announcing their views on disputed legal and political issues violates the First Amendment. Accordingly, we reverse the grant of summary judgment to respondents and remand the case for proceedings consistent with this opinion.

It is so ordered.

Justice Kennedy, concurring.

I agree with the Court that Minnesota's prohibition on judicial candidates' announcing their legal views is an unconstitutional abridgment of the freedom of speech. . . .

Minnesota may choose to have an elected judiciary. It may strive to define those characteristics that exemplify judicial excellence. It may enshrine its definitions in a code of judicial conduct. It may adopt recusal standards more rigorous than due process requires, and censure judges who violate these standards. What Minnesota may not do, however, is censor what the people hear as they undertake to decide for themselves which candidate is most likely to be an exemplary judicial officer. Deciding the relevance of candidate speech is the right of the voters, not the State. The law in question here contradicts the principle that unabridged speech is the foundation of political freedom.

The State of Minnesota no doubt was concerned, as many citizens and thoughtful commentators are concerned, that judicial campaigns in an age of frenetic fundraising and mass media may foster disrespect for the legal system. Indeed, from the beginning there have been those who believed that the rough-and-tumble of politics would bring our governmental institutions into ill repute. And some have sought to cure this tendency with governmental restrictions on political speech. Cooler heads have always recognized, however, that these measures abridge the freedom of speech—not because the state interest is insufficiently compelling, but simply because content-based restrictions on political speech are "expressly and positively forbidden by" the First Amendment. The State cannot opt for an elected judiciary and then assert that its democracy, in order to work as desired, compels the abridgment of speech.

If Minnesota believes that certain sorts of candidate speech disclose flaws in the candidate's credentials, democracy and free speech are their own correctives. The legal profession, the legal academy, the press, voluntary groups, political and civic leaders, and all interested citizens can use their own First Amendment freedoms to protest statements inconsistent with standards of judicial neutrality and judicial excellence. Indeed, if democracy is to fulfill its promise, they must do so. They must reach voters who are uninterested or uninformed or blinded by partisanship, and they must urge upon the voters a higher and better understanding of the judicial function and a stronger commitment to preserving its finest traditions. Free elections and free speech are a powerful combination: Together they may advance our understanding of the rule of law and further a commitment to its precepts. . . .

. . . Even the undoubted interest of the State in the excellence of its judiciary does not allow it to restrain candidate speech by reason of its content. Minnesota's attempt to regulate campaign speech is impermissible.

JUSTICE STEVENS, with whom JUSTICE SOUTER, JUSTICE GINSBURG, and JUSTICE BREYER join, dissenting.

. . . By obscuring the fundamental distinction between campaigns for the judiciary and the political branches, and by failing to recognize the difference between statements made in articles or opinions and those made on the campaign trail, the Court defies any sensible notion of the judicial office and the importance of impartiality in that context.

The Court's disposition rests on two seriously flawed premises—an inaccurate appraisal of the importance of judicial independence and impartiality, and an assumption that judicial candidates should have the same freedom " 'to express themselves on matters of current public importance' " as do all other elected officials. Elected judges, no less than appointed judges, occupy an office of trust that is fundamentally different from that occupied by policymaking officials. Although the fact that they must stand for election makes their job more difficult than that of the tenured judge, that fact does not lessen their duty to respect essential attributes of the judicial office that have been embedded in Anglo-American law for centuries.

There is a critical difference between the work of the judge and the work of other public officials. In a democracy, issues of policy are properly decided by majority vote; it is the business of legislators and executives to be popular. But in litigation, issues of law or fact should not be determined by popular vote; it is the business of judges to be indifferent to unpopularity. . . .

. . . [C]ountless judges in countless cases routinely make rulings that are unpopular and surely disliked by at least 50 percent of the litigants who appear before them. It is equally common for them to enforce rules that they think unwise, or that are contrary to their personal predilections. For this reason, opinions that a lawyer may have expressed before becoming a judge, or a judicial candidate, do not disqualify anyone for judicial service because every good judge is fully aware of the dis-

tinction between the law and a personal point of view. It is equally clear, however, that such expressions after a lawyer has been nominated to judicial office shed little, if any, light on his capacity for judicial service. Indeed, to the extent that such statements seek to enhance the popularity of the candidate by indicating how he would rule in specific cases if elected, they evidence a lack of fitness for the office.

Of course, any judge who faces reelection may believe that he retains his office only so long as his decisions are popular. Nevertheless, the elected judge, like the lifetime appointee, does not serve a constituency while holding that office. He has a duty to uphold the law and to follow the dictates of the Constitution. If he is not a judge on the highest court in the State, he has an obligation to follow the precedent of that court, not his personal views or public opinion polls. He may make common law, but judged on the merits of individual cases, not as a mandate from the voters.

By recognizing a conflict between the demands of electoral politics and the distinct characteristics of the judiciary, we do not have to put States to an all or nothing choice of abandoning judicial elections or having elections in which anything goes. As a practical matter, we cannot know for sure whether an elected judge's decisions are based on his interpretation of the law or political expediency. In the absence of reliable evidence one way or the other, a State may reasonably presume that elected judges are motivated by the highest aspirations of their office. But we do know that a judicial candidate, who announces his views in the context of a campaign, is effectively telling the electorate: "Vote for me because I believe X, and I will judge cases accordingly." Once elected, he may feel free to disregard his campaign statements, but that does not change the fact that the judge announced his position on an issue likely to come before him *as a reason to vote for him*. Minnesota has a compelling interest in sanctioning such statements. . . .

Even when "impartiality" is defined in its narrowest sense to embrace only "the lack of bias for or against either *party* to the proceeding," the announce clause serves that interest. Expressions that stress a candidate's unbroken record of affirming convictions for rape, for example, imply a bias in favor of a particular litigant (the prosecutor) and against a class of litigants (defendants in rape cases). Contrary to the Court's reasoning in its first attempt to define impartiality, an interpretation of the announce clause that prohibits such statements serves the State's interest in maintaining both the appearance of this form of impartiality and its actuality.

When the Court evaluates the importance of impartiality in its broadest sense, which it describes as "the interest in open-mindedness, or at least in the appearance of open-mindedness," it concludes that the announce clause is "so woefully underinclusive as to render belief in that purpose a challenge to the credulous." It is underinclusive, in the Court's view, because campaign statements are an infinitesimal portion of the public commitments to legal positions that candidates make during their professional careers. It is not, however, the number of legal views that a candidate may have formed or discussed in his prior career that is significant. Rather, it is the ability both to reevaluate them in the light of an adversarial presentation, and to apply the governing rule of law even when inconsistent with those views, that characterize judicial open-mindedness.

The Court boldly asserts that respondents have failed to carry their burden of demonstrating "that campaign statements are uniquely destructive of open-mindedness," But the very purpose of most statements prohibited by the announce clause is to convey the message that the candidate's mind is not open on a particular issue. The lawyer who writes an article advocating harsher penalties for polluters surely does not commit to that position to the same degree as the candidate who says "vote for me because I believe all polluters deserve harsher penalties." At the very least, such statements obscure the appearance of open-mindedness. More importantly, like the reasoning in the Court's opinion, they create the false impression that the standards for the election of political candidates apply equally to candidates for judicial office.

The Court seems to have forgotten its prior evaluation of the importance of maintaining public confidence in the "disinterestedness" of the judiciary. Commenting on the danger that participation by judges in a political assignment might erode that public confidence, we wrote: "While the problem of individual bias is usually cured through recusal, no such mechanism can overcome the appearance of institutional partiality that may arise from judiciary involvement in the making of policy. The legitimacy of the Judicial Branch ultimately depends on its reputation for impartiality and nonpartisanship. That reputation may not be borrowed by the political Branches to cloak their work in the neutral colors of judicial action."

Conversely, the judicial reputation for impartiality and openmindedness is compromised by electioneering that emphasizes the candidate's personal predilections rather than his qualifications for judicial office. . . .

The disposition of this case on the flawed premise that the criteria for the election to judicial office should mirror the rules applicable to political elections is profoundly misguided. I therefore respectfully dissent.

A View from the Inside

4.5   **Justice for Sale**
*Interview with Justices Stephen Breyer and
Anthony Kennedy (1999)*

Conducted by Bill Moyers

Moyers: Last year in Philadelphia, at the American
Bar Association, both of you were quite outspoken
on this issue of judicial independence and the
threat of financial contributions and political pressure. Why did you sound the alarm?

Kennedy: We have a special point of view to present. The judiciary as an institution is faced with a
new threat. Democracy is something that you must
learn each generation. It has to be taught. And we
must have a national civics lesson about judicial
independence.

Breyer: It's important to every American that the
law protect his or her basic liberty. We developed a
system of protecting human liberty such that judges
and independent judges are a necessary part of
that protection. I think it's important that Americans
understand that. And if that independence is seriously eroded, it will be hard to protect those things
that this country was based upon.

Moyers: You said in Philadelphia, Justice Kennedy,
that the law makes a promise. The promise is neutrality. What do you mean by neutrality?

Kennedy: You have to remember that we live in a
constitutional democracy, not a democracy where
the voice of the people each week, each year, has
complete effect. We have certain constitutional
principles that extend over time. Judges must be
neutral in order to protect those principles. . . .
There's a rule of law, [and it has] three parts. One:
the government is bound by the law. Two: all peo-

ple are treated equally. And three: there are certain
enduring human rights that must be protected.
There must be both the perception and the reality
that in defending these values, the judge is not affected by improper influences or improper restraints. That's neutrality.

Moyers: And yet, as you said in Philadelphia,
judges don't emerge in a vacuum. You all are products in a way of the political process—not individually, but it's the process that gets you to where you
are, even if appointed. Is neutrality really possible?

Breyer: I think, Yes, it is. Judges are appointed often
through the political process. At least there's a political input, but when you put on the robe, at that
point the politics is over. And, at that point, a judge
must think through each case with the total neutrality that you mentioned. . . . All anyone has to ask
himself is, Suppose I were on trial? Suppose somebody accused me? Would I want to be judged by
whether or not I was popular? Wouldn't I want to be
judged on what was true as opposed to what might
be popular? . . . [O]ur system is based upon what
you described as neutrality and independence.

Kennedy: Our system presumes that there are certain principles that are more important than the
temper of the times. And you must have a judge
who is detached, who is independent, who is fair,
who is committed only to those principles, and not
public pressures of other sort. That's the meaning of
neutrality.

Breyer: I'll give you an example if you want because I often get the question, "Well didn't you go
through a confirmation process?" And in that confirmation process, I sat for 17 hours in front of a
Senate judiciary committee. I mean maybe 17

hours and 30 minutes, who's counting? But they asked me questions and I had to answer. And it was on television. . . . If they were listening and they decided they didn't like what they saw they might communicate with their elected representatives. And perhaps I wouldn't have been confirmed. Well what did I think about that? I thought that that was an effort to inject a popular element, a democratic element into the selection of a person who, once he is selected and confirmed, is beyond electoral control. Now why do we have such a system? Because, on the one hand, people, when they think about it, want judges to be independent. Nobody wants a judge to be subject to the political whim of the moment. At the same time, we do live in a democracy. And for that reason I think it is appropriate to have some element of public control. And that element of public control in the federal system is introduced through the confirmation process and the selection process. But once the person is selected, at that point that person is independent.

Moyers: Do you think that people who make contributions to judicial elections want those judges to be independent?

Breyer: I don't know. I imagine some may, some may not. . . . You can have many different selection systems, but the bottom line has to be a system that, once the judge takes office that judge will feel that he or she is to decide the case without reference to the popular thing or the popular will of the moment.

Moyer: Go back to the confirmation example, for a moment. Do you think the senators wanted you to be independent?

Kennedy: Were they asking questions of Justice Breyer and of me and of our colleagues in order to determine how they would vote on a particular issue? Or were they asking instead to probe the temperament, the judicial qualities, the scholarship of the nominee? I hope it's the latter.

Breyer: It is the latter, it is the latter. . . . They're selecting the person because they think that person will be all right, and they believe and want, once that person is selected, that [the judge] should be independent. I mean, years ago, we heard Russian judges . . . talking about what's called "telephone justice." And telephone justice is where the party

boss calls you up on the telephone and tells you how to decide the case. So they said, Well, don't you have that in the United States? Now, really don't you? So I said, No. And I looked around and I said, Well I know you're thinking that even if we did, I would say no. They said, That's right. And I said, Well how can I explain it? It's just that no one in the United States wants that kind of system and it would be outrageous and beyond belief that someone would call up on the phone.

Moyers: The concern that each of you expressed last year in Philadelphia was in particular about campaign contributions to judicial races. Why do you see that as a threat to independence and neutrality?

Kennedy: Well, in part, it's because the campaign process itself does not easily adapt to judicial selection. Democracy is raucous, hurly-burly, rough-and-tumble. This is a difficult world for a jurist, a scholarly, detached neutral person to operate within. So, the whole problem of judicial campaigns is. . . difficult for us to confront. Now, when you add the component of this mad scramble to raise money and to spend money, it becomes even worse for the obvious reason that we're concerned that there will be either the perception or the reality that judicial independence is undermined.

Moyers: Let me just give you some statistics from a poll conducted by the Texas State Supreme Court and the Texas State Bar Association, which found that 83% of the public think judges are already unduly influenced by campaign contributions. 79% of the lawyers who appear before the judges think campaign contributions significantly influence courtroom decisions. And almost half of the justices on the court think the same thing. Isn't the verdict in from the people that they cannot trust the judicial system there any more?

Kennedy: This is serious, because the law commands allegiance only if it commands respect. It commands respect only if the public thinks the judges are neutral. And when you have figures like that, the judicial system is in real trouble. And that's why we should have a national conversation about it.

Breyer: I agree completely. Independence doesn't mean you decide the way you want. Independence means you decide according to the law and the facts. The law and the facts do not include deciding according to campaign contributions. And if that's what people think, I couldn't agree with you more. The balance has tipped too far, and when the balance has tipped too far, that threatens the institution. To threaten the institution is to threaten fair administration of justice and protection of liberty.

Moyers: Our research shows that the contributions to judicial elections around the country are increasing at a faster percentage than contributions to presidential and congressional races. What do you make of that?

Breyer: I think it's a very good idea to try to look into it empirically. As you know the federal judges are not elected. We are selected, but I grew up in California and in San Francisco and there was a system of electing judges. But it was pretty unusual to find an instance where the position was contested let alone find an instance where there was a lot of campaign money.

Moyers: There was a pre-selection process.

Breyer: Well, just that there would be somebody in the office and the voters—it was more or less an understanding in the entire community, as long as that person was doing a good job on the merits, nobody was going to run against him. And the problem is once you get into this campaign business and begin to have a lot of money, then the person on the bench begins to think—what's going to happen if I decide the case this way or that way? Or at least the public sees it that way.

Kennedy: Decades ago there was an old boy network. And like most old boy networks it worked rather well. . . . The bar defended its judges, the bar was unified. It was run by the old boy network Things have changed. They should have changed. . . . The problem is the bar itself has become fractionated. You have plaintiffs attorneys, you have defense attorneys. So there is no unified bar that will protect a particular judge who has made a courageous decision that's unpopular.

Moyers: We actually talked to a lobbyist in Texas on record, on camera, willing to go on camera to talk about how—it's a lobbyist for the Texas Medical Association who boasted that he had suc-

ceeded in reshaping the philosophy of the Texas supreme court through an all-out political campaign and very large donations. They took [control of the court] from the trial lawyers who had been making contributions and had influenced the court to the other side of the, of the aisle. What does that say about the perception of independence?

Breyer: I think it shows that if you have one group of people doing it, you'll get another group of people doing it. And if you have A contributing to infect, to affect a court one way, you'll have B trying the other way. And you'll have C yet a third way and pretty soon you'll have a clash of political interests. Now, that's fine for a legislature. . . . But if you have that in the court system, you will then destroy confidence that the judges are deciding things on the merits. . . . And as I said our liberties are connected with that.

Kennedy: But when you carry over the political dynamic to the election, fair takes on a different meaning. In the political context fair means somebody that will vote for the unions or for the business. It can't mean that in the judicial context or we're in real trouble. . . . I do not think that we should select judges based on a particular philosophy as opposed to temperament, commitment to judicial neutrality and commitment to other more constant values as to which there is general consensus. . . .

Moyers: I was struck by something you said in Philadelphia, last year. You said that it's wrong for attorneys to make contributions to judicial candidates and expect favorable rulings in return. But would a lawyer make a contribution to a judicial campaign without expecting something? That's not human nature to give without expecting something back.

Kennedy: But the law is a profession and lawyers are committed to uphold the constitutional system and the independence of the judiciary. And I adhere to my statement. If an attorney gives money to a judge with the expectation that the judge will rule in his interest or his client's interest, that is corrosive of our institutions. It's corrosive of judicial independence.

Breyer: Once you're in a system where there are contributions being made, it's certainly not the case that everybody expects something back. I mean those people who are interested in good government will certainly contribute in order to make certain there's some counter-balance to those whose interests in good government is less.

Kennedy: You're hypothesizing the neutral eleemosynary donor. I hope they exist.

Breyer: I think they do.

Kennedy: I'm not sure. . . .

Moyers: Even at the local level some judicial candidates have to raise $250,000 to win and spend a great deal of time not only raising money but making television commercials, being coached by media advisors to walk into the room and look judicial. Now what does this do to the process?

Breyer: It demeans the process. We all know there are other countries where, for various reasons, the public lacks confidence in the judiciary. . . . And where those things have happened, I think there have been bad results for the people who live in the country, not just for the judges, not just for the lawyers, but for the ordinary man and woman who lives in the country. There tends not to be a method of fairly resolving disputes. And that means that it's harder to develop businesses. It's harder to just live an ordinary life in a fair way and it's harder to protect liberty.

Moyers: Have you given any thought to what we could do about this?

Kennedy: First, I hope that there will be enough of a concern by all segments of our community about protecting the independence of the courts that people will seriously consider trying to improve the election climate. That's the first thing. Second, I think the bar association ought to return to its earlier neutral professional attitude. Third, I think other civic groups and the media ought to do the same thing. . . . If we could somehow use elections to educate the public on the meaning of judicial independence, then we could take what is a flaw and turn [it] into a strength, what is a disadvantage and then turn it into advantage.

Breyer: Ultimately, the question of campaign contributions will be decided by the public. We do it in a democracy. Every citizen has to figure out what kind of government he or she wants. The most that we can say is that there is a problem and we hope you'll think about it. . . . And we trust that if people do think about it, they'll come to better solutions. . . .

Moyers: I respect your respect for the public, but I have to say that in states like Louisiana and Texas, where we've been reporting, the public stake in, and awareness of, and involvement in, judicial campaigns is being submerged to the sheer flood of contributions that are coming in. So that the public is less and less aware of what's happening behind the scenes.

Breyer: Judges can't easily defend themselves. We can speak about the institution, but ultimately the bar is the group that both is in touch with the public on the one hand and understands the judicial institution on the other. And I had hoped that the bar associations would take the lead and try and think about the problem and educate the public. . . .

Kennedy: Most of the contributions that you're talking about are by entities that are interested in the civil law, the economic interests. . . . [But] the criminal judge has no basic constituency to support him or her if they are obeying the law and are doing the job in the right way. And so when there's a contested election it then becomes, Who's tougher on crime? And this is very unfortunate because it distorts the idea of judicial independence. A judge sometimes must release a criminal. He doesn't like it, she doesn't like it, but the law requires it. And the context of an election in which you are "soft on crime" betrays a misunderstanding of the judicial process and a misunderstanding of the constitution.

Breyer: And supposing the person didn't do it? It doesn't help to fight crime to put people in prison who are innocent. And if a judge is going to be criticized for letting off a person and it turns out that person was innocent, that would be a pretty bad criticism. Or suppose the person didn't have a lawyer. Well it's fairly important that everyone have a lawyer and so we have a system that you can't convict a person without a lawyer, even if he's guilty. Well the judge might stand up for that principal, which he has to do under the law. And it would be a pity if because he stood up for the correct constitutional principle or decided that a person was innocent, wouldn't be convicted, that some opponent, through a set of advertisements took his job away. That's the problem.

Moyers: Do you think we're losing qualified people because of this system?

Kennedy: I have no recent studies or empirical basis on which to answer that question. . . . We so far, I think, are very lucky. There are some real heroes in the state judicial system, some marvelous judges, who know the law, who love the law, who are serving there for the right reason.

Breyer: I completely agree with Justice Kennedy, and particularly the last comment, because often I used to tell students who come to the court—You'll read in the newspaper about the Supreme Court of the United States. You will read in the newspaper more often about federal courts, but the law that affects people, the trials that affect human beings are by and large in the state courts. That's the bread and butter of the judicial system. Those are the judges who decide where the child should go in the case of divorce. Those are the judges that deal with 90% of the crime. Those are the judges that deal with a person's house, with a person's car, with everything that means something to an individual family. And they don't get lots of publicity and they don't get a lot of salary either. And life in some of those courts is not so easy for the judges. And the walls may have a few cracks and the telephone may not work, and they may have a hard time getting their case recorded because the word processor—well, they don't have one. . . .

Moyers: Do you think that this is a critical moment for examining judicial elections?

Kennedy: A commitment to the Constitution is not something that's genetic, it's not inherited, it's not automatic. It has to be taught. And each generation must learn about the Constitution and the values of constitutional institutions within the context of their own time, within the environment of their own time. And if we are in an era in which there is a loss of confidence in the judicial system—and, even worse, a misunderstanding of the judicial system—then we must take steps to correct it. I do sense that there is a growing misunderstanding, a growing lack of comprehension, of the necessity of independent judges. . . . There must be a rededication to the Constitution in every generation. And every generation faces a different challenge. We weren't talking about this 30 years ago, because we didn't have money in elections. Money in elections presents us with a tremendous challenge, a tremendous problem and we are remiss if we don't at once address it and correct it. . . .

Moyers: Well you remind me of what the historian Plutarch said in the Roman Republic: "The abuse of buying and selling votes crept in and money began to play an important part in determining elections. Later on, this process of corruption spread to the law courts. And then to the army, and finally the Republic was subjected to the rule of emperors."

Breyer: There are loads of countries that have nice written constitutions like ours. But there aren't loads of countries where they're followed. And the reason that they're followed here is not simply because of the judges. It's because of the Civil War. It's because after 80 years of segregation you had a decision of *Brown v. Board* that said people will be treated equally. And then many years before that became real, and gradually over time, 270 million people have learned roughly the importance of following that Constitution and following that law. It's complicated. It's called habit. It's called respect for the Constitution, and it's called respect for the institution of the judiciary. And that grows slowly. People have to be educated and they have to stick to it. If people lose that respect, an awful lot is lost.

4.6 # The Stealth Candidate (1994)

Jane Mayer and Jill Abramson

As the confirmation hearings approached, [Clarence] Thomas continued his intensive study of case law and began preparing for his appearance before the Senate. To his friends, the nominee seemed to be relishing the prospect of a battle. Clint Bolick [former employee at the EEOC, co-founder of the Institute for Justice, and currently research fellow at the Hoover Institute], who had spent the summer rallying conservative support for Thomas, ran into his former boss shortly before the hearings and was buoyed to hear him vow, "I'm going to really take on the opposition! I'm going to be strong. You're going to love my speech!"

But [Kenneth] Duberstein and the White House had a different idea. The final phase of its campaign was the inside-the-Beltway plan, which called for Thomas to "take on" only one group—the U.S. Senate. And the senators would be approached not with cudgels but with carrots.

The Senate was home turf for Duberstein. He had worked there for many years, first as an aide to New York's moderate Republican senator Jacob Javits, and more recently as both a White House political operative and a paid lobbyist. . . . Duberstein did not want to wage holy wars; he wanted to win. "His attitude," said one Democratic aide who dealt with him on the Thomas nomination, "was, 'What do I have to do to sell him?' He wasn't trying to make political points. All he wanted were his fifty-one votes. It was smart, because that's the currency up here."

With a Senate comprising fifty-seven Democrats and forty-three Republicans in 1991, the White House needed to hold every Republican and win over at least seven Democratic senators if Thomas was to be confirmed. (In a deadlock, the tiebreaking vote would be cast by Vice President Quayle.) Few of the needed Democratic votes would come his way if Thomas appeared stridently partisan. And Republican moderates who might be scared off by

From Jane Mayer and Jill Abramson, ch. 9, "The Stealth Candidate" in *Strange Justice: The Selling of Clarence Thomas* (New York: Plume, 1994), pp. 202–220. Reprinted by permission.

Thomas's record at the EEOC would have to be quietly reassured as well.

Some of the most promising Democrats were the six moderate to conservative southern senators who were up for reelection in 1992, all of them heavily dependent on support from the southern Black Belt. Having lost such votes for [Robert] Bork, Bush and Duberstein were determined this time to cut the deals and play the game, if necessary with every chit the White House had.

On its side, the White House had the Senate's traditional deference to a president's choice of nominee. In addition, by 1991, after more than a decade of Republican control of the White House, congressional Democrats were more vulnerable than ever to political pressure. . . . With the low-key George Mitchell as majority leader, Senate Democrats had been unable to muster the votes to overturn a single one of George Bush's vetoes, as moderate southerners often crossed the aisle to vote with their Republican brethren. The House, meanwhile, was now under the control of the muted Thomas Foley.

With no president to offer coattails or political cover and no party bosses with any real clout, the Senate Democrats had become unusually independent. Where they once had depended on the party for money, now many of them raised campaign funds with paid consultants, completely separate from the efforts of the party. As a consequence of these historic changes, Mitchell had little leverage with which to enforce discipline, even without the partisan skills of past leaders.

The Democrats not only lacked discipline; by 1991 most of them also lacked courage. Since losing the 1980 election to Ronald Reagan, liberal Democrats in particular had come to feel like an endangered species. That election had marked a national shift away from their ideology and had also proven beyond a doubt the power of right-wing attack politics. The very word "liberal" became an embarrassment. Senators formerly described as liberal began calling themselves progressive Democrats or, better yet, moderates. They lived in constant fear of being targeted with negative campaigns focusing on single divisive issues such as abortion and gun control.

By the summer of Thomas's nomination, the Democrats had regained control of the Senate, but the fear remained. NCPAC [National Conservative Political Action Committee] had by then fallen apart, but its attack strategy had been adopted by a host of other organizations that had sprung up in its wake, both liberal and conservative. These groups could generate torrents of mail and phone calls from angry constituents. They could also amass huge campaign coffers for opponents: as long as they operated separately from the Republican party, conservative political groups were permitted to finance campaigns against targeted Democrats, raising and spending enormous sums well outside the limits imposed by the federal election laws. Knowing this, Senate Democrats had become extremely leery of taking controversial stands.

In particular, at the time Thomas was bound for the Supreme Court, many Democrats were afraid of the issue of race. They may have had serious questions about Thomas's opposition to affirmative action. But after seeing Bush's landslide victory over Michael Dukakis in 1988, with its racist Willie Horton ad, as well as several 1990 Senate campaigns in which Republicans had obliterated their opponents by making an issue of their embrace of racial quotas, few white liberals were anxious to crusade for such controversial programs, especially against a black nominee. . . .

The party's credibility had been further damaged by several important Democratic senators who were ethically compromised. The dark side of senatorial fund-raising had been recently exposed in the socalled Keating Five scandal, which stung four Democrats (and one Republican) for taking more than a million dollars in contributions from a dishonest savings-and-loan operator. One of those snared in the scandal was Arizona's Dennis DeConcini, a conservative Democratic member of the Judiciary Committee; if any ethical issues arose during the Thomas hearings, DeConcini would hardly be in a position to judge the nominee harshly.

Other senators had been compromised by personal imbroglios, including Virginia's Chuck Robb, the head of the Democratic Senatorial Campaign Committee. Robb was fighting to survive an escapade in which he said he received a back rub from a young woman not his wife as well as allegations that he had attended wild beach parties where drugs were used. Another who could hardly be self-righteous in the face of any irregularities in Thomas's personal life was Ted Kennedy. . . . [T]his important member of the Judiciary Committee would soon be called to testify in the rape trial of his nephew. For the first time in his long political career, Kennedy's liberal activism was shut away behind a stony, embarrassed silence.

The White House also knew that even without these special problems, all senators had vulnerabilities. They were generally obsessed by three worries: avoiding negative publicity, raising money, and appearing invincible to potential opponents back home. Soon after Thomas was nominated, Duberstein, [John] Mackey [DOJ lobbyist], [Fred] McClure [congressional liaison, highest-ranking African American in Bush White House], and the rest of the Bush lobbyists set about the business of gathering fifty-one votes by artfully playing on these and other concerns.

In Georgia, for instance, the freshman Democratic senator, Wyche Fowler, was up for reelection in the fall. He was far more liberal than his senior colleague, Sam Nunn, and even though he and the nominee had the same home state, Fowler's ideology suggested that he was unlikely to cast a positive vote. But the White House realized that with the election very much on Fowler's mind, he would be listening closely to Georgia's blacks to assess their attitude toward Thomas. . . .

Not surprisingly, Fowler was thus high on the list of senators whom the White House targeted for courtesy calls from the nominee. The visit, which occurred soon after Thomas was nominated, was a success: despite large ideological differences, Fowler was quite swayed by Thomas in person. After meeting with Thomas and [John, former senator from Missouri] Danforth for an hour and a half, Fowler later explained, "I had a good impression of his character, the fact he was from Georgia, and the fact that he grew up poor and hard I thought would bring a perspective to a court that was mostly white and privileged."

While these were his stated reasons for supporting Thomas, the White House played other angles as well. Knowing how much the black vote would mean to Fowler's reelection, the White House arranged for sympathetic black leaders in Fowler's state to lobby for Thomas. According to a black pastor at St. Paul's Christian Methodist Episcopal Church in Savannah, Henry Delaney, "A man named Mark Paoletta [Boyden Gray's aide] called me every day for a while. The White House really worked it. They told us to contact Fowler because Senator Fowler didn't know whether there was black support for Thomas." Such stage directions from the White House illustrate how far the administration was willing to go.

And the White House had still more leverage: it had something Fowler wanted. The senator was counting on heavy financial support from the lawyers in his state. The Georgia Bar Association, meanwhile, wanted a federal judgeship for its secretary, a lawyer from Statesboro named James Franklin. Although Franklin was a Republican, Fowler was trying hard to please the state bar, lobbying the White House to appoint him over another Republican candidate. Fowler, who ultimately voted in favor of Thomas, would later disavow any connection between his vote and other issues such as Georgia judgeships. (Franklin was nominated by the White House right after Thomas's confirmation but failed to make it through the Senate.) But two White House aides believe they secured Fowler's vote by nominating his judge. (Ironically, Fowler lost his bid for reelection the following fall, in part because feminist leaders and women withheld their financial and organizational support from him because of his support for Thomas.)

Fowler was one of the six southern Democrats up for reelection that year. Terry Sanford, a progressive from North Carolina, was another who felt the heavy hand of Thomas's Washington supporters in his campaign financing. A liberal former governor, Sanford too was an ideological opposite to Thomas, but the freshman senator was vulnerable to conservative attack, and he needed millions of dollars for his 1992 campaign.

Charles Black, a conservative political strategist in Washington who had been working informally with Duberstein, had special clout in North Carolina. . . . During the summer of 1991, as Sanford was desperately trying to amass funds, Black helped to rally business leaders and Republican contributors in the state to contact the senator on behalf of Thomas. Sanford indeed cast his vote for Thomas; he also succeeded in raising an impres-

sive $2.5 million for his reelection. But in the end Sanford, like Fowler, narrowly lost his reelection, in his case to a better-financed conservative Republican in the Helms mold.

The White House team also contacted major contributors to the coffers of Oklahoma's David Boren, a conservative Democrat whose vote they thought they could win. . . . Not surprisingly, given Oklahoma's economic base, many of his most crucial contributors were leaders of the oil and gas industry, whose interests he fiercely protected.

An old oilman himself, Bush had his own close ties to many of Tulsa's energy executives. In fact, some of Boren's biggest contributors were also members of Bush's Team 100, the wealthy businessmen who gave or raised a minimum of $100,000 for the Republican party. Cross-party contributions were common among Oklahoma's energy interests, providing an obvious opportunity for the White House. And the Bush operatives did not pass it up. According to a former aide to Sununu, "We went to all of Boren's $1,000 contributors who were also Bush contributors and asked them to call Boren on behalf of Thomas. Those oil and gas guys could make the calls." Although a threat was not necessarily expressed, the message was, of course, that Boren's access to oil patch money might run a bit dry if the senator didn't vote with the president.

Because the White House couldn't direct such efforts legally, or appear to be mixing money with votes for Thomas, the arrangements for these lobbying strategies were made at the Republican National Committee in consultation with state party organizations. . . .

Boren, a former Rhodes Scholar and Yale graduate who was considered a thoughtful parliamentarian on Capitol Hill, eventually agreed to support Thomas. His vote was considered especially significant after Anita Hill came forward, because she was a native of his state. But later, after watching Thomas's early performance on the Court, Boren admitted that his support had been a mistake he deeply regretted.

Vice President Quayle also participated in the effort to lobby vulnerable senators. He knew that his golfing buddy Alan Dixon, a Democrat from Illinois who, like Boren, often voted with the Republicans, was running for reelection in 1992 and was worried about who would oppose him. . . . [A]round the time the White House nominated Thomas, a successful Chicago businessman, Gary MacDougal, was poised to throw his hat into the ring. Mac-Dougal had strong ties to Republican officials at both the state and national levels and was thought to be a serious contender who could raise large amounts of money. . . .

Quayle was well aware of Dixon's concern. He also knew that Dixon's was a potential vote for Thomas. According to a White House aide, Quayle called Dixon, emphasizing that his vote for Thomas would be considered a patriotic gesture, something that the Bush White House would value greatly. And when Dixon decided to vote for Thomas, Mac-Dougal found that many of the wealthy Republican business leaders who had pledged to serve on his finance team suddenly began disappearing, asking, for instance, to have their names kept off his campaign letterhead.

Although outsiders could never be sure that Dixon's vote pulled the plug on MacDougal's official Republican support, the suspicion of a deal remained in the air. . . . [L]acking sufficient backing, MacDougal withdrew from the race. The Republicans went on to name a weak replacement whom Dixon seemed sure to defeat. . . .

During August, the Christian Coalition, whose leaders were in touch with Duberstein, also earmarked Dixon for special attention. Action alerts went out to its members in seven states, and television spots backing Thomas were run in twelve markets. In addition, the group sent out two hundred thousand pieces of direct mail and got a hundred thousand Christian activists to sign petitions supporting Thomas, which were delivered by hand to Dixon and other ambivalent senators by Christian Coalition leaders, who met with each senator's legislative assistant: The message was clear: Dixon or any senator who did not heed the Christian Coalition's call to support Judge Thomas would find himself facing a righteous and very angry army at the ballot box, and possibly even a primary challenge from the religious right.

Thus, when Dixon decided to vote for Thomas, it must have seemed politically prudent. Ironically, it turned out to be just the opposite. Dixon never got the chance even to face his weak Republican challenger; in an upset, he was defeated in the Democratic primary by a black woman, Carol Moseley Braun. Her reason for running—and some might suggest winning—was her anger over the Senate's treatment of Anita Hill.

This wheeling and dealing by the White House was cynical but hardly unusual. . . . What was out of the ordinary, however, was the number of deals cut before Thomas had even spent a day testifying as well as the fact that they were brokered for a Supreme Court nominee. . . .

As the summer wore on, the political team at the White House also worked feverishly to polish the candidate himself so that in his first real public debut he would come across winningly. Thomas had to be thoroughly coached, first, to protect himself against allegations that he lacked the legal depth to be a Supreme Court justice, and second, to soften the rougher edges of his ideology. Duberstein instructed Thomas to appear as amiable, flexible, and moderate inside the Beltway as his supporters outside the Beltway had been assured . . . that he was not. . . .

. . . Precisely to raise his stock with influential conservatives, Thomas had given increasingly extreme speeches during his latter years at the EEOC. Now his intellectual flirtations—with the theory of natural law, for instance—would be evident to anyone who made the effort to read the thirty-six thousand documents he and his legal advisers had turned over to the Judiciary Committee.

Characteristically pugnacious, Thomas confided to friends like Bolick and Mackey that he was uncomfortable with Duberstein's stealth approach. Perhaps, left to his own devices, he would have given the Senate and the public a more forthright and illuminating exposition of his views. But honesty was not the best policy, in the view of the White House strategists. As they kept reminding him, their job was to get him to the Supreme Court; once there, he could take on his critics and vote as he pleased.

On the volatile subject of abortion, the White House made a firm decision that Thomas must say nothing definitive. Among other concerns, any indication that the nominee might abrogate a woman's right to an abortion would risk alienating a crucial Republican moderate on the committee, Arlen Specter. A former prosecutor, Specter had led the Republican mutiny against Bork, dooming him with a sharp cross-examination that lasted two days. During 1991, he had voted with George

Bush less than 40 percent of the time, marking himself as a dangerous wild card whom Duberstein's team would need to woo assiduously. The White House knew that the ardently pro-choice Specter was up for reelection in 1992 and was counting on strong support from women's groups. If Thomas were to speak out against abortion, Specter would almost certainly have to vote against him, which is why, as John Mackey, the Justice Department handler, later conceded, avoiding the abortion issue was a calculated decision. . . .

While the conservatism of Thomas was one concern, his lack of depth in constitutional law was another. . . . "With Thomas you had to make sure he substantively came through the hearings," explained a top White House aide. "Thomas hadn't been practicing law, he hadn't been dealing with the law as a judge for very long. All of a sudden the entire Constitution is fair game." Mike Luttig, a young attorney in the Justice Department, was charged with cramming Thomas on the law in a scant few weeks, conducting, in essence, a hectic one-man bar review course.

Luttig's participation was highly unusual and, to some Democratic aides on the Judiciary Committee, ethically offensive. About the same time Thomas was nominated by President Bush, Luttig was appointed to fill a vacancy on the prestigious 4th Circuit Court of Appeals in Virginia. Although he had not yet taken his judicial oath and so technically was still a Justice Department aide, it was virtually unprecedented for a confirmed judicial nominee to work on so blatantly political a matter as the Thomas confirmation. Nevertheless, Luttig was deemed indispensable by the White House. A former clerk for [Justices] Scalia and Burger, he had one of the sharpest legal minds in the administration. . . .

While Luttig conducted his tutorials, it fell to Duberstein to arrange for the "murder boards," the mock trials at which, in a close approximation to the Judiciary Committee's proceedings, Thomas would be grilled on his every speech and ruling. In secret, once before Labor Day and then throughout the week before the September 10 hearings, a select group gathered for these show sessions in Room 180 of the Old Executive Office Building, the ornate former War Department across from the White House. Duberstein chose A. B. Culvahouse, a lawyer who had served as White House counsel

to Reagan, to question the nominee. Boyden Gray was on hand to do a hilarious imitation of Ted Kennedy; [William, editor of the *Weekly Standard*] Kristol and Danforth attended as well.

Thomas also received the help of two Democrats, who agreed to participate in the mock trials as long as they were never publicly identified. Together, they could warn Thomas about what to expect in the way of tough questioning. . . .

The trickiest question clearly was how to duck the issue of abortion. Duberstein hoped that Thomas might finesse this and other issues by personalizing them. He needed to come across as a human being, not a rigid ideologue. During the murder boards, Duberstein thus arranged for one of the questioners to ask Thomas about his sister's abortion. (An article in *USA Today* had briefly mentioned Emma Mae's therapeutic abortion, but no other reporters had picked up on it.) When the question came, Thomas appeared surprised but neither rigid nor judgmental. But evidently it was decided that his apparent acceptance of Emma Mae's choice could not be revealed during the hearings without risk of alienating his supporters in the religious right. So although abortion was one of the most important issues before the Court, neither the Senate nor the public would be allowed even a glimpse of Thomas's views.

In the last week of Thomas's preparation, President Bush himself popped in to wish him luck and express support. All eyes turned to the president as he watched the questioning for a few minutes and then warmly shook hands around the room. . . .

. . .[W]hen his confirmation hearings opened, the nominee was well coached—many would later say overcoached. With dozens of IOUs and armies of well-organized supporters both inside and outside the Beltway, Clarence Thomas now stood ready to face the final hurdle before his life's dream.

In contrast, the Democrats went into the hearings with only the most tenuous of strategies. Overseeing them was the Senate Judiciary Committee's chairman, Joseph Biden of Delaware. Young and handsome, Biden exuded the boyish, informal charm of a popular high school class president.

The chairman had spent much of the long, hot summer in moot court preparations of his own.

After taking turns questioning and playing Thomas in trial runs, he and his aides had concluded that the only matters about which they could afford to question him sharply were his possibly extremist views on abortion and such arcane legal issues as natural law. But if the latter was an acceptable (if tedious) subject, Biden, a pro-choice Catholic from a traditionally anti-abortion state, was not anxious to make a huge ruckus over the former.

Biden had ample reason to raise the issue of Thomas's thin legal experience. The American Bar Association had given Thomas the tepid rating of "qualified"—with a minority voting to rate him "unqualified"—the lowest rating the group had given a Supreme Court nominee in modern times. But the chairman made a strategic decision not to go after Thomas on the issue of either his character or his competence. "The people who were working for Biden concluded that Thomas met the threshold in terms of judicial qualifications, so we made a conscious recommendation that it wasn't legitimate to go after him on those," explained Christopher Schroeder, a Duke University law professor who was hired as a consultant to work with Biden. . . .

Indeed, both personal experience and temperament gave Joe Biden little appetite for pursuing such potentially nasty lines of questioning. In December 1972, he had been about to join the Senate as its youngest member when his wife and infant daughter were killed in a car accident, the Christmas tree still in the back of their car. Biden never publicly discussed this awful loss, let alone exploited it for sympathy votes, but it was one reason he was wary of introducing personal or so-called character issues into politics. . . .

More recently, Biden had been a presidential contender, and the experience had made him even more leery of questions of character or competence. In the midst of the Bork confirmation fight in 1987, Biden had been personally—and he felt unfairly—accused of unethical behavior by the press, which ridiculed him for plagiarizing biographical parts of a campaign speech from Neil Kinnock, a British Labour leader. The accelerating scandal—which included a frenzied search by reporters to document his alleged failure to footnote a source adequately in a law school term paper—had forced Biden to drop out of the race. . . . His background as a defense lawyer had already given him a tendency to sympathize with the accused, but after the 1987 blowout his aversion to delving into personal issues was visceral.

There was another reason—discussed privately among Biden and his staff—for soft-pedaling such questions, in Thomas's case in particular. No white senator, a top Biden aide later acknowledged, wanted to risk the racist image that might result if the second African-American Supreme Court nominee in history were made to look unintelligent. . . .

In an interview, Biden himself confirmed that "some concern was expressed by black leaders about 'How smart is this guy?' But there was in fact a concern about whether or not to make the guy look stupid—what would happen if you embarrassed him?"

For the same reason, the Democrats had no stomach for questioning Thomas about affirmative action. It would have been natural to ask how he could oppose programs that had benefited him so much, but the wealthy white members of the Senate were very uncomfortable cross-examining a black man who had been raised in rural Georgia about his racial views. "How could these ultra-liberal white senators be pro-affirmative action in the face of a self-made black man saying 'We don't need these programs'?" asked one Democratic staff member. This racial dynamic, exactly as the White House had hoped, would shield Thomas's EEOC record from scrutiny.

In truth, harsh treatment was not Biden's style under any circumstances. He viewed his powerful chairmanship as a bipartisan role and prided himself on his friendly relations with the Republican committee members. A moderate Democrat, he was legendary on Capitol Hill for his need—some considered it a compulsion—to be liked by anyone and everyone. . . . An overachiever from way back and an eminently decent man, Biden remained more an emotional, kinetic politician than an intellectual one. But popularity and policy were not always compatible, and sometimes his need to win everyone's affection led him into trouble.

In fact, that is precisely what happened on the opening day of Thomas's confirmation hearings. As Biden walked the nominee and his mother, Leola Williams, toward the hearing room, according to Williams, he misled them about his sympathies. At that point, Biden was still publicly neutral toward Thomas, but he gave assurances in words that later made Williams's blood boil. "Judge Thomas," she remembered Biden saying with his trademark, lightning flash of a brilliant smile, "don't worry about a thing. I'm in your court."

Thus it was a confident Clarence Thomas who on Tuesday morning, September 10, strode into the cavernous Caucus Room in the Senate building named for another Georgia native, the strident segregationist of his youth, the late Richard B. Russell. Short, powerful, and so robust that the buttons were straining on his business suit, Thomas was in every way a perfect counterpoint to the aged Republican committee member, South Carolina's Strom Thurmond, with whom he now walked arm in arm. Thurmond, a former segregationist, had lived long enough to see a new day in the South, one in which cooperation with blacks like Thomas was not just desirable but politically essential.

Danforth, along with Virginia Lamp Thomas and the nominee's son from his first marriage, Jamal, sat directly behind the judge. So did both his mother and his sister, Emma Mae. Only his brother, Myers, was missing from the proud family tableau.

The mood among Thomas's supporters was upbeat. Going into the hearings, Danforth exulted that Thomas already "had it won." Indeed, Duberstein's insistence that the nominee visit more than sixty of Danforth's colleagues had paid off handsomely. Duberstein and Danforth thought Thomas had secured at least sixty votes, including all the Republicans except the notoriously independent and liberal Robert Packwood. Especially important was the indication that, barring disaster, Thomas could count on the support of all six Republicans on the Judiciary Committee, including Specter.

The White House had high hopes of capturing several Democratic votes on the committee as well. While Biden's intentions were hard to decipher, the White House and Danforth thought they had a good chance of winning over two other Democrats, Arizona's Dennis DeConcini and Alabama's Howell Heflin.

Despite his earlier vow to Bolick that he would come on strong, Thomas began the hearings by sticking firmly to the Pin Point script. "My earliest memories are those of Pin Point, Georgia," he said. Wearing a dark suit, red tie, and his signature large

frame glasses, Thomas spoke movingly of "a life far removed in space and time from this room, this day, this moment." At one point, the nominee had his audience near tears as he told of the days when his mother had earned only $20 a week as a maid and had to send her sons to live with their grandparents. "Imagine, if you will, two little boys with all their belongings in two grocery bags," Thomas implored.

While adhering to the bootstraps mythology that Vernon Jordan [former president of the National Urban League and senior partner at Washington law firm Akin, Gump, Strauss, Hauer & Feld] had warned him to avoid, Thomas also demonstrated that he had taken some of Jordan's advice to heart. Next he intoned the names of the civil rights leaders on whose shoulders he stood. "Justice Marshall, whose seat I've been nominated to fill, is one of those who had the courage and the intellect. He's one of the great architects of the legal battles to open doors that seemed so hopelessly and permanently sealed and to knock down barriers that seemed so insurmountable to those of us in the Pin Point, Georgias, of the world."

It was a persuasive, inspiring start. But as soon as the questions began, Thomas was on rockier ground. Biden launched into a long, windy excursion into Thomas's past statements about natural law, focusing in particular on a speech given to the Pacific Research Institute in 1987. In that talk, according to Biden's question, Thomas had endorsed the ideas of Stephen Macedo, a fairly obscure Straussian writer who was a proponent of natural law. Did the nominee still agree with Macedo? asked Biden. Thomas struggled to find an answer. Macedo hadn't been fodder for the murder boards, but Thomas had been warned to steer clear of natural law.

After saying that it had been a long time since he had read Macedo, Thomas fully retreated from his past embrace of natural law theory, saying, "I don't see a role for natural law in constitutional adjudication." He added that he had only been interested in the subject as an academic exercise. He also backed away from the infamous Heritage Foundation speech in which he had praised Lewis Lehrman's treatise against abortion, maintaining that he had only been praising Lehrman's ideas—which were grounded in natural law—as a polite gesture because he was speaking in the auditorium named for the New York conservative, who was also one of the foundation's early benefactors. Thomas also steadfastly refused Biden's invitation to state his position on abortion, going only so far as to endorse a constitutionally protected right to privacy.

By the time Biden banged his gavel for a break, to most observers Thomas looked wooden, unresponsive, and insincere. Some of his old friends, such as his elementary school and college classmate Lester Johnson, were astonished at the transformation in him. "He's so different from the Clarence Thomas who America saw," Johnson later said. "The real Clarence would have told it like it is. He would have laid it out. He's always been an opinionated bastard, always. That epitomizes him." But, Johnson noted, Thomas had told him about ten days before the hearings that he was going to "be out of pocket with this guy Duberstein. He was uncomfortable with it, but I think he and the White House concluded that America would not have liked the real Clarence, so they had to change his image."

It was a wobbly performance, but Thomas's supporters made a valiant stab at "spinning" public opinion in their favor. Duberstein and Danforth had carefully arranged with Biden's staff to be given a signal when the chairman was about to call for a break. That gave Thomas's partisans a chance to get in position for the television cameras. "From Bork the lesson learned was that if you sit in the room, you get painted by the spin doctors outside. At every break we used Danforth, or other surrogates, to go to the mikes," Mackey reflected.

The White House and Justice Department had also arranged for a "response research" team, conducting the confirmation like a presidential campaign. At any given time, at least three Justice Department lawyers from Luttig's Office of Legal Counsel were stationed in a room in Danforth's office one floor below, watching the hearings and matching the questions and answers with the record. In the nearby office of Mississippi's Senator Thad Cochran sat another phalanx of administration officials and political hands—the EEOC's Ricky Silberman; a White House spokeswoman, Judy Smith; the Office of Personnel Management's director and Thomas's friend from the Sullivan Group, Connie Newman; and the right-wing activist Tom Jipping. They were the spin squad, assigned to get views supporting Thomas instantly to the media.

The system worked well. At the first break, Danforth, having been coached by the Justice Department researchers, gave reporters the full text of Thomas's speech on natural law, showing that some lines expressing skepticism about Macedo had been omitted by Biden. One Republican committee member, Orrin Hatch, whose job was to shore up Thomas following hostile Democratic questioning, exploited the issue of the full text when the proceedings resumed. In the opinion of some of Biden's advisers, this surprisingly swift and effective Republican counterattack made the chairman even more wary of cross-examining the nominee.

Despite the intensive effort to manage both the nominee and the response to him, the first day of the hearings went badly. But few thought Thomas's confirmation was really in danger. Even with opposition from the NAACP and other liberal organizations, there was a sense that the Democrats' hearts weren't really in this fight. Kennedy, who had been so devastating to Bork, was silent. Two other liberals, Metzenbaum and Vermont's Patrick [Senator] Leahy, had not made a move.

Even from the more liberal outside interest groups, the opposition to Thomas appeared weak and perfunctory. On many of the ensuing five days of the hearings, the only opponents stalwart enough to remain through the proceedings were Ralph Neas and Joe Rauh, the aging lion of civil rights law. The two white lawyers presented a lonely picture, sitting together outside the hearing room waiting for their own chance to influence the media. Their presence only underscored the absence of leading black civil rights leaders, the men and women who had been so visible and vocal in Bork's fight.

Meanwhile, as the hearings wore on, Biden's queries were sometimes so long and convoluted that Thomas would forget what the question was. Biden had considered the Bork hearings his finest hour, a high-minded discourse that had engaged the country. Bork was defeated fairly, in Biden's view, because of his legal opinions. This time Biden's questioning seemed occasionally to be a vehicle to show off legal acumen rather than to elicit answers.

And the other Democrats on the committee virtually ignored Thomas's speeches and writings on affirmative action. Ironically, only Specter questioned the judge about his controversial views on civil rights, and the inquiries were gentle. Metzenbaum, the one Democrat who dared to tangle with Thomas, failed to get far. Many thought the senator looked petulant and mean-spirited as he badgered the nominee with question after question about abortion. Thomas ducked them all.

Finally Leahy, a skilled former prosecutor, did come close to prying some information out of Thomas. Leahy pointed out that the *Roe* decision, handed down when Thomas was in law school, had been the most fiercely debated decision of the year. Surely, Leahy insisted, it must have been widely discussed at Yale and Thomas must have participated in some of those discussions. The response seemed a blatant obfuscation. Thomas said that he did not recall ever discussing the case and that he hadn't had much time to debate cases because he was married with a child during law school and was busy working to earn his tuition. Leahy retorted that he too had been married and working during law school, but that these responsibilities had not impaired his legal curiosity and availability to discuss important Supreme Court rulings. He pressed again with his question. This time Thomas responded that he had never "debated" the *Roe* decision or publicly discussed his own position on the case. Leahy, the committee, and the public were all incredulous.

The only person who raised what many thought should have been the most salient issue of the hearings—Thomas's lack of qualifications—was a Washington lawyer who was nearly ninety years old. Erwin Griswold, a distinguished former dean of Harvard Law School and a former solicitor general who had argued many cases before the Supreme Court, bluntly told the committee that Thomas had "not yet demonstrated any clear intellectual or professional distinctions." But no one else dared speak out, although Thomas's limited experience and shaky grasp of the law had been apparent to virtually all the people in the room, including many supporters.

Even the White House team was aghast at Thomas's weak performance. "I thought [Thomas] was terrible, wooden," one of the moot court coaches conceded later. But they publicly blamed Duberstein, not the nominee. "He was so overcoached . . . that he didn't show he was a bright and interesting person. We overdid it," one partisan said.

The result was a disservice not only to Thomas but to the entire process. As an aide to Biden with extensive experience in previous confirmation battles put it later, "At the end of Souter, you knew a little more about his philosophy than before it started. But with Thomas, at the end you knew less. It showed that the process had been reduced to a game."

Nevertheless, Thomas's dull and unenlightening performance was followed by an orchestrated stampede of support. The votes that the White House had worked all summer to secure were now ready to be counted. The Pin Point strategy may have been cynical, but it seemed about to pay off.

Thomas himself wryly reflected on the change in his tactics. Rather than "really taking on the opposition," as he had promised Bolick, he told another friend that his credo had become, "Don't get mad. Don't get even. Get confirmed."

4.7   # Statements by Senators Orrin Hatch and Patrick Leahy, Judicial Confirmation Hearings
Senate Judiciary Committee (June 1999–June 2003)

Statement of Senator Patrick Leahy, June 16, 1999

This afternoon the Judiciary Committee holds its first confirmation hearing for judicial nominees this year. I have looked forward to this hearing for some time, as have the outstanding group of nominees who are with us today, their families and those awaiting justice in the States served by the courts to which they have been nominated.

In spite of our efforts last year in the aftermath of strong criticism from the Chief Justice of the United States, the vacancies facing the federal judiciary are, again, topping 70 and the vacancies gap is, again, moving in the wrong direction. We have more federal judicial vacancies extending longer and affecting more people. . . .

The country in now faced with 72 current vacancies. It is now past the middle of June. There are less than 15 weeks left in session this year for the Senate for hearings, Committee consideration and Senate consideration, debate and votes on these nominees and those that continue to be received. Up until this week we have received 42 judicial nominations that are currently pending.

By June 18 last year, the Committee had held seven judicial confirmation hearings and the Senate had confirmed 29 judges. By June 18 in 1991 (President Bush's third year with a Democratic Senate), the Committee had held five hearings and the Senate had confirmed 14 judges. By June 18 in 1987 (President Reagan's third year in his second term with a Democratic Senate), the Committee had held seven hearings and the Senate had confirmed 13 judges. The Committee hearing schedule is behind even the pace of 1996, when the Senate confirmed a record low 17 judges all year and no judges to the Courts of Appeals.

The Committee has found occasion to hold 36 hearings and another 10 business meetings so far this year, for a total of over 45 proceedings. In spite of the fact that the President has been sending us judicial nominations since January 26, this is, regrettably, our first confirmation hearing. . . .

When the President and the Chief Justice spoke out, the Senate briefly got about its business of considering judicial nominations last year. Unfortunately, some have returned to the stalling tactics of 1996 and 1997 and judicial vacancies are again growing in both number and duration. . . . The Senate is not voting on nominees. The Senate is not defeating judicial nominations in up or down votes on their qualifications but refusing to consider them and killing them through inaction.

The Senate is back to a pace of confirming fewer than one judge a month. That is not acceptable, does not serve the interests of justice and does not fulfil our constitutional responsibilities. . . .

During Republican control of the Senate, it has taken two-year periods for the Senate to match the one-year total of 101 judges confirmed in 1994, when we were on course to end the vacancies gap.

What progress we started making last year has been lost and the Senate is again failing even to keep up with normal attrition. Far from closing the vacancies gap, the number of current vacancies has grown from 50, when Congress recessed last year, to 72. Since some like to speak in terms of percentage, I should note that is an increase of over 40 percent in the last eight months. Judicial vacancies now stands at over 8.4 percent of the federal judiciary (72/843). If one considers the 69 additional judges recommended by the judicial conference, the vacancies rate would be over 15.3 percent.

Progress in the reduction of judicial vacancies was reversed in 1996, when Congress adjourned leaving 64 vacancies, and in 1997, when Congress adjourned leaving 80 vacancies and a 9.5 percent rate. No one was happier than I that the Senate was able to make some headway last year toward reducing the vacancies in 1998. I have praised Senator Hatch for his effort. Unfortunately, the vacancies are now growing, again, back up to 72 vacancies and over an 8.4 percent vacancy rate.

Nominees like Marsha Berzon, Justice Ronnie L. White, Judge Richard Paez, and Timothy Dyk deserve to be treated with dignity and dispatch—not delayed for two and three years. We are seeing outstanding nominees nitpicked and delayed to the point that good women and men are being deterred from seeking to serve as federal judges. . . . [B]y all objective accounts and studies, the judges that President Clinton has appointed have been a moderate group, rendering moderate decisions, and certainly including far fewer ideologues than were nominated during the Reagan Administration. . . .

Statement of Senator Orrin G. Hatch, June 16, 1999

Today, we are holding a judicial nominations hearing for 8 nominees: 2 circuit court nominees and 6 district court nominees. This hearing follows the Committee's approval of 2 judges earlier this year. I note that this hearing is approximately 3 months earlier in the year than the first hearing for circuit and district court nominees in 1993, when I was in the minority on this Committee. Also, I note that there was only 1 hearing for circuit and district court nominees in 1993. It is my expectation that the work of the Committee will continue at a reasonable pace throughout this year. . . .

Together, Senator Leahy and I have ensured that the President's nominees receive a fair hearing and the federal courts are adequately staffed to perform their constitutional function. This Committee has been instrumental in the Senate's confirmation of 306 judicial nominees and over 200 other nominees by President Clinton. By conducting thorough but expeditious reviews of nominees and by holding hearings, we should be able to keep the number of vacancies from inhibiting the work of the federal courts and other bodies. I am confident that by the end of the Session, the Committee will have done a fair and even-handed job of evaluating and approving judicial nominees—just as it has done in previous years. And I look forward to working with my colleagues on the Committee to accomplish this.

Statement of Senator Patrick Leahy, September 14, 1999

The Senate has before it ready for action the nominations of Judge Richard Paez, Raymond Fisher and Marsha Berzon to the Ninth Circuit, Justice Ronnie L. White to the District Court in Missouri, and other qualified nominees. For Judge Paez and Justice White, this is their second extended hold on the Senate calender, having been favorably reported by the Committee both last year and earlier this year. . . .

It is September 14 and this is only the Committee's fourth hearing for judicial nominations all year. To put that in perspective, this week the Congress will hold three hearings on the President's recent use of his clemency power. We have only six weeks in which the Senate is scheduled to be in session for the rest of the year. The Chairman has indicated that this is likely to be the third-to-last hearing all year.

By this time last year the Committee had held 10 confirmation hearings for judicial nominees, and 39 judges had been confirmed. By comparison, this year there have been only four hearings and only 17 judges have been confirmed. Thus, the Senate is operating this year at less than half the productivity of last year. We remain miles behind our pace in 1994, when by this time we had held 19 hearings and the Senate had confirmed 63 judges. . . .

I deeply regret that there remain scores of judicial nominees who have yet to be accorded that opportunity. For the last several years I have been urging the Judiciary Committee and the Senate to proceed to consider and confirm judicial nominees more promptly and without the months of delay that now accompany so many nominations. . . .

Statement of Senator Patrick Leahy, February 22, 2000

This afternoon the Judiciary Committee holds its first confirmation hearing for judicial nominees this year and the first confirmation hearing this century. I have looked forward to this hearing for some time. . . .

In spite of our efforts in 1998 in the aftermath of strong criticism from the Chief Justice of the United States, the vacancies facing the federal judiciary are, again, topping 75 and the vacancies gap is, again, moving in the wrong direction. We have more federal judicial vacancies extending longer and affecting more people.

As the Chairman has [noted] in his comments on the constitutional responsibility of this Committee and the Senate to act upon judicial nominations sent to us by the President, our "primary interest must be what is best for the country and the Judicial Branch." Chairman Hatch has noted that "we cannot afford to lose sight of the fact that for each nominations statistic, there is a man or woman whose career has been placed on hold and whose reputation may suffer unwarranted and unintended detriment if we do not perform our duty." I have often said that if this were up to Senator Hatch and me to work out, we could make a good deal of progress very quickly. . . .

The Senate is back to a pace of confirming one judge a month. That is not acceptable, does not serve the interests of justice and does not fulfill our constitutional responsibilities. For the last several years I have been urging the Judiciary Committee and the Senate to proceed to consider and confirm judicial nominees more promptly and without the months of delay that now accompany so many nominations. . . .

During Republican control of the Senate, it has taken more than four years to get to a Senate vote on the nomination of Judge Richard Paez to the Ninth Circuit. It took almost a year and one-half to finally get a vote on the nomination of Judge Sonia Sotomayor to the Second Circuit, a nominee reportedly held up because some feared that she might be nominated to the Supreme Court. . . .

What progress we started making in 1998 has been lost, and the Senate is again failing even to keep up with normal attrition. Far from closing the vacancies gap, the number of current vacancies has grown by more than 50 percent from when Congress recessed in 1998.

I have challenged the Senate to regain the pace it met in 1998 when the Committee held 13 hearings and the Senate confirmed 65 judges. That would still be one fewer than the number of judges confirmed by a Democratic Senate majority in the last year of the Bush administration in 1992. In fact, in the last two years of the Bush administration, a Democratic Senate majority with a Republican President confirmed 124 judges. We now have a Democratic President with a Republican-controlled Senate, and it would take 90 confirmations this year for the Senate to equal that total. . . .

There is a myth that judges are not traditionally confirmed in Presidential election years. That is not true. Recall that 64 judges were confirmed in 1980, 44 in 1984, 42 in 1988 when a Democratic majority in the Senate confirmed 42 Reagan nominees, and 66 in 1992 when a Democratic majority in the Senate confirmed 66 Bush nominees. The 17 confirmations in 1996 were an anomaly that should not be repeated. That has led to years of slower and lower confirmations and heavy backlogs in many federal courts. . . .

Statement of Senator Patrick Leahy, June 15, 2000

I am glad to see the Committee holding a hearing for judicial nominees today. The Committee has reported only 19 nominees and held what amount to four previous hearings all year on judicial nominations. There is growing frustration around the country with this partisan stall. So far this year there have been 99 judicial vacancies and the Senate has acted to fill only 23 of them.

Governor Bush of Texas recently noted:

The Constitution empowers the president to nominate officers of the United States, with the advice and consent of the Senate. That is clearcut, straightforward language. It does not empower anyone to turn the process into a protracted ordeal of unreasonable delay and unrelenting investigation. Yet somewhere along the way, that is what Senate confirmations became—lengthy, partisan, and unpleasant. That has done enough harm, injured too many good people, and it must not happen again.

He proposed that presidential nominations be acted upon by the Senate within 60 days. Of the 42 judicial nominations currently pending, 26 have already been pending for more than 60 days without Senate action. Already this Congress 78 nominees, including 52 eventually confirmed, have had to wait longer than 60 days for Senate action. I urge the Senate to do better. . . .

Opening Statement of Senator Patrick Leahy, August 27, 2001

Today, during the Senate's August recess, the Judiciary Committee is holding another hearing regarding people the President has indicated he intends to nominate to be federal judges next month. The only precedent for this hearing of which I am aware is the hearing I convened last Wednesday. A judicial confirmation hearing during the August recess is otherwise, as far as I am aware or can recall, unprecedented. This is another indication that I am attempting to go the extra mile to help fill the vacancies on the federal courts with qualified, consensus nominees.

This is the second hearing involving judicial nominations we have held during this recess and the fourth hearing involving judicial nominations since the Senate reorganized and the Judiciary Committee's membership was set on July 10, barely seven weeks ago. I regret that no Republican Senators were available to participate at the hearing last week. I welcome the participation of Senator DeWine, the Ranking Republican on the Antitrust Subcommittee and its former Chairman, who I understand will be serving as the Republican representative at this hearing today.

I am sorry that Senator Hatch is not with us today. This hearing was scheduled for this day after extensive consultation with his staff in which they indicated this was a day that he would be able to attend. Apparently, circumstances changed. . . .

I commented last week that for those of us trying to restore dignity and regularity to the nomination and confirmation, the bumps in the road created by the other side are especially frustrating. For example, President Bush's decision to delay the American Bar Association's evaluation of a judicial nominee's qualifications until the nomination is made public, has forced delays in the rest of the process, as well. As a result of this Administration's break with the 50-year-old precedent established under President Eisenhower, the confirmation process of even the least controversial and most qualified candidates is necessarily delayed by several weeks. Likewise this Administration's failures early on to consult with Senators from both parties and to seek nominees who would enjoy broad bipartisan support is a source of concern. . . .

This is the seventh hearing I have held since July 11 to consider presidential nominations and the fourth that includes judicial nominations. Our first hearing was noticed within 10 minutes of the adoption of the reorganization resolution and held the day after the Committee membership was set.

When this Committee reports another nominee to a Court of Appeals vacancy, it will have reported as many Court of Appeals nominees since July of this year as this Committee did under Republican control during all of last year. When the Senate next confirms a Court of Appeals nominee, it will have confirmed as many as were confirmed in the entire first year of the Clinton Administration. . . .

Opening Statement of Chairman Patrick Leahy, October 18, 2001

I begin by thanking Senator Schumer, the Chair of the Courts Subcommittee, for also chairing this hearing on judicial nominations. This is an extraordinary time in the Senate. All three Senate office buildings have been closed in the wake of Senate employees testing positive for anthrax. Nonetheless, the Judiciary Committee is seeking to proceed with this hearing today. . . .

Since the Senate was allowed to reorganize and the Committee membership was set, we have maintained a sustained effort to consider judicial and executive nominees. Today, at our Executive Session, the agenda contained the names of another 13 nominees for United States Attorneys, the Assistant Attorney General for the Office of Legal Counsel and four additional District Court nominees from Oklahoma, Kentucky and Nebraska. We have already confirmed since July more Court of Appeals nominees than were confirmed during the first year of the Clinton Administration and, for that matter, more Court of Appeals nominees than were reported by this Committee in all of last year. With two hearings on two candidates to the 5th Circuit this month, I hope that we will soon be able to send that Circuit some help, as well.

At this hearing we consider five more judicial nominees. Along with Judge Pickering, we have before us nominees for District Court vacancies in Alabama, New Mexico, Nevada and another in Oklahoma. Despite the upheaval we have experienced this year with the shifts in the Senate majority and, more importantly, the need to focus our attention on responsible action in the fight against international terrorism, we are ahead of the pace for hearings and confirmations of judges during the first year of the Clinton Administration and during the first year of the first Bush Administration.

The recent vicious attacks on our people have given all of us a heightened awareness of the critical importance of our civil liberties, of the many possible threats to those freedoms, and of the necessity of responding to the challenge of international terrorism without sacrificing what is best about America. This is serious and important work and our federal judges will be a key component in guarding our freedoms. Our system of checks and balances requires that the judicial branch review the acts of the political branches. I will want to be confident that the nominees before us today will take this responsibility seriously and will rely on their experience and on our rich history of judicial precedent to make wise decisions in the challenging times ahead. . . .

Statement of Senator Orrin Hatch, January 29, 2003

I am pleased to welcome you all to the Committee's first judicial confirmation hearing of the 108th Congress. I first would like to acknowledge and thank Sen. Leahy for his service as Chairman of the Committee over the past 16 months. . . .

Our first panel features three outstanding circuit nominees who were nominated on May 9, 2001, whose hearing was originally noticed for May 23, 2001. I agreed to postpone that hearing for one week at the request of some of my Democratic colleagues who claimed to need the additional week to assess the nominees' qualifications. As we all know, control of the Senate and the Committee shifted to the Democrats shortly thereafter, on June 5, 2001, and these nominees have been languishing in Committee without a hearing ever since. So I am particularly pleased to pick up where we left off in May 2001 by holding our first confirmation hearing for the same three nominees we noticed back then, Justice Deborah Cook, Jeffery Sutton, and John Roberts. It is with great pleasure that I welcome these distinguished guests before the Committee this morning. . . .

Our first nominee is Ohio Supreme Court Justice Deborah Cook, who has established a distinguished record as both a litigator and a jurist. . . . I am proud to have her before us as a nominee who knows first hand the difficulties and challenges that professional women face in breaking the glass ceiling. . . .

. . . She . . . brings to the federal bench more than ten years of appellate judicial experience, which was built on a foundation of fifteen years of solid and diverse litigation experience. There can be little doubt that she is eminently qualified to be a Sixth Circuit jurist, and I commend President Bush on his selection of her for this post.

Our next nominee is Jeff Sutton, one of the most respected appellate advocates in the country today. He has argued over 45 appeals for a diversity of clients in federal and state courts across the country, including a remarkable number, 12 to be exact, before the U.S. Supreme Court. . . .

I feel it necessary for me to comment briefly on some of the recent criticisms we have heard. Of course, to no one familiar with the nominations process's surprise, our usual gang of fringe Washington leftist lobbyists are opposing Republican nominees. Well, their opposition of Jeff Sutton is for all the wrong reasons. But, as people who know me well will attest, I have always been willing to acknowledge a fair point made by the opposition. So in keeping with that principle, I want everyone to know that I found something commendable in

the so-called report published by one of these groups about Jeff Sutton. That report conceded that, "No one has seriously contended that Sutton is personally biased against people with disabilities." That is a very important point—and should be obvious since Jeff Sutton has a well-known record of fighting for the legal rights of disabled people. And he was raised in an environment of concern for the disabled; his father ran a school for people affected by cerebral palsy.

Since the opposition to Jeff Sutton is not personal, then what is it? It seems to come down to a public policy disagreement about some Supreme Court decisions relating to the limits to federal power when Congress seeks to regulate state governments. Those cases include *City of Boerne, Kimel,* and *Garrett,* among others. But in those cases, it was Jeff's job, as the chief appellate lawyer for the State of Ohio, and as a lawyer, to defend his clients' legal interests. As the American Bar Association ethics rules make clear, "[a] lawyer's representation of a client, including representation by appointment, does not constitute an endorsement of the client's political, economic, social or moral views or activities."

Now I don't think anyone on this Committee would actually consider voting against a nominee out of dislike for the nominee's clients. . . .

. . . I think we all agree that anybody involved in a legal dispute has a right to hire a good lawyer—even if that person is guilty of murder. And Jeff's clients are not murderers; they are state governments, defending their legal rights. So let's not beat up on Mr. Sutton just because he worked for the State of Ohio. . . .

. . . I am convinced that Jeff Sutton will be a great judge, and one who understands the proper role of a judge.

Our final circuit nominee today is Mr. John Roberts, who has been nominated for a seat on the D.C. Circuit Court of Appeals. He is widely considered to be one of the premiere appellate litigators of his generation. Most lawyers are held in high esteem if they have had the privilege of arguing one case before the U.S. Supreme Court. Mr. Roberts has argued an astounding 39 cases before the Supreme Court. It is truly an honor to have such an accomplished litigator before this Committee.

The high esteem in which Mr. Roberts is held is reflected in a letter the Committee recently received urging his confirmation. This letter, which I will submit for the record, was signed by more than 150 members of the D.C. Bar, including such well-respected attorneys as Lloyd Cutler, who was White House Counsel to both Presidents Carter and Clinton; Boyden Gray, who was White House Counsel to the first President Bush; and Seth Waxman, who was President Clinton's Solicitor General. . . .

I must say that this panel represents the best of the best, and I commend President Bush for seeking out such nominees of the highest caliber.

Statement of Senator Patrick Leahy, March 12, 2003

This week the Judiciary Committee is holding its fourth and fifth hearings this year involving a total of 20 Article III judicial nominees, three nominees to the Court of Federal Claims and two nominees to the Sentencing Commission. This is so much faster and more extensive than in prior years in which the Republican majority was last in charge, it makes one's head spin. . . . In all of 1996 and in all of 2000, the Republican majority did not hold hearings on as many as six circuit nominees. In 1997 and 1999, Republicans did not hold a hearing for as many as six circuit nominees until September and, in 1995, this mark was not reached until June. Never in any of their most recent six and one-half years in the majority did Republicans hold hearings for as many as six circuit court nominees by March, never. In addition, it was not until the fall of 1997 that Republicans proceeded with hearings [for] as many as 20 Article III judicial nominees of President Clinton and in the three other years in which they were in the majority during the Clinton Administration, they took until the summer to reach that benchmark. The current pace makes the editorial cartoons about assembly line rubber-stamping of lifetime appointments to the federal bench all too accurate. The Senate Judiciary Committee review and hearing process has been changed overnight by the Republican majority as have so many aspects of the confirmation process. Their double standards are showing in the way they approach hearings, Committee debates and floor action on judicial nominees.

We all know that we work better when we work together in a bipartisan manner; when we honor traditions and rules that respect both sides of the aisle; when there is give and take; when there is advising, as well as consenting. I am sorry that the Bush Administration is so resistant to those traditions, those processes and bipartisanship. I believe that we need to uphold the advice prong of our advise and consent responsibilities by involving home-state Senators, this Committee and the Senate. I continue to hear from home-state Senators that they receive little more than notification from this Administration and that it remains most reluctance to consult about potential nominations. When Democrats were in the majority in the 107th Congress, we took many steps in good faith to repair damage done to the confirmation process through the intransigence shown to President Clinton's nominees by a Republican Senate. We confirmed 100 of President Bush's judicial nominees in that time—including to circuits for which Republicans had repeatedly refused to act on Clinton nominees. The Democratic Senate acted far faster and more fairly than the Republican-led Senate had with Clinton nominees. . . .

Statement of Senator Orrin Hatch, March 13, 2003

Welcome to this hearing on the nomination of Justice Priscilla Owen of Texas to the US Court of Appeals for the Fifth Circuit. Justice Owen, we want to welcome you again to the Committee. A lot of people have been looking forward to this Committee's reconsideration of this nomination. . . .

I called this hearing because I believe Justice Owen's treatment in this Committee last September was unfair, unfounded, and frankly a disgrace to the Senate. As several of the Members who voted against her admitted, Justice Owen is a tremendously intelligent, talented and well-credentialed nominee. She earned the American Bar Association's highest rating, unanimously well qualified—and was the first person with that rating ever voted down in this Committee. She is also an honest, decent, fair, principled and compassionate human being and jurist whose service on the Fifth Circuit would be a great benefit to that court and our country. She should have been confirmed last year, and she should be confirmed this year.

I have made these views clear several times, so it should come as no surprise that, after the American voters returned the Senate to the Republicans, and therefore the Chairmanship of this Committee to me, that this Committee will now begin setting straight the mistake it made by halting this nomination in Committee last fall. . . .

Let me be clear about one other thing: I personally do not believe that Justice Owen needs another hearing. Justice Owen gave complete and appropriate answers to all questions. . . .

For the Committee, this hearing is about remedying the wrongful treatment provided to Justice Owen. I don't say this to offend any Member of this Committee—I think they all know that I have deep personal respect for each one of them, and I know they voted according to their best judgment at the time. Nevertheless, as I reviewed the transcript of Justice Owen's last hearing, read her answers to written follow-up questions, and then reviewed the comments made at the markup debate, I was struck at the pervasive way in which Justice Owen's answers were almost totally ignored. The same accusations made by Members at her hearing were repeated at the markup as if Justice Owen's answers did not even exist—as if she was never even before the Committee. . . .

So although we are not beginning anew to review this nomination, and there is no reason simply to rehash old and answered allegations, I nevertheless hope and expect Committee Members—especially those who voted against her—to come to this hearing with a fresh mind, and with a genuine willingness to listen, to consider, and to think again. . . .

Statement of Senator Patrick Leahy, March 13, 2003

Today we meet in an unprecedented session to consider the renomination of Priscilla Owen to the U.S. Court of Appeals to the Fifth Circuit. Never before has a President resubmitted a circuit court nominee already rejected by the Senate Judiciary Committee for the same vacancy. Today, this Committee proceeds to grant Justice Owen a second

hearing having not allowed either Enrique Moreno or Judge Jorge Rangel, both distinguished Texans nominated to the Fifth Circuit, any hearings at all when they were nominated by President Clinton to the same Fifth Circuit vacancy.

This nominee was fairly and thoroughly considered after a hearing only eight months ago, in an extended session chaired so ably and fairly by Senator Feinstein. Justice Owen's earlier nomination was fairly and thoroughly debated in an extended business meeting of the Committee, during which every Senator serving on this Committee had the opportunity to discuss his or her views of the nominee's fitness for the bench. That meeting and that debate was delayed for some time at the request of the Administration and our Republican colleagues. Unlike the scores of Clinton nominations on which Republicans were not willing to hold a hearing or Committee vote or explain why they were being opposed, Justice Owen's earlier nomination was treated fairly in a process that resulted in a Committee vote in accordance with Committee rules that resulted in that nomination's defeat last year. . . .

For Justice Priscilla Owen, a nominee who was afforded every possible courtesy and granted full process, there will be a second hearing. I emphasize the various procedural steps followed by the Committee on Justice Owen's nomination in the Democratic-led 107th Senate to contrast them with the treatment of President Clinton's nominees to this very seat during the previous period of Republican control of the Senate. During that time, two very talented, very deserving nominees were shabbily treated by the Senate. Judge Jorge Rangel, a distinguished Hispanic attorney from Corpus Christi, was the first to be nominated to fill that vacancy. Despite his qualifications, and his rating of Well Qualified by the ABA, Judge Rangel never received a confirmation hearing from the Committee, and his nomination was returned to the President without Senate action at the end of 1998, after a fruitless wait of 15 months.

Frustrated with the lack of action on his nomination, Judge Rangel asked that his name be withdrawn from consideration, and on September 16, 1999, President Clinton nominated Enrique Moreno, another outstanding Hispanic attorney, a Harvard graduate, and a recipient of a unanimous rating of Well Qualified by the ABA, to fill that same vacancy. Mr. Moreno did not receive a hearing on his nomination from a Republican-controlled Senate during its pendency of more than 17 months. President Bush withdrew the nomination of Enrique Moreno and later substituted Justice Owen's name in its place.

. . . Thus, Justice Owen is the third nominee to the vacancy created when Judge William Garwood took senior status so many years ago, but the only one who has been allowed a confirmation hearing. . . .

In examining Justice Owen's record in preparation for her first hearing and, now again, in preparation for today, I remain convinced that her record shows that in case after case involving a variety of legal issues, she is a judicial activist, willing to make law from the bench rather than follow the language and intent of the legislature. Her record of activism shows she is willing to adapt the law to her results-oriented ideological agenda. . . .

I hope that this hearing is not a setting for some to read talking points off the Department of Justice website or argue that there is some grand conspiracy to block all of President Bush's judicial nominees. The consensus nominees are considered expeditiously and confirmed with near unanimity. The nominees selected to impose a narrow ideology on the federal courts remain controversial and some are being opposed. Were the Administration and the Republican leadership to observe our traditional practices and protocols and not break our rules and seek every advantage from the obstruction of Clinton nominees to circuit courts over the last several years, we would be making more progress.

Facts are stubborn and do not change. Written opinions and prior testimony under oath are difficult to overcome. This nomination was examined very carefully a few months ago and rejected by this Committee. To force it through the Committee now based only on the shift in the majority would not establish that the Committee reached the wrong determination last year, but that the process has been taken over by partisanship this year. . . .

Despite the mistreatment of President Clinton's judicial nominees, the Democratic-led Senate of the 107th Congress showed good faith in fairly and promptly acting to confirm 100 of President Bush's judicial nominees. The Senate is now contending over several of President Bush's controversial nominations. This process starts with the President. The President can generate contention in this process,

or he can end it. The President has said he wants to be a uniter and not a divider, yet he has sent this nomination to the Senate, which divides the Senate, which divides the American people, and which even divides Texans. To compound the divisiveness, he has taken the unprecedented step of resubmitting this nomination after it was turned down by this committee.

The President also has said he does not want what he calls "activist" judges. Justice Owen, by the President's own definition, is an activist judge whose record shows her to be out of the mainstream even on the conservative Texas Supreme Court.

In my opening statement at Justice Owen's original hearing last July, I said that the question each Senator on this Committee would be asking himself or herself as we proceeded was whether this judicial nominee met the standards we require for any lifetime appointment to the federal courts. I believe that question has been asked and answered.

Statement of Senator Orrin Hatch, April 1, 2003

It is my pleasure to welcome before the Committee this morning three exceptional nominees for the federal bench.

Our circuit nominee is Carolyn Kuhl, who has been nominated to fill a judicial emergency on the Ninth Circuit, which is the most notoriously liberal federal court in the United States. This is the court that gave us the infamous *Pledge of Allegiance* case, which held that the Pledge of Allegiance is unconstitutional because it contains the word "God.". . .

Unfortunately, the *Pledge of Allegiance* case is not an anomaly. Just last month, the Ninth Circuit decided to ignore and distort controlling Supreme Court precedent in order to skew the playing field in favor of criminal defendants. The court concluded that a key law prohibiting child pornography was unconstitutional as applied to certain criminal defendants. . . .

The Ninth Circuit has also held in recent years that California's so-called three strikes law, which imposes life sentences on career criminals, was unconstitutional. It held that a prisoner who was convicted of making terroristic threats had a right to procreate through artificial insemination. . . . Yet another gem from the Ninth Circuit held that prisoners have a constitutional right to pornography, which had been banned because inmates had used it to harass women guards. Fortunately, saner heads prevailed, and this case was reversed en banc.

Plenty of Ninth Circuit decisions, however, are not corrected en banc, which has led to the Ninth Circuit holding the dubious distinction of having the highest and widest Supreme Court reversal rate in the country among the federal courts of appeals. . . .

I have taken the time to recite the state of affairs on the Ninth Circuit because I think that it will benefit from the confirmation of such an esteemed and experienced jurist as Carolyn Kuhl, whose record demonstrates her commitment to following precedent and steering clear of judicial activism. At the same time, I want to make clear that I, for one, do not believe that the ideological composition of a court should have any determination on whether an otherwise qualified nominee should be confirmed. As I have said before on numerous occasions, I do not believe that ideology has any role, constitutional or otherwise, in the advice and consent process. . . .

Unfortunately, no judicial nominee these days seems to escape criticism by the left-wing special interest groups. Judge Kuhl is no exception. I expect that we will hear attacks on her record as an attorney for the Justice Department during the Reagan Administration, when she was doing her duty to represent the position of the United States. We will probably hear attacks on her record in private practice stemming from the types of clients she represented and the positions she took on their behalf. And I expect that we will hear some unfounded criticism of decisions she has made as a California state court judge.

These types of attacks on President Bush's judicial nominees have become so commonplace, and often bear so little relationship to the nominees' actual records, that they bring to mind the children's story of the boy who cried wolf. After two years of smear campaigns, with each consecutive nominee being declared more anti-this and pro-that than the former, these groups have simply lost credibility, especially when you consider their poor track record in predicting what kind of judges nominees will turn out to be. . . .

Statement of Senator Patrick Leahy, April 1, 2003

Today we meet to consider the nomination of California Judge Carolyn Kuhl to the United States Court of Appeals for the Ninth Circuit, Florida Judge Cecilia Altonaga to the United States District Court for the Southern District of Florida, and Louisiana Judge Patricia Minaldi to the United States District Court for the Eastern District of Louisiana.

The District Court nominees have the support of their home-state Senators, although, as I will discuss in a moment, Senators Graham and Nelson have had a most difficult time getting the White House to agree to continue the tradition of the Florida bipartisan selection commission, and have only recently come to a meeting of the minds with the White House.

The Circuit Court nominee before us today, Judge Carolyn Kuhl, however, is not supported by both of her home-state Senators.

Her appearance before this Committee, despite that clearly stated opposition, is the latest in a string of transparently partisan actions taken by the Senate's new majority since the beginning of this Congress. In each of these actions—each of them unprecedented—Republicans have done something they never did while in the majority from 1995 to 2001. Each provocative step, taken in tandem with the White House, has broken new ground in politicizing the federal judiciary.

The Republican majority has shown a corrosive and raw-edged willingness to change, bend and even break the rules that they themselves followed before when the judicial nominees involved were a Democratic president's choices, instead of a Republican president's choices. Lest some observers wrongly conclude that this sudden and orchestrated series of rules changes is just "politics as usual," it most certainly is not. . . .

Statement of Senator Orrin Hatch, June 11, 2003

I am pleased to welcome to the Judiciary Committee this morning the Attorney General of Alabama, William Pryor, whom President Bush has nominated to fill a judicial emergency on the United States Court of Appeals for the Eleventh Circuit. . . .

During the course of this hearing, we will hear many things about Bill Pryor. We will hear many one-sided half-truths perpetuated by the usual liberal interest groups who will stop at nothing to defeat President Bush's judicial nominees. I want to make sure that this hearing is about fairness, and about telling the full story of Bill Pryor's record.

We will hear that General Pryor is [a] devout pro life Catholic who has criticized *Roe v. Wade,* but the rest of the story is that many prominent Democrats, such as Justice Ruth Bader Ginsburg and former Stanford Dean John Hart Ely, have also criticized *Roe* without anyone questioning their recognition of it as binding Supreme Court precedent.

We will hear claims that General Pryor is against the disabled and elderly, but the real story is that General Pryor has done his duty as Attorney General to defend his state's budget from costly lawsuits. . . .

We will hear claims that General Pryor's criticisms of Section 5 of the Voting Rights Act indicate a lack of commitment to civil rights. But the real story is that General Pryor has a solid record of commitment to civil rights, which includes defending majority-minority voting districts, leading the battle to abolish the Alabama Constitution's prohibition on interracial marriage, and working with the Clinton Administration's Justice Department to prosecute the former Ku Klux Klansmen who perpetrated the bombing of Birmingham's 16th Street Baptist Church, which resulted in the deaths of four little girls in 1963.

We will no doubt hear other claims during the course of this hearing distorting General Pryor's record or presenting only partial truths. I want to urge my colleagues, and everyone here, to listen closely so that the real story is heard. I think those who listen with an open mind may be surprised, and even impressed. I look forward to hearing General Pryor's testimony.

Statement of Senator Patrick Leahy, June 11, 2003

. . . [B]efore I speak about the many positions that Mr. Pryor has taken that raise concerns with regard to his nomination to a federal court, I should make a few observations about procedure. When the possibility was first raised of scheduling Mr. Pryor before his rating from the American Bar Association was received, we raised concerns. While we have all had our disagreements with the ABA's rating of individual judicial nominees, I have long maintained that their evaluations are an important piece of information that should be available early in the process of considering a lifetime appointment to the federal bench.

When Senator Hatch indicated several years ago that he would no longer consider the evaluations of President Clinton's nominees, I differed and continued considering such ratings for what they were worth. When George W. Bush announced that he was removing the ABA Standing Committee from its traditional place in the judicial nominations process, a place it had held for the last 50 years, I objected. I explained then that I thought it was a major mistake because it would chill the candor with which people speak to the ABA about nominees' qualifications and temperament, and because it would give a President little room to back down after finding out one of the nominees it had already announced received a negative rating. Instead of working with the ABA before announcing a nomination publicly, this White House has forced them to do their work in a truncated period of time in a way under restrictive circumstances.

Among the changes made to our process, this year the Committee has scheduled hearings for nominees before any of us knows how the ABA has evaluated them. Today's circuit court nomination is just one example of that sort of mixed-up process which puts the cart before the horse. Mr. Pryor's ABA evaluation was not complete at the time the hearing was noticed last week. It only arrived yesterday afternoon, and he has been determined by some on the ABA's Standing Committee to be "not qualified" to sit on the U.S. Court of Appeals for the 11th Circuit. Now that we have that piece of information, it is not time to rush into a hearing for this nominee. It is time to stop and conduct further investigations, further evaluations, to determine the reason or reasons for the negative rating. . . .

As to the nomination itself, I am concerned about Mr. Pryor's record of ideological rigidity and extremism in a number of areas crucial to the fair administration of justice. I want to know more about his views on the death penalty. I would like to find out more about his views on the so-called "federalist revolution" in which he has been a driving force. I would like to understand how he views discrimination against Americans on the basis of their sexual orientation. I want to know why he disagreed with the Supreme Court of the United States that cuffing a prisoner up to a hitching post in the broiling sun for hours on end was not cruel and unusual punishment. I look forward to learning how he came to believe that the Ameri-

cans With Disabilities Act, the Violence Against Women Act, the Age Discrimination in Employment Act, and even Title VII of the 1964 Civil Rights Act are unconstitutional. Among many other things, I would like to know why someone who has committed his life, both personal and professional, to overturning settled Supreme Court precedent is interested in a job that requires him to uphold it.

I look forward to hearing from Mr. Pryor and to reviewing carefully his answers to the questions of the other Senators. . . .

A Comparative Perspective

4.8 Thoughts on Goldilocks and Judicial Independence (2003)

Frank B. Cross

Introduction

Judicial independence is often treated as if it were an unalloyed good, to be furthered insofar as practically possible. In the traditional telling, an independent judiciary is regarded as if it were the font of justice, the rule of law and individual rights, if not the font of all good things. Such worship of judicial independence is not sustainable, theoretically or empirically. Indeed, the concept of judicial independence potentially flies in the face of our fundamental constitutional concept of checks and balances. While there is no doubt that a measure of judicial independence is a good thing, such independence must be kept in balance with judicial accountability. Increased judicial independence is not always better. . . .

The Concept of Judicial Independence

Understanding the concept of judicial independence requires defining from whom judges are to be independent. While judicial independence is a

From *Ohio State Law Journal* 195 (2003). Reprinted by permission of the author.

dynamic concept that may be defined in different ways, it is generally referred to as a shorthand for the judiciary's independence from the executive and legislative branches of government. The foundation of judicial independence is that "judges *free of congressional and executive control* will be in a position to determine whether the assertion of power against the citizen is consistent with law. . . ." This is the Supreme Court's essential understanding of the phrase. At a minimum, it means that judges cannot be punished physically or economically for the content of the decisions they reach. Consequently, judges need not fear deciding cases on their merits, even when contrary to the interests or desires of the other branches of government. Thus, other branches of government have no power over case outcomes. Judicial independence thereby frees judges to apply the rule of law and do justice in individual cases.

Judicial independence is an instrumental means to an end, not an end in itself. The concept is not attractive because it makes judges happy, but because it protects against other branches forcing unfair judicial outcomes, grounded in self-interest or ideological fervor. Justice Breyer has thus noted that the "question of judicial independence revolves around the theme of how to assure that judges decide according to law, rather than according to their own whims or to the will of the political branches of government." Freed from threats from the other branches, judges may be better able to render dispassionate judgments and apply the law fairly to the facts. They are to be principled decisionmakers impartially deciding cases according to the rule of law. It is against this standard that judicial independence must be measured, and there is no intrinsic guarantee that independence will further the standard.

One potential problem with judicial independence is that judges may have their own self-interests and ideological fervor. An independent, unchecked judiciary may simply decide cases according to its own whims and predilections, rather than according to the rule of law. For example, because of the great independence of the federal life-tenured judiciary, many political scientists believe that they are more ideological in their decisions than elected legislators or executives. Judges may allow corruption and bribery to influence their decisions. They may even be lazy and decide poorly, given the lack of oversight. In these circumstances, the means (independent judiciary) does not advance the end (rule of law). We cannot rely entirely upon judicial self-discipline and restraint to avoid these circumstances.

There is nothing intrinsic in judges that causes them to favor, say, rule-of-law impartiality and the freedoms recognized in the Bill of Rights. Saintliness is not a historic precondition to becoming a judge, nor does the process of doffing judicial robes magically make one saintly. There are surely temptations not to apply the neutral rule of law. . . . In addition to internal political desires, there may even be external pressures to this effect. . . . There is little reason to expect that a wholly independent, unaccountable judiciary would appropriately restrain itself and sincerely seek to apply neutral legal principles to the cases they decide.

If independent judges have more freedom to exercise their own preferences, plus an incentive to do so, we must recognize that those preferences may not involve the protection of individual rights or the rule of law, which is our desired end. The judicial preferences may be arbitrary and antidemocratic. We must worry about checking the judiciary, just as it checks the other branches. These checks, rather than absolute independence, are more likely to enhance the rule of law. Because the federal judiciary need not run for reelection, we must particularly worry about the extent of its independence.

Considering a Truly Independent Judiciary

The Iranian experience offers itself as a case study in true judicial independence. The judicial branch in Iran may be the most independent of any nation. Iran adopted a new constitution in 1979, following the overthrow of the Shah. The constitution provided for separation of powers with an independent judiciary and placed the country's courts within its Ministry of Justice. The High Judicial Council is the highest court, with considerable authority over the law; its members are chosen by the Council of Guardians. Half the members of the Council and the president of the Supreme Court are appointed, not by elected leaders, but by the country's religious leader. Under the constitution, Islamic governance occurs more through the judiciary than through the other branches.

The constitution was revised in 1989, but the independent power of the judiciary was not altered. The Council of Guardians was replaced with the Head of the Judiciary, who is to establish a judicial organization for the implementation of Islamic law. The Head of the Judiciary is appointed for a five year term by the religious Leader of the Islamic Republic but cannot be removed by the executive or legislative branches.

The judiciary in Iran, supervised solely by the Council of Guardians, is charged with ensuring that the nation's law conforms to shari'a—Islamic religious law. The Council of Guardians is an entity like no other in the world, including clerics and representing a true hierocracy. The religious law, as defined and applied by the Council and its subsidiary courts, has the power to trump decisions of the other branches. All laws are reviewed against the standard of fidelity to Islam, and the Council has the authority to strike down laws or executive edicts. The Council also has the authority to supervise elections and disqualify candidates. This gives considerable authority to the judiciary. It is as if, in the West, the common law could override legislation and executive decisions, as well as governing the interpretation of the Constitution. The expansive governmental power of the courts in Iran was combined with formal recognition of their independence from the other branches. In contrast to most other nations, where new judges are appointed by the legislature or executive, the Head of the Judiciary has the power to appoint and promote judges. The Iranian judiciary is not just formally independent, it is functionally as independent as any in the world. . . .

The power and independence of Iranian courts have come under attack recently. Iran's President Khatami has assailed his rivals, especially in the judiciary, as "narrow-minded monopolists and totalitarianists." Ayatollah Ali Khamenei objected to the attack, charging Khatami with "weakening the judiciary." The legislative body even tried to cut the budget for the Council in order to retaliate against its decisions, but failed. The facts present a classic battle between the elected branches, whose will is being frustrated by an unelected judiciary independent of their power. Under the traditional telling, judicial independence must be preserved and the attack on the courts fought back. The Iranian judiciary is "thwarting the democratic will of the people," but this is the fundamental point of having an independent judiciary. The actions of that judiciary, though, require more scrutiny.

President Khatami was reelected with 77% of the vote and is dedicated to expanding democracy, personal freedoms, and civil liberties. Conservatives have used their control of institutions such as the judiciary to wage a counterattack on the President's agenda. . . . The judiciary has readily sacrificed fair judicial processes in the interests of religious conformity. A reformist legislator was jailed for criticizing the courts. In Iran, an independent judicial branch is flexing its powers so as to undermine democracy and personal liberty and has become one of the "main tools of oppression" in the nation.

The questionable actions of the Iranian judiciary cannot be blamed upon the Islamic religion. Like all faiths, Islamic tenets may be interpreted in various ways, and the *Qur'an* did not inevitably compel the decisions of Iranian courts. Rather, the judiciary, freed from accountability to the public or other branches, has seized the power to impose its ideology upon society. While Iranian judges are furthering the cause of the conservative clerics, this apparently is their idea of how best to serve as a judge. In this case, judicial independence seems excessive and unwise. While Iran is by far the most extreme case of excessive judicial independence, it is not alone—the German judiciary has been vigorously criticized for excessive, undemocratic independence.

The Balance of Independence and Accountability

The United States does not have a truly and wholly independent judiciary, which is probably a good thing, as the Iranian experience suggests. Judges in this nation have a large measure of independence but are still constrained. Americans often boast of our judicial independence. Formalistically, the judiciary does have a significant measure of independence. The federal judiciary is life-tenured, and Congress may not reduce its compensation. However, our judicial branch does not have the sort of total independence found in a nation like Iran. In this section, I review the balance of independence and accountability that characterizes the United States judiciary.

Lawyers and legal academics may be somewhat naive about judicial independence, assuming its presence and virtues and rationalizing away evidence to the contrary. Political scientists, by contrast, may be quite cynical about the concept, claiming that judicial independence is no more than a myth. The truth is somewhere in between, as our judiciary has a measure of independence but is not entirely unaccountable to the legislative and executive branches. The relative degree of judicial independence is a descriptive measure that should be settled by accepted tools for finding truth, which may include examples but should focus on more rigorous statistical examination of judicial behavior.

Evidence of Independence

Formalistic guarantees of judicial independence do not demonstrate that the judiciary is in fact independent, though they serve as evidence of this fact. In reality, judges in this nation generally feel free and independent, and able to decide cases as they believe appropriate. Studies of the federal judiciary demonstrate that it has some obvious independence and does not feel too constrained by the political branches of the government. While independence can be difficult to demonstrate directly, empirical evidence can shed light on its existence.

Ideological judging is a sign of independence—if judges were not independent, they would not feel free to exercise their values but would hew to the ideologies of the other branches. Although such political voting by judges may seem contrary to their responsibility and the rule of law, it also evidences their relative independence. Studies of judicial decision-making provide evidence of the existence of judicial independence, in the form of ideological voting. Much empirical research has been conducted on the decision-making of the United States Supreme Court.

An accumulation of the empirical analysis on judicial voting through meta-analysis confirms the importance of ideology. Dan Pinello identified over one hundred empirical analyses that considered judicial votes by party of appointing president and had enough in common that their results could be combined. Virtually every study separately showed a positive association between party and voting practice. The combined analysis considered over 220,000 judicial votes, and the judge's party explained 38% of the variance in their votes. Clearly, there is reason to believe that judges feel free to vote their ideological preferences in a number of cases. That freedom could only come from a measure of independence.

Jeff Segal has conducted a major study of judicial decision-making that concludes that the Supreme Court justices act independently in their voting. He argues theoretically that the judiciary has tools to evade congressional reaction, including the ability to "manipulate issues strategically." Moreover, he stresses the difficulties barring congressional control of the judiciary, even should a majority wish to respond to a decision. Segal also conducts an extensive test of judicial independence, based on the hypothesis that, with a dependent judiciary, "some justices should switch their votes as the political environment changes." Using several theoretical models about congressional decision-making, he then demonstrates that this is not the case. He concludes that "the federal judiciary was designed to be independent, so we should not be surprised that in fact it is." The design of Segal's study did not permit him to prove that the judiciary paid no heed to congressional concerns, but his results demonstrate that justices do not moderate their decisional outcomes in response to legislative preferences, which is a significant finding about judicial independence.

These findings should not come as a surprise to those who follow the Court. It is not difficult to point to particular decisions that demonstrate the independence of the courts. In *Texas v. Johnson,* the Court narrowly held that burning the American flag was protected speech. This produced a storm of public outrage and congressional disapproval, and the legislature "went back and passed a statute authorizing laws which prohibit the burning of flags." The issue returned to the Court and in *United States v. Eichman,* the Court responded to the legislative expression by saying "We don't care," and reaffirming its earlier holding.

Perhaps the most dramatic and clear demonstration of judicial independence came in *City of Boerne v. Flores,* which struck down the Religious Freedom Restoration Act of 1993 ("RFRA"). The statute was passed by Congress to expand the right of free exercise of religion, in response to the Court's decisions limiting the scope of the free exercise right. RFRA had an enormous amount of bipartisan support in Congress. The decision made clear that the justices would adhere to their vision of the Constitution, even in the face of a direct challenge from Congress and the Executive branch. When President Theodore Roosevelt criticized Oliver Wendell Holmes for a decision, Holmes responded: "Now, Mr. President, you can go straight to hell." The Court continues to implicitly respond in this fashion, with decisions such as *City of Boerne* and *Texas v. Johnson.* Clearly, the courts are not slavish followers of the more political branches.

Evidence of Accountability

Judges in this country are not entirely free and unconstrained. The courts rarely challenge the decisions of the legislative and executive branches. Congress and the executive may bring a variety of pressures to bear on even the life-tenured federal judges. Attacks on the judiciary, historically, "inevitably have been political" and "motivated by disagreement with the substance of judicial decisions." When other institutions have significantly disagreed with the substance of judicial decisions, they have taken a variety of measures to attempt to discipline the judiciary. These powers have some effect on judicial decisions.

The congressional power that is most obvious, yet apparently futile, is the authority to impeach judges. Although Congress rarely removes judges from office, threats of impeachment are fairly common. Proponents of the practice believe that the threats are enough, as "just the process of impeachment serves as a deterrent." This was the position of Alexander Hamilton, who argued that the constitutional design meant that a mere threat of impeachment would suffice to deter judges from abusing their powers. Hence, "the low frequency of impeachment should not be seen as evidence of the security of constitutional protection, because this may be due as much to judges' reluctance to make politically controversial decisions as to any display of congressional virtue." Judge Dubois has commented: "I do not think anyone is going to get impeached; but a lot of people are going to be very uncomfortable." Such discomfort surely can influence decision-making at the margin. When Judge Harold Baer came under fire for suppressing drug evidence and criticizing police practices, he vacated his ruling upon reconsideration. Other judges have "publicly worried" about the criticism, and even retired in the face of political criticism.

Congress may also influence the federal courts by eliminating their jurisdiction over certain categories of legal issues. While such jurisdiction-stripping is not common, the threat of action may suffice, as in the case of impeachment. There is historical evidence of this effect. In the late 1950s, after Congress responded to Supreme Court decisions restraining investigation and prosecution of Communist activity with jurisdiction-stripping threats, the Court retreated and issued decisions less protective of the civil liberties of subversives. More disciplined empirical research seems to confirm that jurisdiction-stripping efforts provoke the Court to respond to congressional preferences. Congress need not enact restrictions on jurisdiction because "arousing substantial opposition to the Court may be enough to dominate it." Moreover, there are instances where Congress has actually legislated just short of jurisdiction-stripping but nonetheless curbed the Court's powers. Congress may also devote certain issues to new non-Article III courts that permit them greater "political control" over judicial decision-making. Impeachment and jurisdiction-stripping threats can be seen as part of a continuing dialogue between the political branches and the courts, in which the legislature sometimes sends signals that it expects the courts to heed.

Congress and the President also have control over the resources of the courts. While the Constitution provides some salary protection to judges, salary increases may be withheld. There are no constitutional constraints on appropriations for support staff, facilities and other necessary resources.

Judge Calabresi has remarked on the significance of these appropriations:

> One of the things that has made the judiciary somewhat less independent than it used to be, not perhaps in a dramatic sense but in a subtle way, is that we are, that we have come to be, too dependent on the Administrative Office of the Courts, on fancy offices, on elegant Courthouses, on too many law clerks, on a whole lot of bureaucracy that Congress can take away by not allocating the money to support it. I have actually had a Judge say to me: "Why not take that phrase out of your opinion, you do not need it, and it might offend the Senate. And you know how that could affect the judicial budget."

Indeed, justices often appear before Congress and plead for additional resources and additional pay, or a reduced caseload. Congress may respond favorably or critically and that response may depend in large part on the pattern of judicial decisions.

The desire for promotions is yet another factor that renders judges accountable to the other institutions of government. Because promotions to higher court levels are dependent on the actions of the President and Congress, judges have reason to attend to the preferences of these institutions. Judge Calabresi has noted that "judges want to be promoted," and declared that if he "were to identify the single greatest threat to judicial independence today, it would be the fact that judges want to move up." There is some empirical evidence that promotion potential influenced judicial holdings on the constitutionality of the Sentencing Guidelines.

Finally, the judiciary is limited by its need for assistance in effectively implementing the decisions that it reaches. Implementing any social policy, including those expressed by judicial opinions, requires a variety of resources and tools that the courts lack. The notions of judicial review and judicial independence may be "meaningless unless the executive branch is willing and able to enforce the orders of federal courts." Judges may hesitate to render opinions strongly contrary to the interests of other institutions because they are aware that "they lack the power to enforce broad policy decisions." There have been some "extreme cases of organized opposition" to judicial rulings, such as in the response to the desegregation cases. Steve Griffin has observed that the "Court is aware that its rulings can be difficult to enforce and may be ignored," which "can influence the willingness of the Court to take on certain cases and may limit the remedies the Court applies in cases it does decide."

The culmination of these powers of Congress and the President have the effect of influencing the judiciary at the expense of its perfect independence. Judge Joseph Rodriguez, testifying on behalf of the Judicial Conference, summarized the judiciary's relationship with Congress:

> It is safe to say that the happiness, effectiveness, stability and independence of the federal judiciary depends [sic] to a large extent on Congress. If the legislative branch is responsive to our needs, we shall remain one of the most durable legacies of the founders of this nation. If it is not, then suspicion, underfunding, minute oversight, and capricious additions to workload may become the equivalent of a constitutional amendment effectively repealing Article III.

Congress provides the judiciary with plenty of signals regarding its concerns about trends in decision-making, and wise judges may act with those in mind. Eugenia Toma has investigated the influence of congressional budgetary authority on judicial decisions. She argues that "the relationship between the Supreme Court and the Congress is a contractual one" in which they exchange "budgetary favors" for "politically influenced output." Toma empirically analyzed the association between Court budgets and judicial outcomes for the period between 1946 and 1988. The study found that the larger the difference between the political positions in Court decisions and the Congress, the smaller the budget increase for the Court. For several chief justices, but not Earl Warren, the Supreme Court responded to the budgetary signals by shifting its decisional output in the direction preferred by the legislature.

Judges' overall responsiveness to Congress has not been extensively evaluated. Testing judicial in-

dependence is possible by examining how courts decide cases involving the government. Judicial independence is said to take on "critical significance when the government is one of the parties to a dispute," so examining these cases may be considered one fair yardstick of the concept. While there is evidence of independence—seen in the flag-burning cases, some defendants' rights decisions, and the invalidation of RFRA—there is also empirical evidence of accountability.

It is well established that the Solicitor General, who represents the interests of the federal government before the Court, "is overwhelmingly successful there." This suggests judicial responsiveness to their parallel branches of government. A recent study took the database of Supreme Court decisions used by Segal and others (to demonstrate the ideological independence of the justices) and tested for the Court's deference to the other institutions of government. While the justices' decisions show a significant ideological determinant, virtually every justice significantly modified his or her ideology when reviewing an ideologically contrary decision of another institution. A statistical technique called "proportional reduction in error" enables the testing of whether an additional variable better explains the outcomes observed. For more than 80% of the justices, the consideration of institutional deference produced such a reduction in error. Moreover, nearly every justice showed greater deference to statutes or federal administrative agency decisions than they did to states or lower courts. Much of this deference could not be explained by legal requirements, and the results strongly suggest that the Court tempers its decisions with concern for other institutions.

Even the Court's bravest forays into judicial activism have been hedged by some political concern. The dramatic requirement of school desegregation in *Brown v. Board of Education* was conditioned by the Court's careful caveat requiring desegregation to proceed with "deliberate speed." This condition defused much of the practical political impact of the ruling. It transformed the opinion from a judicial diktat to something more like a gentle nudge to the political processes. The courts have also been loathe to address many important public policy issues, such as the welfare of the poor. Such cases and patterns suggest a measure of judicial deference.

There is also considerable evidence that judges are influenced by general public opinion, either directly or as filtered through the other branches. A study of Supreme Court opinions rendered between 1956 and 1989 concluded that the Court was "highly responsive to majority opinion." Subsequent research found that judicial "decisions do, in fact, vary in accord with current public preferences."

When justices agree with public opinion, it does not prove that they are being directly influenced by public opinion. Judges are drawn from the American public and may simply share the opinions of the majority. However, judges are hardly drawn from a random cross-section of the populace, so this correspondence of attitude is not necessarily the case. It is generally assumed that the elected branches, Congress and the presidency, represent the will of their constituents. When their actions correspond to the will of their constituents, this is presumably evidence of at least some level of responsiveness, and not a simple coincidence of attitudes. Yet the Supreme Court agrees with public opinion about as often as does the legislature.

There is little direct evidence of the influence of public opinion on the Court, but there are hints of its relevance. Chief Justice Rehnquist's history of the Supreme Court suggests that public opinion about our Korean involvement influenced the outcome of *Youngstown Steel*. Justice Souter's opinion in *Planned Parenthood v. Casey* expressly declared that the Court must make "principled decisions under circumstances in which their principled character is sufficiently plausible to be accepted by the Nation." Judges have openly expressed concern about their public standing. Throughout the Court's history, public opinion has informed and influenced its opinions in some cases.

In addition to such direct testimony and case analysis, studies have shown that unpopular precedents are more likely to be overturned than popular ones. Other researchers find that the Court's opinions seem to reflect the opinions of all groups of society, rich and poor, young and old, with varying degrees of education. This is evidence the Court reflects public opinion and not just the attitudes of its members. Judge Dubois cautioned: "Our courts are not completely independent. We are not independent of public opinion. If the court decisions go one way and the country is going another way, we are going to have a calamity." Per-

haps justices are aware, as Judge Irving Kaufman put it, that a level of public support is needed as the "ultimate justification of their power," or perhaps the justices simply want to be popular.

While there is clear evidence that the Court's decisions are more often than not consistent with public attitudes, there is a substantial minority of cases where they are inconsistent, and some decisions are very unpopular. A study of individual rights claims found (a) that the level of public opinion regarding the claim was a significant determinant of the Court's outcome and (b) that for most rights the Court was more likely to favor the claim than the public. Public opinion exerts a pull on the justice but not an insurmountable one. The research suggests that judges are not "weathervanes," but that public opinion exercises some effect on decisions at the margin. The Court does not display anything approaching the slavish devotion to majoritarianism or political preferences that one might expect from a truly dependent institution.

The judiciary has some institutional protection from complete dependency, based on public political preferences. The public, as well as the other institutions of government, desire both an independent judiciary and agreeable ideological decisions. . . . Most of the historic efforts to control the judiciary, such as FDR's Court-packing plan, have been rejected by the public and their representatives. There are political reasons why political institutions would desire an independent judiciary, even though it may sometimes contravene their preferences. Political parties have an incentive to "pre-commit to an institutional apparatus" that will enable their decisions to perpetuate over time. James Rogers suggests that the legislature values judicial independence for informational reasons and permits some political decision-making, so long as it is not too great. There is also a powerful public political constituency for judicial independence but not for total independence, which could seriously threaten democratic preferences.

State Selection Systems Study

The states have a variety of different approaches to selecting judges, and these approaches have been the source of much discussion. They provide an excellent laboratory for evaluating the importance of judicial selection systems and tenure on judicial behavior. One significant concern in choosing among selection systems is judicial independence. It has been suggested that less politicized methods of selection, such as the "merit plan" method, provide greater independence for judges and consequently empower them to more frequently reverse decisions of the state legislature or executive. Logically, the choice of selection systems should have a material effect on the degree of judicial independence of the courts.

The effect of judicial selection systems may be identified through studies of comparative judicial decision-making. To date, most studies have failed to find a clear correlation between the method of selection and judicial decision-making. However, it seems implausible that something so significant as method of selection has no effect on their behavior. The existing studies may have been looking for an effect in the wrong places.

For purposes of the study, I have broken down state judicial selection methods into five categories: partisan elections, nonpartisan elections, legislative appointment, gubernatorial appointment, and merit plan selection. The approaches seem to present a continuum of politicizing the judiciary in the order listed—partisan elections obviously link the judiciary to majoritarianism and party politics, while merit plan selection aims to remove these influences insofar as possible. Each of the states were placed into one of these five categories.

One measure to test the effect of judicial selection systems is judicial activism, which should be correlated with judicial independence. A ruling that a statute is unconstitutional is commonly regarded as a measure of activism, and likewise a measure of independence, because it substitutes the judicial policy choice for that passed by the state legislature. My measure of judicial activism comes from data on the number of statutes declared unconstitutional by courts between 1981 and 1985. The average number of statutes declared unconstitutional during the period was 11.82. Table 1 displays the relative frequency of declarations of statutory unconstitutionality by selection method and the probability that the group's difference from the average was attributable to chance.

Table 1   Selection Methods and Judicial Activism

	Number	Probability
Partisan election	13.92	.26
Nonpartisan election	13.70	.37
Legislative appointment	12.25	.90
Gubernatorial appointment	11.71	.97
Merit plan	9.18	.06[*]

The only statistically significant results were for the merit plan selection method [*], which was associated with fewer declarations of unconstitutionality (and thus less apparent independence). However, the pattern of the results clearly indicates that judiciaries with greater involvement in politics appear to be independent and more likely to declare statutes unconstitutional.

The results presented in Table 1 take no account of other variables that might influence declarations of unconstitutionality and thereby create a spurious association (or obscure a stronger association). The data show that the number of constitutional challenges does not differ much by type of state. However, states with differing selection systems may have other differences that affect the results. I considered the following control variables: the degree of urbanization of the state; the degree of interparty competition in elections; the relative level of public participation (turnout) in elections; and the relative influence of interest groups before the state legislature.

Urbanization was chosen as a control variable because it is the primary demographic difference between merit plan and other states, and it might relate to levels of political conflict. The hypothesized direction of this variable is positive, as such conflict might bring more conflicts before the courts. Interparty competition was chosen because with lower levels of such competition the judiciary is more likely to be ideologically aligned with other branches of government. The hypothesized direction of this variable is negative, both because of the alignment and because legislatures in one-party states have greater reason to reduce the institutional independence of the judiciary. Public participation is a measure of the electorate's interest and involvement and, hence, majoritarianism. Interest group influence is the converse. The hypothesized direction of interest group influence is negative (because those groups will act to preserve their political victories), and the hypothesized direction of public participation is therefore positive. . . .

The results . . . confirm that merit plan judges are less likely to find statutes unconstitutional than are those selected through other methods, even in the presence of significant control variables. The research reveals much else of interest about judicial decision-making. States with lower levels of interparty competition have more statutes declared unconstitutional, as do states with greater interest group influence. Both these results are contrary to the predictions that positive political theory would make, but they are very positive about the role of the judiciary in government. It appears that state judges are more likely to declare a statute unconstitutional when it is the product of flawed majoritarianism in the other branches. This may not reflect judges acting like judges and simply applying the law, but it does suggest that judges are functioning as a desirable, relatively majoritarian government institution, deferring less to legislatures that may not reflect the popular will. This is consistent with a vision that holds that judges should be relatively independent but not entirely unaccountable.

The preceding analysis and results are very preliminary and require much additional investigation. Ideally, one would want to examine each of the judicial declarations of unconstitutionality to determine their nature, whether there was evidence of ideological or interest group influence (and differential levels of ideological influence according to a state's selection system), and whether they were reflecting the true public will in the state or the strength of the legal reasoning supporting the finding of unconstitutionality. However, it is generally well accepted that the cases going to the highest courts are close cases in which both sides can advance reasonably strong cases. It appears that judges selected by the merit plan method are more responsive to the arguments presented by the state in these close cases and thus appear somewhat less independent, contrary to the hypotheses that have been advanced. It also appears that state judges, whatever the selection system, are acting in a generally wise and valuable fashion, responding with some independence to majoritarian weaknesses of the other branches of government.

Conclusion

Judicial independence is not an unalloyed good. Just as a bed may be either too hard or too soft (or just right), judicial independence may be too strong or too weak (or just right). A balance must be struck between independence and accountability. While it would be naive to assert that the United States has it "just right," history suggests that the balance of independence and accountability currently found in this nation is a pretty good one. However, the fact that our arrangements for judicial independence are good does not mean that they cannot be improved. Louis Michael Seidman stresses that the "various decisions to limit— or not to limit—the power or independence of judges reflect the desire to produce different contexts that will yield different outcomes." We must cut through the fog of rhetorical effluvience on judicial independence and examine the matter more closely. The important questions are: what sort of systemic societal outcomes do we wish to advance and what structures of judicial independence are best suited to their advancement? The answers to these questions are not well understood.

While theory is valuable, analysis of appropriate levels of judicial independence would benefit greatly from empirical analyses. Such research is needed first to ascertain the determinants of judicial independence. A simple constitutional declaration that a judiciary is independent is hardly sufficient in itself to protect that status. More specific protections, such as salary protection, presumably further independence but may be inadequate in their own right. We need greater understanding of what institutional features create judicial independence and that understanding would be enhanced by careful empirical analyses.

In addition, empirical research is needed to illuminate the consequences and value of a more independent judiciary. An independent, powerful and unaccountable judiciary plainly frustrates government action that reflects the will of the majority of the people. If it does so in furtherance of some higher principle, such as individual freedom or the rule of law, it may be beneficial for a society. An independent judiciary may also benefit society by generally slowing down the pace of political change and allowing more time for democratic reflection. However, if the independent judiciary only serves to facilitate arbitrary ideological decision-making, that finding might counsel for less independence. The effects of judicial independence should also be investigated more broadly. For example, it would be valuable to know if greater levels of judicial independence contribute to greater economic growth in a society.

The comparative empirical study of state courts should prove enlightening. Differences in selection systems, retention and tenure, and other rules among the states readily enable testing of their institutional effects on judicial decisions and on society more broadly. The differing state judicial systems offer a promising natural laboratory for investigating judicial independence and other aspects of court decision-making. Political scientists are actively engaged in research on state courts and have begun to create large databases to further this study. Legal academics should participate in this investigation more aggressively.

For Further Reading

Goldman, Sheldon. *Picking Federal Judges: Lower Court Selection from Roosevelt Through Reagan.* New Haven, Conn.: Yale University Press, 1997.

Barrow, Deborah J. and Gary Zuk. "An Institutional Analysis of Turnover in the Lower Federal Courts, 1900–1987." *Journal of Politics* 52 (1990): 457.

Moraski, Bryon J. and Charles R. Shipan. "The Politics of Supreme Court Nominations: A Theory of Institutional Constraints and Choices." *American Journal of Political Science* 43 (1999): 1069.

Martinek, Wendy L., Mark Kemper, and Steven R. Van Winkle. "To Advise and Consent: The Senate and Lower Federal Court Nominations." *Journal of Politics* 64 (2002): 358.

Dubois, Philip L. *From Ballot to Bench: Judicial Elections and the Quest for Accountability.* Austin: University of Texas Press, 1980.

Chapter 5

Lawyers and Legal Representation

Introduction

Many Americans are concerned about the conduct of lawyers and the ethical substance of the legal profession. Distrust of lawyers is widespread, and they are often perceived as greedy, unethical, and self-interested. Yet we continue to turn to lawyers to resolve our legal problems. Despite our concerns about the practice of law, lawyers play an important role in our complicated legal and political systems.

Indeed, politics and the legal profession intersect often, so political scientists focus some of their research on a variety of topics related to lawyers. One concern is how lawyers affect the distribution of rights and resources, and this focus leads to investigating how lawyers contribute to the protection of our fundamental rights, what the profession's responsibilities are to society, and how different types of lawyers perform their work as their clients' legal representatives.

Foundations and History

In the early 1800s, Alexis de Tocqueville, a young French nobleman, toured the United States and documented his observations concerning American society and politics. One topic that he addressed was the role of lawyers in the new American democracy. In Chapter 16 of *Democracy in America* (1835), "Causes Which Mitigate the Tyranny of the Majority in the United States," Tocqueville argued that American lawyers were like European aristocrats in that they too provided a critical link between those in power and the governed. As generally conservative elites with an appreciation for the status quo, lawyers moderated the radical tendencies of the populace. At the same time, though, the work of lawyers allowed them regular contact with and service to the people, both of which made lawyers sensitive to the needs and passions of the people. According to Tocqueville, then, the significance of lawyers to balancing power between the people and their government in a democratic polity could not be underestimated.

From the earliest days of the Union, it was understood that lawyers would be very important in the American system of democracy. The best example is the acknowledgment in the Sixth Amendment to the Bill of Rights that lawyers are critical to the distribution of justice. According to that amendment, criminal defendants tried in federal court have the right to counsel. Notably, this right did not extend to defendants in state courts until a series of Supreme Court cases in the early and mid-1900s gradually made the federal right to counsel a fundamental right. Among the most significant of these cases was *Gideon v. Wainwright* (1963), which we include here. Through a process called incorporation, the Court found in the Fourteenth Amendment's Due Process Clause a basis for applying the Sixth Amendment right to counsel to the states.

Prior to *Gideon,* the Court acknowledged that in some criminal cases, the state should provide legal representation for some criminal defendants. However, the Court stopped short of incorporating the Sixth Amendment. Significantly, not all of the justices agreed. Among them was Justice Black, who wrote the majority opinion in *Gideon.* The essence of his argument was quite simple:

> Governments, both state and federal, quite properly spend vast sums of money to establish machinery to try defendants accused of crime. Lawyers to prosecute are everywhere deemed essential to protect the public's interest in an orderly society. Similarly, there are few defendants charged with crime, few indeed, who fail to hire the best lawyers they can get to prepare and present their defenses. That government hires lawyers to prosecute and defendants who have the money hire lawyers to defend are the strongest indications of the widespread belief that lawyers in criminal courts are necessities, not luxuries.

It should not be surprising, then, that the cases that stimulated incorporation of the Sixth Amendment were brought by indigent and otherwise disadvantaged defendants like Gideon. Unable to hire his own attorney, Gideon represented himself at his trial and lost. From prison, Gideon submitted to the Supreme Court a petition for writ of certiorari, which he wrote without assistance of counsel. We include his petition here.

The process of incorporation was and is controversial, in large part because it pits two important American values against each other. There are fundamental rights that are guaranteed to all citizens, regardless of where or how they live. However, there is also a balance of power between federal and state government that requires at least some level of state autonomy. By incorporating the right to counsel, a federal institution required state governments to recognize a fundamental right and in so doing required states to provide counsel to those who could not afford it. However, legitimate concerns surround the states' responsibility to procure counsel, not least of which are the expense involved and the quality of counsel. States, Congress, and the legal profession have spent the years since *Gideon* wrestling with how to manage these impediments to the right to counsel.

Contemporary Judicial Politics

Despite the ultimate victory of the fundamental right to counsel and the court decision that brought it to fruition, the public is not very supportive of the legal profession. In her book *In the Interests of Justice: Reforming the Legal Profession* (2000),

Deborah L. Rhode tackles the disconnect between the public's perception and the legal profession's perception of its failure to serve justice. She argues that as they talk past each other, neither the public nor the legal profession has addressed the fundamental cause of the problems each identifies as important. As a result the discussion has been largely symbolic. The selection here surveys the perceptions, the problems, and the possibility of reforming the legal profession.

Lawyers who are members of the Supreme Court Bar are among the most prestigious practitioners of the law. In his book *The Supreme Court Bar: Legal Elites in the Washington Community* (1993), Kevin McGuire presents a comprehensive analysis of the political impact of these lawyers. They are a demographically homogeneous and very accomplished group, which has an impact on the types of cases that reach the Court and the outcomes that result. The selection here highlights how the Bar influences the Court's decision-making process. In the final analysis, the Supreme Court Bar exercises considerable influence over Court outcomes.

A View from the Inside

Among the most important lawyers in the United States is the solicitor general. In her 1997 report on solicitors general and her interview with former solicitor general Walter Dellinger, National Public Radio's Nina Totenberg presents an informative and interesting look behind the scenes at one of the most powerful attorneys in the country.

There are many other government attorneys who are less prestigious but no less important to the distribution of justice. The journal entries written by Paul Boynton and Dave Rosenberg illustrate vividly the hard work and dedication required of public defenders and district attorneys, as well as the problems associated with representing clients in the "trenches." There are considerable differences between the kind of law practiced by defense and prosecuting attorneys and the lawyers described by McGuire and Totenberg.

A Comparative Perspective

American cynicism about the legal profession is balanced in part by our recognition that lawyers are important to democratic politics. Indeed, as John Burman explains, well-trained lawyers play an essential part in establishing and maintaining the rule of law, a critical component of democracy. In his article "The Role of Clinical Legal Education in Developing the Rule of Law in Russia" (2002), Burman describes the efforts of Americans and Russians to develop strong, hands-on instruction for Russian lawyers so that they may facilitate the growth of democracy in Russia. In the process, he reminds us of the very important, however imperfect, role that lawyers play in our own democracy, a role that we often fail to appreciate.

Foundations and History

5.1

The Temper of the Legal Profession in the United States, and How It Serves as a Counterpoise to Democracy (1835)
Causes Which Mitigate the Tyranny of the Majority in the United States

Alexis de Tocqueville

In visiting the Americans and studying their laws, we perceive that the authority they have entrusted to members of the legal profession, and the influence that these individuals exercise in the government, are the most powerful existing security against the excesses of democracy. This effect seems to me to result from a general cause, which it is useful to investigate, as it may be reproduced elsewhere.

The members of the legal profession have taken a part in all the movements of political society in Europe for the last five hundred years. At one time they have been the instruments of the political authorities, and at another they have succeeded in converting the political authorities into their instruments. In the Middle Ages they afforded a powerful support to the crown; and since that period they have exerted themselves effectively to limit the royal prerogative. In England they have contracted a close alliance with the aristocracy; in France they have shown themselves its most dangerous enemies. Under all these circumstances have the members of the legal profession been swayed by sudden and fleeting impulses, or have they been more or less impelled by instincts which are natural to them and which will always recur in history? I am incited to this investigation, for perhaps this particular class of men will play a prominent part in the political society that is soon to be created.

Men who have made a special study of the laws derive from this occupation certain habits of order, a taste for formalities, and a kind of instinctive regard for the regular connection of ideas, which naturally render them very hostile to the revolutionary spirit and the unreflecting passions of the multitude.

The special information that lawyers derive from their studies ensures them a separate rank in society, and they constitute a sort of privileged body in the scale of intellect. This notion of their superiority perpetually recurs to them in the practice of their profession: they are the masters of a science which is necessary, but which is not very generally known; they serve as arbiters between the citizens; and the habit of directing to their purpose the blind passions of parties in litigation inspires them with a certain contempt for the judgment of the multitude. Add to this that they naturally constitute a body; not by any previous understanding, or by an agreement that directs them to a common end; but the analogy of their studies and the uniformity of their methods connect their minds as a common interest might unite their endeavors.

Some of the tastes and the habits of the aristocracy may consequently be discovered in the characters of lawyers. They participate in the same instinctive love of order and formalities; and they entertain the same repugnance to the actions of the multitude, and the same secret contempt of the government of the people. I do not mean to say that the natural propensities of lawyers are sufficiently strong to sway them irresistibly; for they, like most other men, are governed by their private interests, and especially by the interests of the moment. . . .

I do not, then, assert that all the members of the legal profession are at all times the friends of order and the opponents of innovation, but merely that most of them are usually so. In a community in which lawyers are allowed to occupy without opposition that high station which naturally belongs to them, their general spirit will be eminently conservative and anti-democratic. When an aristocracy excludes the leaders of that profession from its ranks, it excites enemies who are the more formidable as they are independent of the nobility by their labors and feel themselves to be their equals in intelligence though inferior in opulence and power. But whenever an aristocracy consents to impart some of its privileges to these same individuals, the two classes coalesce very readily and assume, as it were, family interests.

I am in like manner inclined to believe that a monarch will always be able to convert legal practitioners into the most serviceable instruments of his authority. There is a far greater affinity between this class of persons and the executive power than there is between them and the people, though they have often aided to overturn the former; just as there is a greater natural affinity between the nobles and the monarch than between the nobles and the people, although the higher orders of society have often, in concert with the lower classes, resisted the prerogative of the crown.

Lawyers are attached to public order beyond every other consideration, and the best security of public order is authority. It must not be forgotten, also, that if they prize freedom much, they generally value legality still more: they are less afraid of tyranny than of arbitrary power, and, provided the legislature undertakes of itself to deprive men of their independence, they are not dissatisfied.

I am therefore convinced that the prince who, in presence of an encroaching democracy, should endeavor to impair the judicial authority in his dominions, and to diminish the political influence of lawyers, would commit a great mistake: he would let slip the substance of authority to grasp the shadow. He would act more wisely in introducing lawyers into the government; and if he entrusted despotism to them under the form of violence, perhaps he would find it again in their hands under the external features of justice and law.

The government of democracy is favorable to the political power of lawyers; for when the wealthy, the noble, and the prince are excluded from the government, the lawyers take possession of it, in their own right, as it were, since they are the only men of information and sagacity, beyond the sphere of the people, who can be the object of the popular choice. If, then, they are led by their tastes towards the aristocracy and the prince, they are

brought in contact with the people by their interests. They like the government of democracy without participating in its propensities and without imitating its weaknesses; whence they derive a twofold authority from it and over it. The people in democratic states do not mistrust the members of the legal profession, because it is known that they are interested to serve the popular cause; and the people listen to them without irritation, because they do not attribute to them any sinister designs. The lawyers do not, indeed, wish to overthrow the institutions of democracy, but they constantly endeavor to turn it away from its real direction by means that are foreign to its nature. Lawyers belong to the people by birth and interest, and to the aristocracy by habit and taste; they may be looked upon as the connecting link between the two great classes of society.

The profession of the law is the only aristocratic element that can be amalgamated without violence with the natural elements of democracy and be advantageously and permanently combined with them. I am not ignorant of the defects inherent in the character of this body of men; but without this admixture of lawyer-like sobriety with the democratic principle, I question whether democratic institutions could long be maintained; and I cannot believe that a republic could hope to exist at the present time if the influence of lawyers in public business did not increase in proportion to the power of the people.

This aristocratic character, which I hold to be common to the legal profession, is much more distinctly marked in the United States and in England than in any other country. This proceeds not only from the legal studies of the English and American lawyers, but from the nature of the law and the position which these interpreters of it occupy in the two countries. The English and the Americans have retained the law of precedents; that is to say, they continue to found their legal opinions and the decisions of their courts upon the opinions and decisions of their predecessors. In the mind of an English or American lawyer a taste and a reverence for what is old is almost always united with a love of regular and lawful proceedings.

This predisposition has another effect upon the character of the legal profession and upon the general course of society. The English and American lawyers investigate what has been done; the French advocate inquires what should have been done; the former produce precedents, the latter reasons. A French observer is surprised to hear how often an English or an American lawyer quotes the opinions of others and how little he alludes to his own, while the reverse occurs in France. There the most trifling litigation is never conducted without the introduction of an entire system of ideas peculiar to the counsel employed; and the fundamental principles of law are discussed in order to obtain a rod of land by the decision of the court. This abnegation of his own opinion and this implicit deference to the opinion of his forefathers, which are common to the English and American lawyer, this servitude of thought which he is obliged to profess, necessarily give him more timid habits and more conservative inclinations in England and America than in France.

The French codes are often difficult to comprehend, but they can be read by everyone; nothing, on the other hand, can be more obscure and strange to the uninitiated than a legislation founded upon precedents. The absolute need of legal aid that is felt in England and the United States, and the high opinion that is entertained of the ability of the legal profession, tend to separate it more and more from the people and to erect it into a distinct class. The French lawyer is simply a man extensively acquainted with the statutes of his country; but the English or American lawyer resembles the hierophants of Egypt, for like them he is the sole interpreter of an occult science.

The position that lawyers occupy in England and America exercises no less influence upon their habits and opinions. The English aristocracy, which has taken care to attract to its sphere whatever is at all analogous to itself, has conferred a high degree of importance and authority upon the members of the legal profession. In English society, lawyers do not occupy the first rank, but they are contented with the station assigned to them: they constitute, as it were, the younger branch of the English aristocracy; and they are attached to their elder brothers, although they do not enjoy all their privileges. The English lawyers consequently mingle the aristocratic tastes and ideas of the circles in which they move with the aristocratic interests of their profession. . . .

In America there are no nobles or literary men, and the people are apt to mistrust the wealthy; lawyers consequently form the highest political class and the most cultivated portion of society. They have therefore nothing to gain by innovation, which adds a conservative interest to their natural taste for public order. If I were asked where I place the American aristocracy, I should reply without hesitation that it is not among the rich, who are united by no common tie, but that it occupies the judicial bench and the bar.

The more we reflect upon all that occurs in the United States the more we shall be persuaded that the lawyers, as a body, form the most powerful, if not the only, counterpoise to the democratic element. In that country we easily perceive how the legal profession is qualified by its attributes, and even by its faults, to neutralize the vices inherent in popular government. When the American people are intoxicated by passion or carried away by the impetuosity of their ideas, they are checked and stopped by the almost invisible influence of their legal counselors. These secretly oppose their aristocratic propensities to the nation's democratic instincts, their superstitious attachment to what is old to its love of novelty, their narrow views to its immense designs, and their habitual procrastination to its ardent impatience.

The courts of justice are the visible organs by which the legal profession is enabled to control the democracy. The judge is a lawyer who, independently of the taste for regularity and order that he has contracted in the study of law, derives an additional love of stability from the inalienability of his own functions. His legal attainments have already raised him to a distinguished rank among his fellows; his political power completes the distinction of his station and gives him the instincts of the privileged classes.

Armed with the power of declaring the laws to be unconstitutional, the American magistrate perpetually interferes in political affairs. He cannot force the people to make laws, but at least he can oblige them not to disobey their own enactments and not to be inconsistent with themselves. I am aware that a secret tendency to diminish the judicial power exists in the United States; and by most of the constitutions of the several states the government can, upon the demand of the two houses of the legislature, remove judges from their station. Some other state constitutions make the members of the judiciary elective, and they are even subjected to frequent re-elections. I venture to predict that these innovations will sooner or later be attended with fatal consequences; and that it will be found out at some future period that by thus lessening the independence of the judiciary they have attacked not only the judicial power, but the democratic republic itself.

It must not be supposed, moreover, that the legal spirit is confined in the United States to the courts of justice; it extends far beyond them. As the lawyers form the only enlightened class whom the people do not mistrust, they are naturally called upon to occupy most of the public stations. They fill the legislative assemblies and are at the head of the administration; they consequently exercise a powerful influence upon the formation of the law and upon its execution. The lawyers are obliged, however, to yield to the current of public opinion, which is too strong for them to resist; but it is easy to find indications of what they would do if they were free to act. The Americans, who have made so many innovations in their political laws, have introduced very sparing alterations in their civil laws, and that with great difficulty, although many of these laws are repugnant to their social condition. The reason for this is that in matters of civil law the majority are obliged to defer to the authority of the legal profession, and the American lawyers are disinclined to innovate when they are left to their own choice.

It is curious for a Frenchman to hear the complaints that are made in the United States against the stationary spirit of legal men and their prejudices in favor of existing institutions.

The influence of legal habits extends beyond the precise limits I have pointed out. Scarcely any political question arises in the United States that is not resolved, sooner or later, into a judicial question. Hence all parties are obliged to borrow, in their daily controversies, the ideas, and even the language, peculiar to judicial proceedings. As most public men are or have been legal practitioners, they introduce the customs and technicalities of their profession into the management of public affairs. The jury extends this habit to all classes. The language of the law thus becomes, in some measure, a vulgar tongue; the spirit of the law, which is produced in the schools and courts of justice, gradually penetrates beyond their walls into the bosom of society, where it descends to the lowest classes, so that at last the whole people contract the habits and the tastes of the judicial magistrate. The lawyers of the United States form a party which is but little feared and scarcely perceived, which has no badge peculiar to itself, which adapts itself with great flexibility to the exigencies of the time and accommodates itself without resistance to all the movements of the social body. But this party extends over the whole community and penetrates into all the classes which compose it; it acts upon the country imperceptibly, but finally fashions it to suit its own purposes. . . .

5.2   ## *Gideon v. Cochran*
Petition for a Writ of Certiorari to the Supreme Court of the State of Florida (1962)

TO: THE HONORABLE EARL WARREN, CHIEF JUSTICE OF THE UNITED STATES

Comes now the petitioner, Clarence Earl Gideon, a citizen of the United States of America, in proper person, and appearing as his own counsel. Who petitions this Honorable Court for a Writ of Certiorari directed to the Supreme Court of the State of Florida. To review the order and Judgement of the court below denying the petitioner a writ of Habeus Corpus.

Petitioner submits that the Supreme Court of the United States has the authority and jurisdiction to review the final Judgment of the Supreme Court of the State of Florida the highest court of the State . . . and Because the "Due process clause" of the fourteenth amendment of the constitution and the fifth and sixth articles of the Bill of rights has been violated. Furthermore, the decision of the court below denying the petitioner a Writ of Habeus Corpus is also inconsistent and adverse to its own previous decisions in paralled cases.

Attached hereto, and made a part of this petition is a true copy of the petition for a Writ of Habeus Corpus as presented to the Florida Supreme Court. Petitioner asks this Honorable Court to consider the same arguments and authorities cited in the petition for Writ of Habeus Corpus before the Florida Supreme Court. In consideration of this petition for a Writ of Certiorari.

The Supreme Court of Florida did not write any opinion. Order of that Court denying petition for Writ of Habeus Corpus dated October 30, 1961, are attached hereto and made a part of this petition.

Petitioner contends that he has been deprived of due process of law Habeus Corpus petition alleging that the lower state court has decided a federal question of substance in a way not in accord with the applicable decisions of this Honorable Court. When at the time of the petitioner's trial he ask the lower court for the aid of counsel. The court refused this aid. Petitioner told the court that this court had made decision to the effect that all citizens tried for a felony crime should have aid of counsel. The lower court ignored this plea.

Petitioner alleges that prior to petitioner's convictions and sentence for Breaking and Entering with the intent to commit petty Larceny, he had requested aid of counsel, that, at the time of his conviction and sentence, petitioner was without aid of counsel. That the Court refused and did not appoint counsel, and that he was incapable adequately of making his own defense. In consequence of which he was made to stand trial. Made a Prima Facia showing of denial of due process of law. *William V. Kaiser* vs. *State of Missouri,* 65 ct. 363 *Counsel must be assigned to the accused if he is unable to employ one, and incapable adequately of making his own defense.* Tomkins vs. *State Missouri,* 65 ct. 370.

On the 3rd June 1961 A.D. your Petitioner was arrested for foresaid crime and convicted for same, Petitioner receive trial and sentence without aid of counsel, your petitioner was deprived Due process of law!

Petitioner was deprived of due process of law in the court below. Evidence in the lower court did not show that a crime of Breaking and Entering with the intent to commit Petty Larceny had been committed. Your petitioner was compelled to make his own defense, he was incapable adequately of making his own defense. Petitioner did not plead nol contender But that is what his trial amounted to.

Wherefore the premises considered it is respectfully contented that the decision of the court below was in error and the case should be review by this court, accordingly the writ prepared and prayed for should be issue.

It is respectfully submitted.

5.3   *Gideon v. Wainwright*
372 U.S. 335 (1963)

MR. JUSTICE BLACK delivered the opinion of the Court.

Petitioner was charged in a Florida state court with having broken and entered a poolroom with intent to commit a misdemeanor. This offense is a felony under Florida law. Appearing in court without funds and without a lawyer, petitioner asked the court to appoint counsel for him, whereupon the following colloquy took place:

The Court: Mr. Gideon, I am sorry, but I cannot appoint Counsel to represent you in this case. Under the laws of the State of Florida, the only time the Court can appoint Counsel to represent a Defendant is when that person is charged with a capital offense. I am sorry, but I will have to deny your request to appoint Counsel to defend you in this case.

The Defendant: The United States Supreme Court says I am entitled to be represented by Counsel.

Put to trial before a jury, Gideon conducted his defense about as well as could be expected from a layman. . . . The jury returned a verdict of guilty, and petitioner was sentenced to serve five years in the state prison. Later, petitioner filed in the Florida Supreme Court this habeas corpus petition attacking his conviction and sentence on the ground that the trial court's refusal to appoint counsel for him denied him rights "guaranteed by the Constitution and the Bill of Rights by the United States Government." Treating the petition for habeas corpus as properly before it, the State Supreme Court, "upon consideration thereof" but without an opinion, denied all relief. Since 1942, when *Betts v. Brady* was decided by a divided Court, the problem of a defendant's federal constitutional right to counsel in a state court has been a continuing source of controversy and litigation in both state and federal courts. To give this problem another review here, we granted certiorari. Since Gideon was proceeding in forma pauperis, we appointed counsel to represent him and requested both sides to discuss in their briefs and oral arguments the following: "Should this Court's holding in *Betts v. Brady* be reconsidered?"

I

The facts upon which Betts claimed that he had been unconstitutionally denied the right to have counsel appointed to assist him are strikingly like the facts upon which Gideon here bases his federal constitutional claim. Betts was indicated for robbery in a Maryland state court. On arraignment, he told the trial judge of his lack of funds to hire a lawyer and asked the court to appoint one for him. Betts was advised that it was not the practice in that county to appoint counsel for indigent defendants except in murder and rape cases. He then pleaded not guilty, had witnesses summoned, cross-examined the State's witnesses, examined his own, and chose not to testify himself. He was found guilty by the judge, sitting without a jury, and sentenced to eight years in prison. Like Gideon, Betts sought release by habeas corpus, alleging that he had been denied the right to assistance of counsel in violation of the Fourteenth Amendment. Betts was denied any relief, and on review this Court affirmed. It was held that a refusal to appoint counsel for an indigent defendant charged with a felony did not necessarily violate the Due Process Clause of the Fourteenth Amendment, which for reasons given the Court deemed to be the only applicable federal constitutional provision. . . .

. . . [T]he Court held that refusal to appoint counsel under the particular facts and circumstances in the Betts case was not so "offensive to the common and fundamental ideas of fairness" as to amount to a denial of due process. Since the facts and circumstances of the two cases are so nearly indistinguishable, we think the *Betts v. Brady* holding if left standing would require us to reject Gideon's claim that the Constitution guarantees him the assistance of counsel. Upon full reconsideration we conclude that *Betts v. Brady* should be overruled.

II

. . . We think the Court in Betts had ample precedent for acknowledging that those guarantees of the Bill of Rights which are fundamental safeguards of liberty immune from federal abridgment are equally protected against state invasion by the Due Process Clause of the Fourteenth Amendment. This same principle was recognized, explained, and applied in *Powell v. Alabama,* (1932), a case upholding the right of counsel, where the Court held that despite sweeping language to the contrary in *Hurtado v. California,* (1884), the Fourteenth Amendment "embraced" those "fundamental principles of liberty and justice which lie at the base of all our civil and political institutions," even though they had been "specifically dealt with in another part of the federal Constitution." In many cases other than *Powell* and *Betts,* this Court has looked to the fundamental nature of original Bill of Rights guarantees to decide whether the Fourteenth Amendment makes them obligatory on the States. Explicitly recognized to be of this "fundamental nature" and therefore made immune from state invasion by the Fourteenth, or some part of it, are the First Amendment's freedoms of speech, press, religion, assembly, association, and petition for redress of grievances. For the same reason, though not always in precisely the same terminology, the Court has made obligatory on the States the Fifth Amendment's command that private property shall not be taken for public use without just compensation, the Fourth Amendment's prohibition of unreasonable searches and seizures, and the Eighth's ban on cruel and unusual punishment. On the other hand, this Court in *Palko v. Connecticut* (1937) refused to hold that the Fourteenth Amendment made the double jeopardy provision of the Fifth Amendment obligatory on the States. In so refusing, however, the Court, speaking through Mr. Justice Cardozo, was careful to emphasize that "immunities that are valid as against the federal government by force of the specific pledges of particular amendments have been found to be implicit in the concept of ordered liberty, and thus, through the Fourteenth Amendment, become valid as against the states" and that guarantees "in their origin . . . effective against the federal government alone" had by prior cases "been taken over from the earlier articles of the federal bill of rights and brought within the Four-teenth Amendment by a process of absorption."

We accept *Betts v. Brady*'s assumption, based as it was on our prior cases, that a provision of the Bill of Rights which is "fundamental and essential to a fair trial" is made obligatory upon the States by the Fourteenth Amendment. We think the Court in *Betts* was wrong, however, in concluding that the Sixth Amendment's guarantee of counsel is not one of these fundamental rights. Ten years before *Betts v. Brady,* this Court, after full consideration of all the historical data examined in *Betts,* had unequiv-ocally declared that "the right to the aid of counsel is of this fundamental character." *Powell v. Al-abama* (1932). While the Court at the close of its *Powell* opinion did by its language, as this Court frequently does, limit its holding to the particular facts and circumstances of that case, its conclu-sions about the fundamental nature of the right to counsel are unmistakable. . . .

. . . The fact is that in deciding as it did—that "appointment of counsel is not a fundamental right, essential to a fair trial"—the Court in *Betts v. Brady* made an abrupt break with its own well-considered precedents. In returning to these old precedents, sounder we believe than the new, we but restore constitutional principles established to achieve a fair system of justice. Not only these precedents but also reason and reflection require us to recognize that in our adversary system of criminal justice, any person haled into court, who

is too poor to hire a lawyer, cannot be assured a fair trial unless counsel is provided for him. This seems to us to be an obvious truth. Governments, both state and federal, quite properly spend vast sums of money to establish machinery to try defen-dants accused of crime. Lawyers to prosecute are everywhere deemed essential to protect the pub-lic's interest in an orderly society. Similarly, there are few defendants charged with crime, few in-deed, who fail to hire the best lawyers they can get to prepare and present their defenses. That govern-ment hires lawyers to prosecute and defendants who have the money hire lawyers to defend are the strongest indications of the widespread belief that lawyers in criminal courts are necessities, not luxu-ries. The right of one charged with crime to counsel may not be deemed fundamental and essential to fair trials in some countries, but it is in ours. From the very beginning, our state and national constitu-tions and laws have laid great emphasis on proce-dural and substantive safeguards designed to assure fair trials before impartial tribunals in which every defendant stands equal before the law. This noble ideal cannot be realized if the poor man charged with crime has to face his accusers without a lawyer to assist him. . . .

The judgment is reversed and the cause is re-manded to the Supreme Court of Florida for further action not inconsistent with this opinion.

Reversed.

Contemporary Judicial Politics

5.4   The Profession and the Public Interest (2000)

Deborah L. Rhode

Lawyers belong to a profession permanently in de-cline. Or so it appears from the chronic laments by

"The Profession and the Public Interest" from *In the Interests of Justice: Reforming the Legal Profession* by Deborah Rhode, copyright © 2001 by Deborah Rhode. Used by permission of Oxford University Press.

critics within and outside the bar. The profession, we are told, has lost its "fine sense of dignity and honor" and has become "contaminated with the spirit of commerce." That complaint came in 1895, but such sentiments were in ready supply a century earlier and later. Today's conventional wisdom is that the profession is "lost," "betrayed," and "in crisis." Such accounts typi-cally feature wistful references to some hypothesized happier era, in which law was less a business than a calling. But if ever there was a true fall from grace, it must have occurred quite early in the profession's history. Over two thousand years ago, Seneca observed advocates acting as accessories to injustice, "smothered by their prosperity," and Plato condemned their "small and unrighteous souls."

Given this historical context, it is tempting to discount the recent chorus of complaints about the profession as familiar variations on familiar themes. But while the novelty of recent critiques should not be overstated, their significance should not be undervalued. Discontent with legal practice is driven by structural factors that are increasingly difficult to challenge. Some of those factors are specific to the market for legal services, such as the bar's growth in size and competitiveness. Other causes reflect more general cultural trends that are reinforcing commercial priorities and eroding a sense of social obligation. All of these forces are widening the distance between professional ideals and professional practice.

Many lawyers are, in Auden's apt phrase, "trudging in tune to a tidy fortune," but they have lost their connection to the values of social justice that sent them to law in the first place. These problems of professionalism are compounded by problems in the justice system. For the vast majority of Americans, that system seems unwieldy, unintelligible, and unaffordable. The last two decades have reflected an increasing gap between rich and poor and a declining willingness to subsidize assistance for those who can least afford it. These inequalities in legal representation have magnified inequalities in adversarial processes. The result is aptly captured in a *New Yorker* cartoon picturing a well-heeled lawyer asking his client: "So, Mr. Pitikin, how much justice *can* you afford?"

Yet what is most disheartening about our current plight is the gap between the profession's and the public's perception of the problem and the failure of both groups to confront its underlying causes. Although lawyers and nonlawyers share some concerns, their central preoccupations and preferred solutions are vastly different. In one respect, however, they are quite similar. Neither the profession nor the public has been willing to address the structural sources of the problems they denounce or to invest the necessary resources in reform. The result has been symbolic crusades and policy paralysis.

. . . Given the centrality of law and lawyers in American life, the problems of legal practice become problems for us all. The central premise of this book is that the public's interest has played too little part in determining professional responsibilities. Too much regulation of lawyers has been designed by and for lawyers.

This is not to suggest that the system is purely self-serving. Without a doubt, the lawyers and judges involved in regulating the profession are committed to protecting the public. And as bar leaders are well aware, the public itself would not continue to delegate such regulatory authority if the profession pursued only its own interests. But no matter how well intentioned, lawyers regulating lawyers cannot escape the economic, psychological, and political constraints of their position. Nothing in the history of the American bar indicates that attorneys are exempt from the natural human tendency to discount interests at odds with their own.

. . . Lawyers are the custodians of American political, social, and economic institutions, and their regulation should be a matter of broad social concern. Yet although lawyer bashing has been in ample supply, thoughtful critiques and constructive responses have not. . . . [T]his chapter surveys the problems facing lawyers from competing perspectives within and outside the bar.

The portrait that emerges is inevitably incomplete. . . . The legal profession is . . . responsible for much that is best in American democratic processes. Lawyers have been architects of a governmental structure that is a model for much of the world. And they have been leaders in virtually all major movements for social justice in the nation's history. But these achievements are not grounds for complacency. Lawyers have also pursued their own and their clients' interests at the expense of broader public concerns. The challenges facing the American bar can only be met through fundamental changes in professional responsibility and regulation.

The Problem from the Public's Perspective

. . . What the public doesn't like about lawyers could fill a lengthy book. And often has. Although the rank order of grievances shifts somewhat over time, certain continuities persist. . . .

Of all the traits that the public dislikes in attorneys, greed is at the top of the list. One classic definition presents a lawyer as "a learned gentleman who rescues your estate from your enemies and keeps it for himself." It is an old quip, but the perception remains widely shared. About three-fifths of Americans describe attorneys as greedy, and between half and three-quarters believe that they charge excessive fees. There is even broader agreement that lawyers handle many matters that could be resolved as well and with less expense by non-lawyers.

The public's other principal complaint about attorneys' character involves integrity. Only a fifth of those surveyed by the American Bar Association (ABA) felt that lawyers could be described as "honest and ethical." And in other studies, the ratings are even lower. Lawyers' ethics rank substantially below those of other occupations, including doctors, police officers, and business executives. Attorneys still edge our used car salesmen, but not by much.

Other character issues involve arrogance, incivility, and inattention to client concerns. Less than a fifth of Americans in the ABA study felt that "caring and compassionate" described lawyers. Neglect of client interests is among the main sources of complaints to bar disciplinary authorities. Unsurprisingly, reports of callous or arrogant treatment are especially common in surveys of disempowered groups, such as indigent criminal defendants, but these criticisms are frequent even among influential business clients. Given these perceptions, it is also unsurprising that 90 to 95 percent of surveyed parents do not want their children to become lawyers.

Of course, what the public dislikes about the legal profession is hard to disentangle from what it dislikes about the law, the legal system, and the lawyer's role within that system. Because the bar exercises so much power over legal institutions, it also is held accountable for their failures. One cluster of complaints focuses on attorneys' amoral advocacy—their willingness to defend causes and clients without regard to the ethical merits. . . . Two-thirds of surveyed Americans believe that attorneys are no longer "seekers of justice" and that they spend too much time finding technicalities to get criminals released.

Attorneys similarly are blamed for perpetuating and profiting from an unnecessarily cumbersome

system. Members of the bar, working as lobbyists, legislators, and judges, have created a structure that seems far too complex, expensive, and open to abuse. As newspaper columnist Art Buchwald once put it, "It isn't the bad lawyers who are screwing up the justice system in this country—it's the good lawyers. . . . If you have two competent lawyers on opposite sides, a trial that should take three days could easily last six months." Most Americans agree. Over three-quarters believe that litigation costs too much and takes too long and that the wealthy receive better treatment than everyone else.

Lawyers are also held responsible for the overload of law in daily life. Over the last half century, legal regulation has become increasingly pervasive, and it is seldom a welcome guest. Everyone hears tales of disputes that are too big for courts, disputes that are too small, and disputes that should never have been disputes at all. Most Americans blame lawyers for filing too many lawsuits, and three-quarters believe that the United States has too many lawyers. Contemporary humor collections replay endless varieties on this theme. "Why does New Jersey have so many toxic waste dumps and California have so many lawyers? Because New Jersey got first choice."

For the profession itself, these public perceptions have been a source of long-standing frustration. When asked to identify the most important problems facing the profession, lawyers consistently have put public image and credibility at the top of the list. Yet a majority of those surveyed believe that the public's negative perception of the profession is "due to ignorance and is fundamentally unjustified." Blame for this sorry state is widely distributed, but attorneys generally single out the media for a generous share. Portraits of vicious and venal lawyering are a Hollywood staple, and journalistic coverage seems similarly skewed. According to New York bar leaders, the fraud and felonies of a few "bad apples" get front page coverage while the profession's "countless other acts of quiet heroism go unnoticed and unpublicized.". . .

There are however problems with the profession's response to public perceptions. . . . [T]he legal profession is unlikely to win a selflessness sweepstakes. Law is the second highest paid occupation, and surveyed lawyers' average pro bono contribution is estimated at under $85 per year. Most practitioners give no money and do no work for the poor or for public interest causes, and the average for the profession as a whole is estimated at less than thirty minutes a week per year. It is also doubtful that lawyers' excessive modesty is at the root of their public image problems. The legal profession is not known for resisting self-promotion. Lawyers spend well over $500 million annually in advertising their own services, and bar organizations devote substantial resources to public relations campaigns.

The premise of such campaigns—that popular ignorance and a bad press are the central problems—is highly dubious. . . . The individuals most likely to have negative impressions of attorneys are those with the most knowledge and personal experience. Corporate clients are among lawyers' harshest critics. By contrast, those who know relatively little about the legal profession and the legal system, and who get their information primarily from television, have the most favorable impressions. . . . The problem, in short, is less with the image of lawyers than with their practices. . . .

Yet finding solutions is more difficult than the public or the profession typically acknowledges. A large part of popular dislike of lawyers stems from aspects of the legal system that are not primarily the fault of lawyers or that are not readily changed. Courts are overburdened and underfunded, and some discontent is inherent in even the best system of dispute resolution. The contexts in which people encounter the profession are often unpleasant: divorce, bankruptcies, personal injuries, or contractual disputes. This unpleasantness inevitably affects perceptions of lawyers who are profiting from others' miseries. Attorneys are also the bearers of unwelcome messages about the law, so they readily become scapegoats when the justice system fails to deliver justice as participants perceive it.

America's adversarial system compounds popular frustration. Litigation is rarely a win-win enterprise, and losers are apt to put some of the blame on lawyers. The targets of resentment are not, however, only—or even primarily—parties' own attorneys. Between two-thirds and three-quarters of surveyed individuals are satisfied with *their* lawyers. The public's major grievances involve perceived abuses by other people's lawyers and a system that fails to prevent those abuses. . . .

It is, however, by no means clear that the public would prefer a substantially different structure in which lawyers played a substantially different role. In fact, Americans are ambivalent. The vast majority believe that, despite the problems in the justice system, it is still the best in the world. And while most people are critical of the zealous representation that attorneys provide to accused criminals and other unpopular defendants, when individuals imagine themselves in litigation, a zealous champion is precisely what they have in mind. In other legal contexts, much of what Americans dislike about opposing counsel is what they value in their own. One of the most positive traits that the public associates with lawyers is that their first priority is loyalty to their clients. Yet one of the most negative traits is lawyers' willingness to manipulate the system on behalf of clients without regard to right or wrong. People hate a hired gun until they need one of their own.

The public is similarly ambivalent about the tension between money and justice. Americans dislike the fact that the best legal representation typically goes to the highest bidder and that law is accessible only to those who can afford it. But Americans also dislike efforts to remedy those inequalities. Equal justice is what we inscribe over courthouse doors, not what we support in social policies. Our nation spends far less than other Western industrial societies on subsidized legal representation. Bar studies estimate that over four-fifths of the legal needs of low-income households and one-third of the needs of middle-income Americans remain unmet. . . . As a culture, we find it more convenient to fault the bar's greed than to acknowledge our own.

Although part of the public's discontent with lawyers reflects misplaced or displaced frustrations, not all of its complaints should be so readily dismissed. . . . [M]any criticisms of professional conduct and regulatory processes have a strong basis in fact. On matters such as excessive fees, unresponsive disciplinary structures, and overbroad protections of the professional monopoly, the public is not ambivalent, and its concerns are not unwarranted. Even on issues like zealous advocacy, where popular opinion is more divided, the individuals who have the most contact with lawyers and knowledge about their practices are the least satisfied.

On most important questions of professional regulation, the problem is not so much that the public is uninformed or undecided but rather that it is unorganized and uninvolved. For the vast majority of Americans, such issues are not a priority. Most people's direct contact with lawyers is limited. Routine users are usually organizational clients, which can deduct excessive legal costs as business expenses. Although egregious abuses or competitors' efforts can occasionally prod the public into action, nonlawyers seldom have sufficient incentives to organize around questions involving regulation of lawyers.

By contrast, the legal profession has every incentive to pursue regulatory concerns and to block initiatives that advanced public interests at the expense of its own. Although such problems are by no means unique to this regulatory context, they are compounded by the bar's pivotal role in American policy making. Unless some substantial constituencies within the profession—lawyers, judges, or legislators—share a reform agenda, its prospects are highly limited. Yet the conditions for advancing such an agenda have seldom been better. Discontent within the profession is substantial. The challenge lies in refocusing that disaffection in more constructive directions and in identifying ways to bridge the gap between professional and public interests.

The Problem from the Profession's Perspective

Recent profiles of legal practice have all the makings of a medieval morality play. In most bar journal accounts, the tone is cheery and the text is worldly; the focus is on power and money, winners and losers, movers and shakers. But at appointed intervals come cautionary subtexts: worries about a decline in ethical values and the loss of professional soul. Prosperity has come at a price, and many lawyers seem to be "searching for their lost wigs."

These competing themes reflect warring trends in contemporary legal practice. By many measures, lawyers have little cause for complaint. No profession offers a greater range of opportunities for financial security and public influence. In no other country do lawyers play such a significant role in social and economic policy. And in no other historical era has the legal profession been more diverse and more open to talent irrespective of race, gender, religion, and ethnicity. When asked directly about their current position, the vast majority of surveyed lawyers express satisfaction. Yet . . . other evidence paints a gloomier picture. A majority of lawyers report that they would choose another career if they had the decision to make over, and three-quarters would not want their children to become lawyers. Only one-fifth of attorneys feel that the law has lived up to their expectations in contributing to the social good. Symptoms of professional malaise are also apparent in health-related difficulties. An estimated one-third of American attorneys suffer from depression or from alcohol or drug addiction, a rate that is two to three times higher than in the public generally.

Although the primary sources of discontent vary somewhat across different areas of practice and demographic groups, common themes emerge. Lawyers are unhappy with the culture of the profession, the structure of their workplaces, and the performance of the justice system. At the most general level, the bar is concerned about the "decline of professionalism." That phrase captures a range of more specific complaints, such as increasing commercialism and competition and decreasing civility and collegiality. The perception of law as a craft and calling is under siege, and the consequence is an eroding sense of public service and cultural authority. . . . Increases in the number of lawyers have increased competition and diminished the force of informal reputational sanctions available in smaller professional communities. Price consciousness among corporate clients, together with the relaxation of bar restrictions on competitive practices within and across professions, have further intensified economic pressures. One result has been a strong emphasis on the bottom line, which squeezes the time available for pursuit of other professional values, such as mentoring and public service.

A further consequence of increased competition has been increased instability in lawyer-client relationships and increased constraints on professional independence. Corporate clients more often shop for representation on particular matters, rather than build long-term relationships. . . . As private practice becomes more competitive, specialized, and transactional, lawyers face more intense pressures to satisfy clients' short-term desires. Without a stable relationship of trust and confidence, it is risky for counsel to protest unreasonable demands or to deliver unwelcome messages about what legal rules or legal ethics require. Part of the dishonesty, incivility, and acrimony that lawyers find troubling in current practice seems driven by these profit dynamics. . . .

Legal practice has become more competitive within as well as among law firms. A steady rise in costs, coupled with instability in demand, have led to greater insecurity in private practice. . . . As working relations become more transient and more strained, fewer lawyers have a stake in investing in their professional culture. These trends are reflected and reinforced by the "eat what you kill" approach to law firm compensation. Partners who attract clients are at the top of the food chain. Lawyers with different priorities—mentoring, public service, quality of life—lack comparable leverage.

Indeed, for too many practitioners, "quality of life" is a nonissue. "What life?" Billable hour requirements have increased dramatically over the last two decades, and what has not changed is the number of hours in the day. Almost half of private practitioners now bill at least nineteen hundred hours per year, and to do so honestly they frequently need to work sixty-hour weeks. . . . [A]ll work and no play is fast becoming the norm rather than the exception. What lawyers lose is not just leisure. They also lose the opportunities for pro bono service, civic involvement, and breadth of experience that build professional judgment and sustain a professional culture.

The scope for crucial personal relationships is also narrowing. Almost half of American attorneys feel that they don't have enough time for their families. For employed women, who still spend about twice as much time on domestic responsibilities as employed men, the puritan ethic run amok poses special difficulties. Excessive hours are the leading cause of professional dissatisfaction among female practitioners. . . . Those with the greatest family commitments often drift off the partnership track, leaving behind a decision-making structure insulated from their concerns. Such patterns help account for the persistent underrepresentation of women in positions of greatest professional status and reward.

Other forces are at work as well. Some sixty recent reports on bias in the profession have chronicled persistent barriers to women and minorities. . . . [U]nconscious stereotypes and inadequate access to mentoring and business development networks compromise the profession's commitments to equal opportunity.

A further source of dissatisfaction involves the quality of work in private practice. Intellectual challenge is the main reason most attorneys choose law as a career, and for a substantial minority it falls well short of expectations. "Doing litigation" in the style to which junior attorneys have become accustomed often means endless cycles of scut work. . . . This lack of larger purpose accounts for the greatest gap between expectations and experience among American lawyers and the widely shared perception that their work is not contributing to the social good.

The reasons lawyers give for that failure partly overlap the ones the public gives. According to both groups, much of the problem involves a justice system that is unduly expensive and unwieldy, and ethical rules that are undemanding and underenforced. Most practitioners are unhappy with regulatory structures and with the incivility, hucksterism, and other misconduct that they seem powerless to prevent. All of these problems have left a growing number of lawyers disaffected or disengaged with their professional lives. . . .

. . . Most bar discussions of the decline of professionalism proceed with a highly selective historical memory. . . . [A]lthough legal practice earlier in this century generally is painted in rosy hues, there is much to dislike about what then passed for professionalism. As Harvard professor Mary Ann Glendon notes, some of the bar's best and brightest made their reputations "using every tactic in the book (and many that were not) to help bust unions, consolidate monopolies, and obtain favorable treatment" from corrupt judges.

Virtually every historical era that modern commentators applaud attracted its own share of critics with concerns similar to those heard today. In 1903, Supreme Court Justice Louis Brandeis warned lawyers that they were losing public respect because they were also losing their commitment to public service and their moral independence from clients. Several decades later, Supreme Court Justice Harlan Fiske Stone worried that the economic pressures of practice had transformed many attorneys into "obsequious servants of business, . . . tainted with the morals and the manners of the market place in its most antisocial manifestations." "More and more," Stone noted, "the amounts of [a lawyer's] income has become the measure of his professional status." Even sweatshop hours, which are usually taken as a distinctively corrosive feature of contemporary practice, have long provoked concern. In 1928, Arthur Train published a novel featuring a Wall Street firm that "never slept," with partners who "arrive early, stay late, and die young." . . .

Moreover, on at least some measures of professionalism, much is getting better. Increased competition also has encouraged increased efficiency and responsiveness to client concerns. The result for many consumers has been higher quality services at lower prices. Lawyers' greater self-consciousness about issues of professional responsibility is itself a sign of progress. So is the attention that these matters now receive in law schools. . . . Lawyers today are at least grappling with problems that in earlier eras were not even acknowledged as problems.

The same is true with issues involving race, gender, and sexual orientation. Washington practitioner Sol Linowitz, in his recent account of the *Betrayed Profession,* recalls that his law school class in the 1950s had only two women. Neither he nor most of his male classmates questioned the skewed ratio at the time, although they did feel somewhat uncomfortable when their two female colleagues were around. And he now acknowledges with rueful candor, "It never occurred to us to wonder whether *they* felt uncomfortable." In today's climate, much progress remains to be made, but at least such questions are on the agenda. . . .[T]hey are attracting reforms from a wide spectrum of bar associations, judicial commissions, and organizations employing lawyers.

We have moved in similar directions on access to legal services. Although . . . lawyers' average pro bono contributions leave much to be desired, efforts to assist those most in need are substantially increasing. Until recently, little pro bono assistance went to systematically underrepresented interests. The vast majority of beneficiaries were family, friends, and organizations serving primarily middle- and upper-income groups, such as hospitals, museums, and Jaycees. No law schools required student pro bono activity, and few made substantial efforts to encourage voluntary involvement. By contrast, today's lawyers and law students are far more likely to engage in pro bono work targeted at poverty and public interest causes.

There is, in short, little evidence for the common view that former Chief Justice Warren Burger expressed: that professionalism is in a "steady decline" or has reached a crisis of "epidemic proportions." The distance between professional ideals and professional practice has always been substantial, and in many respects the present is not demonstrably worse than the past. But neither are current conditions acceptable. And the bar as a whole is disturbingly passive and pessimistic in the face of its own problems. . . .

In short, the central problem facing the American legal profession is its own unwillingness to come to terms with what the problems are. At issue are competing values and concerns. Yet bar commentary on professionalism tends to paper over two central conflicts: the tensions between lawyers' economic and noneconomic interests, and the tensions between professional and public interests. Money is, of course, at the root of both conflicts. . . . [L]awyers have become habituated to "extraordinary incomes." In the process, luxuries have become necessities, wealth has become critical to self-esteem, and relative salaries have become a way of "keeping score."

Yet that process is often self-defeating. . . . [P]eople in general and lawyers in particular overvalue income as a way of achieving satisfaction. . . . But most people overestimate how much money matters. They quickly adjust to higher earnings, and their expectations and desires increase accordingly. And the priority that many lawyers and law firms attach to salaries compromises other goals that are more central to satisfaction, such as time for friends and families and choice of work that is morally and intellectually satisfying.

Lawyers also face a related trade-off that the professionalism debate fails to acknowledge. In the bar's idealized vision of professional life, lawyers can expect both moral independence and worldly rewards, such as power, wealth, and prominence. In actual practice, however, these interests frequently conflict. . . .

The rhetoric of professionalism tends to paper over this conflict by making a virtue out of expedience. Under prevailing views of professional responsibility, lawyers need not choose to exercise moral independence within their professional role. Rather, their preeminent obligation is loyalty to client interests. Over the last century, the bar's codes of conduct have progressively narrowed the ethical discretion that lawyers are expected to exercise once they have accepted representation. . . . [A]n attorney's obligation is to defend, not judge, the client. Under this standard view, good ethics and good business are in happy coincidence. . . .

A final trade-off, similarly unacknowledged in professionalism debates, involves the tension between professional autonomy and public respect. As noted earlier, lawyers put public image at the top of the list of problems facing the profession. . . . Yet despite concerns about their poor public reputation, most lawyers resist efforts to address its sources. They particularly resist seeing any connection between public respect and public accountability or any tension between public accountability and professional autonomy. Rather, the assumption frequently repeated in ethical codes and bar discussions is that self-regulation serves the common good by helping to "maintain the legal profession's independence from government domination."

Almost never do bar leaders acknowledge the possibility that self-interest might occasionally skew lawyers' judgments on matters of professional regulation. . . . No occupational group, however well intentioned, can make unbiased assessments of the public interest on issues that place its own status and income directly at risk. As virtually every expert observes, the greater a profession's control over its own regulation, the greater the risks of tunnel vision. . . .

The American legal profession is no exception. Standards of conduct have been drafted, approved, and administered by bodies composed almost entirely of attorneys. Nonlawyers have had no representation in the adoption of those standards by courts and bar associations and have obtained only token representation on disciplinary bodies. These lay members typically are chosen by the profession and rarely have the backgrounds, resources, or ties to consumer organizations that could create a significant check on professional self-interest.

Given this structure, it is scarcely surprising that studies of bar regulatory processes uniformly find serious flaws in their responsiveness to ordinary consumer grievances. . . . [L]ess than 2 percent of complaints to bar disciplinary agencies result in public sanctions. Yet although the vast majority of

surveyed attorneys concede that the current disciplinary process is inadequate, comparable numbers reject changes in its structure. The bar's unwillingness to confront trade-offs in its regulatory objectives undermines its professionalism agenda. As long as lawyers resist public accountability, they are unlikely to win public confidence.

If lawyers are seriously committed to fostering professionalism, they first must confront the structural reforms it requires. The bar needs a vision beyond the wistful nostalgia and wishful exhortation that dominates current debates.

Recasting the Problem, Rethinking the Responses

Over the last decade, the professionalism problem has launched a cottage industry of efforts: commissions, conferences, courses, centers, creeds, and codes. Despite these efforts, chronic ethical dilemmas remain unresolved. Part of the problem involves the lack of consensus about what the problems are or what trade-offs should be made among competing professional and public interests. Only at the most abstract level do lawyers rally around the same vision. Today's profession has become too diverse and specialized, and its leadership too weak and divided, to enforce any unifying vision of professional ideals. . . . [T]he bar has lurched from project to project, leaving in its wake an overload of soggy lamentations, war-weary clichés, and mixed metaphors. . . .

Any serious response to the dilemmas confronting the American legal profession must begin from different premises. That alternative vision . . . reflects several guiding principles. These involve the ethical responsibilities of lawyers, access to legal services, and bar regulatory structures. . . .

The term *profession* has its origins in the Latin root "to profess" and in the European tradition of requiring members to declare their commitment to shared ideals. The American bar has maintained the form but lost the substance of that tradition. Entering lawyers may still profess to serve justice as officers of the court, but that declaration has little moral content in contemporary practice. Efforts to revive a richer sense of professionalism have foundered on the lack of consensus about what that concept should require and how to reconcile it with more worldly interests.

In this context, it makes sense to view professionalism not as a fixed ideal but rather as an ongoing struggle. The challenge is to work toward understandings of professional responsibility that are both more and less demanding. They must ask for more than current codes and enforcement structures, but they must offer a vision that also

seems plausible in practice. Recent debates on professionalism have suffered from overly idealistic goals and overly limited responses.

That mismatch is by no means inevitable. On matters of public interest not involving their own regulation, lawyers have been crucial in bridging the gap between ideals and institutions. By turning similar energies inward, the bar may give more substantial content to its highest aspirations.

5.5 From *The Supreme Court Bar: Legal Elites in the Washington Community* (1993)

Kevin T. McGuire

An Elite Set of Litigators

The modern Supreme Court lawyer does not closely resemble his counterpart of the nineteenth century. Although these lawyers have assumed the gatekeeping role of their latter-day brethren, the current bar of the high court is quite different from the bar that existed in the dawning days of the republic. Many early litigators, for instance, were members of Congress serving in Washington during legislative sessions. Today, it would be quite unusual for a senator or member of Congress to appear at the podium to argue a case—although members of Congress do, on occasion, participate in Court litigation as amici curiae. In the 1800s, when formal legal training did not exist, attorneys studied law either on their own or under the tutelage of practicing advocates. In contrast, a good many modern Supreme Court lawyers have been trained at the nation's elite law schools. Furthermore, virtually all of the Supreme Court counsel in the nineteenth century were male. In short, historical comparisons reveal a similarity in function but not in form. Still, like their antecedents, the lawyers of the modern Supreme Court remain an elite set of political actors. Why?

In part, the transformation of the Supreme Court bar reflects changes in the legal profession at large.

Legal education has been formalized and is now open to a wide range of students; admission to practice is regulated; the bar in general is increasingly more specialized and stratified. More than anything else, though, the stratification of the bar accounts for the distinctive character of the Court's counsel. At the broadest level, this stratification has resulted in the formation of two major groups—lawyers from lower socioeconomic backgrounds who serve individual clients and smaller economic interests, and lawyers from more privileged backgrounds who represent large organizations and wealthy corporate interests.

These social lines within the bar have a direct bearing upon the nature and quality of legal representation generally and thus affect judicial outcomes. Those who occupy the positions of occupational prestige represent the wealthy and powerful and, like many elites, are advantaged in judicial politics. The consequences of this stratification are exemplified, even magnified, among the litigators who practice in the Supreme Court. In order to grasp the direction and magnitude of their influence as gatekeepers to the Court, one must compare them to their peers in the legal profession, to see what distinguishes those who become active Supreme Court practitioners from those who do not.

Attributes of the Supreme Court Bar

The typical Supreme Court lawyer is a forty-five-year-old, Harvard-educated private practitioner, based in New York, Washington, or Chicago. He

Kevin T. McGuire, "An Elite Set of Litigators" and "The Inner Circle at Work" in *The Supreme Court Bar: Legal Elites in the Washington Community* (Charlottesville: University of Virginia Press, 1993). Reprinted with permission of University of Virginia Press.

specializes in appellate litigation and has at least a half dozen Supreme Court cases to his credit. He is a liberal white Protestant, with strong attachment to the Democratic party. Of course such a general sketch cannot capture the complexity of the full picture. . . .

Size.   The number of lawyers in the United States is fast approaching one million . . .

. . . The official "Bar of the Supreme Court," which consists of those attorneys who have been admitted to practice before the Court, is quite large but of unknown numbers. Since 1925, roughly 134,000 lawyers have been admitted to the bar, with an additional 5,000 attorneys joining the ranks each year. Unfortunately, though, the Court does not purge its rolls. Thus, the size of its actual current membership cannot be established, although it is unquestionably smaller than these figures suggest. Attrition has certainly diminished the numbers. Moreover, the active bar—the subject of our investigation—is only a subset of the official bar, many of whom seek membership as a mark of professional status. Moreover, regardless of the formal bar's size, the likelihood of serving as counsel, even at the case selection stage, remains minimal at best. In any given term, therefore, only a small segment of the legal community participates in Supreme Court litigation.

Employment Setting.   Part of the reason why the Court's counsel tend to be an elite group is that many occupy positions that command considerable social, political, and economic resources. This concentration of legal power is significant, because so much of the practice in the Supreme Court thereby becomes a function of where and for whom one works. Some legal positions inevitably lead to litigation in the Court, the most obvious and notable example being an appointment in the solicitor general's office. Other employment settings, however, are also conducive to interactions with the Court, such as positions that are by design directed toward appellate practice.

The litigators who are engaged in the Court's docket are differentiated much in the manner of the general population of the bar. . . . Private practitioners dominate the bar among both groups. A closer look at the Court's attorneys shows that of the 75 percent who practice law privately, 18 per-

cent are solo practitioners while the remaining 82 percent work in a law firm. . . .

It is here, in the law firms, that one finds many of the Court's active litigators. Attorneys who work in firms—especially large firms—are more likely to serve clients whose business activities make them candidates for litigation in the high court. As one lawyer in a large Washington firm put it,

> If you're an appellate lawyer for a big corporation or another major litigant, sooner or later, you're going to end up in the Supreme Court. And if you continue to be Burlington Northern's appellate lawyer, every time Burlington Northern goes to the Supreme Court, you're going to go, too.

Some 5 percent of all lawyers are employed in state and local government, but at the level of the Supreme Court the proportion of counsel who work in state government is more than three times the national average. Since state and local agencies are so often involved in the issues that dominate the justices' agenda—criminal and constitutional cases, for example—it is not surprising to find that over 15 percent of Supreme Court attorneys represent state governments. . . .

. . . A small but significant minority of lawyers . . . work in the service of organized interests.

. . . [A]mong such organizations one is likely to find some of the Court's most notable practitioners. . . .

Still, whether one focuses on the Court's bar or the distribution of lawyers nationally, the attorneys who work for organized interests do not constitute a large portion of the legal universe.

Members of the legal professoriate often appear in Supreme Court litigation, sometimes in the Court's most visible cases. Laurence Tribe of Harvard University, the scholar whose mammoth constitutional law text is a staple of many law schools, is probably the most renowned academic lawyer. . . .

Gideon v. Wainwright (1963) established the right of criminal defendants to legal counsel, and along with the growing concern the Supreme Court showed for the accused came an acceleration in the number of agencies designed to provide legal assistance to those incapable of paying for such services. Thus, to the extent that consumers of legal aid services have cases that raise constitutional questions, their counsel will appear in Supreme Court litigation. Such participation, proportionally speaking, is not insignificant. . . .

One kind of lawyer clearly underrepresented in the Supreme Court is the corporate in-house counsel, one of the most prestigious positions within the profession. Roughly 10 percent of all lawyers serve as in-house counsel, but their representation in the Court is the smallest for any category of lawyer. . . .

Perhaps the most significant reason has to do with the nature of corporate practice. Office work is endemic to the enterprise of corporate representation; house counsel seldom appear in court and their work is generally not directed toward litigation. . . .

Another reason for the relative scarcity of corporate lawyers among the Supreme Court bar has to do with legal specialization. . . . [C]orporations are among the most likely to seek specialists when they find themselves involved in Supreme Court cases. Business interests, of course, do litigate in the Court, but under such circumstances large corporations often turn to lawyers who have had the greatest experience before the justices. Such lawyers overwhelmingly reside in private practice.

Age. Rising to the top in politics or business takes time, and lawyers in the Court are not exempt from this rule. With age come experience and expertise, both scarce resources in the Supreme Court. One would thus expect the Court's bar to be a more seasoned group, superior in professional maturity. How old are the Court's lawyers? . . .

Some 30 percent of all attorneys are under the age of thirty-five. . . . [M]ore than 80 percent of the Court's bar falls between the ages of thirty-five and sixty-four, with nearly half of all Supreme Court lawyers aged between thirty-five and forty-four. Thus, the Supreme Court bar is dominated by those who have reached a level of professional maturity and who are in the prime years of their legal careers.

This is not the case for American lawyers in general. In recent years, one national transformation within the profession has been the general lowering of age and collective legal experience. . . . On balance, then, the bar of the Court tends to be older than its national counterpart. . . .

Gender. As with many elites, Supreme Court practitioners are overwhelmingly male. Few women

have entered the ranks of attorneys active in litigation before the Court: only 7.3 percent of the Supreme Court bar is female. By contrast, the proportion of women within the national bar is 13.1 percent, nearly twice the percentage of female lawyers in the Court. Still, both figures are modest compared to the number of women in the American population as a whole.

Recent years, however, have witnessed an influx of women into the legal profession. Prior to the mid-1980s, the distribution of the sexes among practicing lawyers was virtually identical to the present gender distribution of the Supreme Court bar. In other words, in terms of gender, the present collection of Supreme Court litigators is a representative cross section of American lawyers a decade ago. One might speculate, then, that as these young female lawyers become established in the profession and gain practical legal experience, they will tend to enter the ranks of the Court's counsel in greater numbers. If the hiring practices of the nation's larger law firms are indicative of a trend toward greater diversity within the legal profession, then women (and racial minorities) will surely have growing representation among the Court's lawyers. . . .

To a certain extent, women have already achieved a visible presence. Several of the Court's more notable practitioners are women, and the solicitor general's office has admitted women in increasing numbers. . . . Indeed, one might suspect that the Court's ongoing willingness to consider women's issues—abortion, the effect of the industrial workplace on reproduction, and so on—will result in an increased reliance upon female litigators. . . .

City of Practice. Baltimore, Philadelphia, and Washington no longer have the primary claim to the bar of the Court. In any given term, petitions will come to the Court bearing the names of attorneys from across the country. Still, like their elite predecessors, the majority of the Supreme Court's lawyers continue to practice in only a few major metropolitan centers.

. . . Taken together, New York, Washington, and Chicago lawyers constitute nearly one quarter of all Supreme Court counsel. . . .

In part, the dominance of these three cities at the bar is a function of the Court's docket. Many large businesses and industries have their headquarters in these locations. Likewise, a multitude of organized interests—many of which are frequent litigators before the Court —are based there. . . .

Another reason that these cities boast such a large share of the Court's bar is related to the demographics of the bar nationally. Indeed, these three cities also contain the largest proportion of the total population of lawyers. . . .

Perhaps most important [is] the dominance of the elite Washington community within the bar of the Court. Washington has more lawyers per capita than any other American city and thus a disproportionate share of the national bar. Interestingly, the capital's share of the Supreme Court bar is not just greater than its share of all lawyers, but dramatically so—almost 50 percent more than its already rich representation of counsel. Although in an absolute sense the Washington bar does not dominate the Supreme Court, the nation's capital stands out as the city making the largest possible contribution to the Supreme Court bar. . . .

Legal Education. . . . [T]he elite law schools have educated a third of the Court's attorneys, with law schools such as Harvard, Michigan, Yale, and Chicago serving as the chief training grounds for those who go on to practice in the Supreme Court. . . . [Seventy] percent of the Court's lawyers attended an above average law school. These numbers suggest that the Supreme Court bar is populated with well-trained practitioners. This in turn raises the question of precisely which law schools future Supreme Court lawyers attended most frequently. . . .

Given the variety and quality of legal education in the nation's capital, one might speculate that many members of the Court's bar are Washington-trained. In fact, fully 5 percent of Supreme Court lawyers graduated from one of four law schools within the federal city—American, Catholic, George Washington, and Georgetown. Overall, 5 percent may seem a modest contribution, but then only 2 percent of American law schools are located in that city. . . . Perhaps predictably, Harvard produces the most Supreme Court lawyers. . . .

In comparison to the legal education of lawyers nationally, the Supreme Court bar has more graduates of the best law schools. The majority of lawyers in both groups—about 51 percent of Supreme

Court lawyers and 56 percent of lawyers nationally—obtained their legal training at . . . average to strong law schools. At the extremes, however, the differences become quite distinct: 32 percent of the Court's lawyers were trained at distinguished law schools, while nationally these institutions train roughly two and a half times fewer advocates. Likewise, nearly one third of the nation's lawyers are trained at below average institutions, almost twice the proportion at the Supreme Court level. . . .

Race. Among those who hold positions of influence in the United States, minorities are clearly underrepresented. Not surprisingly, then, as an elite stratum of the legal population, the Supreme Court bar consists almost entirely of whites—98 percent in fact. That so few minorities practice before the Court must be, in part, a reflection of their small numbers in the bar at large. Although traditionally underrepresented groups, such as blacks and Hispanics, have begun to increase in number within the overall population of lawyers, a similar trend cannot be detected among Supreme Court practitioners. . . .

Blacks have made the greatest gains among minorities, yet they still account for but 2 percent of all lawyers. Among Supreme Court counsel, they appear in a slightly smaller proportion, roughly 1 percent. Of course, their numbers within the Supreme Court bar are clearly not commensurate with their influence. Several black lawyers have distinguished themselves as Supreme Court practitioners, many playing prominent roles in civil rights litigation. . . . [N]otables include former Solicitor General Wade H. McCree and William T. Coleman, Jr., secretary of transportation under President Ford and widely regarded as one of the Court's most skillful advocates. Of course, Justice Thurgood Marshall was an active advocate prior to coming to the Court. During the 1960s his service on behalf of the NAACP Legal Defense Fund as well as his tenure as solicitor general brought him numerous opportunities to brief and argue cases for the Court. . . .

Religion. From the standpoint of religious faith, there is considerable evidence that the influential members of American society are not representative of the United States population as a whole. Lawyers certainly do not mirror the American population on this score. [A]nd the difference is equally glaring for the bar of the Supreme Court. It is therefore instructive to consider how the Supreme Court bar compares not only to the overall population of lawyers but also to the American people in general. . . .

Like most Americans, the majority of American lawyers are Protestants. Further, the proportion of Catholics in the two groups is virtually identical. Among Supreme Court lawyers in particular, however, religious faith is much more evenly distributed than it is among the population overall. Protestants still outnumber members of other faiths but to a significantly smaller degree. Only about a third of Supreme Court lawyers are Protestant, in striking contrast to both American lawyers as a whole and the population generally, where Protestant religions garner well over half the faithful. Catholics, though, account for a relatively comparable portion of all three groups.

It is the Jewish members of the bar who afford the greatest contrast. Six times as many lawyers are Jewish than are Americans generally. Still, Jews comprise barely one-tenth of all lawyers. At the level of the Supreme Court, however, this figure jumps to almost one quarter. Why the disparity? The most likely explanation serves indirectly to reinforce the image of the Supreme Court bar as an elite subset of attorneys.

As I noted earlier, relative to the bar as a whole, the Supreme Court bar claims a disproportionate number of outstanding legal minds, products of the nation's elite law programs. In fact, distinguished law schools stood out as the greatest contributors to the pool of Supreme Court practitioners. Significantly, a majority of the Jewish members of the Supreme Court bar (51 percent) attended the nation's most prestigious law schools. In comparison, only 27 percent of non-Jewish Supreme Court practitioners can boast an elite legal education. The disproportionate Jewish share of the Court's bar, therefore, presumably stems from superior legal training. This finding is consistent with previous research on the nexus between legal education and religious preference.

. . . Beyond the three major religious categories, the only notable distinction of the Supreme Court bar is its substantial number of atheists. This probably reflects the cosmopolitan nature of the respondents: the more elite the sample, the more atheism one would expect to encounter. Although the percentage of Supreme Court lawyers who consider themselves atheists is larger than that observed for the American population, this proportion is more or less congruent with the findings in other studies of the bar. . . . Nonetheless, it is fair to characterize the bar of the Court as one would the bar in general: largely affiliated with traditional religions.

Political Beliefs.   Socioeconomic status correlates strongly with political attitudes. Social elites generally have more education and higher incomes and tend to hold more conservative views than the balance of the population. Our expectation might therefore be that the bar of the Court would be skewed in favor of conservative Republicans. After all, lawyers are among the highest wage earners in America, and existing survey research indicates that such a social cohort would strongly identify with the Republican party. The data . . ., however, tell a different tale.

Broadly speaking, the Supreme Court's lawyers are considerably more pro-Democratic than the American people as a whole Nearly one half the Court's bar identify either weakly or strongly with the Democratic party in comparison to roughly one third of the population nationally. . . .

How do Supreme Court lawyers stack up against the legal profession as a whole? Interestingly, the liberal bias manifests itself even more meaningfully when the Court's counsel are gauged against their brethren. . . . [L]awyers are apt to be conservative; thus, it occasions no surprise to discover that the proportion of Republicans in the legal profession is nearly double that in the population overall. Strikingly, however, despite their sizable preponderance within the bar generally, Republicans within the Court's bar are relatively meager in number. In fact, the ratio between GOP counsel in the two groups is better than two-to-one in favor of the national bar. In contrast, the Democrats' share of the Court's bar—nearly one half of all Supreme Court counsel—is almost 25 percent greater than their proportion in the legal profession at large.

There are several possible reasons for the liberal dominance. Liberal attorneys typically have been interested in using litigation as a means of law reform and thus, all other things being equal, are more likely to become involved in the myriad policy disputes that find their way to the Court. In contrast, lawyers who are only infrequently involved directly in *any* litigation—corporate house counsel, for example—may be inherently sympathetic to business and hence more conservative. Then again, it might be that liberal lawyers responded to my survey with greater alacrity than conservative ones. Regardless of the interpretations one might bring to bear to these data, however, the results do demonstrate that the political preferences of Supreme Court lawyers differ markedly not only from those of the American population but also from those of their peers within the legal profession.

Conclusion

Lawyers are an elite group in American society, and those who litigate before the Supreme Court are even further elevated in the social hierarchy. . . . [I]t is plain that Supreme Court lawyers are not a representative sample of the American legal profession. On the contrary, these lawyers are an elite within an elite. . . .

This stratification has important implications for our understanding of the politics of litigation in the Supreme Court. The modern bar of the Supreme Court has a discrete identity as a legal elite, and its experienced practitioners are the primary power brokers in Supreme Court politics. Issues that make their way through the judicial hierarchy as far as the Supreme Court are likely to be socially and/or politically significant. . . . [T]he nature of the lawyers who argue these issues is equally crucial. . . .

The Inner Circle at Work

. . . Arguments before the justices are the most visible portion of Supreme Court work, but they are only part of a broader range of activities. For every argument a lawyer has made in the Supreme Court, there are nearly twenty cases at the agenda stage in which he has served as counsel; for each amicus brief a lawyer has written on the merits, there are two others he has filed in support of petitions for review. Having noted the significance of the bar's stratification—its division into inner and outer circles—and the strategic importance of how the elite are mobilized in litigation, one can turn attention to the kinds of work, both formal and informal, that the Supreme Court lawyers perform. . . .

Visible and Invisible Participation

Scanning the pages of any volume of the *United States Reports,* one might begin to suspect that only a very few lawyers are active Supreme Court practitioners. After all, in any given term of the Court, only the lawyers in the solicitor general's office are conspicuous for their frequent appearances before the justices. Examining but a single avenue of influence, however—looking only at active participation on the merits—obscures the rich participation of lawyers in Supreme Court politics. If, for example, one considers petitions for certiorari, jurisdictional statements, briefs opposing review, and amicus curiae briefs, one discovers that a good many lawyers participate on a consistent basis. Even the number of arguments, when viewed across a longer period of time, would reflect patterns of frequent involvement by a variety of attorneys.

The participation of these lawyers in Supreme Court litigation can assume a great many forms. Some types of involvement, such as presenting oral arguments, are quite conspicuous. Others are less visible—almost invisible—and are thus apt to be disregarded or dismissed as unimportant. The fact of the matter, however, is that much of the behind-the-scenes work that takes place in Supreme Court litigation is vital to success in the Court, particularly at the agenda stage. No one has a more keen appreciation of this fact than the members of the inner circle.

Let us examine the range of activities of the Court's counsel. Perhaps the most obvious places to begin are the agenda and merits stages. . . .

[A]ppearing before the Court to argue a case is only one component of what these lawyers do. Much of the work done by many Supreme Court practitioners—especially the experienced ones—takes place behind the scenes, as this veteran advocate explained.

> There are various roles in which people like us can help. We can take over a case, but we can also give advice to a lawyer, edit the stuff to make sure that it's presented in the right way to the Court, give moot courts to help the lawyer prepare for oral argument.

. . .Supreme Court lawyers engage in a considerable range of tasks. Of all the individual forms of participation, consultation on the preparation of petitions or oppositions at the agenda stage is the service Supreme Court lawyers most often provide, but, in the aggregate, the bulk of their effort appears to be targeted at preparing their colleagues to argue at the merits. Many of the experienced Supreme Court lawyers in Washington, for example, evaluate one another's oral preparations, criticize their briefs, and school less experienced counsel on what questions to expect from the justices. Prior to her fledgling effort before the Court, one nervous appellate practitioner allowed me to hear the first of her several moot court preparations in a case she was later to argue; among the "justices" were a former advocate for the ACLU and an alumnus of the solicitor general's office. (In fact, just after his first argument before the justices, another lawyer admitted that his appearance at the moot court had actually been more stressful.) Such activities are common. . . .

Far from being restricted to the private bar, similar practices take place among state government attorneys. Indeed, they have been institutionalized. The National Association of Attorneys General (NAAG), with the cooperation of the Justice Department, has implemented a program designed to prime state and local counsel for their appearances in the Court. The State and Local Legal Center has an analogous program. Even lawyers in the experienced public interest bar may provide assistance to outside counsel who are new to the Court. . . .

Providing assistance to colleagues is only part of the story. Lawyers may become active in Supreme Court cases even if they are not serving directly as counsel to one of the parties. Many Supreme Court attorneys are active as writers of amicus briefs, for instance, at both stages of the Court's decision making. . . . [R]oughly one in five Supreme Court lawyers has filed amicus briefs supporting review. The same can also be said for amicus briefs at the merits. . . .

By now it should be clear that much of the work of the Supreme Court bar is dotted throughout the Court's discretionary and plenary dockets. Duties such as behind-the-scenes preparation and the secondary role of writing amicus briefs are not obvious at first glance. Nonetheless, a significant proportion of the Supreme Court bar carries out such tasks quite regularly. This raises the question of which Supreme Court lawyers are most likely to

engage in these less visible activities. Once again, the evidence points to the inner circle as the principal suspect.

Quite apart from lawyers seeking the assistance of their peers, litigants may also turn to the experienced elite to perform these secondary roles. Many parties seek out the specialists specifically for the purpose of helping their inexperienced practitioners navigate the waters of the Supreme Court. Indeed, several Supreme Court experts saw this as a primary function of the Court's bar:

> Often the lawyer is not dumped when the case gets to the Supreme Court. A Supreme Court specialist will come in and work with whoever handled the case in the court of appeals. That's what we do—almost all the time.
>
> If I had only ten thousand dollars to spend, there are two things I would do. First, spend the money and get the people in there to help you write the petition or to write the opposition. It's not only in so much as the writing of it, as it is the strategizing and figuring out what to do. Second, at the merits, don't spend the money to have the expert come and argue the case. Spend it to have somebody read the brief. Not writing the arguments—any good lawyer can write the arguments—but thinking the thing through and doing a moot court. Use it on a consultative basis.

. . . From an economic standpoint, tapping the resources of the elite in this way makes a good deal of sense. Reflecting on how experienced counsel are employed in an advisory capacity, one interest group lawyer with extensive experience litigating in the Court commented:

> If a client has a long-term relationship with a lawyer, and they've never had a case that's gone to the Supreme Court, and if the lawyer's won below, the client is going to be reluctant to quash the lawyer, if the lawyer is able at all. So the more sensible thing may be to get somebody else in to help you out a little bit. That will be undoubtedly much less expensive, and probably get about 90 percent of the benefits of the lawyer with experience, certainly, in terms of preparing for oral argument, reviewing the brief, thinking through a strategy. That's a lot less

time-consuming and expensive than taking over the full representation.

. . . The role of the elite in the filling of amicus briefs is no less dramatic. . . . Amici are an important mechanism whereby the certworthiness of a case can be signaled to the justices, as experienced Supreme Court litigators are well aware. It comes as no surprise, therefore, that those with expertise recognize the value of amici by their willingness to participate in such a capacity. Granted, experienced counsel are fairly likely to file amicus briefs opposing review, but they are considerably more apt to file amici supporting review. This is testament to the political savvy of at least some of the Supreme Court veterans, since briefs opposing review serve only to attract the justices' attention to a case.

Certain parties, such as interest groups and state governments, are frequent litigants before the Court. So one would expect their lawyers to perform a variety of tasks in Supreme Court litigation, including the writing of amicus briefs. Even these litigants, though, will sometimes seek out the Supreme Court specialists. . . . Perhaps, also, clients are prompted to seek a member of the inner circle to draft an amicus brief in the belief that the name of that specialist on the brief may carry some added weight. The elite bar is, in other words, sought as a means of cultivating access to the Court.

As it turns out, having the name of a specialist on your brief can prove no small advantage. On one of my visits to the Justice Department, a current member of the solicitor general's office told me that many amicus briefs are of decidedly questionable value to the Court: "I think a lot of the amicus filings are really trash." As he went on to point out, however, amici written by experienced Supreme Court counsel probably are of genuine worth to the bench:

> The justices really can't spend a lot of time closely scrutinizing all the amicus fillings that are made. They look with some care at the briefs of the parties. I think they glance over the amicus fillings much more lightly. But if they see that there's an amicus filing by a lawyer whose analysis they have found helpful in the past, they are more apt to take a closer look at it.

This opinion is shared by lawyers outside the solicitor general's office. In a perfect description of why parties would benefit from amici written by experienced Supreme Court litigators, one Court veteran said:

> Far too many of them are essentially "me too" briefs. I guess if you wanted your amicus brief read, it might be worth it to hire a Supreme Court practitioner. I think any of the recognized Supreme Court specialists would be unwilling to sign a "me too" brief. So, in that sense, if you've got a brief that you want somebody to read, it is worth it to get a specialist's name on it.

. . . The Court itself has become increasingly less interested in hearing from amici whose substantive contributions to the litigation process are marginal. Thus, the value of elite counsel as writers of and consultants on amicus briefs lies in the fact that their names assist the justices in separating the wheat from the chaff. . . .

Motives for Litigation

As cases make their way to the Supreme Court, lawyers are faced with choices: Should review be sought? Will review be sought, and if so how can the pleading be best supported? The answers to such questions will reflect the lawyer's perspective on the incentives and constraints of the case. . . .

. . . Some lawyers are concerned primarily with securing a legal victory on behalf of their clients. Their main interest turning on the immediate result of a case—did their client win or lose?—they have only incidental concern for the larger ramifications their cases may raise for public policy. Other attorneys may see their cases principally as vehicles for resolving important legal and social questions and thus be relatively less concerned with the fate of an individual client.

Although the application of these two basic orientations among counsel was made originally in the context of civil liberties cases, there is no theoretical reason not to extend a similar classification to the bar as a whole. After all, policies can be economic, as well as social, but invite similar forms of legal involvement. A corporate lawyer, for instance, seeking only to protect a client's patent or secure an exemption from antitrust law, would presumably provide the traditional, results-oriented form of representation. Other lawyers may instead represent a particular long-term policy interest. Labor unions, for example, are among those clients whose basic political interests are economic. Thus, the differentiation between lawyers observed in cases pertaining to social policy may have broader applications.

How important are such considerations to the Supreme Court bar as a whole? Put another way, what motivates lawyers to take cases to the Supreme Court? . . .

Losses in lower courts and client preferences stand out as the most common reasons for seeking review—and not surprisingly. Obviously, a lawyer would not petition the Court had his client not lost in a lower court and considered the case important enough to press on. At the same time, the importance of these two motivations demonstrates that many Supreme Court lawyers do simply serve as advocates on their clients' behalf. Corporate counsel, for instance, are fairly constrained by their clients. Thus, when corporations decide to seek Supreme Court review, counsel probably have little to say in the matter, whether they be in-house lawyers or attorneys from a large law firm. Among the law firm counsel who petitioned the Court, for instance, nearly 60 percent reported that their clients' desire to seek Supreme Court review was a very important consideration. In short, many lawyers can, for the most part, do only what their clients will permit them to do. At best, their influence may be restricted to discouraging the client from seeking Supreme Court review. . . .

Similarly, solo practitioners generally do not have far-reaching social or political goals underlying their litigation strategies. Their interest in Supreme Court policy is incidental to the more immediate concern of a legal victory, as one can readily understand. The solo attorney does not have the stable client base that law firms enjoy. . . . Moreover, these clients often have somewhat unsavory legal problems; they are being pursued by a collections agency, or there's a problem with landlord-tenant relations. Thus, not only does the volatile nature of solo practice perpetuate a short-term view of litigation outcomes but solo practitioners also fail to attract the kinds of clients who care about larger policy considerations. . . . Even

when the solo practitioner does find himself representing a client whose case might raise important social or political issues, he is still likely to assume a short-term perspective. . . .

In this respect, then, the Supreme Court bar is not an equal-opportunity employer. Not all of its members are permitted—or can afford—to pursue issue-oriented work with any regularity. Still, a fair number of private attorneys do seek review because of broader considerations, such as the need for a national standard on the concerns raised by a case, the need to resolve judicial ambiguity, or the presence of a novel issue which has gone unaddressed by the justices. Traditionally, though, it has fallen to counsel to organized interests to address such questions, and quite often their concern extends beyond the immediate outcome of litigation. Rather, they are interested in the degree to which their general public policy goals can be met via the judicial system. Interest groups, such as the ACLU, NAACP, or the AFL-CIO, each have a special set of policy aims, many of which they attempt to achieve through litigation. Of course, interest group cases often arise under circumstances over which the group's attorney exercises little or no control. One former NAACP litigator pointed out that

> when we were involved with some of the civil rights cases, and those young kids were going to jail, we couldn't be selective and say, "Oh, this upsets our strategy."

Nonetheless, organized interests generally enjoy greater flexibility in their selection of cases than do other lawyers. As an alumnus of the ACLU's national office explained:

> We would select cases all the time. A lot of the ACLU cases raise similar issues, all around the country, and we did make judgment calls about which one to push, which one to hold back on, which one to take up, which one not to take up. Fortunately, a lot of the clients that the ACLU represents are "public cause" type clients, and they understand if their case is not the best one to go up.

Such decisions are not always so easy. A lawyer may, for example, be very much concerned with responding to the wishes of the client but also see the case as an excellent opportunity to influence public policy. . . . What course of action will these lawyers follow in such cases?

Strategic Politics: The Case of Amici Curiae

At the level of the Supreme Court, one would not only expect lawyers to employ different strategies in their cases but also suspect that the nature of the case determines the types of strategies they pursue. To put it another way, how do the variables operative in the decision to seek review influence what lawyers actually do in Supreme Court litigation? As an illustration, let us consider the question of whether lawyers solicit amicus support for their pleadings. After all, if an interest group lawyer is concerned with using a certain case to shape national policy, what better way to promote that goal than by demonstrating to the Court that the issues of the case are of serious concern to an outside set of public interests? By way of contrast, a solo practitioner seeking review solely to vindicate the rights of the client might not be aware that garnering external support for the case could be of considerable consequence. Furthermore, what about the lawyer who is guided both by client demand and the desire to promote a policy objective? Is that lawyer any more likely to seek the support of friends at the agenda stage?

It is instructive at this stage to consider the more basic issue of whether *any* Supreme Court lawyers encourage an endorsement from amici curiae. On balance, the answer is that the inner circle does, while the outer circle does not. . . .

If many lawyers at the periphery of the bar have failed to grasp the significance of support from amici, it is common knowledge among both Supreme Court experts and political scientists. . . .

If the elite practitioners actively seek amicus support, then, under precisely what conditions do they seek it? What can the factors that influence the decision to seek Supreme Court review tell us about whether and when lawyers try to find organized interests who will support their petitions? In general, the likelihood of encouraging amici appears to turn on the breadth of the perceived interests in the case. This applies to all kinds of litigation, economic as well as social. For example,

I have sought amici. Particularly when representing a client in an industry where the industry is likely to be adversely affected by the outcome of a case, I have encouraged trade associations to file amicus briefs.

. . . Lawyers whose approach to Supreme Court litigation is dominated by client interests alone are, it turns out, relatively unconcerned with generating outside support for their cases. For instance, there is almost no interest in seeking amici among lawyers whose decision to seek review was motivated primarily by a loss in a lower court. Similarly, lawyers whose clients were anxious to take their cases to the Court do not appear especially eager to activate support from amici. Nor do lawyers typically solicit the assistance of organized interests in a case that has gone to the Supreme Court because of conflicting rulings in the lower courts. In contrast, it makes a great deal of difference whether the petitioner saw his or her case as a vehicle for setting a national policy or addressing a new legal question. In those instances, lawyers are much more likely to seek out amici to reinforce their claims. . . .

It's my personal opinion that the cert stage is the place where amicus briefs are most important, especially if it's a case where cert is based not on conflict between circuits but is based on the nationwide importance of the question. If you've got nationwide organizations saying, "This case is important to us, not just to the parties," that's the most powerful argument you've got. So, if I've got a client who wants to have cert granted, I do encourage amicus briefs at the cert stage.

. . . On the face of it, then, the soliciting of amici support at the case selection stage offers a means to further a client's interests by mustering support for his or her position. At the same time, by effectively acting as a catalyst for interest group involvement, the Supreme Court counsel can influence the Court's decision whether to accept a case for plenary review. . . . This is not to diminish the important independent role of interest groups in Supreme Court litigation; organized interests are no doubt mobilized countless times without the prodding of a practitioner. Nonetheless, as gatekeepers to the Court, the inner circle of Supreme Court lawyers can facilitate access by alerting groups to potential amicus opportunities and letting them know that their voices would be a welcome addition to the pleading. As another Washington practitioner explained:

> Any good Supreme Court lawyer does whatever works in order to win a case. Whenever I have a case that's going up to the Supreme Court on certiorari, I look for amicus help. After it's granted, it's not as important. But [on certiorari] you want something that will flag the Court to the importance of your case.

Amicus solicitation at the merits stage is more common. . . . As the experienced Supreme Court bar will attest, . . . once the Court has granted review, amici tend to make themselves known to counsel. One lawyer observed that, "At the merits, friends are coming out of the wood-work," while another veteran litigator of the Court commented:

> You don't have to do as much encouragement at the merits stage. When cert has been granted, generally amici seek *you* out. At the petition stage, nobody necessarily knows about your case. So you have to sort of inform them about your seeking cert.

Why, then, do so many lawyers try to establish interest group support at the merits? Lacking any specific clue, one might conjecture that lawyers simply view amici on the merits as the norm. For example, one of the Court's most eminent practitioners allowed that:

> We try to get amici because sometimes we're afraid that the absence of them might be noted.

In other words, lawyers may try to locate amici if only because they believe the Court expects amici to participate. Certainly, amicus briefs are present in the vast majority of cases that the Court decides on the merits, and scholars have long speculated on the impact of these briefs at the merits stage. Indeed, evidence suggests that amici do figure prominently in judicial outcomes. . . .

Conclusion

The elite members of the Supreme Court bar are very active in litigation. Of course, even the most experienced counsel are not signing every petition or arguing every case, but that does not mean they are uninvolved. Quite the contrary. The members of the inner circle are frequently engaged, both by litigants and by less experienced counsel, to provide assistance and advice. Their advisory role might be less significant were it not so extensive, but the roots of their activity run quite deep. . . .

Naturally, there are constraints on what these lawyers can and cannot do, and those constraints are reflected in the motives for litigating in the Court. . . .

In sum, there is depth and coherence to the practice of Supreme Court specialists and much of that practice is directed toward gaining access to the Court. Examining the inner circle at work in Supreme Court litigation reveals that the experienced elite are political as well as legal actors in the process of adjudication in the high court.

A View from the Inside

5.6   Interview with Acting Solicitor General of the United States Walter Dellinger (1997)

Conducted by Nina Totenberg

I

The right to die, gun control, religious freedom, abortion clinic protests—all these issues came before the Supreme Court in its last term. And in all of these cases, the government's position was argued by the same man. He is Walter Dellinger, the Acting Solicitor General of the United States.

His name and title are not as well known as those of many people in Washington, but it is the solicitor general who in effect represents the American people before the Supreme Court.

For the past four months, NPR's Nina Totenberg was given access to the solicitor general's office, on condition that she not reveal what she had learned until after the court term had concluded. This is her report.

Nina Totenberg, NPR Reporter: For more than a century, the Office of Solicitor General has been one of the most powerful in government. While outside of the government, the office is little known, the men who have held the job are household names in the law [Archibald Cox, Thurgood Marshall, Irwin Griswold, Robert Bork, Kenneth Starr].

. . .

Totenberg: Of all the nation's public officials, including even the attorney general and the justices of the Supreme Court, the solicitor general, or "SG" as he's known, is the only one required by statute to be learned in the law.

His job is to represent the United States in the Supreme Court; to defend where appropriate presidential actions and laws enacted by Congress and the federal government's interests.

In that capacity this term [1996–1997], the Clinton administration's Solicitor General Walter Dellinger participated in about three-quarters of the cases heard by the court.

Walter Dellinger, Solicitor General of the United States: It is very important for anybody who is in the Office of the Solicitor General to recognize that the president is not your client. Your client is the United States, and the United States has ongoing, continuing interests that precede and post-date any particular administration that's in power.

Totenberg: The idea, he says, is not to make policy, but to defend policy choices if they're defensible.

Dellinger: You're not always going to agree with—certainly not with the policies that Congress has adopted. But you know, the people of the United States are entitled—when their elected representatives pass a law—in a democracy they're entitled to have someone make the best case to the Supreme Court about why the law that the people's representatives have adopted ought to be left standing.

Totenberg: The Office of Solicitor General is steeped in the tradition and the lore of the law. In court, the solicitor general wears a costume of vest and tails that almost matches the quill pens on the desks. He's the only lawyer to have an office at the Supreme Court, though his day-to-day work takes place at his Justice Department office.

From there, the SG presides over a small cadre of lawyers widely viewed as among the best and brightest inside or outside the government. While the accoutrements of the job might seem to be for Thomas Jefferson, Walter Dellinger's approach is more like Bruce Springsteen's.

He bikes to the office, works to music from boogie to the blues, and comes from a background more blue collar than Brahmin. Neither of his parents went further in their education than high school, and when Dellinger was 12, his father died and his mother was left to support three children.

That was the moment, says Dellinger, that he first became a feminist, though he didn't recognize it at the time.

Dellinger: I watched her every day head off to work. She put on a hat and gloves and she would head out, take the bus downtown, and there was almost no job that she could get with—being a woman without a college education. And seeing how hard it was for her to finally get a job as a sales clerk, you know, and she worked six days a week, all day long, trying to support a family.

Totenberg: Eventually, Dellinger won scholarships to college and law school, and became one of the nation's preeminent constitutional scholars teaching at Duke. He met Bill Clinton during the 1992 campaign, and after the election, Dellinger went for a few months to the White House and then to the Justice Department as an assistant attorney general.

Last year, he was appointed the acting solicitor general. At the department, Dellinger is perhaps most famous for enticing the physically self-conscious Janet Reno to dance at the department Christmas party.

Janet Reno, Attorney General of the United States: So Walter got this gleam in his eye and came over and said "you're next." . . .

Totenberg: Dellinger never passes up an opportunity for a joyous bite of life like this, but what goes on in the SG's office most of the time is gruelingly hard work.

Dellinger: Now, when I see the Supreme Court out the window—when I see the lights on, I think if they're still working, I need to still be working.

Totenberg: One of the SG's little known, but important duties is that he must approve every appeal filed by the United States government from any agency, anywhere in the country. Every day, a dozen or so cases arrive on his desk, probably 4,000 or 5,000 a year.

Dellinger: When the solicitor general decides not to appeal a case, it's over.

Totenberg: And the Secretary of Education or the Secretary of Defense or the Secretary of State can be standing there railing at you . . .

Dellinger: Right.

Totenberg: . . . but they don't have any power.

Dellinger: Whoever's in this office, the solicitor general's office, has the final authority to decide and you make a lot of people unhappy, because I think we reject—something like six out of seven requests from cabinet departments to appeal cases are turned down.

Totenberg: The only thing wrong with the job, says Dellinger, is that there's so much of it.

Dellinger: It's like this Lucille Ball program, you know, where the—where she's in this factory and the pies fall off the end of the conveyor belt.

Totenberg: At the same time Dellinger is making daily decisions on which cases to appeal, the SG, like a juggler, must be preparing for his oral arguments before the Supreme Court. There are moot courts—practice sessions where his staff pretends to be the justices grilling him—and there are days of study.

This term, Dellinger argued an extraordinary nine cases—an average of one a month—on subjects ranging from presidential immunity to the right to die, to the constitutionality of the Brady gun control law, the line-item veto, cable TV laws, and a law seeking to expand religious freedom.

Dellinger: The preparation is really very intense. I woke up—you know, you wake up thinking about the case. When you wake up, you wake up thinking of questions.

Totenberg: And with a court that is wont to interrupt any presentation with literally dozens of questions, all plans are likely to go awry, a fact which Dellinger cheerfully jokes about as he's getting dressed to argue a major religious freedom case.

Dellinger: I'm going to have a lottery on how much I get to say before I'm interrupted with a question. . . .

Totenberg: Dellinger seems ebullient, even though, as he notes, his preparation as SG is relatively brief compared to the six months of preparation he took when he argued a case as a private lawyer in 1990.

The next time Dellinger argues a case will be a test of the line-item veto, and this time his nerves are obvious, and possibly an omen. As he sits in his place in the courtroom waiting to begin, the court announces its decision in *Clinton versus Jones,* unanimously rejecting the president's contention that he has temporary immunity from civil lawsuits during his time in office.

Dellinger claims the loss didn't rattle him, but for the second time this term, he makes a mistake of horrific proportions, especially for a lawyer who made a national reputation as an advocate for women's rights. He mixes up the names of the two female justices.

Dellinger: And Justice Ginsburg asked the first question, and it's just like, you know, putting a gun to your head, to turn and say: "Justice O'Connor . . ."

Totenberg: Mimicking Ginsburg's reaction, Dellinger puts his hands to his face.

Dellinger: Of course, Ginsburg goes like this, but she smiles at least. And, you know, fortunately, I stepped back and said, "I can't believe I've done this again."

Totenberg: At least, says Dellinger, the reality is never as bad as his dreams.

Dellinger: I dreamt four nights ago that I showed up 15 minutes late—it was 10:15—and I was in a T-shirt and blue jeans, and I was going to have to go up to the chief justice and say: "I'm really, really sorry. I don't know what happened. Would you rather have me argue in my T-shirt and blue jeans? Or would you all like to wait here another 20 minutes while I rush back and try to get, you know, the outfit on."

And the worst part of it was, I couldn't remember why we thought the act was constitutional.

Totenberg: Walter Dellinger is leaving the Clinton administration next month, returning to Duke and North Carolina, where his wife Anne has a tenured teaching position she loves.

. . .

And what about his personal ambitions? Doesn't he ever think about being appointed to the Supreme Court himself?

Dellinger: Well, a little bit, you know, to be honest. But you know, not much. Because—being on the Supreme Court's like being hit by lightning. It either happens to you or it doesn't, and you know, I go jogging in the rain 'cause I don't think I'm going to get hit by lightning.

Totenberg: As Dellinger knows well, however, the job he holds now is a stormy one—stormy because of the SG's unique relationship with the president and with the Supreme Court.

II

In part two of her report, Nina Totenberg looks at the relationship between the solicitor general and the White House.

Nina Totenberg: The day is May 27 [1997]. The solicitor general, Walter Dellinger, doesn't know it yet, but in less than an hour, the Supreme Court will tell the world that it has ruled against President Clinton unanimously in the *Paula Jones* case.

We are in the car on our way to the court, and Dellinger is preoccupied with the argument he will be making today in defense of the line-item veto.

Have you talked to the president about this bill?

Walter Dellinger: No.

Totenberg: Is he interested in this stuff?

Dellinger: Yeah. But you know, presidents are busy.

Totenberg: Presidents are busy, but not too busy to know or care about Supreme Court cases that will affect their political futures and the way they will be able to govern.

And so it was that President Eisenhower, not a lawyer, personally and in his own hand, wrote language into his solicitor general's brief before it was filed in the famous *Brown versus the Board of Education* school segregation case. That, of course, was unusual, but presidents care what their solicitors general do.

Sometimes the relationship between the SG and the president is close and personal. President Kennedy, for example, knew and trusted Harvard Law professor Archibald Cox, whom he appointed solicitor general. Still, all was not sweetness and light between Cox and the Kennedys. Most notably in the landmark reapportionment case when Cox initially refused to make the argument that the Constitution requires one person/one vote equality. . . . Cox [who died in May 2004] now believes he was wrong to resist, and in the end he deferred, more or less, to the president's wishes. As did Robert Bork when he wanted to challenge the Boston busing decree in 1974. . . . In the end, President Ford decided not to oppose the Boston busing plan.

The conflict in the Reagan administration was more difficult, according to then-solicitor general Rex Lee. Lee found himself constantly at odds with hardliners in the White House who wanted him to argue conservative positions that Lee, himself a conservative, felt could not win in the Supreme Court—positions contrary to long-settled law. . . .

Lee's successor, Charles Freed, argued more fervently for the Reagan administration's agenda—so fervently that some of his career deputies quit. But Freed, too, resisted some of the positions that administration hardliners wanted him to take. . . . So in the last analysis, to whom does the solicitor general owe his loyalty: to the president he's serving and his agenda? Or to the law, the court, and the Constitution?

Dellinger: I think you can't tolerate this job unless you can live with ambiguity about one's role, because you have to believe really contradictory things.

Client is the United States, and therefore I think what you have to do is try to persuade a president and those who work for a president and an attorney general that the positions that you're going to espouse in the Supreme Court have in mind the long-range interests of the United States and they ought to go along with that.

Totenberg: There are, however, some famous cases in which the solicitor general did not succeed in persuading the president, and simply ended up refusing to sign the government's brief or argue its case.

Perhaps the most famous refusal of modern times came during the McCarthy era in the Eisenhower administration, when Solicitor General Simon Sobilov refused to defend the government system of stripping government employees of their jobs based on anonymous and untested accusations.

The case was argued instead by a little-known Justice Department official named Warren Burger. He lost, but when the judicial seat long-promised to Sobilov opened up, Burger got it instead and later was named Chief Justice of the United States.

Because of the solicitor general's unique relationship with the Supreme Court, many of Dellinger's predecessors have tried to insulate the office from outside influences. But cloistering is not Walter Dellinger's style. No issue better illustrated that than the doctor-assisted suicide cases this year.

Dellinger: And I worried a lot about why it was that I was the one that was supposed to or had to decide among all of those choices, so on cases like that, I talked to lots of people and got their views.

Totenberg: He met with constitutional scholars, interest groups, lawyers involved on both sides of the case. And he read the deeply personal letters that many citizens sent to the office, knowing that the SG was in the process of deciding whether to enter the case at all on behalf of the federal government, and on which side.

Dellinger: I sat down with Janet Reno, and wanted to know what she thought about the issue. She'd watched her mother suffer. I'd watched my mother suffer. These are really tough questions.

Totenberg: The Supreme Court term is finished now. Dellinger looks back with some satisfaction, particularly at the right to doctor-assisted suicide cases in which the justices essentially embraced the position he advanced, upholding for now state bans on doctor-assisted suicide.

Dellinger: I thought it was the best moment in the court in a long time, not just this year.

Totenberg: And Dellinger is most unhappy about the court's decision this term striking down the Brady gun control bill.

Dellinger: That is certainly one time this term when I wish I had done a better job of going back to basics. It was our job to attempt to persuade a majority of the court that the framers of the Constitution had a vision of the role and responsibilities of the national government, and we failed to do that.

Totenberg: There were other losses for the solicitor general this term as well. He defended the first law imposing censorship on the Internet to protect children, and he lost. He defended the Religious Freedom Restoration Act, a law passed by overwhelming margins to make it more difficult for states to impose burdens on religious practice.

And he lost the *Paula Jones* case in which the court unanimously rejected the president's argument that he is temporarily immune from civil lawsuits during his time in office.

On the day that Dellinger lost the case, he repaired to the solicitor general's private office at the Supreme Court, where we were waiting to quiz him.

Dellinger: You would prefer to prevail, but really I've kept it firmly in my mind: my job is to present the government's case, not to decide these difficult issues. That's their job, and I did my job back in January when we finished arguing the case, and then it's their turn to do their job and they did it.

5.7   Karen Swenson: Putting in the Hours (2000)

Paul D. Boynton

8 a.m. "Brockton: City of Champions" reads a sign that greets visitors to this gritty city tucked in the northwestern corner of Plymouth County [MA].

A former manufacturing center, Brockton's decades-long downward economic spiral has left it tattered, tough and, at times, dangerous.

But citizens retain their pride in the "City of Champions" mainly due to the prowess of its high school teams on the playing fields.

In truth, Brockton is now enjoying a modest revitalization, the centerpiece of which is a gleaming new courthouse on Main Street.

Public defender Karen L. Swenson frequents the new courthouse, as well as the 109-year-old edifice housing the Superior Court just around the corner.

Out of law school just over two years, Swenson manages her own case assignments, which makes up a lot for her low salary, she says.

On a glorious, sunny day in October, Swenson is the first to arrive at the public defender's office nestled between the courthouses.

She has a busy day ahead of her: a pre-trial conference in District Court first, followed by a hearing in Juvenile Court over her request for

Reprinted with permission of *Massachusetts Lawyer Weekly.*

confidential records. In between she has to gather her thoughts in preparation for *two* trials scheduled the next day. . . .

9 a.m. Swenson's client appearing at the pretrial conference is a college student who was cavorting with a group of fellow college students at a Bridgewater tavern where the drinks were flowing and the dancing was easy.

Caught up in the moment, he apparently started to dance with a disabled female in a wheelchair on the dance floor.

Swenson says the woman had a pitcher of beer in a basket in front of the wheelchair and was apparently enjoying the dancing and drinking.

But then Swenson's client allegedly took it a little too far and essentially engaged in an uninvited "lap dance" involving physical contact.

Her client was eventually charged with "indecent assault and battery." The "indecent" tag means he will have to register with the Sex Offender Registry if convicted, she says.

The pre-trial conference in the criminal session is scheduled for 9 a.m., but Swenson arrives at 9:15 since it's rare that the list is called right on the dot. This allows the assistant district attorneys and defense lawyers to mingle about and talk about possible ways to resolve the various cases.

The courtroom is filled with attorneys milling about, flipping through files, conferring in hushed tones. The gallery is packed with defendants and family members, looking a bit confused and bewildered by the scene.

Not every client will show up for a pre-trial, but Swenson's client is here today.

"That's the start of a good day," she says brightly.

Swenson tracks down the ADA [assistant district attorney] handling her client's case and confers with him at the prosecutor's table.

Shortly thereafter, First Justice David G. Nagle enters the courtroom and the call of the list begins.

The list is called alphabetically and Swenson's client's last name begins with an "S." It could be a long wait.

"I've sat in this session until 2 p.m. waiting to be heard," she mentions.

If parties can reach some sort of plea bargain and place a "green sheet" containing the terms of the settlement into a wooden box at the side of the bench, the chances of being reached sooner are greatly enhanced, she notes.

But there's no settlement in the offing, mainly because the ADA hasn't been able to reach the complaining witness (the wheelchair-confined dancer).

"It's helpful to know that they haven't been having contact with her," Swenson says. "Maybe it means she's not willing to go forward."

So the "green sheet" is put aside and a pre-trial conference report is instead given to the assistant clerk-magistrate.

10:30 a.m.   Swenson's case is finally called.

The assistant district attorney, Thomas J. Flanagan Jr., summarizes the charges, then Swenson makes her pitch that the dancing was basically consented-to by the alleged victim and that the "lap dancing" part of the allegations is false.

Nagle mentions that the defendant "may have a lot of exposure here." He suggests that Swenson confer with her client about the possibility of him accepting a compromise where the case is continued without a finding ("CWOF" in the defense parlance).

Bottom line: if he complies with the terms of probation for a year, the charges would be dropped. But the sticking point is that he would still have to put his name in the Sex Offender Registry.

Swenson and her client mull it over in the hallway, and he decides he'd rather take his chances at trial.

"The reality is that we can always resolve this on the day of trial," Swenson says matter of factly.

They return to the courtroom and get a trial date of Dec. 4.

11:13 a.m.   Swenson arrives back at her office to return phone calls and review the Juvenile Court case file.

She also has to nail down whether a drug case scheduled for trial the next day in Superior Court is going forward. If so, then the District Court trial will have to be rescheduled. (Understandably, in the pecking order of courts, Superior Court cases take precedence.)

Just before noon, Swenson decides to walk to the nearby Superior Court to track down the courtroom clerk.

On the way over, Swenson is joined by her colleague, Cecely A. Reardon.

Swenson finds assistant clerk Brendan P. Sullivan sitting in the courtroom, who informs her that the trial before Superior Court Judge Richard J. Chin is a go for the next day. Swenson will have to contact the District Court about having to reschedule the trial in that court.

Noted criminal defense attorney Robert L. Jubinville happens to be in the courtroom on another matter and has brought pastries to court, as is his custom whenever on trial. Swenson and Reardon sample the goodies. Chin pokes his head out of chambers to ask Sullivan a question.

Swenson then bumps into the assistant district attorney handling the trial.

While they confer, Reardon mentions that Swenson "is what ADAs call a 'true believer.' She's really committed to the work. She's a great trial lawyer."

Swenson, a 1998 graduate of Northeastern Law School, says being a public defender combines her competitive side (she had played field hockey and lacrosse in college), her compassionate side, and her desire to solve legal problems.

(Her job definitely affords her some challenges. Swenson's client in the Superior Court case is Daniel Griffin, an individual later featured in a *Boston Globe* article on solitary confinement. According to the *Globe,* Griffin tried to hang himself after "two stir-crazy months" in solitary.

Griffin was hospitalized but survived, and Swenson defended him in his drug case.)

On the way back to her office, Swenson says her chances of winning the Superior Court drug case are "slim to nil" because it involves a "hand-to-hand" drug transaction where Griffin attempted to sell a $20 rock of crack cocaine to an undercover police officer.

There's no chance for settlement since the prosecution is not willing to reduce the charges, she says.

12:40 p.m. Swenson has lunch in the office "break" room with Reardon and another colleague, John M. Pavlos. They chat about cases and joke around a bit.

1:25 p.m. Swenson has been unable to reach her client in the District Court trial that has to be rescheduled. But she knows that she lives close by.

So Swenson strolls a few blocks to her client's apartment. She is luckily at home. Swenson lets her know that the trial has to be rescheduled and confirms the woman's telephone number.

As she leaves the high-rise apartment building, Swenson mentions that it's unusual for her to visit her clients.

"It can be dangerous," she says flatly. "I wouldn't go alone."

2 p.m. Swenson makes her way to the new courthouse, where the Juvenile Court is located.

The hearing is on a motion to obtain confidential records from a prior case in Juvenile Court involving her client. The current criminal case is in Superior Court and involves horrifying allegations of sexual abuse inflicted by a mother and father on their minor son.

Swenson represents the mother, who, at the time of Juvenile Court proceeding in 1996, was a drug addict. She was declared unfit as a mother and her parental rights were terminated, as was the father's.

The allegations of sexual abuse by their son didn't come to light until a few years after the Juvenile Court proceeding ended.

The attorney for the defendant father is seeking exculpatory evidence in the files of another attorney who represented the father in the Juvenile Court action.

Swenson is taking a different tack. Just before the hearing, she files a motion seeking investigatory

records maintained by the Juvenile Court. She is requesting the court to lift an impoundment order shielding the court file from public view.

Suddenly the relative calm of the courthouse is shattered with the jarring sound of a fire alarm, forcing the lawyers, parties and courtroom personnel to troop out of the building to join a large group of other people who are patiently milling about.

Swenson takes advantage of the fire alarm by speaking with the assistant district attorney handling the rescheduled District Court trial. They work on coordinating the rescheduling of the matter.

After a few minutes, the Brockton Fire Department says it is okay to reenter the building.

The lawyers settle back into the courtroom, and Juvenile Court Judge Robert F. Murray enters to commence the hearing.

The various attorneys assembled—including a lawyer representing the Department of Social Services and the lawyer representing the children—have their say for about one-half hour, but Murray isn't prepared to rule, saying the request beyond the court's investigatory records seems overly broad.

But he might be willing to release certain documents if the requesting attorneys submit a more detailed affidavit spelling out the precise records wanted and why they could assist the mother's and father's defense.

3:10 p.m. The hearing ends, and the attorneys convene in the hallway to hash out further details on what the supplemental affidavits should contain.

Swenson heads back to her office a few minutes later. Her day is far from over.

She now has to refine her preparation for the Superior Court trial the next day.

Swenson has already compiled a trial notebook, but she still wants to fine-tune her opening statement, do more research in support of her evidentiary motions and make sure her jury instructions are ship-shape.

Before the day ends Swenson says she "will practice my opening and closing in the car, in front of the mirror, my husband . . . whoever will listen."

But before she can dig into her last-minute trial preparation, Swenson returns a number of telephone calls. She also updates the case files from the day's activities.

4:30 p.m. Swenson starts the trial preparation. She decides to redo her opening. She also prepares summonses that she then turns over to the investigator in the office for service.

8 p.m. Swenson is finally satisfied with her trial notebook.

But she still has to go to the Plymouth County jail to visit with her client.

9 p.m. Swenson arrives at the jail and spends about 50 minutes with Griffin going over his testimony.

When the day first started, Swenson predicted a late night, and she got it.

It's not until about 10 p.m. that she heads home to eat dinner and watch the World Series game on that night.

What's left of it.

5.8   A Day in the Life of a Yolo County Deputy DA (2001)

Dave Rosenberg

It's always about drugs.

This morning seems like everything has to be attended to at once. I'm already behind the power curve. I've been in trial for two weeks with three defendants who were caught on I-5 heading towards Oregon with approximately one pound of cocaine and one pound of methamphetamine. Yesterday, we finally got through all the pre-trial motions to suppress evidence, at which point, two of the defendants suddenly wanted to plead guilty. I have a policy that I don't plea bargain during trial, unless the case is coming unglued. They pled guilty to all the charges, and threw themselves at the mercy of the court. They got four years each in state prison and they will be facing deportation. Unfortunately, that means I'm behind the power curve on today's cases.

8:30 a.m. Reviewing morning calendar. My morning calendar (9:30 a.m.) has me in two different courtrooms with seven different defendants. They range from a trial readiness conference on the young man accused of breaking a police officer's throat while high on LSD, to a preliminary hearing with a federal parolee accused of manufacturing

methamphetamine in a motel room in West Sacramento, and two young adults accused of possession of several pounds of marijuana for sale. There were also the usual straightforward possession of methamphetamine cases as well.

9:15 a.m. I had to make a quick stop in Department 5 to ask Judge Lebov if I could go up to Department 2 where the bulk of my cases were. He agreed, and as I left the courtroom on my way up to Department 2, I spoke with Tom Purtell, the defense attorney in the LSD case. Though set for trial next week, no courtroom was available, and we agreed that a new trial date would be needed. I asked him to pick a new trial date in an already full trial calendar, and that I would look at my calendar as well (which I always carry with me). If I ever lose my calendar, I'm sunk.

9:30 a.m. Once in Department 2, the attorneys met with the Judge to discuss those cases that could resolve (plea bargain) and those cases that had to be continued. We agreed that two of my cases (possession of methamphetamine) could resolve with pleas of no contest, and an agreement that the defendants would not be sentenced to state prison at the outset. Most likely, they'll receive county jail time and a residential treatment program followed

Excerpt from Judge Dave Rosenberg, "A Day in the Life of a Yolo County Deputy DA." Reprinted with permission.

up by three years probation, which is pretty much a standard sentence for people with drug problems.

The other two cases are more complicated, and involve possession for sale of marijuana, and the other manufacture of methamphetamine. Both were confirmed for preliminary, and both are task force cases with YONET. The defense attorney on the marijuana case doesn't think his client should have to suffer a felony conviction for possession for sale of marijuana, and wants me to plea bargain to "maintaining a place where illegal activities occur." With the evidence found at the scene, including scales, packaging materials, pay-owe sheets and a heat sealer for plastic bags, along with the two pounds of marijuana, I have a hard time agreeing to that request. It's confirmed for hearing.

10:00 a.m.   Back in Department 5 to meet with Judge Lebov and Tom Purtell to pick a new trial date for the kid that broke the officer's throat while high on LSD. I have a triple homicide set in June that is set to last for four weeks. Tom Purtell is booked in July. We agree on August.

10:15 a.m.   Back to Department 2 to meet with the attorneys on the remaining cases and to take pleas to the two possession-of-meth cases.

10:30 a.m.   I had to make a quick call from the clerk's office to federal probation to check on the status of the federal parolee accused of manufacturing methamphetamine. He has a prior federal conviction and is currently awaiting a parole revocation hearing. No luck, so I left a message.

10:45 a.m.   I take the pleas in the two possession cases after the defense attorneys went over the plea forms with their clients. The Judge informs them of their rights and sets sentencing dates. There are other cases ahead of mine, so I have to wait before they are called.

11:30 a.m.   Out of court at 11:30, and back to the office to confirm that the task force agents will be in at 1:30 for the preliminary hearings, and to tell our subpoena clerk to bring in the witnesses on the other two cases.

11:45 a.m.   Telephoned in an order for a sandwich at Togo's which I will pick up and bring back to my desk and work through lunch preparing for preliminary examination at 1:30. Both cases are complicated, and I will have to put on several witnesses in each in order to have the Judge find that there is sufficient evidence to hold the defendants for trial.

11:50 a.m.   Telephone call from policy agency concerning homicide investigation and new information concerning suspect. Can't discuss more since case is pending, and it involves narcotics, and a drug deal gone bad, which is why I'm working it.

11:55 a.m.   Telephone call from Brenda Heng regarding investigation about methamphetamine lab. Wants to know about probable cause for search warrant. We discuss case, and if and when time comes, when to meet and where. I go along with YONET when I can on certain high profile cases or sometimes just so I can learn how they do their jobs.

12:00 noon.   Pick up sandwich. Eat fast.

12:15 p.m.   Back at the office. I pick up the file on a home invasion robbery and shooting in Davis back in 1995. I prosecuted Hoogie Ellis, and he is now in state prison. He and some friends ripped off four drug dealers in Davis, took their pot and shot one of them. We have a second suspect in custody, and I'm set for arraignment and trial setting next week. I'd like to get ready, but with two hearings at 1:30, I give up and put the file down. Later.

12:20 p.m.   Preparing for preliminary hearing on two afternoon cases. One is very complex, and I want to get in enough evidence for conspiracy charges. Prep time until 1:30.

1:30 p.m.   Prelim with marijuana dealers set by court in Department 8. Prelim with meth manufacturer in Department 7. Can't be two places at once. I go to both to coordinate. Prelim with marijuana dealer continued until 3:00 p.m., because Judge Johnson has a juvenile matter to finish up. I go back to Department 7 to meet with the Judge and two attorneys on meth case. (The federal parolee has a co-defendant, thus the two attorneys.) I have four witnesses, including two YONET agents.

2:00 p.m.   Preliminary hearing begins, I call first witness, arresting officer, then move on.

3:00 p.m.   Still doing the meth case. Federal parolee is in custody, his co-defendant is out. Judge Johnson comes into the courtroom to find out why I haven't come down to the marijuana dealing case. There are two co-defendants in that case as well. One of their attorneys wants me to plea bargain to maintaining a place again, since I'm tied up in Department 7. I say no way, we'll stay late if we have to.

3:15 p.m.   Back in preliminary hearing on meth manufacturing case. Defense attorney is raising all kinds of objections, doesn't realize I'm laying a foundation for additional charges for conspiracy to manufacture methamphetamine. Not sure the Judge realizes it either. Sometimes you have to ambush people.

3:45 p.m.   Judge Johnson comes back in, gives file on marijuana case to Judge Warriner. Defense attorneys and their clients get tired of waiting. They agree to continue case until July.

3:55 p.m.   Back in preliminary hearing with meth case.

5:00 p.m.   I'm on my fourth and final witness. Court adjourned until tomorrow at 10:00 a.m. But I have a 9:00 a.m. appearance on a triple homicide involving narcotics in Department 5, and two preliminary hearings in Department 2 at 9:30 a.m.

5:15 p.m.   Meet with YONET agents to discuss pending investigation and search warrant. They've got my home telephone number and beeper number. They'll be in touch.

5:30 p.m.   At my desk, trying to get organized, and trying to return telephone calls and answer mail.

5:45 p.m.   My youngest daughter calls. I need to go home, fix dinner and take care of my two daughters. I'm a single working dad after all.

6:00 p.m.   I have to go home now. Just another typical day in the life of a drug prosecutor.

A Comparative Perspective

| 5.9 |

The Role of Clinical Legal Education in Developing the Rule of Law in Russia (2002)

John M. Burman

Introduction

Anyone with any significant exposure to Russia quickly comes to appreciate Winston Churchill's observation that Russia is a "riddle wrapped in a mystery inside an enigma." Not only has Russia been shielded from outsiders for centuries, it is the world's largest country, making any attempts at generalizations inevitably inaccurate. Any one per-

Reprinted with permission of the *Wyoming Law Review.*

son's observations will necessarily, therefore, be both limited and distorted by his or her preconceptions and experiences. Despite those inherent limitations, let me suggest that while the development of a rule of law in Russia is decades away, at best, and may never happen, the West has a role in trying to foster that development. Part of that role involves legal education. And part of legal education involves clinical legal education. Further, there is a need for a discussion of what the role of clinical legal education should be, and how that role should be played. . . .

The Rule of Law

Nearly two hundred years ago, Chief Justice John Marshall authored the opinion in *Marbury v. Madison,* the seminal decision in which the United States Supreme Court held that Congress may not pass laws which conflict with the Constitution. When that happens, he wrote, "it is emphatically the province and duty of the judicial department to say what the law is." In the same opinion, Marshall declared that "the government of the United States . . . is a government of laws, and not of men." In the United States, in other words, the rule of law, as interpreted by the judiciary, should reign supreme. The promise of *Marbury* has come to fruition.

Almost two centuries later, the United States Supreme Court was called upon to decide what became the critical issue of the Watergate scandal. Must President Nixon obey a subpoena duces tecum in a criminal case requesting that the president surrender to the Watergate special prosecutor audio tape recordings of conversations between the president and his aides? Quoting Marshall's maxim that "it is emphatically the province and duty of the judicial department to say what the law is," the Court said the law is that the president is not above the law and must, just as any American, obey it. He must, therefore, deliver the tapes to the special prosecutor. Nixon, the most powerful man in the world, and the commander-in-chief of the most powerful military force in the world, complied. He complied even though delivering the tapes would reveal his role in the scandal and ultimately force him to resign the presidency in disgrace.

Last December [2000] the same Court ordered a halt to the recount of ballots in Florida, ensuring that Texas Governor George W. Bush would defeat Vice-President Albert Gore, Jr., in that state and thereby emerge victorious in the Electoral College. Two days later the Vice-President conceded the election in a nationwide speech: "Now the U.S. Supreme Court has spoken," he said, "let there be no doubt, while I strongly disagree with the court's decision, I accept it." With those words, the longest, closest presidential election in over a century was over, the bitter dispute resolved without a shot being fired, resolved by the judiciary through its interpretation of what the law is. While a peaceful result was expected by Americans, such an outcome is neither common nor accepted in many other countries, including Russia.

In 1993, Russian President Boris Yeltsin decided the country should have a new constitution. He issued a presidential decree, which contained a plan for constitutional reform. The decree also dissolved the Congress of People's Deputies. The Constitutional Court of Russia pronounced the Decree unconstitutional. As did Vice-President Gore, Yeltsin disagreed strongly with the nation's highest court. Unlike Mr. Gore, he did not accept the ruling. Instead, Yeltsin issued a decree stripping the court of critical powers and ordering the Court "not to convene its sessions until the adoption of the new Constitution of the Russian Federation." Just as Mr. Gore's actions were expected in America, Mr. Yeltsin's were expected in Russia. Why the markedly different results in this country and Russia? The rule of law is alive and well in America; it is not and has never been in Russia.

When the Soviet Union collapsed in 1991, many in the West believed that a democratic, free-market society would quickly and inevitably emerge. After all, that is the system which had won the Cold War, and it was believed to be the only logical and reasonable path for Russia to follow.

Western aid poured into Russia in the early 1990s, along with advice about how to best transform Russian society. . . . Some of that aid and some of that advice was directed at inculcating a rule of law, the precondition to economic reform. Given the enormity of the task of developing a rule of law, it should have been no surprise that developing a rule of law in Russia has come very slowly and erratically. . . .

One area critical to the development of a rule of law, which gets virtually no acknowledgment, is the transformation of Russian legal education. While slow and erratic, that transformation takes many forms; among them is the introduction and growth of clinical legal education. And while the importance and value of that transformation is difficult to measure, and the payoff will be years, if not decades, in coming, the importance of the development is difficult to overstate. Without it, a culture of law, the prerequisite to a rule of law, may never develop.

The American Culture of Law

Shortly after President Clinton was ordered to be deposed in the Paula Jones case, I was in Russia. A Russian judge asked me how a judge could order the president to be deposed, and how could that judge enforce the order? As I groped for an answer, the chasm between America's legal culture and Russia's became clear. I began by trying to explain the independence of the judiciary. Then, I tried to explain that the president obeyed the court because a court order is the law. Neither concept made sense to my Russian acquaintance. As I have pondered the question since then, I have concluded that the answer lies in what we take for granted. The president obeyed because of the American culture of law.

The American culture of law did not, of course, develop overnight, or even over several years. Rather, that culture has been growing and maturing for centuries.

Even before its birth as a nation, the United States was a society founded on the rule of law. The "rule of law" can be defined in a variety of ways, but ultimately whether a society adheres to a rule of law involves three functional questions: Is the society governed by laws openly enacted, equally enforced, and voluntarily accepted by the governed? While it sounds simple, relatively few of the world's nations have truly lived under the rule of law, perhaps because the conditions necessary for the concept to prosper seldom coalesce, and transplanting the rule of law from one society to another has proven to be difficult, at best.

In colonial times, the American colonies were part of the British Empire, the head of which was the British King or Queen. Since King John signed the Magna Carta in 1215, however, the absolute rule of English monarchs had been gradually curtailed. "No freeman," proclaimed the Magna Carta, "shall be taken, imprisoned, disseised, outlawed, banished, or in any way destroyed . . . except by lawful judgment of his peers." The rule of law, in other words, had taken root in the shade of the gracious oaks of Runnymede. From that day to this, law in England has been something very different. Instead of a means for the government to control the governed, law became a means for the governed to control the government.

The rule of law was solidly entrenched by the time Parliament passed the British Bill of Rights in 1689, declaring that "the pretend power of suspending of laws or the execution of laws by regal authority without consent of Parliament is illegal." Not surprisingly, the idea of rule by one's peers, an-

other way of describing representative government, was a central tenet of many colonists. Each of the thirteen American colonies soon had some form of an elected, law-making body, such as the House of Burgesses in Virginia. It should not have been a surprise, therefore, that when King George III attempted to impose taxes on the colonies without their approval, that effort was met with stiff resistance by colonists accustomed to having a say in their government. "No taxation without representation" became the rallying cry for those opposed to the King's efforts.

The rule of law was so ingrained in America by the last quarter of the eighteenth century that King George III's actions led to rebellion. As one would expect, the new nation which emerged was founded on the rule of law. The nation and the notion have flourished ever since. By contrast, the Soviet Union, and the various permutations of the Russian Empire which preceded it, were founded on the rule of men (or women), often culminating in a cult of personality.

The Russian Culture of Lawlessness

Russia has a markedly different history. From its inception, Russia has been ruled by despots; it has "no tradition of the rule of law." Before the 1917 Bolshevik Revolution, Tsars had reigned autocratically for centuries. After the Revolution, the Communist Party, generally acting through its rather innocuous sounding General Secretary, assumed absolute control. Under either system, the law had a place. Whether wielded by a Tsar or the General Secretary of the Communist Party, law in Russia and the Soviet Union was a method of control; it was used by the government to control the governed. Far too often it became a tool of repression. . . .

. . . Despite the Soviet Constitution's flowery guarantees, the Soviet legal system became an important method of government control, not a method of controlling the government through protecting and promoting human rights.

The Soviet Constitution is compelling proof that the rule of law is more than words. A comparison of the constitutions of the Soviet Union and the United States show many similarities. Both guarantee a variety of personal liberties. American and Soviet citizens had constitutional rights to: Free speech; freedom of religion; equality before the law; and privacy. The Soviet constitution actually guaranteed a number of rights which Americans do not have. Soviet citizens enjoyed constitutionally protected rights to health care, education, and housing, none of which are guaranteed by the U.S. Constitution. In the Soviet Union, "women and men had equal rights" under the constitution. An equal rights amendment, of course, was proposed, but failed to win ratification in the United States. Other provisions of the Soviet constitution give pause. "Citizens of the USSR," for example, "are obliged to preserve and protect socialist property." Even so, one who read and compared the Soviet and United States constitutions in a vacuum could well conclude that the Soviet Union had a better rule of law in place than America. When placed in historical context, however, nothing could have been further from the truth. The rights guaranteed by the Soviet Constitution were, unfortunately, literally not worth the paper on which they were written.

Fast-forward to 1991. The Soviet Union has collapsed. After seventy-five years of Communist rule, preceded by centuries of Tsarist rule, Russia lurches uncertainly into an uncharted future. Not prepared by custom or culture for a society founded on the rule of law, Russia and its legal system face breathtaking challenges. Virtually every aspect of society, including the legal system, is in need of fundamental reform if Russia is to survive as a nation and become a functioning part of the increasingly global community. Expecting a rapid transformation to a capitalistic, democratic society, America and other Western countries rush to "help," pouring billions of dollars and mountains of advice into Russia.

Ten years later, Russia is, arguably, worse off than it was under the Soviets. Instead of a democratic, free-market society governed by a rule of law, Russia is astonishingly corrupt, a society which one observer has aptly described as "robber capitalism." The grossly uneven economic effects of "robber capitalism" are evident. . . . Not surprisingly, the great majority of Russians are not happy with their new lives. A recent public opinion poll revealed that seventy-nine percent of Russians surveyed regret the fall of the Soviet Union, up from sixty-nine percent in 1992. . . .

Whither Russia now? At best, "Russia's medium-term prospects are only so-so." Without fundamental changes, Russia "risks going the way of Nigeria—another oil-rich country whose government is thoroughly corrupt and its population impoverished." And one can make the case that "Russia is finished . . . [; it is on] an unstoppable descent into social catastrophe and strategic irrelevance." So what should we (in the West) do?

The conviction that economic and democratic reforms would occur rapidly in Russia has been replaced with the realization that change will come much more slowly and differently than westerners expected. That realization, coupled with the American penchant for instant results, has led powerful voices to urge the U.S. to reduce its commitment of time, energy, and money. To do so now, however, is both simple and simplistic; it ignores both the changes which have occurred, and the time which will be necessary for a rule of law to emerge.

Creating a Rule of Law in Russia

. . . A rule of law will not become a reality, in my view, unless and until four, interrelated conditions coalesce. First, Russia must have sound laws. Second, Russia must have an independent judiciary, which is allowed to interpret and enforce those laws. Third, Russian lawyers must become something more than fighters for communism, or any other "-ism." They must become skilled professionals who are respected by the judiciary, their clients, and society, in general. Fourth, and most difficult, a culture of law must take root and grow in Russia. Any one of those is a tall order; taken together it is tempting to say it is too tall. . . .

. . . Yet one thread binds all areas together. The thread is legal education. The education of the lawyers and leaders of tomorrow is, in my view, the most effective way of creating a culture of law. The reason is simple. . . . A law student has three or four decades ahead of him or her, and students entering law school today were eight years old when the Soviet Union fell. They did not grow up learning that the United States was the evil empire and are much more receptive to American and Western ideas, such as the rule of law. . . .

The Gap Between Legal Education and Legal Reality

Legal education in Russia today must overcome two large, but not insurmountable, hurdles. First, the abysmal legacy of Soviet legal education must be cast aside. Second, law schools need to educate many more and very differently trained lawyers.

Soviet Legal Education

The constitutionally mandated "supreme goal of the Soviet state" was to build a "classless communist society in which there would be public, communist self-government." Education was simply a method of achieving that goal. The Soviet constitution called for "a uniform system of public education that . . . serves the communist education and intellectual and physical development of the youth, and trains them for work and social activity." In accordance with that mandate, legal education was closely regulated by the Soviet Ministry of Education in Moscow; it was, accordingly, both uniform and uniformly directed toward the goal of creating a communist society. Not only were teaching materials prescribed and published by the Ministry of Education, faculty research had to be ideologically consistent with communist doctrine. It was hardly an environment in which critical thinking, legal skills training, or respect for the law would or could thrive. . . .

The methods of instruction also furthered the ideological goal. Students were simply vessels into which the teacher poured prescribed, ideological[ly] correct lectures. The Russian phrase for teaching a class reflects the methodology. Instead of "teaching, a class," a university professor "reads lectures." . . .

The lecture method still predominates in Russian law schools. A Russian friend, who has studied and received law degrees from both a Russian law school and an American one, compared the lecture system and the American system this way: "In the U.S. I had to come prepared for class, in Russia— no need to read anything . . . only professor will be speaking and s/he gives you necessary information." The American system of legal education, he concluded, is "more democratic." . . .

. . . All in all, the legal education system prepared lawyers to perpetuate the Soviet system, not lawyers trained to solve problems through creative thinking, legal analysis, and skillful legal representation.

The Need for More and Differently Trained Lawyers

The need for the Soviet legal system, an important prop of the Communist dictatorship, disappeared with the collapse of the country it had been designed to support. The Soviet Union fractured into fifteen independent nations, each remarkably different from the communist society it replaced, and each with very different legal needs and a need for many more lawyers. Russia was no exception.

With the advent of private property, the privatization of commercial enterprises, private commercial transactions, intra- and international business ventures, and the recognition and enforcement of at least some human rights, lawyers were both in short supply and ill trained for their new roles. They possessed neither the substantive knowledge nor the practical legal skills to function effectively in the new order. . . .

With myriad new legal issues, education which focused on the rote memorization of ideologically correct dogma is clearly inadequate. While such education may have been sufficient for preparing fighters for communism, it neither prepares lawyers to function in a free society—or at least in a society which is something of a free-for-all—nor fosters the development of a rule of law. Changing the names and content of courses to eliminate now-discarded communist ideology is a start, but it is wholly inadequate, too. A massive change in society necessitates a correspondingly massive change in legal education. That change needs to be institutionalized by the Ministry of Education through the establishment of and insistence on appropriate standards for accreditation of law schools, and standards for continuing legal education requirements.

The Role of Lawyers in America or Russia

Any discussion of legal education should begin with a consideration of what lawyers actually do. Only after answering that question is it possible to discuss intelligently how lawyers should be trained. And while lawyers in America and lawyers in Russia will always operate in vastly different cultures, good lawyers in either country will share important, essential attributes.

At the end of the day, lawyers are problem solvers. A would-be client consults a lawyer because he or she has a problem, which is perceived to have a legal aspect, and the would-be client hopes the lawyer can help solve it. Solving a client's legal problem requires much more than knowing the law and/or the ability to think like a lawyer (the oft-heard bromide used to describe and justify legal education in America). A competent lawyer must be able to identify and analyze a client's problem, help the client develop potential solutions, consult with the client about the desired solution to the problem, and take the legal steps necessary to implement the client's desired solution. While an American law student who has sat through three years of law school classes has developed some ability to identify and analyze legal problems, and to formulate some legal solutions, he or she is no more prepared to take the legal steps necessary to effectuate the client's desired goal than a medical student with theoretical knowledge of heart surgery is prepared to perform it on a live patient. Simply put, the law student who has no experience may have learned something about the law, but he or she has not learned to be a lawyer. The only way to do that is to practice law, either during or after law school.

Several years ago, the American Bar Association appointed the Task Force on Law Schools and the Profession. It produced a report, known generally as the Macrate Report. . . .

The Macrate Report identified ten "fundamental lawyering skills." Lawyers should be able to engage in: (1) Problem solving; (2) legal analysis and reasoning; (3) legal research; (4) factual investigation; (5) communication (oral and written); (6) counseling; (7) negotiation; (8) litigation and alternative dispute resolution procedures; (9) the organization and management of legal work; and (10) recognizing and resolving ethical dilemmas. The report also identified four "fundamental professional values. Lawyers should": (1) Provide competent representation; (2) promote justice, fairness, and morality; (3) promote the legal profession; and (4) engage in continuing self development. . . .

Training Lawyers to Fulfill Their Roles Competently

Legal education in America focuses on three and a half of the ten "fundamental legal skills": (2) Legal analysis and reasoning; (3) legal research; (5) written, but not oral, communication; and (10) recognizing and resolving ethical dilemmas; and one of the "fundamental values": Providing competent representation. . . .

The education law students receive in their first two years of law school is critical. It teaches them the fundamental skills of legal analysis and reasoning and legal research, skills without which they could not competently represent clients, even with good supervision. Most third-year students, however, have never interviewed a prospective client or a client, counseled with a client about the client's objectives and the means to be used to achieve those, or the legal or other consequences from the client's proposed course of action. Most have never talked to or written a letter to another lawyer or tried to negotiate a settlement or a contract. Most have never drafted a legal document, or filed one with a court, or served another party, or appeared on behalf of and represented a client in court. Many have never seen the inside of a courtroom. Yet these are all things lawyers do every day. Unless a student is in a clinical program, though, he or she can graduate, pass the bar, and obtain a license to practice law without ever having learned several of the fundamental skills lawyers need. That new lawyer may be lucky and land a job with a law firm or other employer that provides the training and guidance which we have not required the lawyer to receive at law school. Many, unfortunately, do not. They learn at the expense of clients.

Finally, learning to be a lawyer is more than acquiring the fundamental skills necessary to represent a client competently. Values, too, are a fundamental part of clinical legal education. Clinical students scrutinize and imitate their supervisor. If he or she is ethical, in word and deed, the students will be, too. If not, they will not be.

Ultimately, a law student must learn to be a professional. A professional may be defined in many ways. I like Justice Sandra Day O'Connor's definition:

One distinguishing feature of any profession . . . is that membership entails an ethical obligation to temper one's selfish pursuit of economic success by adhering to standards of conduct that could not be enforced either by legal fiat or through the discipline of the market. There are sound reasons to continue pursuing the goal that is implicit in the traditional view of professional life. Both the special privileges incident to membership in the profession and the advantages those privileges give in the necessary task of earning a living are means to a goal that transcends the accumulation of wealth. That goal is public service. . . .

A lawyer, in short, must not just learn to think like a lawyer, he or she must learn to behave like a lawyer. Behaving like a lawyer means being a professional. And a professional has a deep and abiding respect for his or her profession and the rule of law within which the profession operates. That is what students learn in a clinic—how to behave like a lawyer. How do they learn?

The Role of Clinical Legal Education in Training Lawyers

New lawyers or law students, as anyone else, learn by watching and imitating. They watch and imitate other lawyers. It is only natural, therefore, that a budding lawyer watches most carefully and imitates most closely the first lawyer with whom he or she comes into significant professional contact. While it is true that law professors are, for better or worse, role models, much of the modeling we do in the classroom has little or no direct relationship to the practice of law. What clinical supervisors do, by contrast, has a direct bearing on the practice of law because that is what we are doing. Whether we want to be or not, we are often the first, and therefore the most important, lawyer in a new lawyer's life. Everything we say or do makes an impression, and often an indelible one, on our students. . . .

Students in a live-client clinic perform all the tasks lawyers perform, except billing and collecting fees from clients. They interview prospective clients, counsel with clients, negotiate with lawyers, represent their clients in court or in ADR [alternative dispute resolution] proceedings. They

learn how to organize and manage a legal practice, and resolve ethical dilemmas, an almost daily occurrence. . . .

Although clinical legal education has a long history in America, it has really only come of age in the last thirty or forty years. It has become a central part of legal education at virtually every American law school. . . . Not only do law students receive critical training in how to practice law, they provide countless hours of assistance to persons who would otherwise be unable to obtain legal representation. But can that be transplanted to Russia? Yes. It can. And it is happening.

When the Russian law school deans and directors met in November of 2000, they recognized the need for reform. Their report describes the "modern requirements for the legal profession." A lawyer in Russia should: (1) Possess abilities of legal thinking; (2) be able to apply the law creatively; (3) be able to analyze administrative and judicial practice; (4) understand the problems of a market economy; and (5) should have substantive knowledge of a wide spectrum of legal subjects. The report also recognized several barriers to erecting a system of legal education which can provide the requisite training: (1) The absence of clear government policy on legal education; (2) inadequate funding for law schools; (3) low salaries for faculty members; and (4) the proliferation of law schools of doubtful quality.

Despite the hurdles, the deans proposed some solutions. Among them: (1) Develop regional legal teaching methodological centers; (2) use foreign experience; and (3) develop relations with foreign law schools. Perhaps the most important recommendation is the need to "transform the informative character of education into a creative one." To that end, the methods of teaching should be changed to involve discussions, rather than lectures, and active learning, such as through the use of role-plays. Clinical legal education fits the bill to a "T" in Russia, just as it does in America.

Clinical legal education not only prepares lawyers for real life, it has an effect outside the walls of the law school. Persons who would otherwise be unable to obtain legal representation, and are often steamrolled by the system, have a means to obtain representation and fight for their rights.

. . .[A]s the law students gain valuable experience, the clients, invariably for the first time, have a positive experience with the legal system. Rather than imposing yet another burden on them, the legal system often provides them with relief. Even if the clients did not "win," they received something new and different: Due process. And, the perception of having been treated fairly, of having had one's day in court, is often more important than the result. One by one, therefore, clients gain some respect for the legal system. With that respect comes one more victory, however small, in the struggle to create or maintain a culture of law.

The Role of Clinical Legal Education in Promoting a Culture of Law

Although a person in America accused of a crime generally has a right to an attorney provided by the government if the person cannot afford one, no such right exists in civil cases. Accordingly, a person with a civil legal problem, such as a domestic relations case involving the custody of his or her children, has three options. First, a person may always represent him- or herself (proceed pro se). Second, one can try to find a lawyer to provide low cost or free representation (pro bono). Or third, obtain representation from a legal services lawyer.

Proceeding without a lawyer is dangerous, at best. Even a well-informed person with little or no knowledge of the legal system can foul up his or her life for years to come. Lawyers perform a large amount of free or reduced-fee work. The ABA estimates, however, that only fifteen to twenty percent of the legal needs of low-income Americans are being met, suggesting that what is done is far from adequate.

Government-funded legal services are far from adequate. The federally funded Legal Services Corporation, the primary provider of civil legal services to low-income persons, faces almost annual attacks on its very existence and is funded at a level far from adequate to meet the need. Since neither the government nor the private bar meets the need for legal services for low-income persons, the only remaining option is law school clinical programs. And many law school clinics . . . have stepped into the breach. . . .

. . . Many low-income persons have had significant contact with the legal system, but their experience has usually been negative. Representation by a clinic is often the first positive experience with the system that a low-income person has. For once, the person receives the additional measure of respect which legal representation often provides. And not infrequently, legal representation alters the outcome favorably for the client. At a minimum, a person receives due process. Such positive experiences are critical to the maintenance and development of a culture of law. Only when the legal system is thought to be worthy of respect will its decisions be respected and obeyed.

Thankfully, we no longer content ourselves with teaching students to think like lawyers. Rather, we understand that our mission is much broader. Law schools need to help train students to be lawyers. An integral part of that training is helping students to become professionals. At the same time, clinical programs provide a vital method of inculcating respect for the law among non-lawyers.

Clinical Legal Education in Russia

Clinical legal education is not just an American phenomenon. . . . Wherever planted, clinical legal education has grown and prospered, providing valuable experience to law students and much needed legal assistance to under-served populations. Given the changes that have occurred in Russia over the last decade, it is not surprising that the interest in and need for clinical education has grown dramatically in the world's largest nation. . . .

Several clinics in Russia are now well-established, both as part of the educational curriculum and as an important provider of legal services. . . .

In addition to the twin objectives of American clinical education, providing representation to indigent persons and training law students, law school clinics in Russia have a third important role to play. Properly trained and supervised law students in clinical programs can influence the legal system, in general, by elevating the level of practice in Russian courts. They can also assist in monitoring the performance of courts in promoting and protecting human rights. . . .

Summary

With over three hundred law schools in Russia, and only a small fraction of Russian law students receiving appropriate clinical experiences, it is easy for the naysayers to say just that. It is too little, too late. One only has to spend time with students or graduates of clinics to quickly understand how valuable the experience has been to them, and how it will color their legal careers for decades to come (and since Russian law graduates are often in their early twenties, a career of forty or fifty years will be common).

As lawyers who have had a good clinical experience go through their careers, there is both a definable difference in the preparation they have received, as well as an indefinable difference in their attitudes toward law and the legal profession. Instead of soulless lectures, they have experienced the law as a living, breathing thing which can do great good, even if that good is only making sure that the government acts as it should, which is no small accomplishment.

The clients, too, are changed. Instead of a monolithic tool of repression, the law became accessible, and potentially, a friend. And with that change comes a slow change in attitude. For the first time, the law becomes worthy of respect, and respect is the prerequisite to a culture of law. In the world's largest nation, with over 150 million people and a culture of lawlessness, change will be glacially slow, and we are fools to think otherwise. We are even bigger fools if we heed the cries of the new generation of "America firsters," and abandon the chance to affect the future by assisting with the development of clinical legal education in Russia. . . .

The terrorist attacks on New York City and Washington, D.C., showed unequivocally the importance of building and maintaining strong relations between the United States and Russia. Russian President Putin was among the first foreign leaders to contact President George W. Bush after the attacks and pledge his country's support for the United States. That sentiment appears not to be confined to the government. I received several messages from friends and colleagues in Russia, all expressing similar sentiments. They all sounded one theme: "All Russians are shocked and compassionate to Americans."

We have much to offer each other.

For Further Reading

Baum, Lawrence and Corey Ditslear. "Selection of Law Clerks and Polarization in the U.S. Supreme Court." *Journal of Politics* 63 (2001): 169.

Epstein, Cynthia Fuchs. *Women in Law.* New York: Basic Books, 1981.

Lewis, Anthony. *Gideon's Trumpet.* New York: Vintage Books, 1989.

Salokar, Rebecca Mae. *The Solicitor General: The Politics of Law.* Philadelphia: Temple University Press, 1992.

Turow, Scott. *One L: The Turbulent True Story of a First Year at Harvard Law School.* New York: Putnam, 1977.

Chapter 6

Litigation as Political Advocacy

Introduction

Political scientists have long recognized that interest groups play a critical role in judicial politics and litigation involving issues of public importance. Writing in 1908, Arthur Bentley observed that politics enters the judiciary at two crucial points: first, in the selection of judicial nominees to the federal courts; and second, in how the courts decide cases. Turning to the role of the Supreme Court in American politics, Bentley noted that it was a "functioning part of government . . . responsive to group pressures." Like Congress and the executive branch, the Court, wrote Bentley, served as a "mediator of competing group interests."[1]

Although Bentley was the first political scientist to comment on the role of group forces in the judicial process, it was not until 1951 that David Truman offered the first systematic treatment of this issue. In terms more explicit than those of Bentley, Truman commented that "though myth and legend may argue to the contrary, especially concerning our highest courts, the judiciary reflects the play of interests, and few organized groups can afford to be indifferent to its activities." Moreover, Truman wrote that interest groups have a compelling interest in the outcome of constitutional issues and other issues of political significance, "whether . . . to influence the language of a precedent or to contribute to the Court's thinking in expanding or contracting one."[2]

Since Bentley and Truman first opened the door to political scientists interested in the role of interest groups in the judicial process, scholars have developed a substantial literature assessing their participation in all aspects of litigation. Organizations from across the political spectrum representing diverse interests in American society are now regular participants in constitutional litigation. The courts, and the Supreme Court in particular, are aware of the interests that parties not directly involved in a case have in their final decisions. Interest groups unable to sponsor

[1] Arthur Bentley, *The Process of Government* (Chicago: University of Chicago Press, 1908).
[2] David Truman, *The Governmental Process* (New York: Alfred A. Knopf, 1951).

cases themselves often participate as amicus curiae (friend of the court) in order to articulate their interests in a case. The judiciary, like the other branches of government, is now just another forum in which organized interests compete to influence policy outcomes.

Foundations and History

The first three selections in this chapter are from the mid-twentieth century. They highlight the evolution of how interest groups used the courts and of how constitutional litigation became more politicized. In "Private Attorneys-General: Group Action in the Fight for Civil Liberties" (1949), the student editors of the *Yale Law Journal* describe the efforts of the National Association for the Advancement of Colored People (NAACP), the American Civil Liberties Union (ACLU), and the American Jewish Congress (AJC) to advance their civil rights and liberties claims through the courts as the equivalent of "private attorneys-general." The article focuses on the lobbying efforts of three organizations in the executive and legislative branches as well as their willingness to turn to the courts to achieve their policy goals. It also highlights the importance that litigation had begun to assume for groups that frequently found themselves politically disadvantaged in the majority branches. In the years that followed, groups such as the NAACP, the ACLU, and the AJC would win important victories in the courts on matters such as racial desegregation, legal protection for political dissenters, and limitation on religious practices in the public schools. These victories, as the *Yale Law Journal* editors noted then, as would many other scholars after them, were possible because the courts were not accountable to the electorate. By directly invoking the guarantees of the Bill of Rights over electoral accountability, public interest organizations believed they stood a better chance of creating policy change than if they continued often unsuccessful campaigns to win over political majorities.

Clement E. Vose, in "Litigation as a Form of Pressure Group Activity" (1958), notes that interest groups were often much better equipped to handle constitutional litigation on behalf of individuals, who "lack[ed] the time, money, and skill" to pursue their grievances on their own. Moreover, interest groups could represent the interests of their membership and other like-minded parties more effectively by representing aggrieved individuals. Vose also points out the importance of the willingness of an individual to challenge existing law and policy, essentially on behalf of a larger group. To interest groups, this "test case" strategy has since become commonplace for groups that engage in litigation.

In the final piece of this section, "Amicus Curiae Participation in U.S. Supreme Court Litigation: An Appraisal of Hakman's 'Folklore'" (1982), Karen O'Connor and Lee Epstein point out how, by the early 1980s, nearly every area of constitutional law and many areas of civil law attracted interest group attention by the use of amicus briefs. In contrast to some previous studies concluding that sustained and broad interest group activity of the courts was "scholarly folklore," O'Connor and Epstein demonstrate that such activity was anything but an aberration. Interest group politics now characterized Supreme Court litigation, conclude O'Connor and Epstein, and it has ever since.

Contemporary Judicial Politics

What does the contemporary environment of Supreme Court litigation look like? Joseph D. Kearney and Thomas W. Merrill answer this question in "The Influence of Amicus Curiae Briefs on the Supreme Court" (2000). Kearney and Merrill address several important questions: Do amicus briefs influence the outcome of Supreme Court decisions? Do they affect the content of the Court's opinions? Are some groups more successful than others? Does the solicitor general, who represents the United States government before the Supreme Court, have a "special relationship" with the justices that nongovernmental parties do not? In addition to making a sophisticated effort to answer these questions, Kearney and Merrill offer an excellent summation of scholarly efforts addressing interest group use of the courts in the late twentieth century.

A View from the Inside

In 2003, the Supreme Court decided *Grutter v. Bollinger,* which involved a challenge to the University of Michigan Law School's affirmative action program. *Grutter* marked the first time that the Court had agreed to hear a direct challenge to an affirmative action program in higher education since it had decided the landmark case of *Regents, University of California v. Bakke* (1978). And just as *Bakke* set the modern record for the number of organizations participating amicus curiae in a Supreme Court case, so too did *Grutter* attract more briefs than did *Bakke* and the case that eclipsed it twelve years later, *Planned Parenthood v. Casey* (1992). This latter case involved an unsuccessful attempt to dismantle the right to abortion established by *Roe v. Wade* (1973). Here, we excerpt a part of the *Grutter* opinion in which the Court cited several of the amicus briefs that were submitted by parties arguing in support of the law school's affirmative action program. Note how the Court refers to the important societal interests potentially affected by dismantling the constitutional justification for affirmative action. Although literally hundreds of amicus briefs are filed with the Court each year, rarely do the opinions of the justices refer directly to them. *Grutter* demonstrates that the justices are listening and, in some cases, incorporating other voices into their written opinions.

We also include an amicus brief that was filed by the Cato Institute, a libertarian think tank based in Washington, D.C. Cato's participation in *Grutter* is an example of the modern complexion of Supreme Court litigation, which, as we noted earlier, is much more ideologically diverse than it ever has been. Although Cato's views did not prevail in *Grutter,* the institute did have success in *Gratz v. Bollinger* (2003), the case decided along with *Grutter* that invalidated the affirmative action program practiced by the University of Michigan in its undergraduate admissions process. We believe the Cato brief provides an excellent example of opinion on the other side of the affirmative action debate.

A Comparative Perspective

More recently, scholars have begun to explore the role that interest groups play in the relationship between organized pressure and the courts. What, for example, is the nature of the litigation process in other countries? By comparing how the courts operate in other countries, and how such processes compare with those in the United States, we can learn about important similarities and differences between countries operating on democratic principles.

In "So Help Me God: A Comparative Study of Religious Interest Group Litigation" (2002), Jayanth K. Krishnan and Kevin R. den Dulk describe and compare the role that religious interest groups have played in the judicial processes of India, Israel, and the United States.

We also include an amicus brief filed by the government of Canada in a 1999 case involving a dispute between Michigan and the U.S. Environmental Protection Agency over the enforcement of a federal clean air provision. Canada shares an approximately 5,000-mile and largely undefended border with the United States, and so has a vested interest in the environmental policies of its neighbor. We believe the selection offered here is a good example of how foreign governments assert their own interests through the court system rather than through lobbying Congress and executive agencies.

Foundations and History

6.1 ## Private Attorneys-General: Group Action in the Fight for Civil Liberties (1949)

Yale Law Journal

Those who look to the government for protection or gain have long recognized the comparative inadequacy of individual action. They have learned that government will best serve those who merge their efforts into effective organizations.

The law of civil liberties, as developed by courts, legislatures, and administrative agencies over the last two decades, has been profoundly affected by the work of private groups organized either to protect the civil liberties of all or to advance the cause of particular minorities. Representative and most powerful of both kinds of organizations are the American Civil

Liberties Union (ACLU), the National Association for the Advancement of Colored People (NAACP), and the Commission on Law and Social Action of the American Jewish Congress (CLSA). The NAACP and the CLSA entered the civil liberties field as part of their efforts in behalf of minority groups. The ACLU is concerned with defending the civil liberties of all who require assistance. All three came into existence in response to their founders' conviction that in some way American society was not fulfilling its promise of equal opportunity and fair play.

The attempt here will be to analyze the methods of the three organizations, their effect on civil liberties law, and their ability to enter into the more complex civil liberties issues currently facing minority groups and the American people as a whole.

Reprinted by permission of The Yale Law Journal Company and William S. Hein Company from *The Yale Law Journal*, Vol. 58, pp. 574–598.

The ACLU—In Defense of an Idea

The ACLU's key attribute is its willingness to fight for civil liberties for everyone, regardless of cause or circumstances. In the Union's twenty-eight-year history, it has lost many supporters by giving aid to extremists, among them Communists and men of the extreme right like Gerald L. K. Smith, but there has been no deviation from the principle of civil rights for all.

The ACLU's prestige as a non-partisan defender of civil rights has enabled it to command free legal talent and extensive publicity through which it has exercised an influence far out of proportion to its small membership and limited expenditures. It has secured the support and services of outstanding leaders in all walks of life whose prominence has enabled the Union to be an influential behind-the-scenes force constantly considered by legislatures or administrative agencies faced with civil liberties problems. In a field in which public pressure to restrict the activities of an unpopular minority can often become intense, it has been especially effective for an organization to enter the fight not as a minority group trying to defend itself but rather as a non-partisan organization interested in the ideals of free expression and thought.

Organization and Method of Operation

. . . ACLU's chief efforts are exerted in the courts, although it also lobbies. The Union generally enters a case on the appellate level. Individuals who are arrested or sued usually employ their own counsel or are supplied counsel by the court. If the case attracts notice and poses a civil rights question, the local civil liberties committee or national office may intervene. Briefs and arguments are handled by private lawyers who, for the most part, are volunteers. Only one full-time lawyer is employed in the national office and the local civil liberties committees rely almost entirely on volunteer help.

Scope of Activities

The ACLU has compiled an impressive record encompassing the entire field of civil liberties. Its function has been essentially defensive, helping individuals and groups whose civil liberties are threatened by suit, arrest, or the possible passage of restrictive legislation.

In support of free expression, the ACLU has with some success, defended persons prosecuted under various statutes which have attempted to restrict writing and speech. Typical were the state sedition, criminal anarchy, and criminal syndicalism laws which were used to restrict Communist and IWW activity in the 1920's and 1930's. The ACLU has assisted Jehovah's Witnesses, either by direct counsel or by *amicus curiae* briefs, in expanding the right to peddle literature and has been active in the still-befuddled sound truck controversy. In the courts and the legislatures the Union has fought mail, motion picture, and publication censorship.

To protect free thought the Union has defended those upon whom society would impose orthodoxy: conscientious objectors; government employees accused of disloyalty; a pacifist attorney denied admittance to the bar; school children who refused to salute the flag; Communists denied WPA benefits; and alien pacifists denied citizenship for refusal to bear arms. Defending academic freedom, the Union has protested the dismissal of professors because of political expression, but has rarely achieved any real result. ACLU vigorously fought the Tennessee anti-evolution law, teachers loyalty oath bills, and recent attempts to prohibit the teaching of communism in the public schools. . . .

As each group has taken over the major burden of its own struggle, the ACLU's function has become one of assistance through the joint handling of cases, *amicus curiae* briefs, lobbying, or publicity. Today the Union is the chief spokesman and defender only for the unorganized individuals or the groups which are too small or unpopular to have power by themselves.

While the Union's defense activities have been varied and successful, it has done little to enter new areas of civil liberties and attack restrictions on civil rights by instituting test cases and launching effective publicity campaigns. To attack successfully an undemocratic practice by positive campaigns requires a sharper focusing on a particular problem than the Union, with its diverse interests and limited resources, has yet achieved. The results, therefore, are meagre. It has unsuccessfully attempted to eliminate the poll tax by judicial decision. On a local level the Union has shown only occasional initiative in enforcing state civil rights laws. An ACLU test case succeeded in voiding California's attempt to exclude incoming indigents. Test cases have also been instituted involving important new issues which have later been resolved through the efforts of other organizations or private individuals. Notable were the Union's restrictive covenants cases and the cases testing the validity of the wartime forced evacuation of Japanese-Americans from the West Coast. . . .

Both in the courts and the legislatures, the ACLU has rarely succeeded in winning positive victories in new areas of civil rights. But, as a shield for the traditional rights of free expression and thought, the ACLU has made its most significant contribution.

The NAACP—For Negro Equality

The NAACP is the largest and most effective civil rights organization in the United States. Its cause is the advancement of the Negro. Not content with merely holding the line, the Association has struck hard and often to enlarge the scope of Negroes' rights. Its weapons are legal and political action. It has easy access to the Negro press, secures the full cooperation of Negro churches, is highly regarded by the non-Negro community, and is the most militant of all major minority group organizations. . . .

Assisting Negro Criminal Defendants

The NAACP is not a legal aid society for Negroes. It will assist Negroes only where there has been some irregularity of procedure or other discrimination because of color, or where the organization feels that a Negro criminal defendant is innocent. But even where there has been discrimination, branch offices shy away from defending an obviously guilty Negro because of the likelihood of unfavorable publicity and the difficulty of raising special funds to defend a guilty person. The ACLU, on the other hand, would welcome such a case. The difference is perhaps best explained by the fact that the NAACP is interested less in the principles of due process than in furthering the interests of Negroes as a group. For this end it is essential that the Association maintain its respected position in society. . . .

Legal Action to Defeat Discrimination

Recent years have seen vigorous NAACP campaigns to eliminate some of the more patent legal barriers in the path of equal opportunity for the Negro. Until 1936 the legal work of the NAACP consisted essentially of defending criminals or combating other types of discrimination in isolated cases taken principally because a Negro was in trouble and the NAACP could supply help. But the NAACP was not satisfied with the mere defense of the status quo. Many restrictive practices have long been integrated in society and are enforced either through established legislation or accepted private behavior. Southern segregated education is typical. The restrictive pattern has so long been accepted by the minority group that the organization which waits for someone to be sued or arrested will never come to grips with the more accepted patterns of discrimination. Here the minority, by instituting legal proceedings of its own, must carry the fight to the majority or accept the status quo. In 1935 the Association hired its first full-time lawyer and today the national office, with five paid lawyers devotes most of its efforts to affirmative action against discrimination. The local branches and state conferences have undertaken successful campaigns of their own, particularly in the educational field, but the most important work has been by the national office assisted by members of the Association's legal committee throughout the country.

The NAACP court victories have been the result of continued pressure in the courts, on legislatures, and in the press. The cases fought and lost have often provided the publicity to give impetus to continued legal action. In four phases of the fight to destroy segregation and discrimination have the NAACP's legal victories been most notable: defeating the white primary, eliminating segregation in interstate travel, improving Negro education, and ending discrimination in housing. The legal fight has been a slow, whittling process wherein courts have usually decided cases on the narrowest possible grounds, thereby enabling individuals and governments to evade the effect of the decision. Renewed work and further expenditure is then necessary to invalidate the discriminatory practice, under each newer and cleverer disguise, until it is recognized in all its forms as illegal. Only in the case of the white primary, where most southern states have apparently exhausted their evasive tactics, can the victory be considered fairly complete. . . .

Legislative Action

In addition to court action, the Association has lobbied extensively. While unsuccessful this far in terms of bills enacted, lobbying has had an important by-product in the development among Negroes of an awareness of their own rights. Since the NAACP's Washington Bureau has a small staff and limited budget, its effectiveness as a lobbying group depends largely on the strength of the branches and their ability to rally the Negro vote in key areas. The better-organized branches attempt to obtain preelection commitments on civil rights legislation, and the Association, through its *Bulletin*, keeps members informed of Congressional voting records. But the active opposition of the South and the inertia of the North have so far prevented the enactment of any legislation through NAACP efforts. The publicity involved has, however, spurred government action in other ways. It seems likely that both court and administrative action favorable to Negroes has been in part made possible by the gradual shift in the climate of opinion which the NAACP has helped to bring about.

The NAACP has had far greater success in opposing anti-Negro legislation. Its opposition generally is limited to proposed laws which condone some type of segregation. In the last session of Congress, for example, the Association helped defeat Congressional approval of a proposed compact among fourteen southern governors to set up segregated regional colleges. General legislation not specifically related to Negroes may be opposed when it is felt that large numbers of Negroes will be unfavorably affected, as in the case of the Taft-Hartley law.

Thus, the record of the NAACP in attacking discrimination in courts and legislatures is a complete rejection of indirect educational and propaganda techniques in favor of direct legal and legislative action. Without specifically publicizing its own philosophy of action, the NAACP has been the first large civil rights organization to implement, at least in part, that method of attack most clearly defined by the American Jewish Congress as the "law and social action" approach to civil rights.

CLSA—The "Law and Social Action" Approach

Philosophy of Action

The Jewish problem is unique. Discrimination against Jews in the United States is usually non-governmental, non-violent, and extremely subtle. An organization set up to fight defensive legal battles would be virtually useless. Until recently the chief method to combat these anti-Semitic practices was education through good-will propaganda. CLSA breaks from this method in insisting that the best existing means of education is to fight anti-Semitism by direct legal and legislative action, forcing people to support specific bills and work for court victories rather than wait for the slow process of education through propaganda to materialize. To the argument that prejudice cannot be outlawed by court decree or legislative fiat, CLSA answers that prejudice is not the cause but more often the result of discriminatory practices which can be outlawed. The forced segregation of groups into separate neighborhoods or schools, it is argued, creates in the rest of society the feeling of prejudice which will further enforce the segregated pattern.

To implement this philosophy of attacking prejudice by eliminating the discriminatory practices, CLSA was established in November, 1945. Its theoretical means of attack is to merge in one force trained sociological research necessary to uncover discrimination and legal skills and community pressure necessary to fight it. CLSA's activities are always limited, however, by the Federal Government's requirement, as a condition to tax exemption of contributions, that only an insubstantial portion of the organization's work be devoted to influencing legislation. . . .

The main force of CLSA's work has been directed, of course, at problems of particular concern to Jews. But the Commission realizes, perhaps more than any other organization, that a legal principle established by one minority group will often accrue to the benefit of others. It has therefore undertaken affirmative action beyond its own interest group, notably in fighting racial discrimination in the Stuyvesant Town housing project and in supporting Negro complainants before the New York State Commission against Discrimination. In addition, some of its best legal work has been done in support of the more direct campaigns of other organizations. . . .

Evaluation

It is perhaps too soon to pass judgment on the totality of CLSA's efforts. If its cases do not have the significance of NAACP or ACLU court victories it is because the Commission is fighting a set of private discriminatory practices, each one fairly insignificant in itself, which the Commission hopes to eliminate by singling out each practice and fighting it by law suit or by statute. Perhaps because the Jewish local communities are not so closely knit as the Negro communities, CLSA has not been able to produce among Jews the mass group support which the NAACP has created among Negroes.

That the CLSA's methods of direct action have emphasized merging technical social science research with legal skills is due less to a new approach than to the fact that an organization concerned with Jewish problems must employ sociological research to expose the more subtle discrimination to which Jews are subjected. In using sociological research as a basis for legal action CLSA's skills have not always been equal to the task. . . .

While other organizations, notably the NAACP, have employed affirmative and legislative techniques, CLSA has been the chief proponent of this method in the field of Jewish affairs. And it has been the first civil rights organization to clearly formulate and extensively publicize this positive approach which offers to all civil liberties organizations the most effective program yet suggested for meeting the complex civil rights problems of the future.

The Task Ahead

The emphasis in recent years on the development of new areas of civil rights has perhaps overly obscured the vital defensive role that organizations like the ACLU and NAACP must continue to play. The position of the United States in the world struggle for power has created pressures on free thought and expression which can be withstood only by strong organizations, like the ACLU, whose loyalty is beyond question. The task will require every resource that the Union can muster. Legal defenses must be found to combat the effects on free expression of loyalty programs or Congressional investigations into political beliefs. The technique employed in the Taft-Hartley Act of denying economic leadership because of political belief raises issues of free expression which have yet to be explored. The ACLU must employ every legal and propaganda device at its disposal to take a firm stand against those who would scuttle free institutions under the guise of saving them. . . .

In addition to the defensive functions of the organization, however, the new methodology pioneered by the CLSA presents a continuing challenge to all civil liberties organizations. Civil liberties issues have become too complex and their solution too dependent on diverse skills to be properly handled by lawyers on a part-time basis. This is true as much for the problems facing the ACLU as it is for the Jewish and Negro organizations. ACLU, for instance, feels that free expression is seriously endangered by private monopolistic practices in communications industries. If true, this restriction can be fought only after long research and a well-planned legal campaign. And the needs of affirmative action have gone beyond the mere necessity of full-time legal talent. The NAACP brief in the restrictive covenants cases contained a lengthy sociological section; the CLSA brief in the case of the segregation of Mexican schoolchildren recognized the psychological effects of segregation. And the organizations do not doubt the importance of public opinion upon the major civil liberties decisions of legislatures and courts. They must be capable of meeting the problem which Jewish organizations have long faced and which the NAACP has recently attacked—to carve out new and more extensive rights rather than merely to defend an individual against violations of clearly recognized rights. And when the practice sought to be eliminated is in the field of private communication, housing, education, or employment, the problem requires the combined talents of lawyers, social scientists, and publicists. . . .

Litigation as a Form of Pressure Group Activity (1958)

Clement E. Vose

The conventional judicial process is distinguished from legislative and administrative processes by features which forbid, conceal, or control the participation of organized pressure groups. Justice Robert H. Jackson warned that "perhaps the most significant and least comprehended limitation upon the judicial power is that this power extends only to cases and controversies." This limitation has meant that the Supreme Court of the United States refuses to provide advisory opinions and avoids what judges are fond of calling "political questions." It cannot be overstressed that the Supreme Court's only power is to decide lawsuits between adversaries with real interests at stake. Under the case system that marks American jurisprudence, a court is a "substantially passive instrument, to be moved only by the initiative of litigants." This contrasts with the power of the President and the Congress to deal with any subject as desired.

Despite this limiting prerequisite, the Supreme Court does possess considerable control over the particular cases to be decided. The Judiciary Act of 1925 gave the Court almost complete discretionary control of its appellate business through grant or denial of the writ of certiorari. This statute settled the modern principle that the Supreme Court's function was

> not to see justice done in every case, but to decide the more important policy issues presented within the frame of a "case" or "controversy," concerning the federal balance, the relations of the branches of the federal government, or the fundamental rights of the individual in relation to government.

Elaborating upon the function of deciding important policy issues, Chief Justice Fred M. Vinson, in 1949, told the bar that the Supreme Court is interested only in "those cases which present questions whose resolution will have immediate importance beyond the particular facts and parties involved." Vinson

Originally published in *The Annals of the American Academy of Political Science* 319, 1958, pp. 20–31.

added that "what the Court is interested in is the actual practical effect of the disputed decision—its consequences for other litigants and in other situations." This meant that lawyers whose petitions for certiorari were granted by the Supreme Court were representing not only their clients, "but tremendously important principles, upon which are based the plans, hopes and aspirations of a great many people throughout the country."

It is the thesis of this article that organizations—identifiable by letterhead—often link broad interests in society to individual parties of interest in Supreme Court cases. Since the American judicial system is built upon specific cases with specific facts, it is assumed that study of the role of specific organizations is relevant to understanding.

Reasons Organizations Go to Court

Organizations support legal action because individuals lack the necessary time, money, and skill. With no delays a case takes an average of four years to pass through two lower courts to the Supreme Court of the United States. A series of cases on related questions affecting the permanent interest of a group may extend over two decades or more. The constant attention that litigation demands, especially when new arguments are being advanced, makes the employment of regular counsel economical. This may be supplemented by a legal staff of some size and by volunteer lawyers of distinction. Parties also pay court costs and meet the expense of printing the record and briefs. Organizations are better able to provide the continuity demanded in litigation than individuals. Some individuals do maintain responsibility for their own cases even at the Supreme Court level, but this is difficult under modern conditions.

The form of group participation in court cases is set by such factors as the type of proceeding, standing of the parties, legal or constitutional issues in dispute, the characteristics of the organization, and its interest in the outcome. Perhaps the most direct and open participation has been by organizations which have been obliged to protect their own rights and privileges. Robert A. Horn has shown that a modern constitutional law of association has developed out of Supreme Court cases concerning churches, trade unions, political parties, and other organizations. The cases have sometimes placed organizations as parties, but more often the organization supports a member or an officer in litigation. One example must suffice.

The constitutional concept of religious freedom has been broadened in recent years by the Supreme Court decisions in cases involving members of the sect known as Jehovah's Witnesses. Most of the cases began when a Jehovah's Witness violated a local ordinance or state statute. Since 1938, the Witnesses, incorporated as the Watch Tower Bible and Tract Society and represented by its counsel, Hayden Cooper Covington, have won forty-four of fifty-five cases in the United States Supreme Court. As a result Jehovah's Witnesses now enjoy

> the rights to solicit from house to house, to preach in the streets without a license, to canvass apartment buildings regardless of the tenants' or owners' wishes, to be recognized as ministers of an accredited religion and thus be exempt from the draft, to decline to serve on juries, and to refuse to salute or pledge allegiance to the flag.

The NAACP

Since 1909 the National Association for the Advancement of Colored People has improved the legal status of Negroes immeasurably by the victories it has won in more than fifty Supreme Court cases. During its early years, the NAACP relied upon prominent volunteer lawyers like Moorfield Storey, Louis Marshall, and Clarence Darrow to represent Negroes in the courts. Limited success coupled with its failure to win gains from Congress led the NAACP in the 1930's to make court litigation fundamental to its program. A separate organization, the NAACP Legal Defense and Educational Fund, was incorporated for this purpose. The goal of the NAACP was to make Negroes "an integral part of the nation, with the same rights and guarantees that are accorded to other citizens, and on the same terms." This ambition meant that beginning in 1938 Thurgood Marshall as special counsel for the NAACP Legal Defense and Educational Fund held what was "probably the most demanding legal post in the country."

In aiming to establish racial equality before the law on a broad basis, the Legal Defense Fund has not functioned as a legal aid society. Limited resources have prevented the Fund from participating in all cases involving the rights of Negroes. As early as 1935 Charles Houston, an imaginative Negro lawyer who preceded Marshall as special counsel, set the tone of NAACP efforts when he declared that the legal campaign against inequality should be carefully planned "to secure decisions, rulings and public opinion on the broad principle instead of being devoted to merely miscellaneous cases."

By presenting test cases to the Supreme Court, the NAACP has won successive gains protecting the right of Negroes in voting, housing, transportation, education, and service on juries. Each effort has followed the development of new theories of legal interpretation and required the preparation of specific actions in the courts to challenge existing precedent. The NAACP Legal Defense Fund has accomplished these two tasks through the co-operation of associated and allied groups. First, as many as fifty Negro lawyers practicing in all parts of the country have been counsel in significant civil rights cases in the lower courts. Many of these men received their legal education at the Howard University Law School in Washington, D.C., and have shared membership in the National Bar Association since its founding in 1925. These common associations have contributed to the consensus among Negro lawyers on timing their quest for equality through litigation. Second, the NAACP has long benefited from its official advisory group, the National Legal Committee composed of leading Negro and white lawyers. Today Lloyd Garrison is Chairman of the National Legal Committee of forty-five attorneys located in twenty-three cities. This is the nucleus of the many volunteers in many fields who have contributed ideas, often at national conferences, to the planning of litigation. Third, other organizations with no direct connection with the Legal Defense Fund have sponsored a few cases. State and local chapters of the NAACP have often aided Negroes who were parties in cases, especially in the lower courts. The St. Louis

Association of Real Estate Brokers was the chief sponsor of the important restrictive convenant case of *Shelley v. Kraemer*. A Negro national college fraternity, Alpha Phi Alpha, sponsored quite completely the successful attack on discrimination in interstate railway dining cars.

Individual Test Cases

Winning new constitutional protections for Negroes has depended on the development of individual test cases with a Negro as party in each. There is no chronicle of the human interest stories contained in the roles of Negroes in historic Supreme Court cases. But what is known reveals many difficulties to be inherent in improving the legal status of a group of fifteen million persons through individual court cases. In a suit by a single plaintiff, the case may become moot as the passage of time makes the remedy sought inapplicable. This danger, though avoided by the co-operation of state officials, was created in the Missouri Law School case of 1938 when the plaintiff, Lloyd Gaines, disappeared just as the case was completed. Also the concerted efforts of authorities to deny Negroes participation in the Texas white Democratic primary kept Dr. L. A. Nixon from voting even though he was the plaintiff in two Supreme Court victories. Furthermore there is always the temptation for compromise by the original plaintiff which would accomplish his narrow purpose but stop the litigation before the broad constitutional issue was before the appellate court.

These dangers were largely overcome in the School Segregation Cases when federal court actions were instituted by individual plaintiffs both on their own behalf and on behalf of persons similarly situated. Since 1955, in the expanding litigation over race relations, the class action has become a procedural device of growing importance. Rule 23 (a) of the Federal Rules of Civil Procedure provides under certain circumstances that

> if persons constituting a class are so numerous as to make it impracticable to bring them all before the court, such of them, one or more, as will fairly insure the adequate representation of all may, on behalf of all, sue or be sued.

One authority has said that "school segregation is a group phenomenon which is peculiarly suited to resolution in a class action." As Negroes enter a new generation of litigation, their cases are apt increasingly to take the form of the class action. . . .

Organizations as "Friends of the Court"

The appearance of organizations as *amici curiae* has been the most noticed form of group representation in Supreme Court cases. This does not concern the technical office of *amicus curiae* for which an attorney is appointed to assist the court in deciding complex and technical problems. Today, the Supreme Court does sometimes, as in formulating its decree in the School Segregation Cases, issue a special invitation to the Solicitor General or to state Attorneys General to act as *amici curiae*. Of interest here is the rule under which individuals, organizations, and government attorneys have been permitted to file briefs and, or make oral argument in the Supreme Court. During the last decade [1950s] *amici curiae* have submitted an average of sixty-six briefs and seven oral arguments in an average total of forty cases a term.

The frequent entrance of organizations into Supreme Court cases by means of the *amicus curiae* device has often given litigation the distinct flavor of group combat. This may be illustrated by the group representation in quite different cases. In 1943, when a member of the Jehovah's Witnesses challenged the constitutionality of a compulsory flag salute in the schools, his defense by counsel for the Watch Tower Bible and Tract Society was supported by separate *amici curiae*, the American Civil Liberties Union and the Committee on the Bill of Rights of the American Bar Association. The appellant state board of education was supported by an *amicus curiae* brief filed by the American Legion. In 1951, in a case testing state resale price maintenance, the United States was an *amicus* against a Louisiana statute while the Commonwealth of Pennsylvania, the Lousiana State Pharmaceutical Association, American Booksellers, Inc., and the National Association of Retail Druggists entered *amici curiae* briefs in support of the statute.

Many *amici curiae* briefs are workmanlike and provide the Court with helpful legal argument and material. Yet writers who favor their use by organizations and recognize that "the *amicus curiae* has had a long and respected role in our own legal system and before that, in the Roman law" believe that many briefs in recent years display a "timewasting character." Another authority has said that after 1947 there were multiplying signs "that the brief *amicus curiae* had become essentially an instrumentality designed to exert extrajudicial pressure on judicial decisions." Concern over this by the members of the Supreme Court was shown in 1946 when Justice Robert H. Jackson, in a dissenting opinion, criticized an *amicus curiae* brief by the American Newspaper Publishers Association:

> . . .Of course, it does not cite a single authority not available to counsel for the publisher involved, and does not tell us a single new fact except this one: "This membership embraces more than 700 newspaper publishers whose publications represent in excess of eighty per cent of the total daily and Sunday circulation of newspapers published in this country. The Association is vitally interested in the issue presented in this case, namely, the right of newspapers to publish news stories and editorials pending in the courts."

Justice Jackson told his colleagues, "this might be a good occasion to demonstrate the fortitude of the judiciary.". . .

Conclusion

There is a logical relationship of organizational interest in litigation and the importance of courts in forming public policy. Although courts act only in cases between parties with concrete interests at stake, organizations concerned with the impact of the outcome may become quite active participants. Organizations may do this by sponsoring a "test case" brought in the name of a private party, they may aid the government attorney in a case, or they may file a brief as an *amicus curiae.* Considering the importance of the issues resolved by American courts, the entrance of organizations into cases in these ways seems in order. Indeed the essential right of organizations to pursue litigation would appear to follow from the generous attitude of American society toward the freedom of individuals to form associations for the purpose of achieving common goals. Of course, traditional judicial procedures should be followed and the attorneys for organizations, as well as for individuals, must address their arguments to reason. If these standards of conduct are followed, there is no incompatibility between the activity of organizations in litigation and the integrity or independence of the judiciary.

6.3   ## Amicus Curiae Participation in U.S. Supreme Court Litigation: An Appraisal of Hakman's "Folklore" (1982)

Karen O'Connor and Lee Epstein

In 1969 Nathan Hakman published a report of his investigation of the role of interest groups in Supreme Court litigation. He found that interest groups filed amicus curiae briefs in only 18.6 percent of the 1,175 "noncommercial" cases decided by the Supreme Court between 1928 and 1966. Participation as amicus curiae illustrates only one as-

From *Law and Society Review.* Reprinted by permission of Blackwell Publishers.

pect of litigation activity, and at that one of the most limited, but Hakman took this as a reliable indicator that interest group activity in the courts was less frequent than was commonly supposed. Based on these findings, Hakman attacked the view that amicus participation was a form of political action. Such a view, he argued, was mere "scholarly folklore."

Hakman's observations can be understood best in the context of the research tradition which they rejected. Arthur Bentley, writing in 1908, may have been the first social scientist to comment systematically on group influence on the judiciary, but it was David Truman's *The Governmental Process* (1951) which offered the first thorough assessment of group lobbying in the judicial arena. Truman offered no quantitative data, but showed how organized interests promoted the selection of "right"-thinking judges, promoted test cases, filed amicus briefs, and otherwise provided a key linkage between the legislative and judicial arenas. His examples of litigation activity, given the time period he was describing, necessarily focused on cases which involved the clash of economic interests and generally ignored the litigious activities of noncommercial disadvantaged groups. But his discussion of the inevitably political role of the courts made it clear that interests of all kinds would find it useful and even necessary to move into the judicial arena. In particular he noted the tendency of groups, whatever interests they represented, to seek redress in the courts when their political strength elsewhere had diminished.

Clement Vose's study of the NAACP and restrictive housing covenants was probably the first in-depth analysis of a single group's litigation activities. He was able to describe in minute detail the NAACP's strategy to end housing discrimination. He concluded that its effectiveness was the product of several factors, including the selection of appropriate test cases, the hiring and retention of skilled attorneys, and the longevity and stability of the organization. Vose's approach to the study of interest group litigation strategy later was applied to other groups. . . . Hakman argued, however, that these group litigation activities were not representative of Supreme Court cases. He found little evidence that organizations actually select test cases. Most noncommercial litigation, he concluded, is highly technical and not of test-case quality.

Hakman went further to contend that groups generally do not engage in judicial lobbying, and that they rarely have "strategies" for doing so. Based on responses to two questionnaires sent to interest group leaders in 1955 and 1961, Hakman maintained that even "'established' or 'permanent' organizations do not play a significant role in influencing the scope or conduct of courtroom controversies."

Whatever the validity of Hakman's conclusions for the time period he studied, current research on interest group participation casts doubt on their current utility. A legion of scholars has described the judicial lobbying efforts of interest groups. The NAACP Legal Defense Fund's efforts to prevent resumption of capital punishment, the continuing school desegregation and busing controversy, the never-ending issues of separation of church and state, and the more recent controversies over gender discrimination and abortion, all demonstrate continuing, extensive, and significant interest group activity before the courts. . . .

Virtually all recent research, therefore, has found evidence of a significant systematic organizational role in Supreme Court litigation. It is time again to ask, like Hakman, whether these well-documented reports are merely idiosyncratic and thus not representative of Supreme Court litigation as a whole, or whether they are merely the most visible instances of a dynamic now deeply embedded in the litigation process.

Amicus curiae participation is but one facet of interest group participation in litigation; certainly it does not mark the limits of such activity. Nevertheless, it is the measure Hakman used and is probably still the best quantitative indicator available. Since Hakman's study, federal court rules concerning standing and class actions have been liberalized in ways which provide some additional incentives to group litigation. The rules governing amicus submissions to the Supreme Court have remained uniform, however, and thus it is possible to approximate Hakman's study in a later time period. . . .

Hakman divided his sample into three time periods: 1928–1940; 1941–1952; and 1953–1966. He reported that nongovernmental amicus briefs were filed in only 1.6 percent of the noncommercial cases in the first period, 18.2 percent in the second, and 23.8 percent in the third, for an overall rate of amicus participation of 18.6 percent (219 out of 1,175 cases). Because the 1.6 percent figure reported by Hakman for the first time period seemed unduly low, we recounted amicus seemed participation in those cases. The corrected figure, according to our estimates, is 6 percent. Thus, the adjusted "overall" rate of amicus participation from 1928 to 1966 is 19.3 percent.

. . . [I]nterest group amicus participation in noncommercial cases before the Supreme Court was nearly nonexistent until World War II, [but] it rose significantly after the war, and . . . it then accelerated very rapidly in the late 1960s and 1970s. Indeed . . . in some years in the late 1970s participation was exceptionally high. For example, in 1979, interest groups filed amicus curiae briefs in 67.8 percent of the noncommercial cases (59 out of 87) decided by the Court.

. . . If we eliminate criminal cases, which are significantly less likely to attract amicus support for reasons advanced by Hakman and others, we find that the rate of amicus participation has risen substantially, to 63.8 percent. Since there were relatively few criminal cases on the Supreme Court's docket during the first 20 to 25 years covered in Hakman's sample, it seems appropriate to compare his (adjusted) total of 19.3 percent to the current 63.8 percent excluding criminal cases. On the basis of these figures, we can easily conclude that amicus participation today is over three times what it was about 40 years ago.

The increase in amicus participation is seen even more clearly by looking at specific issue categories. Four of our coding categories appear to approximate Hakman's. In each of these, . . . interest group participation is now extensive; indeed, in cases involving labor unions it appears to be a regular part of the litigation process.

Hakman reported that interest groups rarely participated as amicus curiae in noncommercial litigation before the Supreme Court. The term "rarely" might seem inappropriate for describing amicus practice during the last period of Hakman's sample, when such participation occurred in nearly a quarter of the cases. But it seems fair enough to say that amicus participation at that time, though not unusual, was certainly not common. Hakman only measured the number of cases in which at least one amicus brief was filed. Another measure is the average number of amicus briefs filed per case. A measure such as this, which we have not calculated for 1928–1966, would be at least an indicator of the intensity of amicus efforts.

In contrast, we found that amicus briefs are now filed in more than half of all noncommercial full opinion cases, and in two-thirds of the cases when criminal cases are excluded. Multiple submission of amicus curiae briefs also is common. In 26.7 percent of the cases for the 1970–1980 period (n = 120) where at least one brief was filed, four or more amicus briefs were submitted by interest groups. The number of briefs reached as high as 57 in *Regents of the University of California v. Bakke* (1978). It seems fair enough to conclude, even from this brief analysis, that amicus curiae participation by private groups is now the norm rather than the exception. Whether or not Hakman was correct in disparaging the "folklore" of studies of judicial interest group activity, the same conclusion could not be drawn today. Like Hakman, we recognize that there are other indicators of interest besides amicus participation. We are now involved in a systematic and comprehensive study of interest group use of the courts. Our preliminary observations certainly accord with the data reported in this note and with the conclusions of many other contemporary students of the subject.

Contemporary Judicial Politics

6.4   The Influence of Amicus Curiae Briefs on the Supreme Court (2000)

Joseph D. Kearney and Thomas W. Merrill

Introduction and Overview

The last century has seen little change in the conduct of litigation before the United States Supreme Court. The Court's familiar procedures—the October Term, the opening-answering-reply brief format for the parties, oral argument before a nine-member Court—remain essentially as before. The few changes that have occurred, such as shortening the time for oral argument, have not been dramatic.

In one respect, however, there has been a major transformation in Supreme Court practice: the extent to which non-parties participate in the Court's decision-making process through the submission of amicus curiae, or friend-of-the-court, briefs. Throughout the first century of the Court's existence, amicus briefs were rare. Even during the initial decades of this century, such briefs were filed in only about 10% of the Court's cases. This pattern has now completely reversed itself. In recent years, one or more amicus briefs have been filed in 85% of the Court's argued cases. Thus, at the close of the twentieth century, cases without amicus briefs have become nearly as rare as cases with amicus briefs were at the beginning of the century. . . .

The question of how amicus briefs influence judicial outcomes is one as to which, in principle, empirical information can be gathered. Unfortunately, when courts devise policies regarding the filling of amicus briefs, and when lawyers advise clients about filing such briefs, they almost always proceed on the basis of anecdotal information or recent episodes that may be unrepresentative of the larger universe of amicus curiae participation. What is worse, this highly fragmentary information

may be processed through a perceptual lens based on a particular implicit model of judging, which model, again, is untested and may or may not be a reliable guide to underlying realities.

[Here], we present empirical evidence designed to enhance our understanding about the impact of amicus curiae briefs on the Supreme Court and therefore also about the validity of different models of judging. To this end, we have assembled a large database consisting of fifty years of Supreme Court merits decisions—every argued case from the 1946 Term through the 1995 Term. For each decision, we recorded, among other things, the outcome of the case, the number of amicus briefs supporting the petitioner, the number supporting the respondent, and whether certain key institutional litigants filed amicus briefs in the case. We then analyzed these data using standard statistical techniques to try to differentiate between different hypotheses about the influence of amicus briefs on judicial behavior.

Briefly, our principal findings are as follows. First, our study shows conclusively that the incidence of amicus curiae participation in the Supreme Court has increased dramatically over the last fifty years. While the number of cases that the Court has disposed of on the merits has not appreciably increased during this time (indeed it has fallen in recent years), the number of amicus filings has increased by more than 800%.

In terms of the influence of amicus briefs on outcomes, our study uncovers a number of interesting patterns. We find that amicus briefs supporting respondents enjoy higher success rates than do amicus briefs supporting petitioners; that small disparities of one or two briefs for one side with no briefs on the other side may translate into higher success rates but larger disparities do not; that amicus briefs cited by the Court appear to be no more likely to be associated with the winning side than briefs not cited by the Court; and that amicus briefs filed by more experienced lawyers may be more successful than briefs filed by less experienced lawyers. Among institutional litigants that appear frequently before the Court, we confirm the finding of other researchers that the Solicitor General, who represents the United States before the Supreme Court, enjoys great success as an amicus filer. We also track the amicus records of the American Civil Liberties Union ("ACLU"), the American Federation of Labor–Congress of Industrial Organizations ("AFL-CIO"), and the States, and find that they enjoy some success as amicus filers, although less than the Solicitor General.

We cautiously interpret these results as providing more support for the legal model than for either the attitudinal or interest group models. Contrary to what the attitudinal model would predict, amicus briefs do appear to affect success rates in a variety of contexts. And contrary to what the interest group model would predict, we find no evidence to support the proposition that large disparities of amicus support for one side relative to the other result in a greater likelihood of success for the supported party. In fact, it appears that amicus briefs filed by institutional litigants and by experienced lawyers—filers that have a better idea of what kind of information is useful to the Court—are generally more successful than are briefs filed by irregular litigants and less experienced lawyers. This is consistent with the legal model's prediction that amicus briefs have an influence to the extent they import valuable new information. Moreover, the greater success associated with amicus briefs supporting respondents can be explained by the supposition that respondents are more likely than petitioners to be represented by inexperienced lawyers in the Supreme Court and hence are more likely to benefit from supporting amici, which can supply the Court with additional legal arguments and facts overlooked by the respondents' lawyers. . . .

Three Models of Judging and Their Implications . . .

One of the shortcomings of previous quantitative studies of amicus briefs is that they often fail to articulate a clear hypothesis about how information

contained in amicus filings influences the decision making of the Supreme Court. These studies nearly always presuppose some theory of judicial behavior. But often that theory is not made explicit, and only rarely is any linkage established between the theory and a working hypothesis about how information influences the Court. Perhaps further progress can be made in understanding the impact of amicus briefs by delineating more precisely how different models of judicial behavior generate different hypotheses about how amicus briefs influence (or fail to influence) the Court. These hypotheses, in turn, suggest the different types of empirical results we should expect to find in examining large numbers of Supreme Court cases. Whether or not these results [succeed] may shed new light on which model of judging is most accurate. In this Part, we discuss three models of judicial behavior and specify the implications of each model in terms of the pathway of influence of amicus briefs. This in turn suggests, in a general way, the type of empirical results that would tend to corroborate or disprove the model.

The first model, and the one with which lawyers will be most familiar, we call the legal model. As its name suggests, the legal model posits that Justices resolve cases in accordance with their understanding of the requirements of the authoritative sources of law relevant to the question presented. These include the text of the applicable constitutional and statutory provisions, the structure and history of these provisions, precedents of the Court, and arguments about the policy consequences of different outcomes.

The legal model is without doubt the "official" conception of how information, including that provided by amicus briefs, influences judges. . . .

Notwithstanding the legal model's preferred status as reflected in the Court's rules and procedures, political scientists have long been intensely skeptical about whether the legal model has any explanatory power in predicting the outcomes reached by the Court. They note that the legal factors the Court considers are complex and have no fixed ordinal ranking. Thus, they contend, the legal model is open to manipulation and simply serves as a post hoc rationalization for results reached on political grounds.

A proponent of the legal model might respond that it is unrealistic to demand that the law produce highly predictable outcomes, at least at the highest level of appellate litigation. The fact that the cases reaching the Supreme Court are those that produce disagreement among lawyers does not mean that law is irrelevant to the resolution of these disputes. The lawyers appearing before the Court debate these issues in terms of legal doctrine, and they frequently reach a consensus about which outcomes are most appropriate. Indeed, the fact that the Court rules unanimously in nearly 40% of its argued cases suggests either that there is a strong core of agreement among the Justices about the law's requirements in a significant percentage of cases, or at least that their disagreements are not sharp enough to provoke a dissent.

Given the assumption of the legal model that Justices are anxious to resolve the cases before them correctly, in light of the complex norms of the legal profession, they should be eager to explore different legal perspectives on the issue, including different legal theories concerning how the issue should be resolved. These norms include, for many Justices, the social consequences of adopting different legal rules. Thus, these Justices should be receptive to "Brandeis Brief"–type information that sheds light on the wider social implications of the decision.

The legal model therefore generates a clear prediction about what results we should expect from an empirical study of amicus briefs. Amicus briefs should affect the likelihood of a party's success in the Supreme Court, but only insofar as they are of high quality, i.e., they provide new, legally relevant information to the Court beyond that supplied by the parties. The sheer quantity of amicus submissions, on the other hand, should have little impact. Indeed, low-quality briefs that are merely repetitious should have no impact, or perhaps even a negative impact insofar as they "burden the Court," to use the Court's own phrase. Measuring "high quality" in a study that relies on counting large numbers of briefs in large numbers of cases is inherently problematic. Nevertheless, . . . we have attempted in our empirical study to devise various proxies for high-quality briefs in an effort to test this prediction.

The second model of judicial behavior is the attitudinal model, which is today the dominant model used by political scientists studying the Supreme Court. The attitudinal model posits that the Justices decide cases in accordance with their political beliefs. These beliefs are assumed to be fixed by the time a Justice is appointed to the Court; the Justices do not change their ideological predispositions by interacting with their colleagues or by reflecting on the cases they hear or other information they acquire during their years on the Court.

Under the attitudinal model, individual Justices are viewed as each having a package of political "attitudes" that can be ranked along ordinal scales. These are usually scaled from "liberal" to "conservative," but are sometimes expressed more specifically, such as pro- to anti-death penalty or pro- to anti-labor union. The model assumes that as cases presenting facts that implicate these attitudes arise, the outcomes are determined in accordance with the preferences of the majority of the voting Justices. Thus, if the issue involves a conflict between management and labor, and a majority of judges fall on the pro-labor end of the pro- to anti-labor scale, the party representing labor wins.

Lawyers and law professors usually react to the attitudinal model with hostility, regarding it as at best a caricature of the legal process. The proponents of the model acknowledge that it is highly reductionistic, but counter that any model of judicial behavior, if it is to be useful, must be "simple and parsimonious." They maintain that the attitudinal model, for all of its oversimplification, does a better job of predicting the outcomes of Supreme Court cases than any other model. It is this claim to predictive superiority, rather than any subtlety or verisimilitude, that has caused the attitudinal model to become the dominant approach to study of the Court among political scientists. . . .

Recently, some political scientists have begun to question the assumption of the attitudinal model that the Justices do not modify their positions in light of information about how other institutional actors are likely to respond to their decisions. Instead, they have sought to explain judicial behavior in accordance with a "strategic actor" model. This is essentially the attitudinal model with the added assumption that the Justices are rational actors who modify their voting behavior in order to maximize the chances of their ideological preferences actually being adopted as policy. Thus, the Justices do not vote in accordance with their "knee jerk" reaction to the facts of a case, but instead consider how other institutional actors are likely to respond to their decisions. In particular, the Justices will consider whether a given interpretation of a statute is likely to be overruled by Congress, or whether the recognition of a particular constitutional right is likely to be nullified by lackluster executive enforcement.

Although it is difficult to derive testable hypotheses about the influence of amicus briefs from the strategic actor version of the attitudinal model, at least two predictions would seem to flow from this perspective. First, since the interests of the executive branch and of Congress are nearly always represented in the Supreme Court by the Solicitor General, one would expect a strategic Justice to pay very close attention to the amicus briefs filed by the Solicitor General. This might translate into higher success rates for the Solicitor General's amicus briefs relative to those of other filers. Similarly, though less dramatically, one would expect a strategic Justice to pay more than ordinary attention to the amicus briefs filed by the States since the States are often called upon to implement judicial decisions. This might translate into a somewhat higher success rate for the States as amicus filers relative to others.

The third model of judging posits that Justices will seek to resolve cases in accordance with the desires of the organized groups that have an interest in the controversy. We call this the interest group model. Political scientists have long perceived an analogy between interest groups lobbying legislatures and interest groups seeking to influence judicial decisions through the filing of amicus briefs. More recently, some legal scholars influenced by public choice theory have begun to model the judiciary in accordance with the rational-maximizer assumptions of the interest group theory of politics. Indeed, the interest group model may be the dominant conception that amicus filers have today regarding their own efforts.

What has not been perceived is that the interest group model of the judicial process, although it shares with the attitudinal model the basic hypothesis that judicial behavior is political, in fact adopts a very different assumption as to why judges behave politically. In contrast to the attitudinal model, which views judges as having fixed political beliefs and as seeking to advance those beliefs through judicial decisions, the interest group model depicts judges as having no fixed beliefs, but rather as seeking to satisfy the political demands of the best-organized groups appearing before them. The distinction between the attitudinal model and the interest group model of judging thus exactly parallels the distinction in political science between the "ideological" and the "interest group" model of legislative behavior. In both literatures, the former model depicts government actors as utilizing their office in order to advance their view of the public good, while the latter model depicts government actors as utilizing their office in order to maximize their own private good.

The immediate question raised by the interest group model is why Supreme Court Justices, who have lifetime tenure and guaranteed compensation, should care about the political demands of organized groups. . . .

The interest group model generates a clear prediction about what results we should expect from an empirical analysis of amicus briefs. We should expect to find that disparities in amicus support for one side over another would translate into a greater probability of success for the side with the greater support. Such disparities would signal to the Court that organized interest groups, and through them public opinion, are aligned with one side of the controversy rather than another. The greater the disparity of amicus support for one side, the more likely the Court will rule for that side. The quality of the legal analysis contained in amicus briefs, however, would make little difference to the outcome. . . .

Conclusion

Amicus curiae briefs have become an increasingly important phenomenon in Supreme Court litigation. Once a rarity, such briefs are currently filed in the Supreme Court at the rate of about 500 per year. If nothing else, these briefs consume significant amounts of legal resources—and a significant portion of the shelf space devoted to the Court's records and proceedings. As the number of amicus submissions has soared, so have the citations and quotations of amicus briefs found in the Justices' opinions.

The obvious question is whether, or to what extent, these submissions influence the decisions rendered by the Court. Although political scientists and, to a lesser degree, law professors have turned increasingly to empirical analysis in recent years, no one has undertaken to try to answer this question by analyzing the patterns of amicus participation and associated outcomes in a large number of cases decided over a significant span of time. One reason such a study has not been done is that the political scientists who study the Supreme Court overwhelmingly start from the attitudinal model, which explains outcomes in terms of the preexisting political beliefs of the Justices. Such a model suggests that amicus briefs should have little or no impact on outcomes. Perhaps not surprisingly, therefore, the database political scientists use to study the Court (which was developed by attitudinal scholars) does not include information on the number of amicus briefs filed in each case in support of each side or by key institutional litigants. The lack of readily accessible data has undoubtedly discouraged empirical research.

In this Article, we report our efforts to fill this gap in our knowledge by developing and analyzing a database consisting of over 6000 Supreme Court decisions over fifty years. Some of our results confirm the findings of previous, more limited studies. Most prominently, our survey shows that the Solicitor General enjoys a unique degree of success as an amicus filer. We also show that other institutional litigants—the ACLU, the AFL-CIO, and the States—enjoy above-average success, although their success rates fluctuate depending on whether they support petitioners or respondents and never reach the same level achieved by the Solicitor General.

In two respects, however, our study generates results wholly unanticipated by the prior literature. First, we show that amicus filers supporting respondents consistently enjoy more success than do amicus filers supporting petitioners. For example, amicus filers who support respondents are in general 7% more successful than those who support petitioners, and the Solicitor General is 9% more successful when supporting respondents than when supporting petitioners.

Second, we find that although small disparities of amicus support (one or two briefs to none) may be associated with increased success for the supported party, larger disparities (three briefs or more to none) show little sign of increased success and

may possibly even be counterproductive. Undoubtedly one reason we find little support for higher success rates with larger disparities of filings is that there are very few cases that have such disparities. . . .

Regarding the implications our results have in terms of identifying the factors that motivate Supreme Court Justices, we must speak much more tentatively. The attitudinal model, at least in its undiluted form, seems to find the least support in our findings. Amicus briefs clearly do matter in many contexts, and this means that the Court is almost certainly influenced by additional information supplementing that provided by the parties to the case. The strategic actor variation on the attitudinal model fares better, since the Court appears to be more attentive to information supplied by the Solicitor General (representing the executive branch) and, to a lesser degree, to information coming from the States than it is to the information supplied by amicus filers in general. The interest group model, which predicts that the Justices will respond to signals suggesting that organized interest groups disproportionately favor one side over the other, finds only equivocal support. Small disparities of support for one side may matter, although only weakly. Large disparities, however, perhaps because they occur so rarely, cannot be shown to have any impact; indeed, they appear often to work against the interests of the supported party.

We think the explanatory model that fares the best overall is the traditional legal model reflected in the rules and procedures of the Court. Amicus briefs matter insofar as they provide legally relevant information not supplied by the parties to the case—information that assists the Court in reaching the correct decision as defined by the complex norms of our legal culture. This explanation can account for the fact that respondents benefit from amicus support more than petitioners, since it is likely that respondents on the whole are less likely to be represented by experienced counsel. It can also account for the apparent pattern that small disparities of support for one side over the other are associated with greater success on the part of the supported party, since the low-profile nature of these cases may make the Court more attentive to legal arguments. Finally, of course, it is consistent with the remarkable success of the Solicitor General and the significant if less dramatic success of other institutional litigants that employ skilled and experienced Supreme Court advocates. This does not mean that the legal model explains all the

Court's decisions. Nevertheless, we think our findings support the conclusion that legal doctrine matters in at least a significant portion of the Court's business.

A View from the Inside

6.5 *Grutter v. Bollinger*
539 U.S. 305 (2003)

JUSTICE O'CONNOR delivered the opinion of the Court.

This case requires us to decide whether the use of race as a factor in student admissions by the University of Michigan Law School (Law School) is unlawful. . . .

We last addressed the use of race in public higher education over 25 years ago. In the landmark *Bakke* case, we reviewed a racial set-aside program that reserved 16 out of 100 seats in a medical school class for members of certain minority groups. The decision produced six separate opinions, none of which commanded a majority of the Court. Four Justices would have upheld the program against all attack on the ground that the government can use race to "remedy disadvantages cast on minorities by past racial prejudice." Four other Justices avoided the constitutional question altogether and struck down the program on statutory grounds. Justice Powell provided a fifth vote not only for invalidating the set-aside program, but also for reversing the state court's injunction against any use of race whatsoever. The only holding for the Court in *Bakke* was that a "State has a substantial interest that legitimately may be served by a properly devised admissions program involving the competitive consideration of race and ethnic origin." Thus, we reversed that part of the lower court's judgment that enjoined the university "from any consideration of the race of any applicant." . . .

[W]e turn to the question whether the Law School's use of race is justified by a compelling state interest. Before this Court, as they have

throughout this litigation, respondents assert only one justification for their use of race in the admissions process: obtaining "the educational benefits that flow from a diverse student body." In other words, the Law School asks us to recognize, in the context of higher education, a compelling state interest in student body diversity.

We first wish to dispel the notion that the Law School's argument has been foreclosed, either expressly or implicitly, by our affirmative-action cases decided since *Bakke*. It is true that some language in those opinions might be read to suggest that remedying past discrimination is the only permissible justification for race-based governmental action. But we have never held that the only governmental use of race that can survive strict scrutiny is remedying past discrimination. Nor, since *Bakke*, have we directly addressed the use of race in the context of public higher education. Today, we hold that the Law School has a compelling interest in attaining a diverse student body.

The Law School's educational judgment that such diversity is essential to its educational mission is one to which we defer. The Law School's assessment that diversity will, in fact, yield educational benefits is substantiated by respondents and their *amici*. Our scrutiny of the interest asserted by the Law School is no less strict for taking into account complex educational judgments in an area that lies primarily within the expertise of the university. Our holding today is in keeping with our tradition of giving a degree of deference to a university's academic decisions, within constitutionally prescribed limits.

As part of its goal of "assembling a class that is both exceptionally academically qualified and broadly diverse," the Law School seeks to "enroll a 'critical mass' of minority students." The Law School's interest is not simply "to assure within its student body some specified percentage of a particular group merely because of its race or ethnic origin." That would amount to outright racial balancing, which is patently unconstitutional. Rather, the Law School's concept of critical mass is defined by reference to the educational benefits that diversity is designed to produce.

These benefits are substantial. . . . [T]he Law School's admissions policy promotes "cross-racial understanding," helps to break down racial stereotypes, and "enables [students] to better understand persons of different races." These benefits are "important and laudable," because "classroom discussion is livelier, more spirited, and simply more enlightening and interesting" when the students have "the greatest possible variety of backgrounds."

The Law School's claim of a compelling interest is further bolstered by its amici, who point to the educational benefits that flow from student body diversity. In addition to the expert studies and reports entered into evidence at trial, numerous studies show that student body diversity promotes learning outcomes, and "better prepares students for an increasingly diverse workforce and society, and better prepares them as professionals," *Brief for American Educational Research Association, et al. as amici curiae.* . . .

These benefits are not theoretical but real, as major American businesses have made clear that the skills needed in today's increasingly global marketplace can only be developed through exposure to widely diverse people, cultures, ideas, and viewpoints, *Brief for 3M [corporation] et al. as amici curiae.* What is more, high-ranking retired officers and civilian leaders of the United States military assert that, "[b]ased on [their] decades of experience," a "highly qualified, racially diverse officer corps . . . is essential to the military's ability to fulfill its principle mission to provide national security," *Brief for Julius W. Becton, Jr., et al. as amici curiae.* The primary sources for the Nation's officer corps are the service academies and the Reserve Officers Training Corps (ROTC), the latter comprising students already admitted to participating colleges and universities, *Ibid.* At present, "the

military cannot achieve an officer corps that is both highly qualified and racially diverse unless the service academies and the ROTC used limited race-conscious recruiting and admissions policies." *Ibid.* To fulfill its mission, the military "must be selective in admissions for training and education for the officer corps, and it must train and educate a highly qualified, racially diverse officer corps in a racially diverse setting." We agree that "[i]t requires only a small step from this analysis to conclude that our country's other most selective institutions must remain both diverse and selective." *Ibid.*

We have repeatedly acknowledged the overriding importance of preparing students for work and citizenship, describing education as pivotal to "sustaining our political and cultural heritage" with a fundamental role in maintaining the fabric of society. This Court has long recognized that "education . . . is the very foundation of good citizenship." For this reason, the diffusion of knowledge and opportunity through public institutions of higher education must be accessible to all individuals regardless of race or ethnicity. The United States, as amicus curiae, affirms that "[e]nsuring that public institutions are open and available to all segments of American society, including people of all races and ethnicities, represents a paramount government objective," *Brief for the United States as amicus curiae.* And, "[n]owhere is the importance of such openness more acute than in the context of higher education." *Ibid.* Effective participation by members of all racial and ethnic groups in the civic life of our Nation is essential if the dream of one Nation, indivisible, is to be realized.

Moreover, universities, and in particular, law schools, represent the training ground for a large number of our Nation's leaders. Individuals with law degrees occupy roughly half the state governorships, more than half the seats in the United States Senate, and more than a third of the seats in the United States House of Representatives, *Brief for Association of American Law Schools as amicus curiae.* The pattern is even more striking when it comes to highly selective law schools. A handful of these schools accounts for 25 of the 100 United States Senators, 74 United States Courts of Appeals judges, and nearly 200 of the more than 600 United States District Court judges, *Ibid.*

In order to cultivate a set of leaders with legitimacy in the eyes of the citizenry, it is necessary that the path to leadership be visibly open to talented and qualified individuals of every race and ethnicity. All members of our heterogeneous society must have confidence in the openness and integrity of the educational institutions that provide this training. As we have recognized, law schools "cannot be effective in isolation from the individuals and institutions with which the law interacts." Access to legal education (and thus the legal profession) must be inclusive of talented and qualified individuals of every race and ethnicity, so that all members of our heterogeneous society may participate in the educational institutions that provide the training and education necessary to succeed in America. . . .

6.6   Brief of the Cato Institute as Amicus Curiae, *Grutter v. Bollinger*
539 U.S. 305 (2003)

Interest of Amicus Curiae

The Cato Institute was established in 1977 as a nonpartisan public policy research foundation dedicated to advancing the principles of individual liberty, free markets, and limited government. Cato's Center for Constitutional Studies was established in 1989 to help restore the principles of limited constitutional government, especially the idea that the U.S. Constitution establishes a government of delegated, enumerated, and thus limited powers. Toward that end, the Institute and the Center undertake a wide range of publications and programs.

Cato also has had a longstanding interest in circumscribing the use by government of racial and ethnic classifications—a practice fundamentally at odds with constitutional principles of ordered liberty and impartial government, as enshrined in the equal protection and due process guarantees of the Fifth and Fourteenth Amendments. The instant cases raise squarely the continued legality of such racial and ethnic preferences for admission to state universities and colleges and thus are of central concern to Cato and the Center. . . .

Summary of Argument

This litigation involves not a challenge to "affirmative action" simpliciter, whether understood as the use of race-conscious remedies for proven race-based discrimination by state actors or outreach efforts to communicate the University of Michigan's equal opportunity and non-discrimination policies as a means of enlarging the pool of applicants. Rather, seizing on Justice Powell's endorsement of "educational diversity" as a possible compelling state interest for equal protection purposes in *Regents of the Univ. of California v. Bakke (1978)*, the University and its Law School have sought to justify an admissions scheme that explicitly seeks to ensure the admission each year of a "critical mass" of students from selected minority and ethnic groups. The University's undergraduate schools strive to accomplish this objective by automatically awarding 20 points (out of a total of 150 points) for membership in particular minority groups; the Law School pursues this end by monitoring applications to ensure that members from favored minority groups comprise 10–17 percent of its student body. Expert opinion, credited below, indicated that membership in certain racial and ethnic groups increased the odds of Law School acceptance "many, many (tens to hundreds) times" that of similarly situated non-minority applicants.

Respondents' reliance on Justice Powell's *Bakke* position is problematic because Powell's discussion of diversity reflected the views of only one member of the Court and did not state a holding even in that case since a program of the type he suggested he would favor was not before the Court. Moreover, his position that educational diversity might provide a compelling justification for government use of race has never commanded the support of a majority of the Court. But even under the terms of the Powell opinion, the University's pursuit of a "critical mass" of minority students through racial and ethnic preferences cannot be squared with Justice Powell's insistence on a truly

individualized assessment of the merits of applicants in which individuals are treated as individuals; race serves as only one among many factors
potentially contributing to a diverse educational
experience; and all applicants are placed "on the
same footing for consideration" irrespective of race
or ethnicity.

Respondents' "critical mass" rationale is entirely
at odds with the very notion of an individualized
consideration as envisioned in the Powell opinion.
Respondents justify the need for a "critical mass"
in order to provide a supportive environment to enable minority students to discuss freely their experience. Whatever its merits as a pedagogic tool,
"critical mass" calculations inevitably elide into
notions of appropriate group representation. They
have "no logical stopping place," a critical deficiency under "strict scrutiny" analysis as Justice
Powell emphasized in his opinion for the plurality
in *Wygant v. Jackson Board of Educ. (1986),* and
Justice O'Connor reaffirmed in her opinion for the
plurality in *City of Richmond v. J. A. Croson (1989).*
Indeed, if sustained as a matter of equal protection,
they provide the very path to a societal "spoils system," the avoidance of which prompted Justice
Powell in *Bakke* and *Wygant,* the plurality in *Croson,* and the Court in *Adarand Constructors, Inc. v.
Pena (1995)* to insist on "strict scrutiny" whenever
government uses race or ethnicity to allocate public resources or burdens.

Twenty-five years after *Bakke,* it may be time for
the Court to make clear that educational or pedagogic diversity, while a desirable objective, cannot
be pursued through government awards of racial or
ethnic preferences. Because such preferences reflect outright racial stereotyping about how people
will (or should) think or behave on account of their
skin color or ethnicity, they cut against bedrock
constitutional principle that forbids government to
judge individuals as members of racial or ethnic
groups. Whether or not individuals from historically disadvantaged groups may derive some advantage from these programs, the state's awarding
of valuable opportunities on the basis of skin color
or ancestry necessarily diminishes those who are
not benefited and, more importantly, erodes the
national fabric and commitment to equality of opportunity.

Respondents' position is no less constitutionally
infirm even if it were to abandon its doubtful
claim that race is an appropriate proxy for viewpoint diversity and predicate its preferential admissions scheme on the need to provide useful
lessons in group tolerance for non-minority students or, more likely, appropriate representation of
certain minority groups in selective institutions of
higher learning. Because of the availability of a
great many race-neutral means of furthering a
message of tolerance, the University's empathy/tol-
erance rationable simply does not exhibit the element of necessity, of overriding justification,
required of a "compelling" justification that comports with equal protection.

The University's group-representation rationale is
likely what animates preferential admissions policies in the nation's elite institutions of higher learning. Here, preferences serve principally not to
enlarge the supply of qualified minority students
but, rather, to distribute that supply in favor of the
more selective schools. In any event, the use of
race and ethnicity simply to ensure a desired racial
and ethnic representation plainly fails "strict
scrutiny" review, as this Court has made clear in
Croson, Adarand, and Voting Rights Act cases like
Miller v. Johnson (1995).

Respondents and their amici are likely to argue
that legitimate reliance interests will be unraveled
by a ruling striking down the University's racial and
ethnic preferential admissions program. This claim
lacks all merit as (1) Justice Powell's discussion of
the "Harvard Plan" in *Bakke* was not necessary to
resolve the merits of the "reserved places" or "set
aside" plan struck down in that case; (2) respondents' use of race and ethnic preferences exceeds,
by a good margin, the limited consideration of race
envisioned in the Powell opinion; (3) respondents
and other public universities have been put on notice at least since this Court's 1995 ruling in
Adarand that all government classifications based
on race would receive "strict scrutiny" and, in light
of its prior rulings in *Wygant* and *Croson,* nonremedial use of race would likely trigger an especially heavy burden of justification; and (4) the
constitutionality of public university use of race
and ethnicity in admissions decisions has been
heavily contested in the lower courts. In short, respondents simply have taken an aggressive view of
what the Constitution permits, hardly a basis for arguing reliance on well-established constitutional
precedent in their favor.

Argument

I. The Use of Racial or Ethnic Preferences to Achieve a "Critical Mass" of Minority Admissions Exceeds the Limited Privilege, Recognized in Justice Powell's Opinion in *Bakke,* Permitting Consideration of Race as Only One Factor in a Truly Individualized Determination of the Merits of Applicants.

Justice Powell's opinion in *Bakke* reflects the now-established view of the Court that any use by the state of racial and ethnic classifications is subject to the "strict scrutiny" standard of judicial review, even where such classifications purportedly work to the "benefit" of members of minority groups. See, e.g., *Adarand Constructors, Inc. v. Pena (1995); City of Richmond v. J. A. Croson (1989).* There is, however, a substantial question whether that portion of Justice Powell's opinion stating that educational diversity could supply a "compelling" justification for a state university's consideration of the racial and ethnic backgrounds of applicants—a view embraced by none of the other Justices in *Bakke*—constituted a holding even in that case. Because the University of California at Davis set aside specific places for minority students, Justice Powell (and four other members of the Court) voted to strike down the Davis program. A university program that used race or ethnicity as only one factor among many was not before the Court in *Bakke.*

Moreover, it is doubtful that Justice Powell's position on the diversity question has ever commanded the support of a majority of the Court. Indeed, the Court's past rejection of a number of nonremedial justifications for race-based preferences casts considerable doubt on the viability of the diversity rationale. See *Croson* (rejecting "societal discrimination" rationale for use of race which, if sustained, would produce a "mosaic of shifting preferences based on inherently unmeasurable claims of past wrongs"); *Wygant v. Jackson Board of Educ. (1986)* (rejecting "role model" theory for race-based protection of black teachers from layoffs not tied to demonstrated employment discrimination); *Rice v. Cayetano (2000)* (rejecting under the Fifteenth Amendment "self-governance" and fiduciary-beneficiary theories for limiting voting rights to individuals of Hawaiian ancestry concerning elections for state agency administering programs for the benefit of Hawaiian citizenry).

We further note that Justice Powell's *Bakke* opinion was significantly informed by a perceived First Amendment interest in according a measure of "academic freedom" in the running of public institutions of higher learning. That aspect of Justice Powell's opinion is difficult to square, however, with longstanding federal legislation, consistent with the Fourteenth Amendment's Equal Protection Clause, insisting on non-discrimination in all decisions taken by state actors, including universities. It would also seem at least implicitly rejected in *Bob Jones University v. United States (1982).* In that case, seven members of the Court (including Justice Powell) rejected a First Amendment challenge to the federal government's denial of tax-exempt status to a private university that maintained racially discriminatory admissions standards on the basis of religious doctrine. Noting statutes such as Title VI, Chief Justice Burger stated for the Court: "Whatever may be the rationale for such private schools' policies, and however sincere the rationale may be, racial discrimination in education is contrary to public policy. Racially discriminatory educational institutions cannot be viewed as conferring a public benefit within the 'charitable' concept [underlying the federal tax law]."

Nevertheless, because respondents and the Court of Appeals below relied principally on Justice Powell's *Bakke* opinion, and that opinion marks the constitutional frontier respecting the allowable consideration of race in state-university admissions decisions, we assume for purposes of this part of the brief that Justice Powell's view—that a state university's pursuit of educational or pedagogic "diversity" can justify some consideration of the race or ethnic status of applicants—does reflect a majority position on the Court.

Even under Justice Powell's view, however, the University of Michigan's admissions system violates the Equal Protection Clause. Even if diversity can supply a compelling justification for some consideration of race, respondents' preferential admissions programs fail the constitutional test because the means chosen are not "narrowly tailored" to achieving the stated educational objective.

Respondents properly note that, at least in its current form, their deployment of racial and ethnic preferences is subtler than the University of California at Davis's "set aside" or "reserved spaces" approach struck down in *Bakke.* However, they and the appeals court below fail to appreciate that Justice Powell's limited endorsement of the consideration of race presupposed a particular framework for university admissions decisions. Justice Powell assumed such consideration would take place only as part of a truly individualized assessment of the merits of each applicant, including the individual's potential contribution to a diverse student body broadly understood to include all aspects of diversity. The state interest that "would justify consideration of race or ethnic background," Justice Powell wrote, is "not an interest in simple ethnic diversity," but rather "encompasses a far broader array of qualifications and characteristics of which racial or ethnic origin is but a single though important element."

For Justice Powell, the use of race might be justified when it operates as a tie-breaker among otherwise equally qualified applicants enjoying the same measure of individualized assessment. Endorsing Harvard College's self-description of its diversity admissions program (discussed as a matter of judicial notice), Justice Powell observed:

> This kind of program treats each applicant as an individual in the admissions process. The applicant that loses out on the last available seat to another candidate receiving a "plus" will not have been foreclosed from all consideration for that seat because he was not of the right color or had the wrong surname. It would mean only that his combined qualifications, which may have included similar nonobjective factors, did not outweigh those of the other applicant. His qualifications would have been weighed fairly and competitively, and he would have no basis to complain of unequal treatment under the Fourteenth Amendment.

The key, for Justice Powell, was individualized review of the merits of applicants, each placed "on the same footing for consideration":

> The file of a particular black student may be examined for his potential contribution for diversity when compared, for example, with that of an applicant identified as an Italian-American if

the latter is thought to exhibit qualities likely to promote beneficial educational pluralism. . . . In short, an admissions program operated in this way is flexible enough to consider all pertinent elements of diversity in light of the particular qualifications of each applicant, and to place them on the same footing for consideration, although not necessarily according them the same weight.

Respondents and the Court of Appeals stress the fact that, unlike the program in *Bakke,* the University's preferential admissions programs (as presently structured) do not reserve slots for particular minority groups; there is no "set aside" as such; and at all times the merits of applicants from preferred minority groups are assessed against those from non-preferred groups. But, given the findings below, this is merely a formalistic point. Here, there is no dispute that the University's LSA automatically gives each applicant from preferred minority groups an extra 20 points (out of a total of 150 points) that non-minorities do not receive solely because of their race or ethnic origin; the Law School is committed to admitting a "critical mass" of preferred minority students, somewhere along the range of 10 to 17% of the student body every year; and the record evidence is clear that being of a preferred race or ethnic group boosts the odds of acceptance "many (tens to hundreds) times" that of a similarly situated applicant from non-favored groups.

It is thus clear that for the University of Michigan, all applicants are not on "the same footing for consideration" regardless of their race or ethnicity.

Were the situation reversed and, say, a historically black college employed a similar commitment to admitting a "critical mass" of Caucasian students, it would seem highly doubtful that such an admissions program would pass constitutional muster. As Justice Powell made clear in *Bakke* and as expressly affirmed in *Croson* and *Adarand,* "the guarantee of equal protection cannot mean one thing when applied to one individual, and something else when applied to a person of another color."

Whereas the University's LSA practice of automatically awarding favored minority applicants an extra 20 points is quite difficult to reconcile with the tie-breaking, individualized consideration envisioned by Justice Powell, the Law School's "critical mass" concept is entirely at odds with the very notion of individualized consideration. If we put aside for later discussion whether the epistemic or other pedagogic benefits of ensuring classroom representation of members of particular minority groups hold up under analysis, the Law School plainly has engaged in a use of race and ethnicity that cannot plausibly be justified in terms of Justice Powell's *Bakke* opinion.

Respondents' own expert testified in the *Grutter* litigation that if the Law School could not consider race, minority students from the preferred under-represented minority categories would have constituted "only 4% of the entering class instead of the actual enrollment of 14.5%." Given the elusive nature of the diversity rationale, it is difficult to say whether 4% of the entering class would be sufficient to achieve the desired pedagogic benefits. There is no finding below—indeed, respondents do not argue—that it would be insufficient.

Rather, respondents argue that a "critical mass" of minority students is needed to create a protective environment so that those students "do not feel isolated or like spokespersons for their race, and feel comfortable discussing issues freely based on their own personal experiences" (referring to testimony of Dean Lehman). Of course, this stated concern for the comfort level of preferred minority students, viewed as members of groups, is a bit at logger-heads with an individualized conception of the contribution to viewpoint diversity thought to inhere in an individual of a particular race or ethnicity. Moreover, contrary to respondents' sociological assumption, other educators have found that the use of racial preferences to ensure the presence of a "critical mass" of presumably like-minded minority students may serve more to reinforce race-based thinking on the part of those students than to liberate them to consider themselves as individuals. But even if we assume that respondents' views on the pedagogic benefits of achieving a "critical mass" must be accepted, we have moved quite a distance from the individualized inquiry into the content of the character of each applicant approved in Justice Powell's opinion.

"Critical mass" calculations inevitably elide into notions of appropriate group representation. Is every minority group in the student body equally entitled to "critical mass" representation so that those students also do not feel isolated or that they must act as spokespersons for their group? As Judge Boggs, dissenting in *Grutter,* observed:

> Since the Law School gives no principles, sociological or otherwise, by which the "non-representativeness" of individual group members can be judged, we have to assume that a "critical mass" would be of approximately the same size for any designated group. Thus, Afghans, Orthodox Jews, Appalachian Celts, or fundamentalist Christians might also feel that their remarks were being taken as representative, rather than individually, unless they, too, had a "critical mass." Then, the makeup of the entering class could be wholly determined by these groups that the Law School chose to classify as appropriate for worrying about their "under-represented status."

There is "no logical stopping point" for such use of race, a critical deficiency under "strict scrutiny" analysis, as Justice Powell stressed, writing for the plurality in *Wygant,* and Justice O'Connor reaffirmed in her opinion for the plurality in *Croson.* Herein lies the very path to a societal "spoils system," the avoidance of which prompted Justice Powell in *Bakke* and *Wygant,* the plurality in *Croson,* and the Court in *Adarand* to insist on "strict scrutiny" whenever government uses race or ethnicity to allocate public resources or burdens.

II. Pursuit of Educational or Pedagogic Diversity Does Not Provide a Compelling Justification for the Use of Racial or Ethnic Preferences Under the Equal Protection Clause.

Twenty-five years after Justice Powell's opinion in *Bakke* it may be time for the Court to make clear that educational or pedagogic diversity, while a desirable objective, cannot be pursued through government awards of racial or ethnic preferences. This is so even if the Court is not prepared to implement fully the plurality's suggestion in *Croson* that nonremedial use of race is a per se violation of equal protection: "Classifications based on race carry a danger of stigmatic harm. Unless they are strictly reserved for remedial settings, they may in fact promote notions of racial inferiority and lead to a politics of racial hostility."

The "diversity" justification is based on a host of assumptions that reflect outright racial stereotyping—that only black students can provide the necessary critical perspective on the nation's racist past, that only black instructors can teach African-American studies, that only black policemen can instill confidence and evoke a cooperative spirit in minority neighborhoods, that tolerance and the virtues of cultural diversity can be effectively communicated only by persons of the requisite skin color or ethnicity. State action " 'based on the demeaning notion that members of the defined racial groups ascribe to certain 'minority views' that must be different from those of other citizens' " presents "the precise use of race as a proxy the Constitution prohibits." The Constitution, simply put, "provides that the Government may not allocate benefits and burdens among individuals based on the assumption that race or ethnicity determines how they act or think."

After this Court's clear message in *Croson* and *Adarand,* it is no longer adequate to say that the University's use of race as a proxy for desired viewpoints embodies no element of invidious discrimination or stigma simply because it operates for the presumed benefit of previously disadvantaged groups. Invidious comparisons are necessarily made when the state assumes that some people bring more value to an institution than others who are equally if not more qualified (as determined by the institution's own generally applicable standards) simply because they have a certain skin color or ethnicity. Such group-based assumptions about how individuals act or think, however plausible in particular cases, cut against bedrock constitutional principle:

> One of the principal reasons race is treated as a forbidden classification is that it demeans the dignity and worth of a person to be judged by ancestry instead of his or her own merit and essential qualities. An inquiry into ancestral lines is not consistent with a respect based on the unique personality each of us possesses, a respect the Constitution itself secures in its concern for persons and citizens.

. . . In any event, the use of race and ethnicity simply to ensure a desired racial and ethnic repre-

sentation plainly fails "strict scrutiny" review, as this Court has made clear in *Croson, Adarand,* and *Voting Rights Act* cases like *Miller v. Johnson (1995).* "At the same time that we combat the symptoms of racial polarization in politics" or society at large, "we must strive to eliminate unnecessary race-based state action that appears to endorse the disease."

The University of Michigan is, of course, not tied to any particular admissions criteria. As long as it acts in race-neutral manner, and consistent with its pedagogic mission, it can alter its emphasis on aptitude test scores and grade point averages in any way it sees fit. The University also may act to modify criteria that are shown, on an appropriate record, to poorly predict success in college.

But that is not what respondents seek to accomplish here. They wish to retain their emphasis on particular combinations of aptitude test scores and grade point averages, but to vary downward the standard for applicants from preferred minority groups—the University's LSA by awarding an automatic 20 points to "qualified" minorities, the Law School through its pursuit of a "critical mass" of desired minority students. The short answer, as Justice Douglas recognized, dissenting in *DeFunis v. Odegaard (1974),* is that:

> The State . . . may not proceed by racial classification to force strict population equivalencies for every group in every occupation, overriding individual preferences. The Equal Protection Clause commands the elimination of racial barriers, not their creation in order to satisfy our theory as to how society ought to be organized. The purpose of the University of Washington cannot be to produce black lawyers for blacks, Polish lawyers for Poles, Jewish lawyers for Jews, Irish lawyers for Irish. It should be to produce good lawyers for Americans. . . . A segregated admissions process creates suggestions of stigma and caste no less than a segregated classroom, and in the end it may produce that result despite its contrary intentions.

If the University of Michigan's preferential admissions policies are upheld on the basis of the justifications it has offered, such reasoning can readily be employed to " 'justify' race-based decisionmaking essentially limitless in scope and duration."

III. No Legitimate Reliance Interest Privileges the University's Post-1995 Use of Racial and Ethnic Preferences.

Respondents and their amici are likely to argue that they have legitimately relied on this Court's *Bakke* ruling, and that respect for their settled expectations since 1978 should inform this Court's constitutional ruling. To put this contention in proper perspective, it should be noted that the instant cases do not involve class actions, and the claims of the individual plaintiffs go no further back than Jennifer Gratz's 1995 application for admission to the University's LSA.

Respondents' reliance claim lacks merit for several reasons.

First, as previously noted, Justice Powell's discussion of the diversity rationale in *Bakke* reflected the views of only one member of the Court; and his discussion of the "Harvard Plan" was not a holding necessary to resolve the merits of the "reserved places" or "set aside" plan struck down in that case.

Second, as we have attempted to show in Part I above, the University of Michigan's use of racial and ethnic preferences exceeds, by a good margin, the limited consideration of race as part of a truly individualized assessment of the merits of applicants envisioned in Justice Powell's opinion. Hence, Justice Powell's view provides no warrant for respondents' aggressive use of race, as evidenced by the University LSA's automatic conferral of 20 (out of 150 points) to applicants from preferred minority groups and the Law School's pursuit of a "critical mass" of students from such groups amounting to 10–17 percent of each entering class.

Third, respondents, and other state universities employing similar preferential admissions programs, have been put on notice at least since the Court's June 12, 1995 ruling in *Adarand* that all government classifications based on race would receive "strict scrutiny" review, and that under this Court's prior rulings in *Wygant* and *Croson* nonremedial use of racial classifications would likely trigger an especially heavy burden of justification.

Fourth, the permissible use of race and ethnicity in public university admissions decisions has been heavily contested in the lower courts, resulting in rulings of unconstitutionality by the Fifth Circuit in *Hopwood v. Texas (1996)*, and Eleventh Circuit in *Johnson v. Board of Regents of Univ. of Georgia (2001)*.

In sum, respondents can offer no sound basis for arguing that they should not be held accountable for admissions decisions made in 1995 and thereafter. Absent a controlling decision of this Court, respondents certainly had every right to litigate their view of allowable constitutional limits on the use of race and ethnicity in admissions decisions. But like all litigants, they cannot avoid appropriate remedial consequences when their position is not sustained in the courts.

Conclusion

For the foregoing reasons, the decisions of the district court in *Gratz* and of the court of appeals in *Grutter* should be reversed.

A Comparative Perspective

6.7   ## So Help Me God: A Comparative Study of Religious Interest Group Litigation (2002)

Jayanth K. Krishnan and Kevin R. den Dulk

Introduction

It is no accident that religious groups are important political actors in many modern democracies. Most of these democracies were carved out of diverse religious populations, and immigration patterns have only added to the mix. Hence the political systems in these nation-states have had to cope with the peculiar demands of religious citizens—demands which these citizens often voice loudly and with some force in court. Legal advocacy by religious groups, however, is not a self-evident choice as a form of participation. Afte all, modern democracies usually offer organizations multiple points of political access. Moreover, some religious groups might choose to avoid political confrontation altogether, perhaps for uniquely religious reasons.

Our purpose in this article is to examine the factors determining the choice to litigate among religious groups in the United States, Israel, and India. We choose these three countries for important legal and methodological reasons. Each is a modern democracy with a long history of addressing religious matters in civil courts. Due to British influence, each legal system owes much to the common law tradition, and India and Israel have also patterned portions of their legal systems after the American model. Each contains a diverse religious population, albeit to varying degrees. Yet there are also important differences among these nations, and analyzing these differences helps us better understand the myriad forces propelling and/or hindering religious groups in asserting their demands in courts.

From *Georgia Journal of International and Comparative Law* 30 (2002): 233–275. Reprinted by permission.

Our chief focus is legal advocacy through political litigation, that is, advancing broad policy goals by bringing conflicts directly to court for a resolution. Pursuing policy goals in court is rare in all three countries relative to other tactics, but it is nevertheless a factor in interest group politics. Nearly fifty years ago, U.S. Supreme Court Justice Robert Jackson declared it "government by lawsuit" and "the stuff of power politics in America," and its use as a political tactic in the United States has only increased over time. Some scholars have argued that the same is true in Israel and India, though the evidence of the nature and extent of Israeli and Indian political litigation, as we shall see, is less developed in the law and courts literature.

Over time, scholars of law and politics have considered many explanations of interest group litigation, but most have focused on institutional and organizational factors that include: the role of organized groups in the political and legal system, the available legal resources of those groups, and the properties of courts that make them attractive advocacy sites. Each of these factors has well-documented effects on the legal mobilization of organized groups in the United States and abroad, and we do not wish to underestimate their role in structuring the choice to litigate. We argue, however, that another determinant is often omitted from analyses of litigation campaigns. We suggest that adding an ideational factor—that is, the normative and explanatory ideas of the groups themselves—provides a particularly rich insight into motivations for litigation. Ideas reconfigure the strategic terrain: groups see their resources and political environment through a distinctive worldview that influences their political litigation efforts. . . .

Explanatory Framework

. . . The structure of a democratic state's political system may fundamentally affect the type of interaction organizations have with government institutions. The American political system, for example, many believe represents a structure where numerous types of groups have the opportunity to influence policy. Government institutions in the U.S., the argument goes, serve as the playing fields for competing groups to stake their particular claims. The judiciary, of course, is an integral part of the American state, and it therefore serves as an important forum where numerous groups can compete to advance their policy goals. Accordingly, we should not be surprised to find groups within this type of system often engaging the courts.

The political systems of Israel and India are stark contrasts to what we find in the United States. Both Israel and India are strong multi-party systems; in both cases interest groups must compete not only with each other, but also with powerful political parties when attempting to capture the attention of the state. As a result, groups are often "edged-out" by political parties and are unable to represent themselves in such state institutions as the legislature, bureaucracy, or judiciary. For example, in Israel parties control the legislative and bureaucratic branches of government, and as a consequence, control the distribution of social services as well. Parties serve as the main organizations that represent political interests; thus parties (rather than groups) are used as the vehicles for political mobilization. They also set much of the political agenda for the country, and the ruling party, in particular, frequently determines the degree of salience given to an issue. In addition, parties are present at almost every access point of influence in the political system. . . .

In India, too, the presence of powerful parties, particularly the Congress Party, has affected what interest groups have been able to do. From the time of Independence (1947) to 1977, governmental power at the national level was under the leadership of the Congress Party. During this time Congress was the main possessor and distributor of resources. And although there were brief periods when Congress' authority came into question, no other party or organization really was in a position to challenge the seemingly invincible power, prestige, and effectiveness of India's preeminent party.

It was not until after the end of Indira Gandhi's Emergency Rule that India saw an increase in the number of interest groups and social movements. Yet, overall, the nature of the Indian political system has not lent itself to effective interest group mobilization. Little cohesion exists among Indian interest groups. There is high fragmentation and great disunity, even among groups within the same policy sphere. In addition, while parties possess at the very least some resources, most groups struggle to exist; not surprisingly the latter tend to be very ephemeral in nature. Groups are weak institutionally, and their bureaucracy often is inefficient and/or unstructured. The resilience of a group frequently depends upon the personality, charisma, and reputation of one or two major leaders. It is rare to find a developed hierarchy or secondary set of administrators below these few important figures. Therefore, in India, with political parties continuing to have more power than their interest group counterparts, we would expect to find the types of strategies used by an organized group—including litigation—to be highly affected by the relationship it has with existing political parties.

Money and expertise can be devoted to legal activity, the base constituency from which the organization can draw support, organizational structure, and the strength and coordination of pre-existing organizational networks. Each of these resources matters to whether and how organized groups will mobilize the law. Across the ideological spectrum, for example, we might expect that budgetary considerations would affect not only the choice to use legal advocacy, but also the form of legal advocacy a group employs. And, in the realm of U.S. appellate litigation, for example, groups with large budgets might choose the direct control of case sponsorship, while groups with smaller war chests might resort to the less costly amicus curiae brief. An organization's "sunk costs" in staff attorneys can help motivate use of courts as well. Other resources, such as a group's structure and leadership arrangement, can affect how it relates to supporters, how well it divides the labor of advocacy with other groups, and how effectively it chooses its battles. . . .

Social movement theory adds another dimension to the relationship between resources and the development of rights-advocacy organizations. Resources mobilization versions of social movement theory stress that incipient movements can rarely sustain momentum without mobilizing resources and organizing members into some kind of formal arrangement. Drawing from this theory, studies of rights-advocacy movements have detailed the important role of organizational resources at different stages of legal mobilization. Developing an organizational apparatus supports and prolongs a rights-advocacy movement in various ways. Organizations are able to gather intelligence and store information, publicize and establish long-term credibility with constituents and elites, coordinate activities in different legal and political forums, and develop legal expertise beyond the capacities of individual attorneys. . . .

The contextual and resource-centered explanations move us some distance toward explaining religious group legal advocacy. As we shall see, legal mobilization requires attention to all of these factors. But these arguments focus mainly on how groups respond to what they have (or do not have), not on what members of groups believe (or do not believe) about the nature and legitimacy of law and politics themselves. This becomes an important omission when we recognize that worldviews—sets of ideas that help groups explain, evaluate, and engage the social and political world—may either encourage or close off legal advocacy regardless of a group's political context or resources. . . .

It would be impossible to survey the remarkable diversity of religious interest group litigation in the United States within the confines of this study. As illustrations, we examine specific groups associated with two religious traditions that have mobilized law during the past three decades: Roman Catholicism and conservative evangelical Protestantism. To tighten the focus further, we concentrate on their efforts before the Supreme Court from 1971–2000, and we examine two policy areas of particular concern to both traditions: abortion and education. . . .

What accounts for [the rise] in political litigation among evangelical Protestants? The political environment and the availability of resources have factored in the development of evangelical rights advocacy over these decades. Concerns about judicial rulings, support from legislatures and other public officials during the Reagan and Bush administrations, organi-

zational structure, . . . leadership . . . , the [need for] organizational maintenance—all of these factors had varying roles to play in the mobilization of rights-advocacy groups associated with evangelical Protestantism. Yet, taken together, these factors neglect another variable that catalyzed the evangelical movement: religious ideas.

It was not until intellectuals and other elites within the broader world of evangelicalism became convinced that "secular forces" must be confronted in terms of a theology of activist politics that evangelical rights-advocacy groups began to form in the mid-1970s. This argument is consistent with other studies of legal mobilization that reveal the importance of elites in publicizing grievances and opportunities for redress. As evangelical leaders began to nudge their fellow religionists out of apolitical isolation, a small group of evangelical attorneys began to see lawyering as a distinctively religious vocation. . . .

While many Catholics shared evangelical concerns such as moral decay, the ascendancy of secular humanism, desire for more public accommodation of religious education, opposition to abortion rights, they did not generally follow the same trends in legal mobilization. Roman Catholics, whether through the Church's substantial institutional apparatus or myriad lay organizations, had been active legal advocates for many decades. The difference between this advocacy and evangelical legal activity was that Catholic organizations had maintained a relatively constant rate of participation. Though the legal mobilization of evangelical groups increased disproportionately compared to other groups from 1970 to 2000, Catholic organizations maintained consistent amicus participation (between 7 and 14% of total filings in education and abortion cases combined) and case sponsorship across time.

Again, differing ideas explain this variation between the two religious traditions. For over two millennia, the Catholic Church has developed a rich body of social teaching and justifications for engagement in public life and intellectual traditions that evangelicals simply lack. This is not to say that the Catholic Church's considerable institutional resources played little role in its legal advocacy, but rather that the Church would be less likely to mobilize those resources without notions of "common good," "natural law," and "social justice" that enable public engagement. . . .

. . . [K]ey documents—the Declaration of Religious Liberty, Pastoral Constitution, Dogmatic Constitution, and Decree on the Bishop's Pastoral Office of Bishops—created broad frameworks of thought and practice for the global Church. It is important to note, however, that Vatican II was not a meeting about specific tactics of public engagement. Consequently, the link from Vatican II ideas to Catholic rights advocacy is not straightforward. However, the Council provided a set of ideas—explanatory and evaluative beliefs about the role of the Church in public life—that would provide a basis for the U.S. Catholic Conference and other Catholic groups to mobilize the law.

Some of these ideas were translated into a strong sense of partnership with the state. Mark Chopko, the USCC's current General Counsel, describes Vatican II's practical influence as enabling Church agencies to search out ways they could work with government to advance the common good. . . .

Religious Interest Group Litigation in Israel and India

Preliminary evidence from our American case study indicates that religious groups in the United States opt for litigation for both institutional and ideological reasons. In this section of the article, we suggest that Israeli and Indian interest groups use a similar decision calculus.

As we have already discussed, both Israel and India are traditionally thought of as strong multi-party states where groups play a less prominent role in politics. Yet in both countries some groups, including some religious organizations, have indeed turned to the courts as a means of achieving their objectives. In fact, in Israel since the 1980s more social, political, and religious groups are using litigation. And as we shall see, in India too, despite the presence of numerous parties, different interest organizations have occasionally employed the tactic of litigation.

What accounts for this use of courts by specifically religious organizations in these two multi-party states? One explanation may be that in both countries gaining access to the courts is relatively easy. In both countries, court fees are usually minimal, standing requirements are easy to meet, and

in many types of cases representation by a lawyer is not even required. In cases involving the public interest, groups in both Israel and India are permitted to petition directly the respective Supreme Courts for hearings.

Furthermore, groups in both countries have seen an increase in resources during the past two decades. In Israel one non-profit funding agency in particular (The New Israel Fund) has been especially generous in donating different types of resources to certain religiously oriented organizations. The Masorti Movement and the Israel Religious Action Council have been two such benefactors. Likewise, in India several different religious organizations have received new funding, primarily from "non-resident Indians" who live in the United States.

It is only reasonable to assume that easy access to courts and an increase in resources are why certain religious groups are more frequently using the legal process. But are these conditions the only factors that matter? Consider that in spite of these seemingly favorable circumstances there is little record in either Israel or India of religious groups using litigation to the same degree that we find in the United States. Systematic litigation campaigns by Israeli and Indian religious groups are simply not present. So even though in theory it appears favorable for religious groups to use courts, only a select few in these countries regularly engage the judicial process.

Over the last two and one half years the first author of this study has made four visits to Israel and one extended trip to India conducting archival research, content analysis of interest group literature, and performing in-depth, semi-structured interviews of a wide array of groups, including certain religious organizations. The evidence gathered during this fieldwork indicates that in addition to the standard factors typically associated with why religious groups in particular, may or may not choose to litigate, there are other more ideologically-based reasons that affect the decision-making calculus.

The Case of Israel

Within Israel there are those organizations—both religious and non-religious—that have been seeking to reduce the amount of influence the Orthodox Jewish community currently wields over the state.

The Israel Religious Action Center (IRAC) is one such group that combats what it perceives as the Orthodoxy's hegemony over Israeli society. IRAC serves as the legal arm for the Reform Jewish Movement in Israel. Started in 1987, IRAC explicitly rejects—and fights against—the control the rabbinical Orthodoxy has over issues such as marriage, divorce, burial, and conversion. IRAC is intimately involved in the "Who is a Jew" issue. Through a special program known as the Legal Advocacy Centers for Olim (LACO), IRAC helps newly arrived immigrant Jews (who often face discrimination from the Orthodoxy) integrate into Israeli society. . . .

Of course the attorneys agreed that resources play a role in the decision-calculus. But because of the relatively inexpensive costs of litigating in the Supreme Court (where most of their litigation activity takes place), resources, in their view, probably play less of a role in appellate advocacy than in the United States. We also learned that decisions on whether to use litigation depend upon the type of assistance they receive from the country's legislative and bureaucratic institutions. For many issues that concern IRAC, the attorneys stated that neither the Knesset nor the various ministries serve as effective institutions to redress grievances. By contrast, the one attorney pointed to how the Supreme Court has actively been involved in protecting non-Orthodox rights. This particular individual lauded the historic Brother Daniel case, where the Israeli Supreme Court decided that it, not the Orthodox-controlled rabbinical courts, would dictate who could qualify as a Jew for purposes of applying for the country's "Law of Return." Both attorneys expressed satisfaction that the Supreme Court has exhibited the "courage" to venture into legal terrain that many within the Orthodox community believe is beyond the Court's jurisdiction. (In fact, evidence that the Court currently supports non-Orthodox causes is seen by several recent decisions that appear to interpret Judaism in a broader manner.)

Still what is most interesting is that the IRAC attorneys each stated that another factor was involved in the group's decision to pursue litigation as a course of action. One of the attorneys put it most eloquently. The group's inclusive and accepting Judaic beliefs demanded that they fight to secure the rights of all Jews in the country. As this attorney noted, members of IRAC are just as religious as the Orthodox in Israel. IRAC, however, sees Judaism as a pluralistic faith, open to both the Orthodox and non-Orthodox communities. Thus, if certain Jews are being denied the right to have a voice in how they practice their religion, then on both moral and religious grounds, the group believes it must legally do whatever it can to oppose this infringement—whether that means holding rallies, protesting, or going to court.

This comment suggests that religious ideology—in this case, liberal Judaic ideology—indeed plays an important motivational role in the tactical decisions of IRAC. While resources and institutional factors may serve as necessary conditions for understanding litigation strategies, they are simply not sufficient. Religious ideas certainly are key in whether or not IRAC selects litigation as a public policy tactic. . . .

The Case of India

Like Israel, India serves as another optimal case to test the applicability of the standard theories. With good cause there is reason to believe that the country's multi-party system and delay-ridden, overburdened courts contribute to the reason that there are such low rates of interest group litigation. Moreover, the fact that most groups lack sufficient resources to mount continued litigation campaigns is also seen as a huge impediment. But as we mentioned earlier, encoded within the Indian legal system are principles that allow groups to file cases involving issues that impact public policy and the public interest directly in the Supreme Court. Such claims in fact can be done quite cheaply and without even formal legal representation. Perhaps then this explains why some groups have opted to pursue the route of litigation.

But if our focus is on religious organizations, can we explain whether or not these groups litigate solely in terms of institutional and resource factors? To answer this question, we focus on three types of groups in India: a Hindu-based organization, a Muslim group, and a Christian movement. The first of our groups is the Arya Samaj, a Hindu, Vedic organization founded in 1875. The Arya Samaj has multiple branches within and outside of the country. While the group claims not to be steeped in the fundamentalist, Hindutva tradition, it does believe that its members should closely follow the ten basic teachings of the holy Hindu scriptures, the Vedas. The membership of Arya Samaj numbers in the thousands; no accurate figure is currently available. Although often accused of espousing Hindu superiority, the group claims that it only seeks to unify Hindus by abandoning the divisive institution of caste and promoting principles of equality, liberty, education, social welfare, and political representation for all people.

In interviews with one of the leading Swamis (spiritual leaders) in the movement, the first author gathered extensive information on the types of tactics the group practices. To this day, one of the most frequently employed activities includes the holding of public conferences and seminars. Leaders of the organization invite individuals from the grassroots levels and educate them on topics involving religion, politics, economics, and society. In addition, the group publishes and distributes volumes of books, journals, and newspapers. The group occasionally holds rallies and public demonstrations promoting its message. And leaders within Arya Samaj meet with bureaucrats and legislators in an effort to persuade these officials to adopt policies that fall into line with the group's central beliefs.

The Swami being interviewed for this study also noted how there was a "disgust" within his organization over the way that other prominent religious coalitions, including the Sangh Pariwar (of which the ruling Bharatiya Janata Party is a member), have been manipulating the teachings of Hinduism for purely self-interested motives. He stated that his group wished not to be associated with these "character-less" organizations.

The Swami also mentioned that over the past twenty years Arya Samaj has been involved, albeit in infrequent doses, in one type of political tactic: litigation. Arya Samaj, in rare instances, has sponsored cases on behalf of quarry workers and laborers who work primarily on government construction projects. As the Swami noted, his organization observed how these (typically) low-caste individuals were being treated by the government. Their pay was low, their working conditions were abominable, and the risk to their health was immense. Under the principles of the Vedas, it was the duty of Arya Samaj to act on behalf of these underprivileged citizens. According to the Swami,

since the government is filled with self-interested parties and the bureaucracy is highly corrupt, the judiciary remains the only institution to which the group can turn. When pressed on how the group could afford the time (average length of lawsuits in India is one of the longest in the world) or the money to litigate such matters (the group uses one of the country's most expensive Supreme Court attorneys), the Swami indicated these factors were, of course, considerations. But he concluded by saying that he and his fellow members of Arya Samaj feel a deep sense of moral and religious responsibility to act on behalf of those most in need.

Tactical decisions based on religious doctrine can also be seen in the study of the Jamaat-e-Islami Hind (hereinafter Jamaat), arguably the country's largest Muslim interest organization. Started in 1948, Jamaat not only has offices in almost every state in the country and thousands of members, but it is an international organization as well. Its Pakistani branch serves as the world headquarters. During a meeting with Mahmood Khan, a leading policy activist who also is the leader of a state branch, the first author learned the group is involved in four main types of policy activities: (1) holding seminars, (2) sponsoring symposiums with government and societal leaders, (3) publishing materials that promote the group's message, and (4) working at the grassroots level to help the poor build homes, harvest crops, and improve the infrastructure of village life. (Khan vigorously denied his organization performs these social welfare services with the ulterior motive of converting needy individuals to Islam). . . .

The final group in our comparative study involves examining the Christian Institute for Study of Religion and Society (CISRS). CISRS is one of the country's well known Christian-based interest organizations. In addition to its headquarters in New Delhi, CISRS has offices in Bangalore, Calcutta, Madras, and Bombay. The organization claims not to have exact figures on its membership, but it stresses that it has drawn over one hundred thousand supporters in recent CISRS-sponsored peace rallies. CISRS is a member of many Christian umbrella groups in the country, including the Indian National Council of Churches, the World Council of Churches, and the All India Christian People's Forum. . . .

Conclusion

The evidence marshaled in this study supports the general argument that conventional theories of group litigation only partially explain the tactical decision-calculus of religious interest organizations. From our American case study, we see that the noticeably increased presence of evangelical groups in court and the relative constancy of the Catholic Church relates not only to the political environment and available resources but to an additional factor rarely considered by others who study this important area: religious ideas. Whether it is through the sponsorship of cases, submission of amici curiae, or actual participation as litigants, religious convictions help structure the choice to use litigation among these groups. Our Israeli and Indian case studies reveal interesting comparative findings as well. In Israel, the research suggests that the ideas to which a group subscribes also influences whether that group will interact with the

courts. In India, the country with the overall lowest rates of litigation of the three, we see that institutionalist factors (such as lack of resources) certainly account, in large part, for why religious organizations so rarely enter into litigation. As our data indicates, however, it seems that when religious interest groups in India contemplate litigation they often turn to their religious teachings; their ideas and attitudes toward religious beliefs play a crucial role in the decision-making process.

There are many issues that remain to be tackled, including a systematic analysis of the relative weight of institutional, resource, or ideational determinants of legal mobilization. Moreover, this study has been limited to certain religious groups; it leaves open an empirical question regarding the possibility of generalizing to other groups in various national settings. Yet the analysis takes a first step towards introducing a framework for combining a range of factors as explanations for legal mobilization, most importantly the role of ideas in shaping legal activity.

6.8 Brief of the Government of Canada as Amicus Curiae, *Michigan v. United States Environmental Protection Agency* (1999)

Summary of Argument

The Government of Canada respectfully urges the Court to uphold the EPA NOx SIP Call published October 27, 1998 requiring additional controls on the emissions of nitrogen oxides (NOx) from 22 States and the District of Columbia. Canada's brief will show that these emissions contribute significantly to NOx and ozone levels in Canada and have an adverse impact on the health of Canadians and on Canada's ability to attain its own air quality objectives and standards. Canada's experience reinforces the conclusion that there is a rational basis for the EPA NOx SIP Call.

Argument

Identity, Interest and Source of Authority to File

The Government of Canada, the sovereign governing entity for Canada, derives its authority to file this *amicus curiae* brief from the Court's Order of March 19, 1999. Canada has a well-established interest in the U.S. air quality regime, an interest that both the U.S. Congress and Executive Branch have long recognized. Section 115 of the U.S. Clean Air Act requires EPA to control transboundary pollution if it finds that it may "endanger public health or welfare" in Canada. This requirement has been part of the Act since 1965.

In 1991, Canada and the United States entered into a joint Air Quality Agreement that obligates each country to notify the other of actions taken that are likely to have a significant impact on the transboundary flow of emissions and to "coordinate" their air pollution monitoring activities. The Agreement incorporates both the spirit of Section 115 and the rule of international law that protects a country from environmental damage caused by activities in a neighboring country. In September 1999, the two countries will begin negotiating an annex to the Agreement aimed specifically at controlling ground-level ozone.

Canada also filed submissions on three separate occasions when the NOx SIP Call was under consideration by EPA to let EPA know about the significant health effects in Canada caused by U.S.-generated NOx emissions. These comments are part of the administrative record in this case.

Canada's comments in the record demonstrate that Canada will not be able to attain its own air quality objectives and standards if the NOx SIP Call is not upheld.

Health and Environmental Impacts of Ozone

The adverse health and environmental impacts of ground-level ozone are well known. EPA found that these include (i) decreased lung function, primarily in children who are active outside the house, (ii) increased hospital admissions and emergency room visits to treat respiratory problems such as asthma, (iii) possible long-term lung damage and premature death; and (iv) damage to crops, forests and ecosystems.

Epidemiological studies in Canada confirm EPA's findings. In southern Ontario, studies conducted over a six year period by Burnett, *et al.* found that increases in ambient ozone levels of up to 50 parts per billion (ppb) triggered a five percent increase in hospital admissions for asthma, bronchitis, and other respiratory problems on days immediately following the high ozone episodes.

Overall in Canada, ozone and other common air pollutants are estimated to cause as many as 16,000 premature deaths each year. Nitrogen dioxide, a major component of NOx, is one of the pollutants most strongly linked to premature mortality in Canada. . . .

Impact of U.S. Emissions Upon Canada

Unfortunately, because of the substantial flow of NOx emissions from the United States into Canada, the Canadian program alone cannot attain ground-level ozone standards and objectives in Canada, nor can it fully eliminate the adverse health effects of ground-level ozone in Canada. Of the 23 million tonnes of NOx contributed yearly by the United States and Canada to their common airshed, some 21 million tonnes, or 91% of the total, come from the United States. The remaining 9% is of Canadian origin. These NOx emissions travel as much as 300 miles before decaying to one-third of the original concentration.

Recent ozone modeling runs performed for the Canada–U.S. Air Quality Committee show how this transboundary flow affects specific locations in Canada. In London, Ontario, 55% of NOx observed in the ambient environment is from U.S. sources; in Montreal, approximately one-third of NOx is of U.S. origin; and in Saint John, New Brunswick, more than 75% of observed NOx levels come from sources in the United States.

If the NOx SIP Call is fully implemented, there would be a sharp reduction in these figures. Modeling results in the EPA docket show that full implementation would reduce ozone exceedances by 29% in Windsor, Ontario; by 33% in London, Ontario; by 25% in Toronto and the areas just north and west of Lake Ontario; and by 56% in the Bruce Peninsula.

Additional joint modeling runs show that implementing the NOx SIP Call will achieve ozone reductions of 6–14 ppb in the corridor stretching from southwestern Ontario to eastern Ontario, and declines of more than 14 ppb in the region surrounding Sudbury, Ontario.

Thus, the model runs show that the great majority of locations in Canada will be able to attain the objectives and standards of the Canadian control program by 2010 if both the NOx SIP Call and the Canadian NOx and VOC reduction programs are fully implemented. Conversely, if the NOx SIP Call is not permitted to take effect, Canada will not be able to attain its air quality objectives and standards by full implementation of its own program alone.

Conclusion

EPA reached its conclusion that midwestern emissions "contribute significantly" to nonattainment in downwind states after performing its own technical analysis of air quality contributions made by upwind states, and after reviewing the model runs and the technical findings of the Ozone Transport Assessment Group. As this *amicus curiae* brief has shown, U.S. sources of NOx emissions also "contribute significantly" to NOx and ozone levels in Canada. These contributions have an adverse impact on the health of Canadians, and create a much higher burden in achieving the air quality objectives and standards established pursuant to the Canadian Environmental Protection Act. . . .

For Further Reading

Brown, Steven P. *Trumping Religion: The New Christian Right, the Free Speech Clause and the Courts.* Tuscaloosa: University of Alabama Press, 2003.

Derthick, Martha. *Up in Smoke: From Legislation to Litigation in Tobacco Politics.* Washington, D.C.: Congressional Quarterly Press, 2001.

O'Connor, Karen. *Women's Organizations' Use of the Courts.* Lexington, Mass.: Lexington Books, 1980.

Vose, Clement E. *Caucasians Only.* Berkeley: University of California Press, 1959.

Chapter 7

The Politics of Criminal Justice

Introduction

In previous chapters, we have illustrated that judges and lawyers have profound influence over who wins and who loses in legal disputes. This power is particularly obvious in the criminal justice system. However, there are several other powerful political actors and processes at work in the distribution of criminal justice as well. Most obviously, laws are made by elected legislators, who are in turn influenced by their constituents' concerns for personal safety and what constitutes fair processes and outcomes. Juries are also significant, albeit relatively infrequent, sources of authority. And, law enforcement officers must be included among the officials who hold considerable power in the criminal justice system.

Individually and together these actors have a significant impact on outcomes in the criminal justice system. Among the most common methods of influence are the collection of evidence, charge bargaining, plea bargaining, and sentencing. The selections in this chapter illustrate specifically how their behavior affects the distribution of criminal justice.

Foundations and History

In order to understand the workings of our criminal justice system, it is instructive to know at least a bit about the theoretical origins of criminal law. Among the most noteworthy early thinkers was Cesare Beccaria, an Italian aristocrat who wrote, with the help of two colleagues who were also interested in reforming criminal justice procedures, *Of Crimes and Punishments* (1764). Among the selections included here, Beccaria discusses the purpose of criminal laws in society. He proposes ways of proportioning criminal punishment by using scales that measure the significance of crimes against the stability of society. Beccaria also describes the significance of specific and general deterrence as the primary purpose of punishment, and the utility and legitimacy of the death penalty. Finally he outlines measures to prevent crimes by establishing predictable laws that are applied equally to all. You will see in Beccaria's writings many arguments that are fundamental to contemporary debates about our criminal justice system.

Juries play a key role in two proceedings of criminal justice. They determine innocence and guilt and recommend appropriate punishments. They can also generate controversy. In "Trial by Jury in the United States Considered as a Political Institution," Alexis de Toqueville explains that juries are not only legal institutions but also political institutions. As such, juries provide a critical service to democracy. Tocqueville explains that the criminal jury is republican in nature, putting power in the hands of the governed rather than the government. "He who punishes the criminal is . . . the real master of society," he argues, and the responsibility for making the important decision of innocence and guilt is more properly placed in the hands of the people than in those of a judge. Particularly insightful are Tocqueville's observations about the impact of jury service on jurors and society.

Contemporary Judicial Politics

Tocqueville does not specifically address jury selection, but his essay clearly suggests the significance of having juries that are composed of members of the community. Our contemporary view of jury selection, which stems from the Constitution, a series of Supreme Court cases, and Congress, is more specific. That view requires that jurors be selected from a random cross section of the judicial district in which the crime or dispute has occurred. But this process of selection is complicated by the adversarial nature of the justice system, which provides the defense and prosecution with peremptory challenges to eliminate jurors from the jury. Such challenges do not require any explanation since they are designed to give lawyers the opportunity to use their intuition about whether someone will make a supportive juror. This opportunity is limited, however, by the constitutional restrictions on race and sex discrimination in jury selection. Despite a long, and largely recent, line of Supreme Court cases that have established these restrictions, the discussion about what constitutes an unconstitutional use of race in the selection of jurors continues.

In *Miller-El v. Cockrell* (2003), the Court spoke most recently about what constitutes race discrimination in jury selection. While the primary question was procedural, the case provided the opportunity to examine the methods by which the Dallas County district attorney managed *voir dire* and how closely the trial court followed the standards for proving race discrimination that were established in *Batson v. Kentucky* (1986). Note that the Court was not unanimous, and that Justice Scalia and Justice Thomas wrote separate opinions demonstrating their views on the degree to which prosecutors violated Miller-El's constitutional rights.

The problems associated with jury selection are not likely to be resolved any time soon. Nor are a number of other principal but controversial elements of the criminal justice system. Atul Gawande's "Under Suspicion: The Fugitive Science of Criminal Justice" (2001) highlights several of these, including eyewitness testimony, the unanimous jury verdict requirement, prosecutorial discretion, and alibis. This article is particularly interesting because it emphasizes the effort by social scientists to examine the inner workings of the criminal legal system, and the political and legal obstacles scientists face as they study the degree to which the justice system achieves its goals.

A View from the Inside

The politics of criminal justice is particularly obvious in the context of sentencing. Long before he was a nominated to the Supreme Court, Stephen Breyer was one of the first commissioners of the U.S. Sentencing Commission, an agency of the judicial branch created by Congress to establish guidelines that federal judges would be required to use when sentencing. In his article "The Federal Sentencing Guidelines and the Key Compromises Upon Which They Rest" (1988), Breyer discusses the origins of the commission and the guidelincs, detailing the theories of punishment and the political compromises involved in the development of the guidelines that are the basis for federal sentencing. While he does not specifically implicate Beccaria or other historical criminal theorists, note the attention Breyer gives to the theories of punishment that are at the heart of Beccaria's commentary.

The Federal Sentencing Guidelines have been controversial from their inception. Among their most vocal opponents are federal judges, who object to the diminution of judicial discretion. Statements by Chief Justice Rehnquist and Justice Kennedy reported in the media illustrate the concern that the federal judiciary has with the guidelines generally and efforts by the U.S. Department of Justice specifically to further constrict the authority of judges in criminal courts. In the past several years, the Court has created confusion in the criminal justice system by calling into question the role of judges and juries in sentencing through its rulings in *Apprendi v. New Jersey* (2000), *Ring v. Arizona* (2002), and *Blakely v. Washington* (2004).

We include here excerpts from the Court's most recent ruling on the federal sentencing guidelines, *United States v. Booker* (2005),* a case in which a trial judge sentenced the defendant to more prison time than the maximum provided by the guidelines for elements of the crime that were not admitted to by the defendant in his plea bargain. In fact, the Court's decision had two parts, one authored by Justice Stevens (joined by Justices Scalia, Souter, Thomas, and Ginsburg) and the other authored by Justice Breyer (joined by Rehnquist, O'Connor, Kennedy, and Ginsburg). Stevens addressed the constitutional issue in his opinion. He argued, as the Court had previously, that the Sixth Amendment right to a jury trial was violated by sentencing statutes (like the Sentencing Reform Act that established the federal guidelines) that create mandatory sentencing guidelines but also allow judges to increase sentences based on elements of the crime not heard by a jury or admitted in a plea bargain. Breyer addressed the question of how to remedy the conflict between mandatory sentencing guidelines and judicial discretion to depart from mandated sentencing ranges. After dismissing several possible solutions to the constitutional

*The Court actually ruled in two cases in *Booker*. In the second case, *United States v. Fanfan,* the trial judge also found additional elements of the crime that increased the defendant's sentence. However, based on the Court's previous rulings, the judge refused to increase the sentence and instead sentenced the defendant based only on the elements of the crime found by the jury.

problem, Breyer concluded that the appropriate remedy was to remove from the federal sentencing statute the provisions that made the federal guidelines mandatory. In other words, the federal sentencing guidelines are now advisory.

It will take some time to realize the impact of *Booker* on federal sentencing practices. It is, for instance, not known whether judges will continue to use the guidelines in an advisory manner, or whether they will reject the guidelines and exercise judicial discretion as they did before. Furthermore, as Breyer acknowledged in his opinion, the Court's word will not be the last on the subject of federal sentencing. "The ball now lies in Congress' court. The National Legislature is equipped to devise and install, long-term, the sentencing system, compatible with the Constitution, that Congress judges best for the federal system of justice."

A Comparative Perspective

The issue of judicial discretion is important not only in the United States. As Lester W. Kiss explains in "Reviving the Criminal Jury in Japan" (1999), since the 1940s Japan has lacked a jury system. This has led to increased, and perhaps out of control, judicial (and prosecutorial) discretion in criminal trials. The current debate in Japan is whether to reinstitute juries and, if so, in what form to establish them. Kiss's discussion highlights some of Tocqueville's observations and more recent concerns about the relative power of judges, prosecutors, and juries in criminal decision making.

Foundations and History

7.1   From *Of Crimes and Punishments* (1764)

Cesare Beccaria

Of the Origin of Punishments

Laws are the conditions under which men, naturally independent, united themselves in society. Weary of living in a continual state of war, and of enjoying a liberty which became of little value,

Excerpts from Cesare Beccaria, *Of Crimes and Punishments*, chapters 1, 6, 12, 28, and 41. Translated from the French by Edward D. Ingraham, Second American edition. Published by Philip H. Nicklin, 1819.

from the uncertainty of its duration, they sacrificed one part of it, to enjoy the rest in peace and security. The sum of all these portions of the liberty of each individual constituted the sovereignty of a nation and was deposited in the hands of the sovereign, as the lawful administrator. But it was not sufficient only to establish this deposit; it was also necessary to defend it from the usurpation of each individual, who will always endeavour to take away from the mass, not only his own portion, but to encroach on that of others. Some motives therefore, that strike the senses were necessary to prevent the despotism of each individual from plunging society into its former chaos. Such motives are the punishments established, against the infractors of the laws. I say that motives of this kind are necessary; because experience shows, that the multitude adopt no established principle of conduct; and because society is prevented from approaching to that dissolution, (to which, as well as all other parts of the physical and moral world, it naturally tends,) only by motives that are the immediate objects of sense, and which being continually presented to the mind, are sufficient to counterbalance the effects of the passions of the individual which oppose the general good. Neither the power of eloquence nor the sublimest truths are sufficient to restrain, for any length of time, those passions which are excited by the lively impressions of present objects.

Of the Proportion Between Crimes and Punishments

It is not only the common interest of mankind that crimes should not be committed, but that crimes of every kind should be less frequent, in proportion to the evil they produce to society. Therefore the means made use of by the legislature to prevent crimes should be more powerful in proportion as they are destructive of the public safety and happiness, and as the inducements to commit them are stronger. Therefore there ought to be a fixed proportion between crimes and punishments.

It is impossible to prevent entirely all the disorders which the passions of mankind cause in society. These disorders increase in proportion to the number of people and the opposition of private interests. If we consult history, we shall find them increasing, in every state, with the extent of dominion. In political arithmetic, it is necessary to substitute a calculation of probabilities to mathematical exactness. That force which continually impels us to our own private interest, like gravity, acts incessantly, unless it meets with an obstacle to oppose it. The effect of this force are the confused series of human actions. Punishments, which I would call political obstacles, prevent the fatal effects of private interest, without destroying the impelling cause, which is that sensibility inseparable from man. The legislator acts, in this case, like a skilful architect, who endeavours to counteract the force of gravity by combining the circumstances which may contribute to the strength of his edifice.

The necessity of uniting in society being granted, together with the conventions which the opposite interests of individuals must necessarily require, a scale of crimes may be formed, of which the first degree should consist of those which immediately tend to the dissolution of society, and the last of the smallest possible injustice done to a private member of that society. Between these extremes will be comprehended all actions contrary to the public good which are called criminal, and which descend by insensible degrees, decreasing from the highest to the lowest. If mathematical calculation could be applied to the obscure and infinite combinations of human actions, there might be a corresponding scale of punishments, descending from the greatest to the least; but it will be sufficient that the wise legislator mark the principal divisions, without disturbing the order, left to crimes of the *first* degree be assigned punishments of the *last*. If there were an exact and universal scale of crimes and punishments, we should there have a common measure of the degree of liberty and slavery, humanity and cruelty of different nations.

Any action which is not comprehended in the above mentioned scale will not be called a crime, or punished as such, except by those who have an interest in the denomination. The uncertainty of the extreme points of this scale hath produced system of morality which contradicts the laws, multitude of laws that contradict each other, and many which expose the best men to the severest punishments, rendering the ideas of *vice* and *virtue* vague and fluctuating and even their existence doubtful. Hence that fatal lethargy of political bodies, which terminates in their destruction.

Whoever reads, with a philosophic eye, the history of nations, and their laws, will generally find, that the ideas of virtue and vice, of a good or bad citizen, change with the revolution of ages, not in proportion to the alteration of circumstances, and consequently conformable to the common good, but in proportion to the passions and errors by which the different lawgivers were successively influenced. He will frequently observe that the passions and vices of one age are the foundation of the morality of the following; that violent passion, the offspring of fanaticism and enthusiasm, being weakened by time, which reduces all the phenomena of the natural and moral world to an equality, become, by degrees, the prudence of the age, and an useful instrument in the hands of the powerful or artful politician. Hence the uncertainty of our notions of honor and virtue; an uncertainty which will ever remain, because they change with the revolutions of time, and names survive the things they originally signified; they change with the boundaries of states, which are often the same both in physical and moral geography.

Pleasure and pain are the only springs of actions in beings endowed with sensibility. Even amongst the motives which incite men to acts of religion, the invisible legislator has ordained rewards and punishments. From a partial distribution of these will arise that contradiction, so little observed, because so common, I mean that of punishing by the laws the crimes which the laws have occasioned. If an equal punishment be ordained for two crimes that injure society in different degrees, there is nothing to deter men from committing the greater as often as it is attended with greater advantage.

Of the Intent of Punishments

From the foregoing considerations it is evident that the intent of punishments is not to torment a sensible being, nor to undo a crime already committed. Is it possible that torments and useless cruelty, the instrument of furious fanaticism or the impotency of tyrants, can be authorized by a political body, which, so far from being influenced by passion, should be the cool moderator of the passions of individuals? Can the groans of a tortured wretch recall the time past, or reverse the crime he has committed?

The end of punishment, therefore, is no other than to prevent the criminal from doing further injury to society, and to prevent others from committing the like offence. Such punishments, therefore, and such a mode of inflicting them, ought to be chosen, as will make the strongest and most lasting impressions on the minds of others, with the least torment to the body of the criminal.

Of the Punishment of Death

The useless profusion of punishments, which has never made men better induces me to inquire, whether the punishment of *death* be really just or useful in a well governed state? What *right*, I ask, have men to cut the throats of their fellow-creatures? Certainly not that on which the sovereignty and laws are founded. The laws, as I have said before, are only the sum of the smallest portions of the private liberty of each individual, and represent the general will, which is the aggregate of that of each individual. Did any one ever give to others the right of taking away his life? Is it possible that, in the smallest portions of the liberty of each, sacrificed to the good of the public, can be contained the greatest of all good, life? If it were so, how shall it be reconciled to the maxim which tells us, that a man has no right to kill himself, which he certainly must have, if he could give it away to another?

But the punishment of death is not authorized by any right; . . . It is therefore a war of a whole nation against a citizen whose destruction they consider as necessary or useful to the general good. But if I can further demonstrate that it is neither necessary nor useful, I shall have gained the cause of humanity.

The death of a citizen cannot be necessary but in one case: when, though deprived of his liberty, he has such power and connections as may endanger the security of the nation; when his existence may produce a dangerous revolution in the established form of government. But, even in this case, it can only be necessary when a nation is on the verge of recovering or losing its liberty, or in times of absolute anarchy, when the disorders themselves hold the place of laws: but in a reign of tranquillity, in a form of government approved by the united wishes of the nation, in a state well fortified from enemies without and supported by strength within, and opinion, perhaps more efficacious, where all power is lodged in the hands of a true sovereign, where riches can purchase pleasures and not authority, there can be no necessity for taking away the life of a subject.

If the experience of all ages be not sufficient to prove, that the punishment of death has never prevented determined men from injuring society, if the example of the Romans, if twenty years' reign of Elizabeth, empress of Russia, in which she gave the fathers of their country an example more illustrious than many conquests bought with blood; if, I say, all this be not sufficient to persuade mankind, who always suspect the voice of reason, and who choose rather to be led by authority, let us consult human nature in proof of my assertion.

It is not the intenseness of the pain that has the greatest effect on the mind, but its continuance; for our sensibility is more easily and more powerfully affected by weak but repeated impressions, than by a violent but momentary impulse. The power of habit is universal over every sensible being. As it is by that we learn to speak, to walk, and to satisfy our necessities, so the ideas of morality are stamped on our minds by repeated impression. The death of a criminal is a terrible but momentary spectacle, and therefore a less efficacious method of deterring others than the continued example of a man deprived of his liberty, condemned, as a beast of burden, to repair, by his labour, the injury he has done to society, *If I commit such a crime*, says the spectator to himself, *I shall be reduced to that miserable condition for the rest of my life*. A much more powerful preventive than the fear of death which men always behold in distant obscurity.

The terrors of death make so slight an impression, that it has not force enough to withstand the forgetfulness natural to mankind, even in the most essential things, especially when assisted by the passions. Violent impressions surprise us, but their effect is momentary. . . .

The execution of a criminal is to the multitude a spectacle which in some excites compassion mixed with indignation. These sentiments occupy the mind much more than that salutary terror which the laws endeavor to inspire; but, in the contemplation of continued suffering, terror is the only, or at least predominant sensation. The severity of a punishment should be just sufficient to excite compassion in the spectators, as it is intended more for them than for the criminal.

A punishment, to be just, should have only that degree of severity which is sufficient to deter others. Now there is no man who upon the least reflection, would put in competition the total and perpetual loss of his liberty, with the greatest advantages he could possibly obtain in consequence of a crime. Perpetual slavery, then, has in it all that is necessary to deter the most hardened and determined, as much as the punishment of death. I say it

has more. There are many who can look upon death with intrepidity and firmness, some through fanaticism, and others through vanity, which attends us even to the grave; others from a desperate resolution, either to get rid of their misery, or cease to live: but fanaticism and vanity forsake the criminal in slavery, in chains and fetters, in an iron cage, and despair seems rather the beginning than the end of their misery. The mind, by collecting itself and uniting all its force, can, for a moment, repel assailing grief; but its most vigorous efforts are insufficient to resist perpetual wretchedness.

In all nations, where death is used as a punishment, every example supposes a new crime committed; whereas, in perpetual slavery, every criminal affords a frequent and lasting example; and if it be necessary that men should often be witnesses of the power of the laws, criminals should often be put to death: but this supposes a frequency of crimes; and from hence this punishment will cease to have its effect, so that it must be useful and useless at the same time.

I shall be told that perpetual slavery is as painful a punishment as death, and therefore as cruel. I answer, that if all the miserable moments in the life of a slave were collected into one point, it would be a more cruel punishment than any other; but these are scattered through his whole life, whilst the pain of death exerts all its force in a moment. There is also another advantage in the punishment of slavery, which is, that it is more terrible to the spectator than to the sufferer himself; for the spectator considers the sum of all his wretched moments whilst the sufferer, by the misery of the present, is prevented from thinking of the future. All evils are increased by the imagination, and the sufferer finds resources and consolations of which the spectators are ignorant, who judge by their own sensibility of what passes in a mind by habit grown callous to misfortune. . . .

The punishment of death is pernicious to society, from the example of barbarity it affords. If the passions, or the necessity of war, have taught men to shed the blood of their fellow creatures, the laws, which are intended to moderate the ferocity of mankind, should not increase it by examples of barbarity, the more horrible as this punishment is usually attended with formal pageantry. Is it not absurd, that the laws, which detest and punish homicide, should, in order to prevent murder, publicly commit murder themselves?

If it be objected, that almost all nations in all ages have punished certain crimes with death, I answer, that the force of these examples vanishes when opposed to truth, against which prescription is urged in vain. The history of mankind is an immense sea of errors, in which a few obscure truths may here and there be found.

But human sacrifices have also been common in almost all nations. That some societies only it either few in number, or for a very short time, abstained from the punishment of death, is rather favorable to my argument; for such is the fate of great truths, that their duration is only as a flash of lightning in the long and dark night of error. The happy time is not yet arrived, when truth, as falsehood has been hitherto, shall be the portion of the greatest number. . . .

Of the Means of Preventing Crimes

It is better to prevent crimes than to punish them. This is the fundamental principle of good legislation, which is the art of conducting men to the maximum of happiness, and to the minimum of misery, if we may apply this mathematical expression to the good and evil of life. But the means hitherto employed for that purpose are generally inadequate, or contrary to the end proposed. It is impossible to reduce the tumultuous activity of mankind to absolute regularity; for, amidst the various and opposite attractions of pleasure and pain, human laws are not sufficient entirely to prevent disorders in society. Such, however is the chimera of weak men, when invested with authority. To prohibit a number of indifferent actions is not to prevent the crimes which they may produce, but to create new ones, it is to change at will the ideas of virtue and vice, which, at other times, we are told, are eternal and immutable. To what a situation should we be reduced if every thing were to be forbidden that might possibly lead to a crime? We must be deprived of the use of our senses: for one motive that induces a man to commit a real crime, there are a thousand which excite him to those indifferent actions which are called crimes by bad laws. If then the probability that a crime will be committed be in proportion to the number of motives, to extend the sphere of crimes will be to increase that probability. The generality of laws are only exclusive privileges, the tribute of all to the advantages of a few.

Would you prevent crimes? Let the laws be clear and simple, let the entire force of the nation be united in their defence, let them be intended rather to favor every individual than any particular classes of men, let the laws be feared, and the laws only. The fear of the laws is salutary, but the fear of men is a fruitful and fatal source of crimes. Men enslaved are more voluptuous, more debauched, and more cruel than those who are in a state of freedom. These study the sciences, the interest of nations, have great objects before their eyes, and imitate them; but those, whose views are confined to the present moment, endeavor, amidst the distraction of riot and debauchery, to forget their situation; accustomed to the uncertainty of all events, for the laws determine none, the consequences of their crimes become problematical, which gives an additional force to the strength of their passions.

In a nation indolent from the nature of the climate, the uncertainty of the laws confirms and increases men's indolence and stupidity. In a voluptuous but active nation, this uncertainty occasions a multiplicity of cabals and intrigues, which spread distrust and diffidence through the hearts of all, and dissimulation and treachery are the foundation of their prudence. In a brave and powerful nation, this uncertainty of the laws is at last destroyed, after many oscillations from liberty to slavery, and from slavery to liberty again.

7.2 Trial by Jury in the United States Considered as a Political Institution (1835)

Causes Which Mitigate the Tyranny of the Majority in the United States

Alexis de Tocqueville

Since my subject has led me to speak of the administration of justice in the United States, I will not pass over it without referring to the institution of the jury. Trial by jury may be considered in two separate points of view: as a judicial, and as a political institution. . . .

My present purpose is to consider the jury as a political institution; any other course would divert me from my subject. Of trial by jury considered as a judicial institution I shall here say but little. When the English adopted trial by jury, they were a semi-barbarous people; they have since become one of the most enlightened nations of the earth, and their attachment to this institution seems to have increased with their increasing cultivation. They have emigrated and colonized every part of the habitable globe; some have formed colonies, others independent states; the mother country has maintained its monarchical constitution; many of its offspring have founded powerful republics; but everywhere they have boasted of the privilege of trial by jury. They have established it, or hastened to re-establish it, in all their settlements. A judicial institution which thus obtains the suffrages of a great people for so long a series of ages, which is zealously reproduced at every stage of civilization, in all the climates of the earth, and under every form of human government, cannot be contrary to the spirit of justice.

But to leave this part of the subject. It would be a very narrow view to look upon the jury as a mere judicial institution; for however great its influence may be upon the decisions of the courts, it is still greater on the destinies of society at large. The jury is, above all, a political institution, and it must be regarded in this light in order to be duly appreciated.

By the jury I mean a certain number of citizens chosen by lot and invested with a temporary right of judging. Trial by jury, as applied to the repression of crime, appears to me an eminently republi-

can element in the government, for the following reasons.

The institution of the jury may be aristocratic or democratic, according to the class from which the jurors are taken; but it always preserves its republican character, in that it places the real direction of society in the hands of the governed, or of a portion of the governed, and not in that of the government. Force is never more than a transient element of success, and after force comes the notion of right. A government able to reach its enemies only upon a field of battle would soon be destroyed. The true sanction of political laws is to be found in penal legislation; and if that sanction is wanting, the law will sooner or later lose its cogency. He who punishes the criminal is therefore the real master of society. Now, the institution of the jury raises the people itself, or at least a class of citizens, to the bench of judges. . . .

In proportion as you introduce the jury into the business of the courts you are enabled to diminish the number of judges, which is a great advantage. When judges are very numerous, death is perpetually thinning the ranks of the judicial functionaries and leaving places vacant for new-comers. The ambition of the magistrates is therefore continually excited, and they are naturally made dependent upon the majority or the person who nominates to vacant offices; the officers of the courts then advance as do the officers of an army. This state of things is entirely contrary to the sound administration of justice and to the intentions of the legislator. The office of a judge is made inalienable in order that he may remain independent, but of what advantage is it that his independence should be protected if he be tempted to sacrifice it of his own accord? When judges are very numerous many of them must necessarily be incapable; for a great magistrate is a man of no common powers: I do not know if a half-enlightened tribunal is not the worst of all combinations for attaining those ends which underlie the establishment of courts of justice. For my own part, I had rather submit the decision of a case to ignorant jurors directed by a skillful judge than to judges a majority of whom are imperfectly acquainted with jurisprudence and with the laws . . .

In England the jury is selected from the aristocratic portion of the nation; the aristocracy makes the laws, applies the laws, and punishes infractions of the laws; everything is established upon a consistent footing, and England may with truth be said to constitute an aristocratic republic. In the United States the same system is applied to the whole people. Every American citizen is both an eligible and a legally qualified voter. The jury system as it is understood in America appears to me to be as direct and as extreme a consequence of the sovereignty of the people as universal suffrage. They are two instruments of equal power, which contribute to the supremacy of the majority. All the sovereigns who have chosen to govern by their own authority, and to direct society instead of obeying its directions, have destroyed or enfeebled the institution of the jury. The Tudor monarchs sent to prison jurors who refused to convict, and Napoleon caused them to be selected by his agents.

However clear most of these truths may seem to be, they do not command universal assent; and in France, at least, trial by jury is still but imperfectly understood. If the question arises as to the proper qualification of jurors, it is confined to a discussion of the intelligence and knowledge of the citizens who may be returned, as if the jury was merely a judicial institution. This appears to me the least important part of the subject. The jury is pre-eminently a political institution; it should be regarded as one form of the sovereignty of the people: when that sovereignty is repudiated, it must be rejected, or it must be adapted to the laws by which that sovereignty is established. The jury is that portion of the nation to which the execution of the laws is entrusted, as the legislature is that part of the nation which makes the laws; and in order that society may be governed in a fixed and uniform manner, the list of citizens qualified to serve on juries must increase and diminish with the list of electors. This I hold to be the point of view most worthy of the attention of the legislator; all that remains is merely accessory.

I am so entirely convinced that the jury is pre-eminently a political institution that I still consider it in this light when it is applied in civil causes. Laws are always unstable unless they are founded upon the customs of a nation: customs are the only durable and resisting power in a people. When the jury is reserved for criminal offenses, the people witness only its occasional action in particular cases; they become accustomed to do without it in the ordinary course of life, and it is considered as an instrument, but not as the only instrument, of obtaining justice.

When, on the contrary, the jury acts also on civil causes, its application is constantly visible; it affects all the interests of the community; everyone co-operates in its work: it thus penetrates into all the usages of life, it fashions the human mind to its peculiar forms, and is gradually associated with the idea of justice itself.

The institution of the jury, if confined to criminal causes, is always in danger; but when once it is introduced into civil proceedings, it defies the aggressions of time and man. If it had been as easy to remove the jury from the customs as from the laws of England, it would have perished under the Tudors, and the civil jury did in reality at that period save the liberties of England. In whatever manner the jury be applied, it cannot fail to exercise a powerful influence upon the national character; but this influence is prodigiously increased when it is introduced into civil causes. The jury, and more especially the civil jury, serves to communicate the spirit of the judges to the minds of all the citizens and this spirit, with the habits which attend it, is the soundest preparation for free institutions. It imbues all classes with a respect for the thing judged and with the notion of right. If these two elements be removed, the love of independence becomes a mere destructive passion. It teaches men to practice equity; every man learns to judge his neighbor as he would himself be judged. And this is especially true of the jury in civil causes, for while the number of persons who have reason to apprehend a criminal prosecution is small, everyone is liable to have a lawsuit. The jury teaches every man not to recoil before the responsibility of his own actions and impresses him with that manly confidence without which no political virtue can exist. It invests each citizen with a kind of magistracy; it makes them all feel the duties which they are bound to discharge towards society and the part which they take in its government. By obliging men to turn their attention to other affairs than their own, it rubs off that private selfishness which is the rust of society.

The jury contributes powerfully to form the judgment and to increase the natural intelligence of a people; and this, in my opinion, is its greatest advantage. It may be regarded as a gratuitous public school, ever open, in which every juror learns his rights, enters into daily communication with the most learned and enlightened members of the upper classes, and becomes practically acquainted with the laws, which are brought within the reach of his capacity by the efforts of the bar, the advice of the judge, and even the passions of the parties. I think that the practical intelligence and political good sense of the Americans are mainly attributable to the long use that they have made of the jury in civil causes.

I do not know whether the jury is useful to those who have lawsuits, but I am certain it is highly beneficial to those who judge them; and I look upon it as one of the most efficacious means for the education of the people which society can employ.

What I have said applies to all nations, but the remark I am about to make is peculiar to the Americans and to democratic communities. I have already observed that in democracies the members of the legal profession and the judicial magistrates constitute the only aristocratic body which can moderate the movements of the people. This aristocracy is invested with no physical power; it exercises its conservative influence upon the minds of men; and the most abundant source of its authority is the institution of the civil jury. In criminal causes, when society is contending against a single man, the jury is apt to look upon the judge as the passive instrument of social power and to mistrust his advice. Moreover, criminal causes turn entirely upon simple facts, which common sense can readily appreciate; upon this ground the judge and the jury are equal. Such is not the case, however, in civil causes; then the judge appears as a disinterested arbiter between the conflicting passions of the parties. The jurors look up to him with confidence and listen to him with respect, for in this instance, his intellect entirely governs theirs. It is the judge who

sums up the various arguments which have wearied their memory, and who guides them through the devious course of the proceedings; he points their attention to the exact question of fact that they are called upon to decide and tells them how to answer the question of law. His influence over them is almost unlimited.

If I am called upon to explain why I am but little moved by the arguments derived from the ignorance of jurors in civil causes, I reply that in these proceedings, whenever the question to be solved is not a mere question of fact, the jury has only the semblance of a judicial body. The jury only sanctions the decision of the judge; they sanction this decision by the authority of society which they represent, and he by that of reason and of law.

In England and in America the judges exercise an influence upon criminal trials that the French judges have never possessed. The reason for this difference may easily be discovered; the English and American magistrates have established their authority in civil causes and only transfer it afterwards to tribunals of another kind, where it was not first acquired. In some cases, and they are frequently the most important ones, the American judges have the right of deciding causes alone. On these occasions they are accidentally placed in the position that the French judges habitually occupy, but their moral power is much greater; they are still surrounded by the recollection of the jury, and their judgment has almost as much authority as the voice of the community represented by that institution. Their influence extends far beyond the limits of the courts; in the recreations of private life, as well as in the turmoil of public business, in public, and in the legislative assemblies, the American judge is constantly surrounded by men who are accustomed to regard his intelligence as superior to their own; and after having exercised his power in the decision of causes, he continues to influence the habits of thought, and even the characters, of those who acted with him in his official capacity.

The jury, then, which seems to restrict the rights of the judiciary, does in reality consolidate its power; and in no country are the judges so powerful as where the people share their privileges.

Contemporary Judicial Politics

7.3   *Miller-El v. Cockrell*
537 U.S. 322 (2003)

JUSTICE KENNEDY delivered the opinion
of the Court.

In this case we once again examine when a state
prisoner can appeal the denial or dismissal of his petition for writ of habeas corpus. In 1986 two Dallas
County assistant district attorneys used peremptory
strikes to exclude 10 of the 11 African-Americans eligible to serve on the jury which tried petitioner
Thomas Joe Miller-El. During the ensuing 17 years,
petitioner has been unsuccessful in establishing, in
either state or federal court, that his conviction and
death sentence must be vacated because the jury selection procedures violated the Equal Protection
Clause and our holding in *Batson v. Kentucky* (1986).
The claim now arises in a federal petition for writ of
habeas corpus. The procedures and standards applicable in the case are controlled by the habeas corpus
statute codified at Title 28, chapter 153 of the United
States Code, most recently amended in a substantial
manner by the Antiterrorism and Effective Death
Penalty Act of 1996 (AEDPA). In the interest of finality AEDPA constrains a federal court's power to disturb state-court convictions.

The United States District Court for the Northern
District of Texas, after reviewing the evidence before the state trial court, determined that petitioner
failed to establish a constitutional violation war-
ranting habeas relief. The Court of Appeals for the
Fifth Circuit . . . denied a certificate of appealability (COA) from the District Court's determination.
The COA denial is the subject of our decision.

At issue here are the standards AEDPA imposes
before a court of appeals may issue a COA to review a denial of habeas relief in the district court.
Congress mandates that a prisoner seeking post-
conviction relief under 28 U.S.C. §2254 has no automatic right to appeal a district court's denial or
dismissal of the petition. Instead, petitioner must
first seek and obtain a COA. . . . Consistent with

our prior precedent and the text of the habeas corpus statute, we reiterate that a prisoner seeking a
COA need only demonstrate "a substantial showing of the denial of a constitutional right." . . . [W]e
conclude a COA should have issued.

I

A

Petitioner, his wife Dorothy Miller-El, and one Kenneth Flowers robbed a Holiday Inn in Dallas,
Texas. They emptied the cash drawers and ordered
two employees, Doug Walker and Donald Hall, to
lie on the floor. Walker and Hall were gagged with
strips of fabric, and their hands and feet were
bound. Petitioner asked Flowers if he was going to
kill Walker and Hall. When Flowers hesitated or refused, petitioner shot Walker twice in the back and
shot Hall in the side. Walker died from his wounds.

The State indicted petitioner for capital murder.
He pleaded not guilty, and jury selection took
place during five weeks in February and March
1986. When *voir dire* had been concluded, petitioner moved to strike the jury on the grounds that
the prosecution had violated the Equal Protection
Clause of the Fourteenth Amendment by excluding
African-Americans through the use of peremptory
challenges. Petitioner's trial occurred before our
decision in *Batson* and *Swain v. Alabama* (1965)
was then the controlling precedent. As *Swain*
required, petitioner sought to show that the prosecution's conduct was part of a larger pattern
of discrimination aimed at excluding African-
Americans from jury service. In a pretrial hearing
held on March 12, 1986, petitioner presented extensive evidence in support of his motion. The trial
judge, however, found "no evidence . . . that indi-

cated any systematic exclusion of blacks as a matter of policy by the District Attorney's office; while it may have been done by individual prosecutors in individual cases." The state court then denied petitioner's motion to strike the jury. Twelve days later, the jury found petitioner guilty; and the trial court sentenced him to death.

Petitioner appealed to the Texas Court of Criminal Appeals. While the appeal was pending, on April 30, 1986, the Court decided *Batson v. Kentucky* and established its three-part process for evaluating claims that a prosecutor used peremptory challenges in violation of the Equal Protection Clause. First, a defendant must make a prima facie showing that a peremptory challenge has been exercised on the basis of race. Second, if that showing has been made, the prosecution must offer a race-neutral basis for striking the juror in question. Third, in light of the parties' submissions, the trial court must determine whether the defendant has shown purposeful discrimination.

After acknowledging petitioner had established an inference of purposeful discrimination, the Texas Court of Criminal Appeals remanded the case for new findings in light of *Batson*. A post-trial hearing was held on May 10, 1988 (a little over two years after petitioner's jury had been empaneled). There, the original trial court admitted all the evidence presented at the *Swain* hearing and further evidence and testimony from the attorneys in the original trial.

On January 13, 1989, the trial court concluded that petitioner's evidence failed to satisfy step one of *Batson* because it "did not even raise an inference of racial motivation in the use of the state's peremptory challenges" to support a prima facie case. . . .

The Texas Court of Criminal Appeals denied petitioner's appeal, and we denied certiorari. Petitioner's state habeas proceedings fared no better, and he was denied relief by the Texas Court of Criminal Appeals.

Petitioner filed a petition for writ of habeas corpus in Federal District Court. . . . The Federal Magistrate Judge . . . recommended, in deference to the state courts' acceptance of the prosecutors' race-neutral justifications for striking the potential jurors, that petitioner be denied relief. The United States District Court adopted the recommendation. . . . [P]etitioner sought a COA from the District

Court, and the application was denied. Petitioner renewed his request to the Court of Appeals for the Fifth Circuit, and it also denied the COA. . . .

B

. . . Petitioner's evidence falls into two broad categories. First, he presented to the state trial court, at a pretrial *Swain* hearing, evidence relating to a pattern and practice of race discrimination in the *voir dire*. Second, two years later, he presented, to the same state court, evidence that directly related to the conduct of the prosecutors in his case. We discuss the latter first.

A comparative analysis of the venire members demonstrates that African-Americans were excluded from petitioner's jury in a ratio significantly higher than Caucasians were. Of the 108 possible jurors reviewed by the prosecution and defense, 20 were African-American. Nine of them were excused for cause or by agreement of the parties. Of the 11 African-American jurors remaining, however, all but 1 were excluded by peremptory strikes exercised by the prosecutors. On this basis 91% of the eligible black jurors were removed by peremptory strikes. In contrast the prosecutors used their peremptory strikes against just 13% (4 out of 31) of the eligible nonblack prospective jurors qualified to serve on petitioner's jury.

These numbers, while relevant, are not petitioner's whole case. During *voir dire,* the prosecution questioned venire members as to their views concerning the death penalty and their willingness to serve on a capital case. Responses that disclosed reluctance or hesitation to impose capital punishment were cited as a justification for striking a potential juror for cause or by peremptory challenge. The evidence suggests, however, that the manner in which members of the venire were questioned varied by race. To the extent a divergence in responses can be attributed to the racially disparate mode of examination, it is relevant to our inquiry.

Most African-Americans (53%, or 8 out of 15) were first given a detailed description of the mechanics of an execution in Texas:

[I]f those three [sentencing] questions are answered yes, at some point[,] Thomas Joe Miller-El will be taken to Huntsville, Texas. He will be placed on death row and at some time will be taken to the death house where he will be strapped on a gurney, an IV put into his arm and he will be injected with a substance that will cause his death . . . as the result of the verdict in this case if those three questions are answered yes.

Only then were these African-American venire members asked whether they could render a decision leading to a sentence of death. Very few prospective white jurors (6%, or 3 out of 49) were given this preface prior to being asked for their views on capital punishment. Rather, all but three were questioned in vague terms: "Would you share with us . . . your personal feelings, if you could, in your own words how you do feel about the death penalty and capital punishment and secondly, do you feel you could serve on this type of a jury and actually render a decision that would result in the death of the Defendant in this case based on the evidence?"

There was an even more pronounced difference, on the apparent basis of race, in the manner the prosecutors questioned members of the venire about their willingness to impose the minimum sentence for murder. Under Texas law at the time of petitioner's trial, an unwillingness to do so warranted removal for cause. This strategy normally is used by the defense to weed out pro-state members of the venire, but, ironically, the prosecution employed it here. The prosecutors first identified the statutory minimum sentence of five years' imprisonment to 34 out of 36 (94%) white venire members, and only then asked: "If you hear a case, to your way of thinking [that] calls for and warrants and justifies five years, you'll give it?" In contrast, only 1 out of 8 (12.5%) African-American prospective jurors were informed of the statutory minimum before being asked what minimum sentence they would impose. The typical questioning of the other seven black jurors was as follows:

[Prosecutor]: Now, the maximum sentence for [murder] . . . is life under the law. Can you give me an idea of just your personal feelings what you feel a minimum sentence should be for the offense of murder the way I've set it out for you?

[Juror]: Well, to me that's almost like it's premeditated. But you said they don't have a premeditated statute here in Texas.

. . .

[Prosecutor]: Again, we're not talking about self-defense or accident or insanity or killing in the heat of passion or anything like that. We're talking about the knowing—

"[Juror]: I know you said the minimum. The minimum amount that I would say would be at least twenty years."

Furthermore, petitioner points to the prosecution's use of a Texas criminal procedure practice known as jury shuffling. This practice permits parties to rearrange the order in which members of the venire are examined so as to increase the likelihood that visually preferable venire members will be moved forward and empaneled. With no information about the prospective jurors other than their appearance, the party requesting the procedure literally shuffles the juror cards, and the venire members are then reseated in the new order. Shuffling affects jury composition because any prospective jurors not questioned during *voir dire* are dismissed at the end of the week, and a new panel of jurors appears the following week. So jurors who are shuffled to the back of the panel are less likely to be questioned or to serve.

On at least two occasions the prosecution requested shuffles when there were a predominate number of African-Americans in the front of the panel. On yet another occasion the prosecutors complained about the purported inadequacy of the card shuffle by a defense lawyer but lodged a formal objection only after the postshuffle panel composition revealed that African-American prospective jurors had been moved forward.

Next, we turn to the pattern and practice evidence adduced at petitioner's pretrial *Swain* hearing. Petitioner subpoenaed a number of current and former Dallas County assistant district attorneys, judges, and others who had observed firsthand the prosecution's conduct during jury selection over a number of years. Although most of the witnesses denied the existence of a systematic policy to exclude African-Americans, others disagreed. A Dallas County district judge testified that, when he had served in the District Attorney's Office from the late-1950's to early-1960's, his superior warned him that he would be fired if he permitted any African-Americans to serve on a jury. Similarly, another Dallas County district judge and former assistant district attorney from 1976 to 1978 testified that he believed the office had a systematic policy of excluding African-Americans from juries.

Of more importance, the defense presented evidence that the District Attorney's Office had adopted a formal policy to exclude minorities from jury service. A 1963 circular by the District Attorney's Office instructed its prosecutors to exercise peremptory strikes against minorities: "'Do not take Jews, Negroes, Dagos, Mexicans or a member of any minority race on a jury, no matter how rich or how well educated.'" A manual entitled "Jury Selection in a Criminal Case" was distributed to prosecutors. It contained an article authored by a former prosecutor (and later a judge) under the direction of his superiors in the District Attorney's Office, outlining the reasoning for excluding minorities from jury service. Although the manual was written in 1968, it remained in circulation until 1976, if not later, and was available at least to one of the prosecutors in Miller-El's trial.

Some testimony casts doubt on the State's claim that these practices had been discontinued before petitioner's trial. For example, a judge testified that, in 1985, he had to exclude a prosecutor from trying cases in his courtroom for race-based discrimination in jury selection. Other testimony indicated that the State, by its own admission, once requested a jury shuffle in order to reduce the number of African-Americans in the venire. Concerns over the exclusion of African-Americans by the District Attorney's Office were echoed by Dallas County's Chief Public Defender.

This evidence had been presented by petitioner, in support of his *Batson* claim, to the state and federal courts that denied him relief.

II

. . .

B

Since Miller-El's claim rests on a *Batson* violation, resolution of his COA application requires a preliminary, though not definitive, consideration of the three-step framework mandated by *Batson* and reaffirmed in our later precedents. . . . [T]he State now concedes that petitioner, Miller-El, satisfied step one: "[T]here is no dispute that Miller-El presented a prima facie claim" that prosecutors used their peremptory challenges to exclude venire members on the basis of race. . . . Petitioner, for his part, acknowledges that the State proceeded through step two by proffering facially race-neutral explanations for these strikes. Under *Batson,* then, the question remaining is step three: whether Miller-El "has carried his burden of proving purposeful discrimination."

. . . [T]he critical question in determining whether a prisoner has proved purposeful discrimination at step three is the persuasiveness of the prosecutor's justification for his peremptory strike. . . . [T]he issue comes down to whether the trial court finds the prosecutor's race-neutral explanations to be credible. Credibility can be measured by, among other factors, the prosecutor's demeanor; by how reasonable, or how improbable, the explanations are; and by whether the proffered rationale has some basis in accepted trial strategy. . . .

Deference is necessary because a reviewing court, which analyzes only the transcripts from *voir dire,* is not as well positioned as the trial court is to make credibility determinations. . . .

Even in the context of federal habeas, deference does not imply abandonment or abdication of judicial review. Deference does not by definition preclude relief. A federal court can disagree with a state court's credibility determination and, when guided by AEDPA, conclude the decision was unreasonable or that the factual premise was incorrect by clear and convincing evidence. In the context of the threshold examination in this *Batson* claim the issuance of a COA can be supported by any evidence demonstrating that, despite the neutral explanation of the prosecution, the peremptory strikes in the final analysis were race based. It goes without saying that this includes the facts and circumstances that were adduced in support of the prima facie case. . . .

C

Applying these rules to Miller-El's application, we have no difficulty concluding that a COA should have issued. We conclude, on our review of the record at this stage, that the District Court did not give full consideration to the substantial evidence petitioner put forth in support of the prima facie case. Instead, it accepted without question the state court's evaluation of the demeanor of the prosecutors and jurors in petitioner's trial. The Court of Appeals evaluated Miller-El's application for a COA in the same way. . . .

In this case, the statistical evidence alone raises some debate as to whether the prosecution acted with a race-based reason when striking prospective jurors. . . . Happenstance is unlikely to produce this disparity. . . .

In this case, three of the State's proffered race-neutral rationales for striking African-American jurors pertained just as well to some white jurors who were not challenged and who did serve on the jury. The prosecutors explained that their peremptory challenges against six African-American potential jurors were based on ambivalence about the death penalty; hesitancy to vote to execute defendants capable of being rehabilitated; and the jurors' own family history of criminality. In rebuttal of the prosecution's explanation, petitioner identified two empaneled white jurors who expressed ambivalence about the death penalty in a manner similar to their African-American counterparts who were the subject of prosecutorial peremptory challenges. One indicated that capital punishment was not appropriate for a first offense, and another stated that it would be "difficult" to impose a death sentence. Similarly, two white jurors expressed hesitation in sentencing to death a defendant who might be rehabilitated; and four white jurors had family members with criminal histories. As a consequence, even though the prosecution's reasons for striking African-American members of the venire appear race neutral, the application of these rationales to the venire might have been selective and based on racial considerations. Whether a comparative juror analysis would demonstrate the prosecutors' rationales to have been pretexts for discrimination is an unnecessary determination at this stage, but the evidence does make debatable the District Court's conclusion that no purposeful discrimination occurred.

We question the Court of Appeals' and state trial court's dismissive and strained interpretation of petitioner's evidence of disparate questioning. . . . Petitioner argues that the prosecutors' sole purpose in using disparate questioning was to elicit responses from the African-American venire members that reflected an opposition to the death penalty or an unwillingness to impose a minimum sentence, either

of which justified for-cause challenges by the prosecution under the then applicable state law. This is more than a remote possibility. Disparate questioning did occur. Petitioner submits that disparate questioning created the appearance of divergent opinions even though the venire members' views on the relevant subject might have been the same. It follows that, if the use of disparate questioning is determined by race at the outset, it is likely a justification for a strike based on the resulting divergent views would be pretextual. In this context the differences in the questions posed by the prosecutors are some evidence of purposeful discrimination. . . .

As a preface to questions about views the prospective jurors held on the death penalty, the prosecution in some instances gave an explicit account of the execution process. Of those prospective jurors who were asked their views on capital punishment, the preface was used for 53% of the African-Americans questioned on the issue but for just 6% of white persons. The State explains the disparity by asserting that a disproportionate number of African-American venire members expressed doubts as to the death penalty on their juror questionnaires. This cannot be accepted without further inquiry, however, for the State's own evidence is inconsistent with that explanation. By the State's calculations, 10 African-American and 10 white prospective jurors expressed some hesitation about the death penalty on their questionnaires; however, of that group, 7 out of 10 African-Americans and only 2 out of 10 whites were given the explicit description.

There is an even greater disparity along racial lines when we consider disparate questioning concerning minimum punishments. Ninety-four percent of whites were informed of the statutory minimum sentence, compared to only twelve and a half percent of African-Americans. No explanation is proffered for the statistical disparity. . . . It follows, in our view, that a fair interpretation of the record on this threshold examination in the COA analysis is that the prosecutors designed their questions to elicit responses that would justify the removal of African-Americans from the venire. . . .

We agree with petitioner that the prosecution's decision to seek a jury shuffle when a predominate number of African-Americans were seated in the front of the panel, along with its decision to delay a formal objection to the defense's shuffle until after the new racial composition was revealed, raise a suspicion that the State sought to exclude African-Americans from the jury. Our concerns are amplified by the fact that the state court also had before it, and apparently ignored, testimony demonstrating that the Dallas County District Attorney's Office had, by its own admission, used this process to manipulate the racial composition of the jury in the past. . . .

Finally, in our threshold examination, we accord some weight to petitioner's historical evidence of racial discrimination by the District Attorney's Office. Evidence presented at the *Swain* hearing indicates that African-Americans almost categorically were excluded from jury service. . . . Irrespective of whether the evidence could prove sufficient to support a charge of systematic exclusion of African-Americans, it reveals that the culture of the District Attorney's Office in the past was suffused with bias against African-Americans in jury selection. This evidence, of course, is relevant to the extent it casts doubt on the legitimacy of the motives underlying the State's actions in petitioner's case. . . .

To secure habeas relief, petitioner must demonstrate that a state court's finding of the absence of purposeful discrimination was incorrect by clear and convincing evidence, and that the corresponding factual determination was "objectively unreasonable" in light of the record before the court. . . . Our threshold examination convinces us that it was.

The judgment of the Fifth Circuit is reversed, and the case is remanded for further proceedings consistent with this opinion.

It is so ordered.

JUSTICE SCALIA, concurring. . . .

II

In applying the Court's COA standard to petitioner's case, we must ask whether petitioner has made a substantial showing of a *Batson* violation and also whether reasonable jurists could debate petitioner's ability to obtain habeas relief in light of AEDPA. The facts surrounding petitioner's *Batson* claims, when viewed in light of [the] requirement that state-court factual determinations can be overcome only by clear and convincing evidence to the

contrary, reveal this to be a close, rather than a clear, case for the granting of a COA.

Petitioner maintains that the following six African-American jurors were victims of racially motivated peremptory strikes: Edwin Rand, Wayman Kennedy, Roderick Bozeman, Billy Jean Fields, Joe Warren, and Carrol Boggess. As to each of them, the State proffered race-neutral explanations for its peremptory challenge. Five were challenged primarily because of their views on imposing the death penalty (Rand, Kennedy, Bozeman, Warren, and Boggess), and one (Fields) was challenged because (among other reasons) his brother had been convicted of drug offenses and served time in prison. By asserting race-neutral reasons for the challenges, the State satisfied step two of *Batson*. See *Purkett v. Elem* (1995) (per curiam). Unless petitioner can make a substantial showing that (*i.e.,* a showing that reasonable jurists could debate whether) the State fraudulently recited these explanations as pretext for race discrimination, he has not satisfied the requirement of §2253 (c)(2). Moreover, because the state court entered a finding of fact that the prosecution's purported reasons for exercising its peremptory challenges were not pretextual, a COA should not issue unless that finding can reasonably be thought to be contradicted by clear and convincing evidence. . . .

The weakness in petitioner's *Batson* claims stems from his difficulty in identifying any unchallenged white venireman similarly situated to the six aforementioned African-American veniremen. Although petitioner claims that two white veniremen, Sandra Hearn and Marie Mazza, expressed views about the death penalty as ambivalent as those expressed by Rand, Kennedy, Bozeman, Warren, and Boggess, the *voir dire* transcripts do not clearly bear that out. Although Hearn initially stated that she thought the death penalty was inappropriate for first-time offenders, she also said, "I do not see any reason why I couldn't sit on a jury when you're imposing a death penalty." She further stated that someone who was an extreme child abuser deserved the death penalty, whether or not it was a first-time offense. Hearn also made pro-prosecution statements about her distaste for criminal defendants' use of psychiatric testimony to establish incompetency. As for Mazza, her stated views on the death penalty were as follows: "It's kind of hard determining somebody's life, whether they live or die, but I feel that is something that is accepted in our courts now and it is something that—a decision that I think I could make one way or the other."

Compare those statements with the sentiments expressed by the challenged African-American veniremen. Kennedy supported the death penalty only in cases of mass murder. "Normally I wouldn't say on just the average murder case—I would say no, not the death sentence." Bozeman supported the death penalty only "if there's no possible way to rehabilitate a person . . . I would say somebody mentally disturbed or something like that or say a Manson type or something like that." When asked by the prosecutors whether repeated criminal violent conduct would indicate that a person was beyond rehabilitation, Bozeman replied, "No, not really." Warren refused to give any clear answer regarding his views on the death penalty despite numerous questions from the prosecutors. . . . When asked whether the death penalty accomplishes anything, Warren answered, "Yes and no. Sometimes I think it does and sometimes I think it don't [*sic*]. Sometimes you have mixed feelings about things like that." When asked, "What do you think it accomplishes when you feel it does?," Warren replied, "I don't know." Boggess referred to the death penalty as "murder," and said, "whether or not I could actually go through with murder—with killing another person or taking another person's life, I just don't know. I'd have trouble with that." Rand is a closer case. His most ambivalent statement was "Can I do this? You know, right now I say I can, but tomorrow I might not." Later on Rand did say that he could impose the death penalty as a juror. But Hearn and Mazza (the white jurors who were seated) also said that they could sit on a jury that imposed the death penalty. At most, petitioner has shown that one of these African-American veniremen (Rand) may have been no more ambivalent about the death penalty than white jurors Hearn and Mazza. That perhaps would have been enough to permit the state trial court, deciding the issue *de novo* after observing the demeanor of the prosecutors and the disputed jurors, to find a *Batson* violation. But in a federal habeas case, where a state court has previously entered factfindings that the six African-American jurors were not challenged because of their race, petitioner must provide "clear and convincing evidence" that the state

court erred, and, when requesting a COA, must demonstrate that jurists of reason could debate whether this standard was satisfied.

Fields, the sixth African-American venireman who petitioner claims was challenged because of his race, supported capital punishment. However, his brother had several drug convictions and had served time in prison. (Warren and Boggess, two of the African-American veniremen previously discussed, also had relatives with criminal convictions—Warren's brother had been convicted of fraud in relation to food stamps, and Boggess had testified as a defense witness at her nephew's trial for theft, and reported in her questionnaire that some of her cousins had problems with the law. Of the four white veniremen who petitioner claims also had relatives with criminal histories and therefore "should have been struck" by the prosecution—three (Noad Vickery, Cheryl Davis, and Chatta Nix) were actually so pro-prosecution that *they were struck by the petitioner.* The fourth, Joan Weiner, had a son who had shoplifted at the age of 10. That is hardly comparable to Fields's situation, and Weiner was a strong state's juror for other reasons: She had relatives who worked in law enforcement, and her support for the death penalty was clear and unequivocal.

For the above reasons, my conclusion that there is room for debate as to the merits of petitioner's *Batson* claim is far removed from a judgment that the State's explanations for its peremptory strikes were implausible.

With these observations, I join the Court's opinion.

JUSTICE THOMAS, **dissenting.**

. . . Because petitioner has not shown, by clear and convincing evidence, that any peremptory strikes of black veniremen were exercised because of race, he does not merit a certificate of appealability (COA). I respectfully dissent.

II

Because §2254(e)(1) supplies the governing legal standard, petitioner must provide "clear and convincing" evidence of purposeful discrimination in order to obtain a COA. Petitioner's constitutional claim under *Batson* turns on this fact and "reasonable jurists could debate," whether a *Batson* violation occurred only if petitioner first meets his burden under §2254(e)(1). And the simple truth is that petitioner has not presented anything remotely resembling "clear and convincing" evidence of purposeful discrimination.

A

The evidence amassed by petitioner can be grouped into four categories: (1) evidence of historical discrimination by the Dallas District Attorney's office in the selection of juries; (2) the use of the "jury shuffle" tactic by the prosecution; (3) the alleged similarity between white veniremen who were not struck by the prosecution and six blacks who were: Edwin Rand, Wayman Kennedy, Roderick Bozeman, Billy Jean Fields, Joe Warren, and Carroll Boggess; and (4) evidence of so-called disparate questioning with respect to veniremen's views on the death penalty and their ability to impose the minimum punishment.

The "historical" evidence is entirely circumstantial, so much so that the majority can only bring itself to say it "casts doubt on the State's claim that [discriminatory] practices had been discontinued before petitioner's trial." And the evidence that the prosecution used jury shuffles no more proves intentional discrimination than it forces petitioner to admit that he sought to eliminate whites from the jury, given that he employed the tactic even more than the prosecution did. Ultimately, these two categories of evidence do very little for petitioner, because they do not address the genuineness of prosecutors' proffered race-neutral reasons for making the peremptory strikes of these particular jurors.

. . . [T]he reasons that Justice Scalia finds this to be a "close case" are reasons that . . . it is a *losing* case. . . .

. . .

Quite simply, petitioner's arguments rest on circumstantial evidence and speculation that does not hold up to a thorough review of the record. Far from rebutting §2254(e)(1)'s presumption, petitioner has perhaps not even demonstrated that reasonable jurists could debate whether he has provided the requisite evidence of purposeful discrimination. . . . Because petitioner has not demonstrated by clear and convincing evidence that even one of the peremptory strikes at issue was the result of racial discrimination, I would affirm the denial of a COA.

7.4 Under Suspicion: The Fugitive Science of Criminal Justice (2001)

Atul Gawande

In 1901, a professor of criminal law at the University of Berlin was lecturing to his class when a student suddenly shouted an objection to his line of argument. Another student countered angrily, and the two exchanged insults. Fists were clenched, threats made: "If you say another word . . ." Then the first student drew a gun, the second rushed at him, and the professor recklessly interposed himself between them. A struggle, a blast—then pandemonium.

Originally published in *The New Yorker*. Reprinted by permission of the author.

Whereupon the two putative antagonists disengaged and returned to their seats. The professor swiftly restored order, explaining to his students that the incident had been staged, and for a purpose. He asked the students, as eyewitnesses, to describe exactly what they had seen. Some were to write down their account on the spot, some a day or a week later; a few even had to depose their observations under cross-examination. The results were dismal. The most accurate witness got 26 percent of the significant details wrong; others up to 80 percent. Words were put in people's mouths. Actions were described that had never taken place. Events that had taken place disappeared from memory.

In the century since, professors around the world have reenacted the experiment, in one form or another, thousands of times; the findings have been recounted in legal texts, courtrooms, and popular crime books. The trick has even been played on audiences of judges. The implications are not trivial. Each year, in the United States, more than seventy-five thousand people become criminal suspects based on eyewitness identification, with lineups used as a standard control measure. Studies of wrongful convictions—cases where a defendant was later exonerated by DNA testing—have shown the most common cause to be eyewitness error. In medicine, this kind of systematic misdiagnosis would receive intense scientific scrutiny. Yet the legal profession has conducted no further experiments on the reliability of eyewitness evidence, or on much else, for that matter. Science finds its way to the courthouse in the form of "expert testimony"—forensic analysis, ballistics, and so forth. But the law has balked at submitting its methods to scientific inquiry. Meanwhile, researchers working outside the legal establishment have discovered that surprisingly simple changes in legal procedures could substantially reduce misidentification. They suggest how scientific experimentation, which transformed medicine in the last century, could transform the justice system in the next.

For more than two decades now, the leading figure in eyewitness research has been a blond, jeans-and-tweed-wearing Midwesterner named Gary Wells. He got involved in the field by happenstance: one morning in 1974, a packet from a Cincinnati defense attorney arrived at the department of psychology at Ohio State University, in Columbus, where Wells was a twenty-three-year-old graduate student. The attorney had written to see if anyone there could help him analyze a case in which he believed his client had been wrongly identified as an armed robber. Inside the envelope was a large black-and-white photograph of the lineup from which his client had been picked out. Digging around a little in his spare time, Wells was surprised to discover that little was known about how misidentification occurs. He corresponded with the attorney several times during the next year, though he never came up with anything useful. The suspect was tried, convicted, and sent to prison. Wells never did find out whether the client had been falsely identified. But the case got him thinking.

Some months later, he put together his first experiment. He asked people in a waiting room to watch a bag while he left the room. After he went out, a confederate got up and grabbed the bag. Then he dropped it and picked it up again, giving everyone a good look at him, and bolted. (One problem emerged in the initial experiment: some people gave chase. Wells had to provide his shill with a hiding place just outside the room.) Wells knew from all the previous demonstrations that people would often misidentify the perpetrator. Still, he figured, if they did it without great assurance it wouldn't matter much: under directions that the Supreme Court laid out in 1972, courts placed strong weight on an eyewitness's level of certainty. Wells found, however, that the witnesses who picked the wrong person out of the lineup were just as confident about their choices as those who identified the right person. In a later experiment, he assembled volunteer juries and had them observe witnesses under cross-examination. The jurors, it turned out, believed inaccurate witnesses just as often as they did accurate ones.

Wells tried variations on these experiments, first at the University of Alberta and later at Iowa State, where he's now a professor of psychology, but after a time even he found the work discouraging. He did not just want to show how things go wrong; he wanted to figure out how they could be improved. His first clue came after several years, when he noticed an unexpected pattern: having multiple witnesses did not ensure accurate identifications. In his studies, a crime might be witnessed by dozens of people, yet they would often finger the same wrong suspect. The errors were clearly not random.

To investigate further, Wells staged another crime, over and over, until he had gathered two hundred witnesses. The subjects were seated in a room, filling out what they thought were applications for a temporary job, when a loud crash came from behind the door to an adjacent room. A stranger (a graying, middle-aged, mustached local whom Wells had hired) then burst through the door, stopped in his tracks in evident surprise at finding people in the room, and retreated through the same door. Apparently finding a dead end that way, the man rushed in again, dropped an expensive-looking camera, picked it up, and ran out through the exit at the opposite end of the room. Everyone got several good looks at him. At this point, another person dashed in and said, "What happened to my camera?" Wells tested each witness, one by one. Half the group was given a photo lineup of six people—a "six-pack," as the police call it—which included the actual perpetrator. (Police use photo lineups far more frequently than live ones.) In a group of a hundred individuals, fifty-four picked the perpetrator correctly; twenty-one said they didn't think the guy was there; and the others spread their picks across the people in the lineup.

The second group of witnesses was given the same lineup, minus the perpetrator. This time, thirty-two people picked no one. But most of the rest chose the same wrong person—the one who most resembled the perpetrator. Wells theorizes that witnesses faced with a photo spread tend to make a relative decision, weighing one candidate against the others and against incomplete traces of memory. Studies of actual wrongful convictions lend support to the thesis. For example, in a study of sixty-three DNA exonerations of wrongfully convicted people, fifty-three involved witnesses making a mistaken identification, and almost invariably they had viewed a lineup in which the actual perpetrator was not there. "The dangerous situation is exactly what our experiments said it would be," Wells says.

Once this was established, he and others set about designing ways to limit such errors. Researchers at the State University of New York at Plattsburgh discovered that witnesses who are not explicitly warned that a lineup may not include the actual perpetrator are substantially more likely to make a false identification, under the misapprehension that they've got to pick someone. Wells found that putting more than one suspect in a lineup—something the police do routinely—also dramatically increases errors. Most provocative, however, were the experiments performed by Wells and Rod Lindsay, a colleague from Queen's University in Ontario, which played with the way lineups were structured. The convention is to show a witness a whole lineup at once. Wells and Lindsay decided to see what would happen if witnesses were shown only one person at a time, and made to decide whether he was the culprit before moving on. Now, after a staged theft, the vast majority of witnesses who were shown a lineup that did not include the culprit went through the set without

picking anyone. And when the culprit was present, witnesses who viewed a sequential lineup were no less adept at identifying him than witnesses who saw a standard lineup. The innovation reduced false identifications by well over 50 percent without sacrificing correct identifications. The results have since been replicated by others. And the technique is beautifully simple. It wouldn't cost a dime to adopt it.

It has now been fifteen years since Wells and Lindsay published their results. I asked Wells how widely the procedure has been followed. He laughed, because, aside from a scattered handful of police departments, mainly in Canada, it was not picked up at all. "In general," he told me, "the reaction before criminal-law audiences was 'Well, that's very interesting, but . . .'" A Department of Justice report released in 1999 acknowledged that scientific evidence had established the superiority of sequential-lineup procedures. Yet the report goes on to emphasize that the department still has no preference between the two methods.

Among the inquisitive and scientifically minded, there are a few peculiar souls for whom the justice system looms the way the human body once did for eighteenth-century anatomists. They see infirmities to be understood, remedies to be invented and tested. And eyewitness identification is just one of the practices that invite empirical scrutiny. Unfortunately, only a handful of scientists have had any luck in gaining access to courtrooms and police departments. One of them is Lawrence Sherman, a sociologist at the University of Pennsylvania, who is the first person to carry out a randomized field experiment in criminal-enforcement methods. In 1982, with the support of Minneapolis Police Chief Anthony Bouza, Sherman and his team of researchers completed a seventeen-month trial in which they compared three tactics for responding to non-life-threatening domestic-violence calls: arrest, mediation, and ordering the violent husband or boyfriend to leave the home for eight hours. Arrest emerged as the most effective way to prevent repeated acts of violence. The research was tremendously influential. Previously, it had been rare to arrest a violent husband, at least where the assault was considered "non-severe." Afterward, across the country, arrest became a standard police response.

Such cooperation from law enforcement has proved rare. In Broward County, Florida, researchers started a randomized study to see whether counseling for convicted wife-beaters reduced repeat violence—and prosecutors went to court to stop the study. The state of Florida had granted judges discretion in mandating such counseling, and there was a strong belief that it should be assigned broadly, to stop violence, not randomly, for the sake of study. ("No one is suggesting counseling is a panacea and will solve everyone's problems," the lead prosecutor told the local newspaper, "but I think everyone will agree, in a certain percentage of cases it works.") The researchers managed to get most of the men through the study before it was shut down, though, and they discovered not only that counseling provided no benefit but that it actually increased the likelihood of rearrest in unemployed men. (Probably that's because the women misguidedly believed that counseling worked, and were more likely to agree to see the men again.) In the field of law enforcement, people simply do not admit such possibilities, let alone test them.

Consider the jury box. Steven Penrod, a professor of both psychology and law at the University of Nebraska at Lincoln and another lonely pioneer in this area, is happy to rattle off a series of unexplored questions. Are there certain voting arrangements that make false convictions or mistaken acquittals less likely? (Most states require jurors to reach a unanimous verdict for a criminal conviction, but others allow conviction by as few as eight out of twelve jurors.) How would changing the number of jurors seated—say, to three or seventeen or eight—affect decisions? Do jurors understand and follow the instructions that judges give them? What instructions would be most effective in helping juries reach an accurate and just decision? Are there practical ways of getting juries to disregard inadmissible testimony that a lawyer has brought in? These are important questions, but researchers have little hope of making their way into jury rooms.

Lawrence Sherman points out that one of the most fertile areas for work is that of prosecutorial discretion. Most criminal cases are handled outside the courtroom, and no one knows how prosecutors decide whom to prosecute, how effectively they make these decisions, how often they let risky people go, and so on. But he reports that prosecutors he has approached have been "uniformly opposed" to allowing observation, let alone experi-

mental study. "I've proposed repeatedly, and I've failed," Sherman told me. He has a difficult enough time getting cooperation from the police, he says, "but the lawyers are by far the worst." In his view, the process of bringing scientific scrutiny to the methods of the justice system has hardly begun. "We're holding a tiny little cardboard match in the middle of a huge forest at night," he told me. "We're about where surgery was a century ago."

Researchers like Sherman say that one of their problems is the scarcity of financial support. The largest source of research funding is an obscure government agency called the National Institute of Justice, which was modeled on the National Institutes of Health when it was established, in 1968, but has a budget of less than 1 percent of the N.I.H.'s. (The government spends more on meat and poultry research.) The harder problem, though, is the clash of cultures between the legal and the scientific approach, which is compounded by ignorance and suspicion. In medicine, there are hundreds of academic teaching hospitals, where innovation and testing are a routine part of what doctors do. There is no such thing as an academic police department or a teaching courthouse. The legal system takes its methods for granted: it is common sense that lineups are to be trusted, that wife-beaters are to be counseled, and that jurors are not to ask witnesses questions. Law enforcement, finally, is in thrall to a culture of precedent and convention, not of experiment and change. And science remains deeply mistrusted.

"The legal system doesn't understand science," Gary Wells told me. "I taught in law school for a year. Believe me, there's no science in there at all." When he speaks to people in the justice system about his work, he finds that most of his time is spent educating them about basic scientific methods. "To them, it seems like magic hand-waving and—boom—here's the result. So then all they want to know is whose side you're on—the prosecutor's or the defendant's." In an adversarial system, where even facts come in two versions, it's easy to view science as just another form of spin.

For a scientist, Gary Wells is a man of remarkable faith; he has spent more than twenty-five years doing research at the periphery of his own field for an audience that has barely been listening. When I point this out to him, it makes him chuckle. "It's true," he admits, and yet it does not seem to trouble him. "This may be my American optimism talking, but don't you think, in the long run, the better idea will prevail?"

Lately, he has become fascinated with the alibi. "You know," he told me in a recent conversation, "one of the strange things that pop up in DNA-exoneration cases is that innocent people often seem to be done in by weak or inconsistent alibis." And it has got him thinking. Alibis seem so straightforward. The detective asks the suspect, "Where were you last Friday around 11 p.m.?" And if the suspect can't account for his whereabouts—or,

worse, gives one story now and another later—we take that as evidence against him. But should we? Wells wonders. How well do people remember where they were? How often do they misremember and change their minds? What times of the day is a person likely to have a provable alibi and what times not? How much does this vary among people who are married, who live alone, who are unemployed? Are there better ways to establish whether a suspect has a legitimate alibi? "No one knows these things," he says.

A View from the Inside

7.5   The Federal Sentencing Guidelines and the Key Compromises Upon Which They Rest (1988)

Stephen Breyer

Since November 1987, the new Federal Sentencing Guidelines have been law. Now that they have survived constitutional attack, the Guidelines are likely to remain law for many years to come. It is therefore worth explaining some of the key compromises that led to their creation. This discussion is intended to focus the attention of the academic community on the fact that most of these compromises did not involve trade-offs among commissioners with competing points of view. The spirit of compromise that permeates the Guidelines arose out of the practical needs of administration, institutional considerations, and the competing goals of a criminal justice system, all of which combined to bring about a final product quite different from the idealized versions of the Guidelines which were initially envisioned. It is critical to understand the different institutional reasons for compromise, and to comprehend that, in guideline writing, "the best is the enemy of the good." Only after reflection upon these threshold considerations can meaningful academic discussion, criticism, and eventual improvement take place. . . .

Reprinted by permission of *Hofstra Law Review*.

Background

. . .

Comparing State and Federal Guidelines

When the federal Commission began to write the Guidelines in 1985, both Minnesota and Washington had somewhat similar guidelines systems in place. The federal task differed from that of the state commissions, however, in two important ways. First, the federal criminal code had many more crimes than most state codes. Minnesota and Washington state commissions wrote guidelines for 251 and 108 statutory crimes, respectively, such as murder, theft, robbery, and rape. The federal Commission had to deal with 688 statutes. . . . Second, the political homogeneity in individual states may have made it easier to achieve consensus. At the federal level before 1985, scholars and practitioners in the criminal justice community almost unanimously favored the concept of guidelines. Once the Commission reduced that concept to a detailed reality, however, serious political differences began to emerge. . . .

Purposes

Congress had two primary purposes when it enacted the new federal sentencing statute in October of 1984. The first was "honesty in sentencing." By "honesty," Congress meant to end the previous system whereby a judge might sentence an offender to twelve years, but the Parole Commission could release him after four. Since release by the Parole Commission in such circumstances was likely, but not inevitable, this system sometimes fooled the judges, sometimes disappointed the offender, and often misled the public. Congress responded by abolishing parole. Under the new law, the sentence the judge gives is the sentence the offender will serve. . . .

Congress' second purpose was to reduce "unjustifiably wide" sentencing disparity. It relied upon statistical studies showing, for example, that in the Second Circuit, punishments for identical actual cases could range from three years to twenty years imprisonment. . . .

To remedy this problem, Congress created the United States Sentencing Commission, comprised of seven members (including three federal judges) appointed by the President, confirmed by the Senate, and instructed to write, by April 1987, sentencing guidelines which would automatically take effect six months later unless Congress passed another law to the contrary. Congress' statute provides instructions to the Commission listing many factors for it to consider. The statute suggests (but does not require) that the Guidelines take the form of a grid that determines sentencing in light of characteristics of the offense and characteristics of the offender. The resulting Guideline sentence would consist of a range, such as "imprisonment for twenty to twenty-four months," the top of which range cannot exceed the bottom by more than twenty-five percent. The judge might depart from the Guideline range, but if he or she does so, he or she must explain why, and the imposed sentence is subject to appellate review for "reasonableness." . . .

The Two Basic Principles

Two principles guided the Commission. . . . First, in creating categories and determining sentence lengths, the Commission, by and large, followed typical past practice, determined by an analysis of

10,000 actual cases. Second, the Commission remained aware throughout the drafting process that Congress intended it to be a permanent body that would continuously revise the Guidelines over the years. Thus, the system is "evolutionary"—the Commission issues Guidelines, gathers data from actual practice, analyzes the data, and revises the Guidelines over time. The terms "past practice" and "evolutionary" are merely slogans, but they may offer guidance to the user in understanding how the Commission approached its task. . . .

The Compromises

. . . Some compromises were forced upon the Commission by the fundamental features of the criminal justice system, others by the character of the task, and still others by the fact that the Commission was appointed by politically responsible officials and is therefore, at least to some degree, a "political" body. These factors led to six different kinds of compromise.

"Procedural" vs. "Substantive" Justice

The first inevitable compromise which faced the Commission concerned the competing rationales behind a "real offense" sentencing system and a "charge offense" system. It is a compromise forced in part by a conflict inherent in the criminal justice system itself: the conflict between procedural and substantive fairness.

Some experts urged the adoption of a pure, or a nearly pure, "charge offense" system. Such a system would tie punishments directly to the offense for which the defendant was convicted. One would simply look to the criminal statute, for example, bank robbery, and read off the punishment provided in the sentencing guidelines. The basic premise underlying a "charge offense" system is that the guideline punishment is presumed to reflect the severity of the corresponding statutory crime. The judge could deviate from the presumptive sentence, however, in light of certain aggravating or mitigating factors articulated in the sentencing guidelines.

The principal difficulty with a presumptive sentencing system is that it tends to overlook the fact that particular crimes may be committed in different ways, which in the past have made, and still should make, an important difference in terms of the punishment imposed. A bank robber, for example, might, or might not, use a gun; he might take a little, or a lot, of money; he might, or might not, injure the teller. The typical armed robbery statute, however, does not distinguish among these different ways of committing the crime. Nor does such a statute necessarily distinguish between how cruelly the defendant treated the victims, whether the victims were especially vulnerable as a result of their age, or whether the defendant, though guilty, acted under duress. Thus, unless the statutes are rewritten to make such distinctions, the sentencing court is asked to look, at least in part, at what really happened under the particular factual situation before it.

A "real offense" system, in contrast, bases punishment on the elements of the specific circumstances of the case. Some experts have argued for guidelines close to a pure "real offense" system, where each added harm that the offender brought about would lead to an increase in the sentence. The proponents of such a system, however, minimize the importance of the procedures that courts must use to determine the existence of the additional harms, since the relevant procedural elements are not contained in the typical criminal statute. A drug crime defendant, for example, cannot be expected to argue at trial to the jury that, even though he never possessed any drugs, if he did so, he possessed only one hundred grams and not five hundred, as the government claimed. There must be a post-trial procedure for determining such facts. . . . Typically, courts have found post-trial sentencing facts without a jury and without the use of such rules of evidence as the hearsay or best evidence rules, or the requirement of proof of facts beyond a reasonable doubt.

Of course, the more facts the court must find in this informal way, the more unwieldy the process becomes, and the less fair that process appears to be. At the same time, however, the requirement of full blown trial-type post-trial procedures, which include jury determinations of fact, would threaten the manageability that the procedures of the criminal justice system were designed to safeguard. . . .

The upshot is a need for compromise. A sentencing guideline system must have some real elements, but not so many that it becomes unwieldy or procedurally unfair. The Commission's system

makes such a compromise. It looks to the offense charged to secure the "base offense level." It then modifies that level in light of several "real" aggravating or mitigating factors, . . . several "real" general adjustments ("role in the offense," for example) and several "real" characteristics of the offender, related to past record. One can, of course, criticize the Commission for having compromised at the wrong point. Some might believe there should be more real elements, while others argue that there should be fewer. Any valid criticism, however, must first specify which elements should be added or subtracted, and then explain how the factoring of these elements into sentencing considerations affects the workability of the system without compromising either procedural or substantive fairness. It is difficult to contend, therefore, that either a pure unmixed "charge" or "real offense" system would achieve the Commission's objectives.

Administrative Needs

A second, related critical compromise concerns the level of detail appropriate within the system. This compromise was forced on the Commission by the fact that the criminal justice system is an administrative system and, accordingly, must be administratively workable.

The problem of manageability arises in the context of two competing goals of a sentencing system: uniformity and proportionality. Uniformity essentially means treating similar cases alike. Of course, this goal could be achieved simply by giving every criminal offender the same sentence. It can also be approached by creating only several relevant sentencing categories, such as "crimes of violence," "property crimes," or "drug crimes." In order to achieve uniformity, however, a simple category such as "bank robberies" would lump together cases which, in punitive terms, should be treated differently.

To avoid these obvious inequities, the proportionality goal seeks to approach each of the myriad bank robbery scenarios from varying sentencing perspectives. The more the system recognizes the tendency to treat different cases differently, however, the less manageable the sentencing system becomes. The punishment system becomes much harder to apply as more and more factors are considered, and the probability increases that different probation officers and judges will classify and treat differently cases that are essentially similar. Accordingly, it becomes harder to accurately predict how these factors will interact to produce specific punishments in particular cases.

In its initial draft efforts . . . the Commission realized that the number of possible relevant distinctions is endless. One can always find an additional characteristic X such that if the bank robber does X, he is deserving of more punishment. There is no need to distinguish so finely in terms of punishment given how little is known about the effects of punishment and considering the many other arbitrary characteristics of the criminal justice system. Punishment, as the Commission came to see, is more of a blunderbuss than a laser beam. An effort to make fine distinctions among criminal behaviors is like a statistician running out crude statistics to ten decimal places, giving an impression of precision that is false.

Consequently, in later versions, the Commission, often over objections of the Justice Department, limited the number of offense categories incorporated into the Guidelines. As a result, the number of distinctions within each category of offenders increased in comparison to previous versions of the Guidelines. This allowed greater flexibility in recognizing such differences and adjusting for them, where necessary, through a departure from the Guidelines. . . .

The Nature of a Commission

A third important compromise is reflected in the philosophical premises upon which the Commission rested its concept of the Guidelines. . . .

. . . [S]ome students of the criminal justice system strenuously urged the Commission to follow what they call a "just desserts" approach to punishment. The "just desserts" approach would require that the Commission list criminal behaviors in rank order of severity and then apply similarly ranked punishments proportionately. For example, if theft is considered a more serious or harmful crime than pollution, then the thief should be punished more severely than the polluter.

The difficulty that arises in applying this approach is that different Commissioners have different views about the correct rank order of the seriousness of different crimes. . . .

. . . [T]he Commission soon realized that only a crude ranking of behavior in terms of just desserts, based on objective and practical criteria, could be developed. Although guidelines motivated by a just desserts rationale would be cloaked in language and form that evoke rationality, using terms such as "rank order of seriousness," the rankings would not, in substantive terms, be wholly objective. Furthermore, the Commissioners did not abandon their own subjective values by relying on academic methods, such as public opinion polls, which purport to rank crimes objectively in terms of their relative seriousness. The Commissioners believed that public polling was not sufficiently advanced or detailed to warrant its use as accurate sources in ranking criminal behaviors.

An alternative school of thought recommended that the Guidelines be based on models of deterrence. These advocates urged that punishment for each criminal act should reflect the ability of that punishment to deter commission of the crime. This approach, laying less emphasis on the just desserts of the offender, provided important insights. For example, the deterrence theory suggested that very long sentences might not be worth their extra cost, since sentences of medium length might provide nearly equal deterrence. Furthermore, it suggested that in the case of many "white-collar" crimes, a short period of confinement might be preferable to lengthy probation, for the added deterrent value of even a very brief confinement might be high. The empirical work with respect to deterrence, however, could not provide the Commission with the specific information necessary to draft detailed sentences with respect to most forms of criminal behavior.

Faced, on the one hand, with those who advocated "just desserts" but could not produce a convincing, objective way to rank criminal behavior in detail, and, on the other hand, with those who advocated "deterrence" but had no convincing empirical data linking detailed and small variations in punishment to prevention of crime, the Commission reached an important compromise. It decided to base the Guidelines primarily upon typical, or average, actual past practice. The distinctions that the Guidelines make in terms of punishment are primarily those which past practice has shown were actually important factors in pre-Guideline sentencing. . . . The Commission was able to determine which past factors were important in pre-Guideline sentencing by asking probation officers to analyze 10,500 actual past cases in detail, and then compiling this information, along with almost 100,000 other less detailed case histories, in its computers. . . .

Traditional Trade-Offs

A fourth kind of compromise embodied in the Guidelines is more traditional, involving "trade-offs" among Commissioners with different viewpoints and resulting in substantive proposals midway between their differing views. . . .

One important area of such compromise concerns "offender" characteristics. The Commission extensively debated which offender characteristics should make a difference in sentencing. . . . Some argued in favor of taking past arrest records into account as an aggravating factor, on the ground that they generally were accurate predictors of recidivism. Others argued that factors such as age, employment history, and family ties should be treated as mitigating factors.

. . . [T]he Commission decided to write its offender characteristics rules with an eye towards the Parole Commission's previous work in the area. As a result, the current offender characteristics rules look primarily to past records of convictions. They examine the frequency, recency, and seriousness of past crimes, as well as age, treating youth as a mitigating factor. The rules do not take formal account of past arrest records or drug use, or the other offender characteristics which Congress suggested that the Commission should, but was not required to, consider. In a word, the offender characteristics rules reflect traditional compromise.

A second area of traditional compromise involves the Commission's decision to increase the severity of punishment for white-collar crime. The Commission found in its data significant discrepancies between pre-Guideline punishment of certain white-collar crimes, such as fraud, and other similar common law crimes, such as theft. The Commission's statistics indicated that where white-collar fraud was involved, courts granted probation to offenders more frequently than in situations involving analogous common law crimes; furthermore, prison terms were less severe for white-collar criminals who did not receive probation. To mitigate the inequities of these discrepancies, the Commission decided to require short but certain terms of confinement for many white-collar offenders, including tax, insider trading, and antitrust offenders, who previously would have likely received only probation. . . .

Endemic Problems

The Guidelines create a final set of compromises concerning the problems endemic to the criminal justice system. Since no one has yet solved these problems, it is not surprising that the Commission has not solved them either. Take, for example, the defendant who pleads guilty. The Commission's data reveals that a defendant who pleads guilty will typically receive a sentence reduced by thirty to forty percent. A Guideline system that reflects actual past practice should provide such a reduction. Yet, to explicitly write a reduction into the Guidelines based on a guilty plea is to explicitly tell a defendant that a guilty plea means a lower sentence and that insistence upon a jury trial means a higher sentence.

For this reason, some courts have discouraged explicit discussion of this practice by judges. The Guidelines' solution to this problem is to provide a two-level discount (amounting to approximately twenty to thirty percent) for what the Guidelines call "acceptance of responsibility." The Guidelines are vague regarding the precise meaning of "acceptance of responsibility." The Guidelines state that a court can give the reduction for a guilty plea, but it is not required to do so. In effect, the Guidelines leave the matter to the discretion of the trial court.

Plea bargaining presents another controversial issue. Some witnesses argued before the Commission that the practice of plea bargaining should be abolished. Others argued that plea bargaining was highly desirable and practically necessary. . . .

The Guidelines seek to change existing plea bargaining practices only slightly. In a policy statement, the Guidelines maintain that the prosecutor and defense counsel should accurately state the facts. The probation officer will then prepare a report describing the offense accurately on the basis of what counsel have told him. When the parties enter into a plea agreement, the judge will have before him (1) the proposed plea agreement,

(2) the parties' explanation of why the agreement should be accepted, (3) the Guidelines providing the judge with the sentence to be imposed if he or she does not accept the agreement . . ., and (4) if he or she chooses, the probation officer's report. The Guidelines provide that a judge may accept a plea agreement that would depart from a Guide-line-specified range if he or she finds "justifiable reasons" for doing so. Thus, in comparison with pre-Guidelines practice, the judge is likely to be more aware of the true facts, to have a better un-

derstanding of the reasons for the agreement, and to have a standard for comparison of recommended and Guidelines sentences. By collecting the reasons that judges give for accepting plea agreements, the Commission will be able to study the plea bargaining practice systematically and make whatever changes it believes appropriate in future years. With respect to both acceptance of responsibility and plea bargaining, the Commission has basically left the problem, for the present, where it found it. . . .

<h2>7.6   *United States v. Booker*</h2>

543 U.S. _____ (2005)

JUSTICE STEVENS delivered the opinion of the Court in part.

The question presented in each of these cases is whether an application of the Federal Sentencing Guidelines violated the Sixth Amendment. In each case, the courts below held that binding rules set forth in the Guidelines limited the severity of the sentence that the judge could lawfully impose on the defendant based on the facts found by the jury at his trial. In both cases the courts rejected, on the basis of our decision in *Blakely v. Washington,* the Government's recommended application of the Sentencing Guidelines because the proposed sentences were based on additional facts that the sentencing judge found by a preponderance of the evidence. We hold that both courts correctly concluded that the Sixth Amendment as construed in *Blakely* does apply to the Sentencing Guidelines. In a separate opinion authored by Justice Breyer, the Court concludes that in light of this holding, two provisions of the Sentencing Reform Act of 1984 (SRA) that have the effect of making the Guidelines mandatory must be invalidated in order to allow the statute to operate in a manner consistent with congressional intent.

I

Respondent Booker was charged with possession with intent to distribute at least 50 grams of cocaine base (crack). Having heard evidence that he

had 92.5 grams in his duffel bag, the jury found him guilty of violating 21 U. S. C. §841(a)(1). That statute prescribes a minimum sentence of 10 years in prison and a maximum sentence of life for that offense.

Based upon Booker's criminal history and the quantity of drugs found by the jury, the Sentencing Guidelines required the District Court Judge to select a "base" sentence of not less than 210 nor more than 262 months in prison. The judge, however, held a post-trial sentencing proceeding and concluded by a preponderance of the evidence that Booker had possessed an additional 566 grams of crack and that he was guilty of obstructing justice. Those findings mandated that the judge select a sentence between 360 months and life imprisonment; the judge imposed a sentence at the low end of the range. Thus, instead of the sentence of 21 years and 10 months that the judge could have imposed on the basis of the facts proved to the jury beyond a reasonable doubt, Booker received a 30-year sentence.

Over the dissent of Judge Easterbrook, the Court of Appeals for the Seventh Circuit held that this application of the Sentencing Guidelines conflicted with our holding in *Apprendi v. New Jersey* (2000), that "[o]ther than the fact of a prior conviction, any fact that increases the penalty for a crime beyond the prescribed statutory maximum must be submitted to a jury, and proved beyond a reasonable doubt." . . . The court held that the sentence violated the Sixth Amendment, and remanded with instructions to the District Court either to sentence respondent within the sentencing range supported by the jury's findings or to hold a separate sentencing hearing before a jury.

Respondent Fanfan was charged with conspiracy to distribute and to possess with intent to distribute at least 500 grams of cocaine. . . . He was convicted by the jury after it answered "Yes" to the question "Was the amount of cocaine 500 or more grams?" Under the Guidelines, without additional findings of fact, the maximum sentence authorized by the jury verdict was imprisonment for 78 months.

A few days after our decision in *Blakely*, the trial judge conducted a sentencing hearing at which he found additional facts that, under the Guidelines, would have authorized a sentence in the 188-to-235 month range. Specifically, he found that respondent Fanfan was responsible for 2.5 kilograms of cocaine powder, and 261.6 grams of crack. He also concluded that respondent had been an organizer, leader, manager, or supervisor in the criminal activity. Both findings were made by a preponderance of the evidence. Under the Guidelines, these additional findings would have required an enhanced sentence of 15 or 16 years instead of the 5 or 6 years authorized by the jury verdict alone. Relying not only on the majority opinion in *Blakely*, but also on the categorical statements in the dissenting opinions and in the Solicitor General's brief in *Blakely*, the judge concluded that he could not follow the particular provisions of the Sentencing Guidelines "which involve drug quantity and role enhancement." Expressly refusing to make "any blanket decision about the federal guidelines," he followed the provisions of the Guidelines that did not implicate the Sixth Amendment by imposing a sentence on respondent "based solely upon the guilty verdict in this case."

Following the denial of its motion to correct the sentence in Fanfan's case, the Government filed a notice of appeal in the Court of Appeals for the First Circuit, and a petition in this Court for a writ of certiorari before judgment. Because of the importance of the questions presented, we granted that petition, as well as a similar petition filed by the Government in Booker's case. In both petitions, the Government asks us to determine whether our *Apprendi* line of cases applies to the Sentencing Guidelines, and if so, what portions of the Guidelines remain in effect.

In this opinion, we explain why we agree with the lower courts' answer to the first question. In a separate opinion for the Court, Justice Breyer explains the Court's answer to the second question.

II

It has been settled throughout our history that the Constitution protects every criminal defendant "against conviction except upon proof beyond a reasonable doubt of every fact necessary to constitute the crime with which he is charged." It is equally clear that the "Constitution gives a criminal defendant the right to demand that a jury find him guilty of all the elements of the crime with which he is charged." These basic precepts, firmly rooted in the common law, have provided the basis for recent decisions interpreting modern criminal statutes and sentencing procedures. . . .

In *Apprendi v. New Jersey*, the defendant pleaded guilty to second-degree possession of a firearm for an unlawful purpose, which carried a prison term of 5-to-10 years. Thereafter, the trial court found that his conduct had violated New Jersey's "hate crime" law because it was racially motivated, and imposed a 12-year sentence. This Court set aside the enhanced sentence. We held: "Other than the fact of a prior conviction, any fact that increases the penalty for a crime beyond the prescribed statutory maximum must be submitted to a jury, and proved beyond a reasonable doubt."

The fact that New Jersey labeled the hate crime a "sentence enhancement" rather than a separate criminal act was irrelevant for constitutional purposes. As a matter of simple justice, it seemed obvious that the procedural safeguards designed to protect Apprendi from punishment for the possession of a firearm should apply equally to his violation of the hate crime statute. Merely using the label "sentence enhancement" to describe the latter did not provide a principled basis for treating the two crimes differently.

In *Ring v. Arizona*, we reaffirmed our conclusion that the characterization of critical facts is constitutionally irrelevant. There, we held that it was impermissible for "the trial judge, sitting alone" to determine the presence or absence of the aggravating factors required by Arizona law for imposition of the death penalty. . . .

In *Blakely v. Washington,* we dealt with a determinate sentencing scheme similar to the Federal Sentencing Guidelines. There the defendant pleaded guilty to kidnaping. . . . Other provisions of Washington law, comparable to the Federal Sentencing Guidelines, mandated a "standard" sentence of 49-to-53 months, unless the judge found aggravating facts justifying an exceptional sentence. Although the prosecutor recommended a sentence in the standard range, the judge found that the defendant had acted with "'deliberate cruelty'" and sentenced him to 90 months.

. . . The application of Washington's sentencing scheme violated the defendant's right to have the jury find the existence of "'any particular fact'" that the law makes essential to his punishment. That right is implicated whenever a judge seeks to impose a sentence that is not solely based on "facts reflected in the jury verdict or admitted by the defendant." . . .

If the Guidelines as currently written could be read as merely advisory provisions that recommended, rather than required, the selection of particular sentences in response to differing sets of facts, their use would not implicate the Sixth Amendment. We have never doubted the authority of a judge to exercise broad discretion in imposing a sentence within a statutory range. Indeed, everyone agrees that the constitutional issues presented by these cases would have been avoided entirely if Congress had omitted from the SRA the provisions that make the Guidelines binding on district judges; it is that circumstance that makes the Court's answer to the second question presented possible. For when a trial judge exercises his discretion to select a specific sentence within a defined range, the defendant has no right to a jury determination of the facts that the judge deems relevant.

The Guidelines as written, however, are not advisory; they are mandatory and binding on all judges. . . . Because they are binding on judges, we have consistently held that the Guidelines have the force and effect of laws.

The availability of a departure in specified circumstances does not avoid the constitutional issue. . . . The Guidelines permit departures from the prescribed sentencing range in cases in which the judge "finds that there exists an aggravating or mitigating circumstance of a kind, or to a degree, not

adequately taken into consideration by the Sentencing Commission in formulating the guidelines that should result in a sentence different from that described. "At first glance, one might believe that the ability of a district judge to depart from the Guidelines means that she is bound only by the statutory maximum. Were this the case, there would be no *Apprendi* problem. Importantly, however, departures are not available in every case, and in fact are unavailable in most. In most cases, as a matter of law, the Commission will have adequately taken all relevant factors into account, and no departure will be legally permissible. In those instances, the judge is bound to impose a sentence within the Guidelines range. . . .

. . . Booker's case illustrates the mandatory nature of the Guidelines. The jury convicted him of possessing at least 50 grams of crack . . . based on evidence that he had 92.5 grams of crack in his duffel bag. Under these facts, the Guidelines specified an offense level of 32, which, given the defendant's criminal history category, authorized a sentence of 210-to-262 months. Booker's is a run-of-the-mill drug case, and does not present any factors that were inadequately considered by the Commission. The sentencing judge would therefore have been reversed had he not imposed a sentence within the level 32 Guidelines range.

Booker's actual sentence, however, was 360 months, almost 10 years longer than the Guidelines range supported by the jury verdict alone. To reach this sentence, the judge found facts beyond those found by the jury: namely, that Booker possessed 566 grams of crack in addition to the 92.5 grams in his duffel bag. The jury never heard any evidence of the additional drug quantity, and the judge found it true by a preponderance of the evidence. Thus, just as in *Blakely,* "the jury's verdict alone does not authorize the sentence. The judge acquires that authority only upon finding some additional fact." There is no relevant distinction between the sentence imposed pursuant to the Washington statutes in *Blakely* and the sentences imposed pursuant to the Federal Sentencing Guidelines in these cases. . . .

It is quite true that once determinate sentencing had fallen from favor, American judges commonly determined facts justifying a choice of a heavier sentence on account of the manner in which particular defendants acted. In 1986, however, our own cases first recognized a new trend in the legislative regulation of sentencing when we considered the significance of facts selected by legislatures that not only authorized, or even mandated, heavier sentences than would otherwise have been imposed, but increased the range of sentences possible for the underlying crime. Provisions for such enhancements of the permissible sentencing range reflected growing and wholly justified legislative concern about the proliferation and variety of drug crimes and their frequent identification with firearms offences.

The effect of the increasing emphasis on facts that enhanced sentencing ranges, however, was to increase the judge's power and diminish that of the jury. It became the judge, not the jury, that determined the upper limits of sentencing, and the facts determined were not required to be raised before trial or proved by more than a preponderance.

As the enhancements became greater, the jury's finding of the underlying crime became less significant. And the enhancements became very serious indeed. . . .

As it thus became clear that sentencing was no longer taking place in the tradition that Justice Breyer invokes, the Court was faced with the issue of preserving an ancient guarantee under a new set of circumstances. The new sentencing practice forced the Court to address the question how the right of jury trial could be preserved, in a meaningful way guaranteeing that the jury would still stand between the individual and the power of the government under the new sentencing regime. And it is the new circumstances, not a tradition or practice that the new circumstances have superseded, that have led us to the answer . . . developed in *Apprendi* and subsequent cases culminating with this one. It is an answer not motivated by Sixth Amendment formalism, but by the need to preserve Sixth Amendment substance.

. . .

All of the foregoing support our conclusion that our holding in *Blakely* applies to the Sentencing Guidelines. We recognize, . . . that in some cases jury factfinding may impair the most expedient and efficient sentencing of defendants. But the interest in fairness and reliability protected by the right to a jury trial—a common-law right that defendants enjoyed for centuries and that is now enshrined in the Sixth Amendment—has always outweighed the interest in concluding trials swiftly. . . .

Accordingly, we reaffirm our holding in *Apprendi:* Any fact (other than a prior conviction) which is necessary to support a sentence exceeding the maximum authorized by the facts established by a plea of guilty or a jury verdict must be admitted by the defendant or proved to a jury beyond a reasonable doubt.

JUSTICE BREYER delivered the opinion of the Court in part.

. . . We here turn to the second question presented, a question that concerns the remedy. We must decide whether or to what extent, "as a matter of severability analysis," the Guidelines "as a whole" are "inapplicable . . . such that the sentencing court must exercise its discretion to sentence the defendant within the maximum and minimum set by statute for the offense of conviction."

We answer the question of remedy by finding the provision of the federal sentencing statute that makes the Guidelines mandatory incompatible with today's constitutional holding. We conclude that this provision must be severed and excised. . . . So modified, the Federal Sentencing Act makes the Guidelines effectively advisory. It requires a sentencing court to consider Guidelines ranges, but it permits the court to tailor the sentence in light of other statutory concerns as well.

I

We answer the remedial question by looking to legislative intent. We seek to determine what "Congress would have intended" in light of the Court's constitutional holding. . . . In this instance, we must determine which of the two following remedial approaches is the more compatible with the legislature's intent as embodied in the 1984 Sentencing Act.

One approach, that of Justice Stevens' dissent, would retain the Sentencing Act (and the Guidelines) as written, but would engraft onto the existing system today's Sixth Amendment "jury trial" requirement. The addition would change the Guidelines by preventing the sentencing court from increasing a sentence on the basis of a fact that the jury did not find (or that the offender did not admit).

The other approach, which we now adopt, would . . . make the Guidelines system advisory while maintaining a strong connection between the sentence imposed and the offender's real conduct—a connection important to the increased uniformity of sentencing that Congress intended its Guidelines system to achieve.

Both approaches would significantly alter the system that Congress designed. But today's constitutional holding means that it is no longer possible to maintain the judicial factfinding that Congress thought would underpin the mandatory Guidelines system that it sought to create and that Congress wrote into the Act. Hence we must decide whether we would deviate less radically from Congress' intended system (1) by superimposing the constitutional requirement announced today or (2) through elimination of some provisions of the statute. . . .

In today's context . . . we cannot assume that Congress, if faced with the statute's invalidity in key applications, would have preferred to apply the statute in as many other instances as possible. Neither can we determine likely congressional intent mechanically. We cannot simply approach the problem grammatically, say, by looking to see whether the constitutional requirement and the words of the Act are linguistically compatible.

Nor do simple numbers provide an answer. It is, of course, true that the numbers show that the constitutional jury trial requirement would lead to additional decisionmaking by juries in only a minority of cases. Prosecutors and defense attorneys would still resolve the lion's share of criminal matters through plea bargaining, and plea bargaining takes place without a jury. . . .

But the constitutional jury trial requirement would nonetheless affect every case. It would affect decisions about whether to go to trial. It would affect the content of plea negotiations. It would alter the judge's role in sentencing. Thus we must determine likely intent not by counting proceedings, but by evaluating the consequences of the Court's constitutional requirement in light of the Act's language, its history, and its basic purposes.

While reasonable minds can, and do, differ about the outcome, we conclude that the constitutional jury trial requirement is not compatible with the Act as written and that some severance and excision are necessary. . . .

II

. . .

We do not doubt that Congress, when it wrote the Sentencing Act, intended to create a form of mandatory Guidelines system. But, we repeat, given today's constitutional holding, that is not a choice that remains open. Hence we have examined the statute in depth to determine Congress' likely intent *in light of today's holding*. And we have concluded that today's holding is fundamentally inconsistent with the judge-based sentencing system that Congress enacted into law. In our view, it is more consistent with Congress' likely intent in enacting the Sentencing Reform Act (1) to preserve important elements of that system while severing and excising two provisions than (2) to maintain all provisions of the Act and engraft today's constitutional requirement onto that statutory scheme.

Ours, of course, is not the last word: The ball now lies in Congress' court. The National Legislature is equipped to devise and install, long-term, the sentencing system, compatible with the Constitution, that Congress judges best for the federal system of justice.

A Comparative Perspective

7.7   # Reviving the Criminal Jury in Japan (1999)

Lester W. Kiss

I. Introduction

The last decade has spawned a reexamination of the effectiveness of the jury system in the United States. Jury verdicts rendered in certain highly publicized trials have shocked the public and caused journalists and scholars alike to criticize juries as ill-equipped to handle the cases before them. Some critics have even questioned the basic role of the jury as an instrument of democracy and a form of sovereignty of the people. To counter this criticism, others argue that the intense attack on the jury system by scholars and journalists is a result of disgust with unexpected verdicts and is not based on empirical evidence about the system, which shows that juries reach a defensible decision most of the time.

Despite the ongoing debate about the effectiveness of the American jury, several countries have recently adopted or are seriously considering adopting their own jury systems. One of the more heated debates about adopting a jury system is occurring in Japan. Because Japan actually used a jury system for criminal trials from 1928 to 1943, the present-day debate focuses mainly on readopting the jury for criminal cases only.

The purpose of this article is to analyze whether the readoption of criminal jury trials in present-day Japan would be feasible from cultural, societal, and legal viewpoints in light of Japan's prior experience with a jury system. Part II of the article briefly considers why reversion to trial by jury is being considered by Japanese lawyers and judges. Part III

Lester W. Kiss, "Reviving the Criminal Jury in Japan," in *Law & Contemporary Problems* 62 (1999). Reprinted by permission of the author.

describes the jury system used in Japan from 1928 to 1943 and the problems with the system that caused its suspension. Part IV examines the two main types of layperson juries used in other countries. Part V considers the broad question of whether the adoption of one of the jury systems examined in Part IV would be feasible in Japan from cultural, societal, and legal viewpoints.

II. Why the Debate About Trial by Jury?

Just as in the United States, where certain seemingly outrageous jury verdicts have fueled the fire of criticism of the jury system, a similar phenomenon has occurred in Japan regarding its judge-based system. Examples of such highly publicized verdicts by judges include the acquittals of four death row inmates who were imprisoned for over twenty-five years before obtaining new trials.

Two of these controversial cases are *Government v. Akabori* (the Shimada Case) and *Government v. Menda* (the Menda Case). In the Shimada case, Masao Akabori was arrested in May 1954 for the rape and murder of a schoolgirl in Shimada City, Shizuoka Prefecture. After intense questioning by the police, Akabori confessed to the rape and murder. After a four-year trial, Akabori was convicted and sentenced to death in May 1958. His direct appeals to the Tokyo High Court and Supreme Court were fruitless. Twenty-five years later, the Tokyo High Court overturned the Shizuoka District Court ruling rejecting a retrial request and remanded the case to the district court. The district court granted a new trial on May 29, 1986. After nearly a two-year trial, the Shizuoka District Court acquitted Akabori on January 31, 1989. The district court acquitted on the ground that there was no evidence linking Akabori to the crime other than his own confessions, which were shown to be of little reliability.

In the Menda case, Sakae Menda was charged with the hatchet murder of a seventy-six-year old prayer reader and his wife in Hitoyoshi City, Kumamoto Prefecture. Menda confessed to the crime a few days later after detailed questioning. After a year-long trial in the Kumamoto District Court, Menda was found guilty of the murders and sentenced to death on March 23, 1950. The Fukuoka High Court and the Supreme Court upheld the verdict on direct appeal. In 1975, after numerous failed attempts at obtaining a retrial, Menda was successful when the Fukuoka High Court granted his request. The Kumamoto District Court acquitted Menda of both murders on July 15, 1983, approximately thirty-three years after he was convicted. In its ruling, the court rejected Menda's confessions because it found them to be unreliable.

The roots of the debate on the readoption of the jury trial, however, go far deeper than a mere reaction to erroneous verdicts by judges. Although, in theory, the Japanese criminal justice system provides criminal defendants a wide set of legal protections, in reality, these protections are diminished by the practices of judges and prosecutors. In particular, there are questions as to whether judges are effective finders of fact. Proponents of the jury system argue that, in reality, criminal defendants are convicted before the trial even begins. Prosecutors conduct the factfinding and draw legal conclusions, and judges simply "rubber stamp" their results. A jury would be a better finder of fact because juries, unlike judges, do not hear cases on a daily basis and would not simply accept the decision of the prosecutor. Theoretically, juries would be more inclined than a judge would be to listen to the evidence and deliver a fair verdict.

An area that illustrates the poor factfinding that can occur in a Japanese courtroom is the judges' ready acceptance of "voluntary confessions" of criminal defendants. It is doubtful whether such confessions, which occur with great frequency, are truly voluntary. Under the Japanese system, police often have unrestricted power to interrogate a suspect, and many cases of abuse have been reported.

Japanese authorities often demand detailed, corroborated confessions. Such confessions may then be presented at trial, and although they may be attacked by the defendant and defense counsel in court, their corroboration gives judges a basis to accept them even if they are procedurally questionable.

One reason for such easy acceptance of confessions by judges is a peculiarity of trial practice in Japan called "trial by dossier." The confession is submitted to the court in the form of a confession statement which becomes part of a dossier. Judges then read the dossiers and often form factual conclusions in their chambers or homes rather than in open court after having heard witnesses. This practice is problematic because the manner of speech and demeanor of witnesses and of the defendant can have a strong influence on the finder of fact; if these elements are not fully considered, the defendant may not be receiving a fair trial. Proponents of the jury system argue that because there is little hope of judges agreeing to eliminate trial by dossier, the only solution is a switch to an American-style jury system where factual conclusions are formed only after testimony in open court.

Also inhibiting effective factfinding by the Japanese judiciary is that most judges are career judges with little experience in the outside world. One can become a judge after passing the extremely rigorous National Legal Examination (shiho shiken), followed by two years of practical training. The person then has the choice of becoming either a judge, a prosecutor, or an attorney. The result is a highly educated, well-trained elite group of jurists who may have attitudes and experiences quite different from those of the general public. This limited range of life experience may negatively affect the factfinding abilities of these judges.

The idea of readopting the jury system has come to the forefront of possible reforms of the criminal justice system in Japan. Japanese organizations have already conducted in-depth studies of foreign jury systems. For example, a subcommittee of the Osaka Bar Association's Committee for Judicial System Reform toured the United States, Great Britain, and Germany to study citizen participation in the trial process, and the Supreme Court of Japan sent several judges to the United States, United Kingdom, Germany, and France to study juries.

III. The Jury System in Japan from 1928 to 1943

Japan adopted a jury system on April 18, 1923. Although enacted in 1923, the law did not take effect until 1928, and it stayed in effect for fifteen years until it was suspended on April 1, 1943.

Before devising a jury system appropriate for Japan, the Japanese government investigated trial systems in France, Germany, England, and the United States. The result was a uniquely Japanese jury system complementing an otherwise Continental European system of criminal procedure. Therefore, although the Japanese system was influenced by the Anglo-American model of jury trial, it differed in many important respects.

First, not all defendants were entitled to a jury trial. The only cases for which a jury trial was guaranteed were those in which the maximum penalty was death or imprisonment for life or where the maximum penalty was imprisonment for greater than three years and the minimum penalty was imprisonment for not less than one year. In death penalty or life imprisonment cases, the law provided trial by jury unless waived by the accused. In all other eligible cases, the law provided for trial by jury only if the accused specifically requested a jury trial. Furthermore, the law provided that certain crimes were not triable by jury. These crimes included crimes against a member of the imperial family, riot with the purpose of overthrowing the government, violation of the Peace Preservation Act (Chian Iji-ho), espionage, and violation of laws concerning the election of public officials.

Second, the Japanese jury did not return a general verdict of "guilty" or "not guilty." Instead, it responded to questions submitted by the judge (toshin) and related to the existence of facts. These answers were based on the views of a majority of the requisite twelve jurors.

Third, the jurors' responses were not binding. The court, upon finding the jury's answer unwarranted, could disregard it, call another jury, and submit the case anew.

Jury selection resembled the jury selection methods used in the Anglo-American system at that time. The pool of prospective jurors included "male citizens over thirty years of age who had resided in the same city, town or village for two years or longer, who paid not less than three yen in national direct tax for the preceding two consecutive years, and who were literate."

The number of jury trials in Japan decreased drastically from 1928 to 1943. The annual number of cases tried by jury was greatest in 1929, when 143 cases were put to juries. The number dropped to sixty-six the next year and decreased annually until, in 1942, only two jury trials were held. A total of 611 defendants chose jury trials during the fifteen years the system operated. Of these, ninety-four were acquitted. Why did the use of the jury system decline so precipitously during its lifetime?

One reason put forth for the decline of the jury system over this period was the political climate in the late 1920s to 1943. The Jury Act was enacted in 1923 during the period known as "Taisho Democracy." It was primarily because of this nationwide movement toward democracy that Premier Takashi Hara was able to sponsor the Act successfully and allow Japanese citizens an opportunity to participate directly in the justice system. However, by the time the jury system was first used in 1928, the political climate in Japan was moving toward fascism. . . .

This political and cultural environment of rising militarism and fascism countered the rise of the jury system because it encouraged the bourgeoisie to waive the right to trial by jury and prohibited access to trial by jury to those who most needed it: criminal defendants who adhered to communist and socialist ideologies. . . .

Another reason put forth for the decline of the jury system in Japan was the content of the Jury Act itself. Many Japanese scholars observe that it is not surprising that the jury system failed in Japan because the drafters of the Act seemed to have built in various devices to prevent the smooth working of the system. The most important of these is the judge's ability to disregard the jury's answers, seat a new jury, and try the case de novo. The drafters of the Act may have included this provision because they believed that it would be contrary to the judge's responsibility to decide each case if he or she had to give binding effect to the jury's answers. This provision effectively undermined any true power of the jury system and allowed judges to continue to make the final decisions on guilt and innocence. Criminal defendants quickly learned that acquittal by a jury had little meaning, and they would often waive their right to a jury trial from the start or simply not elect trial by jury if given the choice.

Jury trials also cost criminal defendants more money and deprived them of the possibility of bringing a koso appeal on points of fact. Because the sentence of a convicted criminal was usually mitigated upon appeal, criminal defense attorneys understandably would encourage their defendants to preserve the right to this appeal, even if it meant waiving the right to jury trial.

Furthermore, public prosecutors could avoid any request by the accused for a jury trial because the law provided that jury trial was available only if the case underwent a "preliminary investigation" (yoshin).

Finally, the Jury Act did not allow objections to the judge's instructions to the jury. Attorneys and public prosecutors often criticized the instructions given by the judge as "soliciting answers which would lead to the guilt of the accused." Even if the jury did return its special verdicts to the effect that the defendant was not guilty, there was still a great chance that the judge would call for a new trial. Such obstacles frustrated attorneys, sometimes to the point where they would prefer to waive jury trial as a way of expressing piety to the authority of the judge in hopes of leniency in sentencing.

The final factor considered to have led to the unpopularity of the Japanese jury is Japanese culture. Japanese society is often described as "vertical" or "hierarchical," meaning that social relationships are governed by the relative "status" of the parties. This "status" is often determined by, among other factors, age and occupation. . . .

Many scholars are convinced that as a result of the hierarchy in Japanese society, the Japanese people prefer trial by "those above the people" rather than by "their fellows," and that this caused the Japanese to distrust juries from the beginning. . . . Scholars disagree on exactly how much weight should be given to the cultural aspect of the failure of the jury system in Japan, but most agree culture played some part. . . .

IV. Types of Jury Systems

If Japan decided to reintroduce a jury system, it would have to ensure that the new system avoided the systemic defects of the old. This would entail

making jury verdicts binding, allowing defendants who elect jury trial to appeal just as if they had elected nonjury trial, ensuring that election of trial by jury would not be more expensive for the defendant, and allowing defendants to object to the trial judge's jury instructions.

Once these basic facets of any serious jury system were adopted the Japanese would have to decide exactly what form the new jury system would take. . . . This section examines the two models of jury systems that could be implemented in Japan: the Anglo-American jury composed completely of laypersons, and the Continental mixed court composed of both judges and laypersons.

The Anglo-American Jury System

A criminal jury in the Anglo-American system is composed of six to twelve jurors selected at random from the local population. Such a jury can convict or acquit based on either majority or unanimous verdicts. Although the goals of the jury system are numerous, one goal seems to be most important: "The power to condemn citizens to criminal sanctions is potentially so dangerous that it ought not to be left entirely to the hirelings of the state." As Justice White wrote in *Duncan v. Louisiana,*

those who wrote our constitutions knew from history and experience that it was necessary to protect against unfounded criminal charges brought to eliminate enemies and against judges too responsive to the voice of higher authority. The framers of the constitutions strove to create an independent judiciary, but insisted upon further protection against arbitrary action.

Other purposes behind the Anglo-American jury system are to ensure fairness through group decisionmaking, to promote simplicity and better factfinding through lay reasoning and skills, and to allow criminal defendants to be judged by their peers. Unlike judges, laymen have no connection to the criminal justice system other than the fact that they are serving as jurors and therefore lack incentive to abuse their power or misuse the system.

The Continental Mixed Court

The second version of the jury system being considered by the Japanese is the mixed court system, in which laypersons and professional judges sit together in a single panel that deliberates and decides on all issues of verdict and sentence. This mixed court system is widespread in Europe for cases of serious crime. Because the system has been most widely employed in Germany, the rest of this section will look specifically at the German system.

There are two kinds of mixed courts in modern German practice. For more serious crimes, the mixed court consists of five "judges"—two lay and three professional ("two-three court"). For less serious crimes, the court consists of three "judges"—two lay and one professional ("two-one court"). Any decision that disadvantages the accused requires a two-thirds majority vote. This means that in the two-three court, four of the five judges must agree on a verdict of conviction, giving the two laymen a veto power if they act together. In the two-one court, the two-thirds voting rule allows the two laymen either to convict or acquit over the opposition of the professional. Thus, depending on whether the trial is for a serious or minor crime, laymen will have varying power in the decision-making process.

When the trial is over, the mixed court begins deliberations. However, unlike the Anglo-American jury, "the presiding judge (the only professional in the two-one court and the senior professional in the two-three court) 'leads' these in camera proceedings and 'puts the questions and takes the votes.'" This safeguards against the laymen making decisions based on ignorance or bias.

The mixed court system has safeguards against the inexperience of the laypersons. The selection of lay judges is much less random than the selection of jurors in the Anglo-American system. Lay judges are selected for four-year terms, and the selection process is divided into a nomination and a selection phase. German studies on the nomination practices of local authorities have revealed wide variations in practice. Some authorities compile random lists of residents, others delegate the task to the political parties represented on the city council, and still others vigorously seek out volunteers. Some authorities even allow the police to exercise a veto power over the provisional list. In the selection phase, a "selection commission" chooses the new lay judges from the pool of nominees. The number chosen varies from year to year depending on the expected caseload. Considerable variation exists in the functioning of these commissions, and in many cases political parties have a large influence in the process. While it is clear that a goal of the system is for the list of nominees to be representative of "all groups in the population," neither the statutory procedures nor the practices of the local authorities and commissions bears this out. The end result is that lay judges often have educational and social backgrounds more similar to professional judges, which may diminish the effectiveness of the lay role in the mixed court system.

V. Would a Jury System Work in Japan from a Cultural, Societal, and Legal Viewpoint?

Japanese Culture

"Culture" is defined as "the customary beliefs, social norms, and material traits of a racial, religious, or social group." By definition, therefore, culture is a generalization of the beliefs, social norms, and traits of most members of a certain group. When discussing Japanese culture, one must remember that not every Japanese person will act in accordance with the cultural traits described. A generalization of Japanese behavior patterns based on sociological evidence can nevertheless serve as a useful tool in analyzing the probable success of a jury system in Japan.

The hierarchical nature of Japanese society is difficult to miss. The language and behavior one Japanese person exhibits when meeting another for the first time is largely governed by the place each has in Japanese society. This is true both in the business and personal contexts. In the business context, once business cards are exchanged and each person has determined the status of the other, each person can adapt his language and behavior to the situation. . . . Similarly, in the personal context, a student would use honorific Japanese toward a professor, and a younger person would use similar honorific language toward an elder. . . .

Many scholars have pointed out that the Japanese have a higher level of trust for authority figures than do other societies. Such scholars often state as a basis of this trust the Confucian tradition in Japan. They argue that this trust of authority is exemplified by the average Japanese citizen's lack of interest in politics and by his apathy for provoking change in a system with which he is frustrated.

The shudan-ishiki, or "group consciousness," of the Japanese is also a cultural trait that could have profound effects on the actual functioning of the jury system in Japan. . . . [T]he criterion by which Japanese classify individuals socially tends to be that of particular institution rather than that of universal attribute. The institution to which one belongs, therefore, becomes almost the sole criterion for defining one's group. . . .

Maintenance of harmony in the group is another important aspect of Japanese culture. Scholars . . . believe that Japanese society functions effectively only because of the high degree of interpersonal harmony maintained therein. A natural result is that strong, contradictory personal opinions by inferiors are not voiced. . . .

Mixed Court Proposal. The adoption of a mixed court in Japan is problematic. First, because of the hierarchical nature of Japanese society and the Japanese respect for authority, the danger exists that the professional judge or judges would have more than simply their intended "guiding" influence over the laypersons. . . . [T]he layperson juror in a mixed court system in Japan may have difficulty voicing any personal beliefs about the case. Also because a mixed court system contains at least one professional judge, overcoming this problem requires limiting the participation of the judge, which would lead to the Anglo-American jury system.

Furthermore, even if the laypersons were told that they should speak their minds and independently determine the outcome of the case, there is no way of knowing whether a conscious decision to abandon one's cultural instincts could be effective. For example, because it is impolite in Japanese culture to blatantly disagree with a superior (on the principle of maintenance of harmony), how far would a layperson go in voicing disagreement with a professional judge's opinion even after being told he must do so? The layperson would possibly speak up once or twice, but if the judge did not somehow reinforce the viewpoint, only a courageous Japanese juror would press the issue. For these reasons, the adoption of a mixed court system in Japan seems to be undesirable compared to the adoption of a modified Anglo-American jury system.

Anglo-American Proposal. The adoption of an all-layperson jury system modeled on that in the United States would be preferable in Japan because it would create the largest chance for full participation of all jurors. Although the cultural concepts of hierarchy and respect for authority would still play a role in the jury's decisionmaking, there would be more leeway to work around these concepts if no legal authority figures such as professional judges were present. The hierarchical difference between, for example, a policeman and a university professor seems to be much less than that between a policeman and a professional judge, meaning that the policeman may be more candid in expressing his opinion to the professor than to the judge.

The all-layperson system would not be without problems, however. To examine the degree to which an all-layperson system would work in Japanese culture, it is useful to first look at the ideals of the jury system in the United States. According to Samuel Kassin and Lawrence Wrightsman, there are three ideals behind the idea of jury deliberation in the United States. The first ideal is that of independence and equality. "No juror's vote should count more than any other juror's vote," and each person contributes his or her personal opinion. The second ideal is an openness to be influenced by information. Jurors must debate with an open mind and withhold judgment until full deliberation by all of the jurors. "Jurors should scrutinize their own views, be receptive to others', and allow themselves to be persuaded by rational argument." The third ideal is that jurors should not be persuaded by irrational pressures. "No juror should surrender his honest conviction as to the weight or effect of the evidence solely because of the opinion of his fellow jurors, or for the mere purpose of returning a verdict." The reasoning behind this is simple: If a juror changes his vote just to comply with the majority and not because of rational persuasion by new information, his final vote will not reflect his true beliefs.

Scholars do not agree on whether these ideals are properly achieved in juries in the United States.

In one study done by social psychologist Solomon Asch, American subjects were asked to sit around a table and orally give their opinions on various subjects, one after the other. Asch instructed the first five people at the table, who worked for him but acted as subjects, to give an opinion that clearly seemed wrong based on the facts. "Much to Asch's surprise, the sixth person (and real subject) conformed with the incorrect majority 37 percent of the time." There could be two reasons for this result. First, the subject could have publicly voted with the majority because he felt pressure to conform, even though he privately continued to disagree. And, second, the subject could have reevaluated the evidence, truly changed his mind, and voted in accordance with his conscience. The first is a danger to the ideals of the jury system because it could mean that criminals are being convicted by nonunanimous juries. Even in the United States, which has had over 200 years of experience with the jury system, and which is not known as a culture that values "harmony," there is a danger that jurors are not expressing their true opinions in an effort to avoid confrontation.

Nor are jury deliberations in the United States free from hierarchical influences. Many trial attorneys believe that most juries consist of "one or two strong personalities with the rest more or less being followers." The empirical literature on small group discussions supports this assertion: "Participation by the individuals is very uneven, and a few people dominate." Many scholars conclude, therefore, that the ideals are seldom ever realized because of these differences.

Could Japanese society support the three ideals of the Anglo-American jury system? First, to what degree does the hierarchical nature of Japanese culture allow the Japanese juror to maintain his independence and equality and to make an informed and rational decision? Because of the lack of empirical evidence, this question is difficult to answer.

American jurors often lose their independence and acquiesce to the views of the majority even though they privately feel otherwise. Because of the greater importance of hierarchy in Japanese society, this could be a greater problem in the Japanese jury. . . .

In contrast, Japanese "group consciousness" and the desire of Japanese to maintain "harmony" may have less of an effect on the Japanese jury than one would assume. Although it is clear that Japanese culture tends to be more group-oriented than individualistic cultures such as in the United States, the jury may not fit the definition of a "group" as this word is used in the literature discussing Japanese culture. A jury composed of twelve randomly selected individuals, although a group temporarily, is by no means an institution or even a relationship that binds people together. A Japanese would most likely not identify himself as being part of the group that is the jury because he knows that once the case is over, the jury will break up and no longer exist. Therefore, although much literature exists describing the behavior of Japanese when interacting with members of a "group," it is important to keep in mind that because the jury does not seem to qualify as a typical group, Japanese members of the jury may behave more individualistically. "Group consciousness" may not be a threat at all to the effective functioning of the all-layperson jury system in Japan.

The desire to maintain harmony, unlike Japanese group consciousness, is a cultural attribute that could strongly influence jury deliberations. A heated issue at present is whether the desire to maintain harmony in Japan extends past the boundaries of one's immediate group to Japanese society in general. If we assume that the cultural trait of maintaining harmony would continue to exist in the jury room, this could undermine the ideals of independence and equality, openness to be influenced by information, and persuasion only by the substance of arguments. In an effort to maintain harmony, jurors might be willing to give up their personal beliefs and be persuaded for reasons other than substantive reasons. However, the desire to maintain harmony may be thrust aside by Japanese jurors, especially if the judge instructs them to do so, and an open debate could occur where each juror votes his independent mind. Without empirical evidence, it is difficult to say just what part this aspect of Japanese culture would play inside the four walls of the jury room.

Japanese Society

Culture is not the only consideration when discussing whether a jury system should be introduced into a society. One must also look at societal factors such as level of education, race, citizen participation, and other factors to determine whether a jury system could function effectively. J. H. Jearey argues that three conditions are necessary for a jury system to function effectively. First, the society in which it operates must be for the most part racially, culturally, linguistically, and religiously homogeneous. Second, the members of the society must be sufficiently educated to understand their responsibilities as jurors and understand that they must set aside private prejudices when fulfilling these responsibilities. Third, the members of the society must generally agree with the laws which, as jurors, they are required to enforce.

The reasoning behind Jearey's list of conditions is clear. First, the more socially homogeneous a society, the less chance there will be that jurors from that society will base their decisions on racial, religious, or ethnic bias. Second, the more educationally advanced a society becomes, the more jurors will be able to understand their roles and put aside personal views on an issue not based on the facts and law. Furthermore, better educated juries will be able to comprehend more complex evidence used at trial directly, rather than through the statements of a zealous attorney or expert. Finally, if jurors do not agree fundamentally with the laws on which they are supposed to base their decision, jury verdicts may be primarily based on factors other than the law, frustrating the concept of rule of law.

Because all three of these conditions are present in Japanese society, it seems that from a societal perspective, Japan is ripe for the reintroduction of the jury system. First, Japan is overall one of the most socially homogeneous societies in the world. Unlike in the United States, where citizenship is determined by place of birth, in Japan, citizenship is determined by the nationality of one's parents. As a result, except in a few specific instances, almost all Japanese citizens have the same ethnic and historical background. Also, although most Japanese claim to practice Shinto, Buddhism, or both, few are serious about religion. Religion neither unifies nor divides the Japanese people—it simply exists neutrally. Finally, Japan has as little linguistic diversity as can be found in countries in Europe or in different regions of the United States. Japanese is spoken throughout Japan, with varia-

tions in dialect in the North and the South. Japan is also one of the most educationally advanced countries in the world. With a literacy rate of close to ninety-nine percent and a rate of advancement to universities and junior colleges of over thirty-seven percent, the pool of jurors in Japan would allow for well-educated juries. And because over ninety percent of Japanese view themselves as members of the middle class, criminal defendants would, most of the time, truly be receiving a trial by their peers. Finally, because Japan follows the rule of law and the Japanese Constitution puts the power in the hands of the people, Japanese are in basic agreement with the laws they are required to enforce. If this were not so, these laws could be changed by democratic means.

A fourth factor that Jearey does not mention that could affect the success of a jury system is the degree to which a society has allowed or is willing to allow citizen participation in the system. In countries that have had no experience at all with citizen participation in the legal system, a switch to either an all-layperson jury system or a mixed court system could be difficult. On the other hand, societies that have a history of citizen participation in the legal system may be more welcoming of either type of jury system. Traditionally, Japan did not offer laypersons an opportunity to participate in the criminal adjudication process. However, laypersons did have the opportunity to participate in civil conciliation proceedings (chotei) during the Tokugawa period, and they were able to participate on juries during the years 1928 to 1943. During the Allied Occupation, prosecution review commissions (kensatsu shinsakai) were created to allow public participation of Japanese citizens to control abuses of prosecutorial discretion. . . .

Furthermore, certain scholars have noted a change in "law consciousness" of the Japanese from the 1950s to today. This change is simply that more Japanese are willing today to bring their disputes to court than in the 1950s, signaling a more active role for citizens in the system. The formation of popular movements, the use of prosecution review commissions in certain highly publicized cases, and the increase in academic writings and programs concerning forms of citizen participation evidence the citizen participation that is currently occurring. . . .

Japanese Legal System

There is no technical legal barrier preventing Japan from readopting the jury system. The Jury Act was never repealed; rather, it was suspended until World War II was over. The Japanese Diet could either repeal the Act to Suspend the Jury Act or enact a new law altogether establishing jury trial for criminal cases.

From a practitioner's perspective, the reintroduction of the jury system would change life drastically. One significant change would be that of timing. Under the present system, a long trial is not conducted in one continuous sitting. Rather, the case is tried in short sessions, usually for a few hours each month. The introduction of juries would require cases to be tried in one continuous time period, certainly changing the method of preparation of the attorneys.

Another significant change would be that a trial by dossier would be replaced by bouts of live witness testimony. The predictability of the old system would be gone. Japanese attorneys would have to learn the art of trying a case in front of laypersons rather than experienced career judges. The focus will be shifted from the papers to the live witnesses testifying.

Adoption of a jury system would also certainly affect the appellate system in Japan. Presently, a defendant may appeal both factual and legal findings to the first level of appeal (koso appeal). The Jury Act of 1923 abolished the koso appeal for jury trials on points of fact. Any law readopting the jury system would probably do the same, or risk undermining the factual determinations of the jury. . . . For defense attorneys, the primary effect would be to curtail opportunities for appeal or post-conviction review on factual grounds. However, presumably the better factfinding by juries would make up for this.

It is also likely that, through the adoption of a jury system in Japan, the near 100% conviction rate would decline. Prosecutors may also push for the adoption of a U.S.-like plea bargaining system, which could be used to save the courts time by preventing many cases from reaching the jury.

Also, from a purely practical perspective, although some Japanese courtrooms continue to have jury boxes and jury rooms, the great majority do not. Certainly the cost and effort of adding such necessities for jury trials, in addition to juror wages and travel, are factors to be considered in how smoothly a jury system could be adopted in Japan.

Thus, although there is no legal obstacle preventing Japan from bringing back the jury in criminal trials, reintroduction of the jury system would take time and effort on the part of both the Japanese government and attorneys. At least one commentator has stated that the need for such efforts, in addition to skepticism about the jury system, may be enough to prevent adoption of the jury system in Japan in the near future. . . .

For Further Reading

Abramson, Jeffrey. *We the Jury: The Jury System and the Ideal of Democracy.* New York: Basic Books, 1994.

Gilliam, Franklin D. and Shanto Iyengar. "Prime Suspects: The Influence of Local Television News on the Viewing Public." *American Journal of Political Science* 44 (2000): 560.

Gordon, Sanford C. and Gregory A. Huber. "Citizen Oversight and the Electoral Incentives of Criminal Prosecutors." *American Journal of Political Science* 46 (2002): 334.

Stith, Kate and Jose A. Cabranes. *Fear of Judging: Sentencing Guidelines in the Federal Court.* Chicago: University of Chicago Press, 1998.

Tonry, Michael. *Thinking About Crime: Sense and Sensibility in American Penal Culture.* New York: Oxford University Press, 2004.

Chapter **8**

Politics and Civil Justice

Introduction

Because criminal cases often bring with them a great deal of notoriety, the American public is exposed to the workings of the criminal justice system. Spectacular criminal cases often raise complex constitutional questions that highlight the competing interests of prosecutors, judges, and criminal defendants. Depending on the outcome, these cases can spark a sense of outrage, both individual and collective, in a way that few other issues do. Civil litigation, though seldom receiving as much media attention, is also important since it resolves disputes between individuals, or between individuals and large institutions, such as corporations, educational institutions, and nonprofit organizations. Civil law compensates individuals who have been injured financially. These injuries can arise from many areas, such as fraudulent corporate behavior, defamation, devaluation of property, or harm to physical well-being. Earlier chapters in this volume have emphasized the "reform" nature of constitutional litigation, and how such lawsuits can help bring about social and political change. The theme continues in this chapter. We offer selections that demonstrate how civil litigation can be a catalyst for policy change on important matters that affect the everyday lives of citizens in the United States and beyond.

Foundations and History

Few would dispute the idea that some lawyers are more competent than others. But does it follow that these lawyers always win, or does winning in court have as much to do with superior resources, specialization, and other institutional advantages beyond mere professional skill? Marc Galanter, in his classic article "Why the Haves Come Out Ahead: Speculations on the Limits of Legal Change" (1974), argues that "repeat players"—individual lawyers, firms, and so on—possess a clear advantage over what he calls "one-shotters" in civil litigation. Galanter's article also offers an important theoretical explanation for the success—or lack thereof—of lawyers, groups, and specialized legal practices beyond civil litigation. The article has remained a benchmark for scholars interested in why some litigants succeed and others do not. In *Rights at Work: Pay Equity Reform and the Politics of Legal Mobilization* (1994), Michael W. McCann presents a systematic explanation of how and why civil litigation functions as an element of reform politics, and notes that lawsuits need not succeed in court in order to contribute to political reform. By attracting attention to an issue through litigation or pushing the resolution of a problem from legal channels into the political arena, lawsuits can serve as crucial elements of reform outside the courtroom.

Contemporary Judicial Politics

Lawyers in civil cases often work on a contingency fee basis. That is, they do not get paid unless they win their case. This is far different from attorneys who work for firms that bill their clients on an hourly basis and get paid regardless of whether they win or lose a particular legal battle. Lawyers who work on behalf of plaintiffs in high-profile civil cases, such as those involving lawsuits against tobacco companies, gun companies, or the pharmaceutical industry, come to their task with expectations of a big payday. But how much money is enough? In "Fistful of Fees" (2000), Richard Zitrin and Carol M. Langford explore this question by talking about the new breed of "hired gun" who chooses clients based on fee expectations and not necessarily commitment to the cause being fought over.

A View from the Inside

Have you ever wondered how tobacco litigation rose from obscurity into high media attention, seemingly overnight? The answer stems from the Supreme Court's decision in *Cipollone v. Liggett Group, Inc.* (1992). In *Cipollone,* the constitutional doctrine of federal preemption, the legal principle giving Congress the power to supersede state laws that conflict with a national policy interest, came into play. The Court ruled that the doctrine of federal preemption did not prevent plaintiffs from bringing lawsuits against tobacco companies under state personal injury law. The excerpt from *Cipollone* offers an explanation of the Court's ruling that opened the door for lawsuits against the tobacco companies and, since the mid-1990s, has remained a staple of civil litigation intended to reform this major issue in public policy.

Regardless of how the ongoing campaign against the tobacco companies turns out, one thing is certain: The lawyers involved in defending the tobacco companies and the lawyers representing former smokers will all make a considerable amount of money. The question for many in the legal profession and those interested in legal ethics is just how much money represents fair compensation for their efforts. Massachusetts was one of the first states to reach an agreement with the tobacco companies, restricting their marketing and advertising abilities, and requiring them to pay health care costs associated with smoking. In "Greed on Trial" (2004), Alex Beam, a reporter for *Atlantic Monthly,* provides a description of greed at work in this tobacco-fee settlement trial.

A Comparative Perspective

In "Class Action Lawsuits" (2004), Ian Bell examines a theme familiar from our earlier readings in this chapter. It illustrates the rise of the class action lawsuit as a means to recover damages from a personal injury sustained at the hands of a large corporation, from the perspective of the Scottish legal system. Americans are divided on the wisdom of "tort reform" to restrict the money damages that juries may award civil plaintiffs, with some seeing large awards as an appropriate way to punish wealthy but negligent companies. Others see such awards as encouraging unethical lawyers to extract massive fees from deep-pocket defendants, driving up legal costs and allowing lawsuits to be filed for absurd reasons. Other countries find themselves facing the same dilemmas. Do you find the issues raised in this piece about class action lawsuits in Scotland similar to those raised in the United States?

Foundations and History

8.1 Why the "Haves" Come Out Ahead: Speculations on the Limits of Legal Change (1974)

Marc Galanter

. . . I would like to try to put forward some conjectures about the way in which the basic architecture of the legal system creates and limits the possibilities of using the system as a means of redistributive (that is, systemically equalizing) change. Our question, specifically, is, under what conditions can litigation be redistributive, taking litigation in the broadest sense of the presentation of claims to be decided by courts (or court-like agencies) and the whole penumbra of threats, feints, and so forth, surrounding such presentation. . . .

Most analyses of the legal system start at the rules end and work down through institutional facilities to see what effect the rules have on the parties. I would like to reverse that procedure and look through the other end of the telescope. Let's think about the different kinds of parties and the effect these differences might have on the way the system works.

Because of differences in their size, differences in the state of the law, and differences in their re-

From *Law and Society Review* 9 (Fall 1974): 95–160. Reprinted by permission of Blackwell Publishers.

sources, some of the actors in the society have many occasions to utilize the courts (in the broad sense) to make (or defend) claims; others do so only rarely. We might divide our actors into those claimants who have only occasional recourse to the courts (one-shotters or OS) and repeat players (RP) who are engaged in many similar litigations over time. The spouse in a divorce case, the auto-injury claimant, the criminal accused are OSs; the insurance company, the prosecutor, the finance company are RPs. Obviously this is an oversimplification; there are intermediate cases such as the professional criminal. So we ought to think of OS-RP as a continuum rather than as a dichotomous pair. Typically, the RP is a larger unit and the stakes in any given case are smaller (relative to total worth). OSs are usually smaller units and the stakes represented by the tangible outcome of the case may be high relative to total worth, as in the case of injury victim or the criminal accused). Or, the OS may suffer from the opposite problem: his claims may be so small and unmanageable (the shortweighted consumer or the holder of performing rights) that the cost of enforcing them outruns any promise of benefit.

Let us refine our notion of the RP into an "ideal type" if you will—a unit which has had and anticipates repeated litigation, which has low stakes in the outcome of any one case, and which has the resources to pursue its long-run interests. . . . An OS, on the other hand, is a unit whose claims are too large (relative to his size) or too small (relative to the cost of remedies) to be managed routinely and rationally.

We would expect an RP to play the litigation game differently from an OS. Let us consider some of his advantages:

1. RPs, having done it before, have advance intelligence; they are able to structure the next transaction and build a record. It is the RP who writes the form contract, requires the security deposit, and the like.
2. RPs develop expertise and have ready access to specialists. They enjoy economies of scale and have low start-up costs for any case.
3. RPs have opportunities to develop facilitative informal relations with institutional incumbents.
4. The RP must establish and maintain credibility as a combatant. His interest in his "bargaining reputation" serves as a resource to establish "commitment" to his bargaining positions. With no bargaining reputation to maintain, the OS has more difficulty in convincingly committing himself in bargaining.
5. RPs can play the odds. The larger the matter at issue looms for OS, the more likely he is to adopt a minimax strategy (minimize the probability of maximum loss). Assuming that the stakes are relatively smaller for RPs, they can adopt strategies calculated to maximize gain over a long series of cases, even where this involves the risk of maximum loss in some cases.
6. RPs can play for rules as well as immediate gains. First, it pays an RP to expend resources in influencing the making of the relevant rules by such methods as lobbying. (And his accumulated expertise enables him to do this persuasively.)
7. RPs can also play for rules in litigation itself, whereas an OS is unlikely to. That is, there is a difference in what they regard as a favorable outcome. Because his stakes in the immediate

outcome are high and because by definition OS is unconcerned with the outcome of similar litigation in the future, OS will have little interest in that element of the outcome which might influence the disposition of the decision-maker next time around. For the RP, on the other hand, anything that will favorably influence the outcomes of future cases is a worthwhile result. The larger the stake for any player and the lower the probability of repeat play, the less likely that he will be concerned with the rules which govern future cases of the same kind. Consider two parents contesting the custody of their only child, the prizefighter vs. the IRS for tax arrears, the convict facing the death penalty. On the other hand, the player with small stakes in the present case and the prospect of a series of similar cases (the IRS, the adoption agency, the prosecutor) may be more interested in the state of the law.

Thus, if we analyze the outcomes of a case into a tangible component and a rule component, we may expect that in case 1, OS will attempt to maximize tangible gain. But if RP is interested in maximizing his tangible gain in a series of cases 1 . . . n, he may be willing to trade off tangible gain in any one case for rule gain (or to minimize rule loss). We assumed that the institutional facilities for litigation were overloaded and settlements were prevalent. We would then expect RPs to "settle" cases where they expected unfavorable rule outcomes. Since they expect to litigate again, RPs can select to adjudicate (or appeal) those cases which they regard as most likely to produce favorable rules. On the other hand, OSs should be willing to trade off the possibility of making "good law" for tangible gain. Thus, we would expect the body of "precedent" cases—that is, cases capable of influencing the outcome of future cases— to be relatively skewed toward those favorable to RP.

Of course it is not suggested that the strategic configuration of the parties is the sole or major determinant of rule-development. Rule-development is shaped by a relatively autonomous learned tradition, by the impingement of intellectual currents from outside, by the preferences and prudences of the decision-makers. But courts are passive and these factors operate only when the process is triggered by parties.

The point here is merely to note the superior opportunities of the RP to trigger promising cases and prevent the triggering of unpromising ones. It is not incompatible with a course of rule-development favoring OSs (or, as indicated below, with OSs failing to get the benefit of those favorable new rules).

In stipulating that RPs can play for rules, I do not mean to imply that RPs pursue rule-gain as such. If we recall that not all rules penetrate (i.e., become effectively applied at the field level) we come to some additional advantages of RPs.

8. RPs, by virtue of experience and expertise, are more likely to be able to discern which rules are likely to "penetrate" and which are likely to remain merely symbolic commitments. RPs may be able to concentrate their resources on rule-changes that are likely to make a tangible difference. They can trade off symbolic defeats for tangible gains.

9. Since penetration depends in part on the resources of the parties (knowledge, attentiveness, expert services, money), RPs are more likely to be able to invest the matching resources necessary to secure the penetration of rules favorable to them.

It is not suggested that RPs are to be equated with "haves" (in terms of power, wealth and status) or OSs with "have-nots." In the American setting most RPs are larger, richer and more powerful than are most OSs, so these categories overlap, but there are obvious exceptions. RPs may be "have-nots" (alcoholic derelicts) or may act as champions of "have-nots" (as government does from time to time); OSs such as criminal defendants may be wealthy. What this analysis does is to define a position of advantage in the configuration of contending parties and indicate how those with other advantages tend to occupy this position of advantage and to have their other advantages reinforced and augmented thereby. This position of advantage is one of the ways in which a legal system formally neutral as between "haves" and "have-nots" may perpetuate and augment the advantages of the former. . . .

We may think of litigation as typically involving various combinations of OSs and RPs. . . .

One-Shotter vs. One-Shotter

The most numerous [parties in this litigation] are divorces and insanity hearings. Most . . . are uncontested. A large portion of these are really pseudo-litigation, that is, a settlement is worked out between the parties and ratified in the guise of adjudication. When we get real litigation [between these parties] it is often between parties who have some intimate tie with one another, fighting over some unsharable good, often with overtones of "spite" and "irrationality." Courts are resorted to where an ongoing relationship is ruptured; they have little to do with the routine patterning of activity. The law is invoked *ad hoc* and instrumentally by the parties. There may be a strong interest in vindication, but neither party is likely to have much interest in the long-term state of the law (of, for instance, custody or nuisance). There are few appeals, few test cases, little expenditure of resources on rule-development. Legal doctrine is likely to remain remote from everyday practice and from popular attitudes.

Repeat Player vs. One-Shotter

The great bulk of litigation is found [between these parties]—indeed every really numerous kind except personal injury cases, insanity hearings, and divorces. The law is used for routine processing of claims by parties for whom the making of such claims is a regular business activity. Often the cases here take the form of stereotyped mass processing with little of the individuated attention of full-dress adjudication. Even greater numbers of cases are settled "informally" with settlement keyed to possible litigation outcome (discounted by risk, cost, delay).

The state of the law is of interest to the RP, though not to the OS defendants. Insofar as the law is favorable to the RP it is "followed" closely in practice (subject to discount for RP's transaction costs). Transactions are built to fit the rules by creditors, police, draft boards and other RPs. Rules favoring OSs may be less readily applicable, since OSs do not ordinarily plan the underlying transaction, or less meticulously observed in practice, since OSs are unlikely to be as ready or able as RPs to invest in insuring their penetration to the field level.

One-Shotter vs. Repeat Player

All of these are rather infrequent types except for personal injury cases which are distinctive in that free entry to the arena is provided by the contingent fee. In auto injury claims, litigation is routinized and settlement is closely geared to possible litigation outcome. Outside the personal injury area, litigation between these parties is not routine. It usually represents the attempt of some OS to invoke outside help to create leverage on an organization with which he has been having dealings but is now at the point of divorce (for example, the discharged employee or the cancelled franchisee). The OS claimant generally has little interest in the state of the law; the RP defendant, however, is greatly interested.

Repeat Player vs. Repeat Player

Let us consider the general case first and then several special cases. We might expect that there would be little litigation here, because to the extent that two RPs play with each other repeatedly, the expectation of continued mutually beneficial interaction would give rise to informal bilateral controls. This seems borne out by studies of dealings among businessmen and in labor relations. Official agencies are invoked by unions trying to get established and by management trying to prevent them from getting established, more rarely in dealings between bargaining partners. Units with mutually beneficial relations do not adjust their differences in courts. Where they rely on third parties in dispute-resolution, it is likely to take a form (such as arbitration or a domestic tribunal) detached from official sanctions and applying domestic rather than official rules.

However, there are several special cases. First, there are those RPs who seek not furtherance of tangible interests, but vindication of fundamental cultural commitments. An example would be the organizations which sponsor much church-state lit-

igation. Where RPs are contending about value differences (who is right) rather than interest conflicts (who gets what) there is less tendency to settle and less basis for developing a private system of dispute settlement.

Second, government is a special kind of RP. Informal controls depend upon the ultimate sanction of withdrawal and refusal to continue beneficial relations. To the extent that withdrawal of future association is not possible in dealing with government, the scope of informal controls is correspondingly limited. The development of informal relations between regulatory agencies and regulated firms is well known. And the regulated may have sanctions other than withdrawal which they can apply; for instance, they may threaten political opposition. But the more inclusive the unit of government, the less effective the withdrawal sanction and the greater the likelihood that a party will attempt to invoke outside allies by litigation even while sustaining the ongoing relationship. This applies also to monopolies, units which share the government's relative immunity to withdrawal sanctions. RPs in monopolistic relationships will occasionally invoke formal controls to show prowess, to give credibility to threats, and to provide satisfactions for other audiences. Thus we would expect litigation by and against government to be more frequent than in other RP vs. RP situations. There is a second reason for expecting more litigation when government is a party. That is, that the notion of "gain" (policy as well as monetary) is often more contingent and problematic for governmental units than for other parties, such as businesses or organized interest groups. In some cases courts may, by proffering authoritative interpretations of public policy, redefine an agency's notion of gain. Hence government parties may be more willing to externalize decisions to the courts. And opponents may have more incentive to litigate against government in the hope of securing a shift in its goals.

A somewhat different kind of special case is present where plaintiff and defendant are both RPs but do not deal with each other repeatedly (two insurance companies, for example.) In the government/monopoly case, the parties were so inextricably bound together that the force of informal controls was limited; here they are not sufficiently bound to each other to give informal controls their bite; there is nothing to withdraw from! The large one-time deal that falls through, the marginal enterprise—these are staple sources of litigation.

Where there is litigation in the RP vs. RP situation, we might expect that there would be heavy expenditure on rule-development, many appeals, and rapid and elaborate development of the doctrinal law. Since the parties can invest to secure implementation of favorable rules, we would expect practice to be closely articulated to the resulting rules.

On the basis of these preliminary guesses, we can sketch a general profile of litigation and the factors associated with it. The great bulk of litigation is [between RPs vs. OSs], much less [between OSs vs. RPs]. Most of the litigation [in these cases] is mass routine processing of disputes between parties who are strangers (not in mutually beneficial continuing relations) or divorced—and between whom there is a disparity in size. One party is a bureaucratically organized "professional" (in the sense of doing it for a living) who enjoys strategic advantages. Informal controls between the parties are tenuous or ineffective; their relationship is likely to be established and defined by official rules; in litigation, these rules are discounted by transaction costs and manipulated selectively to the advantage of the parties. On the other hand, [between OSs vs. OSs and RPs vs. RPs] we have more infrequent but more individualized litigation between parties of the same general magnitude, among whom there are or were continuing multi-stranded relationships with attendant informal controls. Litigation appears when the relationship loses its future value; when its "monopolistic" character deprives informal controls of sufficient leverage and the parties invoke outside allies to modify it; and when the parties seek to vindicate conflicting values. . . .

Implications for Reform: the Role of Lawyers

We have discussed the way in which the architecture of the legal system tends to confer interlocking advantages on overlapping groups whom we have called the "haves." To what extent might reforms of the legal system dispel these advantages? Reforms

will always be less total than the utopian ones envisioned above. Reformers will have limited resources to deploy and they will always be faced with the necessity of choosing which uses of those resources are most productive of equalizing change. What does our analysis suggest about strategies and priorities?

Our analysis suggests that change at the level of substantive rules is not likely in itself to be determinative of redistributive outcomes. Rule change is in itself likely to have little effect because the system is so constructed that changes in the rules can be filtered out unless accompanied by changes at other levels. In a setting of overloaded institutional facilities, inadequate costly legal services, and unorganized parties, beneficiaries may lack the resources to secure implementation; or an RP may restructure the transaction to escape the thrust of the new rule. Favorable rules are not necessarily (and possibly not typically) in short supply to "have-nots"; certainly less so than any of the other resources needed to play the litigation game. Programs of equalizing reform which focus on rule-change can be readily absorbed without any change in power relations. The system has the capacity to change a great deal at the level of rules without corresponding changes in everyday patterns of practice of distribution of tangible advantages. Indeed rule-change may becom a symbolic substitute for redistribution of advantages. . . .

The contribution of the lawyer to redistributive social change, then, depends upon the organization and culture of the legal profession. We have surmised that court-produced substantive rule-change is unlikely in itself to be a determinative element in producing tangible redistribution of benefits. The leverage provided by litigation depends on its strategic combination with inputs at other levels. The question then is whether the organization of the profession permits lawyers to develop and employ skills at these other levels. The more that lawyers view themselves exclusively as courtroom advocates, the less their willingness to undertake new tasks and form enduring alliances with clients and operate in forums other than courts, the less likely they are to serve as agents of redistributive change. Paradoxically, those legal professions most open to accentuating the advantages of the "haves" (by allowing themselves to be "captured" by recurrent clients) may be most able to become (or have room for, more likely) agents of change, precisely because they provide more license for indentification with clients and their

"causes" and have a less strict definition of what are properly professional activities.

8.2

From *Rights at Work: Pay Equity Reform and the Politics of Legal Mobilization* (1994)

Michael W. McCann

. . . This . . . exercise [in theory building] provides a foundation for the second endeavor implied by my title—that of developing a general framework for conceptualizing how rights themselves "work" as cultural conventions in social practice. Just as my focus on legal advocacy seeks to offer new insights into the politics of pay equity struggles, therefore, so does the pay equity experience provide a valuable case study for developing a distinctive analytical approach applicable to legal reform activity in a variety of contexts. The remainder of this [article] will outline the contours of this "legal mobilization" framework and its role in structuring my study of pay equity politics.

Legal Mobilization and Political Struggle: Toward a General Theory

It should be acknowledged at the outset that the "legal mobilization" theory employed in this study signifies less a discrete analytical model than a tradition of loosely allied interpretive approaches crafted by scholars with quite different conceptual concerns and empirical applications. For example, much of the best known scholarly work has focused attention primarily on mobilization of the law by individuals seeking resolution of mostly "private" disputes. This work is valuable in many ways, but it has only limited relevance for analyzing the ways in which organized movements seek broad changes in public policies and social practices. Other scholars, by contrast, have developed the legal mobilization approach specifically to address social reform activ-

Reprinted by permission of The University of Chicago Press and the author.

ity. These important works figure prominently in the following pages, although they tend to be speculative or silent about some themes at the heart of my analysis. At the same time, other recent works on law and social movements have contributed ideas that parallel and enrich the legal mobilization perspective, even though they do not explicitly align themselves with the approach. One task undertaken in the following pages thus is to construct a workable framework for analyzing legal mobilization by social movements that builds on, synthesizes, and yet transcends the groundbreaking efforts of many others.

Law as Social Practice

The starting point for this theory building enterprise is the basic definition offered by Frances Zemans: "The law is . . . mobilized when a desire or want is translated into a demand as an assertion of rights." From this simple premise we can elaborate a number of themes that inform a broad and somewhat novel vision of law. For one thing, the legal mobilization model emphasizes an understanding of law as identifiable traditions of symbolic practice. As Marc Galanter puts it, law should be analyzed more capaciously "as a system of cultural and symbolic meanings than as a set of operative controls. It affects us primarily through communication of symbols—by providing threats, promises, models, persuasion, legitimacy, stigma, and so on."

This does not mean that law is simply a set of abstract concepts informing our attitudes and preferences. Rather, legal discourses are viewed more fundamentally as *constitutive* of practical interactions among citizens. As such, legal conventions provide some of the most important "strategies of action" through which citizens routinely negotiate social relationships. This understanding implies, on the one hand, that legal knowledge to some degree prefigures social activity; inherited legal conventions shape the very terms of citizen understanding, aspiration, and interaction with others. E. P. Thompson's classic description of how law mediates class relations captures this dynamic well:

> Class relations were expressed, not in any way one likes, but *through the forms of law;* and the law, like other institutions which from time to time can be seen as mediating (and masking) existent class relations . . . has its own characteristics, its own independent history and logic of evolution.

Among the most important of such legal conventions are discourses regarding basic *rights* that designate the proper distribution of social burdens and benefits among citizens.

On the other hand, it is important to understand that these inherited legal symbols and discourses provide relatively malleable resources that are routinely reconstructed as citizens seek to advance their interests and designs in everyday life. In particular, legal discourses offer a potentially plastic medium both for refiguring the terms of past settlements over legitimate expectations and for expressing aspirations for new terms of entitlement. "'Rights' can give rise to 'rights consciousness' so that individuals and groups may imagine and act in light of rights that have not been formally recognized or enforced" by officials, notes Martha Minow. *Legal (or rights) consciousness* in this sense refers to the ongoing, dynamic process of constructing one's understanding of, and relationship to, the social world through use of legal conventions and discourses.

Such reconstructive activity in practice is neither boundless nor entirely "free," of course. Growing out of learned conventions and long developing power relations, even highly innovative legal practices carry with them their own limitations, biases, and burdensome baggage. Legal "cultures provide symbols and ideas which can be manipulated by their members for strategic goals," agrees Sally Engle Merry, "but they also establish constraints on that manipulation." Hence the primary project of the legal mobilization model outlined here: to analyze the constitutive role of legal rights both as a strategic resource and as a constraint for collective efforts to transform or "reconstitute" relationships among social groups.

This particular conception of legal mobilization builds on several other assumptions. First, it is important to emphasize that legal practices and rights discourses are not limited to formal state forums. After all, citizens routinely mobilize legal strategies for negotiating exchanges and resolving disputes in many social settings without relying on direct official intervention. "Efforts to create and give meaning to norms, through a language of rights, often and importantly occur outside formal legal institutions such as courts . . . [and constitute] an activity engaged in by nonlawyers as well as by lawyers and judges," affirms Minow. Indeed, this shift in the focus of legal analysis away from the initiative of state officials and to the initiative of citizens engaged in everyday struggles is a trademark of the legal mobilization theory developed here.

A second related assumption is that the legal order is pluralistic rather than monolithic. Not only is official state law a maze of diverse, indeterminate, and often contradictory legal traditions, but in addition a multitude of relatively autonomous "indigenous" law traditions contend for preeminence within the many subcultures and institutional terrains of society. Moreover, even when contending groups embrace common legal conventions, we should be sensitive to the fact that the understandings and usages of those conventions often vary quite dramatically. Because legal conventions are inherently indeterminate and people's experiences are heterogenous, legal consciousness itself is variable, volatile, complex, and even contradictory. We thus should expect that differently situated people at different times interpret and act on law in quite different ways. As Santos puts it, "our legal life is constituted by an intersection of different legal orders, that is, by interlegality."

This in turn suggests a third proposition—that both official and indigenous legal norms and practices generally contribute only limited, partial, and contingent constitutive influences in most domains of citizen activity. In other words, law is rarely an exclusive force in actual social practice, whether for judges on the bench or citizens in the street. Rather, legal conventions usually constitute just one highly variable dimension in the complex mix of interdependent factors that structure our understandings and actions. And it is this pluralistic, contingent character of legal consciousness in practice that renders law a dynamic but elusive force in social life.

Legal Mobilization and Reform Movement Politics

These basic premises provide the legal mobilization approach with a more expansive, subtle, and complex view of law's role in political struggle than most studies focusing on reform-oriented litigation alone offer. One important point follows directly from the previous premises. That is, the pluralistic character of law provides reform activists with some measure of choice regarding both the general institutional sites and the particular substantive legal resources that might be mobilized to fight policy battles and advance movement goals. This by no means is intended to refute the general thrust of critics who emphasize the conservative character of institutionalized legal practices in most official state forums. Indeed, legal mobilization theory is rooted in the assumption that law is a primary medium of social control and domination. Authoritative legal forms and relational logics by definition are the products of long evolving historical struggles in which some interests, groups, norms, and arrangements have tended to prevail in relatively systematic fashion. . . .

. . . [Here, I] will demarcate four general stages of movement action in which legal mobilization can figure somewhat differently:

1. *the movement building process* of raising citizen expectations regarding political change, activating potential constituents, building group alliances, and organizing resources for tactical action;
2. *the struggle to compel formal changes in official policy* that address movement demands at least in principle;
3. *the struggle for control over actual reform policy development and implementation* that evolves among the various interested parties; and
4. *the transformative legacy of legal action* for subsequent movement development, articulation of new rights claims, alliance with other groups, policy reform advances, and social struggle generally.

This typology of stages can be revised to fit different trajectories of conflict, but its general emphasis on temporal contingency defines an enduring component of the legal mobilization framework. . . .

. . . Liberal legal reform action often is modest in design and impact, to be sure. However, this generally is due to the limited resources and strategic opportunities for defiant action available to movement activists as much as to fatal flaws in their understanding of their situation. In sum, it is worth reiterating that the legal mobilization framework envisions law as essentially neither just a resource nor just a constraint for defiant political action. Rather, the approach encourages us to focus on how, when, and to what degree legal practices tend to be both at the same time.

Contemporary Judicial Politics

8.3   ## Fistful of Fees: The Hired Gun or Lawyer Is Due What He's Been Promised, But No More (2000)

Richard Zitrin and Carol M. Langford

It is morning. The stranger rides into town on a horse as black as a moonless night, a woolen poncho concealing the gunbelts strapped across his chest. He says nothing to the poor, worried townsfolk who crowd the streets to catch a glimpse of him. Everyone knows why he is here. He has been asked to do the impossible, though no one dares ask how. The odds are long, and his price is high: If he prevails, his bounty will be taken from the spoils he recovers from those who have ravaged and pillaged the town for years. . . .

We are hardly the first to compare contingency fee lawyers to hired guns. At their best, these lawyers boast skills and special talents needed by many but possessed by few. The gunfighters are willing to risk their lives—the lawyers their livelihoods—by taking on seemingly hopeless causes for the chance to leave with a sack of gold.

But how much reward should these gunslingers get? Are they entitled to whatever their clients are willing to pay, even if the clients agree out of sheer desperation? What if the hired gun looks to the vanquished for payment?

What are even the best attorney's skills worth, and when does a fee stop being compensation for services performed and become the product of unabashed greed?

Same as Carnival Wager?

Judge H. Lee Sarokin compares contingency fees to a carnival wager: the barker offers $100 to anyone who can climb to the top of a greased pole and puncture a balloon. Those who climb halfway are

not entitled to $50 for the time and effort they devoted. They get nothing at all. Only total victory results in the prize.

But the barker can't merely pay those who succeed for the time they spent. The bargain calls for a substantial payment, measured by the difficulty of success and the skill required to achieve it.

Sarokin did not come to this conclusion lightly. He had the unique vantage point of a New Jersey federal judge who presided over the first two trials against tobacco companies a decade ago. He watched tobacco lawyers stonewall discovery, finally concluding that "the tobacco industry may be the king of concealment and disinformation."

Even after his special master [a professional appointed by the Court with expertise in a particular field who is charged with searching for documentary evidence] uncovered smoking-gun evidence against the industry, the tobacco interests appealed, getting discovery disclosures reversed and the judge thrown off the cases. As for the plaintiffs' lawyers—those who took their best shot at cleaning up the town—it was a gallant try, but they wound up with nothing.

To the Ultimate Victors

So Judge Sarokin reasoned that to the ultimate victors—those who through massive litigation by individual states ultimately drove Big Tobacco from town—the spoils go. We agree. Without states importing high-powered legal talent—lawyers lured by a great pot of gold—there may have been no spoils to share. Significantly, these lawyers' paydays were exactly what their contingency fee contracts called for. The states—like townsfolk who hired the gunfighter—knew the deal. With hindsight, one could call these fee contracts bargains with the devil. But those that bargained got what they paid for.

The analogy between the contingency fee lawyer and the hired gun goes only so far, of course.

First, while some may disagree, lawyers are not generally killers; Big Tobacco may have retreated to the hills outside of town, but it's not dead.

Second, lawyers still have fiduciary duties to their clients. Judge Sarokin suggests that while the tobacco litigation fee contracts are valid, those lawyers excessively enriched should consider making reasonable adjustments to their fees. Many, in fact, have.

Third, it's clear that not every contingency case involves a foe as daunting and difficult to challenge as the tobacco industry. Where a huge and unexpected settlement occurs in a more ordinary case, there may be a duty for the lawyer to reduce a fee so out of proportion that it becomes unconscionable. Still, the default proposition is—and should be—that if the contingency fee contract calls for a particular sum, the lawyer is entitled to that.

Three keys are related to this proposition. First is the informed consent of the client—not just consent but informed consent. Second is the sophistication of the client, which often affects how well that client is informed. Third is the lawyer's objective evaluation of the difficulty of the task—an evaluation that must be shared with the client. There's a far cry between attorneys general agreeing to pay a hired gun to rid their states of Big Tobacco, and a group of naive townspeople who think they face terrorists when they're really just a bunch of rowdies. Where plaintiffs have few resources and victory is all but certain, the conscionability of a fee should be tied to the degree of difficulty of the enterprise—just as it is for the "impossible" jobs.

This sharing separates the best contingency lawyers from gunslingers. Not only do they share information, but they share, rather than take, the spoils of victory—so that both lawyer and client truly benefit. . . .

The other extreme? Lawyers who train their guns on their own client. In a recent sidebar to the Orange County bankruptcy litigation, the Southern California firm of Hennigan, Mercer & Bennett did exactly that. Hennigan agreed with the county's court-appointed litigation representative to charge an hourly fee, which it raised three times between its July 1996 agreement and the final resolution of litigation in 1999. In that time, Hennigan billed

and was paid over $26 million at its so-called "benchmark" hourly rates.

Self-Serving Language

Three times, the firm had asked the Orange County representative to share in the spoils of victory with a contingency fee, but the representative steadfastly refused. Still, the firm's fee contract included this self-serving language: "It is our firm's practice to charge our clients for services rendered based upon not only the total number of hours charged at benchmark billing rates, but also upon such other factors. . . ."

These factors included everything from the complexity of the case and the skill of the lawyering to firm lawyers working "after normal business hours and the extent of risk in being paid."

And who got to decide how much of the spoils of victory the law firm would receive? "When our representation is ended, the firm will determine the amount of the total fees and will send the Representative a final statement."

Theoretically, this language called for a raising or lowering of the firm's benchmark rate. Not surprisingly, however, Hennigan decided that it was entitled to more—in fact, an additional fee of over $48 million, making its total fee almost three times its benchmark bill.

Federal Judge Gary L. Taylor was enraged by the Hennigan firm's audacity: "The lawyers had gotten a career-defining dream case, and while the issues were novel and the stakes were high," it was also true that "the work was steady, . . . all expenses were paid, . . . all fees were promptly paid in full and there was no risk of delay or non-payment. . . ."

Taylor saved his most vitriolic criticism for this claim by the firm in its fees motion against its own client: "If lawyers in cases like these are paid only their 'straight hourly rates' they have less reason to maximize results for clients or to expedite resolution." Taylor called the idea that a lawyer is justified doing less than one's best for a client "a flawed and cynical philosophy," a "repugnant" concept "contrary to a lawyer's oath and duty."

Flawed and cynical as this might be, it is unfortunately too prevalent in a profession that is supposed to adhere to ethical standards higher than those used by the average gunslinger. The Hennigan firm, not satisfied to be well paid for its time and efforts, sought to plunder its own client's spoils.

To us, the most incredible part of this story is that Judge Taylor—after excoriating the lawyers for failing to recognize their duties and pointing out that their efforts involved virtually no risk and "legal results that were mixed"—nevertheless awarded the firm $3 million over its benchmark fees.

To be sure, he rejected the vast majority of the firm's claims. But by validating the fee contract and even paying the firm a sweetener, he tacitly gave

credence to the idea that lawyers are not so different from gunfighters after all—and that when the townspeople make a deal with the devil, the devil will get his due.

The town was more peaceful, but still poor. The threat to the village was gone. But most of the plunder stolen from the town had left with the stranger. Also gone was the protection that lasted only as long as the stranger was in town. He rode off to fight other battles, unconcerned that the townspeople remained to face the next threat alone.

A View from the Inside

8.4   *Cipollone v. Liggett Group, Inc.*
505 U.S. 504 (1992)

JUSTICE STEVENS delivered the opinion of the Court.

Article VI of the Constitution provides that the laws of the United States, "shall be the supreme Law of the Land; . . . any Thing in the Constitution or Laws of any state to the Contrary notwithstanding." Thus, since our decision in *McCulloch v. Maryland* (1819), it has been settled that state law that conflicts with federal law is "without effect." Consideration of issues arising under the Supremacy Clause, "start[s] with the assumption that the historic police powers of the States [are] not to be superseded by . . . Federal Act unless that [is] the clear and manifest purpose of Congress." Accordingly, "'[t]he purpose of Congress is the ultimate touchstone'" of preemption analysis.

Congress' intent may be "explicitly stated in the statute's language or implicitly contained in its structure and purpose." In the absence of an express congressional command, state law is preempted if that law actually conflicts with federal law, or if federal law so thoroughly occupies a legislative field "'as to make reasonable the inference that Congress left no room for the States to supplement it.'" . . .

When Congress has considered the issue of preemption and has included in the enacted legislation a provision explicitly addressing that issue, and when that provision provides a "reliable indicium of congressional intent with respect to state authority," "there is no need to infer congressional

intent to preempt state laws from the substantive provisions" of the legislation. Such reasoning is a variant of the familiar principle of expression *unius est exclusio alterius:* Congress' enactment of a provision defining the preemptive reach of a statute implies that matters beyond that reach are not preempted. In this case, the other provisions of the 1965 and 1969 Acts offer no cause to look beyond Section 5 of each Act. Therefore, we need only identify the domain expressly preempted by each of those sections. As the 1965 and 1969 provisions differ substantially, we consider each in turn.

In the 1965 preemption provision regarding advertising, Congress spoke precisely and narrowly: "No *statement* relating to smoking and health shall be required *in the advertising* of [properly labeled] cigarettes." Section 5(a) used the same phrase ("No *statement* relating to smoking and health") with regard to cigarette labeling. As Section 5(a) made clear, that phrase referred to the sort of warning provided for in Section 4, which set forth *verbatim* the warning Congress determined to be appropriate. Thus, on their face, these provisions merely prohibited state and federal rulemaking bodies from mandating particular cautionary statements on cigarette labels or in cigarette advertisements.

Beyond the precise words of these provisions, this reading is appropriate for several reasons. First, as discussed above, we must construe these provisions in light of the presumption against the pre-emption of state police power regulations. This presumption reinforces the appropriateness of a narrow reading of Section 5. Second, the warning required in Section 4 does not, by its own effect, foreclose additional obligations imposed under state law. That Congress requires a particular warning label does not automatically preempt a regulatory field. Third, there is no general, inherent conflict between federal preemption of state warning requirements and the continued vitality of state common law damages actions. For example, in the Comprehensive Smokeless Tobacco Health Education Act of 1986, Congress expressly preempted State or local imposition of a "statement relating to the use of smokeless tobacco products and health" but, at the same time, preserved state law damages actions based on those products. All of these considerations indicate that Section 5 is best read as having superseded only positive enactments by legislatures or administrative agencies that mandate particular warning labels.

This reading comports with the 1965 Act's statement of purpose, which expressed an intent to avoid "diverse, nonuniform, and confusing labeling and advertising regulations with respect to any relationship between smoking and health." Read against the backdrop of regulatory activity undertaken by state legislatures and federal agencies in response to the Surgeon General's report, the term "regulation" most naturally refers to positive enactments by those bodies, not to common law damages actions. . . .

For these reasons, we conclude that Section 5 of the 1965 Act only preempted state and federal rulemaking bodies from mandating particular cautionary statements, and did not preempt state law damages actions. . . .

[The Court then turned to consider each of the damage claims brought by Cipollone.]

Failure to Warn

. . . In this case, petitioner offered two closely related theories concerning the failure to warn: first, that respondents "were negligent in the manner [that] they tested, researched, sold, promoted, and advertised" their cigarettes; and second, that respondents failed to provide "adequate warnings of the health consequences of cigarette smoking."

Petitioner's claims are preempted to the extent that they rely on a state law "requirement or prohibition . . . with respect to . . . advertising or promotion." Thus, insofar as claims under either failure to warn theory require a showing that respondents' post-1969 advertising or promotions should have included additional, or more clearly stated, warnings, those claims are preempted. The Act does not, however, preempt petitioner's claims that rely solely on respondents' testing or research practices or other actions unrelated to advertising or promotion.

Breach of Express Warranty

Petitioner's claim for breach of an express warranty arises under [a New Jersey statute], which provides:

Any affirmation of fact or promise made by the seller to the buyer which relates to the goods and becomes part of the basis of the bargain creates an express warranty that the goods shall conform to the affirmation or promise.

Petitioner's evidence of an express warranty consists largely of statements made in respondents' advertising. . . . [T]he appropriate inquiry is not whether a claim challenges the "propriety" of advertising and promotion, but whether the claim would require the imposition under state law of a requirement or prohibition based on smoking and health with respect to advertising or promotion. . . .

That the terms of the warranty may have been set forth in advertisements, rather than in separate documents, is irrelevant to the preemption issue (though possibly not to the state law issue of whether the alleged warranty is valid and enforceable), because, although the breach of warranty claim is made "with respect to advertising," it does not rest on a duty imposed under state law. Accordingly, to the extent that petitioner has a viable claim for breach of express warranties made by respondents, that claim is not preempted by the 1969 Act.

Fraudulent Misrepresentation

Petitioner alleges two theories of fraudulent misrepresentation. First, petitioner alleges that respondents, through their advertising, neutralized the effect of federally mandated warning labels. Such a claim is predicated on a state law prohibition against statements in advertising and promotional materials that tend to minimize the health hazards associated with smoking. Such a *prohibition,* however, is merely the converse of a state law requirement that warnings be included in advertising and promotional materials. Section 5(b) of the 1969 Act preempts both requirements and prohibitions; it therefore supersedes petitioner's first fraudulent misrepresentation theory. . . .

Petitioner's second theory, as construed by the District Court, alleges intentional fraud and misrepresentation both by "false representation of a material fact [and by] conceal[ment of] a material fact." The predicate of this claim is a state law duty not to make false statements of material fact or to conceal such facts. Our preemption analysis requires us to determine whether such a duty is the sort of requirement or prohibition proscribed by Section 5(b).

Section 5(b) preempts only the imposition of state law obligations "with respect to the advertising or promotion" of cigarettes. Petitioner's claims that respondents concealed material facts are therefore not preempted insofar as those claims rely on a state law duty to disclose such facts through channels of communication other than advertising or promotion. Thus, for example, if state law obliged respondents to disclose material facts about smoking and health to an administrative agency, Section 5(b) would not preempt a state law claim based on a failure to fulfill that obligation.

Moreover, petitioner's fraudulent misrepresentation claims that do arise with respect to advertising and promotions (most notably claims based on allegedly false statements of material fact made in advertisements) are not preempted by Section 5(b). Such claims are not predicated on a duty "based on smoking and health," but rather on a more general obligation—the duty not to deceive. This understanding of fraud by intentional misstatement is appropriate for several reasons. First, in the 1969 Act, Congress offered no sign that it wished to insulate cigarette manufacturers from longstanding rules governing fraud. To the contrary, both the 1965 and the 1969 Acts explicitly reserved the FTC's authority to identify and punish deceptive advertising practices—an authority that the FTC had long exercised and continues to exercise. . . .

Moreover, this reading of "based on smoking and health" is wholly consistent with the purposes of the 1969 Act. State law prohibitions on false statements of material fact do not create "diverse, nonuniform, and confusing" standards. Unlike state law obligations concerning the warning necessary to render a product "reasonably safe," state law proscriptions on intentional fraud rely only on a single, uniform standard: falsity. Thus, we conclude that the phrase "based on smoking and health," fairly but narrowly construed, does not encompass the more general duty not to make fraudulent statements. Accordingly, petitioner's claim based on allegedly fraudulent statements made in respondents' advertisements are not preempted by Section 5(b) of the 1969 Act.

Conspiracy to Misrepresent or Conceal Material Facts

Petitioner's final claim alleges a conspiracy among respondents to misrepresent or conceal material facts concerning the health hazards of smoking. The predicate duty underlying this claim is a duty not to conspire to commit fraud. For the reasons stated in our analysis of petitioner's intentional fraud claim, this duty is not preempted by Section 5(b), for it is not a prohibition "based on smoking and health" as that phrase is properly construed. Accordingly, we conclude that the 1969 Act does not preempt petitioner's conspiracy claim.

To summarize our holding: the 1965 Act did not preempt state law damages actions; the 1969 Act preempts petitioner's claims based on a failure to warn and the neutralization of federally mandated warnings to the extent that those claims rely on omissions or inclusions in respondents' advertising or promotions; the 1969 Act does not preempt petitioner's claims based on express warranty, intentional fraud and misrepresentation, or conspiracy.

The judgment of the Court of Appeals is accordingly reversed in part and affirmed in part, and the case is remanded for further proceedings consistent with this opinion.

It is so ordered.

| 8.5 | # Greed on Trial (2004) |

Alex Beam

My favorite moment during last winter's $1.3 billion Massachusetts tobacco-fee trial came near the end, when Ronald Kehoe, an avuncular, white-haired assistant attorney general, was questioning the state's star witness, Thomas Sobol. Sobol was describing how his former law firm, Brown Rudnick Berlack & Israels, prepared in 1995 to sue Big Tobacco on behalf of the Commonwealth.

Sobol testified that to reduce its risk on what looked like a long-shot lawsuit, Brown Rudnick hired a bunch of cheapo "contract" lawyers, at $25 to $35 an hour, and also cut back on its pro bono commitment, redirecting $1 million worth of work to the anti-tobacco litigation.

Kehoe: Was the tobacco litigation seen by the firm as a form of pro bono activity in part?

Robert Popeo [*Brown Rudnick's attorney, jumping out of his chair*]: Objection, your Honor.

Judge Allan Van Gestel: Sustained.

Did Brown Rudnick view the anti-tobacco lawsuit, which would later pay out the largest legal fee in the Commonwealth's history, as pro bono work? I asked Sobol that question over hot chocolate at Johnny's Luncheonette, in Newton, Massachusetts. Both on and off the stand the forty-six-year-old Sobol cuts a bold figure, closely resembling Bruce Springsteen before the Boss started showing his age. For want of a better term, Sobol—not unlike Jan Schlichtmann, the Boston lawyer who litigated the toxic-waste case made famous in the book and movie *A Civil Action*—has star quality. In one of several tendrils linking the two cases, which were tried in the same downtown courtroom, Schlichtmann and Sobol were briefly colleagues, before quarreling over the—yes—fees in a high-profile class-action suit, unrelated to tobacco.

Sobol told me that some of his Brown Rudnick colleagues did view the tobacco project as pro

bono work. "It wasn't considered 'real lawyering,'" he said, "because we were suing corporate America, not defending corporate America. And we weren't making any money on a day-to-day basis." He added, "But this was a fee transaction. We weren't rendering services for free."

No, not exactly. Brown Rudnick and four other firms representing Massachusetts had secured a 25 percent contingency fee in the tobacco litigation. And that litigation paid off hugely. In 1998 a master settlement agreement (MSA) between forty-six states and Big Tobacco awarded Massachusetts $8.3 billion over twenty-five years, in purported Medicaid losses resulting from smoking. The tobacco companies also agreed to pay the states' legal fees, in many cases relying on an arbitration panel to decide how much each legal team deserved. As the lead law firm for the Commonwealth, Brown Rudnick hit the jackpot. Having invested about $10 million in time and expenses, it won $178 million from the panel, which awarded Massachusetts, of all the states covered by the MSA, the highest legal fees—$775 million in all. In court the state noted that Brown Rudnick's chief of litigation, Frederick Pritzker (also the chairman of its ethics committee), had siphoned off $14 million for seventy hours of work: a rate of $200,000 an hour. Sobol, the lead lawyer, received $13 million. On paper each Brown Rudnick partner stood to make an average of $140,000 a year from this case alone.

But the big numbers equaled only 9.3 percent of the $8.3 billion award. Brown Rudnick asked the state for a compromise between the 9.3 percent and the promised 25 percent fee. Attorney General Thomas Reilly refused to pay a penny more than the arbitration award. Now Brown Rudnick and the four other firms were back in court, asking for the full 25 percent: $1.3 billion more in fees. Brown Rudnick and the others were actually making the tobacco companies look good.

The events that landed the lawyers in Judge van Gestel's cavernous Art Deco courtroom had not exactly heaped honor on either side. Lawyers for

Alex Beam, "Greed on Trial," in The Atlantic Online, June 2004. Reprinted by permission of the author. Alex Beam is a columnist at the *Boston Globe*.

every state in the Union had collected unheard-of fees from the lawsuits that led up to the MSA; Big Tobacco had signed the agreement, which reimbursed the forty-six states for $206 billion worth of smoking-related medical costs, in exchange for protection from further litigation by the states. In Florida, one of four states that settled outside the MSA process, lawyers had also negotiated a 25 percent contingency fee; that fee equaled $2.8 billion, a sum that "simply shocks the conscience of this court," one Florida judge observed. A year after Florida settled, arbitrators awarded its eleven law firms an even larger fee: $3.4 billion—or an average of $300 million each.

The MSA fee arbitration resulted in the doling out of checks on a generous if unscientific basis. The first states to sue won a bonus for getting the ball rolling; the Massachusetts lawyers' $775 million (which amounted to an average of more than $7,700 an hour) reflected the state's role as one of the key participants. In other states lawyers lifted their fingers to the wind of public opinion and eventually settled for the arbitration awards, which were by any reasonable standard gargantuan. (Lawyers in Texas ended up accepting "only" $3.3 billion. They had asked for $25 billion—more than the state's settlement amount—but soon came around. The former Texas attorney general is in jail for trying to defraud the tobacco fund; but that, as they say, is another story.) Brown Rudnick and a co-plaintiff, the San Francisco partnership of Lieff Cabraser, Heimann & Bernstein, decided to sue for their full fees.

While the lawyers were grubbing, the state was hardly covering itself in glory. Scott Harshbarger, who as the Massachusetts attorney general signed the contingency-fee deal in 1995, ran for governor three years later. His opponent, the incumbent Paul Cellucci, made the "obscene" tobacco fees a campaign issue—as did Governor George W. Bush in Texas. In the heat of the campaign Harshbarger pulled Massachusetts out of the increasingly controversial MSA negotiations. He lost the election anyway, and the state joined the agreement. This allowed Cellucci and his Republican successors to feast on the multimillion-dollar settlement revenues.

By 2000 the word was out across the country that many states were squandering the vast sums raining down on them from the MSA. In theory the money was earmarked for medical care, or for anti-smoking education targeted especially at young

people. In practice most legislatures used it for budget balancing or more exotic purposes. In Los Angeles some of the money was designated for improving wheelchair access on sidewalks; and then-mayor Richard Riordan proposed using some to settle abuse claims filed against the Los Angeles Police Department. In Massachusetts the governor and the legislature pillaged the tobacco awards in short order to balance the state budget.

Perversely, the tobacco money proved to be addictive. In 2003 the attorneys general of thirty-three states sided with Philip Morris against an Illinois court that wanted the company to post a $12 billion bond after it lost a huge class-action case. Philip Morris loudly proclaimed that posting the bond would bankrupt it, thus threatening its MSA payments to the states. The litigating lions saved the shorn tobacco lamb; at the behest of the states, the court reduced the bond to a more manageable $6.8 billion.

During the course of *Brown Rudnick, et al. v. The Commonwealth of Massachusetts,* in a sidebar conversation with Robert Popeo and the Commonwealth's lead attorney, Dean Richlin, the sixty-eight-year-old Judge van Gestel, an old-fashioned lawyer who referred to the law in wistful tones as a "learned profession," expressed shock at the states' plumping for Big Tobacco.

Van Gestel: That's, in my view, a very sad event, in that the states have to keep the evil empire, as it's been called, afloat.

Richlin: Exactly so.

Van Gestel: The next thing you know, the states will be having Joe Camel as the logo. I mean, I only meant that partly facetiously. . . . To me, it's an outrage.

The humorist Dave Barry had great sport with the tobacco litigation, noting,

> [The states] are distributing the money as follows: (1) Legal fees; (2) Money for attorneys; (3) A whole bunch of new programs that have absolutely nothing to do with helping smokers stop smoking; and (4) Payments to law firms. Of course, not all the anti-tobacco settlement is being spent this way. A lot of it also goes to lawyers.

. . . I have served on a jury, and in my experience nothing is more powerful than a Friday deadline. Not surprisingly, this jury announced its verdict before lunch on a Friday. A reasonable fee, it concluded, would be 10.5 percent. The cap on annual payments by the tobacco firms virtually ensured that the lawyers would never receive their full fee. Frederick Pritzker's grandchildren would have to go out and earn a living, just as their grandfather had.

It must have been a good decision, because both sides claimed victory, and neither party appealed the verdict. Brown Rudnick and Mintz Levin contended that they had won another $100 million in fees. "I don't have many cases with verdicts of $100 million," Popeo crowed. "If that's not a victory, you have great expectations." But Richlin's boss, Tom Reilly, pointed out that the extra money would probably never reach the lawyers, because the payment stream would be halted in 2025, before the full fee had been paid. "The state of Massachusetts doesn't owe a dime to the law firms," Reilly said. "They got what they deserved."

If Reilly runs for higher office, he may lose twelve potential votes—those of the jurors. When she read the quotation in the newspaper, JoAnn Schwartzman told me, "It all hurt. We had a very difficult job, and we weren't trying to make a political statement. We weren't trying to reward or punish anyone."

I've said the trial was boring, and it was. But it was the kind of ennui that commercial airline pilots describe—boredom punctuated by rare moments of intense concentration. During [expert witness Charles] Silver's lengthy testimony Richlin introduced an excerpt from one of Silver's articles that spoke of the "war . . . waged for control of the civil justice system."

Richlin: Sir, did you feel then that a war was being waged for control of the civil justice system?

Silver: I felt then that the war was waged, and I know today that the war continues to be waged. It's being fought in this courtroom in front of this jury.

Richlin: You feel that what we are doing here is part of the war for the civil justice system, sir?

Silver: Absolutely. I think you would have to be blind not to recognize the political overtones in this lawsuit.

I caught up with Silver . . . in Austin. . . . What, exactly, had he and Richlin been talking about? "Well, you have the trial lawyers on one side, and the insurance companies, the tobacco companies, and the other product defendants on the other side," he said. Richlin agreed, and was even willing to fill in some details of Silver's vision: trial lawyers are generous financial supporters of the Democratic Party, and their opponents in industry, as a rule, support Republicans.

Not for nothing did Joe Rice, a veteran of the asbestos and tobacco wars, donate to the presidential campaign of the Democratic Senator John Edwards, himself an accomplished plaintiff's lawyer. Likewise, Rice also opposed the recent failed effort by Senate Republicans to confiscate all legal fees collected after June 1, 2002, by plaintiffs and class-action lawyers. Officially proposed as the Intermediate Sanctions Compensatory Revenue Adjustment Act, it was nicknamed the "one-yacht-per-lawyer bill." Rice called the bill "the greatest attack on civil rights that's occurred in this century outside of racial [issues], obviously," according to *The American Lawyer* magazine.

The war never ends, this line of theorizing goes. Yesterday the lawyers bankrupted the silicone-breast-implant and asbestos industries. Today they have targeted cigarette and handgun manufacturers. Tomorrow, as everyone knows, they will take on the nefarious merchants of trans fat: McDonald's, Frito-Lay, Taco Bell.

The Richlin-Silver exchange made for great theater, and ever since I have been wondering: Did I sit in a courtroom off and on for six weeks watching lawyers battle for the heart and soul of our civil justice system? Was the case, as Popeo explained to me afterward, a unique test of the separation of powers, of the sanctity of the contract—indeed, of the integrity of the state?

Or was I simply watching some of the best litigators on the East Coast wrangle over astronomical sums of money—sums that few of us laypeople could even understand?

I think I know the answer.

A Comparative Perspective

8.6   Class Action Lawsuits (2004)

Ian Bell

You'll have seen the adverts. Trip over in the street: sue someone. Drop a hammer on your foot: sue someone. Spill hot coffee in your lap: sue everyone in sight. What the lawyers call a legal remedy is becoming a panacea for anyone hoping to make a few bob from a minor grievance. It is an American habit, one we have imported over the last decade, and it is a habit that even eternally litigious Americans are coming to regret. They call it the compensation culture.

The problem it raises is threefold. First, as the cheesy ads show, the growing desire to sue or claim compensation for loss or injury, real or imagined, is bringing out the worst in some members of the legal profession. Justice and cash, as so often, are becoming confused.

Secondly, nuisance claims are a costly waste of valuable time that only push up insurance premiums for everyone and lead to absurd institutional precautions. Individuals, shops, local government, companies large and small: nobody wants to get sued and everyone is looking for ways to avoid taking what ought to be proper responsibility for their actions.

Thirdly, and most importantly, trivial claims and the reaction to them create the danger that real injustices will go unanswered. In America, the Bush administration is already pushing for "tort reform" with the clear intention of making it harder for individuals to sue big companies. This might have the welcome result of deterring someone from suing a food company because they ate too much and got fat. It might just as easily—and this is probably the idea—make it harder to bring corporate criminals to book.

The issue of compensation, in any case, confuses the relationship between the individual and soci-

ety. A financial settlement might be good for the individual who lands it, but does nothing for the common good. Take the smaller of England's teaching unions, the National Association of Schoolmasters Union of Women Teachers [NASUWT]. Amazingly, it currently advises its 220,000 members not to take pupils away on school trips for fear teachers could be sued or prosecuted if anything goes wrong.

This is clearly scarcely an advance for education, particularly where deprived children are concerned. It is, nevertheless, a typical effect of the compensation culture. Things which were once taken for granted, simple, innocent things, are now deemed too dangerous to risk. Nobody would argue that a negligent teacher should go unpunished. The NASUWT's position instead is that thousands of perfectly competent teachers should avoid any risk of even being involved in a simple accident.

The irony of this became clear when the union held its annual conference in Llandudno [Wales] last week. Not content with attempting to render themselves immune to compensation claims, its members decided that they wanted a piece of the action. Aggrieved at the number of accusations of physical or sexual abuse made against them that turn out to be malicious, the teachers voted to demand the right to sue their own pupils for compensation.

In one sense the reaction is understandable. If the NASUWT is to be believed, only 69 out of 1782 allegations made against its members over the last decade led to convictions. Delegates also argued, rightly, that such accusations are horribly damaging to innocent teachers, their families and their schools. Even when innocence can be demonstrated, mud sticks. Proceedings can go on for months, sometimes years, with teachers suspended and under constant suspicion. Schools and children's services, meanwhile, tend to take children at their word, not least in the current climate of fear generated by paedophilia.

But suing pupils? Aside from the fact that legal actions cannot be brought against minors, how would compensation clear anyone's name? It also seems obvious that the threat of legal action would be a useful means of intimidation in the hands of a real abuser. There are well-documented reasons, after all, why allegations made by children are taken seriously. The few that are true are vastly more important than the many that are malicious— however painful the experience for innocent teachers.

NASUWT members want more. Last week they also demanded that teachers facing allegations should be guaranteed anonymity until a conviction is secured. This, like compensation, is another legalistic fad that is growing in popularity. The logic of it in the case of children or rape victims is easy to demonstrate. But why should a teacher facing serious allegations be any different from anyone else who has been accused of a crime? If stigma and public humiliation are the issues, why shouldn't every accused be anonymous? Because, simply put, the principle that justice must be seen to be done would be destroyed.

Yet again the demand for a right to compensation corrupts the argument. The real danger is of the entire notion that some people in some circumstances certainly do deserve recompense for falling into disrepute. The legal status of children gives teachers a particular problem, but if the NASUWT has its way then other professions, particularly in the social services, would surely follow. Why not? The teaching union's policy on school trips is the perfect example of where compensation culture leads. Yet the same union wants to extend that culture. If everyone got in on the act the result would be social paralysis.

Governments would not allow that, of course. The trouble is that by acting to prevent nuisance claims governments will also be able to prevent truly wronged individuals seeking redress. If it comes to a choice between big business and ordinary people we know how politicians here, as much as in America, will jump. No more Erin Brockovich, no more compensation for industrial malpractice, no more attempts to at least obtain a little limited satisfaction after corporate wrongdoing. Company directors in this country are already able to avoid personal responsibility when their firms' health and safety failures lead to injury and death. "Tort reform," Bush-style, would render them all but immune.

That, though, is the direction in which we are heading. The NASUWT clearly feels there is an inherent unfairness in the way allegations against its members are handled. They believe there is more than a whiff of "guilty until proven innocent" in the way such cases are processed. But in demanding the right to claim compensation they exchange self-protection for self-interest. An innocent teacher suffers no financial loss and you do not end mental torment with a bundle of fivers.

On the other side of the coin, you wonder what will remain if such trends continue. No more school sports? No more swimming lessons? No more cutting paper for Christmas decorations? A society lapsing into the insane belief that the world should contain no possible risks? Or a society in which the idea of redress is banished because stupid, greedy people have rendered the system unworkable and given governments the excuse to hobble legitimate litigants?

The chances are that the British government will soon have to take a long and hard look at the laws governing compensation. Something like the legislation governing criminal injuries or Legal Aid might be required to standardize claims procedures and put an end to frivolous complaints. At least it would give certain lawyers something useful to do.

Teachers like the members of the NASUWT are, to some extent, stuck with their problem. Their profession is paying the price for society's necessary vigilance towards child abuse. You can sympathise with their desire to have some protection against the little beasts who are simply vicious or who fail to understand the consequences of their actions. But teachers are not miners; fighting for years for justice after their jobs and their employers ruined their bodies. Neither are teachers alone in believing themselves to be innocent victims of a grim social phenomenon. But the idea of a teacher suing a pupil is as wrong-headed as it is dangerous.

Malicious and serious complaints should always carry a penalty, whatever the age of the accuser. Punishments could be devised within the school system. Why is the union not calling for that reform, rather than the chance to put a cash price on hurt and humiliation? Perhaps because increasingly money is the only language our society understands. The irony, if such is your taste, is that we will pay a heavy price for it.

For Further Reading

Katz, Sanford N. *Family Law in America.* New York: Oxford University Press, 2004.

Kluger, Richard. *Ashes to Ashes: America's Hundred-Year Cigarette War, the Public Health, and the Unabashed Triumph of Philip Morris.* New York: Vintage Books, 1997.

Kritzer, Herbert and Susan S. Silbey. *In Litigation: Do the "Haves" Still Come Out Ahead?* Stanford, Calif.: Stanford University Press, 2003.

Sarat, Austin, ed. *The Social Organization of Law: Introductory Readings.* Los Angeles: Roxbury, 2004.

Chapter 9

The Politics of Appellate Courts

Introduction

As their name suggests, appellate courts hear appeals from lower courts. This function has two primary purposes. One is to evaluate the outcomes of lower courts; if a litigant is dissatisfied with the lower court's ruling, the appellate court may review the ruling for mistakes made in the application of the law. In so doing, appellate courts facilitate justice by regulating the processes by which litigants are found responsible for wrongdoing. The other purpose of appellate courts is to clarify the law. Laws are often open to interpretation, and inconsistent application of laws by judges, juries, and lawyers may mean that different litigants are treated differently. The significance that we place on equal justice requires that there be some method of resolving conflicts among competing interpretations of law. Thus, while most cases are not appealed from trial courts, those that are provide appellate courts with the significant responsibility of continually fine-tuning legal processes and laws, and promoting greater consistency and equality in the justice system.

How appellate courts go about their work is the focus of much legal and scholarly attention, as the readings in this chapter reveal. Our selections highlight many of the issues related to the business of appellate courts, among them the origin of circuit courts, the processes by which decisions are made, the factors relevant to decision making, and the relative success of litigants. While the emphasis is on the federal appellate courts, many of the concepts, ideas, and arguments are also applicable to state appellate courts.

Foundations and History

The Supreme Court of the United States is the only federal court that is mandated by the Constitution. According to Article III, the creation of other federal courts was left to Congress: "The judicial Power of the United States, shall be vested in one supreme Court, and in such inferior Courts as the Congress may from time to time ordain and establish." In the Judiciary Act of 1789, Congress established the organization of the federal courts, creating district and circuit courts. But at that time these lower courts had very different functions than they do now. District courts dealt with admirality and maritime cases, while circuit courts functioned largely as trial courts. It took over one hundred years for Congress, in the Evarts Act of 1891, to create a system of circuit courts of appeals. We include the text of the Evarts Act in this chapter.

One of the primary purposes of the Evarts Act was to reduce the workload of Supreme Court justices. In his article, "On the Road: The Supreme Court and the History of Circuit Riding" (2003), Joshua Glick elaborates on the work required of the justices before and after the creation of the circuit courts of appeals. As the title suggests, Glick emphasizes the practical difficulties associated with the requirement that justices sit on circuit courts across the country. He also describes the role that the Court played in lobbying Congress for an end to riding the circuit.

Contemporary Judicial Politics

Appellate courts are important sources of policy at both the state and federal level. Most of us are aware of the policy significance of supreme courts, but intermediate appellate courts can be quite powerful too. These courts include the federal circuit courts of appeals. Among the most newsworthy federal circuit court rulings of the past several years is *Newdow v. U.S. Congress et al.* (2002), also known as the Pledge of Allegiance case, which was ruled on by the Ninth Circuit Court of Appeals. Notwithstanding the Supreme Court's reversal of that ruling, we include it here as an example of the significant constitutional conflicts that intermediate appellate courts may be asked to resolve. This case also demonstrates the role of hierarchy and precedent in appellate court decision making as the Ninth Circuit argues about the significance of adhering to Supreme Court rulings in other religion cases.

While Newdow won at the Ninth Circuit against the United States, empirical research by Donald R. Songer, Reginald S. Sheehan, and Susan B. Haire suggests that this is not typical. In their article, "Do the 'Haves' Come Out Ahead Over Time? Applying Galanter's Framework to Decisions of the U.S. Courts of Appeals" (1999), they find that in most appellate cases, litigants who have the most resources (including money, time, and expertise) and who are repeat players in the justice system tend to win. This is particularly true for the U.S. government when it is a party to a case.

Another conclusion of Songer et al. is that the partisanship of judges influences case outcomes. Similarly, in their article, "Judging by Where You Sit" (2003), David A. Schkade and Cass R. Sunstein argue that judicial ideology matters in appellate court decision making. Specifically, the data demonstrate that the debate about judicial selection is not merely political rhetoric or symbolism. Not only do Republican judges make more conservative decisions than do Democrats (and vice versa), but different combinations of Republicans and Democrats on the three-judge circuit panels influence case outcomes.

A View from the Inside

We have selected two articles written by judges that discuss the significance of the appellate opinion-writing process for the legitimacy of the courts' rulings. In "Speaking in a Judicial Voice" (1992), then District of Columbia Circuit Court of Appeals Judge Ruth Bader Ginsburg discusses what it means for appellate courts to speak authoritatively from the bench. She argues that it is important for courts that hear cases in panels of multiple judges—three-judge panels at the circuit level and a nine-judge panel at the Supreme Court—to be collegial. This is not to say that judges who disagree with the majority opinion should not dissent, but that they should do so in a way that does not detract from the efforts of the court to legitimize its rulings. Similarly, in "The Work of Appellate Judges" (2001) Judge Dennis J. Sweeney emphasizes the need for judges to do their own research and writing to increase the legitimacy of their courts.

There is some debate about whether oral arguments before appellate benches influence judicial rulings. Nevertheless, lawyers do make oral arguments and we have included two short articles written by lawyers, one by David I. Bruck and one by J. Thomas Sullivan. Each describes his experiences arguing for the first time before the U.S. Supreme Court. Not only are their stories fascinating but their perceptions provide an interesting glimpse into this part of the Court's decision-making process.

A Comparative Perspective

The nature of appellate court decision making has attracted the attention of many political scientists who focus on courts in other countries. In their article, "Judicial Decisionmaking and the Use of Panels in the Canadian Supreme Court and the South African Appellate Division" (2003), Lori Hausegger and Stacia Haynie use the research on American circuit courts and the Supreme Court to inform their study of Canadian and South African appellate courts. Specifically, they test the hypothesis that policy preferences influence judicial behavior. They do not look at case outcomes, however. Rather, they examine the factors that affect the processes by which appellate judges are selected to sit on the panels that make the decisions. In so doing, they demonstrate that political behavior by judges is not unique to American courts.

Foundations and History

9.1   The Evarts Act: Establishment of the U.S. Circuit Courts of Appeals (1891)

CHAP. 517.

An Act to establish circuits courts of appeals and to define and regulate in certain cases the jurisdiction of the courts of the United States, and for other purposes.

Be it enacted by the Senate and House of Representatives of the United States of America in Congress assembled, That there shall be appointed by the President of the United States, by and with the advice and consent of the Senate, in each circuit an additional circuit judge, who shall have the same qualifications, and shall have the same power and jurisdiction therein that the circuit judges of the United States, within their respective circuits, now have under existing laws, and who shall be entitled to the same compensation as the circuit judges of the United States in their respective circuits now have.

Sec. 2.   That there is hereby created in each circuit a court of appeals, which shall consist of three judges, of whom two shall constitute a quorum, and which shall be a court of record with appellate jurisdiction, as is hereafter limited and established. . . .

The court shall have power to establish all rules and regulations for the conduct of the business of the court within its jurisdiction as conferred by law.

Sec. 3.   That the Chief-Justice and the associate justices of the Supreme Court assigned to each circuit, and the circuit judges within each circuit, and the several district judges within each circuit, shall be competent to sit as judges of the circuit court of appeals within their respective circuits in the manner hereinafter provided. In case the Chief-Justice or an associate justice of the Supreme Court should attend at any session of the circuit court of appeals he shall preside, and the circuit judges in attendance upon the court in the absence of the Chief-Justice or associate justice of the Supreme Court

shall preside in the order of the seniority of their respective commissions.

In case the full court at any time shall not be made up by the attendance of the Chief-Justice or an associate justice of the Supreme Court and circuit judges, one or more district judges within the circuit shall be competent to sit in the court according to such order or provision among the district judges as either by general or particular assignment shall be designated by the court: *Provided*, That no justice or judge before whom a cause or question may have been tried or heard in a district court, or existing circuits court, shall sit on the trial or hearing of such cause or question in the circuit court of appeals. A term shall be held annually by the circuit court of appeals in the several judicial circuits at the following places: In the first circuit, in the city of Boston; in the second circuit, in the city of New York; in the third circuit, in the city of Philadelphia; in the fourth circuit, in the city of Richmond; in the fifth circuit, in the city of New Orleans; in the sixth circuit, in the city of Cincinnati; in the seventh circuit, in the city of Chicago; in the eighth circuit, in the city of St. Louis; in the ninth circuit, in the city of San Francisco; and in such other places in each of the above circuits as said court may from time to time designate. The first terms of said courts shall be held on the second Monday in January, eighteen hundred and ninety-one, and thereafter at such times as may be fixed by said courts. . . .

Sec. 5.   That appeals or writs of error may be taken from the district courts or from the existing circuit courts direct to the Supreme Court in the following cases:

In any case in which the jurisdiction of the court is in issue; in such cases the question of jurisdiction alone shall be certified to the Supreme Court from the court below for decision.

From the final sentences and decrees in prize causes.

In cases of conviction of a capital or otherwise infamous crime.

In any case that involves the construction or application of the Constitution of the United States.

In any case in which the constitutionality of any law of the United States, or the validity or construction of any treaty made under its authority is drawn in question.

In any case in which the constitution or law of a State is claimed to be in contravention of the Constitution of the United States.

Nothing in this act shall affect the jurisdiction of the Supreme Court in cases appealed from the highest court of a State, nor the construction of the statute providing for review of such cases.

Sec. 6.   That the circuit courts of appeals established by this act shall exercise appellate jurisdiction to review by appeal or by writ of error final decision in the district court and the existing circuit courts in all cases other than those provided for in the preceding section of this act, unless otherwise provided by law, and the judgments or decrees of the circuit courts of appeals shall be final in all cases in which the jurisdiction is dependent entirely upon the opposite parties to the suit or controversy, being aliens and citizens of the United States or citizens of different States; also in all cases arising under the patent laws, under the revenue laws, and under criminal laws as in admiralty cases, excepting that in every such subject within its appellate jurisdiction the circuit court of appeals at any time may certify to the Supreme Court of the United States any questions or propositions of law concerning which it desires the instruction of that court for its proper decision. And thereupon the Supreme Court many either give its instruction on the questions and propositions certified to it, which shall be binding upon the circuit courts of appeals in such case, or it may require that the whole record and cause may be sent up to it for its consideration, and thereupon shall decide the whole matter in controversy in the same manner as if it had been brought there for review by writ of error or appeal.

And excepting also that in any such case as is hereinbefore made final in the circuit court of appeals it shall be competent for the Supreme Court to require, by certiorari or otherwise, any such case to be certified to the Supreme Court for its review and determination with the same power and authority in the case as if it had been carried by appeal or writ of error to the Supreme Court.

In all cases not hereinbefore, in this section, made final there shall be of right an appeal or writ of error or review of the case by the Supreme Court of the United States where the matter in controversy shall exceed one thousand dollars besides costs. But no such appeal shall be taken or writ of error sued out unless within one year after the entry of the order, judgment, or decree sought to be reviewed. . . .

Sec. 10.   That whenever on appeal or writ of error or otherwise a case coming directly from the district court or existing circuit court shall be reviewed and determined in the Supreme Court the cause shall be remanded to the proper district or circuit court for further proceedings to be taken in pursuance of such determination. And whenever on appeal or writ of error or otherwise a case coming from a circuit court of appeals shall be reviewed and determined in the Supreme Court the cause shall be remanded by the Supreme Court to the proper district or circuit court for further proceedings in pursuance of such determination. Whenever on appeal or writ or error or otherwise a case coming from a district or circuit court shall be reviewed and determined in the circuit court of appeals in a case in which the decision in the circuit court of appeals is final such cause shall be remanded to the said district or circuit court for further proceedings to be there taken in pursuance of such determination.

Sec. 11.   . . . [A]ll provisions of law now in force regulating the methods and system of review, through appeals or writs of error, shall regulate the methods and system of appeals and writs of error provided for in this act in respect of the circuit courts of appeals, including all provisions for bonds or other securities to be required and taken on such appeals and writs of error, and any judge of the circuit courts of appeals, in respect of cases to be brought to that court, shall have the same powers and duties as to the allowance of appeals or writs of error, and the conditions of such allowance, as now by law belong to the justices or judges in respect of the existing courts of the United States respectively.

Sec. 12. That the circuit court of appeals shall have the powers specified in section seven hundred and sixteen of the Revised Statutes of the United States.

Sec. 13. Appeals and writs of error may be taken and prosecuted from the decisions of the United States court in the Indian Territory to the Supreme Court of the United States, or to the circuit court of appeals in the eighth circuit, in the same manner and under the same regulations as from the circuit or district courts of the United States, under this act. . . .

Sec. 15. That the circuit court of appeal in cases which the judgments of the circuit courts of appeal are made final by this act shall have the same appellate jurisdiction, by writ of error or appeal, to review the judgments, orders, and decrees of the supreme courts of the several Territories as by this act they may have to review judgments, orders, and decrees of the district court and circuit courts; and for that purpose the several Territories shall, by orders of the Supreme court, to be made from time to time, be assigned to particular circuits.

Approved, March 3, 1891.

9.2   On the Road: The Supreme Court and the History of Circuit Riding (2003)

Joshua Glick

Introduction

Circuit riding—the system of sending Supreme Court Justices around the country to serve as judges of the various federal circuit courts—is not a topic that is given much direct attention in Supreme Court history, constitutional law scholarship or in law school classes on constitutional law. Indeed, Chief Justice William H. Rehnquist, remarking that the practice of circuit riding is not often discussed, said, "few lawyers and law students are aware that the Judiciary Act of 1789 created circuit courts but no circuit judges."

Nevertheless, circuit riding was officially part of the Supreme Court for the first 121 years of its history. Throughout this time, the practice was reviled by most justices, who complained bitterly about having to travel and having less time to spend attending to their duties in the nation's capital. In fact, the first Court even agreed to take a reduction in salary in exchange for Congress appointing a separate circuit judiciary.

Congress viewed the practice differently. For the majority, circuit riding transformed the justices into

"republican schoolmasters" who brought federal authority and national political views to the states. Equally important, circuit riding enhanced the justices' ability to contribute to the formation of national law by exposing them to local political sentiments and legal practices.

For years, the many efforts to abolish the practice that came before Congress all failed. Indeed, the history of circuit riding can just as easily be called the "history to abolish circuit riding." Throughout its existence, two main criticisms of the practice stand out. First, the justices disliked riding circuit because they loathed the traveling. The practice caused serious physical hardships during the burgeoning days of the Republic. Second, the justices found it impossible to attend simultaneously to the ever-growing docket of the Supreme Court and to their circuit duties. This was especially true of the Court in the latter part of the nineteenth century.

For a long time Congress showed a complete unwillingness to come to the aid of the Court and abolish circuit riding. Most members of Congress held firm to the belief that circuit riding benefited the justices and the populous, and they turned a deaf ear to the corps of justices that desired to abolish the practice. Alone, the judicial branch lacked the influence to effectuate change.

Reprinted by permission of *Cardoza Law Review.*

Gradually, however, circuit riding lost support. The Court's increasing business in the nation's capital following the Civil War made the circuit riding seem anachronistic and impractical and a slow shift away from the practice began. The Judiciary Act of 1869 established a separate circuit court judiciary. The justices retained nominal circuit riding duties until 1891 when the Circuit Court of Appeals Act was passed. With the Judicial Code of 1911, Congress officially ended the practice. The struggle between the legislative and judicial branches over circuit riding was finally concluded.

In general, this struggle over circuit riding was fought on practical, not constitutional grounds. The two main criticisms of traveling and the ever-increasing docket formed the basis of most of the complaints that the justices laid before Congress. Indeed, the constitutionality of the practice was raised on rare occasion by several justices including Chief Justice John Jay and Chief Justice John Marshall, but when the question came before the Court in 1803 in the case of *Stuart v. Laird,* the justices held the practice constitutional. They did so not by looking at the Constitution, but by looking at the institutional practice of the Court since 1789. The Court, declared the justices, had acquiesced and ridden circuit for too many years for the practice to be deemed unconstitutional. . . .

The Practice of Circuit Riding

Article III of the United States Constitution established the authority and scope of the federal judiciary, but it was not a self-executing provision. For the first eleven months of its existence, the federal government had no judiciary. However, the Senate's first order of business was to enact the necessary legislation to formally establish a system of federal courts, and Senate Bill Number One ultimately became the Judiciary Act of 1789. The system created consisted of a Supreme Court comprised of five associate justices and one chief justice, as well as a two-tiered system of inferior courts comprised of three circuit courts, situated in the eastern, middle and southern portions of the country, and district courts, one located in each state.

The Judiciary Act of 1789 did not provide for separate circuit court judges. Instead, it required that the justices of the Supreme Court also serve as judges of the circuit courts. The Act required two Supreme Court Justices to "ride" twice each year to one of the three circuits where they would sit as a panel with the district judge from the state of original jurisdiction.

Circuit riding was established for several important reasons. First were the cost factors: circuit riding saved money for both the federal government and for the litigants. Only two sets of national judges were created and the first Congress felt that the early federal payroll could not accommodate a separate set of circuit judges. Additionally, giving litigants two Supreme Court Justices at their trial heightened the finality of those trials, thereby lessening the litigants' need to take appeals to a distant Supreme Court, which would have been prohibitively expensive for most people. In fact, the Act's principle drafters explained that the circuit riding provisions had been written to answer such concerns.

Second, since the early circuit courts were courts of original jurisdiction, circuit riding involved the Supreme Court Justices directly at the trial of most of the earliest federal cases. It was important at the time that authorative and correct answers be given to the critical legal questions that were expected to come before the federal courts. Having the justices ride circuit allowed cases to receive immediate attention from the nation's highest judges. This was especially necessary for federal criminal trials because the Judiciary Act of 1789 did not allow for appeals in criminal cases; it vested the circuit courts with exclusive jurisdiction in all criminal matters involving a violation of a federal statute.

Third, circuit riding "[kept] the Federal Judiciary in touch with the local communities," and "brought home to the people of every state a sense of national judicial power through the presence of the Supreme Court Justices." . . . Favorable public opinion was necessary to ensure the survival of the young Republic and the active and visible presence of the justices would help foster loyalty toward the new form of government and somewhat weaken the people's previous allegiance to their state's government.

Fourth, circuit riding by the highest judges of the land enhanced the uniformity of federal law by having the justices review erroneous decisions of state courts that had denied federal rights asserted.

This was an end much desired by Federalists. Furthermore, circuit riding allowed the justices to stay attuned to local law. The justices were assigned to the circuit where they lived and had practiced law in order to ensure that they were familiar with relevant state law. This was necessary because much of the circuit court trial work was in diversity cases where state law was applicable. . . .

Lastly, circuit riding facilitated the development of a unified judicial branch. The Framers were "troubled by the notion of a stationary, geographically-isolated Supreme Court exercising appellate review over a sprawling contingent of atomized judges scattered across the United States." Circuit riding allowed the Supreme Court Justices to keep in touch with the dispersed district courts judges.

Nevertheless, circuit riding was not without its problems. For over 100 years, the Supreme Court had no power to pick and choose the cases that it wanted to adjudicate. . . . Cases came to the Supreme Court's docket from either the district or the circuit courts for mandatory review on a writ of error, rather than a writ of certiorari. This was problematic because the justices sitting together as the Supreme Court heard on appeal the same cases that they had heard on the circuit bench. Although the first Judiciary Act entrusted some appellate jurisdiction to the circuit courts, the circuit courts were primarily trial courts of original jurisdiction; hence, the justices could be, in effect, trial and appellate judges in identical controversies. While the Court had informally adopted a practice by which justices would not adjudicate cases in which they had been involved below, it was sometimes necessary for all available justices to participate in order to have a quorum. Additionally, because the justices rode circuit in rotation beginning in 1792, different justices frequently heard the same cases in their various stages. This made uniformity of practice and decision difficult.

Another problem with circuit riding stemmed from the practice of assigning a justice to the circuit where he lived and practiced. By implication, a president was not free to choose anyone he wanted to fill a Court vacancy. The nominee had to come from the circuit where the previous justice was assigned; otherwise the circuit would be deprived of someone knowledgeable of its state law. . . .

The History of Circuit Riding

The First Court's Struggle with Riding Circuit

The Supreme Court of the United States met for the first time in the Royal Exchange Building in New York City on Monday, February 1, 1790. During that session and the following two terms, there were no cases on the docket and the justices had little to do. Nevertheless, the justices said of their appointment "The duty will be severe." This was due to their circuit duties.

Circuit riding was an arduous task but, because of the landscape of the thirteen original states, it varied from circuit to circuit. Travel through the Eastern Circuit was fatiguing. Travel through the large Middle Circuit was "strenuous but not as bad as it might have been, since judicial travel was entailed only from court city to nearby court city. . . ." However, "the Southern Circuit required long trips through rough, unpopulated, and even unknown terrain" at times in "unpredictably bad nasty weather" with lodgings "uncertain and often unpleasant." . . .

Difficult for healthy men in the prime of life, circuit riding was even more difficult for several of the justices who were aging. Furthermore, because the justices had to spend almost six months a year attending to their circuit duties, they were prevented from spending much time at home or engaging in other pursuits such as the study of law. . . .

Starting in the first term of the Supreme Court, the justices complained bitterly about their circuit duties, and circuit riding became a matter of intense and continual preoccupation for them. The justices of the 1790s were "seasoned politicians" well connected to the political elite. They regularly exchanged correspondence with political figures in the hope of advancing the interests of the Court. As expected, most of the justices' efforts were concentrated in one area: trying to persuade Congress to eliminate or overhaul the circuit riding system.

When the justices returned to New York from their first circuit riding assignments in August of 1790, the question of proposing changes to Congress was the focal point of their session. . . . [They] agreed on the general premise of a letter that Chief Justice John Jay wrote on their behalf to the President. The letter bluntly stated that the circuit riding provision in the Judiciary Act of 1789 was unconstitutional. . . . First, he argued that by instituting circuit riding, Congress had impermissibly extended the de facto original jurisdiction of the Supreme Court. Second, Jay contended that the Supreme Court was created primarily to act as a court of last resort and should not normally sit in judgment of the work that its members had preformed as circuit riding justices of inferior tribunals. . . . Finally, Jay objected to the legislature appointing judges to offices for which they were neither nominated nor confirmed. . . . Without mentioning any of the practical difficulties of circuit riding, Jay requested that Washington ask Congress to repeal the provision. It is unclear whether the final version of this letter was sent to the president. Nevertheless, Congress recognized right from the outset that the Judiciary Act was imperfect and that it would need to be revised. . . .

In his . . . report to Congress the following December, Attorney General Edmund Randolph argued in favor of terminating the justices' circuit riding duties. Randolph advocated that the district court judges be turned into circuit riders, rather than staff the circuit courts separately. . . .

The Chief Justice and other justices were optimistic. . . . In fact, even President Washington was convinced that the system would be modified. . . . Nevertheless, Congress surprised the justices and the President by not acting on the proposal. Randolph's report was buried in committee, where it died. . . .

By 1792, the justices were desperate to eliminate their circuit assignments. On March 15, 1792, Justice James Iredell wrote to Chief Justice Jay to say that the justices should informally suggest to Congress that they each forfeit $500 of their salary in return for being relieved of their circuit riding duties. Considering the Chief Justice earned $4,000 per year and the Associate Justices $3,500 per year, from which traveling expenses had to be deducted, the proposal was not insignificant. . . . There is no evidence that Iredell's salary reduction proposal was ever presented to Congress. . . .

Iredell, however, did use his political connections to obtain some relief from Congress. The Judiciary Act was silent regarding assignments to the circuit courts. . . . Iredell, assigned to the arduous Southern circuit, had urged his brethren on several

occasions that the circuits should be rotated among the justices; however, the other justices were not receptive. . . . Frustrated, he contacted his brother-in-law Senator Johnston. At Johnston's behest, a bill was drafted by the Senate on March 22, 1792. It was approved by the House . . . and the Senate. . . . President Washington signed the bill into law . . . , and the Judiciary Act of 1792 was enacted. The first substantive alteration of the Judiciary Act of 1789, the Act required that "no judge, unless by his own consent, shall have assigned to him any circuit which he hath already attended, until the same hath been afterwards attended by every other of the said judges." . . . The change . . . was able to pass Congress only because it was inherently uncontroversial; it did not fundamentally alter circuit riding's place within the federal judiciary. . . .

To make matters worse, a few weeks prior Congress had passed the Pension Act. The Act, which granted pensions to disabled revolutionary soldiers, thrust upon the justices the new duty of deciding pension claims in the circuit courts and reporting those findings to [the] Secretary of War. Consequently, the justices would be required to increase the amount of time they would have to devote to their circuit duties.

While the justices decided many cases when riding circuit, "the vast majority were the kind of mundane contract and property squabbles that today would be relegated to small claims court." However, the passage of the Pension Act spawned a case of constitutional proportions. Hayburn's Case (and other like cases) was the first instance in which Supreme Court Justices expressed a view on the constitutionality of an act of Congress. In fact, all six justices believed that Congress could not constitutionally use circuit courts to process the veterans' pension applications.

William Hayburn applied for a pension in Pennsylvania. Justices Wilson and Blair, riding circuit, and District Judge Peters refused to consider his claim. They did not file an opinion, but simply entered an order. . . . The justices and district judge recognized that pension administration was an executive task that, delegated to the judiciary, violated the principles of separation of powers. Following the decision, they wrote a letter to President Washington explaining that "it is a principle important to freedom, that, in Government, the judicial should be distinct from, and independent of the legislative department." It is interesting to note that the justices seemed apologetic when writing to Washington. They wrote: "Be assured, that, though it became necessary, [refusing to render a decision] was far from being pleasant. To be obliged to act contrary either to the obvious direction of Congress, or to a Constitutional principle, in our judgment equally obvious, excited feelings in us which we hope never to experience again."

Several months after the justices had rebuffed the pension law, they made their first formal request to Congress to alter the circuit riding system. . . .

They enclosed a separate letter addressed to Congress. . . .

. . . While Congress did respond to the justices, they provided only partial relief. The Judiciary Act of 1793 decreased the justices' circuit riding duties by requiring only one member of the Court to sit on each circuit and decreasing the amount of circuits that each justice would have to ride from two to one per year. . . .

In 1794, the justices again wrote to Congress. While they did not make any direct suggestions because any suggestions they made would be "be capable of being ascribed to personal Considerations," it was clear that they were requesting that circuit riding be abolished. . . .

Upon receiving no assistance from Congress, the justices resorted to self-help in February of 1794. They informally agreed to each pay the justice who rode the Southern Circuit $100 in order to ease his burden. . . .

Nevertheless, the justices still continued to hope for legislative reform. In January of 1796, the Senate appointed a committee to consider alterations of the judicial system. Samuel Johnston wrote to Justice Iredell that he "hoped they will at last see the necessity of having a separate set of Circuit Judges leaving the Judges of the Supreme Court to hold that Court only. . . ." Johnston speculated that the only objection to the plan would be expense. Again, the Justices' hopes were dashed; the committee made no report. Justice Iredell wrote to his wife Hannah, "We are still doomed, I fear, to be wretched Drudges."

In 1797 the justices continued their perennial reform effort. Their letters suggest that they may have drafted the Circuit Court Act of 1797, which revised and streamlined the order of circuit riding in the Eastern, Middle and Southern Circuits. . . .

The next year Chief Justice Oliver Ellsworth was "optimistic about prospects for change." The Senate considered a bill that would have relieved the justices of their circuit riding duties and provided five new districts and two new district judges for the circuit courts. . . . His hopes proved to be false; . . . the Senate voted to postpone further consideration of the bill. It was never brought up again. Not until the Judiciary Act of 1801 did the justices get legislative relief, albeit temporary.

Between the years 1789 and 1799, ten federal judges resigned and several prominent colonial men declined federal judgeships outright. Four of those ten resignations were from Supreme Court Justices who, at least in part, were dissatisfied with their circuit riding responsibilities. As Senator Gouverneur Morris would later remark, candidates for the bench required "less the learning of a judge than the agility of a post-boy."

Chief Justice Jay decided in 1792 that he would leave the Court if changes were not made to the circuit system; purportedly he said that "almost any other Office of suitable Rank and Emolument was preferable" to continuing as Chief Justice. After learning that Congress had failed to abolish circuit riding, Jay decided to make an ultimately unsuccessful bid for the New York governorship. He then changed his mind and remained on the Court, concluding that remaining was tolerable enough because of the partial relief granted by Congress in 1793. Nevertheless, he remained discontented. . . .

Ultimately, Jay was renominated and elected. He resigned from the Court in 1795 and was succeeded by John Rutledge, who was in turn succeeded by Oliver Ellsworth. In 1801, Jay was reappointed to the position of Chief Justice by President John Adams; but he declined the appointment. In a letter to Adams, Jay remarked that given the circuit riding requirements of the office, "independent of other Considerations, the State of my Health removes every Doubt—it being clearly and decidedly incompetent to the fatigues incident to the office." Jay's refusal to accept his commission led Adams to appoint John Marshall as Chief Justice. . . .

The Marshall Court and the Judiciary Act of 1801

In 1801, the outgoing Federalist Congress passed the Judiciary Act of February 19, 1801, modifying the entire judicial system. The Act finally abolished circuit riding. Furthermore, it reduced the number of justices on the Supreme Court from six to five, and established a new set of six circuit courts staffed with sixteen new judges. The Act also "eliminated the embarrassment and apparent impropriety of justices reviewing their own lower court decisions." In creating the new courts, Congress made it more feasible for the Supreme Court to become an institution, regularly meeting in Washington, without being bogged down by the travel required to perform circuit duties.

The Republicans (or Democratic Republicans as they called themselves) quickly denounced the Act, arguing that the dockets of the federal courts did not warrant such an increase in the number of judges; that the bill created new unwarranted federal jobs; and that the great increase of federal power was an infringement upon states' rights and a step toward the complete consolidation of government.

Above all else, the Republicans' worst fear was that all of the newly created judgeships would be filled with Federalists appointed by the outgoing president, John Adams. Their fears were realized; within thirteen days of the bill's enactment, President Adams sent to the Senate a complete list of nominations for the new judgeships. By March 2, the Senate had confirmed all of the appointments. Many of the commissions for these judges were finalized on the President's last day in office; hence they became known historically as the "midnight judges."

The Republicans were furious. President-elect Thomas Jefferson and his party's leaders were determined to repeal the Judiciary Act when the new Congress convened. However, they had more in mind than merely turning back the clock and ridding the judiciary of the new Federalists judges. . . . The Republicans had three contentions: first, the lack of necessity of any increase in the number of federal judges in view of an alleged decrease in the dockets of the federal courts; second, the desirability of the performance of circuit duties by the Supreme Court Justices; and third, the constitutionality of the proposed legislation. Specifically, circuit riding was defended on the ground that the practice acquainted the justices with local law and custom.

The Federalists responded that the Act could not be repealed because of the constitutional provision that grants judges life tenure. They argued that the

independence of the judiciary would be destroyed, because if Congress had the power to wipe out a judge's position whenever it disagreed with its decision, the judiciary would become an unequal branch of government, acting under fear of legislative action. Further, the Federalists claimed that the Act was needed to relieve the Supreme Court Justices of their arduous circuit riding duties. They argued that they "were not convinced that the best way to study law was to ride rapidly from one end of the country to another." It was also contended that most cases decided in the federal courts were predicated on common law, and therefore knowledge of local customs was not required to adjudicate cases.

Predictably, the Republicans (who controlled Congress) ultimately prevailed and the Repeal Act passed the Senate on February 3, 1802, by a vote of sixteen to fifteen. The House . . . passed it by a vote of fifty-nine to thirty-two on March 3, 1802. President Jefferson signed the bill into law on March 31, 1802. The Act eliminated the sixteen newly created judgeships, transferred cases back to the courts where they otherwise would have been heard, and restored the justices' circuit riding duties. Seven weeks later, Congress passed the Judiciary Act of 1802, which divided the country into six circuits. This Act also altered the justices' circuit riding responsibilities by assigning each circuit a separate justice who, together with a district court judge, would compose a circuit court that would convene twice a year.

. . . Fearing that the question of the Repeal Act's constitutionality would immediately be questioned in the courts and presented to the Supreme Court for final decision, the Republicans in Congress resolved to prevent or postpone any such decision until the time when the political power of the administration was stronger. Immediately after the passage of the Repeal Act, yet another bill was introduced that proposed to abolish the new June and December terms of the Supreme Court (created by the Act of 1801), and restore the old February term. . . .

. . . [T]he bill passed the Senate on April 8, the House on April 23, and became law on April 29. With this "legislative maneuver," an adjournment of the court was enforced for fourteen months (December, 1801 to February, 1803). . . .

. . . The judicial branch seemed powerless and at the mercy of a truly vengeful Congress.

The only way that the Court could have stood up to Congress was by not performing its circuit duties. Indeed, since the repeal went into effect during the Court's congressionally-imposed adjournment, the question of performance was the immediate question facing Chief Justice John Marshall and the Court in April 1802. To ride circuit would be to concede the constitutionality of the Repeal Act. On the other hand, choosing not to ride circuit would put the Court in direct opposition to President Jefferson and the Republican majority in Congress. On April 19, 1802, Marshall asked the Associate Justices, via written communication, whether they should comply with the new statute by performing their circuit duties. . . .

Marshall doubted the validity of the Repeal Act and believed that the Constitution required distinct appointments and commissions for Supreme Court Justices and circuit court judges. He wished that the Court would have an opportunity to hear a challenge to the legislation. Nevertheless, as the leader of the Court he stated that he would be guided by the views of his Associates. In light of the overall negative attitude that Congress had taken toward the judiciary in the repeal debates and its success in preventing the Court from meeting for fourteen months, he emphasized the seriousness of the matter about to be decided. . . .

. . . [T]he Chief Justice and his Associates proceeded to hold their circuit courts as usual in the autumn of 1802. It was not until February of 1803 that the Court met again in Washington.

While riding circuit that fall the justices encountered Federalist lawyers who argued that the Repeal Act was unconstitutional. In cases that had been continued from the preceding term when the circuit courts had been staffed by "midnight judges," it was contended that the new circuit court (consisting of a Supreme Court Justice and a district judge) lacked jurisdiction, having been commissioned by a law that unconstitutionally removed life-tenured judges. In all cases but one, the result was the same. Upon hearing the jurisdiction claim and before it could be argued, the court adjourned overnight, the judges and the lawyers then conferred, and the next day the plea was withdrawn or passed over without comment.

The one exception to this pattern was the Fourth Circuit contract case of *Laird v. Stuart*. Plaintiff Laird had obtained a judgment from one of the circuit courts created by the 1801 Act, and sought to enforce it in the court to which jurisdiction had been transferred by the 1802 Repeal Act. The defendant Stuart argued that the court hearing the case following the Repeal Act had no jurisdiction because the statutes replacing the 1801 Act were unconstitutional. Chief Justice Marshall, sitting alone on circuit, heard Stuart's plea to jurisdiction and ruled against him, and in favor of constitutionality, without issuing an opinion. An appeal was taken to the Supreme Court and the constitutionality of the Repeal Act and the practice of circuit riding ultimately came before the Court in *Stuart v. Laird.* The case served as the engine for the Court to finally set to rest the bitter political struggle over the legislation and circuit riding. Marshall recused himself from reviewing his own decision and six days after *Marbury v. Madison* was handed down, the Supreme Court, in a three-paragraph opinion by Justice Paterson, affirmed the circuit court decision.

Stuart presented two constitutional questions: whether Article III judges could be removed from office and whether the Supreme Court Justices could constitutionally sit on circuit courts. Just as Marshall had done in his earlier correspondence, the Court avoided the first question, but decided the second. Federalist Charles Lee, attorney for the defendant and former Attorney General, advanced three arguments as to why it was unconstitutional for the justices to sit on circuit courts. The first argument he offered was that a litigant had the right to have his case determined by six unbiased Supreme Court Justices. Second, he argued that the statute assigning circuit duties to the justices also appointed them as circuit judges and hence was in direct conflict with Appointments Clause, which states that appointments are to be made by the President with advice and consent of the Senate. His third argument stemmed from *Marbury;* the justices could not sit on circuit because the cases they would try there were outside the original jurisdiction of the Supreme Court, as defined by Article III.

The Court, by a unanimous vote, upheld the Repeal Act, but did so without directly addressing the constitutional issues raised by Mr. Lee. . . .

Thus, the Court upheld circuit riding in the face of a constitutional challenge. In contrast to *Marbury,* the opinion was pragmatic and invoked the Court's own acquiesce in circuit riding since 1789. The justices had rode circuit in the past, and therefore did not require specific commission to ride again. In upholding the Repeal Act, the Court avoided getting itself involved in a political battle with the Republican Congress and the President. . . . Despite the Court's on-going struggle with Congress over circuit riding, it showed deference to the legislature's interpretation of the Constitution and thereby failed to forever rid itself of the reviled practice.

Once the controversy subsided, the justices returned to their normal routines. The life of a Marshall Court justice was a strenuous one and salary was relatively low for men of comparable education and prominence. The justices only spent between six weeks and two months a year in Washington. A much larger portion of their time was spent performing their circuit duties where they were forced to be away from their families and homes for extended periods of time and travel through a largely undeveloped country. Justice Joseph Story's travels on the First Circuit provide an overview of circuit riding during the Marshall Court era. Story's spring circuit duties began with the holding of court in Boston on or about May 1. It ended in Providence or Newport, Rhode Island, on or about June 27. Overall, Story had to travel about 2,000 miles to complete his circuit duties. Other justices with less compact circuits needed to allocate much more time to travel. For instance, Justice John McKinley, assigned to the Ninth Circuit, had to allocate approximately six months out of the year to accomplish his judicial duties in Washington and on circuit.

. . . During the latter part of Chief Justice Marshall's tenure, some members of Congress sympathized with the plight of the justices. Bills were introduced to relieve the justices of their circuit riding duties, appoint additional justices, and increase the number of circuits to provide for the growing judicial activity in the West and Southwest.

Many of the opponents of these judicial reform bills were opposed to the elimination of circuit riding. They feared, as Senator William Smith did, that the justices, once relieved of their circuit duties, would become "completely cloistered within the city of Washington, and their decisions, instead of emanating from enlarged and liberal minds, will assume a severe and local character." Senator Abner Lacock warned that Washington lawyers would acquire undue influence and control over the Court, and the justices would be subjected to "dangerous influences and strong temptations that might bias their minds and pollute the streams of national justice."

In 1826, the Court's docket was so heavily congested that some form of legislative relief became imperative; the Court seemed unable to cope with the burden of its dual duties. . . .

The debates for and against abolishing circuit riding were argued with vigor and with "considerable extravagance and often in picturesque language.". . .

Despite the prevailing sentiment favorable to judicial reform, nothing was accomplished by the debate of 1826; Congress was still not willing to abolish circuit riding and the bill was defeated. It is interesting to note that around the same time the bill was defeated the Supreme Court was subject to criticism regarding its decisions affecting the power of the states vis-à-vis the federal government and attempts were being made to contract the Court's jurisdiction. Congress, clashing with the Court over its federalism jurisprudence, was able to use its power to thwart a reformation of the system. . . .

. . . As the Court entered its next era with unchanged obligations, the stage was set for more Congressional battles over circuit riding.

The Middling Years

Roger B. Taney succeeded John Marshall as Chief Justice in 1836. Members of the Taney Court, like those of earlier periods, spent more than half of their time traveling and attending to their circuit duties. At the beginning of the Taney period there were seven circuits with one justice assigned to each. District judges sat with the Supreme Court Justice to hold the circuit courts.

In March of 1837, Congress turned its attention to the judiciary and divided the United States into nine circuits, and added two members to the Supreme Court to perform circuit duties for the new circuits and help the Court deal with its increasing workload. This Act finally gave the West and Southwest two circuits, and eight states were added to the circuit system. It was the duty of every justice to ride circuit once each year for each district within his circuit. . . .

While the justices no longer traveled by horseback, their journeys were still hazardous. . . .

Concurrently, the rapid increase in the dockets of the Supreme Court and circuit courts proved extremely burdensome to the justices. Although it did not produce any immediate responses, the infamous mileage summary and complaints from Justice McKinley (and other justices who thought themselves over-worked), as well as from constituencies who felt that they were inadequately served, prompted another long discussion and attempts at legislation to amend or abolish the circuit system. . . .

In 1853, the Baltimore and Ohio Railroad was completed, promising greater speed and comfort in circuit travel. With a new mode of transportation expanding rapidly, there was a renewed attempt to reform the judicial system by adding additional circuits. The reform was deemed urgent because of the great expansion of the United States' territory, and the large increase in the Court's docket. . . . In 1855, a bill was again introduced that would have added two new circuits and relieved the justices of circuit court duty. The bill was met with the same opposition and arguments as previous bills dealing with the subject matter, but . . . the bill probably would have passed had it not encountered another element of opposition. This opposition came from the opponents of slavery, who feared that if the Court was expanded, President Pierce would appoint two pro-slavery justices.

On the eve of the Civil War, President Abraham Lincoln was determined to improve the federal judicial system. In his first annual message to Congress, he remarked that the federal judicial system had become outgrown and was in need of alteration. . . . Despite the call of President Lincoln and like-minded Senators, circuit riding was not reformed during Lincoln's time in office.

However, during the War, Congress did realize that the judicial system was outgrown and in need of change. It passed the Act of March 3, 1863, which officially established the tenth circuit comprising California and Oregon. . . .

During the War Between the States, the justices did not hold circuit courts in the states that seceded from the Union. However, the justices continued to ride circuit within the Union and encountered cases involving mundane legal matters and war-related issues. In fact, war-related problems arose more often in circuit cases than they did in Supreme Court cases. As a result, justices would first reveal their views on war-related issues on circuit. For instance, Chief Justice Taney was averse to hearing circuit cases that involved arrest for trea-

sonous pro-Southern activities, and deliberately took steps to postpone or delay the cases. . . .

The Union's victory in the Civil War gave rise to new notions of nationalism and national organization. Coupled with an expanding population and industrialization these notions provided an impetus for judicial reform. As the number of cases that came before the Court dramatically increased, the need for an intermediate tier of courts with full appellate jurisdiction became apparent. Change, however, did not happen quickly.

On March 8, 1869, Senator Trumbull again introduced a bill to reform the judicial system. . . . [I]t called for the creation of a circuit judgeship for each circuit, thus providing some relief to the circuit riding justice. Despite moderate opposition, Trumbull's bill passed the Senate on April 23, 1869. After debate in the House, the bill was approved by a vote of ninety to fifty-three. Upon the President's approval, the bill became the Act of April 10, 1869. Congress had at last provided "a long-desired and long-contested judicial reform." The Act established a separate circuit court judiciary. The circuit courts remained the primary court of first instance, and nine new circuit judges were appointed. They had the same powers and jurisdiction as a Supreme Court Justice sitting on circuit. A circuit court could be held by a Supreme Court Justice, the circuit judge, the district judge in his district, or by two sitting together. Under the new system, it was the duty of each Supreme Court Justice to attend at least one term of the circuit court in each district of his circuit once every two years.

While the appointment of specific circuit judges provided the Supreme Court Justices some relief, they were not entirely relieved of their circuit riding duties. . . . Thus, although the stage was being set for its complete abolition, circuit riding entered its final era with a still uncertain fate.

The End of the Road

History demonstrates that as the years progressed, the Supreme Court was unable to deal with its ballooning docket. . . . When examining the period spanning from 1869 to 1911, the arguments for and against circuit riding and broader judicial reform reappear. Indeed, it can be said that since 1790, the same arguments had been advanced over and over. This time, however, the outcome was different. The Supreme Court finally got relief from the legislative branch.

In May 1881, former Justice William Strong published an article in the *North American Review* on "The Needs of the Supreme Court." The article advocated the abolition of circuit riding duties and an overall reorganization of the federal judicial system. Justice Strong bemoaned the increase in the number of cases on the Court's docket. Indeed, for the October 1880 term, the Court had 1212 cases on its docket and because the court lacked discretion over its docket, it was obliged to decide all of the cases. This was an unprecedented increase since in the five years ending in 1880 an average of 391 cases had come to the docket. The justices, he wrote, spent eight to twelve hours a day hearing, conferring, and deciding cases from the opening of the term in October to its conclusion in May. After that, each justice still had to attend to circuit duties. . . .

[Chief Justice Melville] Fuller realized that active circuit duty contributed to the problem of the ever-increasing Supreme Court docket. For more than ten years, various bills for the relief of the Supreme Court had been pending, but Congress had not taken action. Fuller, encouraged by President Benjamin Harrison's first annual message to Congress in 1889, was determined to change the system; three years after he became Chief Justice he succeeded in doing just that.

Fuller was aware that Senator William M. Evarts was the Senate's leading advocate for the creation of federal courts of appeal. In January of 1890, Fuller gave a dinner at his home in honor of the recently appointed justice, David Brewer. The guests were the justices of the Court, as well as Senators William Evarts, George F. Edmunds and other members of the Senate Judiciary Committee. With hopes of immediate reform, Fuller spoke to his guests about the backlog of cases that had accumulated on the Court's docket. His efforts soon paid off. A few weeks after the dinner, the Senate Judiciary Committee ordered that copies of all of the pending bills for the relief of the Supreme Court be sent to Fuller. The Committee wrote that it would "be agreeable to the Committee to receive . . . the views of the Justices." Fuller asked Justice Horace Gray to prepare a report on the bills. With the unanimous consent of the justices, Gray drafted a letter to the Senate Judiciary Committee dated March 12, 1890. The letter recommended that intermediate circuit courts of appeal be established. However, despite over 100 years of complaining about circuit riding, the Fuller Court justices did not seek to abolish the practice. Fuller biographer James W. Ely characterizes this a tactical decision on the part of the justices. . . .

In March of 1891, under a bill sponsored by Senator Evarts, Congress set up the circuit courts of appeal. The statute broke the stalemate that had thwarted efforts at judicial reform since the Civil War, granted substantial relief to the Supreme Court, and made a "lasting and important contribution to the federal judicial structure." The Circuit Court of Appeals Act expanded the federal court system from two to three tiers. The district courts retained their trial jurisdiction and the Act assigned the two appellate functions to two separate courts. The new circuit courts of appeal played the error correction role and took appeals as of right from the district courts. The Supreme Court would hear appeals from the circuit courts and was still responsible for the interpretation of the U.S. Constitution, the enunciation of national law, and the supervision of the lower federal courts. . . .

The Act introduced the concept of discretionary review by "writ of certiorari." This allowed the Supreme Court to pick and choose the cases it wanted to hear. It was the direct opposite of the old "writ of error," which, since it provided for appellate review as a matter of right, was responsible for the exponential increase of the Court's docket. The framers of the Act thought that the writ of certiorari would be issued only for the purpose of resolving conflicts of judgments among the different courts of appeal in cases where the judgment of the court would be final. The goal was to achieve nationwide uniformity of law. However, in its first decision on the matter, *Lau Ow Bew v. United States,* the Court gave a broad interpretation to its new-found power. In an opinion by Chief Justice Fuller, the Court opined that in considering which cases it should grant review to, it was permitted to consider the "gravity and importance" of the case.

On the topic of the creation of the circuit courts of appeal and the introduction of the concept of certiorari, Chief Justice Rehnquist has written: "From this point on the Supreme Court was no longer at the disposal of every losing litigant in a federal court who had the time and money to take an appeal to the "highest court in the land." The Court's case load was transformed. Whereas in 1890, there were 623 new cases docketed, in 1891 (with the new Act only a few months in operation) there were only 379, and by 1892, just 275.

While earlier versions of the Act called for the complete abolition of the old circuit courts, in order to satisfy the Congressional traditionalists, the Evarts Act did not abolish the courts. Even though the circuit courts no longer had any appellate jurisdiction over the district courts, they retained original trial jurisdiction over capital cases, tax cases, and diversity cases where the amount in controversy exceeded the district court's limit. Essentially, the circuit courts and district courts had concurrent jurisdiction; this resulted in much confusion for litigants and attorneys.

"As a gesture to tradition," the justices' circuit duties were not eliminated, but little was expected of them. It was unclear, however, exactly what the circuit riding responsibilities of the justices were after the Evarts Act was passed. Under the Act, the justices of the Supreme Court were made "competent to sit as judges of the circuit court of appeals within their respective circuits"; however, nothing mandated that they sit as judges on the old circuit courts or the new Circuit Courts of Appeals. To the chagrin of those in Congress who still believed in the virtues of circuit riding, after the new Act was passed, most justices ceased riding circuit.

Biographer James Ely cites Fuller's circuit attendance in order to dispel the "casual assumption" that circuit riding "abruptly disappeared" after the passage of the Evarts Act. While he may be correct, it is clear that a majority of the justices gave up circuit riding after the passage of the Act. Congress was aware of the situation and the legislative branch, ironically not at the request of the justices, eventually became convinced that the old circuit

courts and circuit riding were officially obsolete. In the Judicial Code of 1911, circuit riding died a quiet death. Congress officially abolished the circuit courts and made the district courts the exclusive federal trial courts.

Circuit Riding Postscript

Much to the satisfaction of the Supreme Court, circuit riding was abolished in 1911; however, two remnants of the practice remain part of the institution. First, justices still act as Circuit Justices for each circuit. At the beginning of each term the Court assigns to each justice one or more of the thirteen federal circuits, and applications in cases arising in such circuits are within the jurisdiction of the justice assigned thereto. A justices' authority is limited to granting temporary relief, such as a temporary injunction, a stay of judgment or execution, and the granting of bail.

Second, retired justices can ride circuit pursuant to 28 U.S.C. 294(a) which states: "Any retired Chief Justice of the United States or Associate Justice of the Supreme Court may be designated and assigned by the Chief Justice of the United States to perform such judicial duties in any circuit, including those of a circuit justice, as he is willing to undertake." Indeed, several justices have elected to continue their judicial service after retirement by sitting by designation on various Courts of Appeals. These justices include Byron White, Lewis Powell, Potter Stewart, William Brennan, Thurgood Marshall, Stanley Reed, and Harold Burton. Justice Tom Clark, who retired from the Court in excellent health at the relatively young age of sixty-seven, spent the remaining ten years of his life riding circuit. He remains the only retired justice to have sat by designation on all of the circuits. . . .

Contemporary Judicial Politics

9.3　*Newdow v. U.S. Congress et al.*
328 F.3d 466 (2002)

OPINION BY Alfred T. Goodwin.

Goodwin, Circuit Judge: Michael Newdow appeals pro se a judgment dismissing his challenge to the constitutionality of the words "under God" in the Pledge of Allegiance to the Flag. Newdow argues that the addition of these words by a 1954 federal statute to the previous version of the Pledge of Allegiance (which made no reference to God) and the daily recitation in the classroom of the Pledge of Allegiance, with the added words included, by his daughter's public school teacher are violations of the Establishment Clause of the First Amendment to the United States Constitution.

Factual and Procedural Background

Newdow is an atheist whose daughter attends public elementary school in the Elk Grove Unified School District ("EGUSD") in California. In accordance with state law and a school district rule, EGUSD teachers begin each school day by leading their students in a recitation of the Pledge of Allegiance ("the Pledge"). The California Education Code requires that public schools begin each school day with "appropriate patriotic exercises" and that "[t]he giving of the Pledge of Allegiance to the Flag of the United States of America shall satisfy" this requirement. . . .

The classmates of Newdow's daughter in the EGUSD are led by their teacher in reciting the Pledge codified in federal law. On June 22, 1942, Congress first codified the Pledge as "I pledge allegiance to the flag of the United States of America and to the Republic for which it stands, one Nation indivisible, with liberty and justice for all." On June 14, 1954, Congress add[ed] the words "under God" after the word "Nation." The Pledge is currently codified as "I pledge allegiance to the Flag of the United States of America, and to the Republic for which it stands, one nation under God, indivisible, with liberty and justice for all."

Newdow does not allege that his daughter's teacher or school district requires his daughter to participate in reciting the Pledge. Rather, he claims that his daughter is injured when she is compelled to "watch and listen as her state-employed teacher in her state-run school leads her classmates in a ritual proclaiming that there is a God, and that our's [sic] is 'one nation under God.' "

Newdow's complaint in the district court challenged the constitutionality, under the First Amendment, of the 1954 Act, the California statute, and the school district's policy requiring teachers to lead willing students in recitation of the Pledge. He sought declaratory and injunctive relief, but did not seek damages. . . .

The magistrate judge reported findings and a recommendation that the district court hold that the daily Pledge ceremony in the schools did not violate the Establishment Clause. District Judge Edward J. Schwartz approved the recommendation and entered a judgment of dismissal. This appeal followed.

Discussion

. . .

Establishment Clause

The Establishment Clause of the First Amendment states that "Congress shall make no law respecting an establishment of religion," a provision that "the Fourteenth Amendment makes applicable with full force to the States and their school districts." Over the last three decades, the Supreme Court has used three interrelated tests to analyze alleged violations of the Establishment Clause in the realm of public education: the three-prong test set forth in *Lemon v. Kurtzman,* the "endorsement" test, first articulated by Justice O'Connor in her concurring opinion in *Lynch v. Donnelly,* and later adopted by a majority of the Court in *County of Allegheny v. ACLU,* and the "coercion" test first used by the Court in *Lee [v. Weisman].*

In 1971, in the context of unconstitutional state aid to nonpublic schools, the Supreme Court in *Lemon* set forth the following test for evaluating alleged Establishment Clause violations. To survive the *"Lemon* test," the government conduct in question (1) must have a secular purpose, (2) must have a principal or primary effect that neither advances nor inhibits religion, and (3) must not foster an excessive government entanglement with religion. The Supreme Court applied the *Lemon* test to every Establishment case it decided between 1971 and 1984, with the exception of *Marsh v. Chambers,* the case upholding legislative prayer.

In the 1984 *Lynch* case, which upheld the inclusion of a nativity scene in a city's Christmas display, Justice O'Connor wrote a concurring opinion in order to suggest a "clarification" of Establishment Clause jurisprudence.

Justice O'Connor's "endorsement" test effectively collapsed the first two prongs of the *Lemon* test:

> The Establishment Clause prohibits government from making adherence to a religion relevant in any way to a person's standing in the political community. Government can run afoul of that prohibition in two principal ways. One is excessive entanglement with religious institutions. . . . The second and more direct infringement is government endorsement or disapproval of religion. Endorsement sends a message to nonadherents that they are outsiders, not full members of the political community, and an accompanying message to adherents that they are insiders, favored members of the political community.

The Court formulated the "coercion test" when it held unconstitutional the practice of including invocations and benedictions in the form of "nonsectarian" prayers at public school graduation ceremonies. . . . [I]t relied on the principle that "at a minimum, the Constitution guarantees that government may not coerce anyone to support or participate in religion or its exercise, or otherwise to act in a way which establishes a state religion or

religious faith, or tends to do so." The Court first examined the degree of school involvement in the prayer, and found that "the graduation prayers bore the imprint of the State and thus put school-age children who objected in an untenable position." The next issue the Court considered was "the position of the students, both those who desired the prayer and she who did not". Noting that "there are heightened concerns with protecting freedom of conscience from subtle coercive pressure in the elementary and secondary public schools," the Court held that the school district's supervision and control of the graduation ceremony put impermissible pressure on students to participate in, or at least show respect during, the prayer. The Court concluded that primary and secondary school children may not be placed in the dilemma of either participating in a religious ceremony or protesting.

Finally, in its most recent school prayer case, the Supreme Court applied the *Lemon* test, the endorsement test, and the coercion test to strike down a school district's policy of permitting student-led "invocations" before high school football games. . . . Applying the *Lemon* test, the Court found that the school district policy was facially unconstitutional because it did not have a secular purpose. The Court also used language associated with the endorsement test.

We are free to apply any or all of the three tests, and to invalidate any measure that fails any one of them. Because we conclude that the school district policy impermissibly coerces a religious act and accordingly hold the policy unconstitutional, we need not consider whether the policy fails the endorsement test or the *Lemon* test as well.

In the context of the Pledge, the statement that the United States is a nation "under God" is a profession of a religious belief, namely, a belief in monotheism. The recitation that ours is a nation "under God" is not a mere acknowledgment that many Americans believe in a deity. Nor is it merely descriptive of the undeniable historical significance of religion in the founding of the Republic. Rather, the phrase "one nation under God" in the context of the Pledge is normative. To recite the Pledge is not to describe the United States; instead, it is to swear allegiance to the values for which the flag stands: unity, indivisibility, liberty, justice, and—since 1954—monotheism. A profession that we are a nation "under God" is identical, for Establishment Clause purposes, to a profession that we are a nation "under Jesus," a nation "under Vishnu," a nation "under Zeus," or a nation "under no god," because none of these professions can be neutral with respect to religion. The school district's practice of teacher-led recitation of the Pledge aims to inculcate in students a respect for the ideals set forth in the Pledge, including the religious values it incorporates. . . .

The school district's policy here . . . , places students in the untenable position of choosing between participating in an exercise with religious content or protesting. The defendants argue that the religious content of "one nation under God" is minimal. To an atheist or a believer in non-Judeo-Christian religions or philosophies, however, this phrase may reasonably appear to be an attempt to enforce a "religious orthodoxy" of monotheism, and is therefore impermissible. . . .

The coercive effect of the policy here is particularly pronounced in the school setting given the age and impressionability of schoolchildren, and their understanding that they are required to adhere to the norms set by their school, their teacher and their fellow students. . . . [E]ven without a recitation requirement for each child, the mere presence in the classroom every day as peers recite the statement "one nation under God" has a coercive effect. The coercive effect of the Pledge is also made even more apparent when we consider the legislative history of the Act that introduced the phrase "under God." These words were designed to be recited daily in school classrooms. President Eisenhower, during the Act's signing ceremony, stated: "From this day forward, the millions of our school children will daily proclaim in every city and town, every village and rural schoolhouse, the dedication of our Nation and our people to the Almighty." All in all, there can be little doubt that under the controlling Supreme Court cases the school district's policy fails the coercion test. . . .

The only other United States Court of Appeals to consider the issue is the Seventh Circuit, which held . . . that a policy similar to the one before us regarding the recitation of the Pledge of Allegiance containing the words "one nation under God" was constitutional. . . .

It . . . concludes . . . that . . . the First Amendment "[does] not establish general rules about speech or schools; [it] call[s] for religion to be treated differently." We have some difficulty understanding this statement; we do not believe that the Constitution prohibits compulsory patriotism as in *Barnette,* but permits compulsory religion as in this case. If government-endorsed religion is to be treated differently from government-endorsed patriotism, the treatment must be less favorable, not more.

The Seventh Circuit makes an even more serious error, however. It not only refuses to apply the *Lemon* test because of the Supreme Court's criticism of that test in *Lee,* but it also fails to apply the coercion test from *Lee.* Circuit courts are not free to ignore Supreme Court precedent in this manner. Instead of applying any of the tests announced by the Supreme Court, the Seventh Circuit simply frames the question as follows: "Must ceremonial references in civic life to a deity be understood as prayer, or support for all monotheistic religions, to the exclusion of atheists and those who worship multiple gods?" For the reasons we have already explained, this question is simply not dispositive of whether the school district policy impermissibly coerces a religious act.

In light of Supreme Court precedent, we hold that the school district's policy and practice of teacher-led recitation of the Pledge, with the inclusion of the added words "under God," violates the Establishment Clause. . . .

The judgment of dismissal is vacated with respect to Newdow's claim that the school district's Pledge policy violates the Establishment Clause and the cause is remanded for further proceedings consistent with our holding. Plaintiff is to recover costs on this appeal.

Reversed and remanded.

9.4   Do the "Haves" Come Out Ahead Over Time? Applying Galanter's Framework to Decisions of the U.S. Courts of Appeals (1999)

Donald R. Songer, Reginald S. Sheehan, and Susan B. Haire

[Marc] Galanter's watershed analysis (1974) made a compelling case for the proposition that the "haves" tend to come out ahead in litigation. Since the publication of this analysis, Galanter's methods and theoretical insights have spawned numerous studies that have examined the advantages of some litigants in a wide variety of courts. Several studies of trial courts have confirmed Galanter's basic findings. Generally, these findings indicate that classes of litigants with the greatest resources and the lowest relative stakes in litigation have the highest rates of success in trial courts; governments have been more successful in litigation than have business or other organizations, and organizations have been more successful than individual litigants. Galanter (1974) suggests that these "haves" will win more frequently because they are likely to have favorable law on their side, superior material resources, and better lawyers and because a number of advantages accrue to them as a result of their "repeat player" status. Superior resources allow the "haves" to hire the best available legal representation and to incur legal expenses, such as those associated with extensive discovery and expert witnesses, that may increase the chances of success at trial. In addition, as repeat players, they will reap the benefits of greater litigation experience, including the ability to develop and implement a comprehensive litigation strategy that may involve forum shopping and making informed judgments regarding their prospects of winning at trial or on appeal.

The question of who wins and loses in U.S. courts may be the most important question we seek to answer as judicial scholars. In fact, "Who gets what?" has traditionally been viewed as one of the central questions in the study of politics more generally. In the United States, the courts are widely viewed as key institutions for the legitimate settlement of a wide spectrum of conflicts between individuals and groups that have important implications for the dis-

tribution of material and symbolic goods. Therefore, understanding who wins in the courts is an essential component of a full appreciation of "the authoritative allocation of values" in society. Moreover, because the courts of appeals are the final arbiters for the vast majority of federal litigation, it is important to determine how different types of litigants have been received by these courts. In this article, we assess whether particular types of litigants win, or lose, more frequently in the U.S. Courts of Appeals than other types and whether their success varies over time. Drawing from Galanter's work, our comparison includes examining the success rates of repeat players, the "haves," and one shotters, who are usually "have nots," in the U.S. Courts of Appeals from 1925 to 1988. . . .

Data and Measures

To examine the success of "haves" and "have nots" in cases decided by the U.S. Courts of Appeals, we selected data from the recently released appeals court database. The database includes data on the nature of the appellant and respondent, the issue, the party of the judges on each panel, and the outcome of all cases from a random sample of published decisions from each circuit for each year from 1925 through 1988.

To facilitate the analysis of change over time, the 64 years of data included in the U.S. Courts of Appeals Data Base were divided into five periods. The periods capture significant changes in the legal and political history of the twentieth century that might plausibly affect the relative likelihood of success by certain categories of litigants. In the first period, 1925–1936, the legal system was dominated by conservative, probusiness judges at all levels of the judicial system. Our second period, 1937–1945, begins with the "switch in time that saved nine" that marked the beginning of the Roosevelt Court and its aggressive pro–New Deal policies. Throughout this

From *Law and Society Review* 811 (1999). Reprinted by permission of Blackwell Publishing.

period, the courts came to be dominated by Roosevelt judges who were selected in large part for their devotion to New Deal economic policies that had a decidedly pro-underdog orientation. The third period, 1946–1960, was characterized by economic prosperity and the selection of lower court judges (by Truman and Eisenhower) without much regard for their policy preferences. The fourth period, 1961–1969, was most notable for the leadership of the judiciary by the Warren Court (perhaps the most liberal Supreme Court in our history), a pair of Democratic presidents in the White House, dramatic agitation in Congress and on the streets for expansion of civil rights, and strident advocacy for the welfare of poor people that culminated in President Johnson's "War on Poverty." During our final period, 1970–1988, the Supreme Court became steadily more conservative as the appointees of Nixon, Ford, and Reagan ascended to the high bench. These general trends suggest that in two periods (1937–1945 and 1961–1969), the courts should have been staffed by a considerable number of judges who were sympathetic to the interests of one-shot "have not" litigants (especially the poor), whereas in our first and last periods (1925–1936 and 1970–1988), the courts appear to have been dominated by political conservatives who presumably had probusiness proclivities. Our middle period, 1946–1960, would appear to represent a time of moderation. The analysis here examines whether the different political orientations that characterized these five periods were marked by different levels of success in courts for litigants with different status.

As prior attempts to operationalize and apply Galanter's concepts have pointed out, specific information about the wealth of particular parties in a given case or the relative litigation experience of those parties is often not available in court opinions. Because the data for this study, like the data for these earlier studies, were derived from court opinions, there was rarely enough information to unambiguously classify one of the parties as having greater litigation experience, wealth, or other relevant resources than their adversary. Consequently, we adopted the strategy . . . of assigning litigants to general classes and then making assumptions about which class was usually the stronger party.

Each appellant and each respondent were classified as belonging to one of five major classes: individual litigants, businesses, state and local governments, the U.S. government, or other. "Other" included unions; nonprofit (private) organizations; nonprofit (private) schools; social, charitable, or fraternal organizations; political parties; and litigants who could not be unambiguously categorized. Into this "other" category fell 7.8% of the appellants and 6.3% of the respondents. They were excluded from analysis because they could not be categorized in terms of litigation resources. If the party listed in the case citation was a named individual, but his or her involvement in the suit was due directly to his or her role as an official of a government agency or as an officer, partner, or owner of a business, the code was based on the organizational affiliation and not as an individual. For example, if the chief executive officer of a multinational corporation was appealing a criminal conviction for personal income tax evasion, the appellant was coded as an individual. If the chief of police was the subject of a . . . suit for damages because of an alleged torture of a prisoner held in that chief's jail, however, the defendant would be classified in the local government category. All government agencies, even those who are "independent" of the chief executive, and government corporations were categorized in the appropriate government class (for example, the National Labor Relations Board and the Tennessee Valley Authority were classified in the federal government class). . . . [W]e assume that individuals usually have less experience and fewer resources than either businesses or units of governments. When business and governmental parties oppose one another, we assume that governments will usually be stronger because even when the financial resources of government are no greater than those of the business, the government agency is more likely to be a repeat player (or a more frequent repeat player in the particular issue area involved in the suit).

We defined winners and losers by looking at "who won the appeal in its most immediate sense, without attempting to view the appeal in some larger context." Thus, for example, if the decision of the district court or the administrative agency was "reversed," "reversed and remanded," "vacated," or "vacated and remanded," the appellant was coded as winning, regardless of whether the opinion announced a doctrine that was broad or narrow and regardless of whether that doctrine might be supposed in general to benefit future haves or have nots. Also, . . . we excluded from analysis all cases with ambiguous results (e.g., those in which the court affirmed in part and reversed in part).

Our focus is on whether or not any relative advantage accrues to those classes of parties with superior litigation experience and resources. In the federal court system, the trial court loser enjoys a constitutional right of appeal. Although rational calculations of the chances of winning may exert a substantial impact on some decisions about whether or not to appeal, it will be rational for many litigants to appeal even if their chances of obtaining a reversal are substantially less than 50%. Appeals are brought by trial court losers after decisionmakers (judge and jury) at trial made initial interpretations of the facts and the law. Therefore, even if appellate justice is blind and litigation resources are irrelevant, one would expect that respondents would prevail against the majority of appeals. In the data used in this study, the courts of appeals affirmed 72% of the decisions appealed to them. Therefore, to assess whether the hypothesized relative advantage of repeat players with superior wealth and status exists, it is not enough to know whether or not the "haves" won more frequently in an absolute sense. Instead, we must also explore whether they "were better able than other parties to buck the basic tendency of appellate courts to affirm." Therefore, we used the index of net advantage . . . because it provides a better measure of litigant success in courts over different time periods than a simple measure of the proportion of decisions won by a given class of litigants would.

Appellant Success and Net Advantage

The beginning point of analysis was to examine the appellant success rate for each of the four basic categories of litigants . . . for the 64-year period. . . . There were wide disparities in the relative success of different classes of appellants in the courts of appeals, and those differences were quite consistent with the expectations derived from Galanter. Despite the general propensity of the circuit courts to affirm, the federal government was successful on 51.3% of its appeals and had an overall rate of success (from its participation as an appellant and as a respondent) of 70%. At the other end of the spectrum, individuals won only 26.1% of their appeals and had an overall rate of success of only 35.1%. Moreover, the rank order of the success rates was exactly the order that would be predicted from Galanter's theory. Individuals had the lowest rate of success, followed, in order, by business, state and local government, and the federal government. Overall, the United States was twice as successful as individuals and one and a half times as successful as businesses.

As noted earlier, the net advantage index may be a better indicator of litigation success than the raw rate of success because it is unaffected by the relative frequency that a given class of litigant appears as an appellant rather than as a respondent. Thus, if there is a propensity to affirm in the courts of appeals, this propensity will not affect the index of net advantage. This net advantage for each class of litigant . . . reinforces the picture suggested by the raw measures of success. Individuals suffered a sharply negative net advantage, businesses were slightly below zero, and both levels of government enjoyed strong positive numbers for their net advantage. The federal government, which won 51.3% of the cases it appealed, held adversaries to only a 25.7% success rate in the cases they appealed (i.e., the federal government won 74.3% of the cases in which it appeared as respondent), giving the United States a net advantage of 25.6%. State and local governments had a net advantage of 15.6%, whereas businesses had a slightly negative net advantage of −2.8%. At the bottom were individuals whose net advantage was −12.6%, a finding that reflects that those who filed appeals against individuals won substantially more often than individuals did when they appealed. . . .

Turning to the analysis of change over time, it is evident from the data . . . that the haves win consistently throughout the 64-year period examined.

Looking first at the overall success rates of each category of litigant, . . . individuals had the lowest rates of success in all five periods and businesses had lower rates of success than either category of government in every period. Moreover, the success of each category of litigant remains remarkably consistent over time. In every time period, the success of individuals falls within the 31% to 39% range, whereas the success of business litigants varies between 45% and slightly under 49%. Although the gap between individual and business success varies over time, the highest degree of success achieved by individuals remains 6 percentage points below the lowest level of success achieved by business litigants.

The thesis that the stronger, repeat player litigants should prevail also receives strong support from the data on changes in the net advantage of different classes of litigants. . . . The net advantage scores, like the overall success rates, show that the "haves" were generally more successful than one shotters presumed to have fewer resources. In all five periods, individuals, presumably most of whom are one shotters whose stakes are large relative to their resources, had sharply negative net advantage rates. Business litigants, a category of litigants that presumably contains nontrivial numbers of both repeat players and one-shot players, had net advantage rates near zero. In contrast, the repeat player government litigants had strongly positive net advantage rates. Predictions derived from Galanter's work appear to be least satisfactory as an explanation of outcomes in the 1937–1945 period. During this period, which includes the height of the New Deal and the ascendancy of the Roosevelt Court, individuals appeared to fare about as well as businesses (slightly lower on overall success rates but with a slightly higher net advantage score). Whereas businesses and individuals fared substantially worse than either level of government, state and local governments were more successful than the federal government on both measures of success.

. . . To further explore the advantage that the stronger party appears to have in cases before the federal circuit courts, we . . . elected only those cases in which parties in different categories confronted each other. . . .

When specific matchups are examined, the findings strongly support Galanter's theory. Individuals have low rates of success against all other categories of respondents, whereas the success rate of the United States as appellant remains high against all other parties. In every matchup, the repeat player party presumed to be stronger enjoyed a substantial net advantage. The matchups involving individuals are particularly revealing. As the presumed strength and litigation experience of the opponent of the individual litigants increase, the size of the net advantage going to the stronger party

rises steeply. The 6.3% net advantage that businesses enjoy over individuals rises to 19.5% when individuals faced state governments and increases to a 34.5% advantage for the United States when it faces individuals.

. . . [F]or each of the five periods used in the prior analyses. . . . there was only one matchup in which the stronger party did not enjoy a positive net advantage over its opponent. In the 1961–1969 period, individuals enjoyed a 6.4% net advantage over business litigants they faced as appellants and respondents. In all other matchups across time periods, however, the litigant with presumed greater litigation experience and resources enjoyed a strong net advantage (at least 8% in all other cases). For all matchups, the stronger party enjoyed an average net advantage of 22.7%. Most striking is the 33.6% net advantage enjoyed by businesses in their matchups with individuals in the 1937–1945 period. . . .

Appellant Strength in a Multivariate Analysis

Although the analysis of bivariate relationships presented above produced results that are consistent with the thesis that litigant status and strength are significantly related to rates of appellant success, the thesis can be only provisionally supported until the effects of potential intervening variables are examined. For example, the apparent success of the presumptively stronger parties may be due in large part to the number of criminal appeals in the sample. Criminal appeals typically match an individual (especially a poor individual) against some level of government. Because many criminal appeals appear to have very little legal merit, the government usually wins. Alternatively, because judicial ideology, as measured by party affiliation or identity of the appointing president, has been found to be related to outcomes in the federal courts, the relative success of the "haves" may be due to the relative number of Democrats and Republicans that were on a court at a particular time. . . .

The variable measuring the status of the appellant is positively related to the likelihood of appellant success, and the relationship is significant. . . . [T]he measure of experience and resources of the respondent was also related to appellant success to a statistically significant degree. The results also indicate that the ideological makeup of the panel will affect case outcomes. . . . [P]anels with majorities appointed by Democratic presidents are more likely to support appeals from conservative decisions below, whereas panels with a majority of judges appointed by Republican presidents are more likely to support appeals from liberal decisions. . . . [T]he effects of litigant experience and resources. . . . remain strong even after controls for partisan preferences are included in the model.

The strong and statistically significant effects of litigant status in this multivariate model of decisionmaking over 64 years suggest that the nature of the litigant has had an enduring effect on the probability of appellant success that is independent of the policy preferences of the judges and the predisposition to affirm criminal convictions. . . .

Conclusion

At its most basic level, the findings of this study reaffirm Galanter's thesis that the "haves come out ahead." The parties that may be presumed to be repeat players with superior resources consistently fared better than their weaker opponents and the disparity in success rates was greatest when the disparity in strength was greatest. Although there was a strong propensity of the federal courts of appeals to affirm, the greater success of stronger parties could not be attributed to the number of times they appeared as respondent rather than as appellant.

The most notable addition of this analysis to the fairly extensive literature that has been built on Galanter's insights is the discovery that this tendency of repeat player "haves" to win more frequently than their less advantaged opponents has been remarkably stable over much of the twentieth century. Since 1925, individuals lost more than 60% of their cases, businesses had success rates slightly under 50%, and governments won a commanding majority (over 68%) of the cases in which they participated. . . .

On the courts of appeals (and, presumably, on state supreme courts), there have been significant changes in the partisan and ideological composition of the judiciary over time. The definition of the time periods used in this analysis was determined in large part by a desire to examine whether these changes were related to changes in the influence of repeat player status and litigant resources on outcomes. Our results suggested that there may have been a relatively modest increase in the propensity of the "have nots" to win in the period in which these partisan balances were most favorable to liberal interests (i.e., 1937–1945 period), but even major partisan shifts on the courts do not appear to fundamentally change the patterns predicted from Galanter's theoretical framework. The years since 1925 have also brought several institutional changes that might have been expected to benefit the litigation prospects for the "have nots." Most notable are the advent of a constitutional right of free legal counsel for the poor in some criminal appeals and the dramatic expansion of legal services available to the poor in civil contests. The efforts to provide access to the judicial process for those less fortunate, however, did not appear to significantly diminish the odds of success for governments, and to a lesser degree businesses, in these appellate courts over time.

Although it is thus apparent that the "haves" come out ahead in the U.S. Courts of Appeals to an impressive degree and that they have been coming out ahead throughout most of the twentieth century, we can only suggest, somewhat tentatively, why. . . . It may be that there has always been some normative tilt in the law toward the interests of business and governments, but major changes have affected the tilt since 1925. For example, from the mid 1950s until the early 1970s, the Supreme Court increasingly favored claims made by individuals asserting violations of their rights. Prior to that time, the Court was not sympathetic to individuals raising civil liberties and rights issues. Congress passed numerous statutes in the 1960s establishing Great Society programs and guaranteeing civil rights in employment, housing, and transportation. These changes may have contributed to the success of individuals in appeals involving business litigants during the 1960s. Overall, however, these changes did not appear to significantly affect the relationship between litigant strength and case outcomes in the courts of appeals. The second possibility . . . [is] that the success of stronger parties might be due to judicial attitudes that favored them. The findings of our multivariate model, however, reinforce the earlier conclusions that, on the federal circuit courts, the effect of litigant status is independent of partisan-based influences.

The most probable explanation for the long-term success of the "haves" in the U.S. Courts of Appeals appears to be related to those factors suggested by Galanter (1974); our analysis found that parties presumed to be repeat players with greater resources came out ahead when pitted against presumptively weaker parties even after controlling for other influences affecting case outcomes. Unfortunately, the data are not sufficient to enable us to determine which of the specific characteristics of the stronger parties are the key ingredients of success. . . .

Thus, the limitations of opinion-derived data make it difficult to determine conclusively the basis of the success of the "haves." One piece of data uncovered in the analysis, however, is relevant to the assessment of whether the successes enjoyed by the "haves" are due more to their wealth and status than to the advantages derived from their repeat player status. Whereas the wealth of litigants would reflect on their ability to hire better lawyers and finance more extensive research, repeat player status of litigants would influence their ability to estimate the odds of success on appeal and skill in selecting probable winners. It also might reflect

their willingness to absorb trial court losses to avoid the risk of adverse precedent being created on appeal. Such litigants would be more interested in "playing for rules" rather than immediate material gain. If the success of the "haves" was due to wealth alone, one would expect that the effect of litigant status would be the same for appellants and respondents. Our multivariate analysis of appellant success, however, suggested that the status of appellants had a greater impact than the status of respondents. Such a finding may indicate that litigation experience is more important than material resources. The advantages that can be secured by wealth and prestige should benefit both appellants and respondents, but only the potential appellants (i.e., the party that lost in the court below) can take full advantage of a sophisticated litigation strategy that Galanter suggests is characteristic of repeat players. . . .

. . . [T]he results of this study clearly indicate that Galanter's insights on the relationship between party capability and litigation in the trial courts may be extended to explain patterns of litigants success in the U.S. Courts of Appeals. Moreover, these patterns have been enduring, as the "haves" were more likely to prevail over a half century of appellate litigation in the federal courts.

9.5   Judging by Where You Sit (2003)

David A. Schkade and Cass R. Sunstein

Ideology matters when choosing judges—perhaps too much, as the battles between President Bush and Senate Democrats show. But how much does ideology matter once judges are on the bench?

As it turns out, it matters a lot. We have studied thousands of votes by federal appellate judges, who are randomly assigned to three-judge panels, which then make decisions by majority vote. According to our research, judges appointed by Republican presidents show more conservative voting patterns, while Democratic appointees are more liberal.

These findings may not be surprising. The most striking lesson of our research, however, is the

influence of what might be called the majority ideology. For both Democratic and Republican appointees, the likelihood of a liberal vote jumps when the two other panel members are Democrats, and drops when the two other panel members are Republicans.

The effect of ideology on panel decisions is clear. Consider, for example, a case in which a woman has complained of sex discrimination. In front of an appellate panel of three Democratic appointees, she wins 75 percent of the time. But if the panel has fewer Democratic appointees, her chances decline. With two Democratic and one Republican appointee, she wins 49 percent of the time; with one Democratic and two Republican appointees, she wins 38 percent of the time. And with a panel of three Republican appointees, she wins just 31 percent of the time.

Or consider cases in which a company has claimed that an environmental regulation is unlawful. Before an all-Democratic panel, the company wins about a quarter of the time. But before an all-Republican panel, the company wins about three-quarters of the time. Or consider a case in which white people are challenging an affirmative action program; they win two times out of three before three Republican appointees—but only one time in six before three Democratic appointees. The same pattern can be found in many other areas of the law.

Of course, judges are not politicians or ideologues. If the facts and the law argue strongly for one side, it will prevail, regardless of the political affiliation of the president who appointed the judges. But in the hardest cases that make their way to the federal appellate courts, the evidence is clear: Republican-appointed judges tend to vote like Republicans and Democratic-appointed judges tend to vote like Democrats.

There are some interesting exceptions. In criminal appeals, Republican and Democratic appointees do not differ. Contrary to the stereotype, Democratic appointees are not "softer on crime." And in cases involving abortion and capital punishment, judges appear not to be influenced by their colleagues. No matter what the composition of the panel, Republican appointees are much more likely to vote to uphold restrictions on abortion and to permit executions to go forward.

Ideology also has a more subtle effect on individual judges: in general, both Republican and Democratic appointees are affected by their panel colleagues. A Republican appointee sitting with two other Republicans votes far more conservatively than when the same judge sits with at least one Democratic appointee. A Democratic appointee, meanwhile, shows the same tendency in the opposite ideological direction.

For example, on an all-Republican panel, Republican judges are far more likely than not to vote to strike down affirmative action and campaign finance reform—and also to rule against people claiming that they have been discriminated against on the basis of sex or disability. But in the very same areas, Republican appointees show a much more moderate pattern of votes when there is at least one Democrat on the panel. The same holds true for Democratic appointees, who show extremely liberal voting patterns when sitting with fellow Democratic appointees, a tendency that shifts in the conservative direction when they sit with one or more Republican appointees.

These findings explain what the current battle is all about. Even on the lower federal courts, judicial ideology matters, and in a way that is crucial to the development of the law. The ideology of a judge is important not only because of how that judge will vote, but also because of the judge's effect on his or her colleagues.

Thus the fight over judicial nominations is no symbolic battle. The debate between President Bush and Democratic senators, between the executive and the legislative branches, is about more than politics. It about the future shape of the law.

A View From the Inside

9.6 Speaking in a Judicial Voice (1992)

Ruth Bader Ginsburg

Collegiality in Appellate Decisionmaking

. . . I turn now to the first of the two topics this lecture addresses–the style of judging appropriate for appellate judges whose mission it is, in Hamilton's words, "to secure a steady, upright, and impartial administration of the laws." Integrity, knowledge, and, most essentially, judgment are the qualities Hamilton ascribed to the judiciary. How is that essential quality, judgment, conveyed in the opinions appellate judges write? What role should moderation, restraint, and collegiality play in the formulation of judicial decisions? As background, I will describe three distinct patterns of appellate opinion-casting: individual, institutional, and in-between.

The individual judging pattern has been characteristic of the Law Lords, who serve as Great Britain's Supreme Court. The Lords sit in panels of five and, traditionally, have delivered opinions seriatim, each panel member, in turn, announcing his individual judgment and the reasons for it.

In contrast to the British tradition of opinions separately rendered by each judge as an individual, the continental or civil law traditions typified and spread abroad by France and Germany call for collective, corporate judgments. In dispositions of that genre, disagreement is not disclosed. Neither dissent nor separate concurrence is published. Cases are decided with a single, per curiam opinion generally following a uniform, anonymous style.

Our Supreme Court, when John Marshall became Chief Justice, made a start in the institutional opinion direction. Marshall is credited with establishing the practice of announcing judgments in a single opinion for the Court. The Marshall Court, and certainly its leader, had a strong sense of insti-

This speech was originally published in *New York University Law Review,* Vol. 67, no. 6, December 1992. Reprinted by permission.

tutional mission, a mission well served by unanimity. Marshall was criticized, in those early days, for suppressing dissent. Thomas Jefferson complained: "An opinion is huddled up in conclave, perhaps by a majority of one, delivered as if unanimous, and with the silent acquiescence of lazy or timid associates, by a crafty chief judge, who sophisticates the law to his own mind, by the turn of his own reasoning."

But even Marshall, during his long tenure as Chief Justice, ultimately dissented on several occasions and once concurred with a separate opinion. We continue in that middle way today. Our appellate courts generally produce a judgment or opinion for the court. In that respect, we bear some resemblance to the highly institution-minded civil law judges, although our judges individually claim authorship of most of the opinions they publish. In tune with the British or common law tradition, however, we place no formal limit on the prerogative of each judge to speak out separately. . . .

But overindulgence in separate opinion writing may undermine both the reputation of the judiciary for judgment and the respect accorded court dispositions. Rule of law virtues of consistency, predictability, clarity, and stability may be slighted when a court routinely fails to act as a collegial body. Dangers to the system are posed by two tendencies: too frequent resort to separate opinions and the immoderate tone of statements diverging from the position of the court's majority.

Regarding the first danger, recall that "the Great Dissenter," Justice Oliver Wendell Holmes, in fact dissented less often than most of his colleagues. Chief Justice Harlan F. Stone once wrote to Karl Llewellyn (both gentlemen were public defenders of the right to dissent): "You know, if I should write in every case where I do not agree with some of the views expressed in the opinions, you and all my other friends would stop reading [my separate opinions]." In matters of statutory interpretation,

Justice Louis D. Brandeis repeatedly cautioned: "[I]t is more important that the applicable rule of law be settled than that it be settled right." "This is commonly true," Brandeis continued, "even where the error is a matter of serious concern, provided correction can be had by legislation.". . .

Separate concurrences and dissents characterize Supreme Court decisions to a much greater extent than they do court of appeals three-judge panel decisions. In the District of Columbia Circuit, for example, for the statistical year ending June 1992, the court rendered 405 judgments in cases not disposed of summarily; over eighty-six percent of those decisions were unanimous. During that same period, the Supreme Court decided 114 cases with full opinions; only 21.9% of the decisions were unanimous. A reality not highlighted by a press fond of separating Carter from Reagan/Bush appointees accounts in considerable measure for this difference: the character of cases heard by courts of appeals combines with our modus operandi to tug us strongly toward the middle, toward moderation and away from notably creative or excessively rigid positions. . . .

Concerning the character of federal cases, unlike the Supreme Court, courts of appeals deal far less frequently with grand constitutional questions than with less cosmic questions of statutory interpretation or the rationality of agency or district court decisions. In most matters of that variety, as Justice Brandeis indicated, it is best that the matter be definitively settled, preferably with one opinion. Furthermore, lower court judges are bound more tightly by Supreme Court precedent than is the High Court itself.

Turning to the way we operate, I note first that no three-judge panel in a circuit is at liberty to depart from the published decision of a prior panel; law of the circuit may be altered only by the court en banc. To assure that each panel knows what the others are doing, the District of Columbia Circuit, and several other federal circuit courts of appeals, circulate opinions to the full court, once approved by a panel, at least a week in advance of release.

Second, in contrast to district judges, who are the real power holders in the federal court system—lords of their individual fiefdoms from case filing to first instance final judgment—no single court of appeals judge can carry the day in any case. To attract a second vote and establish durable law for the circuit, a judge may find it necessary to

moderate her own position, sometimes to be less bold, other times to be less clear. We can listen to and persuade each other in groups of three more effectively than can a larger panel.

On the few occasions each year when we sit en banc—in the District of Columbia Circuit, all twelve of us when we are full strength—I can appreciate why unanimity is so much harder to achieve in Supreme Court judgments. Not only do the Justices deal much more often with constitutional questions, where, in many cases, only overruling or constitutional amendment can correct a mistake. In addition, one becomes weary after going round the table on a first ballot. It is ever so much easier to have a conversation—and an exchange of views on opinion drafts—among three than among nine or twelve.

In writing for the court, one must be sensitive to the sensibilities and mindsets of one's colleagues, which may mean avoiding certain arguments and authorities, even certain words. Should institutional concerns affect the tone of separate opinions, when a judge finds it necessary to write one?

I emphasize first that dissents and separate concurrences are not consummations devoutly to be avoided. As Justice William J. Brennan said in thoughtful defense of dissents: "None of us, lawyer or layman, teacher or student, in our society must ever feel that to express a conviction, honestly and sincerely maintained, is to violate some unwritten law of manners or decorum." I question, however, resort to expressions in separate opinions that generate more heat than light. Consider this sample from an April 1991 District of Columbia Circuit decision. The dissenter led off: "Running headlong from the questions briefed and argued before us, my colleagues seek refuge in a theory as novel as it is questionable. Unsupported by precedent, undeveloped by the court, and unresponsive to the facts of this case, the . . . theory announced today has an inauspicious birth." That spicy statement, by the way, opposed an en banc opinion in which all of the judges concurred, except the lone dissenter.

It is "not good for public respect for courts and law and the administration of justice," Roscoe Pound decades ago observed, for an appellate judge to burden an opinion with "intemperate denunciation of [the writer's] colleagues, violent invective, attributi[on]s of bad motives to the majority of the court, and insinuations of incompetence, negligence, prejudice, or obtuseness of [other judges]." Yet one has only to thumb through the pages of current volumes of United States Reports and Federal Reporter Second to come upon condemnations by the score of a court or colleague's opinion or assertion as, for example, "folly," "ludicrous," "outrageous," one that "cannot be taken seriously," "inexplicable," "the quintessence of inequity," a "blow against the People," "naked analytical bootstrapping," "reminiscent . . . of Sherman's march through Georgia," and "Orwellian.". . .

The most effective dissent, I am convinced, "stand[s] on its own legal footing"; it spells out differences without jeopardizing collegiality or public respect for and confidence in the judiciary. I try to write my few separate opinions each year as I once did briefs for appellees—as affirmative statements of my reasons, drafted before receiving the court's opinion, and later adjusted, as needed, to meet the majority's presentation. Among pathmarking models, one can look to Justice Curtis's classic dissent

in the *Dred Scott* case, and, closer to our time, separate opinions by the second Justice John Marshall Harlan. . . .

Concerned about the erosion of civility in the legal profession, the Seventh Circuit, commencing in the fall of 1989, conducted a "study and investigation into litigation practices and the attending relationships among lawyers, among judges, and between lawyers and judges." The Final Report of the committee in charge of the study, released in June 1992, urges judges to set a good example by staying on the high ground. Specifically, the Report calls on judges to avoid "disparaging personal remarks or criticisms, or sarcastic or demeaning comments about another judge," and instead to "be courteous, respectful, and civil in opinions, ever mindful that a position articulated by another judge [generally] is the result of that judge's earnest effort to interpret the law and the facts correctly." To that good advice, one can say "amen.". . .

9.7   The Work of Appellate Judges (2001)

Dennis J. Sweeney

Justice Louis Brandeis once boasted that the Supreme Court was one of the few Washington institutions that did its own work. Although many fine and capable jurists pass through the courts of appeals and the supreme courts of the states and the nation, the appellate judiciary has slid a bit from Justice Brandeis's ideal. There are certainly many appellate judges who continue to do their own work. But just as many relegate the most fundamental and most important function of the job to law clerks. So much so that writing, research, and analytical thought are no longer absolute requirements for a job on an appellate bench. And while this may seem like an innocuous development, it is not.

The very heart of the work of appellate judges is principled decision making. They make choices among competing choices. And then, through the vehicle of a written opinion, explain to the world why they did what they did. Many solid appellate

Reprinted by permission of *Judicature,* the Journal of the American Judicature Society.

judges have sat down following conference and tried to justify a tentative decision reached at conference, only to be unable to write a principled opinion supporting the conclusion. "It won't write." The reason is simple—you've got the wrong result, stupid; reach the result the analysis dictates. But how can the judge do this when the judge doesn't work through the analysis by him or herself?

There are many important functions that appellate judges serve, but none more important than this: Writing is the sine qua non of what they do. No administrative committee, no conference, no meeting, no class, no media event, and no social function is more important than the written opinion.

Relegating the very heart of what it is to be an appellate judge to law clerks relieves the judge of a difficult and, sometimes, tedious, time consuming, frustrating task, but it also leads to unprincipled decisions. Richard Posner, in *Overcoming Law* (1995), compares the arts to judging and makes the point:

But the arts remain a bastion (albeit an embattled one) of artisanship, and to its votaries law is an art. So acknowledgment that neophytes can, after only three years of professional instruction and no professional experience, do much of the principal work of judges more or less satisfactorily, or at least not shockingly badly, still has the capacity to undermine professional self-esteem. It is a little as if brain surgeons delegated the entire performance of delicate operations to nurses, orderlies, and the first-year medical students—and patients were none the worse for it.

But suggesting that neophytes can do this work as well as judges does more than just undermine professional self-esteem. It undermines the very rule of law.

Judges face enormous political pressures today. Particularly those who must stand for popular election every four or six years. Only by taking the time to work through legal analysis to a decision on a pad of paper, or a computer screen, can the judge, the lawyers, and ultimately the public be assured that the rule is a rule of law rather than a justification for a popular, newsworthy, or biased result.

Like other government employees, appellate judges must be held accountable. But it is not accountability in the popular political sense. It is accountability of a different sort, one not easily understood. Simply put, the accountability question is: Did you sit down and work through the difficult task of reaching this result? Did the judge, in the words of Justice Richard Traynor, "wrestle with the devil"?

Earning Respect

There has been a long, gradual decline in public respect for the courts. And both bench and bar spend time, effort, and money to understand why. Many, even very thoughtful citizens, view appellate courts as just another politically powerful branch of government, free to exercise authority as they see fit. But judges are not just another politically powerful branch of government. They are different. They must justify decisions by law, by logic, and against state and federal constitutions—in short, by principle.

The comparison between judges and other politicians is tempting but must be rejected. How a legislator or executive gets to a result is really not very important. We elect legislators, governors, and presidents precisely because of their agenda. And we expect them to do everything within their power to advance that agenda. They cut deals and cut corners. We appropriately measure their success by their ability to advance that agenda.

Judges make an implicit pact with the public to lay aside agendas. Cardozo says so in his epic work, *The Nature of the Judicial Process* (1921):

> The judge, even when he is free, is still not wholly free. He is not to innovate at pleasure. He is not a knight-errant roaming at will in pursuit of his own ideal of beauty or of goodness. He is to draw his inspiration from consecrated principles. He is not to yield to spasmodic sentiment, to vague and unregulated benevolence. He is to exercise a discretion informed by tradition, methodized by analogy, disciplined by system, and subordinated to "the primordial necessity of order in the social life." Wide enough in all conscience is the field of discretion that remains.

Relegating the important work of reasoning and writing to law clerks promotes unprincipled, ideologically oriented decision making, for which the courts should be criticized. It relieves the judge of the difficult burden of justifying a legal conclusion with anything more than her or his own visceral instincts or, worse yet, his or her own social, economic, or political ideology. And it justifies the very kind of criticism from both the public and the legal community that we want to avoid. How much appropriate cynicism about the decisions by the judicial branch of government is bred by results that were forgone conclusions, with a law clerk filling in the reasons, rather than the result of a careful and principled opinion?

Both the bench and the bar spend vast sums of money on conferences and programs calculated to improve the image of the judiciary when the answer may be easy—do our own work. And encourage the press, the public, and politicians to promote appointment or election of lawyers and judges who are both capable of and interested in, the service of law. This job is no different from any other. If you want respect, then do your job.

9.8   # First Arguments at the Supreme Court of the United States: A Rarefied Kind of Dread (2003)

David I. Bruck

There's always anxiety involved in representing death-row inmates. But when the Supreme Court grants certiorari in a death-sentenced client's case, nightmare scenarios begin to loom.

Of course, there's the fear of losing, and in a capital case, that's no small matter. But if the legal claim that the Supreme Court has agreed to consider seems very strong, you're likely to encounter a different, more rarefied kind of dread. After all, your claim only seems strong because Supreme Court precedent suggests that you're going to win. But what if the Court took your case not simply to apply its own precedents (as you claim the lower courts had boneheadedly refused to do), but to overrule or weaken them? Then your Supreme Court case will turn out not only to have been a personal disaster for your client, but also to be a historic catastrophe for scores, even hundreds, of other death row inmates.[1]

In *Skipper v. South Carolina*[2] the Supreme Court had granted review (I hoped) to consider whether South Carolina was violating the Court's most well-established Eighth Amendment protection—the right to have sentencing juries or judges consider all the reasons why the death penalty should not be imposed.[3] The South Carolina Supreme Court had held that juries deciding whether to sentence a convicted murderer to death should not be allowed to consider evidence that he'd make a well-adjusted, non-violent prisoner if sentenced to life imprisonment instead. It seemed obvious to me that a jury could reasonably decide not to impose the

death penalty simply because the defendant had shown that he'd do all right in prison if allowed to live, but the state supreme court found it just as obvious that a capital defendant's post-trial behavior was "irrelevant," and that his jury could be prevented from hearing evidence bearing on that issue.[4]

At the time (and for many years before and since) I devoted most of my solo law practice to defending capital clients at trial and on appeal. . . . I was gratified and excited when the Court granted my certiorari petition.[5] And the cert grant in *Skipper* was all the sweeter because exactly six months earlier, the Court had denied the cert petitions I'd filed on behalf of two other death-row clients raising the identical claim.[6]

As I worked on the merits brief, writing and circulating draft after draft to about a dozen members of an informal network of capital defense attorneys and law professors around the country, I tried to reassure myself that the Court had simply granted review to straighten out an aberrant state court that had not read its previous death-penalty decisions closely enough. But those earlier Supreme Court decisions were life-lines to which hundreds of death-row inmates were clinging. So I couldn't help brooding over the fact that the more obviously the state court's decision seemed at odds with Supreme Court precedent, the more disastrous a Supreme Court loss would be. A win for my client would help maybe half a dozen other inmates. But a loss would greatly weaken one of the few constitutional protections—the right to present mitigating evidence—that the Supreme Court had not already watered down.

What's more, just six weeks before the *Skipper* argument, I had seen first-hand what it means to lose a capital case. Terry Roach was a mentally impaired South Carolina prisoner who'd been sentenced to

---

Editor's Note: Footnotes have been included at the request of the author.

This essay first appeared at *5 Journal of Appellate Practice & Process, 75* (2003).

[1] *Wainwright v. Witt,* 469 U.S. 412 (1985) was such a setback. By repudiating the rule of *Witherspoon v. Ill.,* 391 U.S. 510 (1968), that any ambiguity about the propriety of excluding jurors who oppose capital punishment required reversal of the death penalty, Witt doomed jury-selection claims in capital cases, and contributed to the upsurge in executions during the late 1980s and early 1990s.

[2] 476 U.S. 1 (1976).

[3] See *Lockett v. Ohio,* 438 U.S. 586 (1978).

[4] *State v. Koon,* 298 S.E.2d 769, 773–774 (S.C. 1982).

[5] *Skipper v. S.C.,* 474 U.S. 900 (1985).

[6] *Patterson v. S.C., Koon v. S.C.,* 471 U.S. 1036 (1985) (Marshall & Brennan, JJ., dissenting from denial of certiorari).

death for his part in two murders committed when he was 17.[7] I had not been one of his lawyers, but I spent the final six hours keeping him company before he was electrocuted early on the morning of January 10, 1986. After his body had been hoisted from the electric chair onto a gurney and rolled out of the death chamber, I took a small bundle of his belongings (a comb, a Bible, some flip-flops) to his family, who had been waiting in a borrowed apartment a few miles from the prison. Anyone who doubts that there are innocent victims on both sides of every death-penalty case would have been convinced by the scene of stunned devastation that greeted me that morning.

So as the Supreme Court argument approached, I began to feel a little like someone who'd staked his family's life savings on a risky stock in hopes of a three-percent return. I was reasonably sure the Court would rule for my client. But for everyone except him and his family, a loss would hurt a lot more than a win would help. Of course a lawyer puts his own client first, but one can't (and shouldn't) handle a death-penalty case in the Supreme Court without giving a lot of thought to how many people will be hurt (killed, actually) if the case goes bad.

Once the briefs were done, the only way to channel all that anxiety into something constructive was to do a couple of moot argument sessions. I doubted that anything I said or didn't say at oral argument was likely to affect the outcome; whatever the Court's reason for granting review was probably how the case would come out. But I wasn't going to turn down a chance to get grilled by some of the most experienced capital litigators and appellate advocates in the country (including several former Supreme Court law clerks), and after two such sessions, I'd had my chance to stammer through responses to just about every question that would come up during argument before the Court.

February 24, 1986, was a day of brilliant sunshine on newly fallen snow. Shoes freshly shined, I picked my way through the drifts and slush outside the Court, hoping that the unexpected snowfall didn't foreshadow any other obstacles that I'd failed to foresee.

Nowadays, the Clerk, William Suter, conducts a helpful (and reassuring) orientation cum pep-talk for all arguing counsel just after nine o'clock in the lawyer's lounge off the Courtroom. But in the mid-1980s, counsel's only initiation was a sign-in at the Clerk's ground-floor office, followed by a brief introduction to Mr. Spaniol, then the Clerk of the Court, and as much small-talk as the Clerk and eight nervous lawyers on both sides of four unrelated cases could manage (which, as I recall, wasn't much). Then it was on into the Courtroom, where (since I had the third argument), my co-counsel Jack Boger and I waited till about 11:00 to take our places at the "on-deck" table on the petitioner's side of the aisle.

The longest part of the wait was the last minute or so. As counsel for the petitioner, I'd been instructed to take my place at the podium and then to stand and wait for as long as it took the Courtroom to quiet down after the previous case, at which point the Chief Justice would recognize me and I could begin. I was surprised at how intimate the courtroom seemed: The lawyers are just a few feet from the bench and the Justices, and I stood and gazed up at the Chief Justice in a state of suspended animation for what seemed like a very long time. It reminded me of the ski racing I'd done as a kid, standing in the gate waiting for the signal at the top of the slalom course. The trick, our coach had told us, was not to forget to breathe. So I took deep breaths until Chief Justice Burger intoned in his deep baritone voice, "We will hear arguments now in *Skipper against South Carolina*. Mr. Bruck, I think you may proceed when you are ready."

After that, it was a pretty easy run. The state had set up some procedural defenses rather than engage the merits of the South Carolina rule at issue, so I plodded through those, helped by some gentle questioning from Justice O'Connor. At one point I started to insist that there were two things wrong with the state's procedural argument, and the first thing was. . . .

"That it is wrong," Justice White interjected with a smile. There was laughter in the courtroom behind me, and I knew that this was not going to be nearly as hard as I'd feared.

Ten minutes into my argument, the Court recessed for its one-hour lunch break. The sensation was like a time-out in the middle of an Olympic bobsled run. Nothing could provide any greater advantage to one side in a Supreme Court argu-

---

[7] *Roach v. Aiken,* 474 U.S. 1039 (1986) (Brennan & Marshal, JJ., dissenting from denial of stay).

ment. (It's an advantage that no one gets anymore, because with only half as many cases on the Court's current argument calendar as in the mid-1980s, the Court almost never hears more than two arguments on any given day, and both arguments are almost always over by lunch.) Now I had a whole hour to sit with Jack Boger (a brilliant lawyer and gentle soul who then directed the NAACP Legal Defense Fund's Capital Punishment Project), and get his take on how things were going (fine, he thought) and whether I'd answered the Chief's hypothetical questions well enough. By the time the argument resumed, I felt sure the votes were there to reverse, and the rest of my half hour felt like a high-powered but enjoyable (albeit, on my side, slightly manic) conversation with the Justices.

After the argument was over, Jack and I headed out into the first floor hallway where there were congratulations to be had and some decompressing to do, while Court officers patiently but firmly tried to get everyone quieted down and moving towards the exits. But as soon as I could, I needed to get to a pay phone to call my client and let him know how the argument had gone.

The officers on South Carolina's death row had assured me that they'd get Ronnie Skipper to the phone when I called from Washington, and when the time came, they did. I tried not to be overconfident in predicting the outcome, and I'd watched enough Supreme Court arguments by then to know that Justices' questions and comments don't always reveal how a case will turn out. But this argument had gone well, and while I no longer remember exactly what we said, I must have sounded reassured, and I know that I tried to be reassuring.

What I do recall was the sense of incongruity between the majesty and pageantry of the Supreme Court proceedings and the dingy squalor of the death-row cell-block on the other end of the line. It was hard to believe that one could be so intimately connected to the other.

My client's mother had come to Washington for the argument, and I felt almost embarrassed that she was there to witness the elegant, dignified spectacle to which the ruinous calamity of her son's crime and sentence had somehow given rise. I don't encourage family members of condemned clients to attend appellate arguments, because I worry about how it must feel to realize that a son's or a brother's fate turns on the sorts of arcane legal points that are usually at issue. But this time it turned out okay, because when the argument was over and we headed out into the snowy city, we all felt pretty sure that her son was going to get another chance at life.[8] What's more, after having endured a South Carolina prosecutor's shouting and hollering about how Ronnie ought to die, and a jury agreeing, now she'd seen the Supreme Court of the United States calmly considering whether he had been treated fairly, and I suppose there must have been some comfort in that.

---

[8]Sure enough, the Court unanimously reversed the death sentence nine weeks later, Justice White's opinion for the majority sustaining both the Eighth Amendment and due process claims. *Skipper*, 476 U.S. at 2–9. Justice Powell's concurrence, joined by the Chief Justice and Justice Rehnquist, rejected the Eighth Amendment claim but agreed that the death sentence had been obtained in violation of the Due Process Clause. Id. at 9–15 (Powell, J., Burger, C.J., & Rehnquist, J., concurring). That November, Ronnie Skipper was re-sentenced to life imprisonment by a South Carolina court.

9.9 First Arguments at the Supreme Court of the United States: Twice Grilled (2003)

J. Thomas Sullivan

I was fortunate enough to argue two cases before the Court in successive years, a circumstance that I

Editor's Note: Footnotes have been included at the request of the author.

This essay first appeared at 5 *Journal of Appellate Practice & Process*, 151 (2003).

suspect is quite rare for an unknown private practitioner. The experiences have blurred in my memory over time, likely due in no small part to the fact that I lost both cases, but I will try to separate the highlights here.

I do remember that any trip to the Court is indeed an awesome experience. My labor law professor,

Charles J. Morris, had commented in class about the honor of arguing before the Court and then tossed out the suggestion that we, too, would be able to argue a case before the Court one day. His rather simplistic assurance on this point came back to me when I was notified that my first cert petition had been granted. I also remember the sleepless night before that argument; my premature attempts to awaken so that I would be sure to avoid being late; the back-up wake-up call my wife, Suzy, gave me that morning. How foolish she was to ask if I had slept well.

The concerns common to most counsel arguing before the Court were complicated before my first argument by a problem that I can say with some assurance is unique. Three days before my flight to Washington, I was playing with my then one-year-old daughter Molly. A toy she particularly liked had a suction cup on it, and I plopped it onto my forehead to make her laugh. She laughed enthusiastically, bouncing the toy in every which direction trying to pull it off while I steadfastly remained in control of the device for some matter of minutes. When I finally dislodged the thing, it had left a large, well-defined red circle in the middle of my forehead that looked exactly like a target. For the next two days, we tried everything to make the mark go away, but nothing seemed to work. I was worried that the Court might observe me as some kind of nut showing up pre-targeted for oral argument, but thankfully, it disappeared the day of my flight to Washington.

I remember that once I saw it, and then stepped inside it, the Court's impressive building gave me the feeling that this is a place where something very important happens. I think I would have had that feeling even if I had not been a lawyer, even if I had not been there to argue a case that morning. I realized again how much was at stake for my client, and imagining worst-case scenarios, I was quite relieved when I saw a sign indicating that the Supreme Court has a full-time tailor in residence. I put my fears about a ripped seam aside.

I still recall my first appearance at the Court as the worst oral argument I have ever delivered, and one of the worst experiences of my life. I should have won, because I was able to rely on *Brown v. Ohio,*[1] a decision favorable to my client that was almost directly on point. I was also sustained in my optimism

by two other decisions, *Waller v. Florida*[2] and *Robinson v. Neil,*[3] written by Chief Justice Burger and then-Justice Rehnquist, respectively. Both supported my client's argument that his conviction for driving while intoxicated barred a later prosecution for vehicular manslaughter based on the same incident. Regrettably, Justice Powell, who had written the majority opinion in *Brown,* was ill on the day I argued, and I have always wondered whether his absence made a difference, because I lost on a split decision.[4]

Once the case [*Fugate v. New Mexico*] was called, I found myself a total wreck. While my friend and co-counsel Henry Quintero[5] sat comfortably at counsel table after pocketing one of the quill pens, I drank most of the water available at the podium in a vain attempt to moisten my dry throat, and focused on willing my knees to hold me up. I was not in good shape, and I remember that Justice White didn't provide much help. Referring to *Illinois v. Vitale,*[6] another leading case that supported our position, I pronounced *Vitale* using two syllables, just as Dick Vitale, the omnipresent basketball commentator, pronounces his name. Justice White, after pointedly spearing me during my opening sentence to the Court,[7] used a three-syllable approach to *Vitale* when he mentioned the case. Things went downhill from there.

Justice Marshall, whom I shall always respect as a lawyer who not only served on the Court, but argued before it, pointed out that the accident victim had not died until after the resolution of the DUI case, and asked the understandable question: "How can you have a homicide if no one's dead?"[8] I could only tell him that this was just the

---

[1] 432 U.S. 161 (1977).

[2] 397 U.S. 387 (1970).

[3] 409 U.S. 505 (1973).

[4] *Fugate v. N.M.,* 470 U.S. 904 (1985) (per curiam).

[5] Henry Quintero has recently been appointed a district judge for the Sixth Judicial District of New Mexico.

[6] 447 U.S. 410 (1980).

[7] I was stating the issue when he abruptly asked, "Isn't that why we're here?"

[8] One of the recognized exceptions to the application of double jeopardy arises when a critical evidentiary fact—in this case, for example, the victim's death—occurs after the initial prosecution on the lesser offense. Oddly, the New Mexico vehicular homicide statute provided when *Fugate* was decided that a defendant could be prosecuted for causing either death or serious bodily injury. Because the victim had been seriously injured in the accident, Fugate could have been prosecuted for manslaughter when the DUI was pending.

way the New Mexico legislature had written the vehicular homicide statute. It wasn't a convincing response.

I couldn't later explain to my client the four votes to affirm the New Mexico Supreme Court's holding, which relied on a 1912 decision from the occupation of the Philippines that seemed to have been overruled by implication in the large body of far more recent double-jeopardy law. I can't explain it now either, but I do know that *Fugate* remains a constitutional rule that may well apply only in New Mexico.

The following year, New Mexico's Attorney General Paul Bardacke and I met in the Court again when we argued *New Mexico v. Earnest*.[9] General Bardacke, as Justice Rehnquist called him during questioning, had asked me some weeks before if I planned to use the reserved seats to which I was entitled. I had not even been aware that I had reserved seats, having overlooked that part of the instructions to counsel. When I indicated that I had no use for the tickets, he asked if I might cede them to him, and I agreed. Then he explained that Michael Douglas, who had been his roommate at Berkeley, wanted to attend the argument. If only I had been able to finish my script by then! But instead of writing dialogue, I had been writing briefs. I even forgot to ask Paul if he would introduce me to Douglas.

My other clear memory of the events leading up to the argument in *Earnest* is of the pre-game that takes place in the Clerk's chambers, where the lawyers scheduled for the grill that day assemble, get some basic directions, and say their prayers. I know I said one. Then the fellow standing in line before me remarked that the only advice he had been given by the senior partners in his law firm was that the Chief Justice despised button-down collars. He frowned with mild dismay as he suddenly noticed the button-down collar on my brand-new white shirt, and said, "I guess I shouldn't have mentioned that."

Well, it didn't matter. I gave as good an appellate argument as I can, relying on Supreme Court au-

thority indicating that a non-testifying co-defendant's confession could not be admitted as substantive evidence at trial in the absence of a meaningful opportunity for cross-examination. When asked if the New Mexico trial courts had applied the penal-interest exception to admit accomplice confessions in other cases, I looked over at my co-counsel and friend, Susan Gibbs. She shook her head no, allowing me to give a negative answer. She also took one of the quill pens, but this time I drank no water, and my knees held up.

I remember that I found it hard to sit quietly in my seat at counsel table during Bardacke's rebuttal. I almost always represent criminal defendants who have lost in the lower court, so I cherish rebuttal. Yet on the day when I delivered my best and most important argument, I was denied the opportunity for one last plea. I wish I had been given the chance, because the Court vacated the reversal I had won at the New Mexico Supreme Court, and I lost on remand.[10]

Unlike *Fugate*, in which no great issues of constitutional consequence were actually implicated in the argument, the *Earnest* litigation grew out of a longstanding question in Confrontation Clause analysis: Should the statements of accomplices be admitted into evidence when the defendant has had no opportunity to cross-examine those witnesses? Four members of the Court concluded later in *Lilly v. Virginia*[11] that accomplice statements cannot be admitted in the absence of cross-examination. And Justice Scalia, concurring, noted that he would not allow such statements to be admitted if made to the police.[12]

I was heartened by the result in *Lilly*, but also disappointed. It seems clear to me that Ralph Earnest would win if his case came to the Supreme Court today. He wouldn't be serving a life sentence. He would be free.

---

[9]477 U.S. 648 (1986).

[10]*State v. Earnest*, 744 P.2d 539 (N.M. 1987), cert. denied, 484 U.S. 924 (1987). Earnest also lost on his Confrontation Clause claim when he raised it later in a federal habeas proceeding. *Earnest v. Dorsey*, 87 F.3d 1113 (10th Cir. 1996), cert. denied, 519 U.S. 1016 (1996).

[11]527 U.S. 116 (1999).

[12]Id. at 143 (Scalia, J., concurring).

A Comparative Perspective

9.10   Judicial Decisionmaking and the Use of Panels in the Canadian Supreme Court and the South African Appellate Division (2003)

Lori Hausegger and Stacia Haynie

Studies of judicial decisionmaking over the last several decades have significantly increased our understanding of the behavior of the U.S. Supreme Court and the justices who compose it. In an attempt to increase our understanding of courts and of judging more broadly, there recently has been an emphasis on the expansion of comparative judicial research. Such an emphasis will allow scholars to develop truly generalizable theories of judicial decisionmaking that apply to courts beyond the borders of the United States. With this comparative focus in mind, we explore the primary assertions of previous research on appellate court behavior: Judges are affected by their policy preferences, and decisions are made that benefit those preferences. To test our assertions, we analyze the behavior of individuals in two appellate courts: the Supreme Court of Canada in the post-Charter years and the Appellate Division of the Supreme Court of the apartheid-era Republic of South Africa. More specifically, we focus on the behavior of the chief justices in panel assignments, exploring the role of tenure, issue, and ideology.

Interest in panel assignments in the United States has been primarily confined to studies of the federal courts of appeal (the only federal courts to hear cases in panels) during the desegregation era. Several studies of possible influences on these assignments discovered that while assignments were thought to be random in most courts, in the Fifth Circuit at least, the chief justice appeared to be influenced by his policy preferences when assigning justices. Further, scholars have suggested that while

From *Law and Society Review* 37 (2003): 635–654. Reprinted by permission of Blackwell Publishing.

policy preferences may not have an impact in all courts, the panel assignment process could still be classified as nonrandom since considerations of seniority and expertise may influence chief justices.

Although work on panel assignments has been largely abandoned in recent years, research on the opinion assignments of U.S. Supreme Court chief justices can provide insight into possible influences on panel assignments as well. The opinion assignment literature has found differences among the chief justices. Thus, while Chief Justice Rehnquist has been found to consider workload factors most prominently, earlier chief justices were found to consider their own policy preferences when making opinion assignments—those with similar preferences to the chief justice were more likely to be assigned an opinion. Other factors such as judicial expertise, efficiency, experience, and the importance of the case have also been suggested as possible influences by some of this literature. These factors inform our own study of panel assignments—the additional power held by chief justices in our countries of interest. Despite the decreased attention paid to the panel assignment decision in the United States in recent years, we believe this behavior has the potential to significantly affect the outcome of cases. Thus, the factors influencing the chief justice in his assignments need to be explored.

Judging in Comparative Perspective

If we assume that judges are universally drawn from similarly situated populations of elite political actors, we can also assume that some behaviors will be consistently demonstrated across social systems. To test the generalizability of this assertion, analyses must evaluate behaviors across a wide variety of social systems. To explore the assertion that judges will exhibit similar behaviors even in differing polities, we deliberately chose two very diverse countries: Canada and South Africa. Thus, we compare one country with a long, stable democratic tradition beginning a new era of articulated protection of rights and liberties with an authoritarian regime that lacked any pretense of equality among its population. Politically, socially, and economically, these two countries differ dramatically. We argue that if judges exhibit similar behaviors in these two disparate systems, scholars can have greater confidence in the underlying assertions of judicial behavior theory. Moreover, for comparative theory and methodology to develop in public law research, scholars must inevitably include a wide variety of legal systems where differences exist but where the similarities between the courts in each country invite comparison.

We argue that judges, like other political actors, have policy preferences they seek to have adopted by the court in its decisions. Further, we argue that chief justices, in particular, have unique opportunities to shape outcomes. To that end, we chose to study two countries in which the chief justices have greater power than that exercised by the chief justice of the U.S. Supreme Court. In both Canada and South Africa, the court hears disputes in panels, the membership of which is determined by the chief justice. Chief justices may use panel assignment to appoint like-minded judges in an attempt to influence the ultimate decision of the court. We hypothesize that chief justices in both Canada and South Africa will demonstrate such behavior and assign members to panels in a nonrandom manner.

In both countries included in our study, the high courts sit atop a professionalized judiciary and comprise well-trained legal minds. Judges have secure tenure at both courts, and other political institutions give deference to the courts and their decisions. Moreover, both legal systems have been similarly influenced by their British colonial heritages. Despite the enormous differences in the social structures in Canada and South Africa, if our theories of judging are generalizable, we expect similar factors to influence judicial behavior.

The Canadian and South African Courts

Court History and the Exercise of Power

The Supreme Court of Canada and the Appellate Division of the Supreme Court of South Africa (at least for the time period of study) both stand at the apex of their judicial systems—they are courts of last resort. Both courts are part of an integrated judicial system and hear appeals for both provincial and federal law. The South African court exists in a mixed legal system based on both the Roman-Dutch civil law heritage, which arrived with the white settlers of the Dutch East Indian Company in 1652, and the English common law system introduced by the British colonials. Similarly, the Canadian Supreme Court is familiar with both common and civil law as a result of the country's history of English and French settlement. While it is an overstatement to suggest that Canada has a dual legal system (given the dominance of common law), one Canadian province, Quebec, has retained a civil law system. This division within the country has led to the requirement that three of the nine Supreme Court judges on the bench at any given time must come from Quebec.

The South African Appellate Division and the Canadian Supreme Court have experienced varying levels of power. When the Afrikaner National Party ascended to power in South Africa in 1948, bringing with it a devotion to segregation of the races, the courts were originally considered by the opposition to be a harbor of hope. While the Appellate Division of the Supreme Court did not have the ability to exercise traditional powers of judicial review, it did have the capacity to declare acts of Parliament and government officials *ultra vires*.* The opposition saw the courts as a possible avenue to stem the National Party's efforts to obliterate the few rights remaining to people of color, and in a number of cases in the early 1950s the Appellate Division did rule against the government. These rulings brought the court into direct conflict with

---

*Declaring an act or action *ultra vires* is to rule it beyond the scope of the legitimate powers afforded to that level of government (or a particular government official) by the enabling statute or constitutional provision.

the National Party regime. After several exchanges, the government responded by increasing the size of the court from six to 11 and proceeded to pack the court with Afrikaners. Further, in 1956, a newly expanded Senate enabled the Parliament to add a clause to the constitution that specifically denied South African courts the power of judicial review. When this new clause was challenged, the newly expanded Appellate Division sided with Parliament ten to one. From that point, the Appellate Division remained deferential to the government in most of the major disputes before it.

The Canadian Supreme Court, by contrast, became increasingly powerful in the latter half of the twentieth century. In 1949, the court formally became Canada's court of last resort when appeals to the British Judicial Committee of the Privy Council were finally eliminated. In the decades following, the court gained both power and prestige. Although Canada subscribed to the British tradition of parliamentary supremacy, the Canadian court was able to exercise a limited form of judicial review. Canada's federal structure meant the court was often asked to rule on the powers of the provincial and federal governments—keeping each within its own sphere of influence by declaring actions *ultra vires* if necessary. The passage of the Constitution Act in 1982 increased this power for the courts through its entrenchment of constitutional supremacy and its introduction of the Charter of Rights and Freedoms, Canada's own bill of rights. The Canadian Supreme Court now has final responsibility for interpreting the constitution, including the ability to strike down laws and actions it deems inconsistent with the constitution. The court enjoys the full power of judicial review and, with it, increased policymaking power. . . .

The Courts' Cases

The cases analyzed here are drawn from the published decisions of the South African Appellate Division from 1950 to 1990 and of the Canadian Supreme Court from 1986 to 1997. The Canadian Supreme Court and the South African Appellate Division hear appeals of civil and criminal cases with procedural and substantive challenges, based on both common law and statutory grounds. A large portion of each court's docket is composed of crim-

inal cases. The South African court also sees a heavy concentration of economic cases but only a small but increasing number of civil liberties cases. The agenda of the Canadian Supreme Court has undergone a shift. While about 50% of the court's issue agenda was composed of tax cases and ordinary economic disputes in the 1970s, this was reduced to less than 10% by 1990. Instead, civil liberties and civil rights cases increased from barely 10% in the 1970s to comprise about 60% of the court's docket in the 1990s.

The path these cases take to each court differs. In South Africa, appeal is a matter of right, significantly limiting the discretionary control of the court over its docket. Judges on the lower courts are responsible for granting leaves to appeal, but leave should not be granted unless there is a reasonable likelihood that the appellant will prevail. Thus, although the Appellate Division must accept cases that the lower court has granted leave to appeal, these cases should be those involving some controversy. Parties denied leave can appeal that denial to the Appellate Division, which can vote to grant the leave despite the lower court's refusal.

In Canada, the Supreme Court has wide discretionary power on which cases it chooses to hear. Applications for leave to appeal are heard by a panel of three judges and decisions are made by a majority vote. Still, "appeals of right" do exist in Canada for some criminal cases and continue to make up about one-fifth of the Canadian court's agenda.

Court Structure and Judges

The Appellate Division of South Africa consists of a chief justice and a number of judges of appeal. In 1950, the first year of this study, the court consisted of six judges of appeal. By the end of the study (in 1990), there were 18 judges of appeal. However, we note that statutory provisions allow the chief justice occasionally to appoint acting judges of appeal for short periods (from a few months to a few years) to serve during illnesses, absences, or interim periods between appointments. By contrast, the Canadian Supreme Court has consisted of nine members, including the chief justice, since 1949.

Judges on the South African Appellate Division and the Canadian Supreme Court are chosen by the Prime Minister after consultation with the Minister of Justice. In South Africa, the chief justice has significant input on appointments. The Canadian Prime Minister's choice is constrained by the requirement that three members of the Court must come from the province of Quebec to ensure that the court will have members who are familiar with Quebec's civil code. Besides the three seats for judges from Quebec, three seats on the Canadian Court are typically designated for judges from Ontario, the most populous province, while the remaining three seats are shared by judges from the western and Maritime provinces. Only one female judge sat on the Canadian Court until 1987. She was joined by two others by 1989. This number decreased to two in 1991 and remained there until 2000, when it again increased to three. The South African Appellate Division did not have any female judges during the time period of interest, and no judges of color served on either court during the years included in the study.

Judges serve on the South African Appellate Division until retirement at age 70 and on the Canadian Supreme Court until age 75. Both the Canadian and South African constitutions allow Parliament to remove a judge on grounds of incompetence or misbehavior, but no judge has ever been removed in this manner in either nation.

For years in both Canada and South Africa, the most senior judge traditionally was elevated to the position of chief justice when the seat was vacated. A judge's first language was also considered in making the appointment. However, these conventions have been violated in both countries. . . .

The Use of Panels

Unlike their American counterparts, judges on these courts of last resort do not have to sit en banc to hear cases. Instead, judges may decide cases in panels. Indeed, the South African Appellate Division has done so on all but three occasions during the time period of interest. On the Appellate Division, the quorum is five for civil cases and three for criminal cases, although criminal cases considered particularly complex may be assigned to a five-judge panel. The Canadian Supreme Court sits as a panel of five or seven, or as a full Court of nine to hear cases. The most common panel size appears to be seven, despite an apparent preference by recent chief justices to have more cases heard by the full court.

In both countries, the chief justice of the court assigns judges to panels. Very little is known about the panel process itself. For Canada, it appears that the panel assignment is made several weeks before the case is heard—usually after the court has received all submissions in the case. In South Africa, all panel assignments are made before the beginning of the session. Only urgent cases, three to four per year, are added after the close of the roll. However, in both countries, the assignment decision is not announced publicly until the day the case is heard.

There is speculation in South Africa that various chief justices have manipulated their panel assignments to maximize the likelihood of decisions that are closest to their preferred policy positions or their own conceptions of good policy. . . .

In Canada, the few studies addressing possible influences on panel assignments rely mainly on anecdotal evidence. . . .

Comparative Inquiry and Theory Building

One of the basic questions facing students of judicial behavior remains: Why do judges make the choices that they do? In American courts, this question has traditionally been explored through individual voting behavior via the attitudinal model. Judges are presumed to be rational decision makers with specific policy preferences. Though the law and the facts are not irrelevant in the decisionmaking calculus, interpretation of the law and the facts is presumed to be affected by personal preferences. Given that we argue that judges are similar across systems, how can we explore the hypothesis that judges act to further their own policy preferences?

We argue that the assignment of judges to panels provides an opportunity to explore this hypothesis across our two systems. Specifically, we argue that it is important to determine whether South African and Canadian chief justices eschew the advantage of the potential power of panel assignment to further their own preferences or utilize this power to manipulate panel composition and potential outcomes. What does, in fact, influence their panel assignments? Do different factors have a different influence in each country? As mentioned above, we believe answers to these questions are important because the composition of panels may significantly impact—even determine—the outcome of cases. More important, this analysis can provide support for the underlying theoretical assertion of judicial behavior research that judges are affected by nonlegal factors in their choices.

Hypotheses

Both the chief justice of the South African Appellate Division and the chief justice of the Canadian Supreme Court are considered "first among equals." Indeed, their ability to assign members of the court to panels provides additional power not possessed by the U.S. Supreme Court chief justice. What affects the panel assignment choice? This section outlines some possible influences on a chief justice's decision.

Because we argue that judges prefer to see their own perceptions of good policy adopted, the hypotheses expect chief justices in each country to use their leadership resources to influence panel composition rather than to assign randomly. Thus, assignments are expected to be at least partially dictated by the policy preferences of the chief justice. Research on the U.S. Supreme Court has demonstrated empirically that judges' behavior is motivated, in large part, by their individual attitudes or judicial philosophies. And research on the U.S. chief justice's opinion assignments suggests that ideology plays a role in this behavior: those whose preferences are more closely aligned with the chief justice will be assigned to author opinions. Opinion and panel assignments may provide similar opportunities for policy-minded chief justices, and thus both behaviors may be affected by similar variables. That is, chief justices may be more likely to assign to panels individuals whose preferences are more closely aligned with their own. As detailed above, several researchers have investigated the possibility of this type of behavior

on the U.S. Courts of Appeals during the desegregation era. These studies find some evidence of the chief judges of the Fifth Circuit gerrymandering panels. Thus, judges with policy preferences that the chief justice assumes to be closer to that of his own should be more likely to be assigned to panels.

Operationalizing policy preferences requires that the variables be reliable and valid across both systems. We believe that despite the systemic differences between Canada and South Africa, it is nonetheless feasible to create a valid and reliable measure of policy preferences. First, policy preferences indicate a tendency to support particular outcomes in particular issue areas. For U.S. courts, this has been measured as support for or against the underdog. However, including support for all those classified as underdogs in the United States would not be appropriate here because certain issue areas are not comparable across countries. For example, cases supporting government regulation of businesses are generally coded as supportive of the government as the underdog versus businesses as the upperdog. But coding support for the South African government's regulation of a segregated commercial enterprise is obviously not comparable to government regulation in Canada. Instead, we argue that support for those accused of crimes can be used as a comparable measure. Measuring judicial support for the accused in Canada and South Africa should similarly distinguish attitudes among judges because the salience and direction of outcome in this issue area translates across countries. For both countries, these cases involve the social control activities of the state. Individuals accused of violating society's rules are universally less sympathetic to the general population. Evaluating a judge's sympathy for these individuals may generally measure a judge's support for procedural or substantive due process, the issues at bar in criminal disputes in both countries. Second, while measures of judicial policy preferences based on support for the criminally accused are not completely interchangeable with measures based on other types of issues, greater support for procedural or substantive due process translates to more egalitarian or liberal attitudes in both countries. Each judge's policy preference is operationalized as the percentage of votes he or she casts in favor of the accused in criminal cases. . . . We hypothesize that *the closer the judge's score is to that of the chief justice, the more likely he or she will be assigned to a panel.*

While we assert that chief justices consider policy preferences in all cases, they may be particularly attentive in cases involving more politically salient issues. Workload pressures may require the chief justice to distribute panel assignments fairly evenly. The opinion assignment literature has found that the chief justice attempts to equalize the judges' workload when assigning opinions. Some of this same pressure may motivate a chief justice's panel assignments. If chief justices do, in fact, assign judges to panels nonrandomly, we would expect them to reserve like-minded judges for the more salient issues. . . . We expect *those closer to the chief justice's policy preferences to be more likely to be selected for cases involving issues salient to the public, the government, and the judges themselves.*

In Canada, this was operationalized as the presence of a Charter of Rights and Freedoms issue, since these types of civil rights or liberties issues (a subset of the total civil rights and liberties issues heard by the court) were expected to be most salient. The charter involves fundamental issues such as equality rights, language rights, and the rights of criminal defendants. Litigation under the charter has impacted electoral, legislative, and administrative politics. Thus, these cases tend to receive the most attention from the media, the public, and the court itself—they are the "high profile and headline-grabbing" cases.

In South Africa, operationalizing salient issues appears more difficult because there were no constitutionally delineated rights and liberties in that country during the period examined. Nonetheless, as in many countries with parliamentary supremacy and no formal bill of rights, there are certain due process protections via the common law and statutory delineation. The South African courts recognized certain protections for individual liberties, derived from the Roman–Dutch legal traditions and the English law. Therefore, individuals brought challenges when speech, religion, press, association, and even equality were limited. And rights of the accused were also recognized. Attentive publics were particularly cognizant of the rights and liberties cases. Thus, in both countries,

our measure of salience includes the types of civil rights and liberties cases that tend to attract the attention of the public, the elite, and the regime.

While attitude compatibility is expected to be one of the main influences on a chief justice's assignment decision, other factors are expected to constrain his choice. Some research on the opinion assignments of chief justices of the U.S. Supreme Court has found that more experienced judges are more likely to receive opinion assignments than their junior colleagues. Chief justices are expected to give junior judges time to acclimatize to their new, perhaps overwhelming, role. Indeed, Chief Justice Hughes is quoted as saying, "[t]he community has no more a valuable asset than an experienced judge. It takes a new judge a long time to become a complete master of the material of his Court." And Chief Justice Stone is said to have thought that "a new judge beginning the work of the Court should be put at his ease in taking on the work until he is thoroughly familiar with it."

These same sentiments may motivate panel assignments, with chief justices preferring to assign more senior and experienced judges to panels. However, the differences between opinion and panel assignments might also lead to a different expectation. Opinion assignments are a more significant delegation of power. The individual assigned to craft the opinion has the opportunity to shape the specific language of the policy the court has adopted. Opinions can be shaped to restrict the applicability of the outcome or to broaden its significance in the resolution of future conflicts. Merely participating in a panel, however, should not require the same experience as writing the opinion, and any one individual should not have as significant an impact on the outcome of the case. As a result, chief justices may feel less inclined to disproportionately assign senior judges to panels. Indeed, workload pressures may require chief justices to distribute a significant number of panel assignments to junior judges. They may not have the luxury of granting these judges a "transition period" during their early years on the bench.

Therefore, although seniority may affect panel assignments, we do not have firm expectations for the performance of this variable. While following some of the opinion assignment literature would lead one to hypothesize that senior judges may be assigned to panels more frequently, it is also possible that the chief justice will assign junior judges more frequently to panels. Although we lack a strong hypothesis, we expect that *more junior judges may be more likely to be impaneled than senior judges for cases as a whole.*

However, while workload pressures may result in junior judges being assigned to as many or more cases than senior ones, these cases may be the less complex or less salient ones. Chief justices may want to reserve their more experienced colleagues for the most salient cases—cases that are likely to be important to a wider audience and that may benefit from the higher skill levels of senior judges. Thus, we anticipate that *more senior judges will be more likely to be assigned to a panel hearing a salient civil rights or civil liberties case. . . .*

Much of the opinion assignment literature has focused on the effect of freshman judges in particular. This literature emphasizes a "transition time" that freshman judges need to acclimatize to their new position. Because these judges may be assigned to panels differently from other junior judges, we also include a variable measuring whether the judge in question was a freshman on the Court (within their first year of appointment). While junior judges as a whole may not experience the benefits of a "transition period," chief justices may treat new appointees differently. In addition, their recent ascent to the court may make them unavailable to hear cases arriving from lower courts on which they recently served. Thus, we expect *freshman judges to be assigned less frequently to panels.*

The Models

We use multivariate models to determine the factors influencing the composition of panels in Canada and South Africa. . . .

We coded all published cases from 1986 to 1997 for Canada and from 1950 to 1990 for South Africa. For every panel, we created a variable for each judge sitting on the court when the case was heard. Thus, for the dependent variable, each judge received a (1) if he or she participated in a case, that is, if he or she was selected for the panel. A judge received a (0) if he or she was on the bench

but did not participate, that is, if he or she could have been picked but was not. . . .

Results

. . . The results suggest that even in systems as disparate as Canada and South Africa, similar behaviors are evident in the panel assignments of the chief justices. . . . [M]any of the variables are significant and in the predicted direction. The overall models are significant at the 0.001 level. . . .

The variable measuring ideological distance between the chief justices and every sitting judge on their court does appear to have the same effect in each country, but it is in an unexpected direction. For our full range of cases, each country's individual results suggest that the chief justice is actually significantly more likely to select individuals who are further from the chief justice ideologically. . . . Why would the chief justice more often assign judges with whom he disagrees to panels? In Canada, at least, this disparity may be influenced by the chief justice's inclination to assign himself to fewer panels, preferring to participate in en banc hearings (an option possible in Canada but not South Africa). Thus a judge with identical ideology is left off a panel frequently. For both countries, it is also possible that workload pressures require the chief justice to use colleagues with distant preferences for cases as a whole.

However, this assignment disparity does not eliminate ideological considerations by the chief justice. While ideologically distant judges may be assigned to more cases, those closer to the chief justice may be assigned disproportionately to the more salient cases. The results . . . suggest that this may indeed occur. For cases involving salient civil rights and liberties issues, the Canadian and South African chief justices are more likely to assign judges with similar preferences. . . . These results suggest that chief justices may be saving judges with close policy preferences for particular cases. Thus, chief justices may prefer to assign judges with close policy preferences but may be unable to routinely do so across all cases.

The seniority variable does not appear to have the same effect in both countries. In South Africa, senior judges generally are more likely to be placed on panels . . . , while in Canada, junior judges are more likely to be selected. . . . We did not have a strong expectation for this variable's effect, and these results do not help settle the question of influence. It may be that workload pressures are stronger in Canada due to the larger panel sizes (five and seven judges in Canada versus three and five in South Africa) and, therefore, junior judges are pressed into service more often. However, interestingly, in Canada, as in South Africa, junior judges are not more likely to be assigned to the more salient cases. . . . Unable to focus on experience in every case, the chief justice may save his more experienced judges for the most important cases before the court.

The related variable measuring whether a judge was a freshman on the court is significant in both countries and in the expected direction: freshman judges are less likely to be placed on panels. . . . Thus, even in Canada, it appears that chief justices do manage to shield at least first-year judges from some of the heavy workload. . . .

Discussion and Conclusions

We believe that comparative research should encompass multiple-country studies evaluating individual behavior. Such studies will allow scholars to build general theories for certain hypothesized relationships in judicial research. We assert that countries, even those as diverse as Canada and South Africa, can be compared. Judging is a political behavior that exhibits similar actions affected by similar influences. These results suggest that panel assignment is one such behavior. . . .

Examining chief justices' decisions across countries provides one avenue for examining behavior among judicial actors. Using comparable measures of dependent and independent variables, we find that chief justices in both Canada and South Africa do not assign their colleagues randomly. In both countries, policy preferences have an impact on those decisions. Chief justices appoint those further from their preferences for cases as a whole, with Canadian chief justices more likely than South African chief justices to assign those further from them to panels. However, when panels concern salient issues, both Canadian and South African chief justices appoint judges closer to them more often. In addition, seniority has an impact in both countries, albeit in a different direction for each.

Future research must attempt to delineate the relationships we assessed even more precisely. Because we measured preferences as the absolute value of the distance from the chief justice, extremely conservative judges and extremely liberal judges will have the same score. The Canadian chief justices have larger panel sizes and may appoint both extremely conservative and extremely liberal judges to the panels alongside members who are more closely aligned with the chief justice. The ideologues will then be marginalized, and the panel median will remain closer to the chief justice. Such ideologues may be less common in South Africa, giving the chief justice a simpler decisionmaking calculus in panel choices.

Future research should also expand our simplistic model to include other potential influences such as issue specialization or other indicators of case importance. Finally, future research should evaluate the effect of chief justices' panel assignments on outcomes. It may be that the chief justices are attempting to wield greater influence over court decisions but futilely so. Conversely, chief justices' behavior may be significant in terms of policy outcomes of high courts.

Beginning with a simple plan to test the feasibility of cross-country studies exploring judicial behavior, we selected a common behavior, panel assignment, across very diverse countries. Our analysis suggests that some aspects of existing judicial theory can be used to explain behaviors beyond the borders of the United States. The addition of other countries is obviously necessary to increase our confidence in that assertion, but this research demonstrates the feasibility of analyses across widely differing social systems, an important finding for the future of comparative research.

For Further Reading

Baum, Lawrence, Sheldon Goldman, and Austin Sarat. "Evolution of Litigation in Federal Courts of Appeals: 1895–1975." *Law and Society Review* 16 (1981): 291.

Coffin, Frank M. *On Appeal: Courts, Lawyering, and Judging.* New York: Norton, 1994.

Howard, J. Woodford, Jr. "Role Perceptions and Behavior in Three U.S. Courts of Appeals." *Journal of Politics* 39 (1977): 916.

Klein, David E. *Making Law in the United States Courts of Appeals.* New York: Cambridge University Press, 2002.

Songer, Donald R., Stephanie A. Lindquist, and Susan B. Haire. "One Principal and Multiple Agents: Supreme Court Auditing of the United States Courts of Appeals." *Law and Society Review* 37 (2003): 143.

Chapter 10

Courts and Public Opinion

Introduction

The relationship between courts and the American public is complex and demonstrates vividly the political nature of the judiciary. Courts are unique institutions of American government because they are inherently less democratic than legislatures and executives. All federal judges and many state judges are unelected officials who often make countermajoritarian decisions. They can and do make such decisions because they are relatively independent of the public demands that elected officials face. At the same time, however, and as Alexander Hamilton observed in *Federalist* No. 78, courts have neither the purse nor the sword to enforce their decisions. Compliance with judicial rulings depends on support from the American public. If the public believes that courts and judges are not operating appropriately or effectively, the institutional legitimacy of courts may be diminished. The media play a critical but controversial role in the relationship between the public and courts. Not only are they the primary source of information for most Americans, but their access to the public is protected, at least to some degree, by the First Amendment.

The readings in this chapter suggest that scholars, judges, and other legal actors are aware of the conflict that can exist between judicial independence and public support. Students of the Supreme Court have been primarily interested in the Court's willingness to exercise judicial review and its ability to confer legitimacy upon its rulings in the absence of public support. Additionally, they have asked, how are judges to be independent of but also attentive to public support? What should and does the American public know about courts and the justice system, and how influential is their knowledge on the business of courts? How do restraints on the dissemination of information affect public knowledge and opinions about the judiciary? How do the media contribute to public awareness and perceptions of the courts and law? And, how can courts maintain their legitimacy when they are confronted by public disapproval?

Foundations and History

In "The Court and American Life" (2003), David M. O'Brien presents a thoughtful and thorough discussion of how the Supreme Court manages the balance between independence and public confidence. He emphasizes the Court's ruling in *Brown v. Board of Education* (1954) as an example of how the Court struggles with making policy while attending to the needs and desires of the American public as it strives to maintain its institutional legitimacy. In so doing, O'Brien directly addresses the conundrum of an undemocratic Court in a democratic political system.

Political science research examining the relationship between the judiciary and the American public has a long history, much of it focusing on the legitimacy of the Supreme Court. Given the power of judicial review, early scholars emphasized normative questions such as whether the Court *should* exercise review. Later research is more empirical, asking how and when the Court does exercise review and whether this exercise affects its legitimacy. We have included a seminal piece of research by Richard Funston. "The Supreme Court and Critical Elections" (1975) follows and precedes several groundbreaking articles in this line of research. Funston systematically examines the Court's countermajoritarian behavior in connection with political party systems and realigning elections. Does the Court follow the election returns? Does it attend to the will of the public by supporting legislation passed by the people's representatives, or are there times when the Court rejects majority preferences in support of minority's? His analysis demonstrates that the Court is most likely to exercise judicial review when the party system is in transition, and is most likely to uphold the will of the lawmaking majority during periods of electoral stability.

Contemporary Judicial Politics

While Funston's work focuses on the connection between the Supreme Court and elite opinion in the form of congressional and executive lawmaking majorities, other research focuses on the relationship between courts and the public. Again, much of the earliest work is normative. It asks whether the courts *should* be attentive to or affected by public opinion. In the last several decades, though, the primary question has become empirical: *Are* courts attentive to public opinion? Are the courts influenced by public opinion or, conversely, do they influence the public? Most of the research focuses on the Supreme Court, and the selection that we include here is no exception. Jeffrey L. Yates and Andrew B. Whitford's research, presented in "The Presidency and the Supreme Court After *Bush v. Gore:* Implications for Institutional Legitimacy and Effectiveness" (2002) is particularly interesting. It addresses the controversial 2000 presidential election and the question of whether the Court's legitimacy was negatively affected by its decision in *Bush v. Gore* (2000). Using Gallup Poll data to measure public support for the Court, they find that, despite claims to the contrary, the Court's legitimacy and effectiveness appear not to be diminished by its role in the election.

If the Supreme Court is to maintain its legitimacy by influencing public opinion, it follows that the public must know something about the Court. Elliot E. Slotnick and Jennifer A. Segal examine television news coverage of the Supreme Court in "Television News and the Supreme Court: Opportunities and Constraints" (1998) in an effort to understand the difficulties that the media face when gathering information to deliver to the public. Through interviews with several former and current Court reporters, Slotnick and Segal illustrate the contrasts between the needs of the media and the interests of the Court, and how they interact to affect the type of information that the American public receives about the work of the Court.

A View from the Inside

Much of the discussion about courts and the public occurs in the context of trial courts where the impact of the media and the public on court processes can be great. Long before the O. J. Simpson and Rodney King cases, Sam Sheppard was tried for allegedly bludgeoning his wife to death in their home. We have included in this first section the Supreme Court's ruling in *Sheppard v. Maxwell* (1966) because it provides an excellent discussion of many of the issues related to the interaction between courts and the public. It establishes important precedent for the fundamental issue in the case: What constitutes a fair trial? To answer the question, the Court provides a detailed description of the events surrounding the trial, including who collected the evidence and how it was collected, how the judge and lawyers behaved throughout the trial, how the jury was selected and treated, and how the media participated in and influenced the trial. The appropriate balance between the defendant's right to a fair trial and the public's right to be informed was critical to the Court's decision. In the end, the Court found that despite the rights of the public and the media, the balance can never tip against the interests of the defendant.

In the past several years, several Supreme Court justices have commented on the role of public opinion in death penalty decisions. We include here one of the most articulate views on this topic, made by Chief Justice Rehnquist in his dissent in *Atkins v. Virginia* (2002). In this case involving the constitutionality of the death penalty for mentally handicapped defendants, Rehnquist argued that it is no less than "judicial fiat" for the Court to look past legislative directives and jury verdicts to public opinion polls, international laws, and the views of interest groups in determining the constitutionality of the death penalty. Particularly notable is Rehnquist's discussion about the reliability and validity problems associated with public opinion data. More recently, these arguments have been reiterated in the dissenting opinions in *Roper v. Simmons* (2005), a case involving the execution of minors.

A Comparative Perspective

The concern about institutional legitimacy is not confined to the United States. As James L. Gibson and Gregory A. Caldeira demonstrate in "Defenders of Democracy? Legitimacy, Popular Acceptance, and the South African Constitutional Court" (2003), the role of courts in emerging democracies is of great interest insofar as they are critical to the success of democratic politics. Through an extensive survey of South Africans, Gibson and Caldeira examine the degree to which legitimacy leads to compliance. Their research explains theories of legitimacy and describes the creation and function of the South African Constitutional Court. The results of their data analysis suggest that the Constitutional Court has not met with the same degree of support as have courts in other democratic countries, thus inhibiting the Court's ability to promote its rulings and defend democracy in South Africa.

Foundations and History

10.1 The Court and American Life (2003)

David M. O'Brien

"Why does the Supreme Court pass the school desegregation case?" asked one of Chief Justice Vinson's law clerks in 1952. *Brown v. Board of Education of Topeka, Kansas* had arrived on the Court's docket in 1951, but it was carried over for oral argument the next term and then consolidated with four other cases and reargued in December 1953. The landmark ruling did not come down until May 17, 1954. "Well," Justice Frankfurter explained, "we're holding it for the election"—1952 was a presidential election year. "You're holding it for the election?" The clerk persisted in disbelief. "I thought the Supreme Court was supposed to decide cases without regard to elections." "When you have a major social political issue of this magnitude," timing and public reactions are important considerations, and, Frankfurter continued, "we do not think this is the time to decide it." Similarly, Tom Clark recalled that the Court awaited, over Douglas's dissent, additional cases from the District of Columbia and other regions, so as "to get a national coverage, rather than a sectional one." Such political considerations are

by no means unique. "We often delay adjudication. It's not a question of evading at all," Clark concluded. "It's just the practicalities of life—common sense."

Denied the power of the sword or the purse, the Court must cultivate its institutional prestige. The power of the Court lies in the persuasiveness of its rulings and ultimately rests with other political institutions and public opinion. As an independent force, the Court has no chance to resolve great issues of public policy. *Dred Scott v. Sandford* (1857) and *Brown v. Board of Education* (1954) illustrate the limitations of Supreme Court policy-making. The "great folly," as Senator Henry Cabot Lodge characterized *Dred Scott*, was not the Court's interpretation of the Constitution or the unpersuasive moral position that blacks were not persons under the Constitution. Rather, "the attempt of the Court to settle the slavery question by judicial decision was simple madness. . . ."

A hundred years later, political struggles within the country and, notably, presidential and congressional leadership in enforcing the Court's school desegregation ruling saved the moral appeal of *Brown* from becoming another "great folly."

Because the Court's decisions are not self-executing, public reactions inevitably weigh on the minds of the justices. Justice Stone, for one, was furious at Chief Justice Hughes's rush to hand down *Powell v. Alabama* (1932). Picketers protested the Scottsboro boys' conviction and death sentence. Stone attributed the Court's rush to judgment to Hughes's "wish to put a stop to the [public] demonstrations around the Court." Opposition to the school desegregation ruling in *Brown* led to bitter, sometimes violent confrontations. In Little Rock, Arkansas, Governor Orval Faubus encouraged disobedience by southern segregationists. The federal National Guard had to be called out to maintain order. The school board in Little Rock unsuccessfully pleaded, in *Cooper v. Aaron* (1958), for the Court's postponement of the implementation of *Brown's* mandate. In the midst of the controversy, Frankfurter worried that Chief Justice Warren's attitude had become "more like that of a fighting politician than that of a judicial statesman." In such confrontations between the Court and the country, "the transcending issue," Frankfurter reminded the others, remains that of preserving "the Supreme Court as the authoritative organ of what the Constitution requires." When the justices move too far or too fast in their interpretation of the Constitution, they threaten public acceptance of the Court's legitimacy.

The Court's institutional prestige and role in American politics occasionally weighs heavily on the justices, particularly when confronting major controversies. The plurality opinion issued by Justices Kennedy, O'Connor, and Souter in *Casey*, declining to overrule "the essence of *Roe v. Wade*" while rejecting much of its analysis, . . . illustrates that concern. So too, the Court sought to avoid igniting another major controversy in its 1997 rulings in *Washington v. Glucksberg* and *Vacco v. Quill*. There, the Court refused to extend its 1990 ruling in *Cruzan v. Cruzan,* recognizing the right of terminally ill patients to have life-support systems withdrawn, to embrace a right to physician-assisted suicide. Chief Justice Rehnquist's opinion for the Court, and several concurring opinions, emphasized that that claim of the so-called right to die with dignity movement should continue to play out in state legislatures and the political process, while not completely ruling out in the future the Court's reconsideration of such a constitutional claim.

The political struggles of the Court (and among the justices) continue after the writing of opinions and final votes. Announcements of decisions trigger diverse reactions from the media, interest groups, lower courts, Congress, the president, and the general public. Their reactions may enhance or thwart compliance and reinforce or undermine the Court's prestige. Opinion days thus may reveal something of the political struggles that might otherwise remain hidden within the marble temple. They may also mark the beginning of larger political struggles for influence in the country.

Opinion Days

The justices announce their decisions in the courtroom, typically crowded with reporters, anxious attorneys, and curious spectators. When several decisions are to be handed down, the justices delivering the Court's opinions make their announcements in reverse order of seniority. Authors of concurring or dissenting opinions are free to give their views orally as well. Before 1857, decisions were announced on any day the Court was in session. Thereafter the practice was to announce decisions only on Mondays, but in 1965 the Court reverted to its earlier practice. In 1971, the Court further broke with the late-nineteenth-century tradition of "Decision Mondays." On Mondays, the Burger Court generally released only orders and summary decisions and admitted new attorneys to its bar. The Rehnquist Court followed that practice until 1995, when it decided that it would immediately release (but not announce in the courtroom) which cases were granted after the Friday conference, instead of waiting until Mondays, so it could speed up the scheduling of oral arguments. In those weeks when the justices hear oral arguments (October through April), the Court usually announces opinions on Tuesdays and Wednesdays, and then on any day of the week during the rest of the term (May and June). By tradition, there is no prior announcement as to when cases will be handed down.

Even as late as Warren's last term, in 1968–1969, entire days were devoted to the delivery of opinions and admission of attorneys. In 1971, Burger managed to persuade the others, over the strong objections of Black, to make only brief summary announcements. But he failed to get the justices to agree to put an end to what he considered an "archaic practice" of orally announcing opinions from the bench. Justices now announce most opinions in two to four minutes, merely stating the result in each case.

The erosion of the practice of reading the full text of opinions was only partly due to its time-consuming nature. The practice sometimes occasioned outbursts and caustic exchanges among the justices, publicly dramatizing the struggles within the Court. Once, when vigorously dissenting, McReynolds hit the bench with his fist, exclaiming, "The Constitution is gone!" and then explained why he thought so. Frankfurter tended to monopolize opinion days, just as he liked to dominate oral arguments and conference discussions. In one instance, after he had ad-libbed at length when delivering the Court's opinion, Chief Justice Stone snidely remarked. "By God, Felix, if you had put all that stuff in the opinion, never in my life would I have agreed to it." On another occasion, in a relatively minor case, Frankfurter took nearly fifteen minutes to attack the majority's ruling as nonsense. His sharp criticism prompted Chief Justice Warren, who had not even written an opinion in the case, to offer a rebuttal in open Court. Warren then turned to Frankfurter and invited him to respond. Not to be outdone, the latter told the courtroom, "The Chief Justice urges me to comment on what he said, but of course I won't. I have another case." Such extemporaneous exchanges are rare now, with the prevalence of summary announcements.

Communicating Decisions to the Media

"Sir, we write the opinions, we don't explain them." That was the response of New Jersey State Supreme Court Chief Justice Arthur Vanderbilt to a reporter's request that he explain a passage in an opinion. Members of the Supreme Court generally agree with that motto. Opinions, Brennan has observed, "must stand on their own merits without embellishment or comment from the judges who write or join them." Justice White was notorious for simply announcing that the lower court was re-

versed or affirmed "for reasons on file with the Clerk." By contrast, when Justice Ginsburg announces a decision she reads from a prepared text that is later given to reporters. Reporters nonetheless complain about the secrecy surrounding the Court's decision making, while justices complain that their decisions are distorted by the media.

Justices appreciate that compliance with their decisions depends on public understanding of their opinions. Sometimes they are particularly sensitive to this consideration. Chief Justice Hughes, for instance, permitted President Roosevelt to run a telephone line from the White House to the Court in order to learn immediately the Court's decision in the *Gold Clause* cases (1935). This decision was vital to the New Deal in upholding FDR's removal of the gold standard and the devaluation of the dollar. . . . When *Brown v. Board of Education* was decided, Warren insisted that "the opinion should be short, readable by the lay public, non-rhetorical, unemotional and, above all, non-accusatory."

Media coverage of the Court has grown in the last seventy years. In the 1930s, less than half a dozen reporters covered the Court on a regular basis. During Hughes's chief justiceship, a "Press Office" was established in the Office of the Marshal. The single "press officer"—a former reporter—would announce those cases on the Court's conference list and those set for oral argument. Later, in the 1940s, he began distributing an edited list of the cases. Reporters had six small cubicles on the ground floor, just below the courtroom, where they received copies of opinions sent down through a pneumatic tube. By the late 1950s, there were full-time reporters from the United Press International (UPI), the Associated Press (AP), a few major newspapers, and a couple of more specialized legal periodicals, such as *U.S. Law Week*. In the last three decades, the number of reporters steadily increased to about thirty, with a core group of regular journalists about half that number. However, all three major television networks, along with Cable News Network, once had regular reporters at the Court, but dropped them in the 1980s and 1990s.

Despite the growing media attention, the justices remain somewhat indifferent to the problems of journalists who try to make the Court's decisions understandable for the public. Inevitably at odds with the Court's traditions, journalists are at times frustrated by their limited access to the justices. Shortly after coming to the Court, Burger was confronted with a petition of grievances by the corps of reporters covering the Court. . . . "so that the public may be better informed about the Court." Not all of the demands appeared reasonable from the Court's perspective. The Court was unreceptive to demands for reasons that justices sometimes disqualify themselves from cases and for "access to the staff of the justices." The Court also rejected a proposed press privilege of having—"on a confidential basis"—advance notification and copies of the opinions to be handed down.

But changes have been made, though not without opposition from some justices. On opinion days, journalists now receive copies of the headnotes—prepared by the Reporter of Decisions and summarizing the lineup of the justices and the main points of a decision. Justice Black disapproved on the ground that "the press will understand the opinions better." The Court also now has an expanded Public Information Office, which makes available all filings and briefs for cases on the docket, the Court's conference lists and final opinions, as well as speeches made by the justices. Reporters thus may follow cases from the time of filing to acceptance for oral argument, and then listen to oral arguments and the delivery of decisions as well as immediately read the final published opinions. Even so, the media's access to the justices remains limited. No cameras are permitted in the courtroom when the Court is in session, nor does that prospect appear likely in the near future. As Justice Souter put it in 1996 when testifying before a House of Representatives appropriations committee hearing: "I think the case [against cameras in the courtroom] is so strong that I can tell you that the day you see a camera coming into our courtroom, it's going to roll over my dead body."

In light of these changes, Burger felt that "except for its decision conferences, the Supreme Court literally operates 'in a goldfish bowl.' " But reporters feel differently. They do not have the kind of access to the Court that they do to Congress, the president, and the executive branch. As the *New York Times*' Linda Greenhouse observed, "Sources, leaks, casual contact with newsmakers—none of these hallmarks of Washington journalism exists on the Court beat." To some the secrecy within the marble temple is disturbing, though others are less troubled by it. "It is more valuable to have a Justice on the record [in a printed opinion] saying what he or she means than hearing some Hill aide anonymously explain the actions of a senator or congressman." As the former *Washington Post* reporter Fred Barbash remarked, "No other institution explains itself at such length, such frightening length."

Some of the difficulties of covering the Court are inherent in the business of journalism—press deadlines, the problems of condensing complex decisions into a 180-second "news slot" or "soundbite," and possibly, even the training of reporters. The Court has tried to address even such practical matters. For example, in opening the session at ten in the morning rather than at noon, the Warren Court provided a couple of extra hours so as to relieve some of the pressures of reporters' deadlines. "Decision Mondays" were also abandoned in response to complaints that the "massing of opinions" on a single day made conscientious reporting virtually impossible. Reporters continue to complain that the Court hands down too many of its major decisions during the last week of the term.

The public learns through the media something about only a few of the Court's rulings each term. Usually, only the most controversial rulings by the Court are reported. Studies of media coverage of the Court's rulings indicate that the major television networks report on no more than half of the most important decisions each term, and the bulk of the Court's work receives no attention.

Within a short period of time, both print and broadcast reporters must condense often complex and lengthy opinions in an understandable way for the public. Only about half of the reporters who cover the Court have law degrees. Not surprisingly, they disagree about the importance of formal legal education. "Lawyer-reporters tend to use less jargon," claims NBC's former Court reporter Carl Stern. "Non-lawyers fear to stray from the literal words used by the Court." By contrast, the veteran reporter Lyle Denniston maintains, "A law degree inhibits one's ability to cover the Court." Law schools, he insists, "train you to have too much respect for authority" and "teach you to be-lieve that things are done better the higher you go."

Regardless of whether reporters have a legal background, the interpreting of opinions remains difficult. Some decisions are "literally impossible to decipher," the *New York Times* reporter Linda Greenhouse has noted. Some problems in com-municating decisions are of the Court's own mak-ing. Since opinions for the Court must meet the approval of a majority of the justices, ambiguity results from the negotiations and compromises necessary to reach agreement. . . . Ambiguities may also be prudent. They leave problems open for later cases, and the Court preserves its policy-making options. For example, reporters, school boards, and citizens celebrated or cursed *Brown v. Board of Education* for not mandating integration rather than merely ending segregation. But justices like Stanley Reed had no doubt about that "big distinction." They would never have gone along with a ruling mandating integration. As Warren later emphasized, the justices "decided only that the practice of segregating children in public schools solely because of their race was unconsti-tutional. This left other questions to be an-swered"—answered in later cases, after the justices had gauged public reactions and further deliberated among themselves.

Misunderstanding also results when opinions in-clude extraneous matter, statements of personal philosophy, and other forms of *obiter dicta*—words entirely unnecessary for the decision of the case. These problems are exacerbated by longer, more heavily footnoted opinions. The justices are partic-ularly confusing when they divide five to four and issue numerous concurring and dissenting opin-ions.

Implementing Rulings and Achieving Compliance

When deciding major issues of public law and pol-icy, justices must consider strategies for getting public acceptance of their rulings. When striking down the doctrine of "separate but equal" facilities in 1954 in *Brown v. Board of Education (Brown I)*,

for instance, the Warren Court waited a year before issuing, in *Brown II*, its mandate for "all deliberate speed" in ending racial segregation in public edu-cation.

Resistance to the social policy announced in *Brown I* was expected. A rigid timetable for deseg-regation would only intensify opposition. During oral arguments on *Brown II*, devoted to the ques-tion of what kind of decree the Court should issue to enforce *Brown*, Warren confronted the hard fact of southern resistance. The attorney for South Car-olina, S. Emory Rogers, pressed for an open-ended decree—one that would not specify when and how desegregation should take place. He boldly pro-claimed:

> Mr. Chief Justice, to say we will conform de-pends on the decree handed down. I am frank to tell you, right now [in] our district I do not think that we will send—[that] the white people of the district will send their children to the Negro schools. It would be unfair to tell the Court that we are going to do that. I do not think it is. But I do think that something can be worked out. We hope so.

"It is not a question of attitude," Warren shot back, "it is a question of conforming to the de-cree." Their heated exchange continued as follows:

> *Chief Justice Warren:* But you are not willing to say here that there would be an honest attempt to conform to this decree, if we did leave it to the district court [to implement]?

> *Mr. Rogers:* No, I am not. Let us get the word "honest" out of there.

> *Chief Justice Warren:* No, leave it in.

> *Mr. Rogers:* No, because I would have to tell you that right now we would not conform—we would not send our white children to the Negro schools.

The exchange reinforced Warren's view "that reasonable attempts to start the integration process is [*sic*] all the court can expect in view of the scope of the problem, and that an order to immediately admit all negroes in white schools would be an absurdity because impossible to obey in many areas. . . .

The Court's problem, as one of Reed's law clerks put it, was to frame a decree "so as to allow such divergent results without making it so broad that evasion is encouraged." The clerks agreed that there should be a simple decree but disagreed on whether there should be guidelines for its implementation. . . .

At conference, Warren repeated these concerns. Black and Minton thought that a simple decree, without an opinion, was enough. As Black explained, "the less we say the better off we are." The others disagreed. . . .

Agreement emerged that the Court should issue a short opinion-decree. In a memorandum, Warren summarized the main points of agreement. The opinion should simply state that *Brown I* held racially segregated public schools to be unconstitutional. *Brown II* should acknowledge that the ruling created various administrative problems, but emphasize that "local school authorities have the primary responsibility for assessing and solving these problems; [and] the courts will have to consider these problems in determining whether the efforts of local school authorities" are in good-faith compliance. The cases, he concluded, should be remanded to the lower courts "for such proceedings and decree necessary and proper to carry out this Court's decision." The justices agreed, and along these lines Warren drafted the Court's short opinion-decree.

The phrase "all deliberate speed" was . . . inserted in the final opinion at the suggestion of Frankfurter. Forced integration might lead to a lowering of educational standards. Immediate, court-ordered desegregation, Frankfurter warned, "would make a mockery of the Constitutional adjudication designed to vindicate a claim to equal treatment to achieve 'integrated' but lower educational standards." The Court, he insisted, "does its duty if it gets effectively under way the righting of a wrong. When the wrong is deeply rooted state policy the court does its duty if it decrees measures that reverse the direction of the unconstitutional policy so as to uproot it 'with all deliberate speed.' As much an apology for not setting precise guidelines as a

recognition of the limitations of judicial power, the phrase symbolized the Court's bold moral appeal to the country.

Ten years later, after school closings, massive resistance, and continuing litigation, Black complained: "There has been entirely too much deliberation and not enough speed" in complying with *Brown*. "The time for mere 'deliberate speed' has run out." *Brown's* moral appeal amounted to little more than an invitation for delay. . . .

With no federal leadership, implementation of *Brown* was deliberately slow and uneven. . . . The Department of Justice had little role in ending school segregation before the passage of the Civil Rights Act of 1964. . . .

By the mid-1960s, the Departments of Justice and HEW [Health Education and Welfare] had assumed leadership in implementing *Brown*. But it took time to build records and evidence of segregation in northern and western school districts and to challenge local authorities in the courts. Not until the summer of 1968 did the outgoing Johnson administration initiate the first school desegregation cases in the North and the West and try to achieve the national coverage that the Court envisioned in *Brown*.

In 1969, Black impatiently observed "There is no longer the slightest excuse, reason, or justification for further postponement of the time when every public school system in the United States will be a unitary one. . . ."

. . . Black concluded that the Court's emphasis on "all deliberate speed" had been a "self-inflicted wound." "The duty of this Court and of the others," he implored, "is too simple to require perpetual litigation and deliberation. That duty is to extirpate all racial discrimination from our system of public schools NOW." . . .

Twenty years after *Brown*, some schools remained segregated. David Mathews, secretary of the Department of Health, Education, and Welfare, reported to President Ford the results of a survey of half of the nation's primary and secondary public schools, enrolling 91 percent of all students: of these, 42 percent had an "appreciable percentage" of minority students, 16 percent had undertaken desegregation plans, while 26 percent had not, and 7 percent of the school districts remained racially segregated.

For over four decades, problems of implementing and achieving compliance with *Brown* persisted. Litigation by civil rights groups forced change, but it was piecemeal, costly, and modest. The judiciary alone could not achieve desegregation. Evasion and resistance were encouraged by the reluctance of presidents and Congress to enforce the mandate. Refusing publicly to endorse *Brown,* Eisenhower would not take steps to enforce the decision until violence erupted in Little Rock, Arkansas. He then did so "*not* to enforce integration but to prevent opposition by violence to orders of a court." Later the Kennedy and Johnson administrations lacked congressional authorization and resources to take major initiatives in enforcing school desegregation. Not until 1964, when Congress passed the Civil Rights Act, did the executive branch have such authorization.

Enforcement and implementation required the cooperation and coordination of all three branches. . . . The simplicity and flexibility of *Brown* . . . invited evasion. It produced a continuing struggle over measures, such as gerrymandering school district lines and busing in the 1970s and 1980s, because the mandate itself had evolved from one of ending segregation to one of securing integration in public schools. Republican and Democratic administrations in turn differed on the means and ends of their enforcement policies in promoting integration.

Over forty years after *Brown,* over 500 school desegregation cases remained in the lower federal courts. At issue in most was whether schools had achieved integration and become free of the vestiges of past segregation. . . . [T]he Court declined to review major desegregation cases from the mid-1970s to the end of the 1980s. During that time the dynamics of segregation in the country changed, as did the composition and direction of the Court.

In the 1980s support for mandated school desegregation waned and the Reagan and Bush administrations encouraged localities to escape the "burdens" of *Brown* by fighting courts' desegregation orders. The federal bench also grew more conservative and integration proved elusive. By the 1990s resegregation was on the rise in many parts of the country, particularly in the Midwest and Northeast for blacks and in the West for Hispanics. . . . However, the South became one of the most integrated regions in the country. Whereas 99 percent of blacks in the South attended all-black schools in 1963, only 24 percent went to schools enrolling 90–100 percent minorities in the 1990s. By comparison, 48 percent in the Northeast attended predominantly nonwhite schools, 42 percent in the Midwest, and 28 percent in the West. Although the Northeast and Midwest have less than half the old Confederacy's proportion of black students, they have twice the South's level of intense segregation. As a result, a "black family moving from Michigan or New Jersey to Georgia or Tennessee is more likely now to see their child grow up in integrated schools than if they had remained in the North.". . .

Brown, nonetheless, dramatically and undeniably altered the course of American life. . . . Neither Congress nor President Eisenhower would have moved to end segregated schools in the 1950s, as their reluctance for a decade to enforce *Brown* underscores. The Court lent moral force and legitimacy to the civil rights movement and to the eventual move by Congress and President Johnson to enforce compliance with *Brown.* . . .

Public Opinion and Partisan Realignment

Public opinion serves to curb the Court when it threatens to go too far or too fast in its rulings. The Court has usually been in step with major political movements, except during transitional periods or critical elections. It would nevertheless be wrong to conclude, along with Finley Peter Dunne's fictional Mr. Dooley, that "th' supreme court follows th' iliction returns." To be sure, the battle over FDR's "Court-packing" plan and the Court's "switch in time that saved nine" in 1937 give that impression. Public opinion supported the New Deal, but after his landslide reelection in 1936, turned against FDR when he proposed to "pack the Court" by increasing its size from nine to fifteen. In a series of five-to-four and six-to-three decisions in 1935–1936, the Court had struck down virtually every important measure of FDR's New Deal program. But in the spring of 1937, while the Senate Judiciary Committee considered FDR's proposal, the Court abruptly handed down three five-to-four rulings upholding major pieces of New Deal legislation. Shortly afterward, FDR's close personal friend and soon-to-be nominee for the

Court, Felix Frankfurter, wrote Justice Stone confessing that he was "not wholly happy in thinking that Mr. Dooley should, in the course of history turn out to have been one of the most distinguished legal philosophers." Frankfurter, of course, knew that justices do not simply follow the election returns. The fact that the Court abandoned its opposition to the New Deal when it did, moreover, significantly undercut public support for FDR's Court-packing plan. . . . In this instance at least, as political scientist Gregory Caldeira concludes, the Court "outmaneuvered the president" and by retreating from its defense of conservative economic policy shaped public opinion in favor of preserving its institutional integrity. . . .

Life in the marble temple is not immune from shifts in public opinion. For one thing, [Justice] Scalia emphasizes, "it's a little unrealistic to talk about the Court as though it's a continuing, unchanging institution rather than to some extent necessarily a reflection of the society in which it functions. Ultimately, the justices of the Court are taken from the society, [and] if the society changes, you are going eventually to be drawing judges from that same society, and however impartial they may try to be, they are going to bring with them those societ[al] attitudes."

The justices, however, deny being directly influenced by public opinion. . . .

The Court's prestige rests on preserving the public's view that justices base their decisions on interpretations of the law, rather than on their personal policy preferences. Yet complete indifference to public opinion would be the height of judicial arrogance. Even one so devoted to the law as Frankfurter was not above appealing to the forces of public opinion. When the Warren Court debated the landmark reapportionment case, Frankfurter asked Stewart—who had the pivotal vote—to consider that *Baker v. Carr* could

> bring the Court in conflict with political forces and exacerbate political feeling widely throughout the Nation on a larger scale, though not so pathologically, as the Segregation cases have stirred. The latter . . . resulted in merely regional feeling against the Court, with the feeling of most of the country strongly in sympathy with the Court. But if one is right about the widely scattered assailable apportionment disparities, . . .

clash and tension between Court and country and politicians will assert themselves within a far wider area than the Segregation cases have aroused.

Baker v. Carr, Frankfurter feared, would turn the whole country against the Court. But after there was a clear majority for the overturning of laws that denied equal voting rights, Douglas pushed for an early announcement of the decision with the comment "This is an election year."

Changes in the composition of the high bench, as Justice Scalia suggests, appear to register broader changes in the country. . . .

. . . Whether the Court should or does stay in step with the opinion of dominant national political coalitions remains problematic. . . . As an unelected body, the Court's role is basically counter-majoritarian and therefore whether it ought to "stay in tune with the times" is highly debatable. Whether the Court assumes the role of a majoritarian-reinforcing institution also seems doubtful. Vacancies on the bench occur almost randomly and at times are unrelated to shifts in electoral politics. Moreover, it is unclear that the Court always confers legitimacy on the policies of other nationally democratically accountable institutions.

The Court's bearing on shifts in the electorate and public opinion is complicated and reveals no historically prescribed role. American electoral politics periodically undergoes partisan realignment coinciding with the rise and fall of majority parties. . . .

During critical elections in 1860, 1896, 1932, 1960, and 1964, some political scientists argue, the Court supported the reigning party by helping shape its positions on critical issues. Other scholars contend, however, that after critical elections the Court stands firm and does battle with the newly emergent majority party. Yet, as political scientist John B. Gates has shown, "neither role appears inevitable," nor has the Court played the same role in each realignment.

Before the 1860 election, *Dred Scott* fanned the flames of sectional conflict over slavery, and prior to the 1896 election, the Court reinforced the laissez-faire economic policies of the old Republican party by overturning federal income tax legislation and restricting the enforcement of antitrust laws. Still, after Lincoln's victory and his securing a new majority of Republican justices on the bench, the Court did not invariably side with him or his party's policies. Prior to the New Deal realignment the Court sent mixed signals on progressive economic policies, yet after the 1932 election virtually went to war with FDR and Congress over the New Deal. During the subsequent constitutional crisis in 1937 the Court then abruptly reversed course, despite no changes in membership. In the 1960s the Warren Court's rulings reinforced the liberal-egalitarian social policies promoted by the Democratic party. At the same time, the Court thereby contributed to the defection of white middle-class voters, especially in the South, and to the breakup of the old New Deal coalition. Already angry over LBJ's pushing the Civil Rights Act of 1964 through the Democrat-controlled Congress, voters grew increasingly bitter over forced integration, rising crime rates, affirmative action, and higher taxes. "Liberal judicial activism," "crime control," and quotas became powerful symbols for Republican presidential candidates from Nixon to Bush. In short, the Court has not consistently played a prescribed role either before or after partisan realignments.

The relationship between the Court and public opinion remains subtle, complex, and difficult to measure. Unlike *Brown, Roe, Casey,* and *Bush v. Gore,* most of the Court's decisions attract neither media nor widespread public attention. The public tends to identify with the Court's institutional symbol as a temple of law rather than of politics—impartial and removed from the pressures of special partisan interests. Yet there is a strong relationship between diffuse public support for the Court and agreement with its recent rulings, political ideology, and partisanship. Issues like school desegregation and abortion focus public attention and may mobilize public support for or opposition to the Court. In the last fifty years, public confidence in the Court has ebbed and flowed with changes in the direction of its policy-making on major issues affecting American life. From the mid-1960s to the mid-1980s, confidence declined in relation to the Court's rulings protecting the rights of the accused, invalidation of state and federal laws, and to presidential popularity. But the Court's composition changed dramatically with Reagan's, Bush's, and Clinton's appointees. The Court continues to be generally held in high regard by the public and polls indicate that the Court's move in more conservative directions—on the rights of the accused, for instance—is in accord with public opinion. That point is underscored by the fact that the Court's public approval rating remained virtually unchanged after the decision in *Bush v. Gore* was handed down, contrary to predictions by the dissenters and critics that the Court's institutional reputation would be badly damaged.

Does the Court influence public opinion or does the latter influence the Court? There is no simple answer. Much depends on the Court's composition, what and how it decides particular issues, and its salience for the public in the short and long run; in Calderia's words, "Sometimes opinion moves against the Court; at other times it follows the Court; and at still others it scarcely moves at all. . . ."

10.2   The Supreme Court and Critical Elections (1975)

Richard Funston

Among judicial agencies throughout the world, past and present, the Supreme Court of the United States stands out as a uniquely powerful political institution. No other court has ever been so continuously, consistently, and intimately involved in the policy-making processes of government. Foremost among the Court's interpretive and thus political powers is its power to nullify an act of Congress by declaring it to be unconstitutional.

This uniquely American institution of judicial review, placing the ultimate power of constitutional policy making in the hands of a small group of un-

From *American Political Science Review* 69, no. 3 (September 1975): 795–811. Reprinted with the permission of Cambridge University Press.

elected individuals, has for decades created a dis-quietude among American legal and political theo-rists. These scholars have produced a voluminous body of literature, largely impressionistic and pre-scriptive, seeking to account for the existence of ju-dicial review and, more importantly, attempting to create a consistent theory of its appropriate scope. . . . [I]n very general terms the analysts of judicial re-view have tended to divide, on normative grounds, into two schools of thought, commonly referred to as judicial activism and judicial self-restraint.

It is important to recognize, however, that at base both the activists and the advocates of restraint share a similar conception of the Supreme Court's function in the American political system: Both see the Court as the protector of minority rights against a majority tyranny. The problem, then, to which both the theorists of judicial activism and the philosophers of judicial self-restraint address them-selves is: When should the Court interfere with the popular will? Or, put differently, what constitutes unconstitutional action? The advocates of judicial restraint believe that "unconstitutional" must be de-fined narrowly. In their view, the Constitution is a vague, imprecise charter which allows great leeway to the dominant political forces. The Court must on occasion move to protect a minority, . . . but, for reasons of democratic principle or of political pru-dence, these instances must be infrequent and well justified. Activists, on the other hand, believe the Constitution to be a more precise document; there-fore, they define "unconstitutional" more broadly. As a consequence, they believe that the Court must interfere with the popular will more frequently. Moreover, they are more optimistic about the Court's political strengths than are the advocates of restraint, and so they believe that the Court not only *should* but *can* interfere more frequently. . . .

The Dahl-Dooley Hypothesis

Several years ago in a justly famed article Professor Robert Dahl argued that the traditional concern of public lawyers about the Supreme Court's power of judicial review was largely unfounded. The Court cannot and does not, Dahl argued, function to pro-tect minorities. With admirable rigor, he demon-strated that seldom, if ever, had the Court been

successful in blocking the will of a law-making ma-jority on an important policy issue.

. . . National politics in the United States, Dahl tells us, has been dominated by relatively cohesive alliances that endure over long periods of time. Be-cause the Court is a political institution whose members are recruited with their political prefer-ences and prejudices in mind, it is inevitably part of the dominant political alliance, except for transi-tional periods during which the old alliance is crumbling and a new one rising to take its place. During these periods, presumably, the Court, by virtue of the life tenure of the Justices, will be out of step with the political times. . . . When the Court strikes down congressional legislation as unconsti-tutional, Dahl demonstrated, it is seldom success-ful in the long run in thwarting the majority policy. *But the crucial point is that most of the time the Court will not be striking down national legisla-tion.* Dahl did not examine this point at length, nor, therefore, did he consider when the Court would be most likely to act in a counter-majoritarian fash-ion.

. . . I propose . . . to do what Dahl did not—that is, to test the following hypothesis: Over long peri-ods of time, the Supreme Court reflects the will of the dominant political forces; however, during tran-sitional periods, in which the Court is a holdover from the old coalition, the Court will be more likely to perform the counter-majoritarian functions as-cribed to it by traditional theory. The hypothesis, in other words, is that, as Mr. Dooley so cryptically put it, "the Supreme Court follows the election returns."

. . . Essentially the problem we are addressing is: When are Supreme Court decisions most likely to conflict with the will of a national majority? As Dahl himself noted, in any strict sense, there is simply no way of establishing with any high degree of confidence whether a given policy alternative was or was not supported by a majority of Ameri-cans. But let us assume, as did Dahl, that one may equate the "law-making majority" with the "na-tional majority." In other words, . . . there is at least *some* relation between a voter's preference among candidates or parties and his preferences among alternative public policies. . . .

. . . If we take the preferences of the law-making majority to represent the will of the national majority, and if we take as our operational definition of the preferences of the law-making majority federal legislation passed by majorities in the House and Senate and signed by the president, then we may conclude that the Supreme Court is out of line with the majority will when it holds congressional statutes unconstitutional. We may then examine over time the behavior of the Court in exercising its power to declare congressional statutes unconstitutional in order to determine if this behavior occurs randomly, as the traditional conception of the Court's function would suggest, or if it tends to occur at given, identifiable intervals, as Dahl's thesis implies.

Electoral Realignment and the Party System

To examine the hypothesis that the Supreme Court follows the election returns, the first thing to which we should turn are the election returns. . . .

. . . If we construct a simple, chronological chart of the ebb and flow of electoral patterns and compare it with the behavior of the Court in exercising its power of judicial review, we shall then be able to test the Dahl-Dooley thesis that the Court is never long out of line with the dominant political coalition, except during transitional periods, which we shall identify as realignment phases.

First, however, an intermediate step may be taken. It may be useful to determine for whom and for what the electorate voted, since our operational definition of the majority will is not simply the electoral preference but rather the action of the law-making majority. . . . [William] Chambers and [Walter Dean] Burnham's study of the history of American voting alignments reveals that over time American party politics has experienced five major patterns of party competition or, as Chambers and Burnham call them, five national party systems.

The first national party system . . . existed from 1789 until 1820. This really was a transitional phase between the establishment of the American State and the acceptance of and regularization of its political patterns. . . .

Chambers and Burnham, like most contemporary American historians, discount the importance of Jefferson's election in 1800. It certainly did not constitute a realignment with any significance for national policy making. Despite Jefferson's liberal,

laissez-faire statements, there was no appreciable change in national economic policy . . . [T]he Republican leadership appears to have been hardly less elitist than that of the Federalists. These similarities, coupled with the fact that national elections remained largely undemocratized, may account for the collapse of the first party system. By 1820, when Monroe ran unopposed for the presidency, there evidently were insufficient points of political conflict to sustain a system of national, multiparty competition.

The emergence of recognizably modern parties occurred during the second American party system, following a partisan realignment in response to the election of John Quincy Adams. The growing popular demand for democratization of the franchise coincided with popular revulsion at the "deal" by which Adams was elected from within the House of Representatives and coalesced around the charismatic figure of Andrew Jackson. The resulting system of partisan competition contributed to the decentralization of political power in America. The period saw the rise of the convention and the decline of the centralized congressional caucus as a mechanism for the selection of presidential candidates. Under Jackson and his successors, the federal government progressively declined in power vis-à-vis the states, eventually completely withdrawing from intervention in the economic sector. In part this was due, of course, to the rise of slavery as a political issue. The pursuit of any active federal economic policy necessarily exacerbated the emerging sectional conflict. As a corollary, the presidency experienced a decline in prestige at the expense of the locally-elected Congress. . . . Because the two national parties lacked consistent, coherent principles the second American party system was extremely unstable. Both the Whigs and the Democrats were motley collections of contradictory elements which were incapable of reconciling within themselves the divisive influence of the sectional conflict over slavery.

For this reason, an entirely sectional party emerged. The central reality of the realignment which produced the Republican party was the restructuring of all political relationships along sectional lines. Were the cancer of slavery to be contained in order that it might be removed from the body politic, this was the only institutional arrangement possible. By the 1850s, a textbook example of a prerevolutionary situation had developed in the United States. New elites, representing the urban, industrial Northeast, were challenging the hegemony of the old, southern, agrarian elite which had dominated national policy making under the Jacksonian system. Were the Union to survive, entirely new ways of doing things had to be adopted, created, or invented. Certainly the period immediately following the Civil War was one of great ferment, experimentation, and change. Not only was slavery abolished but also, for a time, attempts were made to involve the national government in a program of elevating the freedman to a position of first-class citizenship, while simultaneously the federal government initiated a series of measures designed to foster economic expansion.

By the 1870s, however, the radical phase of the third party system had collapsed. This collapse was ratified in the infamous bargain of 1876 by which, in exchange for the White House, the Republican party abandoned its efforts to create a viable Republican structure in the South. For the next twenty years, the division of partisan competition was so close that national political life was virtually stalemated. At the same time, political institutions generally were declining in significance relative to, or were being overshadowed by, the changes being wrought in the society at large by the corporate-industrial revolution.

These changes were, in turn, rendering the arrangements of the third party system obsolete. The old politics was structured in such a way that it was incapable of taking into account certain demographic and economic changes of major importance. The result was to exclude by definition certain groups from participation in the political process. . . . For complex reasons of structural weakness, one of the excluded groups, the western farmers, managed to capture one of the two major parties, the Democratic, without the assistance of the immigrants in the Northeast. . . . The immigrants responded by shunning a Democratic party openly prejudiced against them. Moreover, in 1893 the country's worst economic depression to that date occurred while a Democrat was President. The response of the industrial workers was the same as it was to be in 1932, an electoral abhorrence of the party in power. The consequent political realignment produced a system of noncompetition, nonparticipation, one-party states, one-party sections, and Republican dominance which lasted until the late 1920s.

The realignment that produced the winning coalition of rural and urban underprivileged, labor, ethnic minorities, and the academic elite which we associate with Franklin Roosevelt actually was presaged by the Smith campaign of 1928. The "Happy Warrior" was able to wrest control of the Democratic party from the southern-rural-colonial forces which had dominated it; his campaign attracted a huge bloc of new immigrant voters into the political system, precipitating a realignment in the urban Northeast. . . .

The consequences of this last realignment in American politics are familiar to all. A bureaucratized, welfare-warfare state became the major reality of American politics. The Democratic party replaced the GOP as the dominant party in a system of partisan competition based upon appeals to economic self-interest and group identification. . . .

Periodicity in Supreme Court Behavior

. . . [M]any students of the Court have remarked that its history has been delimited by five fairly specific periods. . . . In each of these five periods of the Court's history, certain characteristic doctrines have prevailed, only to be abandoned in a later period. The Court seems always to have some special interest to protect or value to advance. Have these interests or primary legal norms been opposed to or consonant with the primary values expressed within the larger political system?

The first and formative period of the Supreme Court's history is identified with the Chief Justiceship of John Marshall. Under Marshall, the primary legal norms advanced by the Court were national supremacy, judicial power, and the protection of private property. During Marshall's tenure, the Court labored to establish the supremacy of the national government over the states through broad interpretations of such constitutional provisions as the commerce clause and the necessary and proper clause. Similarly, it asserted its own power to review the validity of state legislative and judicial actions, thereby increasing not only the power of the federal government generally but also the power of the federal judiciary in particular. Nationalism also proved to be a useful tool for the protection of vested rights. Since most of the statutes which interfered with private property during this era were state laws, interpretations that severely limited states' rights were frequently employed to invalidate such statutes.

There would indeed seem to be a certain coincidence between the values asserted or advanced by the Court under Marshall and the dominant norms of the first American party system identified by Chambers and Burnham. That party system was characterized by the centrality of its organization, and, although more moderate in their elitism than the Federalists, the Republicans were nonetheless committed to the protection of aristocratic privilege, a part of which involved the protection of property rights. Thus, the harmony which developed between Marshall's Supreme Court and Jefferson's successors may have been less than accidental.

Perhaps not surprisingly, Marshall's successor was none other than Andrew Jackson's right-hand man, Roger Brooke Taney. Just as Jackson and his successors dismantled the neomercantilist system and withdrew the federal government from the economic sector, so the Taney Court was less inclined to invalidate state legislation and viewed corporate enterprise with a less hospitable eye than had Marshall. During this period, the federal government declined in power vis-à-vis the states, and the presidency experienced a precipitate drop in prestige. Although the Court under Taney did not suffer an equivalent decline, it did behave similarly in that it withdrew to a position somewhat more like an impartial arbiter between states and nation, rather than functioning, like the Marshall Court, as an active champion for the central government. Finally, just as the second party system was characterized by an extreme sectionalism of voting patterns, so too the Court under Taney increasingly came to divide along sectional lines in its disposition of cases, with the southerners, as in the other two branches, holding a slim but stable majority.

The infamous *Dred Scott* decision and its subsequent repudiation upon the battlefield brought about a decline in the Court's prestige which lasted throughout the decade of the 1860s. As a result, the Supreme Court did not participate in the radical phase of the third party system. The program which was initially followed by the Republican victors of the realignment of 1852–1860 was twofold: on the one hand, a policy of federal protection of civil rights, especially those of the newly freed blacks; on the other, a policy of federal intervention in the economy in order to encourage the development of commercial and corporate enterprise. By 1870, the first half of this program had been abandoned. This abandonment of the black man by the Republican leadership was formalized in the bargain of 1876 which produced a sectional, partisan deadlock that lasted for the next decade and a half. This solution came to be tacitly accepted by public opinion, and in the 1880s was recognized as legitimate by the Supreme Court in a series of decisions which emasculated most of the comprehensive radical program for the protection of the Negro. On the other hand, the Court, having regained its strength and prestige, did its part in advancing the second half of the Republican program, federal encouragement of industrial capitalism. Not only did the Court thus validate the practices of the dominant political coalition but also it laid the groundwork for new doctrines of constitutional limitation which might be employed to protect corporate property if the dominant political values were to change.

If anything, the Supreme Court *anticipated* the electoral realignment which brought about the fourth party system. By 1893, as already noted, the stage was set for a political coalition between the western farmers and the immigrant laborers. Such a coalition, of course, did not occur. But, before it was clear that this would be the case, while the industrial elite still feared such a coalition might prevail, the Supreme Court in a series of classic decisions in 1894–95 did what it could to undermine the legitimacy of a massive assault on established elite rule. When it became clear, however, that the feared coalition would not emerge and that the result of the realignment of 1888–1896 was to elevate McKinley Republicanism to a position of preeminence in the political system, the

Court began a campaign completely in consonance with the values represented by the dominant party: laissez-faire at home and imperial dominance abroad. With respect to the latter, the Court, in a series of decisions at the turn of the century, validated America's rise to the position of imperial power, holding in essence that the Constitution allowed Americans to "take up the white man's burden." As for the domestic principle of laissez-faire economics, this period saw the Court employ the due process clause of the Fourteenth Amendment as a formidable weapon against an assortment of state legislation that sought to protect consumers, unions, farmers, unorganized labor, women, and children against the abuses of business enterprise. The high point of the Court's attempts to control public policy was, of course, reached during seventeen months in 1935–36, when the Court launched a frontal attack upon the New Deal. Public opinion, though opposed to "packing" the Court, was outraged, and the Court beat a strategic, if belated, retreat, abandoning its role as economic policy maker.

In the most recent period of the Court's history, constitutional law has been brought into accord with the norms of the New Deal Democrats. The precedents of economic due process have been scuttled, and the authority of the government to intervene in the economy is virtually undisputed. From the New Deal to the Great Society, the Court has sustained the welfare state. At the same time, the Court has liberalized the constitutional law of civil liberties and, in particular, has advanced on many fronts the value of egalitarianism, the doctrine of the "common man."

On the basis of this cursory analysis, it would certainly seem that the Supreme Court does follow the election returns over time. . . . [S]ome of the Court's most notable collisions with the elected branches have indeed occurred during periods of partisan realignment. The analysis, however, may be advanced with somewhat more rigor by examining the data statistically.

First of all, it should be made clear that the time span to be used for this exercise begins in 1801, with the appointment of the great Chief Justice, John Marshall, and ends in June, 1969, with the retirement of Mr. Chief Justice Warren. Thus, the overall period covers approximately 168 years. . . .

According to the way in which I count the cases, there have been ninety-four during this 168-year period which are of interest to us, i.e., cases in which the Court declared federal legislation to be unconstitutional either in whole or in part. . . . During realignment phases or, as they might be called, critical periods, was the tendency of the Court to declare federal legislation unconstitutional significantly greater than during noncritical periods of stable party competition? To answer that question, all that is necessary is to calculate the arithmetic mean for the total years of critical and noncritical periods. . . . As expected, . . . during critical periods the Court was slightly more likely to behave in a counter-majoritarian manner—but not very much more likely.

By using *all* cases in which federal legislation has been held unconstitutional in whole or in part, however, we are not really measuring what we set out to measure. For example, in *Myers v. U. S.,* decided in 1926, the Court declared unconstitutional an act which had been passed fifty years earlier. In other words, here we have a Court on the eve of the realignment of 1928–36 declaring void a statute passed many years before the realignment of 1888–1896. What can one conclude from this case about the relationship between the *Myers* Court and the law-making majority? Obviously, nothing. Therefore, as did Dahl, let us confine ourselves to cases which held provisions of federal legislation to be unconstitutional within four years of their enactment. We may then assume with a fair degree of confidence that the law-making majority which passed the legislation is not a dead one and that, if the Court acts against that sort of majority it is in fact acting counter to prevailing majority sentiment.

Within the 168 years with which we are concerned, there have been 38 cases in which the Court has declared provisions of federal legislation unconstitutional within four years of enactment. . . . Sixteen have occurred during the 32 years of partisan realignment identified by Chambers and Burnham as critical periods. Twenty-two have occurred during the other 136 years. If one now calculates the central tendencies of the Court, one arrives at an index for critical periods of 0.50 and an index for noncritical periods of only 0.16. Which is to say that, as hypothesized, there has been a significantly greater tendency on the part of the Court during realigning periods to utilize its power to declare federal legislation unconstitutional, i.e., to oppose the law-making majority will, than during periods of political stability, when the Court is part of the dominant political majority.

How much greater? To answer this question we need but to compute a measure of relative variability. . . . This coefficient, . . . I shall label in this case the Coefficient of Counter-Majoritarianism, is obtained by dividing one index by the other. . . . Statistically-speaking the Court has been more than three times as likely to declare recently enacted federal legislation unconstitutional during the realignment periods identified by Chambers and Burnham than it has been during the vast majority of its history.

. . . It is not merely that during critical periods of partisan realignment the Court is more likely to declare recently enacted federal legislation unconstitutional than at other times, but that during realigning periods this is the very sort of congressional legislation which is most likely to be nullified by the Court!

One might suppose that this finding would justify acceptance of the Dahl-Dooley hypothesis. But a further modification may elaborate the point. Just as the scope of cases which would be accepted as evidence that the Court was out of line with a prevailing majority was narrowed by limiting it to those cases in which legislation not more than four years old was held unconstitutional, the scope of the critical periods may be expanded. If the Court is out of line with the will of the law-making majority during realignment periods, it would be reasonable to expect that, as the realignment takes place and the newly dominant coalition begins to consolidate its position, the Court will gradually come back into line with that majority by virtue of the recruitment process; or, put in statistical terms, the Coefficient of Counter-Majoritarianism will decrease over time.

In order to examine this proposition, it is necessary to introduce the concept of a lag period. We have been examining the behavior of the Court only during realigning periods when the Court, because of the life tenure of the Justices, is out of step with the dominant trends of the political times. During and immediately following these realigning periods, however, appointments are being made to the Court which serve to bring it back into line

with the dominant political coalition. If we take as our definition of "lag period" that period of time which is required for a new majority to be appointed to the Court, we have the possibility of calculating two different lag periods. The first possibility is to calculate the lag periods as ending with the fifth or majority appointment to the Court after the *beginning* of the realigning period. Using this possibility, the lag periods end in 1835, 1864, 1896, and 1938. The second possibility is to calculate the lag periods as ending with the fifth or majority appointment to the Court after the *end* of the realignment period. Using this possibility, the lag periods end in 1836, 1864, 1909, and 1940. If the hypothesis is valid, we would expect that the Coefficient of Counter-Majoritarianism would be greatest when one uses as the measure of critical periods only the periods of partisan realignment. The coefficient should be smallest when one uses as the measure of critical periods the expanded eras produced by modifying the periods with the second possible and longest lag period. And it should be somewhere in between these two using the first possible calculation of lag period. In other words, one would suspect that the greater the length of the critical periods, the more the Coefficient of Counter-Majoritarianism would decrease as the Court comes back into line with the dominant law-making majority.

In fact, this is exactly what we do find. . . . [D]uring periods of electoral and partisan realignment, the Court, as a result of its life tenure, is most likely to be out of line with the new, dominant law-making majority. . . . As time passes, the new majority is enabled to appoint its own adherents to the Supreme bench, and the Court increasingly returns to harmony with the new law-making majority. Not only is this true logically but also, . . . it is empirically demonstrable. . . .

It must be admitted, however, that this study represents but a very tentative first step. Not only does it suggest ways in which concepts and research from other areas of the discipline of political science can be utilized to address one of the classic problems in public law, it also illustrates the methodological and conceptual problems involved in such borrowing. Much more work can and should be done in this area. Different and more sophisticated statistical techniques might be employed to analyze the data presented here; different definitions of realignment periods could be utilized; and Supreme Court behavior in relation to different categories of cases might be correlated with the electoral realignment data. . . .

Conclusion

The question remains, of course, apart from being an interesting statistical exercise, what significance this has for an understanding of the judicial function. First of all, it suggests that Professors Dahl and Charles Black have been correct in emphasizing the Court's function as a legitimating agency. The traditional concept of the Court as the champion of minority rights against majority demands is *largely* incorrect. In order to bring theoretical concepts of the Court's function into line with empirical reality, emphasis should be placed upon the Court's "yea-saying" power rather than upon its "nay-saying" power. Put more cryptically, *McCulloch v. Maryland* is the most important case in American constitutional law—not *Marbury v. Madison*. Historically, of course, the "nay-saying" power, the power of judicial review, has attracted more scholarly attention because it is so unique. But in both quantitative and qualitative terms the "nay-saying" power is the less important aspect of Supreme Court policy making.

The "yea-saying" power, on the other hand, involves two aspects. The Court can either expand or it can confine or mitigate the operation of statutes. This means that students of judicial policy making should be paying more attention to the Court's statutory, as distinct from its constitutional, interpretation. In the areas of selective service, welfare, and civil rights, to cite but a few recent examples, the Court has been making public policy of tremendous consequence, though without raising any issues of constitutional dimensions. This policy making, however, has tended to escape most political scientists, if not attorneys. Confining the attention to judicial findings of unconstitutionality ignores, as did Dahl, the decisions most pertinent in practice to the questions of whether and how much the Court has succeeded in imposing its own will in the place of Congress's. A systematic study of statutory interpretation might very well yield richer results.

This, in turn, suggests that students of the judicial process should stop equating "activism" with "judicial creativity." Several years ago, Mr. Justice Felix Frankfurter delivered an address in which he claimed that John Marshall had actually been a practitioner of judicial restraint. The reaction of the legal profession was one of general hilarity. Everyone *knew* Marshall had been an activist. But, according to a more complex way of looking at the judicial function, was not Frankfurter correct? After all, in thirty-five years on the bench, Marshall declared only one portion of one fairly limited congressional statute to be unconstitutional. But he was a *very creative* judge.

Finally, however, it must be emphasized that this analysis suggests that the traditional concept of the Court as the protector of minorities is not entirely incorrect. The debate between the judicial activists and the advocates of judicial restraint is particularly relevant during transitional phases of partisan realignment. In fact, by focusing the debate on these periods of political instability, one actually heightens the saliency of that debate, making it more crucial for both the Court and the country. But most of the time that debate will be irrelevant to the actual configurations of political power within the American constitutional system. . . .

If, then, the Court is normally in line with popular or, at least, law-making majorities, what function could it possibly serve? Traditional theory had a role for the Court to play, the protector of minority rights against the potential tyranny of the majority of the moment. If the Court does not normally play that role, does it serve any function at all which is distinctive to it? Because, if it does not, it is an absurd example of governmental "featherbedding" and should be abolished. In fact, it may be argued that the Court does play a role that differs from the legislative and executive functions and is peculiarly suited to its capabilities. That argument rests on the distinction between expediency and principle and begins with the premise that all governmental actions have two kinds of effects. The first is their immediate, intended effects. For example, faced with a major national economic crisis, we pass legislation which infringes upon agreements entered into between private individuals, i.e., contracts. The second kind of effect of any public program or policy is its bearing upon principles or values which we believe to be fundamental and of general applicability; or, to take our example again, we believe in the right of the majority to determine the course of government and in the right of the nation to protect its existence in times of crisis, either military or economic. We are all able to perceive the relation between our immediate needs or desires and a particular governmental action, and it is these perceptions which we transmit, by virtue of the electoral process, to our representatives. But we are not always able to perceive, because we do not always care about, the relation of a given policy, program, or action to our long-term values.

Assuming that we wish to have principled government, some agency must, in the normal operation of the policy process, be primarily concerned with society's fundamental, underlying values; and practical, if not philosophic, reasons dictate that this agency be one or another of the branches of the federal government. Which one? I submit not only that it should be but also that, in the American constitutional system, it can only be the Supreme Court. The Court, by virtue of its institutional position, is able to deal with matters of principle, whereas Congress and the president, because they are responsible to the electoral whims of the moment, cannot. The Justices "have, or should have, the leisure, the training, and the insulation to follow the ways of the scholar in pursuing the ends of government." This situation and the marvelously functional mystique of the judicial process—those seemingly esoteric institutional customs—allow the Court to appeal to our principled good sense, which may be forgotten in the heat of the moment. It is true, as Dahl points out, that the Court cannot withstand us when we are determined, but through the exercise of its power of judicial review it may entreat us to take a sober second thought about the course which we have set for ourselves.

. . . It is the Court's function to legitimate, if possible, contemporary public acts by demonstrating their consonance with fundamental constitutional principles. . . .

The Court . . . may be conceived of as an educational institution. The Justices of the Supreme Court, as Professor Eugene Rostow has put it, "are inevitably teachers in a vital national seminar." They are in a better position to conduct such a seminar than any other officials in American government.

Finally, in this respect, it may be noted that this concept of the Court as an institution which brings our short-run, expedient means into accord with our long-run ends or principles is also grounds for justifying the Court's power of judicial review. For what would be the good of a declaration of legitimacy from an institution which had no choice but to validate everything that was brought before it? It is only because the Court has the power to annul that its validation is worthwhile. . . .

Contemporary Judicial Politics

10.3   ## The Presidency and the Supreme Court After *Bush v. Gore:* Implications for Institutional Legitimacy and Effectiveness (2002)

Jeffrey L. Yates and Andrew B. Whitford

Introduction

The 2000 presidential election between Albert Gore, Jr., and George W. Bush was the closest race for the executive office in recent times; Gore's margin over Bush in the popular vote was 0.51 percent and the electoral vote margin was four votes in favor of Bush. Bush's inauguration on January 20, 2001 made him the first president since Benjamin Harrison in 1888 to win the electoral vote but lose the popular vote.

While these statistics show the national electorate's complete division in choosing the next president, they mask the underlying mechanisms of governance that came into play during the months required to reconcile the competing claims of the candidates. Traditional studies of presidential election politics concentrate on the months preceding the single day on which the nation expresses its opinion about the national leadership of the country for the next four years. In this case, studies must grapple with those months that followed November 7, 2000 to explain how our constitutional mechanisms of governance and conflict resolution interpreted national opinion.

The election and the Court's decision are now more than a year behind us, and we have witnessed a new national focus following the traumatic events of Sept. 11, 2001, through which we may view the political repercussions of the Court's decision in *Bush v. Gore.* In this article we assess the ramifications of the Court's decision for the le-

gitimacy and effectiveness of the presidency and the Court. . . .

Institutional Perspectives in Light of *Bush v. Gore*

Bush v. Gore's effect on the institutional legitimacy of the Court, as well as the institutional legitimacy of the presidency, is the primary potential long-term problem for balancing the relative powers of the three branches. Just as Congress and the presidency rely on their legitimacy for creating opportunities for policy change, the Court relies on its reservoir of institutional legitimacy for obtaining its institutional goals and maintaining its position as one of three coequal and separated powers.

Moreover, the legitimacy of the Court has special importance for understanding the presidency. The Court helps maintain the balance of power between the president and Congress. The Court's power to intervene and allocate power essentially depends on its social standing and tacit authority, i.e., the nation's acceptance of the Court as a final arbiter. As such, the balance of power between the two overtly political institutions also depends on that acceptance.

Of all of the dissenters in *Bush v. Gore,* Justice Breyer seemed most concerned with the impact of the case on the Court's legitimacy and efficacy. In his dissent, Breyer questioned the Court's decision to take on the case by noting the distinction between political and legal importance: "Of course, the selection of the President is of fundamental national importance. But that importance is political, not legal. And this Court should resist the

Reprinted by permission of *Stanford Law & Policy Review.*

temptation unnecessarily to resolve tangential legal disputes, where doing so threatens to determine the outcome of the election." Breyer makes reference to the Hayes-Tilden 1876 election and Justice Bradley's role as one of five Supreme Court Justices serving as members of the electoral commission that voted along partisan lines. This involvement of the justices in a partisan conflict did not, in Breyer's mind, lend credibility to the outcome, but simply undermined the credibility of the Court and the judicial process. However, an important distinction between these two instances is that in Hayes-Tilden the justices were working individually in extra-judicial roles, and thus in a quasi-political function; in *Bush v. Gore,* rather than lending merely their individual voices to a political result, they lent the credibility of the institution. In other words, while Breyer's analogy may not be exactly on point, the actions of the Court in *Bush v. Gore* actually may be potentially more damaging than in Hayes-Tilden because the Court's institutional credibility was leveraged to achieve a desired political outcome.

Breyer's concern over the Court's involvement and legitimacy brings to mind Justice Felix Frankfurter's well-known admonition concerning the impact of the Court's political involvement on the Court's legitimacy in his dissent in *Baker v. Carr:*

> The Court's authority—possessed of neither the purse nor the sword—ultimately rests on sustained public confidence in its moral sanction. Such feeling must be nourished by the Court's complete detachment, in fact and appearance, from political entanglements and by abstention from injecting itself into the clash of political forces in political settlements.

But is it the case that the Court always loses credibility when the justices dictate an important political result, or does the context matter? The Court also took a hand in a political outcome of national importance in *United States v. Nixon.* In this, the last significant time that the Court decided who would occupy the White House, the justices initially divided over whether to even hear the case and then, in discussions on the merits, disagreed about the scope of executive privilege. Nixon, however, had indicated through

counsel that he was keeping open the option of defying the Court and that the question of compliance had not yet been decided. Thus, the need for the Court to provide a "definitive decision" was evident.

Justice Powell's retrospective analysis of the Nixon situation in 1988 underscored the Court's curious potential enforcement dilemma and its inherent reliance on public legitimacy to give force to its decisions: "one has to wonder what would have happened if Nixon had said what President Jackson said on one occasion, 'You have your decree, now enforce it.' Of course, there was no way we could have enforced it. We had 50 'police' officers, but Nixon had the First Infantry Division." In the end, the justices came together for an eight to zero decision against the beleaguered executive, and Nixon, though highly upset with the voting of his appointees to the Court, complied. Hence, by presenting a united front against a president who lacked public support, the Court was able to prevent a potentially serious threat to its institutional authority.

While it clearly lacks enforcement personnel, the Court can rely on popular sentiment in making decisions involving presidential power conflicts. Indeed, quantitative analyses of Supreme Court cases dealing with presidential power indicate that the Court generally responds to executive prestige in the eyes of the public when making decisions to promote or constrain the parameters of presidential power. In *United States v. Nixon.* Nixon's declining public approval may not have determined the Court's decision, but at a minimum, it removed a potentially important obstacle to the Court's intervention in a matter of allocating power among the branches of government.

Bush v. Gore draws a finer distinction. In this case the members of the Court were undoubtedly aware that they were treading on "sacred ground" in determining the outcome of the election by a split decision. Certainly, Justice Breyer was cognizant of the potential effect of not presenting a united front. He worried that "above all, in this highly politicized matter, the appearance of a split decision runs the risk of undermining the public's confidence in the Court itself." However, fears of constitutional crisis resulting from its decision, compliance problems from Congress or the executive branch, or public opposition to the decision did not ultimately dissuade the five-member majority in *Bush v. Gore* from ending the election. As we detail below, this occurred because the Court, an institution that is mindful of the prevailing public mood and Washington politics, had clear signs that its decision to end the election (thus placing Bush in the White House) would not yield serious repercussions from the public or other political actors.

. . . [A] Gallup poll taken directly after the initial ballot count found a broad-based majority of the public willing to recognize either candidate as the legitimate president, although as we might expect, voters were considerably more willing to accept their chosen candidate as the legitimate president.

A second Gallup poll taken directly before the decision found a majority of the public (again extending across partisan attachments) saying it would accept the Court's ruling as legitimate regardless of the outcome of the Court's decision.

A third poll (also taken December 12) showed that most respondents—including both Bush (64 percent) and Gore (59 percent) voters—said they would favor the Court to decide the election over other political institutions with actual or potential involvement in the conflict (including Congress, the Florida legislature, and the Florida Supreme Court). Moreover, before the decision, both Bush and Gore publicly expressed that they would respect the outcome of the Court's deliberations.

[This] evidence . . . suggests that the Court's taking the case and deciding the election would ostensibly yield no reasonably foreseeable repercussions from other elite political actors or the public and no potential diminution of its authority or institutional sovereignty. Hence, the Court, an institution well attuned to the political mood of the general public and Washington elites, was likely willing to hear the case and to decide the fate of the election (even with a contentious five to four vote) essentially because public and elite sentiment clearly indicated that this would be an acceptable action by the Court. In fact, the Court predicted correctly, as we show below, that the majority of the public would accept the decision as legitimate, even though some may have disagreed with the outcome. Moreover, Vice President Gore kept his

word and acknowledged the legitimacy of the Court's decision, notwithstanding the outcome, in his concession speech.

Institutional Legitimacy and Effectiveness

Political scientists and social theorists alike recognize the broad importance of a political institution's legitimacy (or credibility). For a social institution to have force, it must have support among members of a population. In that population, each person's support partly depends on their expectation and understanding that others will support the institution. The resulting complexity of this web of contingent support makes it very difficult to explain how, why, and when any given political institution gains and retains legitimacy with the public. It is clear, however, that institutional legitimacy can be fragile. If enough members of a population lose faith that an institution has social value—in the Supreme Court's case, as an impartial social arbiter of disputes—its social support can evaporate when individuals withdraw their support in a cascade. Constitutional theorists, political scientists, and politicians have long acknowledged the peculiar and fragile role of institutional legitimacy for the presidency and for the Supreme Court. . . .

. . . [P]ublic support is also very important to the policy-making viability of the Supreme Court. Although the Court was designed to be insulated from the pressures of electoral politics (e.g., justices have life tenured positions), the Court nevertheless lacks its own enforcement bureaucracy and must rely on public acceptance to legitimize its authority over the lower courts, legislators, bureaucrats at all levels, and the public itself. . . .

The Court also implicitly depends on a degree of public deference in order to protect itself from intrusion by the other two branches. Chief Justice Rehnquist recently cited the need for legitimacy in the eyes of the public as an ingredient for the preservation of the Supreme Court as a coequal branch. After recounting a number of historical instances in which the Court's authority and independence were challenged, but ultimately survived, he concluded: "I suspect the Court will continue to encounter challenges to its independence and authority by other branches of government because of the design of our Constitutional system. The degree to which that independence will be preserved will depend again in some measure on the public's respect for the judiciary."

It is clear that *Bush v. Gore* critically affected the short-term legitimacy of the presidency, if not the Court. While overall public approval for President Bush remained about average for the start of a presidential administration, that average masked specific divergence from the norm as the administration suffered from the highest ever initial disapproval ratings measured by a Gallup poll. However, this all changed following the events of September 11. Bush's public approval rating shot up from a relatively lackluster 51 percent public approval just days prior to the terrorist attacks to 90 percent public approval on polls taken September 21–22, the highest approval ever recorded for a president by Gallup. Similarly, his disapproval ratings plummeted over the same time span, going from his highest recorded level, 39 percent, to only 6 percent.

The level of general public support for the Supreme Court has remained fairly constant despite the decision in *Bush v. Gore*. . . . [O]verall support for the Court in the period from August 29 to September 25, 2000 was 59 percent, and after *Bush v. Gore* (poll taken January 10–14) it actually rose to 62 percent.

But this average masks a shift from broad-based public support to a highly politically polarized landscape of opinion. Support among Republicans rose from 60 percent to 80 percent, but support among Democrats fell from 70 percent to 42 percent. This separation extends to public confidence in the Court. Polls also revealed that the public's agreement with the Court's decision, its perception of the fairness of the decision, and its perception of the basis of the decision (legal versus political) all fell along partisan lines.

. . . [W]hile the majority considers Bush to be legitimately elected, there is specific divergence on the issue by both party and race. Taken together, these findings suggest that, for the Court, public support for the institution hinges to some degree upon agreement with the ideological nature of its decisions. As Caldeira and Gibson [1992] show, the underlying structure of public support for institutions such as the Court or the presidency—that is, whether that support is contingent or diffuse—is as determinative of institutional legitimacy, and hence institutional vitality and viability, as is the overall level of public support.

It is clear that after September 11 and at the time this article went to press, the President enjoys high overall public approval as well as broad-based support from all political and racial subgroups. While there is little information available to discern how the public feels about the 2000 presidential election and the Court's decision in *Bush v. Gore* in the aftermath of the terrorist attacks, recent polls as of press time do provide some clues. . . . [L]ittle has changed in the way the public feels about the integrity of the process that placed Bush in the executive office. About one-half of those polled feel Bush won the election fair and square, with the rest saying that he either stole the election or won on a technicality. However, this overall finding obscures the actual partisan rift involved. More than 80 percent of Republicans feel that the election was won fairly, as opposed to a mere 18 percent of Democrats, with little change after September 11. . . .

Conclusion: The Impact of *Bush v. Gore*

The analyses presented above reveal that the Court's decision yielded clear short-term effects for both presidential and Supreme Court legitimacy. However, these short-term effects have diminished over time and will likely continue to fade. While some public concerns over the election and the case remain, we argue that the long-term effect of *Bush v. Gore* will not be deterministic; the Supreme Court's long-term legitimacy and effectiveness have not been irreparably damaged. . . .

10.4 # Television News and the Supreme Court: Opportunities and Constraints (1998)

Elliot E. Slotnick and Jennifer A. Segal

. . . [T]he Court presents a unique setting for reporters covering the institution and, indeed, . . . some facets of the beat have important and similar implications for both print and broadcast journalism outlets. It remains important to recognize, however, that all journalistic venues are not created equal and, clearly, are not the same. In this chapter we shall examine the inherent strengths and weaknesses of the television medium for covering the Court. What are the journalistic constraints imposed by the Court itself as well as those associated with the imperatives of nightly newscasts? What changes have occurred in network newscast coverage of the Court in past years and what does the future hold for the relationship between the Supreme Court and nightly newscasts? We shall pay particular attention in this chapter to the issues and concerns raised for television reporters who must cover the Court in "the age of infotainment."

The Strengths and Weaknesses of Television News for Covering the Court

The inherent strengths of television newscasts for covering the Court have been well summarized by the [late] Toni House, the [former] Court's Public Information Officer, who commented, "What television is able to do is put a human face on the decisions when they are allowed to. They go out and put the people who were involved on camera.". . . For Carl Stern [former NBC News Supreme Court reporter], television can offer "the drama of human experience":

Many of these cases involve highly emotional issues in which passions run high. Television is able to convey the intensity of these situations

From *All the News That's Fit to Air: Television News and the Supreme Court* by Elliot Slotnick and Jennifer A. Segal. Reprinted with permission of Cambridge University Press.

and perhaps even more clearly explain what's at issue than print can. With print you have to figure the words out. So television can transport you to the scene and can tell you quickly what is at issue in a rather simple way.

Foreshadowing what we will later discuss as a generic problem for television coverage of the Court, however, Stern continued, "Of course, many cases are not simple."

In a similar vein, Tim O'Brien [former ABC News Supreme Court reporter] noted that television can be an ideal medium for covering events combining human interest with a concern for explaining relevant legal principles—that is, of course, when reporters have sufficient time:

A lot of people think that the Supreme Court deals primarily on abstract legal issues, principles that are beyond [and] don't really affect people, something for academics to debate. And that, of course, we know is not true. In a sense, I found it to be an ideal beat for television. The cases that come up here . . . many of them are almost tailor-made for television. When you talk to the people who bring them and what their stake in the cases are. . . . It does, unfortunately, require time that television doesn't always have to spend. What I've done, and what . . . they [newscast producers] very much like me to do, is to go out and interview the people who bring the cases. That makes the principle relevant. It makes the issue relevant to the viewer. . . .

In the commentaries of television journalists such as Carl Stern and Tim O'Brien we see clearly how what television does "best," that is, explain legal principles simply and with a focus on the human consequences of the Court's actions, also plants the seeds of what the medium may do most poorly. Legal principles are not always simple, and a good deal more may be at stake in Supreme Court cases than the consequences of the rulings for the litigants involved. And, as alluded to above, television rarely offers its journalists sufficient time to sort out details and nuance. . . .

At times, particularly when really major cases are handed down, the lack of time is joined with a call for immediacy in reporting and instant analysis. Toni House recalled one instance when NBC's desire for a "rush to judgment" from Carl Stern resulted in his on-air refusal to distill the meaning of a complicated decision. Stern was simply not yet ready when the network interrupted regular programming with a news bulletin. . . .

Interestingly, some of the major constraints faced by television news reflect the fact that the Court's work is primarily reflected in its words, which, as Pete Williams [NBC News Supreme Court and justice correspondent] pointed out, is the forte of print, not broadcast, journalism:

> It may be that the print media have an enormous advantage because the Court basically handles the flow of words. I mean it's words in briefs that come in and it's words in opinions that go out. . . . So the print media are kind of well matched to that flow of words. . . .

In the sections that follow . . . we shall explore, in greater depth, the constraints on television news coverage of the Court that are imposed by the rules and procedures of the Court itself, as well as those constraints that flow from the imperatives of network television news.

Constraints on Supreme Court Coverage: Supreme Court Rules, Norms, and Procedures

Two related areas in which the Court's own rules, norms, and procedures place an especially heavy burden on television are its propensity for issuing multiple rulings, often several important ones, on the same day, and its habit of deciding cases, en masse, at or near the very end of the term. Historically, all Supreme Court decisions were announced during a series of "decision Mondays" with the Court convening at noon. Marginal reforms moved the Court's starting time to 10 A.M. in 1961, a time considerably more conducive to the demands of the news day. In 1965, the exclusivity of Mondays

for announcing decisions was abandoned, making newsworthy rulings less likely to pile up on a given news day. While such reforms have been somewhat beneficial, they have not sufficiently alleviated the problems they address in the eyes of Court reporters. Despite the formal demise of decision Monday, rulings are still not spread equally across the news week. Even more importantly, a disproportionate number of the Court's rulings (and the preponderance of its important ones) are announced in June, reflecting the difficulties of reaching decision closure as well as the demands of opinion writing. . . .

. . . Fred Graham [former law correspondent for CBS News] recalled a day when "the Warren Court handed down enough decisions and new Court rules to fill an entire 991 page volume of the Supreme Court's official case reports. There was no way for us even to read so many pages, much less write coherent stories about them."

Tim O'Brien labeled such scenarios a "travesty," suggesting that it is not only the reporters and the viewing public who suffer because of it:

> For one, anybody who doesn't think the quality of the opinions suffers is mistaken. . . . And then we can't explain . . . to the viewer . . . if there's three or four major decisions on the same day, who's going to read all that? And the Court seems to feel that "[it's] not my job, man," and some of the justices say that should not be any of our concern. "Personally," a justice tells me, "personally, I sympathize with you. But I think it would be wrong to take your interest into consideration."

One reporter who feels that the Court should alter its procedures not, necessarily, to take television's interests into account but, rather, to be more responsive to the public's interest is Pete Williams:

> I'm old-fashioned enough to believe we should cover the news and the Supreme Court should do its thing and we should do our thing and that's the way it is. And if the Supreme Court chooses to hold all the decisions until the last day and announce them all at once, then we just have to do the best we can. But if, and I think the Court does care about this a little bit . . . if the Court really cares about . . . people understanding what they do, and I think that's impor-

tant, I mean the Court doesn't want to become either so seemingly irrelevant or so mysterious and remote, that's not a good thing. I think it is in the Court's interest to . . . think of themselves as part of the government. . . .

Other suggestions made by some reporters over the years range from being given advance notification that a decision was to be announced, to some procedure for gaining advance access to opinions. . . .

Discussing such suggestions from the Court's perspective, Toni House explained, "The Court believes that once it has reached a conclusion it has an obligation to the parties involved to resolve the issue as quick[ly] as it can. And that speaks to not even holding something back for a day." Of the justices she added, "Most assuredly, they do not care about whether it gets on television or not. They just don't."

Evidence that this is the case can be gleaned from an anecdote told by Linda Greenhouse: [Supreme Court correspondent for the *New York Times*]:

One time in an encounter with the Chief Justice, I said to him . . . "Why does the Court do this? Why don't you just spread it out a little more? Not . . . even for our convenience but just so the public will have access to more information about the Court." And he looked at me, I think he was kidding, maybe he wasn't kidding, and he said, "Well, just because we hand it down on a certain day doesn't mean you have to write it on that day. You could just save it for a day . . ." which, actually, from the Court's point of view, I'm sure, makes perfect sense. But from our point of view, of course, makes no sense at all.

. . . As a consequence of multiple decision days and the end-of-term decision deluge, Court reporters are left, according to Tim O'Brien, with a "whirlwind at the end of June. . . . All that time you spend shooting the material, you can only do one or two of them." The situation often results in television journalists having to make a tough call regarding how to play their story. . . .

. . . As Pete Williams observed,

it's sad when, if there's only five or six really good cases that term, and they do two of them

the same day. It just breaks your heart because you think, "Wow, I can only do one of these." And if they are both really, really good barnburner cases, then I will do one and some other reporter . . . will do the other. . . . Or the network will say, "Well, we're only going to do one and which is it going to be?" And you have to make the decision. And it's just sort of sad because the other one begs to be told, but it's just not going to happen. . . .

. . . One example, June 27, 1990, proved to be a particularly harrowing day for the network newscasts as they attempted to deal, not very successfully, with three rulings . . . among the Court's leading decisions of the term.

The cases decided on that day included *Metro Broadcasting v. FCC,* dealing with an affirmative action program in broadcast licensing, *Maryland v. Craig,* a Sixth Amendment case centering on whether children could testify on closed-circuit television to avoid a potentially traumatic face-to-face confrontation with alleged child abusers, and *Idaho v. Wright,* another Sixth Amendment case concerning whether a doctor could testify at a trial about his meeting with a child abuse victim in lieu of the victim testifying directly at the trial. ABC was the only network to cover all three decisions, however sketchily. Thus, *Craig* aired for 1:50, while *Wright* received forty seconds of airtime, and *Metro Broadcasting* only twenty seconds. On CBS, no coverage was given to the *Wright* decision, *Craig* was covered for twenty seconds, and *Metro Broadcasting* received a mere ten-second mention. On NBC, only the *Craig* case received any mention at all, airing for well under thirty seconds.

This all occurred, we should note, merely two days after the Court had decided *Cruzan v. Director, Missouri Department of Health,* an emotionally laden case first raising the issue of the right to die, and *Hodgson v. Minnesota* and *Ohio v. Akron Center for Reproductive Health,* two cases dealing with somewhat different state laws touching on parental notification and abortion rights. Clearly, all three cases warranted coverage. The networks tended to solve the dilemma by blending the Minnesota case (*Hodgson*) and the Ohio case (*Akron*) without drawing any distinctions between them. *Cruzan* coverage received the most prominence, while coverage of the now "collapsed" abortion cases was substantial as well. On both of these late-term decision days, while things were clearly difficult for the press, they were undoubtedly equally problematic for a viewing public left reeling from the announcement of six prominent rulings, among the term's most important, in a matter of days.

Gaining sufficient airtime for worthy cases is not the only problem facing Court reporters as a consequence of the Court's rules, norms, and procedures. Another, as Carl Stern developed, was the need for reporters to translate greater numbers of opinions and, in addition, more obtuse opinions over time as a consequence of the bureaucratization of the Court and the increased staffing enjoyed by each justice:

> . . . Justice [Louis] Brandeis was asked what makes the Supreme Court great. He said it's because we do our own work here. And so it used to be. And the justices wrote relatively brief and compact decisions because they didn't have a lot of help. And that made life relatively easy for reporters. . . . But it also meant things were clearer. . . . [J]ust as the Court has reduced the size of its calendar . . . if it were to reduce the number of clerks so decisions would be simpler, less heavily footnoted, less everybody writing their own thing, then life would be immeasurably easier for reporters. And the law, I think, would be immeasurably clearer for the practitioners . . . and the judges who have to apply the law. . . . Today, you have to struggle for hours to read them and . . . each footnote is a sword hanging over your head . . . that may take away from the broad principles being announced elsewhere in the body of the decision. . . . And trying to figure out these coalitions and the parts they joined and the parts they didn't join, you need a nuclear physicist to figure these out. . . . The plain fact is that Supreme Court decisions today look like the periodic tables in chemistry.

The Issue of Cameras in the Supreme Court

If there is one facet of the Court's rules that, in the public eye as well as in the eyes of many Court reporters, has created the greatest constraints for tele-

vision journalists, it would clearly be the ban on cameras in the Supreme Court. The refusal to allow cameras to cover oral argumentation and the announcement of decisions flies in the face of the trend in many state court settings as well as the experimental use of cameras in the past by lower federal courts and the current "home rule/local option" approach adopted by the U.S. Judicial Conference for the Courts of Appeals. While many critics of allowing television in courtrooms base their objections on the circus atmosphere associated with trial court settings such as the O. J. Simpson murder trial, the issues and concerns are, understandably, different in appellate court settings and, in particular, in a venue such as the U.S. Supreme Court.

Gilbert Merritt, Chief Judge of the Sixth Circuit Court of Appeals and the Chair of the U.S. Judicial Conference's committee that examined the cameras in the courts issue, summarized the fundamental pros and cons of allowing cameras in appellate courts as developed in his committee's deliberations:

> The primary arguments against cameras in appellate courts was that this was a foot in the door, that it will expand from here. A lot of judges are opposed to cameras for a number of reasons. They think it creates a theatrical situation. That lawyers and judges will react to the cameras in an unnatural way by changing their conduct and that this wouldn't be in the interest of justice.

Recognizing that trial and appellate court settings are quite different, Merritt admitted that "the arguments on the one side are not so much that . . . it is bad to have cameras in appellate courts, because there are no witnesses and there are no jurors in the appellate courts. . . . But the argument was more that this is a nose of the camel under the tent argument. A foot in the door."

In summarizing the arguments for allowing cameras in federal appellate courts, Merritt emphasized their putative public benefits:

> There were a number of arguments on the other side. One, that cameras have the potential for getting a good bit of information to the public about how the judicial system works. That if

they are carefully handled in appellate courts we don't run the risk of the theater entertainment problem. And that the federal judiciary . . . a life tenured institution, unelected, without term limits, needs to justify itself and it needs for the press to understand better how it works and to translate better to the American people . . . the functions of the federal judiciary . . . and that there are reasons why we are life tenured, unelected. . . . And one thing that having some cameras, hopefully under the control of favorable circumstances will do, perhaps, over time, is to educate better the American people about the judiciary.

. . . In contemplating why the Supreme Court remains unwilling to allow cameras, reporters often stressed motivations that were highly personal, which didn't, necessarily, flow from the concerns often aired publicly about the supposed impact of cameras on the delivery of justice. Fred Graham, for example, asserted:

Television cameras are in virtually every other Supreme Court, state supreme court, and many, many trial courts, and it's just no problem. . . . I think there are some control freaks on the Supreme Court . . . and they want to control the system. I think they enjoy their anonymity. I think it must be quite a thrill to have the power that goes with being a justice and to be able to walk down the street and not have anyone harass you. I once saw a very raucous antiabortion demonstration . . . around the corner from the Supreme Court . . . and Harry Blackmun was taking his noonday stroll. Strolled right up and stood and watched, and they were screaming, shouting. No one noticed the author of *Roe v. Wade,* and he padded off after a while shaking his head.

. . . An argument often raised about camera coverage of the Court underscores that in the sound-bite world of television, there would inevitably be distortion and misinformation cast out over the airwaves. Characterizing newscast coverage of the Court, Judge Merritt opined that "most of the time the sound bite is this. There is a picture of a participant in the courtroom on the stand and a headline reader. An anchor or a reporter tells you in fifteen to thirty seconds what that means, and the picture is used to authenticate oftentimes a false . . . or inaccurate . . . statement. That is the problem. It's not COURT TV. It's the problem of how it's used in the sound-bite world."

. . . [P]rint reporter Lyle Denniston summarized his position, a stance derived from an adamant belief in First Amendment values of open access:

The judiciary in . . . the federal system now treats the broadcast media as if it had no rights to be present in that courtroom in the only way it can be present because the judiciary does not trust how it will use those rights. . . . Do not assume that we have an obligation to report on the judiciary in the way the judiciary would like, and if we fail in that obligation, then we're going to have our rights taken away from us.

Confronted with Judge Merritt's comments, Denniston argued even more vehemently:

When was the last time that a court told a reporter from *USA Today,* "You may not come in my courthouse because your coverage will be too brief or too selective"? . . . But when the judiciary turns to the broadcast media, it says, "Your right of access depends on whether we like what you say about us." And nobody has ever said to me as a print [journalist] when I walk up to a courthouse, "Denniston, you can't come in here unless you give forty inches to this. You can't come in here unless you cover it gavel to gavel. You can't come in here unless you run the transcript." Nobody has the guts to tell me that I can't cover a public institution because of the way I cover it. . . . But . . . the judiciary around this country . . . they sit there on their high-and-mighty bench and decide that if the coverage is not what I'm going to like, you can't even be in the courtroom. And judges need to understand that . . . if television and radio people can't bring their mikes and their cameras, they are not there. They are simply not there. And there is no reason to assume that anybody is going to ultimately tolerate a judiciary that says coverage of our court as a right of access depends upon our agreement with the scope of your coverage. And judges have got to get that straight. It's not their call. It is just not their call.

As a practical matter, Denniston's strong First Amendment position can be supplemented by the recognition that venues such as COURT TV and C-SPAN now do exist so that much television coverage of the Court would take on the comprehensiveness that Judge Merritt seeks. Further, as Tim O'Brien observed of cameras in the Court: "They're now unobtrusive [and] television has developed in such a way, the proliferation of channels and networks, that you really can cover the arguments from beginning to end. . . ."

The consequences of the absence of cameras in the Court for television news are, of course, easily stated. . . . [C]overage of the Court is less substantial than it might otherwise be, and just as importantly, the nature of Court coverage is different as well. Fred Graham elaborated on these two effects for television news:

> . . . So I think the fact that they don't have cameras in courts, first of all, they don't cover as many stories. And I think it does change what they say, what they focus on, because they can get a picture, let's say, of the scene that's involved in the case, so they'll talk about that rather than what the justice said.

As far as the prospects for cameras entering the Supreme Court to cover arguments and decisions in the future, Graham . . . sees both a small window for optimism as well as major obstacles:

> I used to think it was going to be just a very few years. . . . I think the personalities and beliefs of the Chief Justice are very important, and we've now had three straight Chief Justices who had very little regard for informing the public. And I think if the next Chief Justice were . . . a more modern person, a person who was more comfortable with modern means of communication. . . . Then I think a process would go on . . . after a justice or two backed out. . . . The fly in the ointment here is Justice [Antonin] Scalia, who . . . is hostile to the media. And he's young and strong-minded. So I really wonder whether Scalia would ever change his mind. . . . [T]his is the sort of thing that the justices tend to want to have unanimity over.

. . . Indeed, . . . it appears to miss the mark to even talk in terms of a "debate" about cameras in the Court: "There is no debate about cameras in the Court. . . . The Court has steadfastly stood by its policy that cameras are not welcome during session."

Constraints on Supreme Court Coverage: The Imperatives of Television Journalism

While many of the constraints that affect how the Court is covered on nightly newscasts are derived from rules, norms, and procedures that can be traced to the Court's own doorstep, other circumstances that have an impact on coverage can be seen in the very nature of contemporary television journalism and the way in which the nightly network newscasts are produced. In the heyday of television coverage of the Court the three major networks all had professional journalists who were also attorneys (Tim O'Brien at ABC, Fred Graham at CBS and Carl Stern at NBC), who followed the Court as a full-time beat. . . . [M]uch has changed. . . .

Pete Williams, who covers the Justice Department as well as the Court for NBC, estimated that he spends about a third of his time on Court coverage. . . . [T]he scope of CBS's coverage has diminished radically in recent years. This has not escaped the attention of the network's former law correspondent, Fred Graham: "In a very distressing way, CBS has gone full circle to where they were when they hired me." Graham explained that until his hiring, nobody paid close attention to the Court, but George Herman served as a "designated reporter," who "had no training. He would wait, and when a story came across on the wires that there had been an important decision, they would send him up. . . . They hired me to prepare in advance and to know and to cover it from a basis of some preparation and knowledge." Now, in Graham's view, CBS's coverage once again resembles the earlier model.

This theme was repeated by both NBC's and ABC's current law correspondents. Pete Williams noted that "there's only two of us that regularly hang out at the Court, me and Tim [O'Brien]. . . . CBS has a producer there now. But they don't listen to the arguments as much as we do, so their coverage is declining." Tim O'Brien commented, "CBS does not appear to have any commitment at all," which, he felt, was somewhat ironic because, in the aftermath of Graham's departure from CBS and before Jim Stewart's ascension to the beat, Rita Braver (now the network's White House correspondent) kept the Court at a relatively high profile:

> When she was there, they gave her tons of time. . . . I've since come to conclude it's not so much that they cared about the Court—it's that they were promoting Rita. I felt it was the only network to truly treat the Court right, and now it's the only network to truly treat it wrong.

When asked how much time he spent covering the Court, CBS's Jim Stewart admitted, "Not a great deal, to be honest with you. I think we did seven to eight pieces last year. We'll be doing about the same this year." Even more so than NBC's Williams, Stewart's beat covers a wide landscape:

> I was on 110 times last year. I covered the Justice Department, law enforcement, law, if you will. And, quite frankly, the events of the day, given Oklahoma City, given the organized crime problem they've uncovered among immigrants, given the immigration problems America has, that is the . . . lion's share of this beat. For me to read every brief, every filing that comes in on every case is a waste of time.

Ultimately, while Stewart admits that something has been lost by the general trend on network newscasts to move away from the utilization of highly specialized correspondents, he appears to defend today's approach both as a matter of sound economics and sound journalistic practice:

> Beats are what generate the best stories in journalism, whether it be television or newspaper. That's only common sense. The more you're steeped in your subject matter the better you can explain it and the better you pick up on the nuance and the trends. But it is true across the board for all the networks that I think there has been less of that. To that extent, I think we should be faulted. . . . [W]hen I came to CBS just six years ago, we had a full-time State Department reporter, we had a full-time environmental reporter. We don't have those any longer. And that's a loss. . . . Some days I think

we'd be much better off having a legally trained correspondent who carefully watched that because this is important. This is, make no mistake about it, serious business. But at the same time . . . whoever . . . took the job would go fucking nuts before very long because they wouldn't get on the air more than ten or twelve times a year. There is just no way that the events of the day at that Court are going to drive him on the air anymore. So is that a proper allocation of resources? And that's a question every news organization has to ask itself.

Perhaps answering that question for himself, Stewart continued, "I mean, should I go up there and spend every day just to watch to see if Clarence Thomas ever asks a question?"

The answer to that question has also been clearly given. . . . The reasons for the diminished interest appear to reflect, in part, changes in the Court's behavior. As Toni House commented, "I think the Court . . . is doing things that are less interesting to television." These "less interesting" things can be categorized under a number of continually resonating themes. For one, in an absolute sense the Court is deciding fewer and fewer cases and, consequently, since it is a potential source for news less often, it receives, as a matter of course, less attention. Second, the nature of the questions the Court is visiting has been met with diminishing interest as has its tendency to treat issues, increasingly, by relying on narrow legalisms. . . . In addition, television perceives a contemporary Court that appears to be comfortable with its role, one that does not often take the initiative to strike out boldly in new and controversial policy directions. . . .

If, indeed, it is the Court's output that is primarily responsible for the institution's diminishing coverage, it is, of course, possible that the pendulum could swing the other direction in the future. This was suggested by Pete Williams:

> We've had fewer stories on the air this year than we have in past years and it may just be the quality of the term. . . . Yes, coverage of the Court is . . . declining right now. But that may change. Coverage of Congress was . . . declining too until Newt Gingrich came along, and then it got very different.

Pete Williams's suggestion to the contrary, there are ample reasons to suggest that a significant increase in coverage of the Court, regardless of its output, will not be in the cards. Given the commercial imperatives that drive network newscasts, particularly in an era that Fred Graham characterized as moving from a serious concern with journalistic standards to the age of infotainment, this is simply not likely to occur. It is to a consideration of infotainment, its impact on network newscasts, and its consequences for coverage of the Supreme Court that we now turn.

Covering the Court in the Age of Infotainment

The very notion of infotainment itself is suggestive of some of the fundamental differences between broadcast and print journalism and the environments in which they operate. Clearly, both newspapers and networks are business enterprises, yet ostensibly the "product" through which newspapers attract their readership is the news. Television news, however, is much less central to the network's operation. . . . Entertainment can be as important a requisite for television news as it is for the remainder of the broadcast day. This has important implications for the reporting of governmental affairs and, particularly, for an institution such as the relatively "invisible" Supreme Court, where it can be argued that "proceedings are so dull that it is a public service to keep them off the tube" and where much of what goes on "rocks along at the excitement level of watching cement set."

In discussing the emergence of infotainment in the early 1980s, Graham begins with Eric Sevareid's tongue-slightly-in-cheek comment, "The trouble started . . . when CBS News began to make a profit." In Sevareid's view, "People forget . . . that television news started out as a loss leader. It was expected to lose money." Expectations began to change, however, when CBS News's *60 Minutes* began to show a profit: "Once CBS News became an engine of profits . . . then the goal was no longer quality but ratings. Television news had become a victim of its own success," and, in Graham's view, there was a "fundamental change in values" as

"ratings replaced journalistic principles as the guiding force of the News Division.". . .

. . . While the word *infotainment* quickly became an embarrassment and left "official" usage at CBS, "it remained the underlying technique for presenting the news." At bottom, the approach "boiled down to two new marching orders: First, make the news appeal to the heart by capturing . . . 'magic moments,' and second, make CBS News look, as much as possible, like entertainment TV." These new imperatives changed fundamentally the role of the journalist: "Traditionally, journalists had understood that news was what the public needed to know and wanted to know. Infotainment changed that by making the central focus 'what will keep them watching our network.' "

The move to infotainment had important consequences for covering the Court, as Graham related:

> They decided that their definition of what they wanted and what was news changed. And they decided that what people wanted to see was very visual, and courts, the Supreme Court, you couldn't show, and so it made it almost by definition . . . not newsworthy. The Supreme Court was not newsworthy. . . . [T]here was very little interest in my superiors.

In Graham's view such a development was not "healthy for the legal system and it certainly wasn't good for the prospects of a correspondent who hoped to make a career broadcasting legal news on TV." This point was brought home when Graham attempted to report on the Court's decision declaring unconstitutional the automatic spending-cut provisions of the Gramm-Rudman deficit reduction law in 1986:

> The Court relied on the tortured reasoning that Congress had violated the separation of powers by giving authority to trigger across-the-board spending cuts to the Comptroller General, an official who theoretically could be fired by Congress. To me, the conservative Reagan court had scuttled an innovative effort at fiscal control on a technicality and I thought it important to explain how the Court had tied the logic in knots to agree with the Reagan administration's position. But the grown-ups decreed that I could not utter the words "Comptroller General" or ex-

plain the firing problem on the ground that television viewers couldn't handle such detail. My resulting report—that the law was thrown out because it violated the separation of powers—was simple and easy to grasp. It also didn't burden our viewers with an understanding of what had actually happened. I learned that straight news could be harmful to your professional health.

. . . Graham learned, too, that even "less than straight" news might sometimes have difficulty seeing airtime when it was focused on the Court. Frustrated at not getting stories aired, Graham admitted that "an increasing portion of my effort went into sifting through the Supreme Court docket in search of whiz-bang fact situations that might make it on." Once he thought he had a "sure winner" in the case of Grendel's Den, a restaurant near Harvard that was denied a liquor license because of objections from the local Catholic parish. The case somehow found its way to the Court:

> As Supreme Court cases go, this one seemed made for the age of infotainment. There were boozy college students, a prudish priest, a famous liberal law professor, and a carefully muted question of Church and State. I had cannily concealed the constitutional issue amid scenes of noisy students and aggrieved parishioners; thus, the legal point did not get in the way of a good yarn. To me, Grendel's Den became the benchmark of legal reporting in the infotainment era. "If this one can't make it," I thought, "no Supreme Court case is a good bet."

The Grendel's Den story never made it on to the *CBS Evening News.* The piece was killed, according to Graham, because it was to air on a Friday night and it would not leave the viewers in an appropriate frame of mind to approach the weekend's television viewing.

Concerns about infotainment could play as important a role in the stories that did air and how they were played as they could in stories that did not. Graham recounted the scenario "when *Miami Vice* was very popular and our producers at CBS got the idea that the public . . . wanted to see young, good-looking people and . . . they wanted

to see a place that was bright and sunshiny and maybe with a little surf out there:"

> I was covering a . . . decision that had to do with affirmative action among police [and fire] departments. And there were several different police departments that were involved, and I traveled around to the various places to talk to the people . . . who were actually involved in those cities. On the day the Supreme Court decided the case, it was decided at CBS that I wouldn't do the story based on actually having gone to the cities where these disputes arose, but it would be done from Miami. Because Miami had police, although it was not one of the cities involved in this dispute . . . they did have police and they had black police and white police and . . . there were young good-looking people that would be shown and a sunny background and even some water. And so that story was done. It was a Supreme Court decision. Dan Rather came on and said, "The Supreme Court has issued a decision today involving affirmative action in police and fire departments, and now we go to Miami with, whoever the reporter is, for the story." And he did it.

. . . While we have been focusing on infotainment in a critical vein, it is equally important to underscore that it is not only television news' desire to entertain, per se, that constitutes the problem. Rather, it is what appears to be missing from the brew. This point was reiterated by Carl Stern:

> It's not just this silly business about happy talk and infotainment. . . . I think TV is entitled to get a little silly if it wants, and if it doesn't meet these Olympian goals we all set for it. . . . That's not the part that hurts. The part that hurts is that at least at bottom there's supposed to be some sort of unwritten contract between people who describe themselves as journalists and the public that they serve that they're going to do their level best to ensure that the public gets the truth, the whole truth, nothing but the truth. And that's not what's happening. . . . Lenin, a peculiar source of information to be quoted at this point, said truth is that which serves. Well, we don't believe that. We believe truth is truth

whether it serves or doesn't serve. Well, unfortunately, TV these days, I'm not suggesting that they've become Leninists but, essentially, truth is that which serves the production sense of the people who put the show on the air. And it is a show. It's a show. . . . And that's the loss of it for those who took it seriously.

The news "show," as James Fallows [correspondent for *Atlantic Monthly*] has observed, needs "stars" and operates on the belief that "the delivery system—that is the reporter as an entertainment instrument—is more important than the substance of the story":

> . . . The sin . . . is not being inaccurate. The sin is being boring.

It is important to be clear about what Stern, Fallows, and others are charging and what they are not about the changing nature of the evening newscasts that began to take hold through the middle and late 1980s. Clearly, editors and producers have a legitimate and important role to play and often improve the stories that do get chosen for airtime. . . .

Further, nobody is suggesting that news producers do not have a legitimate and important professional role to play in making critical choices in putting together the evening news. As Pete Williams explained, "There are more correspondents that want to get on the air than can possibly get on the air in a given day. . . . [A] producer of a nightly newscast is thinking. . . . 'Well, okay, I have those people in the waiting room that want to get on the air. Well, what . . . should we be doing?'" Tim O'Brien admitted that in a reporter's effort to get on the air, a Supreme Court story can often legitimately come out the loser in the contest: "If I have a . . . case that I think might belong on, and I have some editors who might think not, what I'll look at is what's in the lineup, what else are they planning to run. And there are times when I'll say, 'This is an incredibly important story' [and] I looked at what I was competing with and said, 'You know, they were right. They still had bigger fish to fry.' ". . .

Such a reality may, at times, be both regrettable and, perhaps, unavoidable. There are instances, however, where the dictates of the news "show" create the result. As Carl Stern related, there were times when

you would call them [newscast producers] up at 10:30 in the morning. You know in your gut that this is a story that has got to go. You know your competitors are going to do it, and you know it is going to be all over page one tomorrow. And you can't persuade the producer to go with it because he's got an eight-minute piece booked into the show on pedophile priests that they've been promoting for three days. That's the one that really gets to you. When you know something important has happened and you're not going to be able to tell the public about it. . . .

The real journalistic problem that developed in the infotainment era as it applied to the Supreme Court particularly (and newscasting more generally) often went beyond such gaffes (if they were inadvertent) and even went beyond the increased propensity to cover only the biggest and most sensational cases that could be made to fit the new approach. As Carl Stern asserted, "If it was simply a matter to be entertaining, I suppose I wouldn't feel so badly about it. But it's worse than that." He continued, "I could live with the fact that they cover only occasionally and that they cover only the cases that seem to be the sizzlers. I understand that. . . . But what I agonize over is distortion and untruth, and quite often I see stories that I believe are . . . conveying to the public an untrue perception of what happened. And that's not done negligently. It's done intentionally, and I think that's unforgivable. I think that is the highest sin in journalism, and I see it all around." In our extended interview, Stern framed the fundamental issue regarding the disjuncture between the Court's action and its portrayal on the air:

> You have written extensively about different things that television people did on the air. You reasonably believed that what you heard coming across the television was their thoughts, their analysis, their best efforts to communicate what the Court had done. That is a somewhat simplistic view. And it doesn't take into account the enormous changes that occurred in television journalism in the late 1980s.

These comments, we think, underscore some of the reasons why the serious professional journalists revealed in these pages often fall far short in their coverage of the Court. . . . The changes that Stern alludes to are touched on in some of the examples offered by Fred Graham discussed above. They relate to the fundamental altering of the journalistic relationship between the Court reporters and the news producers, and the increasing role the producers took on in determining the very *content* of news reports on the Court. Prior to the triumph of the infotainment approach, reporters' professional judgments held the key to understanding what was sufficiently newsworthy to justify coverage. . . .

[But] newscast content in the age of infotainment became, in a sense, a competition. As Stern explained it, "news is merchandise just as surely as being in the car business or retail clothing. It is a business of merchandising, and the explanation that may satisfy a reporter trying to be precise may not satisfy the producer trying to excite an audience". . . .

A major consequence of these developments for journalists covering the Court became the need to engage in protracted "demoralizing" negotiations to get a story on the air and to get it told in a manner that did justice to the actual event being covered. Fred Graham described the scene at CBS:

> The editing process loomed larger and larger. And what happened was, you would write the story in conjunction with your producer and late in the afternoon, say 4:30 or 5:00, that goes to New York. Then there are two levels of editing there, and then they would come back and they would say do so and so. Sometimes the so and so they want you to do is either incomprehensible or flat wrong. And then you have to get on the phone and negotiate that. And quite often you're negotiating. The deadline, of course, is 6:30 for the evening news, and it's 6:00. It was a maddening process and . . . a very demoralizing thing.

The picture Stern draws of what happened at NBC is painted in remarkably similar tones:

> Over and over again on a daily basis when I was writing, at least in the latter years of being on the air at NBC, I frequently was obliged to change what the Court had said to meet the requirements of a producer even though I didn't believe that that's what the Court had said. It ba-

sically got down to a contest every night about a quarter of six between what I knew the Court had said and what I knew the producer would accept. And then it got down to a question as to whether we were going to do the story at all. Frequently, more often than not, that meant having to . . . just take down the producer's words, the producer having very little knowledge of what the Court had actually done, and going to a microphone and reciting those words. . . . I'm not talking about an isolated incident. I am talking about every report.

Frequently, the subject of the negotiations would revolve around Stern's efforts to quote from the Court's decision or to paraphrase what it had said:

> There's many a time . . . that I took . . . if not a verbatim quote at least the essence of what a justice had said and was told by a producer to change it to this or that. And I would say, "But that's not what he said," and they would say, "Well, that's what he really meant." And I would say, "No, that's not what he meant, and that's not correct." And then it came down to, "Do you want to get on the air tonight or don't you want to get on the air tonight?" As you can see by my present circumstance [at the time of our interview, Stern was the Director of the Office of Public Affairs at the Department of Justice], I don't want to get on the air tonight because it reached a point where I no longer believed in some instances that we were accurately describing what the Court had said.

. . . Graham noted that at one point, "I refused to do one story. I just said I won't do it because you're insisting that I make it wrong. This is wrong and I won't do it." Graham's action may have had some effect, since "several times after I refused to do the story, they realized that if I felt that strongly, maybe it was wrong and they permitted me to change it." Nevertheless, Graham continued, "there were other times when they required me to say things that were nonsensical or that were inconsistent with other things I had said. And despite my arguments, they insisted, and I did it." Carl Stern offered a similar assessment: "I would occasionally, I say occasionally . . . find myself in a position where I didn't know what I was saying. I didn't know what the piece meant because I was, well, following instructions.". . .

The Nuts and Bolts of Covering the Court on Network Television Newscasts

. . . [S]tyles of reporting on the Court by television journalists developed largely as a necessary response to the predicament that reporters found themselves in covering a low-priority, visually staid beat. Fred Graham pioneered the approach to coverage that continues to this day as the prototype for television's Supreme Court analysts: "My approach was to go to the community where each dispute arose, take pictures of the scene, interview the people involved, and present the legal question through the stories of the people who raised it." Graham recognizes that this approach seems "obvious now, as it is the way all the networks do it," and he admits that "while it was TV legal journalism at its best, as long as we were excluded from the courtroom it was not good enough.". . .

Supreme Court cases, of course, offer several decision points for possible coverage ranging from the filing of a petition for certiorari through the granting of certiorari, oral argument, and the actual decision itself. Decisional coverage is, logically, the point at which most cases will make it into a newscast since, at that stage, the reporter has the best chance of gauging accurately the case's importance. Stories on petitioning for certiorari or even the granting of certiorari are quite rare since there is a good chance that the case will not pan out down the road in its ultimate decision. Thus, as Pete Williams underscored, spending a good deal of his time on the various facets of the certiorari process is "just not a very productive expenditure of my time. . . . There's already a high homework-to-getting-on-the-air ratio for the Supreme Court, and that would just make it a lot higher." Inevitably, however, there will be isolated cases that do receive coverage through all stages of Supreme Court processing. As Williams noted, "It just depends on how big the case is. . . . [T]he term limits case we covered every step of the way. We covered it when they granted cert, we covered it when it was argued, we covered it when it was decided."

Coverage of oral argumentation, while not as frequent as decisional coverage, is a favored stage of Supreme Court processes for television for a number of reasons. As Toni House observed:

> Probably what they do best is oral arguments. . . . [I]t tells the story. Also, it's a drama. It's this side against the other side. The advocates most likely are out front after the argument telling their side. You can quote the justices speaking from the bench. . . . [I]t gives it elements that make it televisable and entertaining.

As a practical matter, there is a strong element of scheduling predictability in oral argumentation that raises its stock for reporters. As Fred Graham explained, "you don't get squeezed out on a day where there are multiple decisions. You know you've got that day. You know when it's coming. . . . So that . . . permits you to lay out your thinking a lot better than on the day of decision." Tim O'Brien indicated that he sometimes preferred to do a story the evening before oral argument was to take place:

> We have so little time, I sometimes think it's better spent listening to the people involved in the case and the experts than putting up drawings of justices and questions that they ask. . . . [O]ften . . . I will not have any shot in my piece from Washington, maybe a shot of the Supreme Court only to say this is where the case is going to be argued tomorrow.

We have stressed throughout that because of the Court's relative isolation, coupled with the inaccessibility of the justices to the media, television coverage of the institution focuses almost exclusively on its work output. Little attention is placed on the justices themselves, save for the relatively brief period of their coming on or going off the Court. Pete Williams mused on this seeming irony:

> [W]hen . . . it comes time to appoint a new justice, it is the biggest god damn story in town. All the jockeying, who might it be? We crowd around everybody who comes to town. . . . When Stephen Breyer came here the first time, the stakeouts of him walking through Union Station with his broken collarbone. . . . And we

pay a little attention to the confirmation hearing . . . because it is a test of the president. And that is why it becomes such a big story. And then there are all these stories about their judicial philosophy. . . . Then they go on the Court and we proceed to ignore them.

. . . Rarely do stories focus on the justices per se, and when they do, it is most often a reflection of reporting on appointment politics and processes. This is not to suggest that stories concerning malfeasance or scandal would not be covered heavily. Rather, it underscores that such information about the justices is rarely forthcoming.

Interestingly, despite the fact that Supreme Court reporters work in a domain where they have less access to decision makers and decision processes than in other governmental beats, the truth of the matter is that they have such complete access to documentary information about what they are covering that they have an unusual opportunity to prepare for stories and are rarely caught off guard by a case decision. When the networks all covered the Court with full-time legal correspondents, their preparation was quite extensive. As Carl Stern described it, "The sort of stuff we did then would be unheard of today for a TV . . . reporter."

> For example, at the start of the Court and through the term I would do the conference lists. . . . [T]hat could be doing a couple thousand cases. Why? Because you only know where the Court is going . . . if you have some idea what kinds of cases they are hearing or what kinds of cases they aren't hearing. . . . [A]nd, also, you spot things early. And once you identify those cases that you think the Court is likely to take—obviously, it will be a small list for television that you care about—you would go out and you would start collecting visuals.

If Stern were uncertain about whether the Court would actually hear a case, or if a potentially attractive case remained several stages from the Supreme Court, he might call the network's affiliates and seek copies of any footage they might have "on cases that I thought would come along. There were cases where it would take years.". . .

. . . Pete Williams, who characterized the Court as having "the highest homework-to-actually-get-

ting-on-the-air ratio in town," described the winnowing process he goes through in covering cases:

> Of the . . . eighty signed opinions we are going to have this year . . . we will keep our eye on . . . fifteen to twenty cases that are potentially of interest to us. So you have to read the briefs in all those cases, you have to call the lawyers, talk to the lawyers, talk to the law school professors. . . . Then we have to in probably ten of those cases go out and shoot a lot of tape.

Williams will also attend the oral argument in the cases that "we are peripherally interested in. . . . I tend not to go to oral argument for every single case. I don't think anyone does that. That would just be a phenomenal waste of time." Regarding his advance preparation, Williams estimated that about half of it does not see the light of day and never leads to airtime and inclusion in a story. . . .

One source of information relied on somewhat by the Court reporters in their preparation is *Preview*, a publication underwritten largely by the American Bar Association, which offers summaries and insights on the issues and arguments before the Court. Maximum use is not made of it, however, because, as Pete Williams explained, "the trouble is it comes out so late. It is always good to read, and I invariably read it if there is a case I'm covering because . . . it is another brain on that case. But I need to know a lot of things before that comes out, so there's just no substitute for reading the briefs." . . .

As a consequence of having so much documentary information on the public record, coupled with aids such as *Preview*, the willingness of interest groups to serve as sources for reporters, and the multistepped processes through which cases proceed at the Court before a decision is announced, television reporters, even today, are rarely caught off guard or unprepared for a ruling. Indeed, Fred Graham asserted that the dictates of preparing footage for broadcasting made him better prepared as a television journalist than he had been at the *New York Times*:

> You could almost always look at the case at the time the Court took it, even before, and see pretty much what its potential was to be important. And the ones that showed that potential, you knew that when it was decided it was going

to be important news, so you had to go out with your camera well before it was due to be decided and interview all the people and take pictures of the scenes. . . .

Earlier, we alluded to elements of a story that made it newsworthy in the eyes of reporters generally. Now we will turn to the more narrow concern of what makes a case sufficiently newsworthy to receive coveted airtime on the nightly newscasts. . . . Interestingly, part of the answer may be dictated by the nature of a case's outcome. As Fred Graham noted, "There are some cases in which if it went one way, big story, but if it went the other way, no story." Carl Stern drew a distinction between statutory and constitutional cases, the latter of which were easier to get on the air, other things being equal: "On the constitutional stuff there are red flags all over it. If this is a case about reading the bible in class or . . . burning the American flag it doesn't take a genius. . . . I always said to myself, half jokingly, 'Does it meet the bar-stool test?' Is this the kind of thing people are going to argue about in bars, saloons? And they're just intellectually interesting. It's something we can really argue about. . . . Those you can spot very easily."

Clearly, the sheer magnitude of some stories alone will get them on the newscast. Pete Williams asserted that "big stories are as television worthy as they are newspaper worthy." Thus, "decisions on term limits . . . affirmative action decisions, the gun in school decisions . . . were as big for us as they were for newspapers. So the big cases are always going to get on television." Other stories that are less "big" will receive airtime when they have "more compelling visual elements . . . or [something] that . . . everybody can identify with." . . .

Regarding the importance of visuals for making a case television worthy Lyle Denniston observed, "I used to sit in a cubbyhole between Carl Stern and Tim O'Brien and on big decision days I was always amazed at how much of their conversation focused on the pictures that they had available as opposed to discussing the substance of what the Court had done."

In the final analysis, gauging newsworthiness for the network newscasts involves a fine balancing act. Tim O'Brien assessed some of the elements in the balance:

The case you cover is the one you believe to be the most newsworthy and the most important. Sometimes, you can sacrifice some of the importance if it is an extremely interesting case. And sometimes you can sacrifice some of the interest. It can be a rather dull case, if it is extremely important. But how it affects people generally and its interest to people are both considerations.

As Pete Williams has lamented, too often in drawing the balance even interesting cases with the potential for widespread impact do not get on the air. Offering a particular example, he pointed out that "it's very hard to get . . . pure First Amendment cases on television. . . . The lady in Iowa with the antiwar sign in her window, or the woman in . . . Ohio who wanted to pass out anonymous campaign literature. And the little community that prided itself on being sort of special and a little bit snooty that wanted to have no signs." These cases, among others, did not meet the network's criteria.

Some cases do, of course, make it on to the evening news. . . . Perhaps the first imperative noted by several reporters is to actually be in the courtroom when the decision is released. As Pete Williams stressed:

I like to hear what it is that the justice says is important about the case, partly because if I want to use a quote from them speaking it, I can be right there to get the quote. And if they make some gesture. And sometimes they do unusual things, like Ruth Bader Ginsburg reads her whole opinion or something. You just want to be there. . . . And it also provides a little review and it sort of keys me to things to watch out for in the opinion.

Carl Stern concurred: "You've got to sit there and listen to them. Oral announcements are more truncated these days but, in the old days, when Hugo Black was railing against his colleagues . . . or even when Blackmun did some of his famous dissents and so on with passion, you pick up a good sense of the case by listening to oral announcements of it."

Not all of the television reporters enjoy the luxury of "being there" for all of the decisions they cover. Tim O'Brien, for example, often has to file an immediate radio report, which may lead him to obtain a copy of a decision from the Court's Public Information Office as it is announced:

> Consider this. . . . The decision comes down at ten after ten and they want something they can put on the air at eleven o'clock. They can record it half an hour after I have the decision, so what I usually do is I read the syllabus, which will say whether the lower court decision was affirmed, reversed, affirmed in part, [or] reversed in part and will summarize why. Then I go to the dissent, read the beginning and end of the dissents or dissent, and then, if time permits, I go back and read more of the majority opinion. Before I go on the evening news, I like to have the whole decision read cover to cover, and usually I can do that but not always.

Carl Stern, too, had to prepare pieces for radio with great dispatch and, looking back, he takes some credit for the syllabus now appended to decisions at the time of their announcement:

> When I came to the Supreme Court there was no syllabus, there was no headnote, and it was a terrible time. There was one day . . . when the Court came down with 544 pages of printed decisions in about twenty minutes, and I had to file to radio at 11:00. And all you could do was flip over to the last page and see what the Court said because there was no way to know. And I'd come from Ohio which has a syllabus. . . . [Once] I had to do . . . six decisions in one spot, and I did fine except on one of them . . . I got it backwards, I got it wrong on the air. . . . I told Warren Burger that story . . . and . . . Burger ordered the reporter . . . to start putting these headnotes, which they used to prepare after the fact for publication in the bound volume of *U.S. Reports,* to do it ahead of time and to put them out informally with the decision so that people could get a quick summary of it. And that was the result of my conversation with Burger.

Interestingly, to the extent that Court procedures have changed through the years to respond, in part, to journalistic needs, many of these reforms occurred during the watch of staunch media critic Warren Burger. Fred Graham explained:

Burger never conceded that there was a legitimate public interest in such matters as the justices' health, their finances, their reasons for disqualifying themselves from cases, their votes on deadlocked appeals and their off-the-bench activities. Thus, Burger became an enthusiastic reformer of the mechanics of covering the Supreme Court, perhaps in hopes that by facilitating our efforts to cover the formalities we would be less likely to fritter away our energies on personalities and gossip.

In this sense the Chief Justice sought to bring added efficiency to dissemination of the information already distributed by the press officer. In no sense was the scope of distributed information altered. The irony of Burger's role, however, was not lost on Graham: "It was amazing how enlightened Burger could appear simply by changing some of the musty old procedures that his predecessors hadn't bothered to question."

For reporters who do not have to worry about preparing an early piece for radio, the drill may be somewhat different. Thus, Pete Williams will contact the news desk in Washington and the appropriate production people in New York to alert them that a decision has been rendered that warrants coverage. Usually, at that time, he will be given the go-ahead. Then, in conjunction with his producer and researcher, he will begin to track down appropriate people to interview about the case, often including efforts to reach the litigants directly.

. . . As Jim Stewart described the process, he does not spend time at the Supreme Court waiting for decisions to come down as do the reporters for the other networks:

> We have two people there every time decisions are announced. They quickly scan. They call me, I'm listening to them as they're listening to the case as it's announced and called out there. We make a snap judgment on whether these are dog cases or whether these are cases that might have a chance. . . . We know in advance, obviously, cases that we have considered bellwether cases. And if that decision comes down, we immediately hit the red phone and tell New York and start blocking time out.

. . . In between arranging and conducting interviews or having one's producer doing so, the reporter will often be in contact with the newscast's sketch artist to discuss what drawings are needed. At this juncture, Pete Williams explained:

> You start thinking about the graphic elements and you start envisioning what the story is going to be. . . . And then all that stuff starts to come back to you, and they tell you what the people said in the interviews and you choose those things, and the crew comes down and you do your standup. You quibble with them on the script and, finally, get the script approved. And you go in that little room under the Court bench and you voice the track part, and then it all comes together.

Summing Up and Looking Forward

. . . [W]e have taken an extended look at the world in which the Supreme Court reporter operates with a particular focus on the job of a network television correspondent covering the Court. We have relied mostly on the reporters' own perceptions of what their jobs entail and how they define their journalistic as well as their public responsibilities. Our exploration has examined the resources at the Court reporter's disposal including consideration of the roles played by interest groups, the Court's Public Information Office, the justices themselves, and the Supreme Court journalist's own colleagues in performing the job. We have paid considerable attention to the uniqueness of the Supreme Court beat, while exploring the constraints imposed on journalists by the institution of the Court itself as well as by the nature of the television news business. Much of our focus has been on changes in the television news industry that culminated in the 1980s in what Fred Graham characterized at CBS News as the triumph of infotainment over news substance. Along the way we have explored several possible reforms that have been proffered from many sources, including reporters themselves, to help facilitate "better" coverage of the Court that would, it is argued, lead ultimately to a better informed public. Special attention was placed on the issue of cameras in the courtroom.

The portrait that emerged from our consideration of the task of the television Supreme Court reporter is quite a sobering one. Their job is quite complex, and in the absence of visual access to the decision-making process and routine interviews with the decision makers, they must find alternative ways of convincing their superiors that airtime is warranted. Once gaining valuable airtime, they must present as much as they can in an attenuated time frame. [As] Tim O'Brien admits, . . . television news can be a "headline service" with very little in-depth legal reporting:

> If you are really concerned about quality news reporting on the law, you should not be watching television. . . . Every line is a headline on television. And we sometimes wind up just reading headlines when we read Supreme Court stories and that is frustrating.

Much more recently, however, O'Brien added, "Well, things are relative."

> I think we do a reasonably good job. It could be a hell of a lot better, but given the restrictions that we have inherent in the nature of the business and the restrictions imposed on us by the Court, problems that we have, I think we do a reasonably respectable job. But it could be better, of course.

A View from the Inside

 Sheppard v. Maxwell
384 U.S. 333 (1966)

MR. JUSTICE CLARK delivered
the opinion of the Court.

This federal habeas corpus application involves the question whether Sheppard was deprived of a fair trial in his state conviction for the second-degree murder of his wife because of the trial judge's failure to protect Sheppard sufficiently from the massive, pervasive and prejudicial publicity that attended his prosecution. The United States District Court held that he was not afforded a fair trial and granted the writ subject to the State's right to put Sheppard to trial again. The Court of Appeals for the Sixth Circuit reversed by a divided vote. We granted certiorari. We have concluded that Sheppard did not receive a fair trial consistent with the Due Process Clause of the Fourteenth Amendment and, therefore, reverse the judgment.

Marilyn Sheppard, petitioner's pregnant wife, was bludgeoned to death in the upstairs bedroom of their lakeshore home in Bay Village, Ohio, a suburb of Cleveland. On the day of the tragedy, July 4, 1954, Sheppard pieced together for several local officials the following story: He and his wife had entertained neighborhood friends, the Aherns, on the previous evening at their home. After dinner they watched television in the living room. Sheppard became drowsy and dozed off to sleep on a couch. Later, Marilyn partially awoke him saying that she was going to bed. The next thing he remembered was hearing his wife cry out in the early morning hours. He hurried upstairs and in the dim light from the hall saw a "form" standing next to his wife's bed. As he struggled with the "form" he was struck on the back of the neck and rendered unconscious. On regaining his senses he found himself on the floor next to his wife's bed. He rose, looked at her, took her pulse and "felt that she was gone." He then went to his son's room and found him unmolested. Hearing a noise he hurried downstairs. He saw a "form" running out the door and

pursued it to the lake shore. He grappled with it on the beach and again lost consciousness. Upon his recovery he was lying face down with the lower portion of his body in the water. He returned to his home, checked the pulse on his wife's neck, and "determined or thought that she was gone." He then went downstairs and called a neighbor, Mayor Houk of Bay Village. The Mayor and his wife came over at once, found Sheppard slumped in an easy chair downstairs and asked, "What happened?" Sheppard replied: "I don't know but somebody ought to try to do something for Marilyn." Mrs. Houk immediately went up to the bedroom. The Mayor told Sheppard, "Get hold of yourself. Can you tell me what happened?" Sheppard then related the above-outlined events. After Mrs. Houk discovered the body, the Mayor called the local police, Dr. Richard Sheppard, petitioner's brother, and the Aherns. The local police were the first to arrive. They in turn notified the Coroner and Cleveland police. Richard Sheppard then arrived, determined that Marilyn was dead, examined his brother's injuries, and removed him to the nearby clinic operated by the Sheppard family. When the Coroner, the Cleveland police and other officials arrived, the house and surrounding area were thoroughly searched, the rooms of the house were photographed, and many persons, including the Houks and the Aherns, were interrogated. The Sheppard home and premises were taken into "protective custody" and remained so until after the trial.

From the outset officials focused suspicion on Sheppard. After a search of the house and premises on the morning of the tragedy, Dr. Gerber, the Coroner, is reported—and it is undenied—to have told his men, "Well, it is evident the doctor did this, so let's go get the confession out of him." He proceeded to interrogate and examine Sheppard while the latter was under sedation in his hospital room. On the same occasion, the Coroner was given the clothes Sheppard wore at the time of the tragedy together with the personal items in them. Later that afternoon Chief Eaton and two Cleveland police officers interrogated Sheppard at some length, confronting him with evidence and demanding explanations. Asked by Officer Shotke to take a lie detector test, Sheppard said he would if it were reliable. Shotke replied that it was "infallible" and "you might as well tell us all about it now." At the end of the interrogation Shotke told Sheppard: "I think you killed your wife." Still later in the same afternoon a physician sent by the Coroner was permitted to make a detailed examination of Sheppard. Until the Coroner's inquest on July 22, at which time he was subpoenaed, Sheppard made himself available for frequent and extended questioning without the presence of an attorney.

On July 7, the day of Marilyn Sheppard's funeral, a newspaper story appeared in which Assistant County Attorney Mahon—later the chief prosecutor of Sheppard—sharply criticized the refusal of the Sheppard family to permit his immediate questioning. From there on headline stories repeatedly stressed Sheppard's lack of cooperation with the police and other officials. Under the headline "Testify Now In Death, Bay Doctor Is Ordered," one story described a visit by Coroner Gerber and four police officers to the hospital on July 8. When Sheppard insisted that his lawyer be present, the Coroner wrote out a subpoena and served it on him. Sheppard then agreed to submit to questioning without counsel and the subpoena was torn up. The officers questioned him for several hours. On July 9, Sheppard, at the request of the Coroner, re-enacted the tragedy at his home before the Coroner, police officers, and a group of newsmen, who apparently were invited by the Coroner. The home was locked so that Sheppard was obliged to wait outside until the Coroner arrived. Sheppard's performance was reported in detail by the news media along with photographs. The newspapers also played up Sheppard's refusal to take a lie detector test and "the protective ring" thrown up by his family. Front-page newspaper headlines announced on the same day that "Doctor Balks At Lie Test; Retells Story." A column opposite that story contained an "exclusive" interview with Sheppard headlined: "'Loved My Wife, She Loved Me,' Sheppard Tells News Reporter." The next day, another headline story disclosed that Sheppard had "again late yes-

terday refused to take a lie detector test" and quoted an Assistant County Attorney as saying that "at the end of a nine-hour questioning of Dr. Sheppard, I felt he was now ruling [a test] out completely." But subsequent newspaper articles reported that the Coroner was still pushing Sheppard for a lie detector test. More stories appeared when Sheppard would not allow authorities to inject him with "truth serum."

On the 20th, the "editorial artillery" opened fire with a front-page charge that somebody is "getting away with murder." The editorial attributed the ineptness of the investigation to "friendships, relationships, hired lawyers, a husband who ought to have been subjected instantly to the same third-degree to which any other person under similar circumstances is subjected. . . ." The following day, July 21, another page-one editorial was headed: "Why No Inquest? Do It Now, Dr. Gerber." The Coroner called an inquest the same day and subpoenaed Sheppard. It was staged the next day in a school gymnasium; the Coroner presided with the County Prosecutor as his advisor and two detectives as bailiffs. In the front of the room was a long table occupied by reporters, television and radio personnel, and broadcasting equipment. The hearing was broadcast with live microphones placed at the Coroner's seat and the witness stand. A swarm of reporters and photographers attended. Sheppard was brought into the room by police who searched him in full view of several hundred spectators. Sheppard's counsel were present during the three-day inquest but were not permitted to participate. When Sheppard's chief counsel attempted to place some documents in the record, he was forcibly ejected from the room by the Coroner, who received cheers, hugs, and kisses from ladies in the audience. Sheppard was questioned for five and one-half hours about his actions on the night of the murder, his married life, and a love affair with Susan Hayes. At the end of the hearing the Coroner announced that he "could" order Sheppard held for the grand jury, but did not do so.

Throughout this period the newspapers emphasized evidence that tended to incriminate Sheppard and pointed out discrepancies in his statements to authorities. At the same time, Sheppard made many public statements to the press and wrote feature articles asserting his innocence. During the inquest on July 26, a headline in large type stated: "Kerr [Captain of the Cleveland Police] Urges Sheppard's Arrest." In the story, Detective McArthur "disclosed that scientific tests at the Sheppard home have definitely established that the killer washed off a trail of blood from the murder bedroom to the downstairs section," a circumstance casting doubt on Sheppard's accounts of the murder. No such evidence was produced at trial. The newspapers also delved into Sheppard's personal life. Articles stressed his extramarital love affairs as a motive for the crime. The newspapers portrayed Sheppard as a Lothario, fully explored his relationship with Susan Hayes, and named a number of other women who were allegedly involved with him. The testimony at trial never showed that Sheppard had any illicit relationships besides the one with Susan Hayes.

On July 28, an editorial entitled "Why Don't Police Quiz Top Suspect?" demanded that Sheppard be taken to police headquarters. It described him in the following language:

> Now proved under oath to be a liar, still free to go about his business, shielded by his family, protected by a smart lawyer who has made monkeys of the police and authorities, carrying a gun part of the time, left free to do whatever he pleases. . . .

A front-page editorial on July 30 asked: "Why Isn't Sam Sheppard In Jail?" It was later titled "Quit Stalling—Bring Him In." After calling Sheppard "the most unusual murder suspect ever seen around these parts," the article said that "[e]xcept for some superficial questioning during Coroner Sam Gerber's inquest he has been scot-free of any official grilling. . . ." It asserted that he was "surrounded by an iron curtain of protection [and] concealment."

That night at 10 o'clock Sheppard was arrested at his father's home on a charge of murder. He was taken to the Bay Village City Hall where hundreds of people, newscasters, photographers and reporters were awaiting his arrival. He was immediately arraigned—having been denied a temporary delay to secure the presence of counsel—and bound over to the grand jury.

The publicity then grew in intensity until his indictment on August 17. Typical of the coverage during this period is a front-page interview entitled:

"DR. SAM: 'I Wish There Was Something I Could Get Off My Chest—But There Isn't.' " Unfavorable publicity included items such as a cartoon of the body of a sphinx with Sheppard's head and the legend below: " 'I Will Do Everything In My Power To Help Solve This Terrible Murder.'—Dr. Sam Sheppard." Headlines announced, inter alia, that: "Doctor Evidence Is Ready For Jury," "Corrigan Tactics Stall Quizzing," "Sheppard 'Gay Set' Is Revealed By Houk," "Blood Is Found In Garage," "New Murder Evidence Is Found, Police Claim," "Dr. Sam Faces Quiz At Jail On Marilyn's Fear Of Him." On August 18, an article appeared under the headline "Dr. Sam Writes His Own Story." And reproduced across the entire front page was a portion of the typed statement signed by Sheppard: "I am not guilty of the murder of my wife, Marilyn. How could I, who have been trained to help people and devoted my life to saving life, commit such a terrible and revolting crime?" We do not detail the coverage further. There are five volumes filled with similar clippings from each of the three Cleveland newspapers covering the period from the murder until Sheppard's conviction in December 1954. The record includes no excerpts from newscasts on radio and television but since space was reserved in the courtroom for these media we assume that their coverage was equally large.

II

With this background the case came on for trial two weeks before the November general election at which the chief prosecutor was a candidate for common pleas judge and the trial judge, Judge Blythin, was a candidate to succeed himself. Twenty-five days before the case was set, 75 veniremen were called as prospective jurors. All three Cleveland newspapers published the names and addresses of the veniremen. As a consequence, anonymous letters and telephone calls, as well as calls from friends, regarding the impending prosecution were received by all of the prospective jurors. The selection of the jury began on October 18, 1954.

The courtroom in which the trial was held measured 26 by 48 feet. A long temporary table was set up inside the bar, in back of the single counsel table. It ran the width of the courtroom, parallel to the bar railing, with one end less than three feet from the jury box. Approximately 20 representatives of newspapers and wire services were assigned seats at this table by the court. Behind the bar railing there were four rows of benches. These seats were likewise assigned by the court for the entire trial. The first row was occupied by representatives of television and radio stations, and the second and third rows by reporters from out-of-town newspapers and magazines. One side of the last row, which accommodated 14 people, was assigned to Sheppard's family and the other to Marilyn's. The public was permitted to fill vacancies in this row on special passes only. Representatives of the news media also used all the rooms on the courtroom floor, including the room where cases were ordinarily called and assigned for trial. Private telephone lines and telegraphic equipment were installed in these rooms so that reports from the trial could be speeded to the papers. Station WSRS was permitted to set up broadcasting facilities on the third floor of the courthouse next door to the jury room, where the jury rested during recesses in the trial and deliberated. Newscasts were made from this room throughout the trial, and while the jury reached its verdict.

On the sidewalk and steps in front of the courthouse, television and newsreel cameras were occasionally used to take motion pictures of the participants in the trial, including the jury and the judge. Indeed, one television broadcast carried a staged interview of the judge as he entered the courthouse. In the corridors outside the courtroom there was a host of photographers and television personnel with flash cameras, portable lights and motion picture cameras. This group photographed the prospective jurors during selection of the jury. After the trial opened, the witnesses, counsel, and jurors were photographed and televised whenever they entered or left the courtroom. Sheppard was brought to the courtroom about 10 minutes before each session began; he was surrounded by reporters and extensively photographed for the newspapers and television. A rule of court prohibited picture-taking in the courtroom during the actual sessions of the court, but no restraints were put on photographers during recesses, which were taken once each morning and afternoon, with a longer period for lunch.

All of these arrangements with the news media and their massive coverage of the trial continued during the entire nine weeks of the trial. The courtroom remained crowded to capacity with representatives of news media. Their movement in and out of the courtroom often caused so much confusion that, despite the loud-speaker system installed in the courtroom, it was difficult for the witnesses and counsel to be heard. Furthermore, the reporters clustered within the bar of the small courtroom made confidential talk among Sheppard and his counsel almost impossible during the proceedings. They frequently had to leave the courtroom to obtain privacy. And many times when counsel wished to raise a point with the judge out of the hearing of the jury it was necessary to move to the judge's chambers. Even then, news media representatives so packed the judge's anteroom that counsel could hardly return from the chambers to the courtroom. The reporters vied with each other to find out what counsel and the judge had discussed, and often these matters later appeared in newspapers accessible to the jury.

The daily record of the proceedings was made available to the newspapers and the testimony of each witness was printed verbatim in the local editions, along with objections of counsel, and rulings by the judge. Pictures of Sheppard, the judge, counsel, pertinent witnesses, and the jury often accompanied the daily newspaper and television accounts. At times the newspapers published photographs of exhibits introduced at the trial, and the rooms of Sheppard's house were featured along with relevant testimony.

The jurors themselves were constantly exposed to the news media. Every juror, except one, testified at voir dire to reading about the case in the Cleveland papers or to having heard broadcasts about it. Seven of the 12 jurors who rendered the verdict had one or more Cleveland papers delivered in their home; the remaining jurors were not interrogated on the point. Nor were there questions as to radios or television sets in the jurors' homes, but we must assume that most of them owned such conveniences. As the selection of the jury progressed, individual pictures of prospective members appeared daily. During the trial, pictures of the jury appeared over 40 times in the Cleveland papers alone. The court permitted photographers to take pictures of the jury in the box, and individual pictures of the members in the jury room. One newspaper ran pictures of the jurors at the Sheppard home when they went there to view the scene of the murder. Another paper featured the home life of an alternate juror. The day before the verdict was rendered—while the jurors were at lunch and sequestered by two bailiffs—the jury was separated into two groups to pose for photographs which appeared in the newspapers.

III

We now reach the conduct of the trial. While the intense publicity continued unabated, it is sufficient to relate only the more flagrant episodes:

1. On October 9, 1954, nine days before the case went to trial, an editorial in one of the newspapers criticized defense counsel's random poll of people on the streets as to their opinion of Sheppard's guilt or innocence in an effort to use the resulting statistics to show the necessity for change of venue. The article said the survey "smacks of mass jury tampering," called on defense counsel to drop it, and stated that the bar association should do something about it. It characterized the poll as "non-judicial, non-legal, and nonsense." The article was called to the attention of the court but no action was taken.

2. On the second day of voir dire examination a debate was staged and broadcast live over WHK radio. The participants, newspaper reporters, accused Sheppard's counsel of throwing roadblocks in the way of the prosecution and asserted that Sheppard conceded his guilt by hiring a prominent criminal lawyer. Sheppard's counsel objected to this broadcast and requested a continuance, but the judge denied the motion. When counsel asked the court to give some protection from such events, the judge replied that "WHK doesn't have much coverage," and that "[a]fter all, we are not trying this case by radio or in newspapers or any other means. We confine ourselves seriously to it in this courtroom and do the very best we can." . . .

4. . . . .[T]he jury viewed the scene of the murder on the first day of the trial. Hundreds of reporters, cameramen and onlookers were there, and one representative of the news media was permitted to accompany the jury while it inspected the Sheppard home. The time of the jury's visit was revealed so far in advance that one of the newspapers was able to rent a helicopter and fly over the house taking pictures of the jurors on their tour.

5. On November 19, a Cleveland police officer gave testimony that tended to contradict details in the written statement Sheppard made to the Cleveland police. Two days later, in a broadcast heard over Station WHK in Cleveland, Robert Considine likened Sheppard to a perjurer and compared the episode to Alger Hiss's confrontation with Whittaker Chambers. Though defense counsel asked the judge to question the jury to ascertain how many heard the broadcast, the court refused to do so. The judge also overruled the motion for continuance based on the same ground, saying:

Well, I don't know, we can't stop people, in any event, listening to it. It is a matter of free speech, and the court can't control everybody. . . . We are not going to harass the jury every morning. . . . It is getting to the point where if we do it every morning, we are suspecting the jury. I have confidence in this jury. . . .

7. When the trial was in its seventh week, Walter Winchell broadcast over WXEL television and WJW radio that Carole Beasley, who was under arrest in New York City for robbery, had stated that, as Sheppard's mistress, she had borne him a child. The defense asked that the jury be queried on the broadcast. Two jurors admitted in open court that they had heard it. The judge asked each: "Would that have any effect upon your judgment?" Both replied, "No." This was accepted by the judge as sufficient; he merely asked the jury to "pay no attention whatever to that type of scavenging. . . . Let's confine ourselves to this courtroom, if you please.". . .

9. After the case was submitted to the jury, it was sequestered for its deliberations, which took five days and four nights. After the verdict, defense counsel ascertained that the jurors had been allowed to make telephone calls to their homes every day while they were sequestered at the hotel. Although the telephones had been removed

from the jurors' rooms, the jurors were permitted to use the phones in the bailiffs' rooms. The calls were placed by the jurors themselves; no record was kept of the jurors who made calls, the telephone numbers or the parties called. The bailiffs sat in the room where they could hear only the jurors' end of the conversation. The court had not instructed the bailiffs to prevent such calls. By a subsequent motion, defense counsel urged that this ground alone warranted a new trial, but the motion was overruled and no evidence was taken on the question.

IV

The principle that justice cannot survive behind walls of silence has long been reflected in the "Anglo-American distrust for secret trials." A responsible press has always been regarded as the handmaiden of effective judicial administration, especially in the criminal field. Its function in this regard is documented by an impressive record of service over several centuries. The press does not simply publish information about trials but guards against the miscarriage of justice by subjecting the police, prosecutors, and judicial processes to extensive public scrutiny and criticism. This Court has, therefore, been unwilling to place any direct limitations on the freedom traditionally exercised by the news media for "[w]hat transpires in the court room is public property." The "unqualified prohibitions laid down by the framers were intended to give to liberty of the press . . . the broadest scope that could be countenanced in an orderly society." And where there was "no threat or menace to the integrity of the trial," we have consistently required that the press have a free hand, even though we sometimes deplored its sensationalism.

But the Court has also pointed out that "[l]egal trials are not like elections, to be won through the use of the meeting-hall, the radio, and the newspaper." And the Court has insisted that no one be punished for a crime without "a charge fairly made and fairly tried in a public tribunal free of prejudice, passion, excitement, and tyrannical power." "Freedom of discussion should be given the widest range compatible with the essential requirement of the fair and orderly administration of justice." But it must not be

allowed to divert the trial from the "very purpose of a court system . . . to adjudicate controversies, both criminal and civil, in the calmness and solemnity of the courtroom according to legal procedures." Among these "legal procedures" is the requirement that the jury's verdict be based on evidence received in open court, not from outside sources. . . .

Only last Term in *Estes v. Texas,* we set aside a conviction despite the absence of any showing of prejudice. . . .

And we cited with approval the language of Mr. Justice Black that "our system of law has always endeavored to prevent even the probability of unfairness."

V

It is clear that the totality of circumstances in this case also warrants such an approach. Unlike Estes, Sheppard was not granted a change of venue to a locale away from where the publicity originated; nor was his jury sequestered. The Estes jury saw none of the television broadcasts from the courtroom. On the contrary, the Sheppard jurors were subjected to newspaper, radio and television coverage of the trial while not taking part in the proceedings. They were allowed to go their separate ways outside of the courtroom, without adequate directions not to read or listen to anything concerning the case. . . .

At intervals during the trial, the judge simply repeated his "suggestions" and "requests" that the jurors not expose themselves to comment upon the case. Moreover, the jurors were thrust into the role of celebrities by the judge's failure to insulate them from reporters and photographers. The numerous pictures of the jurors, with their addresses, which appeared in the newspapers before and during the trial itself exposed them to expressions of opinion from both cranks and friends. The fact that anonymous letters had been received by prospective jurors should have made the judge aware that this publicity seriously threatened the jurors' privacy.

The press coverage of the Estes trial was not nearly as massive and pervasive as the attention given by the Cleveland newspapers and broadcasting stations to Sheppard's prosecution. Sheppard stood indicted for the murder of his wife; the State was demanding the death penalty. For months the virulent publicity about Sheppard and the murder had made the case notorious. Charges and counter-charges were aired in the news media besides those for which Sheppard was called to trial. In addition, only three months before trial, Sheppard was examined for more than five hours without counsel during a three-day inquest which ended in a public brawl. The inquest was televised live from a high school gymnasium seating hundreds of people. Furthermore, the trial began two weeks before a hotly contested election at which both Chief Prosecutor Mahon and Judge Blythin were candidates for judgeships.

While we cannot say that Sheppard was denied due process by the judge's refusal to take precautions against the influence of pretrial publicity alone, the court's later rulings must be considered against the setting in which the trial was held. In light of this background, we believe that the arrangements made by the judge with the news media caused Sheppard to be deprived of that "judicial serenity and calm to which [he] was entitled." The fact is that bedlam reigned at the courthouse during the trial and newsmen took over practically the entire courtroom, hounding most of the participants in the trial, especially Sheppard. At a temporary table within a few feet of the jury box and counsel table sat some 20 reporters staring at Sheppard and taking notes. The erection of a press table for reporters inside the bar is unprecedented. The bar of the court is reserved for counsel, providing them a safe place in which to keep papers and exhibits, and to confer privately with client and co-counsel. It is designed to protect the witness and the jury from any distractions, intrusions or influences, and to permit bench discussions of the judge's rulings away from the hearing of the public and the jury. Having assigned almost all of the available seats in the courtroom to the news media the judge lost his ability to supervise that environment. The movement of the reporters in and out of the courtroom caused frequent confusion and disruption of the trial. And the record reveals constant commotion within the bar. Moreover, the judge gave the throng of newsmen gathered in the corridors of the courthouse absolute free rein. Participants in the trial, including the jury, were forced to run a gantlet of reporters and photographers each time they entered or left the courtroom. The total

lack of consideration for the privacy of the jury was demonstrated by the assignment to a broadcasting station of space next to the jury room on the floor above the courtroom, as well as the fact that jurors were allowed to make telephone calls during their five-day deliberation.

VI

There can be no question about the nature of the publicity which surrounded Sheppard's trial. . . . Indeed, every court that has considered this case, save the court that tried it, has deplored the manner in which the news media inflamed and prejudiced the public. . . .

Nor is there doubt that this deluge of publicity reached at least some of the jury. . . . Despite the extent and nature of the publicity to which the jury was exposed during trial, the judge refused defense counsel's other requests that the jurors be asked whether they had read or heard specific prejudicial comment about the case, including the incidents we have previously summarized. In these circumstances, we can assume that some of this material reached members of the jury.

VII

The court's fundamental error is compounded by the holding that it lacked power to control the publicity about the trial. From the very inception of the proceedings the judge announced that neither he nor anyone else could restrict prejudicial news accounts. And he reiterated this view on numerous occasions. . . .

The carnival atmosphere at trial could easily have been avoided since the courtroom and courthouse premises are subject to the control of the court. As we stressed in *Estes,* the presence of the press at judicial proceedings must be limited when it is apparent that the accused might otherwise be prejudiced or disadvantaged. Bearing in mind the massive pretrial publicity, the judge should have adopted stricter rules governing the use of the courtroom by newsmen, as Sheppard's counsel requested. The number of reporters in the courtroom itself could have been limited at the first sign that their presence would disrupt the trial. They certainly should not have been placed inside the bar. Furthermore, the judge should have more closely regulated the conduct of newsmen in the courtroom. For instance, the judge belatedly asked them not to handle and photograph trial exhibits lying on the counsel table during recesses.

Secondly, the court should have insulated the witnesses. All of the newspapers and radio stations apparently interviewed prospective witnesses at will, and in many instances disclosed their testimony. . . . Although the witnesses were barred from the courtroom during the trial the full verbatim testimony was available to them in the press. This completely nullified the judge's imposition of the rule.

Thirdly, the court should have made some effort to control the release of leads, information, and gossip to the press by police officers, witnesses, and the counsel for both sides. Much of the information thus disclosed was inaccurate, leading to groundless rumors and confusion. That the judge was aware of his responsibility in this respect may be seen from his warning to Steve Sheppard, the accused's brother, who had apparently made public statements in an attempt to discredit testimony for the prosecution. . . .

Defense counsel immediately brought to the court's attention the tremendous amount of publicity in the Cleveland press that "misrepresented entirely the testimony" in the case. Under such circumstances, the judge should have at least warned the newspapers to check the accuracy of their accounts. And it is obvious that the judge should have further sought to alleviate this problem by imposing control over the statements made to the news media by counsel, witnesses, and especially the Coroner and police officers. The prosecution repeatedly made evidence available to the news media which was never offered in the trial. Much of the "evidence" disseminated in this fashion was clearly inadmissible. The exclusion of such evidence in court is rendered meaningless when news media make it available to the public. For example, the publicity about Sheppard's refusal to take a lie detector test came directly from police officers and the Coroner.

From the cases coming here we note that unfair and prejudicial news comment on pending trials has become increasingly prevalent. Due process requires that the accused receive a trial by an impartial jury free from outside influences. Given the pervasiveness of modern communications and the difficulty of effacing prejudicial publicity from the minds of the jurors, the trial courts must take strong measures to ensure that the balance is never weighed against the accused. And appellate tribunals have the duty to make an independent evaluation of the circumstances. Of course, there is nothing that proscribes the press from reporting events that transpire in the courtroom. But where there is a reasonable likelihood that prejudicial news prior to trial will prevent a fair trial, the judge should continue the case until the threat abates, or transfer it to another county not so permeated with publicity. In addition, sequestration of the jury was something the judge should have raised sua sponte with counsel. If publicity during the proceedings threatens the fairness of the trial, a new trial should be ordered. But we must remember that reversals are but palliatives; the cure lies in those remedial measures that will prevent the prejudice at its inception. The courts must take such steps by rule and regulation that will protect their processes from prejudicial outside interferences. Neither prosecutors, counsel for defense, the accused, witnesses, court staff nor enforcement officers coming under the jurisdiction of the court should be permitted to frustrate its function. Collaboration between counsel and the press as to information affecting the fairness of a criminal trial is not only subject to regulation, but is highly censurable and worthy of disciplinary measures.

Since the state trial judge did not fulfill his duty to protect Sheppard from the inherently prejudicial publicity which saturated the community and to control disruptive influences in the courtroom, we must reverse the denial of the habeas petition. The case is remanded to the District Court with instructions to issue the writ and order that Sheppard be released from custody unless the State puts him to its charges again within a reasonable time.

It is so ordered.

10.6 *Atkins v. Virginia*
536 U.S. 304 (2002)

CHIEF JUSTICE REHNQUIST, with whom JUSTICE SCALIA and JUSTICE THOMAS join, dissenting.

The question presented by this case is whether a national consensus deprives Virginia of the constitutional power to impose the death penalty on capital murder defendants like petitioner, *i.e.,* those defendants who indisputably are competent to stand trial, aware of the punishment they are about to suffer and why, and whose mental retardation has been found an insufficiently compelling reason to lessen their individual responsibility for the crime. The Court pronounces the punishment cruel and unusual primarily because 18 States recently have passed laws limiting the death eligibility of certain defendants based on mental retardation alone, despite the fact that the laws of 19 other States besides Virginia continue to leave the question of proper punishment to the individuated consideration of sentencing judges or juries familiar with the particular offender and his or her crime.

I agree with *Justice Scalia* that the Court's assessment of the current legislative judgment regarding the execution of defendants like petitioner more resembles a *post hoc* rationalization for the majority's subjectively preferred result rather than any objective effort to ascertain the content of an evolving standard of decency. I write separately, however, to call attention to the defects in the Court's decision to place weight on foreign laws, the views of professional and religious organizations, and opinion polls in reaching its conclusion. The Court's suggestion that these sources are relevant to the constitutional question finds little support in our precedents and, in my view, is antithetical to considerations of federalism, which instruct that any "permanent prohibition upon all units of democratic government must [be apparent] in the operative acts (laws and the application of laws) that the people have approved." The Court's uncritical acceptance of the opinion poll data brought to our attention, moreover, warrants additional comment, because we lack sufficient information to conclude that the surveys were conducted in accordance with generally accepted scientific principles or are capable of supporting valid empirical inferences about the issue before us.

In making determinations about whether a punishment is "cruel and unusual" under the evolving standards of decency embraced by the Eighth Amendment, we have emphasized that legislation is the "clearest and most reliable objective evidence of contemporary values." The reason we ascribe primacy to legislative enactments follows from the constitutional role legislatures play in expressing policy of a State.

Our opinions have also recognized that data concerning the actions of sentencing juries, though entitled to less weight than legislative judgments, "'is a significant and reliable index of contemporary values,'" because of the jury's intimate involvement in the case and its function of "'maintain[ing] a link between contemporary community values and the penal system.'"

In my view, these two sources—the work product of legislatures and sentencing jury determinations—ought to be the sole indicators by which courts ascertain the contemporary American conceptions of decency for purposes of the Eighth Amendment. They are the only objective indicia of contemporary values firmly supported by our precedents. More importantly, however, they can be reconciled with the undeniable precepts that the democratic branches of government and individual sentencing juries are, by design, better suited than courts to evaluating and giving effect to the complex societal and moral considerations that inform the selection of publicly acceptable criminal punishments.

In reaching its conclusion today, the Court does not take notice of the fact that neither petitioner nor his *amici* have adduced any comprehensive statistics that would conclusively prove (or disprove) whether juries routinely consider death a disproportionate punishment for mentally retarded offenders like petitioner. Instead, it adverts to the fact that other countries have disapproved imposition of the death penalty for crimes committed by mentally retarded offenders. . . . I fail to see, however, how the views of other countries regarding the punishment of their citizens provide any support for the Court's ultimate determination. While it is true that some of our prior opinions have looked to "the climate of international opinion" to reinforce a conclusion regarding evolving standards of decency, we have since explicitly rejected the idea that the sentencing practices of other countries could "serve to establish the first Eighth Amendment prerequisite, that [a] practice is accepted among our people.". . .

To further buttress its appraisal of contemporary societal values, the Court marshals public opinion poll results and evidence that several professional organizations and religious groups have adopted official positions opposing the imposition of the death penalty upon mentally retarded offenders. . . . In my view, none should be accorded any weight on the Eight Amendment scale when the elected representatives of a State's populace have not deemed them persuasive enough to prompt legislative action. . . . For the Court to rely on such data today serves only to illustrate its willingness to proscribe by judicial fiat—at the behest of private organizations speaking only for themselves—a punishment about which no across-the-board consensus has developed through the workings of normal democratic processes in the laboratories of the States.

Even if I were to accept the legitimacy of the Court's decision to reach beyond the product of legislatures and practices of sentencing juries to discern a national standard of decency, I would take issue with the blind-faith credence it accords the opinion polls brought to our attention. An extensive body of social science literature describes how methodological and other errors can affect the reliability and validity of estimates about the opinions and attitudes of a population derived from various sampling techniques. Everything from variations in the survey methodology, such as the choice of the target population, the sampling design used, the questions asked, and the statistical analyses used to interpret the data can skew the results.

The Federal Judicial Center's *Reference Manual on Scientific Evidence 221-271* and its *Manual for Complex Litigation* offer helpful suggestions to judges called upon to assess the weight and admissibility of survey evidence on a factual issue before a court. Looking at the polling data in light of these factors, one cannot help but observe how unlikely

it is that the data could support a valid inference about the question presented by this case. For example, the questions reported to have been asked in the various polls do not appear designed to gauge whether the respondents might find the death penalty an acceptable punishment for mentally retarded offenders in rare cases. Most are categorical (*e.g.,* "Do you think that persons convicted of murder who are mentally retarded should or should not receive the death penalty?"), and, as such, would not elicit whether the respondent might agree or disagree that all mentally retarded people by definition can never act with the level of culpability associated with the death penalty, regardless of the severity of their impairment or the individual circumstances of their crime. Second, none of the 27 polls cited disclose the targeted survey population or the sampling techniques used by those who conducted the research. Thus, even if one accepts that the survey instruments were adequately designed to address a relevant question, it is impossible to know whether the sample was representative enough or the methodology sufficiently sound to tell us anything about the opinions of the citizens of a particular State or the American public at large. Finally, the information provided to us does not indicate why a particular survey was conducted or, in a few cases, by whom, factors which also can bear on the objectivity of the results. In order to be credited here, such surveys should be offered as evidence at trial, where their sponsors can be examined and cross-examined about these matters.

There are strong reasons for limiting our inquiry into what constitutes an evolving standard of decency under the Eighth Amendment to the laws passed by legislatures and the practices of sentencing juries in America. Here, the Court goes beyond these well-established objective indicators of contemporary values. It finds "further support to [its] conclusion" that a national consensus has developed against imposing the death penalty on all mentally retarded defendants in international opinion, the views of professional and religious organizations, and opinion polls not demonstrated to be reliable. Believing this view to be seriously mistaken, I dissent.

A Comparative Perspective

10.7 ## Defenders of Democracy? Legitimacy, Popular Acceptance, and the South African Constitutional Court (2003)

James L. Gibson and Gregory A. Caldeira

Those responsible for the "Third Wave" of democratization place an extraordinary degree of confidence in judicial institutions as guardians of democracy. Courts are often cast as "veto-players"—institutions designed to protect democracy from the excesses of executive power, majority tyranny, corruption, and a myriad of social and political ills. Many seem to regard strong and independent courts as an essential palliative for the potential afflictions of the democratic body politic.

At least some courts in the new democracies of the world have been surprisingly effective in policing the contours of the new regimes. . . . [T]he constitutional courts of Hungary and Poland have been quite influential, and relative success has characterized the first few years of the courts in Bulgaria, Slovakia, Slovenia, the Czech Republic, and the Baltic states (but with relative failure in Russia and failure of the high courts in Kazakhstan, Belarus, Albania, and Romania). Some courts in the emerging democracies have apparently started "out of the gate" with effective decisions of enormous political consequence.

How do these courts get away with making such consequential and controversial judgments? In particular, how do these courts get their decisions respected, accepted, implemented, and complied with, even when most people disagree with their decisions? The paradox is that though courts have fewer formal powers than most other political institutions—possessing the power of neither the purse nor the sword—some courts seem to have an uncommon ability to get people to abide by disagreeable rulings. This is precisely the power of a veto player—an institution that can go against what is

popular (especially in a democracy) and do so effectively, making its decisions stick.

Political scientists have developed some understanding of why some courts are effective at getting their decisions accepted and others are not. . . . [M]ost believe that theories of *institutional legitimacy* provide the most comprehensive account of the efficacy of legal institutions. According to legitimacy theory, under some circumstances courts achieve a moral authority that places them above politics and allows them the freedom to make unpopular decisions. This moral authority—or legitimacy—means that people accept judicial decisions, even those they bitterly oppose, because they view courts as appropriate institutions for making such decisions. In this sense, commitment to procedure and process trumps concern over outcomes; dedication to the long-term health and efficacy of an institution overrides dissatisfaction with its immediate outputs; and, consequently, courts can effectively perform their assigned function within the political system.

Within the context of established democracies, legitimacy theory is widely accepted by scholars. Unfortunately, however, few attempts to test this theory outside such polities have been reported, and it is unclear that extant findings, mostly on the U.S., are generalizable to other political and legal systems. Not all cultures perceive courts as above politics—certainly this was not true of the old Communist regimes in Central and Eastern Europe—and in many legal systems the rule of law is not a deeply and widely shared cultural value. Subcultural differences within heterogeneous systems (e.g., Muslims in Western Europe) may render compliance especially problematic. Is it reasonable to assume that powerful political actors in regimes undergoing democratic reform will accept court

From *Journal of Politics* 65, no. 1 (February 2003): 1–30. Reprinted by permission of Blackwell Publishers, Ltd.

decisions vetoing their programs? . . . The theory claiming that courts have special abilities to generate acquiescence, and thus that they can act as referees for political wars, may be applicable only to stable, democratic regimes, where the theory has been examined and tested empirically.

. . . [T]he purpose of this article is to investigate the legitimacy of one of the newest of these high courts, the South African Constitutional Court. Based on a survey of the South African mass public, we ask whether the Court can function as a guardian of South Africa's nascent democracy. More specifically, we test hypotheses about the *consequences of institutional legitimacy for acceptance of unpopular court decisions.* We do so within the context of a civil liberties dispute over the rights of political minorities. . . .

Theories of Institutional Legitimacy

Considerable agreement exists among political scientists on most of the major elements of legitimacy theory. For instance, nearly all agree that legitimacy is a normative concept, having something to do with the right (moral and legal) to make decisions. "Authority" is sometimes used as a synonym for legitimacy. Institutions perceived to be legitimate are those with an authoritative mandate to render judgments for a political community. This understanding of institutional legitimacy is widely accepted among those studying judicial institutions in the United States, especially the U.S. Supreme Court.

To serve effectively as veto players in a democracy, courts must have some degree of legitimacy. Indeed, the very notion of *vetoing* the actions of another institution implies that the court is going against popular opinion, at least as opinion is represented in majoritarian institutions. Thus, legitimacy takes on importance primarily in the presence of an *objection precondition.* When people approve of a decision, the legitimacy of the decision maker is of little consequence since people are getting what they want. When the decision is unpopular, its efficacy hinges upon the perceived legitimacy of the decision-making process and institution. Some may ask, for instance, whether the institution has the authority, the "right," to make

the decision, thereby challenging the outcome. Institutions short on legitimacy are thought not to be capable of vetoing the actions of more representative (and hence more legitimate) institutions of government.

At this point in the theory, an important disagreement over definitions arises. Some scholars *equate* legitimacy with compliance; others treat legitimacy as one of many possible causes of compliance. We take the latter tack, conceptualizing the decision to obey or not obey a law or accept or challenge a decision as *conceptually* independent of whether an institution is judged to have the authority to make the decision. . . . To treat compliance as *evidence of* legitimacy makes tautological the relationship between perceived legitimacy and compliance and precludes consideration of any determinants of compliance that are not grounded in legitimacy. . . .

Despite voluminous research on the legitimacy-acquiescence linkage, it is unclear to what degree findings from long-established democratic polities can be generalized to the world's emerging democracies. Courts such as the U.S. Supreme Court and the German Federal Constitutional Court have enormous stores of legitimacy, developed over a long time. How do courts in fledgling democracies acquire this ability to make their decisions "stick"? Do, and how do, people in political systems with little history or tradition of democratic governance come to accept granting counter-majoritarian powers to relatively unaccountable political institutions? Although the legitimacy-acquiescence linkage is widely accepted by scholars, the generalizability of the theory must be more thoroughly investigated.

Once we broaden our concern beyond established democracies, it is reasonable to hypothesize that a variety of factors influence the degree to which courts are able to make their decisions stick. For instance, as the size of the stakes in the litigation increases, we expect the likelihood of compliance to decrease. When fundamental political values are at risk, acquiescence would be expected to be less widespread. To the extent that a polity is characterized by heterogeneous subcultures, including perhaps variability in fundamental commitments to the rule of law, judicial effectiveness would likely be more limited. More generally, the legitimacy of democracy itself—not just majority rule, but institutionalized respect for minority rights as well—may influence acquiescence to court decisions. Many Western courts are able to capitalize on deep-seated support for the rule of law, individual liberty and liberalism, limited government, and political tolerance through respect for minority rights. But some new democracies tend toward the "illiberal democracy" model, and systems in which minority rights are not much respected are increasingly commonplace, even among nominally democratic regimes. Studies limited to established Western democracies, therefore, in effect hold constant many of the variables determining the legitimacy-conferring abilities of courts.

The end of apartheid in South Africa provides a valuable opportunity to test legitimacy theory within a transitional regime. We begin our analysis with a description of the activities of the Constitutional Court and how South Africa might contribute to understanding better the hypothesized processes.

The Constitutional Court in South African Politics

South Africa's Constitutional Court has struggled from its inception in 1995 to create a separate and distinct identity as a *legal* institution, in contrast to South African *political* institutions. . . . [T]he creation of the Constitutional Court was enveloped in intense and highly political conflict, in part because all actors were able to foresee the power and importance of the Court in South African politics. Conflict over the Court's structure was publicized widely, which probably undermined the initial legitimacy of the institution to at least some degree.

Perhaps recognizing the precariousness of its situation, the Court has been highly consensual in its decision making, with dissents in fewer than 5% of its cases. . . .

At the same time, the Court has not been reluctant to enter the political fray, often handing down politically controversial decisions. Though it may not be surprising that the Court struck down many statutes from the apartheid regime, it also came down in many cases against the strongly held views of the new majority and various political and legal elites, and it has even challenged President Mandela and the African National Congress (ANC). For instance, in the face of widespread public concern about rampant crime and violence, the Court broadened protections of those accused or convicted of a crime, as in its decision to strike down the death penalty (*State v. Makwanyane and Another,* 1995), and in its ruling reversing the presumption that a confession made to a magistrate is voluntary and therefore admissible in court (*State v. Zuma and Others,* 1995). . . .

If the Court took bold steps in some areas, it has, in the views of many, moved too cautiously in defining and expanding the social and economic rights in the Constitution. Thus, for example, in *Soobramoney v. Minister of Health of KwaZulu-Natal* (1997), the Court found the provincial government's refusal to fund extraordinary medical measures consistent with the constitutional right to health care and emergency treatment. More generally, some scholars and activists on the left have taken the Constitutional Court to task for failing to force the national government to deliver on the promises of the social and economic clauses of the Bill of Rights. . . .

Racial conflict over the judiciary has also been pervasive, with some of the residue rubbing off on the Constitutional Court. Many see the courts as the last bastion of white domination, especially since blacks make up only a small percentage of the bench in the ordinary courts and since only three blacks sit on the Court. . . .

In sum, the Constitutional Court was conceived in controversy, continues to be involved in the most contentious social issues, and has not been timid in offending various constituencies. Ironically, it suffers at once from an understandable identification with the ANC, which undoubtedly undermines its legitimacy among whites, and from an image in some quarters as much too timid in its approach to constitutional development, too willing to protect the white minority, allied with the regular judiciary, and too slow to reflect the racial diversity of the society at large. Moreover, the Court is a young institution and inevitably is tainted by its linkage to the apartheid past. Thus, we expect the Court to enjoy a limited store of institutional legitimacy, to have little capacity to bring about acquiescence to its controversial decisions, and to be unable to play a major role as a veto player in South African politics.

The Special Meaning of Legitimacy in a Deeply Divided Society

Unfortunately for the Court, legitimacy takes on particular importance in a deeply divided society like South Africa. In such polities, differences in history, culture, values, and interests can produce dramatically different views of the duties of political institutions, as well as assessments of whether they are functioning properly. Such polities face enormous difficulties when it comes to consolidating democracy. If the legitimacy of democratic institutions—including the Constitutional Court—varies across the major ascriptive groups, then it is difficult to confine political conflict to ordinary issues of public policy and to keep it from spilling over to struggle over the very nature of the political regime itself. Thus, in the analysis that follows, we are especially attentive to the attitudes toward the Court held by South Africa's various racial communities.

Research Design

Our analysis is based on a panel survey of South Africans conducted in 1996 and 1997. The first wave was fielded in the fall (April through June) of 1996. Interviews were completed with roughly 94% of the 3,258 South Africans in the sample. The respondents were interviewed in their language of choice. Versions of the instrument were prepared and validated (i.e., translated, back-translated, and reconciled) in Zulu, Xhosa, Tswana, North Sotho, South Sotho, and Afrikaans (in addition, of course, to English). The sample is representative of all major ethnic/racial/linguistic groups in South Africa (i.e., via over-sampling . . .).

The reinterview—in which the items measuring the legitimacy of the Constitutional Court were asked—was conducted in 1997. The response rate was 53%. This compares favorably with panels conducted in other parts of the world.

In our analysis, we distinguish among the various subcultures in South Africa, adopting the traditional racial categories used by survey researchers and others. When we report figures for the entire South African population, we weight the data so as to render the number of respondents in each group proportionate to the size of the group in the population. Although 1,518 reinterviews were completed, the weighted N is 1,285 (since many minority groups, like whites and Coloureds, were oversampled).

The Institutional Legitimacy of the Constitutional Court

. . . South Africans hold ambivalent attitudes toward their Constitutional Court. A majority believes that the Court can generally be trusted, but it is a slim majority, and a plurality asserts that if the Court started making unpopular decisions it should be abolished. Most respondents were simply confused by the item on jurisdictional change. Very few South Africans actively distrust the Court, but the reservoir of goodwill for this institution is not particularly deep or solid. In the minds of many South Africans, the Court seems to be on a sort of probation, based on a cautious and somewhat suspicious trust. This is not surprising in light of the newness of the Court at the time of the interview (1997).

Racial differences in attitudes toward the Court are inconsistent . . ., in part due to the large percentage of respondents who have not yet formed views toward the institution. . . . Generally, Africans are the most supportive constituency for the Court, with whites, Coloureds, and Asian South Africans extending somewhat less legitimacy to the institution.

From a comparative perspective, the South African Constitutional Court has failed to develop a very deep reservoir of goodwill among the South African mass public. The South African average is among the lowest [compared to many European countries]. To put this further into perspective, consider the statement about doing away with the Court (since it so directly reflects our theoretical concern with institutional loyalty). The 27.9% of South Africans who would stand by their Court even when it makes unpopular decisions compares with a support figure of 76.0% for the U.S. Supreme Court. . . .

The Consequences of Institutional Legitimacy

Does institutional legitimacy have consequences for the ability of courts to serve as veto players in politics? The central hypothesis of research on institutional support is that legitimacy contributes to acquiescence. . . .

Whether people accept actual court decisions of which they disapprove has rarely been analyzed, in large part due to the difficulty of studying heavily contextual behaviors such as the decision to accept a court ruling or not. Nonetheless, experimental research provides a method by which acquiescence can be studied. Following earlier research we included in this survey a "Legitimacy Experiment" designed to assess whether loyalty toward the South African Constitutional Court contributes to the willingness of citizens to accept its unpopular decisions.

The Structure of the Legitimacy Experiment

The experiment focused on tolerating a political enemy and began by asking the respondents to "imagine that [a disliked political enemy] was planning to make a public speech in your community." Since such speeches are a common part of political life in South Africa, we doubt that many respondents had difficulty conjuring up an image of such an event. Indeed, a tactic often used by political parties in South Africa is to make recruiting speeches in "enemy" territory, including so-called no-go areas. The initial responses of the South Africans to a proposed speech by a disliked political enemy are, in general, fairly *intolerant*. Indeed, nearly 51% of the respondents strongly support banning the speech, with another 18% supporting the ban but not strongly. Since 9% of the respondents were uncertain of their own position, only 21% of the South Africans gave a tolerant reply when asked about an opponent's desire to express its views. To reiterate, in the experiment, 70% of the sample, the intolerant, were presented with institutional decisions allowing the speech to take place; the tolerant 21% were confronted with a court decision banning the speech. Once the South Africans had indicated their tolerance or intolerance, they were told that what they did not want to happen in the dispute was about to happen and were asked whether they would do anything about it. The next question posited that the local political authorities had made a decision on the controversy that was contrary to the respondent's own preferences. For instance, those who would *allow* the speech to take place were told that the local authorities had decided to *ban* the speech. They were then asked whether they would accept or contest the decision of the local authorities. Finally, the subjects were told that the Constitutional Court had made a decision contrary to the respondent's own view. Thus, for each of the survey respondents, we measured the preference prior to any institutional intervention, the initial behavioral propensity, the willingness to accept a contrary decision of the local authorities, and the willingness to accept a contrary decision of the Court. . . .

Most tolerant South Africans would *not* join in a movement to try to get the speech allowed, although racial differences in this propensity are large. Whereas only 38.4% of the Africans would not act to protect the rights of their political enemy, fully 78.9% of the whites would accept the decision. Coloureds and South Africans of Asian origin are similarly inclined to do nothing to support the speech taking place, although not to the degree of whites. The differences across race are moderately strong and highly statistically significant. The passivity of the whites stands out clearly. . . .

By contrast, *intolerant* South Africans are much more prone to action—only 29.5% would not join in efforts to *ban* the speech. Again, racial differences are substantial, with only one-quarter of the Africans claiming they would do nothing, but nearly two-thirds of the whites similarly inclined toward inactivity.

Thus, . . . tolerant South Africans are less likely than their intolerant fellow citizens to act upon their initial preferences. This is true of each of the racial groups, although the difference is considerably smaller for South Africans of Asian origin. This finding is consistent with more general research showing those with tolerant attitudes as having characteristics that make them less likely to be influential in politics, when compared to those with intolerant attitudes. This finding does not bode well for the protection of civil liberties in South Africa.

. . . Among tolerant South Africans, the decision of the local authorities increases acceptance of an *intolerant* outcome by about 12 percentage points; the Constitutional Court's intervention results in roughly 18% more acceptance of a decision to ban the speech. Among those initially intolerant, the effect is weaker, with the Court able to convince about 11% more of the South African mass public to tolerate the speech. Across all South Africans, irrespective of their tolerance or intolerance, the effect of a Constitutional Court decision is not large—12.4% would acquiesce to the outcome (whatever it is) due to a ruling by the Court [data not shown]. That is, if we combine both the tolerant and the intolerant, 34.7% would accept the initial decision on whether to allow the speech; a total of 47.1% would accept the outcome after the Court ruled.

The Total Effect of the Court's Intervention

How successful would the Constitutional Court be in getting acquiescence to an unpopular decision? With the aid of a few simple assumptions, we can simulate the effects on the South African mass public of a ruling by the Court.

Before the intervention of the Constitutional Court, 69.7% of the South Africans were intolerant; 21.3% were tolerant. Let us assume that a Court decision with which the respondent *agrees* does not change her or his initial opinion. Thus, those who are tolerant remain tolerant after the Court makes a tolerant decision. Let us also assume that a Court decision has no effect on those without an opinion on the dispute. Thus, those agnostic about whether a speech should be allowed remain agnostic after the Court decides the case. With these two simple assumptions, we need only examine the reactions of those who oppose the decision in order to estimate public opinion as it would exist after the Court intervened in the dispute.

Assume that the Court makes a tolerant decision. Neither the 21.3% who are tolerant nor the 9.0% who are agnostic would change their views. Among the 69.7% who are initially intolerant, the Court decision converts some to grudging tolerance, converts others to uncertainty, and does not influence the views of yet another portion of the sample. If we apply the calculations, a tolerant court decision would result in 48.8% of the South Africans accepting/supporting the decision, 16.2% being uncertain, and 35.0% persisting in their intolerance. Thus, the Court would be able to boost tolerance from 21.3% to 48.8%, an increase of 27.5%.

Now, let us assume the Court makes an intolerant decision. Then, the tolerant segment of society shrinks to 5.5%, while intolerance (real or grudging) balloons to 84.1%. Thus, the effect of the Court in this situation is to diminish political tolerance by 15.8 percentage points and to increase intolerance by 14.4 percentage points.

These simulations demonstrate that the effect of a Court decision can be rather dramatic. Indeed, the "tolerance interval"—the range of opinion depending on what the Court decides—varies from 5.5% to 48.8%, a sizable and politically meaningful interval. Even though not all of this effect can properly be attributed to the legitimacy of the institution (because acceptance may result from a variety of factors—see below), the Court decision makes a politically significant difference.

These figures represent the total effects of a Court ruling. But to what degree is acquiescence a function of the perceived legitimacy of the Court? Some have argued that legitimacy has little to do with accepting court decisions, and rational choice theorists would surely be loathe to endorse anything but instrumental calculations about whether to comply with a court ruling. Thus, we now turn to consideration of the legitimacy hypothesis and to tests of alternative explanations for the persuasiveness of the Court's decisions.

The Effect of Institutional Legitimacy

. . . Consider first those who are initially tolerant. . . . Among Africans, greater support for the Constitutional Court is associated with more acceptance of the Court's decision (which is in this instance, of course, a decision favoring *intolerance*). Even at the lowest level of support, a majority (51.4%) of tolerant Africans would acquiesce, but among strong supporters of the Court, about two-thirds (66.7%) would accept a court decision with which they disagreed. This is a moderate and highly significant relationship ($r = .21$).

By contrast, among whites, *we observe no such effect* (although note that small numbers of respondents are involved in this analysis, since tolerance is not very widespread in South Africa). Whites overwhelmingly accept a court decision, and it *matters not at all* whether they are supportive of the Court or not. Something other than the legitimacy of the Court causes whites to be willing to (or resigned to) accept a decision with which they disagree.

A weak tendency for legitimacy to contribute to acquiescence can be found among Coloured South Africans, although again we must be especially cautious in analyzing only 41 people. Among South Africans of Asian origin, however, court legitimacy matters little: 77.8% of the least supportive and 82.4% of the most supportive Asians would not challenge an unpopular court decision, and the correlation, though not statistically significant, is even in the wrong direction.

Several conclusions emerge from analysis. First, great majorities of tolerant whites, Coloureds, and those of Asian origin are likely to accept a court decision contrary to their preferred position. Because acquiescence is so widespread, the legitimacy of the Court matters little. One might speculate that these South Africans would accept a decision of most political institutions, legitimate or not. This finding reinforces the view that legitimacy is not the only cause of acquiescence.

Second, tolerant Africans are not nearly so inclined to acquiesce. Only a bare majority of Africans would accept such a court decision. Nonetheless, institutional legitimacy makes a difference—those who perceive the institution as more legitimate are more likely to desist from challenging the decision. Yet, to put this into perspective, even among Africans extremely supportive of the Court, the proportion accepting the decision is lower than the proportions among non-Africans who are the *least supportive* of the Court.

. . . [F]or those who stated initially that they would support a ban on the speech. Among Africans, perceptions of the Court *have nothing to do with acquiescence*. Similar conclusions characterize Coloured South Africans and those of Asian origin. Among whites, however, some (positive) relationship exists. Moreover, except among whites, levels of acceptance of the Court's decision (in this instance, a tolerant decision) are considerably lower than those found among the tolerant. Generally, *for the intolerant, the hypothesis that perceived Court legitimacy contributes to acquiescence must be rejected for all but white South Africans.* . . . [P]erceptions of a legitimate Court only have a substantively significant effect on three groups: Africans and Coloureds who are tolerant, and intolerant whites. This is quite limited support for the central hypothesis of research on institutional legitimacy.

The substantive implications of these findings are important from the point of view of political tolerance. Among white South Africans, tolerance is ob-

durate and intolerance is pliant. That is, tolerant whites are likely to resist an intolerant decision from the Constitutional Court; their tolerance trumps their support for the institution, resulting in a tolerant conclusion. Moreover, intolerant whites can be persuaded by a tolerant Court decision. Combining the initial preferences and acceptance of the Court decision, the scenario represented by this experiment is associated, in the end, with a fairly high level of tolerance among white South Africans.

The results among Africans are *entirely the opposite*. Intolerant Africans are not persuaded by a tolerant Court decision; tolerant Africans allow their support for the Court to trump their tolerance. Thus, among Africans, the effect of the Constitutional Court's legitimacy is to exacerbate *intolerance*, the opposite of the tendency among whites. Coloured South Africans react somewhat similarly to Africans. A legitimate court can persuade the tolerant to accept an intolerant outcome; it has little effect on those initially intolerant. *Thus, among whites, the Court has the capacity to foster democratic practices; among most of the South African population, the Court can do little to convert those opposing the exercise of democratic freedom to a more tolerant and democratic position.* . . .

Summary and Concluding Remarks

. . . [W]e conclude that theories of the legitimacy-acquiescence linkage do not work well in South Africa; the findings from research on stable democracies do not seem to be easily and directly generalizable to transitional regimes. Future research should specifically address the conditions under which institutional legitimacy contributes to acquiescence and, thus, to institutional effectiveness.

In terms of broader theories of courts and transitional politics, this analysis suggests several conclusions. First, courts are not always born with an endowment of legitimacy. Especially where legal institutions have been at the center of political struggles, as they were in South Africa, newly created courts must earn the respect and trust of their constituents. Second, when a society is riven by cleavages, even disagreements over the desirability of democratic institutions and processes, achieving broad-based legitimacy may be difficult indeed. For many ordinary people, courts are the least "democratic" institutions, the most difficult to understand and grasp. That people would differ over extending legitimacy to largely unaccountable judicial institutions seems inevitable, especially in deeply divided polities.

Moreover, a legitimacy shortfall may be exacerbated if a court fails to appreciate the need for mass legitimacy (a common failing of judges, given the elitist nature of lawyers) and therefore seeks anonymity rather than publicity for the institution's work. Judges have access to powerful symbols—even if they are only symbols of authority—that can contribute mightily to legitimacy, especially since extant research so strongly suggests that "to know" courts is "to love them." Failure to mobilize these resources can only limit the effectiveness of judicial institutions.

Finally, courts may require some time to acquire legitimacy. Because they are typically denied the legitimizing imprimatur of the ballot box, courts in transitional regimes may begin with a legitimacy shortfall. At present, we understand precious little about how courts build legitimacy, in part because longitudinal studies are virtually nonexistent. Returning to the South African Constitutional Court to examine whether and how it succeeds in building legitimacy is therefore a crucial research task.

South Africa is greatly in need of a strong, legitimate (and independent) Constitutional Court. The country is badly divided by race and class, and politics currently provides little hope of bridging that gap. Moreover, a serious potential threat to the country's fledgling democracy is unchecked majoritarianism. The hegemony of the ANC—with its as yet unused ability to mobilize its supermajority to modify the Constitution—frightens many, including those who support the substantive (as opposed to procedural) goals of the party. A strong constitutional court may at some point be essential to "veto" popularly supported governmental excesses (e.g., government efforts to combat the recent escalation of crime and urban terrorism). If the Constitutional Court is to become an effective defender of democracy, it must build a stronger and deeper reservoir of goodwill among ordinary South Africans.

For Further Reading

Dahl, Robert. "Decision-Making in a Democracy: The Supreme Court as a National Policy-Maker." *Journal of Public Law* 6 (1958): 279–295.

Hoekstra, Valerie J. *The Supreme Court and Local Public Opinion.* New York: Cambridge University Press, 2003.

Marshall, Thomas R. *Public Opinion and the Supreme Court.* Boston: Unwin Hyman, 1989.

McGuire, Kevin T. and James A. Stimson. "The Least Dangerous Branch Revisited: New Evidence on Supreme Court Responsiveness to Public Preferences." *Journal of Politics* 66 (2004): 1018–1035.

Mishler, William and Reginald S. Sheehan. "Public Opinion, the Attitudinal Model, and Supreme Court Decision Making: A Micro-Analytic Perspective." *Journal of Politics* 58, no. 1 (1996): 169–200.

Chapter 11

Judicial Impact

Introduction

In January 1829, President Andrew Jackson, in his first inaugural address, articulated his position on the status of Indian tribes in the eastern and southern regions of the United States. To clear out land for American settlers, President Jackson proposed relocating tribes such as the Cherokees, Chickasaws, Choctaws, Creeks, and Seminoles to regions west of the Mississippi. Congress endorsed President Jackson's vision the following year by enacting the Indian Removal Act of 1830, which forced more than 10,000 American Indians living east of the Mississippi to migrate to land provided for them in Oklahoma. Moreover, many states passed their own laws permitting the confiscation of Indian lands, as well as denying Indians the right to sue in court, mine for gold or other valuable minerals, or enjoy other basic rights of citizenship. Since 1819, Georgia had attempted to displace the Cherokees, a process that intensified after gold deposits were discovered on their tribal lands. The Cherokees refused to comply with state directives, and passed tribal laws forbidding the sale of property to Georgia authorities. In 1828, the Georgia legislature passed a law outlawing the Cherokee tribal authority and seized their lands. The Cherokees' appeal to President Jackson, who by then had signed the Indian Removal Act, was rejected, and the tribe sued Georgia for violating their sovereign tribal authority under federal law. Ultimately, the United States Supreme Court, in *Worcester v. Georgia* (1832), ruled that Georgia had acted unlawfully in seizing the Cherokees' land. Upon receiving the news, an unsympathetic President Jackson reportedly said, "Chief Justice John Marshall has made his decision; now let him come enforce it."

The federal government ignored the Court's decision in *Worcester,* and ordered the removal of the Cherokees, without compensation, from their Georgia lands. By the mid-1830s, the Cherokees joined other Indian tribes on the Trail of Tears to Oklahoma. Thousands of them died from famine, disease, and exhaustion during their forced march westward. According to the highest court in the land, the Indians had the law on their side. However, they did not have the support of the political branches of government or of public opinion. President Jackson's response to *Worcester* is often cited as an example of Alexander Hamilton's admonition in

Federalist No. 78 that the judiciary, possessing neither the power to make laws nor the power to enforce them, was indeed the weakest branch of government. Conversely, open defiance of the Court's rulings, illustrated by episodes such as the one in *Worcester,* have been relatively rare in American political history. Judicial scholars, for the most part, are persuaded that the courts, and especially the Supreme Court, are an important venue in which to resolve social and political disputes, and the decisions handed down by legal tribunals often have a profound impact on public policy. How much they matter, however, has not been resolved. Some scholars suggest that the courts are only as successful as the political branches of government and public opinion will allow them to be.

This, our final chapter, is devoted to the issue of judicial impact. By judicial impact, we do not mean merely the degree to which lower courts follow the opinions of courts of last resort, although that is one question we do consider. We have selected readings that offer a much broader definition of judicial impact, from considering how and why lawyers select certain cases to the ripple effect that legal opinions have on policy innovation outside the courts.

Foundations and History

The conflict between President Andrew Jackson and Chief Justice John Marshall offers an early example of the limits of judicial power. Even now, after we read newspaper headlines about the impact that some momentous Supreme Court opinion will have on law and public policy, we cannot always be sure that the individuals and institutions affected by such a decision will follow it to the letter. Our first selection in this chapter is an excerpt from Kenneth M. Dolbeare and Phillip E. Hammond's pioneering book on judicial impact, *The School Prayer Decisions: From Court Policy to Local Practice* (1971). Dolbeare and Hammond examine to what extent several local communities followed two of the Court's most controversial twentieth-century decisions, *Engel v. Vitale* (1962) and *Abington v. Schemp* (1963), which outlawed state-sponsored prayer and Bible reading, respectively, in the public schools. The authors found that noncompliance was quite common in the communities they surveyed; yet few schools believed that they had actually failed to follow the Court's decisions. Moreover, they noted noncompliance did not result in additional lawsuits demanding that schools follow the law. Dolbeare and Hammond explain why these communities chose to behave as they did, and provide a way of thinking about impact and compliance that has become influential in later studies.

In "Supreme Court Impact on Compliance and Outcomes: *Miranda* and *New York Times* in the United States Courts of Appeals" (1990), Donald R. Songer and Reginald S. Sheehan examine another dimension of judicial impact: the degree to which lower courts follow and implement the rulings of the Supreme Court. Like Dolbeare and Hammond, Songer and Sheehan selected two landmark cases, *Miranda v. Arizona* (1966), which required police officers to warn criminal suspects of their right to remain silent and their right to counsel, and *New York Times v. Sullivan* (1964), which created the law of libel. Songer and Sheehan found that lower courts continued to accept the Court's landmark decisions as binding, even as it changed or modified those decisions in subsequent rulings. Together, these studies offer examples of how political scientists define judicial impact and how they attempt to measure and explain it.

Contemporary Judicial Politics

Bradley C. Canon and Charles A. Johnson have introduced many students to the judicial process through their textbook, *Judicial Policies: Implementation and Impact* (1998). We provide an excerpt here that offers an outline of the framework they have developed to study the response to judicial rulings. Using the Court's historic *Roe v. Wade* (1973) decision, Canon and Johnson provide a description of how different populations respond to a Supreme Court ruling. Ultimately, Canon and Johnson conclude that compliance with a Supreme Court decision is determined by the cooperation of an interrelated set of interpreting, implementing, consumer, and secondary populations.

In 1991, Gerald Rosenberg published *The Hollow Hope: Can Courts Bring About Social Change?* Since then, legal scholars and political scientists have debated his conclusion that the courts, and the Supreme Court in particular, have little impact on social change. Rosenberg did not deny that the Court had a singular and unique authority to define the meaning of constitutional rights, but he argued that the Court was much more constrained in producing reform than previous scholars had believed. Rosenberg also suggested that organizations should not always look to the courts to achieve reform through "impact" litigation. Indeed, they would be much better off airing their grievances through the political process. Our excerpt here offers Rosenberg's view on the "dynamic" and the "constrained" Court, and what conditions are likely to produce social reform. Do you believe that Rosenberg makes a persuasive argument that the courts are not the best venue for reform? Or do you believe instead that the courts are capable of producing sweeping social change based on a new interpretation of the Constitution?

A View from the Inside

Beyond the empirical question of whether lower courts, abortion providers, public schools, or any other affected parties follow Supreme Court decisions is the question that begets the study of judicial impact: What is the appeal of impact litigation—a lawsuit designed to create some major change or innovation through a judicial mandate? Are such lawsuits effective? What is the wisdom of having the courts "make" law rather than affecting change by going through the legislative process? Peter H. Schuck addresses these questions in "Benched" (2000). There he examines several contemporary waves of "impact" litigation—civil rights, tobacco, and school desegregation—and offers some provocative analyses of the consequences that impact litigation has on the legal structure and the evolution of rights in a democratic society.

In February 2003, the Supreme Judicial Court of Massachusetts ruled that the Massachusetts constitution could not be interpreted to prohibit civil marriage between same-sex couples. This decision came less than a year after the court of appeals in Ontario, Canada, ruled that the Canadian Charter of Rights required the recognition of same-sex marriages by law. The Canadian federal government decided not to appeal the decision, clearing the way for the issuance of marriage licenses to gay couples in Canada's largest province. In July 2005, the Canadian parliament approved a federal law granting gay couples the right to marriage. In the United States, however, the reaction was much different. Cities and small towns with large gay populations, such as San Francisco and New Paltz, New York, applied the logic of the Massachusetts court to their own municipal laws and began issuing marriage licenses to same-sex couples. But President George W. Bush announced his opposition to the practice and his support for a constitutional amendment defining legal marriage as being between a man and a woman. Curious about what the firestorm was all about? We excerpt the Massachusetts decision in *Goodridge v. Department of Public Health* (2003) here.

A Comparative Perspective

Contemporary scholarship on American courts has revealed a great deal about the impact that judicial decisions have on legal development and social change. But what do we know about the relationship between the courts and civil society in other countries? Is there something unique about the American Constitution that encourages litigation to achieve change that is seemingly unavailable through the political process? Do differences in the legal and political cultures of different countries affect the degree to which judicial decisions reverberate throughout society? We offer an excerpt from Charles R. Epp's book, *The Rights Revolution: Lawyers, Activists, and Supreme Courts in Comparative Perspective* (1998), which examines how lawyers perceive the capacity of the courts in the United States, Canada, Great Britain, and India to create social change, and the impact that such decisions have on their respective societies. Compare Epp's discussion with the lessons drawn from the other readings in this chapter.

Foundations and History

11.1   The Law of the Land: Myth and Reality (1971)

Kenneth M. Dolbeare and Phillip E. Hammond

Even in tranquil times, the United States government annually generates numbers of new laws, regulations, and decisions which require citizens to modify their behavior in important ways. In the past decade, some sweeping changes were mandated by congressional statutes, presidential orders, and Supreme Court decisions. Dramatic newspaper headlines follow every major action of this kind. Commentators speculate profoundly on their significance and implications. Politicians, corporations, interest groups, and powerful individuals struggle determinedly over specific details of draftsmanship, appropriations, and implementation. Citizens react with enthusiasm, denunciation, or indifference, according to their perceptions and preferences.

But there is often a great gap between the official legal requirement and the actual experience of citizens' lives. Though things *appear* to change, they *actually* remain the same. Noble ideals are emblazoned on the statute books in Washington— promising much, but often providing little, to the ordinary citizen. We are all aware of this gap, at least in the abstract. Illustrations readily spring to mind. Racial discrimination alone, recently the subect of so much national rule-making, provides hundreds of examples every day. It is the gap between rhetoric and reality, symbol and substance, and the gap exacerbates already strained social and political relationships.

That such a gap exists is all too clear, but its incidence, causes, and implications are not. We know little of a systematic or comprehensive nature about the impact of national rule-making; frequently, not even the people supposed to be affected by new legislation are aware of its actual

consequences. Some research has been directed at the administrative processes by which national policies are implemented, but little at the social and political barriers which absorb or deflect change-inducing national requirements before they reach the local behavioral level.

The implications of the rhetoric-reality gap are often the subject of confident assertions, but of quite contrasting kinds. To some the gap is the inevitable product of man's incapacity to conform the real world to his high ideals. To others it is a functional means whereby political brokers can preserve the fragile accommodations that hold the society together. To others it is an illustration of a cynical carrot-and-stick process by which powerful elites manage deprived masses. To still others it is a source of mass apathy or alienation. No doubt it is all of these in some combination in most real-life situations. But we do not really know, because evidence has not often been brought to bear on the effects of specific and perceived "gaps" on popular attitudes and behavior.

With this general framework in mind, we have attempted a modest contribution to understanding barriers to change. As a result of several different types and levels of analysis, we have focused on the ways in which state and local leaders, bearing official responsibility for carrying out the Supreme Court's mandate regarding elimination of schoolhouse religious activities, managed to avoid taking action and to preserve the status quo of prayers and other religious observances —all without arousing controversy. If the impact of these decisions were to be measured by the extent of change in the classrooms of Midway, our anonymous Midwestern state, that impact could only be called negligible. But this means that state and local officials and others holding power were successful both in deflecting the national mandate for change and in

From *The School Prayer Decisions from Court Policy to Local Practice,* pp. 3–11. Reprinted by permission of University of Chicago Press.

discouraging local efforts to use that mandate to bring change about. This process of managing the Midway state and local political agendas so as to avoid conflict and preserve the status quo reveals some crucial aspects of the linkage between national action and local consequences. In short, we shall gain insight into one important component of the rhetoric-reality problem. To be sure, the subject of Supreme Court rulings on schoolhouse religion involves some unique features. But as we shall see, the principal effect of using this subject probably is to highlight the discretion of state and local leaders, thereby making possible fuller understanding of the techniques and perceptions of those leaders than would be possible in situations where their discretion is less. . . .

Inertia in Midway: An Overview

We shall tell the story of five Midway towns where, five years after the Court's outlawing of the practice, the schools have continued to say prayers, read from the Bible, and conduct many other forms of supposedly unconstitutional religious observances. Local leaders are not deliberately defying the Court; they have simply found it congenial and possible to continue established local practice without regard to the Court's decisions. Those who might have wanted to follow the law of the land were discouraged, isolated, or rendered impotent. School superintendents, even some who agreed with the Court's rulings, have participated in their schools' religious activities and, incidentally, soberly declared in questionnaire surveys that their schools are in full compliance with the Court mandate. Law enforcement and state educational officers with years of experience and close local contacts sincerely deny that they know of any violations of the Court's holdings. During this entire five-year period, moreover, *not a single lawsuit* challenging the ongoing practices in the schools has been initiated by *any* parent or taxpayer in the state.

We think that there are four paramount reasons for this flagrant noncompliance with the Court's constitutional ruling on school prayers and Bible reading, each bearing on the larger problem of the gap between national policy and local consequences.

The first explanation is that every state and local official has what is to him a good reason for not assuming responsibility to act consistently with the Court's decision. Each public official starts, of course, with his own value preferences and sense of what he should do because of the job he holds. But he acts in a context of other people's power and preferences. Therefore he must set up priorities among his goals, expecting to submerge some in order to achieve others. In such a context, every official could be in agreement with the Court's ruling, even perceiving it as part of his job to carry it out, but still actually do nothing because doing something is simply not important enough to jeopardize his chances of getting other more crucial goals achieved. To an individual official, it may just not be worth risking loss of the higher priority items to do anything about the Supreme Court's requirement. The citizen who would like his child to be free of prayers and other people's Bibles, or who thinks that his community should abide by the law of the land, may not find this set of circumstances a very satisfying explanation. However "understandable" refusal to act may be in the case of an individual official—or all state and local government officers generally—it may be small consolation to the man in the street to find that those in authority have such "good" reasons for not complying with national policy. Yet such reasons do exist; they are the first factor in explaining the inertia in Midway.

The second explanation is that officials and other leaders, having tacitly committed themselves to ignoring the Court's mandate as long as possible, apparently develop perceptual screens which enable them to avoid knowledge threatening or conflicting with the accommodation they have made. In this way their inactivity and the resultant noncompliance is rationalized away. State education officials, for example, apparently can become genuinely ignorant of the practices in their schools; leaders of such concerned interest groups as the Civil Liberties Union or the Council of Churches may acquire the same blinders. In another manifestation, responsible officials at all levels begin to misinterpret the requirements of the Court's ruling: they see it as outlawing only state-prescribed prayers or prohibiting only explicit local requirements for religious observances, and therefore as not reaching teachers' discretionary practices in the classroom. They see it as a question of voluntarism, of the right of the majority to exercise their religion. Thus superintendents of unquestioned integrity, for example, can indicate in mail questionnaire responses that their districts are in full compliance with the Court's rulings when they are actually engaging in every form of religious activity known to the American public school system.

The third major explanation, and perhaps the most important one, is that the basic operating principle of local leaders calls for the avoidance of conflict at almost any cost. In all five of the towns we studied, local power structures thoroughly permeate their communities and both subtly and openly discourage controversy of any kind. Although in most cases key members of local power structures only marginally favor schoolhouse religion on its merits, and acknowledge the abstract duty to obey the Court, they are unanimous in wanting to avoid public airing of the issue and hence are entirely committed to maintaining the status quo of religious practices. Their preference is to keep decision-making within their ranks and thus to suppress all issues that threaten such smooth-working processes. It is not even necessary for local powerful figures to give explicit instructions to school boards or superintendents; the latter know well what is expected of them and what it would cost in support for other educational goals if they failed to keep the lid on the potentially incendiary schoolhouse religion issue. Conflict avoidance, of course, when elevated to the level of a basic operating principle, not only becomes managed quiescence but can also be a far-reaching denial of democratic participation. It may come as news to some, though hardly to many, that small town governance frequently falls far short of the democratic ideal which it is so often said to embody.

Fourth, there were no regular channels through which the issue could be raised to official visibility. Neither state nor local officials could be forced to take a stand on this question through any institutionalized procedure. At the state level, relevant interest groups such as the Civil Liberties Union or the Council of Churches saw no available and economically feasible public route to put the issue onto an official agenda. At the local level, there were not even any potentially interested groups or prominent individuals who might have raised the issue of compliance. Local ministers, not very well

integrated into the decision-making apparatus of their communities in any event, were further neutralized by disagreement among themselves over mechanics and by their perception of opposition from parishioners. And if the ministers did not take action on a religious issue, lay citizens were even less inclined to do so on their own initiative.

The absence of channels or arenas through which the issue might be legitimately and routinely raised means that an individual's only recourse is to initiate a lawsuit. The social and psychological costs of doing so, and the possible isolation or ostracism which might follow, make this an unlikely course in a small town setting. The procedural opportunities for challenging the acts of a public official in Midway are not as readily invoked or as effective as they are in some states, and so the overall context would be discouraging for even the most determined advocate of separation of church and state.

Court Decisions in State and Local Context: Some Special Circumstances

So far we have been using words like *leaders, officials,* or *power holders* more or less interchangeably. In place of these words we shall be using a single term, *elite,* meaning those persons who, for whatever reason, have more than the usual power or responsibility in a given context. Presently we shall discuss the matter of who constitutes the elite in educational affairs in Midway, and the state level elite will be distinguished from elites at a local level. Whether the educational elites are elites in other realms as well is a question we shall address later on, but our usage here is quite independent of the answer to that question. Our purpose, in other words, is not to prejudge the case of who rules in the state and communities of Midway but is merely to call by a single name those who in fact are found to rule.

Ours, then, is a study of the responses of state and local elites to a Supreme Court decision requiring change in their communities' practices. But such a study involves some specialized circumstances and creates related analytical needs. We must be alert, for example, to any special implications of the fact that the national mandate in this instance flows from the Court rather than the Congress or the president. It is possible, too, that the issue of schoolhouse religion engages a peculiar set of elite and public reactions and thus is very untypical. We must remember also that the setting for the study is small-town, midwestern America. Each of these facts requires some care in analysis and imposes some constraints on the scope of interpretations which may emerge. But we can adapt our inquiry to such limitations reasonably well, and make profitable use of the opportunities offered.

The fact that this national thrust toward change emanated from the Supreme Court is of course a basic structuring element in our inquiry. The phrasing of the opinion itself left some ambiguities available for exploitation by those so inclined, and no comprehensive or specific standards of conduct were prescribed. More important, no agency of the national or state governments carries responsibility for implementing Court decisions; no bureaucracy with overseeing, investigative, or enforcement responsibilities was charged with supporting the ruling. If there is to be enforcement (in the strict sense) under such circumstances, it must usually come through the lower courts. In this instance, of course, the courts would have to be invoked by local taxpayers or parents. Such courts would not be routinely involved in the subject area, as is the case in regard to the recent Supreme Court initiatives regarding the rights of defendants in criminal

cases. (In the latter situations, the new rights are readily claimed by defendants at their trials and can be insisted upon by higher courts, with resulting impetus toward conformance with Supreme Court requirements.) Enforcement is rendered even more difficult by the fact that actual implementation is in the hands of a large number of people—the classroom teachers of the nation, subject, we may assume, to the close and sometimes emotional attention of some parents.

Although the mechanics of enforcement are thus distinctive, they imply no unique situation in American politics. Behavior-changing requirements emanating from the Supreme Court are neither new nor different in kind from those produced by the other institutions of government. Their political character, in the sense of allocating burdens and benefits within the society, are too evident to require comment. Further, under the long-settled principles of American federalism, state and local officials bear responsibility for carrying out the provisions of the United States Constitution and laws along with their other duties. There are, in other words, many potential agents and means for putting Court decisions into effect, just as there are for other national mandates. What is *really* different about the reception of all such national policies by state and local officials, elites, and the public is the extent to which they happen to share the goals being fostered. . . .

11.2   **Supreme Court Impact on Compliance and Outcomes: *Miranda* and *New York Times* in the United States Courts of Appeals (1990)**

Donald R. Songer and Reginald S. Sheehan

A series of studies in the past two decades, usually referred to as "judicial impact" studies, have vitiated the traditional assumption that lower courts automatically adopt and diffuse the constitutional interpretations announced by the Supreme Court. In fact, several scholars have concluded that these judicial impact studies suggest that constitutional rules as announced by the Supreme Court often have little influence on the behavior of judges and other officials in the legal system.

But there is reason to doubt that the judicial impact literature presents an accurate appraisal of the overall significance of Supreme Court interpretations of the Constitution for lower courts. Extant empirical research deals primarily with a highly biased sample of controversial civil liberties decisions, especially those of the Warren Court. In effect, the studies to date may have been biased because they are limited to the small portion of the court's output for which the chances for significant impact were the smallest. Moreover, most research on judicial impact has examined the response of state courts because that is where scholars expected to find noncompliance. Much less attention has been given to the impact of the Supreme Court on the lower federal courts. This suggests that one should expect to find greater impact if federal court decisions, especially those dealing with economic issues or even less highly charged civil liberties decisions (e.g., libel cases), are examined. . . .

Impact studies have also been handicapped by excessive attention to the relatively narrow and artificially dichotomous concept of compliance. Much of the literature on the impact of the Supreme Court on lower courts has dealt with their compliance with specific decisions of the Supreme Court. But compliance is only a subset of the broader concern with the impact of judicial policies. In contrast, political scientists' concerns extend beyond mere compliance to include a wide array of political consequences in the implementation of judicial policies.

Although compliance studies have illuminated some significant problems, such a focus inevitably misses much of the dynamic of the relationships between courts in our federal system. Lower courts may fail to support the basic policy of the Supreme Court without being overtly noncompliant with any specific decision. Therefore, to gain a more complete understanding of the significance of the constitutional and statutory rules announced by the Supreme Court, a broader concept of impact needs to be used.

The focus on a few selected decisions is too narrow to gauge the impact of the Court on a given policy area. The central significance of the Court is not the specific decisions it makes but the broad policies it fashions from a series of decisions. . . .

The criticisms noted above of defining the impact of the Supreme Court on lower courts solely in terms of compliance suggest the need to investigate the extent to which the substantive outcomes (who wins and who loses) in the lower courts are affected by the decisions of the Supreme Court. The impact of the Court in this framework may be conceived of as the extent to which policy changes announced by the Supreme Court produce changes in the outcomes of cases decided by the lower courts. . . .

The present study undertakes such a dual analysis of the response of the United States Courts of Appeals to the criminal procedure and libel decisions of the Supreme Court during a period stretching from 1952 through the mid 1970s. In addition to shedding some light on the question of whether a different picture of impact will result from the use of different methods of conceptualizing impact, the focus on the courts of appeals will help to fill one of the gaps in the impact literature. Prior to this point the response of the courts of appeals to policy changes announced by the Supreme Court has received relatively little attention compared to the more extensive literature on impact on state courts.

The focus of the compliance analysis was the response of the courts of appeals to the decisions of the United States Supreme Court in the landmark cases of *Miranda v. Arizona* and *New York Times v. Sullivan.* The selection of these two cases was designed to permit a comparison of the impact of the Supreme Court in one highly controversial area and in an area in which a significant policy change generated less intense opposition. The *Miranda* case resulted in one of the most controversial criminal procedure decisions of the Warren Court. Under the decision, no incriminating statement which was the product of custodial interrogation could be admitted at trial unless the defendant had previously been warned of four specific rights and had voluntarily and knowingly waived those prior to questioning.

In *New York Times,* the Court abandoned its earlier reluctance to review state libel laws and ruled that Alabama's libel law did not provide sufficient leeway for exercising First Amendment rights. Under the new test for libel announced by the Court, public officials could recover damages for defamatory statements relating to their official conduct only if they could show "actual malice" by the defendant. Although the *Times* case and subsequent libel decisions were "not without controversy," the libel area did not "generate the heat that the areas of school desegregation and police practices do."

Both decisions remain as valid precedent today. But while neither decision has been overturned, the general policy implicit in the decisions met with a different fate in subsequent Court decisions. In a series of decisions for a full decade after the *Times* case the Court consistently expanded First Amendment protection from libel suits by extending the actual malice test to an increasingly broad array of defendants. In contrast, while the court continued to support the basic pro-defendant position announced in *Miranda* in most cases it reviewed for the next five years, it did not significantly expand the scope of the original landmark decision. . . .

At the most basic level of compliance analysis, it may be noted that none of the decisions of the courts of appeals examined directly defied either the *Times* or *Miranda* decisions. In every case that discussed either precedent the court of appeals opinion indicated that the Supreme Court decisions were accepted as binding. Moreover, a number of appeals court opinions cited the Supreme Court decisions to justify making pro-defendant decisions in cases in which it may be inferred the defendants would have lost before these new precedents were announced by the Court. . . .

Our analysis of libel decisions in the first five years after *New York Times* produced similar results. In the eighteen cases discovered . . . there were no cases of noncompliance. Fifteen of the decisions were in full compliance and four of the decisions correctly anticipated the Supreme Court's extension of the actual malice test to cover persons who were public figures but not public officials.

In three cases, however, the courts of appeals indicated their acceptance of the new Supreme Court precedents but nevertheless interpreted key portions of the precedent in such a narrow manner that defendants actually received little added protection for their rights of expression. In each of these three decisions, the courts of appeals gave a narrow interpretation to the requirement that plaintiffs prove "actual malice." While none of these three decisions unequivocally violated the letter of the Supreme Court mandate, they each appear to be attempts to evade the most reasonable inference about what the "intent" of the Supreme Court decisions probably would be in regard to the particular fact situations involved.

Overall then, 83.7 percent of the appeals court decisions appeared to be both fully compliant with the letter of the *Times* decision and supportive of general policy of expansion of the protection of expression which may be inferred from the decision and the subsequent extensions of the actual malice rule. On the other hand, three decisions, 16.7 percent of the total, may be viewed as decisions which are technically or narrowly compliant with the Supreme Court precedent but which attempt to provide an unsympathetic interpretation which will limit the scope of the Court's impact.

It might be noted that this rate of narrow compliance is more than twice as high as [previously] reported. . . .

Although the *Miranda* decision evoked substantially more controversy than the libel decisions of the Supreme Court, analysis of response by the courts of appeals reveals high levels of compliance with this decision as well. Of the 250 cases decided by the courts of appeals in our sample which dealt with the *Miranda* decision, only one instance of possible noncompliance and twelve decisions which could be classified as narrow compliance were discovered. This 94.8 percent full compliance rate essentially matched the 93.1 percent rate of compliance reported by [previous scholarship] for libel decisions and is actually higher than our own findings for full compliance with *New York Times*.

This generally compliant response by the courts of appeals was most directly illustrated by the case in which a decision of the district court which appeared to be in compliance with pre-*Miranda* decisions was reversed for failure to comply with the new rules announced in *Miranda*. In the remaining cases the court upheld the conviction for reasons which were not inconsistent with the *Miranda* rule. The most frequent bases for affirming the district court were the findings that the trial occurred before *Miranda* and was therefore not bound by the ruling or that the *Miranda* warnings had been properly given. In all of the cases, the court of appeals at least implicitly accepted the *Miranda* decision as binding and in none of the cases did the court announce an interpretation of law that was clearly at odds with *Miranda*. There were no cases of open defiance.

Nine of the twelve decisions labeled as narrow compliance involved the refusal of the lower courts to require Miranda warnings prior to interrogation because they concluded from the facts of their case that the defendant was not in custody. In six of these cases, the courts narrowly interpreted the *Miranda* ruling as applying only to interrogation conducted by law enforcement officers. Consequently they held that the warnings were not required when the questions came from investigative agents of the IRS or from a psychologist who was charged with preparing a report on whether the defendant was psychologically unfit to stand trial. In the remaining three cases of narrow compliance the question was whether the defendant had been taken into custody by police at the time of questioning. Additionally, there were three cases that involved situations not specifically covered by *Miranda* in which the court presumably had enough discretion to decide the case either way and in each case ruled against the defendant's position.

Overall then, the rates of compliance with both *Miranda* and *New York Times* are impressively high in light of the dismal picture of lower court defi-

ance painted by much of the literature on judicial impact. The high level of compliance with *Miranda* is particularly surprising since a number of scholars have suggested that noncompliance is most likely to occur in response to Supreme Court decisions which represent significant new directions in policy and which evoke widespread controversy. Therefore, if the impact of the Supreme Court on the courts of appeals is to be conceptualized in terms of compliance, the inescapable conclusion to be drawn from these analyses is that the impact of the Court is quite substantial. . . .

Contemporary Judicial Politics

11.3   Responses to Judicial Policies (1998)

Bradley C. Canon and Charles A. Johnson

. . . In virtually all instances, courts that formulate policies must rely on other courts or on nonjudicial actors to translate those policies into action. Inevitably, just as making judicial policies is a political process, so too is the implementation of the policies—the issues are essentially political, and the actors are subject to political pressures.

Studying Responses to Judicial Policies

[Here, we] examine . . . the implementation and impact of judicial policies. There are important substantive and theoretical reasons for studying what may at first appear to be a very narrow part of the judicial process and for studying it as a political process instead of as a legal process. From the substantive perspective, few areas of the American political system remain untouched by judicial deci-

Bradley C. Canon and Charles A. Johnson, "Respones to Judicial Policies," in *Judicial Policies: Implementation and Impact.* Copyright © 1998 CQ Press, a division of Congressional Quarterly, Inc.

sion making. In our litigious society many disputes that have public policy ramifications are decided by the judiciary. Although judicial policies differ from legislative actions and executive orders in their origin, they are also public policies: they too must be implemented before disputes or problems are resolved, and they have an impact on the public. Racial segregation, for example, did not end with the announcement of *Brown v. Board of Education* in 1954. Ten years after the Supreme Court decided that "separate but equal" is inherently unequal, a great majority of the South's black students continued to attend overwhelmingly black schools. The Court's policy was given meaning only after considerable efforts by lower courts; the Department of Justice; the Department of Health, Education and Welfare; Congress; and civil rights groups. Our knowledge about desegregation and the judiciary would be quite incomplete if we limited our analysis to the *Brown* decision. Knowing how events lead to a judicial decision and what the decision itself means gives us an incomplete picture of the judicial process.

Studying the reaction to judicial policies is also important from a theoretical perspective. To a certain degree, evaluating the implementation of judicial policies is in the mainstream of the field of policy analysis. Important theoretical questions in this field may be answered by studying the aftermath of judicial decisions: Why are some policies implemented while others are not? Why do some organizations change policies while others do not? Why do some policies have the intended impact while others fail to do so or have unintended consequences? The varied outcomes of judicial policies provide ample opportunities to examine the impact of public policies.

Responses to some court decisions have been immediate and implementation almost complete. For example, in the years following the Supreme Court's 1973 abortion decision in *Roe v. Wade,* several million women ended their pregnancies with legal abortions and new pro-choice and pro-life groups emerged as powerful forces in our political system. By contrast, the events following *Brown v. Board of Education* demonstrate that the implementation of other decisions may be prolonged.

Still other decisions meet with varied responses across the country. The Supreme Court's decision in *Gregg v. Georgia* (1976), for example, cleared the way for states to impose the death penalty after serious challenges in the 1970s. Although some states passed no legislation reauthorizing the death penalty, others chose to adopt new legislation on death penalties. Today there are many prisoners on death row.

The aftermath of these decisions and others raises important questions about the ability of the judiciary to make public policy effectively and about how individual citizens and political institutions relate to the judiciary. Moreover, studying the implementation of judicial decisions may shed some light on such longstanding issues as the relationship between law and human behavior and the role of the judiciary in our political system.

If studying the implementation of judicial policies is important, then we must study it as a political process. In a general sense, the implementation of *any* public policy is a political process. The notion that the administration of policy is apolitical has long since been discarded (if it was ever in vogue) . . . .

. . . [M]any judicial decisions afford a great deal of latitude for interpretation and implementation. Political actors and institutions who follow through on the decisions make the judicial policy. Cer-

tainly, the judges who enforced civil rights decisions were subject to political pressures from a variety of sources. Similar pressures affected public and private institutions after court decisions on affirmative action. Even presidential politics may become intertwined with judicial policies, as did Richard Nixon's 1968 "law and order" presidential campaign criticizing the Supreme Court's criminal justice decisions or the explosive issue of abortion in virtually every presidential election since 1980.

Like Congress and the president, the Supreme Court and other courts must rely on others to translate policy into action. And like the processes of formulating legislative, executive, and judicial policies, the process of translating those decisions into action is often a political one subject to a variety of pressures from a variety of political actors in the system.

Roe v. Wade: A Case Study of Judicial Impact

The best way to illustrate the political nature of the events that follow a judicial decision is to review the implementation and impact of a decision that remains controversial decades after its announcement by the U.S. Supreme Court. We will use the Supreme Court's 1973 abortion decision in *Roe v. Wade* to show what may happen after a judicial policy is announced. Later in this [article] we will suggest a conceptual scheme by which the events following any judicial decision may be effectively organized and compared with the events following other judicial decisions.

The Decision

On Monday, January 22, 1973, Associate Justice Harry Blackmun announced the decision of the Court in two cases concerning the rights of women to end unwanted pregnancies with legal abortions, *Roe v. Wade* and *Doe v. Bolton*. . . . The justices fully expected a public outcry after the decision was announced. They were not disappointed.

The cases before the Court challenged the laws prohibiting abortion in Texas and Georgia. In both cases the Court decided in favor of the plaintiffs—women who were identified only as Jane Roe and Mary Doe. The direct effect of the decision was to void the antiabortion laws in these two states. Indirectly, of course, the Court also voided laws in forty-four other states that prohibited or limited abortion. . . .

In effect, the Supreme Court had given women the right to abortion on demand during the first two trimesters of pregnancy and had allowed the state to regulate abortions only to protect the mother's health during these two trimesters. The Court held that during the third trimester the state could regulate or even prohibit abortions, except where the life or the health of the mother was endangered.

Immediate Responses

The reactions from several corners of the political system were immediate, and they were mostly negative. . . .

But not all reactions were negative. The president of Planned Parenthood, Alan F. Guttmacher, called the decision a "courageous stroke for right to privacy and for the protection of a woman's physical and emotional health." A similar reaction came from women attorneys at the Center for Constitutional Rights, who cited the decision as a "victory for [the] women's liberation movement." . . . Several months after the abortion decision Justice Blackmun gave a speech at Emory University Law School, in Atlanta, Georgia, where a woman embraced him after his speech, saying, "I'll never be able to thank you for what you have done. I'll say no more. Thank you." Unknown to Blackmun at the time, this rare positive response came from "Mary Doe," the woman from Texas who had challenged the Texas abortion law.

Reactions also came from members of Congress. . . . By November 1973, more than two dozen resolutions to overturn some aspect of the Court's decision were introduced in Congress. Two of the proposals eventually enacted into law were added to the Health Programs Extension Act of 1973, which was amended to permit institutions receiving federal funds to refuse to perform abortions, and the 1973 Foreign Assistance Act, which was amended to prohibit the use of U.S. funds to pay for abortions overseas.

Response was also immediate from women who sought abortions. In the first three months of 1973, over 180,000 abortions were performed in the United States; during the first year following the Supreme Court's decision a total of 742,460 abortions were performed nationwide. . . .

Whether a woman secured an abortion depended heavily on whether there was a physician or medical facility willing to provide abortion services. [One] study . . . found that fewer than half of the hospitals in their national sample changed abortion policies after *Roe.* Indeed, for many hospitals in the sample (85.6 percent), the abortion issue was not a subject of heated staff or board discussions. Whether hospitals provided abortion services depended strongly on whether the hospital staff was in favor of abortions; factors such as community need or demand for abortion services were largely unrelated to the hospitals' decisions.

A national survey by the research division of Planned Parenthood, the Alan Guttmacher Institute, in 1973 revealed that less than one-third (30.1 percent) of the non-Catholic short-term general hospitals in the United States provided abortion services. Another survey revealed that 75 percent of the hospitals providing abortion services were privately controlled, rather than publicly controlled or government operated. In the year following the abortion decision, a relatively small number of nonhospital clinics provided abortion services (178 nationwide), and only a few physicians (168 nationwide) reported performing abortions in their offices. Nonetheless, in the first year after the decision, the largest percentage of abortions occurred in clinics (44.5 percent), and most of the remaining abortions (41.1 percent) were performed in private hospitals.

The Alan Guttmacher Institute concluded that in the twelve months following the Supreme Court's abortion decision, "the response of health institutions in many areas to the legalization of abortion in 1973 was so limited as to be tantamount to no response at all." This widespread non-response had a considerable effect on *Roe v. Wade*'s impact— after being granted the *constitutional* right to an abortion, many women could not exercise that right, at least locally, because medical facilities in their communities refused to provide such services.

Later Responses

Despite the limited availability of abortion providers noted in reports by the Alan Guttmacher Institute, the number of abortions nationwide continued to increase for several years after the Supreme Court's abortion rights decision. . . .

Although the abortion rate data are subject to interpretation, there has been a clear and continuing shift in the kinds of facilities providing abortion services after *Roe*. An increasing number of abortions are provided by clinics rather than hospitals. Indeed, the number of clinics providing abortions doubled in the three years following *Roe*. In 1992, two-thirds of the nation's abortions were provided by these non-hospital clinics. Regardless of the type of providers, however, national data also reveal that the number of abortion providers has declined after an initial growth following *Roe*. . . .

Another way to consider abortion rates (number of abortions per 1,000 women aged fifteen through forty-four) after *Roe v. Wade* is to examine the same data at state and local levels. In 1994, for example, the abortion rate varied from a low of 2 per 1,000 women in Wyoming to a high of 42 per 1,000 women in California. The trends within states over time also vary considerably. Abortion rates in Colorado and Pennsylvania, for example, increased substantially after *Roe v. Wade*. In Pennsylvania, where state law had limited abortions, the increase is not surprising. In Colorado, however, a relatively liberal abortion law was in place before the *Roe* decision. However, in contrast to the national trends, Colorado and Pennsylvania's abortion rates after 1978–1980 declined to roughly 1973 rates. These trends differ dramatically from the experience in California, which prior to *Roe* had a permissive law allowing abortions under many circumstances. Abortion rates in California were largely unaffected by *Roe* through 1983. . . . The important point here is to appreciate that there are variations in abortion rates across time, in different kinds of facilities, in different kinds of communities, and in different parts of the country.

Politics and Abortion Rights

The Supreme Court's decision in *Roe v. Wade* brought the issue of abortion rights to center stage in American politics. In national institutions, in state and local governments, in political parties, in some interest groups, in some religious denominations, and among the general public, battles were fought between the decision's supporters and its detractors. In many instances, these battles and resulting

government actions substantially affected the implementation and impact of the Court's decision.

Congressional Actions.   Within a year of *Roe*'s announcement, fifty constitutional amendments were introduced pursuing a variety of strategies for revising the Court's decision. A subcommittee of the Senate Judiciary Committee held sixteen days of hearings on the proposed amendments in 1974 and 1975, after which the Judiciary Committee voted not to report any of the proposed amendments to the floor for a vote because of legal questions about the proposals. Subsequent attempts to amend the Constitution also failed at various stages of the legislative process, including a vote in 1983 on an amendment that read: "A right to abortion is not secured by this Constitution. The Congress and the several States shall have concurrent power to restrict and prohibit abortion." An attempt to pass ordinary legislation in 1981 called the Human Life Bill (which defined "persons" protected by the Fourteenth Amendment to include fetuses from the point of conception and would have removed federal court jurisdiction in abortion cases) also failed to garner enough congressional support to pass.

Opponents of abortions and the Supreme Court's decisions achieved greater success in Congress with legislative initiatives aimed at curtailing federal involvement in providing or paying for abortions and protecting physicians and hospitals who refused to provide them. Poor women's access to abortion services was significantly diminished by a series of legislative riders to appropriations bills that effectively ended payments through the federal Medicaid program. Passage of this legislation, generally referred to as the Hyde Amendment (for its chief sponsor, Rep. Henry Hyde, R., Ill.), resulted in an almost complete cessation of federally funded abortions—from approximately 250,000 in 1976 to fewer than 2,500 in 1978. While there is evidence that many poor women found alternative funding for abortions, Eva Rubin notes that poor women often "postponed abortions for two or three weeks . . . [which] might mean that the abortion was performed in the second trimester . . . [and with funds] diverted from household money."

A new tactic by pro-life forces in Congress emerged in the mid-1990s with congressional attempts to ban abortions in particular circumstances. The passage in 1996 and 1997 of legislation banning an infrequently used late-term abortion procedure called "partial birth abortion" by abortion opponents and "intact dilation and extraction" by abortion rights proponents marked a new level of proposed federal regulation. This legislation was vetoed twice by President Clinton and became a political issue in the 1996 presidential election. One leader of a pro-life lobby group, Ralph Reed of the Christian Coalition, indicated that this legislation would be followed by other attempts to "outlaw other procedures . . . like a ban on abortion in the last month, and so on. . . ."*

Abortion Politics at the State and Local Levels

Most of the legislation in the United States concerning abortions is state-level legislation. In 1973 *Roe v. Wade* invalidated most laws that flatly prohibited abortions, but states have continued to be prominent players in U.S. abortion policy. [T]hirty-two states had passed sixty-two laws relating to abortion. Almost all of these laws were aimed at limiting access to abortions, regulating abortion services, or stopping abortions under certain conditions. They are especially frequent in a handful of states that have a strong antiabortion political culture (Pennsylvania, Ohio, Minnesota, Missouri, Louisiana, Utah, and Idaho). . . .

Interest Groups and Abortion Politics. As has happened with other major issues in American politics, the Supreme Court's establishment of abortion rights in *Roe v. Wade* led to considerable activity by organized interests in the United States. While a few interest groups could be found on either side of the abortion issue before the Court's 1973 decision, their number and the variety of their activities increased dramatically after *Roe.*

Groups opposed to the decision grew rapidly in number, often organizing public demonstrations against the decision and, later, picketing clinics.

Opposition groups, more so than supporters, included many people who had the time to picket, orchestrate letter-writing campaigns, call legislators, and participate in other political activities. The orientation and composition of these groups often produced large demonstrations, such as the annual March for Life rallies in Washington, D.C., on the anniversary of the *Roe* decision. . . .

Organized interests opposing abortion were often linked to religious organizations—usually either the Catholic Church or fundamentalist Christian organizations. . . .

Organized groups that supported the Court's abortion decision were initially happy about *Roe* and did not mobilize a political campaign to support the decision's implementation. As Congress, state legislatures, and other government bodies passed new restrictive legislation, these groups sought to influence abortion policy primarily through litigation. Although the supportive groups organized some public demonstrations and contacted legislators, their most obvious efforts focused upon the courts. . . .

Abortion Policy Questions Return to the Courts. The actions taken by Congress, state legislatures, and various administrative agencies at all levels of government, as well as the activities of private organizations, often led to the consideration of new policy questions by the courts. The Supreme Court's decision in *Roe v. Wade* had invalidated state laws prohibiting abortion, but it had left unanswered questions about restrictive legislation, especially with regard to the latter stages of pregnancy. Similarly, the Court was silent on policy questions regarding the state's obligation to provide abortion services in public hospitals or to pay for abortions for women who could not afford them. Courts often and necessarily leave important questions open when deciding a core issue; addressing them in subsequent cases gives the judiciary a continuing role in the implementation of its policies. . . .

. . . [I]n *Planned Parenthood of Southeastern Pennsylvania v. Casey* (1992) . . . the Court [again] upheld the right to abortion in a fragmented decision, but with six justices signaling that state legislatures could enact laws regulating the circumstances under which women could have abortions,

---

*In *Stenberg v. Carhart* (2000), the Supreme Court invalidated a Nebraska late-term abortion law on the grounds that it did not contain a provision permitting an exception for the life of the mother and banned a procedure commonly used in pre-viability abortions. This decision nullified thirty-one state laws.

as long as the laws did not place an "undue burden" on the right to obtain an abortion. . . .

Nonetheless, the impact of . . . *Casey* is uncertain. The number of abortions has declined slightly, from a high of 1.43 million to 1.27 million, in the mid-1990s, but how much of the change is attributable to the Court cases as opposed to greater sex education, more frequent use of contraceptives, or a rise in abstinence is not known. Fluctuations aside, the number of abortions in the United States each year remains large.

Even more cases concerning abortion services were addressed in lower courts. A few even involved criminal prosecutions of physicians, as did the case of Dr. Kenneth C. Edelin of Massachusetts. Edelin was convicted of manslaughter after he performed an abortion in the sixth or seventh month of pregnancy. His conviction was later overturned on appeal, but reports in the popular press after the conviction suggested that hospitals in several cities began limiting abortions in later stages of pregnancy so as to avoid similar charges. . . .

A Model of the Implementation and Impact of Judicial Policies

Chronicling the events that followed the Supreme Court's abortion decision gives some idea of the range of reactions and actors that may become involved in the implementation of a judicial decision. Similar case histories could be supplied for other court decisions. But our aim is not to study the aftermath of every judicial decision; instead, we want to make general statements about what has happened or may happen after any judicial decision. That is, we hope to move away from idiosyncratic, case-by-case or policy-by-policy analyses and toward a general theoretical understanding of the events that may follow a judicial decision. (The remainder of this [reading] is devoted to explaining the responses one may encounter to any given judicial decision—who may react to the decisions and how; what types of reactions may occur; and what effects those reactions may have on the implementation of the judicial policy.)

The first step in understanding any political process is to develop a conceptual foundation upon which explanations may be built. We will or-

ganize our presentation of what happens after a court decision around two major elements: *the actors* who may respond to the decision and *the responses* that these actors may make. Focusing on these two elements enables us to define more precisely who is reacting and how. In studying the responses to judicial policies, we describe and attempt to explain the behavior following a court decision—specifically, what the behavior is, its antecedents, and its consequences. Hence, when we discuss impact, we are describing the general reactions and changes (or lack thereof) that follow a judicial decision. When we discuss implementation, we are describing the behavior of lower courts, government agencies, or other affected parties as it relates to enforcing a judicial decision. When we discuss what many would call compliance/noncompliance or evasion, we are describing behavior that is in some way consistent or inconsistent with the behavioral requirements of the judicial decision.

. . . [D]ifferent sets of actors, referred to as populations, may respond to a judicial policy. The organization of these populations is essentially a functional one, in which their roles in shaping the impact of judicial decisions and their influence on the ultimate impact of judicial policy differ. We now turn to a discussion of these populations and their responses, illustrated with examples drawn from the events after the Supreme Court's abortion decision as well as other recent court decisions.

The Interpreting Population

For any appellate court decision, the actor most often charged with responding to a decision is a particular lower court, often a trial court. Moreover, in our common law system many appellate court decisions become policies used in deciding future cases. In a general sense, therefore, a higher court's policy affects all lower courts within its jurisdiction. This set of courts is known as the interpreting population. (This population may include state attorneys-general or other non-judges who have an official role in interpreting the law.) The interpreting population, as the name implies, responds to the policy decisions of a higher court by refining the policy it has announced. Such refinements can have the effect of enlarging or limiting the original policy. This population, in other words, interprets the meaning of the policy and develops the rules for matters not addressed in the original decision. Of course, all populations must "interpret" the decision in order to react to it. Interpretations by lower courts, however, are distinguished from other interpretations since theirs are viewed as authoritative in a legal sense by others in the political system. Hence, this population provides "official" interpretations of a court policy applicable to the other populations under its jurisdiction.

The Supreme Court's *Roe* decision launched the judiciary into a new area of the law, which required considerable refining before complete implementation. Shortly after the decision was announced, lower state and federal courts began hearing cases presenting issues that had not been directly addressed in *Roe.* In Florida, for example, the issue of a father's rights were raised by a father who brought legal action to restrain the mother of his unborn child from obtaining an abortion. The lower court denied relief and the Florida Supreme Court affirmed that decision, arguing that the U.S. Supreme Court's abortion decision was based on the mother's "right of privacy." The decision to terminate a pregnancy was, therefore, purely the right of the mother and could not be subject to interference by the state or private individuals.

Meanwhile, in Arizona, another matter was before the courts. Arizona law prohibited the advertisement of any medicine or procedures that facilitated abortions. New Times, Inc., a local publisher, was convicted under this statute and appealed to the state supreme court. The conviction was reversed, since the Arizona abortion statutes were found to be similar to the Texas statute struck down in *Roe v. Wade,* even though the issue before the court was different from that decided in the original abortion cases.

In each of these instances, and in others . . . , the issue before the court had not been addressed directly in the original decision. Consistent with the common law tradition, the lower courts had the responsibility of making authoritative interpretations of policy in light of the original Supreme Court decision. In their interpretations these courts could limit the application of the original policy, as did the Arizona trial court in convicting the publisher, or could facilitate its implementation, as did the Florida courts. . . .

The Implementing Population

The lower courts apply a higher court's policy only in cases that come before them. Higher court policies, however, usually affect a wider set of actors than those involved in lawsuits. We refer to this set of actors as the implementing population. In most instances, this population is made up of authorities whose behavior may be reinforced or sanctioned by the interpreting population. The implementing population usually performs a policing or servicing function in the political system—that is, implementors apply the system's rules to persons subject to their authority. Prominent examples of this population are police officers, prosecutors, university and public school officials, and welfare and social security workers. In many instances, the original policy and subsequent interpretations by lower courts are intended to impose requirements or set limits on the behavior of the implementing population. A clear example of this activity involves decisions concerning police behavior with regard to the rights of criminal suspects.

When the services or practices of private concerns are subject to a judicial policy, the implementing population is composed of private individuals or institutions. For example, court decisions may require or strongly suggest that corporations implement policies against racial or gender discrimination or harassment. . . . [H]owever, when a private organization has a choice (is not obligated to follow a policy), it is part of the consumer population.

The implementing population will vary from decision to decision. For criminal justice decisions, prosecutors, police officers, and defense attorneys are the primary implementors. For environmental protection decisions, the implementors are most often federal and state environmental protection agencies. Reapportionment decisions usually involve legislators as the implementing population. When judicial decisions require no action by government agencies, nongovernmental service agencies may be the implementors. Sometimes there is no implementing population at all. For example, no one is charged with implementing a case such as *New York Times Co. v. Sullivan* (1964), which significantly decreased the applicability of libel law to public officials. The decision held that when public officials initiated libel suits against the media, they had to show a much greater degree of fault than did private persons who filed libel suits. *Sullivan* is implemented solely through court rulings made in the course of litigation.

The degree to which a court decision actually benefits those it was intended to benefit depends on the implementing actors and institutions whose activities are affected by the decision. Implementors' reactions may range from full compliance to doing nothing. These reactions have been extensively studied by social scientists and legal scholars . . .

The Consumer Population

Those for whom the policies are set forth by the court are identified as the consumer population. This population is the set of individuals (usually not affiliated with the government) who would or should receive benefits or suffer disabilities as a result of a judicial decision; that is, they gain or lose desired rights or resources. Criminal suspects, for example, benefit from judicial policies announced by the Supreme Court in a series of decisions in the 1960s. African American students presumably benefited from school desegregation decisions following *Brown v. Board of Education* (1954). But they were disadvantaged by more recent judicial decisions limiting affirmative action programs in many public universities. Thus, some consumer populations do not benefit from a judicial policy. For example, juvenile court defendants suffer because they do not have the right of trial by jury; stockholders can suffer when their corporation is split up as a result of an antitrust ruling. And there are decisions under which members of the consumer population may either benefit or suffer, depending on their attitudes toward the policy. When led prayer was banned in the public schools (*Abington School District v. Schempp,* 1963), children who wanted to pray became disadvantaged and those who did not want to pray became advantaged.

The consumer population, depending on the policy involved, may include the entire population of the political system, as with judicial decisions concerning general tax legislation. For some decisions, however, a very limited population may be directly involved, such as criminal suspects under arrest. When the policy affects a specific sector but supposedly is for the public good (for example, an-

titrust decisions), a distinction between direct and indirect consumption must sometimes be made. Also, for some decisions there are two levels of consumer population, those who have to decide whether to offer some previously prohibited service and those who decide whether to use the service. For example, after *Roe* women could still not obtain legal abortions unless hospitals, clinics, and physicians were willing to perform them. As we noted, most medical facilities and doctors choose not to offer abortion services.

Specifying the consumer population exactly may be troublesome in some cases. For example, while few would dispute that women with unwanted pregnancies are the consumers for the Supreme Court's abortion decision, opponents would likely argue that unborn children are also consumers and receive catastrophic negative benefits from the abortion decision. Others might argue that fathers of unborn children or parents of underage, pregnant girls are part of *Roe*'s consumer population.

In studying the reactions of consumers to judicial policies, several questions need to be addressed. Do the potential consumers of a judicial policy know of the policy? If they know of the policy, why and how do they modify their attitudes or behavior because of it? What effect, if any, does the policy have on the attitudes and behavior of the consumer with regard to the judiciary or other political institutions? . . .

The Secondary Population

The populations we have discussed so far are those directly (at least potentially) affected by a judicial policy or its implementation. The secondary population is a residual one. It consists of everyone who is not in the interpreting, implementing, or consumer population for any given decision. Members of the secondary population are not directly affected by a judicial policy; however, some members may react to a policy or its implementation. This reaction usually takes the form of some type of feedback directed toward the original policy maker, another policy maker, the implementing population, or the consumer population.

The secondary population may be divided into four subpopulations: government officials, interest groups, the media, and the public at large. First, there are government officials. This subpopulation includes legislators and executive officers who are not immediately affected by the decision. Though usually unaffected directly, these individuals are often in a position to support or hinder the implementation of the original policy. This subpopulation is distinguished from other secondary subpopulations in that its members have direct, legitimate authority in the political system, and they are often the recipients of political pressure from the public. Clearly, for example, Congress and state legislatures substantially affected implementation of *Roe v. Wade* with the passage of laws restricting the funding of abortions.

The second subpopulation is interest groups, which are often activated by court policies even when they are not directly affected by them. Subsequent pressures by these groups may help facilitate or block effective implementation of the judicial policy. National, state, and local pro-life organizations have worked diligently to discourage providers from offering abortion services and women from obtaining abortions. These groups have also maintained considerable pressure on public officials and the courts to limit the implementation of pro-choice policies.

The third subpopulation is the media, which communicate the substance of judicial policies to potentially affected populations. Included here are general and specialized media, which may affect implementation or consumption by editorial stance or simply by the way they report (or do not report) judicial policies. Media attention to a policy, descriptions of reactions to it, and support or criticism of it can play a large role in determining the amount and direction of feedback courts and implementors get. Media reports of activities by pro-choice and pro-life groups have helped keep the abortion issue at the forefront of American politics.

The fourth subpopulation consists of members of the public at large, insofar as they do not fall within the consumer population. The most important segment of this subpopulation is attentive citizens—those who are most aware of a judicial policy. This segment includes individuals who may be related to the consumer population (e.g., parents of teenage girls seeking an abortion), politically active people (e.g., political party workers), or just people who follow the news pretty regularly. . . .

Fluidity and Linkage Among Populations

The basis for the foregoing classification of populations is primarily functional. We may, therefore, on some occasions find that particular individuals are members of different populations in different circumstances. For example, it is entirely possible for a state attorney general to be an interpreter for one judicial policy and an implementor for another. In the former instance, the attorney general would be issuing an authoritative, legally binding statement interpreting a judicial decision; in the latter instance, the attorney general would be charged with the responsibility of applying a judicial policy to some consumer population or of carrying out some order of the court. School boards or superintendents may be implementors of a schoolhouse religion decision and consumers of a court decision changing the way the state finances the schools. Media outlets are consumers of a libel decision like *Sullivan,* but more often they are in the secondary population. Obviously, private citizens are in both the consumer and secondary populations, depending on the nature of the judicial policy.

Attorneys constitute a special set of participants whose function may vary from one setting to another. They assist the interpreting population when they argue for a particular interpretation of a higher court's decision in briefs or oral arguments before lower court judges. They have a role in implementation when they insist that agencies follow policies promulgated by a higher court. When they advise clients to take advantage (or not to do so) of a judicial policy, attorneys are playing a role as quasi-members of the consumer population.

Perhaps even more often, attorneys are called upon to give their interpretations of judicial policies to potential consumers, implementing groups, and, occasionally, secondary groups such as interested citizens or legislative bodies. Such interpretations are not official like those of the interpreting population. Often, however, their interpretations can be final, since paying clients usually act on lawyers' advice; so it is reasonable to assume that such interpretations play an important role in accounting for the reactions of others to judicial policies. As we have mentioned, attorneys also assist in interpreting higher court policies for lower courts.

In a broad sense, as they perform these functions, attorneys serve as links between various populations. They provide a means for the communication of decisions downward from higher courts to relevant actors, as well as being unofficial interpreters of these decisions. Their linkage activities may also prompt new litigation or feedback to the courts or other agencies, which, in turn, may affect the implementation of a decision.

Acceptance Decisions and Behavioral Responses

In this [reading], we focus on the responses to judicial policies by all of the populations we have identified. We may observe a large variety of responses to judicial decisions, so precise distinctions are difficult to make. Nonetheless, we believe two general categories of responses are captured in the concepts of acceptance decisions and behavioral responses. The *acceptance decision* involves psychological reactions to a judicial policy, which may be generalized in terms of accepting or rejecting the policy. An individual's acceptance decision is shaped by several psychological dimensions: intensity of attitude, regard for the policy-making court, perceptions of the consequences of the decision, and the person's own role in society.

The *intensity of a person's attitude* toward the policy prior to the court's decision can be important. Most white southerners, for example, were extremely hostile toward policies of racial integration before *Brown;* thus their unwillingness to accept the decision was not surprising. Many people had similarly intense attitudes about abortion and about prayers in the public schools. Many minority groups felt strongly about affirmative action. For most policies, though, feelings are not so intense. Few people feel strongly about such issues as the size and composition of juries, whether a high school newspaper can be published without the principal's approval, or the application of the First Amendment guarantees to commercial advertising. In such instances the acceptance decision is less likely to be governed by prior attitudes.

Another dimension of acceptance reflects people's *regard for the court* making the decision. People who view the U.S. Supreme Court favorably may be more inclined to accept a decision as legitimate and proper. Those who generally view the Court negatively or who believe it has taken on too much authority may transfer their views to particular decisions of the Court.

A third psychological dimension takes into account a person's *perception of the consequences of a decision.* Those who may not quarrel with a decision in the abstract but believe it will have a serious and detrimental effect on society may be reluctant to accept it. In the 1950s, for example, many citizens feared that communism would expand in the United States as a result of the Supreme Court's decisions granting due process to persons suspected of engaging in subversive activities. In the late 1990s many people worry that court decisions voiding affirmative action programs will make it more difficult for minority applicants to obtain jobs.

Finally, acceptance decisions are shaped by a *person's own role in society.* An ambitious judge, school superintendent, or police chief may be reluctant to accept (publicly, at least) an unpopular judicial policy for fear that it will harm his or her career. Corporate officers or citizens may be unwilling to accept a decision if they think it will reduce their profits or cause them great inconvenience. Conversely, people may accept quite willingly decisions that are popular with the public or that bring them financial or other benefits.

Behavioral responses involve reactions that may be seen or recorded and that may determine the extent to which a court policy is actually realized. These responses are often closely linked to acceptance decisions. Persons who do not accept a judicial policy are likely to engage in behavior designed to defeat the policy or minimize its impact. They will interpret it narrowly, try to avoid implementing it, and refuse or evade its consumption. Those who accept a policy are likely to be more faithful or even enthusiastic in interpreting, implementing, and consuming it. Of course, nonacceptors may not always be in a position to ignore a decision or to refuse completely to comply with it. Malapportioned state legislatures, for instance, had little choice but to reapportion themselves after the Supreme Court established a "one person, one vote" criterion for legislative representation in the 1960s. People may adjust some of their behavioral responses to meet the decision's requirements while they have other, less visible, behavioral responses that may more truly reflect their unwillingness to accept the decision. Conversely, acceptors may for reasons of inertia never fully adjust their behavioral responses to a new judicial policy.

Changes in policy often entail *changes in rules or formal directives* within an organization. But at the day-to-day level, norms, informal understandings, or even behavioral habits within an organization may set the tone. Public and private employers may, for example, adopt formal policies prohibiting sexual harassment, but many informally tolerate violations of those policies. Policy changes may also lead to changes in organizational structure or function. As we have indicated, the delivery of abortion services changed after *Roe v. Wade* to the extent that currently most abortions are performed in clinics, not hospitals.

Another type of behavioral response is the *actions or inaction* of those who consume the policy. Consumption decisions can be affected by the way the interpreting and implementing populations act. Consumers may respond to a court decision by using, ignoring, or avoiding it. For example, many lawyers do not advertise, even through the Supreme Court has ruled that they can do so (*Bates v. Arizona Bar,* 1978). We must examine actual behavior, in addition to policy changes of corporations and agencies, if we are to better understand the consumption of judicial policies.

Feedback is another behavioral response to judicial policies. It is directed toward the originator of the policy or to some other policy-making agency. The purpose of feedback behavior is usually to pro-

vide support for or make demands upon political actors (including judges) regarding the judicial policy. Feedback is often communicated through interest groups or the media. Almost immediately after the Supreme Court announced its abortion decision, feedback in the form of letters to the justices began. Also, some members of Congress let the Court know of their displeasure with the abortion decision by introducing statutory restrictions or constitutional amendments to overturn *Roe.* Manifestations of displeasure or support by various interest groups have been directed at the Court and other political institutions, such as Congress and state legislatures. In varying degrees, these types of feedback have led to modifications of the policy—as we can see in the Court's *Webster* and *Casey* decisions abandoning the trimester system and allowing the states greater leeway in regulating abortion.

[Here,] we have introduced the notion that judicial decisions are not self-implementing; courts must frequently rely on lower courts or on nonjudicial actors in the political system to turn law into action. Moreover, the implementation of judicial decisions is a political process; the actors upon whom courts must rely are usually political actors and are subject to political pressures as they allocate resources to implement a judicial decision. . . .

11.4 The Dynamic and the Constrained Court (1991)

Gerald Rosenberg

What is the role of U.S. courts in producing significant social reform? When and under what conditions will U.S. courts be effective producers of significant social reform? When does it make sense for individuals and groups pressing for such change to litigate? What kinds of effects from court victories can they expect? Which view best captures the reality of American politics? Given the alleged success of the social reform litigation of the last four decades, and Americans' attachment to the Dynamic Court view, it is tempting to suggest that it *always* makes sense

From *The Hollow Hope: Can Courts Bring About Social Change?,* pp. 9–36. Reprinted by permission of University of Chicago Press.

for groups to litigate. On the other hand, our attachment to the vision of the Constrained Court, as well as a knowledge of legal history, can suggest that courts can *never* be effective producers of significant social reform. But "always" and "never" are claims about frequency, not conditions. To fully understand the role of the courts in producing significant social reform, we must focus on the latter. . . .

[Here], I flesh out the two views. My aim is to make each view plausible, if not enticing. Then, critically examining evidence for their plausibility, I develop a set of constraints and conditions under which courts can produce significant social reform. These suggest that both views oversimplify court effectiveness.

Structural Constraints: The Logic of the Constrained Court View

The view of courts as unable to produce significant social reform has a distinguished pedigree reaching back to the founders. Premised on the institutional structure of the American political system and the procedures and belief systems created by American law, it suggests that the conditions required for courts to produce significant social reform will seldom exist. Unpacked, the Constrained Court view maintains that courts will generally not be effective producers of significant social reform for three reasons: the limited nature of constitutional rights, the lack of judicial independence, and the judiciary's inability to develop appropriate policies and its lack of powers of implementation.

The Limited Nature of Rights

The Constitution, and the set of beliefs that surround it, is not unbounded. Certain rights are enshrined in it and others are rejected. In economic terms, private control over the allocation and distribution of resources, the use of property, is protected. "Rights" to certain minimums, or equal shares of basic goods, are not. Further, judicial discretion is bound by the norms and expectations of the legal culture. These two parameters, believers in the Constrained Court view suggest, present a problem for litigators pressing the courts for significant social reform because most such litigation is based on constitutional claims that rights are being denied. An individual or group comes into a court claiming it is being denied some benefit, or protection from arbitrary and discriminatory action, and that it is *entitled* to this benefit or that protection. Proponents of the Constrained Court view suggest that this has four important consequences for social reformers.

First, they argue, it limits the sorts of claims that can be made, for not all social reform goals can be plausibly presented in the name of constitutional rights. For example, there are no constitutional rights to decent housing, adequate levels of welfare, or clean air, while there are constitutional rights to minimal governmental interference in the use of one's property. This may mean that "practi-

cally significant but legally irrelevant policy matters may remain beyond the purview of the court.". . . Further, . . . "the legal forms we use set limits on what we can imagine as practical outcomes." Thus, the nature of rights in the U.S. legal system, embedded in the Constitution, may constrain the courts in producing significant social reform by preventing them from hearing many claims.

A second consequence from the Constrained Court perspective is that, even where claims can be made, social reformers must often argue for the establishment of a new right, or the extension of a generally accepted right to a new situation. In welfare rights litigation, for example, the Court was asked to find a constitutional right to welfare. This need to push the courts to read the Constitution in an expansive or "liberal" way creates two main difficulties. Underlying these difficulties is judicial awareness of the need for predictability in the law and the politically exposed nature of judges whose decisions go beyond the positions of electorally accountable officials. First, the Constitution, lawyers, judges, and legal academics form a dominant legal culture that at any given time accepts some rights and not others and sets limits on the interpretation and expansion of rights. Judicial discretion is bound by the beliefs and norms of this legal culture, and decisions that stray too far from them are likely to be reversed and severely criticized. Put simply, courts, and the judges that compose them, even if sympathetic to social reform plaintiffs, may be unwilling to risk crossing this nebulous yet real boundary. Second, and perhaps more important, is the role of precedent. . . . Constrained by precedent and the beliefs of the dominant legal culture, judges, the Constrained Court view asserts, are not likely to act as crusaders.

Third, supporters of the Constrained Court view note . . . that to claim a right in court is to accept the procedures and obligations of the legal system. These procedures are designed, in part, to make it difficult for courts to hear certain kinds of cases. As the Council for Public Interest Law (CPIL) puts it, doctrines of standing and of class actions, the so-called political question doctrine, the need to have a live controversy, and other technical doctrines can "deter courts from deciding cases on the merits" and can result in social reform groups being unable to present their best arguments, or even have their day in court. Once in court, however, the legal process tends to dissipate significant social reform by making appropriate remedies unlikely. This can occur . . . because policy-based litigation aimed at significant social reform is usually "disaggregate[d]. . . into discrete conflicts among limited actors over specific individual entitlements." Remedial decrees, it has been noted, "must not confuse what is socially or judicially desirable with what is legally required." Thus, litigation seldom deals with "underlying issues and problems" and is "directed more toward symptoms than causes."

Finally, it has long been argued that framing issues in legally sound ways robs them of "political and purposive appeal." In the narrow sense, the technical nature of legal argument can denude issues of emotional, widespread appeal. More broadly, there is the danger that litigation by the few will replace political action by the many and reduce the democratic nature of the American polity. James Bradley Thayer, writing in 1901, was concerned that reliance on litigation would sap the democratic process of its vitality. He warned that the "tendency of a common and easy resort" to the courts, especially in asking them to invalidate acts of the democratically accountable branches, would "dwarf the political capacity of the people." This view was echoed more recently by [Michael] McCann, who found that litigation-prone activists' "legal rights approach to expanding democracy has significantly narrowed their conception of political action itself." Expanding the point, McCann argued that "legal tactics not only absorb scarce resources that could be used for popular mobilization . . .[but also] make it difficult to develop broadly based, multi-issue grassroots associations of sustained citizen allegiance." For these reasons, the Constrained Court view suggests that the nature of rights in the U.S. constrains courts from being effective producers of significant social reform. Thus,

> Constraint I: The bounded nature of constitutional rights prevents courts from hearing or effectively acting on many significant social reform claims, and lessens the chances of popular mobilization.

Limits on Judicial Independence— The Institutional Factor

. . . [R]eformers have often turned to courts when opposition to significant social reform in the other branches has prevented them from acting. Thus, much significant social reform litigation takes place in the context of stalemate within, or opposition from, the other branches. For courts to be effective in such situations, they must, logically, be independent of those other branches. Supporters of the Constrained Court view point to a broad array of evidence that suggests the founders did not thoroughly insulate courts or provide them with unfailing independence.

To start, the appointment process, of course, limits judicial independence. Judges do not select themselves. Rather, they are chosen by politicians, the president and the Senate at the federal level. Presidents, while not clairvoyant, tend to nominate judges who they think will represent their judicial philosophies. Clearly, changing court personnel can bring court decisions into line with prevailing political opinion (and dampen support for significant social reform). Thus, the Constrained Court perspective sees the appointment process as limiting judicial independence.

Judicial independence requires that court decisions, in comparison to legislation, do not invariably reflect public opinion. Supporters of the Constrained Court view note, however, that Supreme Court decisions, historically, have seldom strayed far from what was politically acceptable. Rather than suggesting independence, this judicial unwillingness to often blaze its own trail perhaps suggests, in the words of Finley Peter Dunne's Mr. Dooley, that "th' supreme coort follows th' iliction returns."

In at least two important ways, the Constrained Court view suggests, Congress may constrain court actions. First, in the statutory area, Congress can override decisions, telling the courts they misinterpreted the intent of the law. That is, Congress may rewrite a provision to meet court objections or simply state more clearly what it meant so that the courts' reading of the law is repudiated. Second, although Congress cannot directly reverse decisions based on constitutional interpretations, presumably untouchable by the democratic process, it may be able to constrain them by threatening certain changes in the legal structure. A large part of the reason, of course, is the appointment process. But even without the power of appointment, the Court may be susceptible to credible threats against it. Historical review of the relations of the Court to the other branches of the federal government suggests that the Court cannot for long stand alone against such pressure. From the "Court-packing" plan of FDR to recent bills proposing to remove federal court jurisdiction over certain issues, court-curbing proposals may allow Congress to constrain courts as producers of significant social reform.

American courts, proponents of the Constrained Court view claim, are particularly deferential to the positions of the federal government. On the Supreme Court level, the solicitor general is accorded a special role. The office has unusual access to the Court and is often asked by the Court to intervene in cases and present the government's position. When the solicitor general petitions the Court to enter a case, the Court almost invariably grants the request, regardless of the position of the parties. The government is also unusually successful in convincing the Court to hear cases it appeals and to not hear those it opposes. . . .

That does not comport with notions of independence and a judicial system able to defy legislative and political majorities. Thus, the Constrained Court view's adherents believe,

> Constraint II: The judiciary lacks the necessary independence from the other branches of the government to produce significant social reform.

Implementation and Institutional Relations

For courts, or any other institution, to effectively produce significant social reform, they must have the ability to develop appropriate policies and the power to implement them. This, in turn, requires a host of tools that courts, according to proponents of the Constrained Court view, lack. In particular, successful implementation requires enforcement powers. Court decisions, requiring people to act, are not self-executing. But as Hamilton pointed out two centuries ago in *The Federalist Papers* (1787–88), courts lack such powers. Indeed, it is for this reason more than any other that Hamilton emphasized the courts' character as the least dangerous branch. Assuaging fears that the federal courts would be a political threat, Hamilton argued in *Federalist 78* that the judiciary "has no influence over either the sword or the purse; no direction either of the strength or of the wealth of the society; and can take no active resolution whatever. It may truly be

said to have neither FORCE nor WILL, but merely judgment; and must ultimately depend upon the aid of the executive arm even for the efficacy of its judgments." Unlike Congress and the executive branch, Hamilton argued, the federal courts were utterly dependent on the support of the other branches and elite actors. In other words, for Court orders to be carried out, political elites, electorally accountable, must support them and act to implement them. Proponents of the Constrained Court view point to historical recognition of this structural "fact" of American political life by early Chief Justices John Jay and John Marshall, both of whom were acutely aware of the Court's limits. President Jackson recognized these limits, too, when he reputedly remarked about a decision with which he did not agree, "John Marshall has made his decision, now let him enforce it." More recently, the unwillingness of state authorities to follow court orders, and the need to send federal troops to Little Rock, Arkansas, to carry them out, makes the same point. Without elite support (the federal government in this case), the Court's orders would have been frustrated. While it is clear that courts can stymie change, though ultimately not prevent it, the Constitution, in the eyes of the Constrained Court view, appears to leave the courts few tools to ensure that their decisions are carried out. . . .

This constraint may be particularly powerful with issues of significant social reform. It is likely that as courts deal with issues involving contested values, as issues of significant social reform do almost by definition, they will generate opposition. In turn, opposition may induce a withdrawal of the elite and public support crucial for implementation. Thus, proponents of the Constrained Court view suggest that the contested nature of issues of significant social reform makes it unlikely that the popular support necessary for implementation will be forthcoming.

A second claim made by proponents of the Constrained Court view about courts effectively implementing decisions is that the legal system is a particular type of bureaucracy that has few of the advantages and many of the disadvantages of the ideal Weberian type. For example, important components of the Weberian bureaucracy include a hierarchical command structure, a clear agenda, little or no discretion at lower levels, stated procedures, job protection, positions filled strictly by merit, area specialization, and the ability to initiate action and follow-up. While on the surface the U.S. judicial system is hierarchical, has stated procedures, and provides job protection, closer examination under a Constrained Court microscope complicates the picture. For example, although orders are handed down from higher courts to lower ones, there is a great deal of discretion at the lower levels. Decisions announced at the appellate level may not be implemented by lower-court judges who disagree with them or who simply misunderstand them. Similarly, procedures designed to prevent arbitrary action may be used for evasion and delay. Further, unlike the ideal bureaucratic type, courts lack a clear agenda and any degree of specialization. Rather, judges and clerks go from case to case in highly disparate fields. This means that area expertise and planning, often crucial in issues involving significant social reform, are seldom present, making it uncertain that the remedy will be appropriate to the problem. . . .

Through the eyes of the Constrained Court view, the decentralized nature of the judicial system may constrain courts from producing significant social reform for several reasons. In a nutshell, the structure of courts opens the possibility for bias and misinterpretation to influence lower-court decisions. Further, the entrepreneurial nature of many lawyers makes it difficult for groups seeking significant social reform through the courts to present a coherent strategy. And the nature of the legal bureaucracy makes delay endemic. These claims merit brief attention.

The American judicial system vests considerable discretion in lower-court judges. Only rarely do appellate courts issue final orders. In almost all cases, they remand to the trial court for issuance of the final order. This leaves lower-court judges with a great deal of discretion. The objective judge will conscientiously attempt to follow the higher court's orders. However, misinterpretation of those orders, especially if they are vague, is possible. Further, the biased judge has a myriad of tools with which to abuse discretion. These include the "delay endemic to legal proceedings," narrow interpretation, and purposeful misinterpretation. In this kind of case, litigants must follow procedure and re-appeal the case to the higher court for help, further delaying change.

This structural aspect of the American judicial system, those in the Constrained Court camp argue, may pose a particular problem for litigants seeking significant social reform. Bias and misinterpretation aside, it may be difficult for groups seeking reform to present a coherent strategy. Access to the legal system can be gained in any one of hundreds of courts (in the federal system) by any one of hundreds of thousands of lawyers. In particular, . . . interest groups planning a litigation strategy may find themselves faced with a host of cases not of their doing or to their liking. There is no way to prevent other lawyers, individuals, and groups from filing cases. And if these cases are not well-chosen and well-argued, they may result in decisions that wreak havoc with the best-laid plans. Thus, groups are sometimes on the defensive, forced to disassociate themselves from the legal arguments of purported allies and sometimes even to oppose them.

Although in practice federal judges have life tenure, this does not mean they are free from constraints. In asking for significant social reform, litigants are asking judges to reform existing institutions. However, judges may be unwilling to take on this essentially non-judicial task. To the extent that lower-court judges are part of a given community, ordering massive change in their community may isolate them and threaten the respect of the court. Also, the judicial selection process for lower federal court judges is designed to select people who reflect the mores and beliefs of the community in which the court sits. Therefore, adherents to the Constrained Court view argue, it is unlikely that lower-court judges will be predisposed to support significant social reform if the community opposes it. . . .

A further obstacle for court effectiveness, assert believers in the Constrained Court view, is that significant social reform often requires large expenditures. Judges, in general prohibited from actively politicking and cutting deals, are not in a particularly powerful position to successfully order the other branches to expend additional funds. . . .

. . . Courts, it can be argued, are not structured to produce significant social reform. Thus, proponents of the Constrained Court view propose,

Constraint III: Courts lack the tools to readily develop appropriate policies and implement decisions ordering significant social reform.

To sum up, the Constrained Court view holds that litigants asking courts for significant social reform are faced with powerful constraints. First, they must convince courts that the rights they are asserting are required by constitutional or statutory language. Given the limited nature of constitutional rights, the constraints of legal culture, and the general caution of the judiciary, this is no easy task. Second, courts are wary of stepping too far out of the political mainstream. Deferential to the federal government and potentially limited by congressional action, courts may be unwilling to take the heat generated by politically unpopular rulings. Third, if these two constraints are overcome and cases are decided favorably, litigants are faced with the task of implementing the decisions. Lacking powerful tools to force implementation, court decisions are often rendered useless given much opposition. Even if litigators seeking significant social reform win major victories in court, in implementation they often turn out to be worth very little. Borrowing the words of Justice Jackson from another context, the Constrained Court view holds that court litigation to produce significant social reform may amount to little more than "a teasing illusion like a munificent bequest in a pauper's will."

Court Effectiveness: The Logic of the Dynamic Court View

The three constraints just presented are generated from the view of courts as unable to produce significant social reform. That view appears historically grounded and empirically plausible. Yet, on reflection, it has two main difficulties. First, it seems to overstate the limits on courts. After all, since the mid-twentieth century or so courts have been embroiled in controversies over significant social reform. Many lawyers, activists, and scholars have acted or written with the belief that the constraints are weak or non-existent and can easily be overcome. Indeed, the whole modern debate over judicial activism makes no sense if the Constrained Court view is correct. If courts are as impotent as the constraints suggest, then why has there been such political, academic, and judicial concern with the role of courts in modern America? Theory

and practice are unaligned if the Constrained Court view is entirely correct. Second, examined carefully, its claim is that courts are *unlikely* to produce significant social reform; it does not deny the possibility. However, that doesn't help us understand when, and under what conditions, courts can produce significant social reform. The Constrained Court view is not the complete answer.

The Dynamic Court view may help. It maintains that courts can be effective producers of significant social reform. Its basic thrust is that not only are courts not as limited as the Constrained Court view suggests, but also, in some cases, they can be more effective than other governmental institutions in producing significant social reform. As Aryeh Neier puts it, "[s]ince the early 1950s, the courts have been the most accessible and, often, the most effective instrument of government for bringing about the changes in public policy sought by social protest movements." The constraints of the Constrained Court view, then, may oversimplify reality.

Political, Institutional, and Economic Independence

Proponents of the Dynamic Court view argue that the Constrained Court view entirely misses key advantages of courts. At the most fundamental level, key to the Dynamic Court view is the belief that courts are free from electoral constraints and institutional arrangements that stymie change. Uniquely situated, courts have the capacity to act where other institutions are politically unwilling or structurally unable to proceed. For example, one of the great strengths of courts is the ability to act in the face of public opposition. Elected and appointed officials, fearful of political repercussions, are seldom willing to fight for unpopular causes and protect the rights of disliked minorities. Courts, free of such electoral accountability, are not so constrained. From civil rights to women's rights, from protecting the rights of the physically and mentally challenged to ensuring that criminal defendants are treated constitutionally, the courts have acted where other institutions have refused. . . .

The ability of courts to act is particularly clear with issues of significant social reform. With such issues, entrenched interests often have the institutional base to prevent change in other political bodies. In civil rights in the 1950s, for example, . . . the key position of Southern Democrats in Congress virtually ensured that no civil rights legislation would be forthcoming. If change was to come, proponents of the Dynamic Court view argue, it could come only from the courts. Similarly, examining school desegregation in the years 1968–72, [Jennifer] Hochschild argues that "were it not for the courts, there would be little reduction in racial isolation [in the public schools]." And with reapportionment, legislators from malapportioned districts had no incentive to reform the electoral system and vote themselves out of office, until the courts acted. In other words, the Dynamic Court view proposes that courts are free from the obstacles that lead to "a partial failure of executive or legislative government institutions to do their jobs in a satisfactory and legal way."

A similar argument applies to bureaucratic and institutional change. Proponents of the Dynamic Court view suggest that insulation, institutional inertia stemming from routinized procedures, and group pressure make it difficult for non-judicial institutions to reform themselves. Looking at "entrenched bureaucracies," environmental lawyer Victor Yannacone saw "self-perpetuating, self-sufficient, self-serving bureaus [which] are power sources unto themselves, effectively insulated from the people and responsible to no one but themselves." Where there is little incentive to change, it is only an outside force such as a court, uninvolved in daily operations, that may have the will to force change. Organizations contemplating reform also must confront the desires of their constituencies. "In the face of pressures from many diverse constituencies and interests," [another researcher] writes, "it is unlikely that even public institutions headed by cooperative administrators will reform themselves without the outside coercive force of the court providing the impetus for specific change." Courts simply do not face such pressures. Court decisions will not adversely affect the court's ongoing relations with elected officials, interest groups, financial backers, and the like, whose cooperation is essential for getting work done, for the simple reason that courts are not structured to need or maintain such ongoing relations. Courts do not depend on carefully worked out institutional arrangements because they do not specialize in any one area. Unlike bureaucracies and large institutions, the parties they deal with vary from case to case. Here, too, courts are uniquely situated.

The "inadequacy" of the political process is an essential basis for the Dynamic Court view because "policy formulation in our society is too often a one-sided affair—a process in which only the voices of the economically or politically powerful are heard." In the legislative and executive branches, not all affected interests are heard and not all voices carry the same weight. The predictable result of this systematic exclusion of the "public" is that "government agencies cannot adequately represent all facets of the public interest." However, courts, it is contended, can rectify this exclusion because, "unlike the hierarchical statist view of entrenched elite rule, the judicial view guarantees the independence of citizen groups contending for influence within the adversary process." Neither access nor influence depends on connections or position. Access to all affected interests is guaranteed by judicial rules, and influence depends on strength of argument, not political position. . . . The judiciary, with "no corrupting links to anyone," affords "equality of both access and influence to citizens" more "completely" than any "other institutional form." And this means that it is able to respond to social reform claims of ordinary citizens where other institutions are not. . . .

The underlying claim here of the Dynamic Court view is that access and influence are not dependent on economic and political resources. The kind of professional lobbying that is required to be effective in influencing bureaucracies or enacting legislation is not necessary for winning court cases. Groups lacking key resources can use courts not only directly to change the law but also to strengthen their voices within the other branches of government and authoritatively present their positions. Thus, proponents of the Dynamic Court view claim, courts offer the best hope to poor, powerless, and unorganized groups, those most often seeking significant social reform.

The judicial process may also provide a powerful forum for gathering and assessing information. In contrast to legislative and bureaucratic proceedings, wide participation in legal proceedings makes it likely that the full range of relevant information will be brought to bear on the final decree. Where crucial information is being withheld, or is hard to obtain, the judicial process of discovery, supported by the coercive powers of the court, may help bring it to light. Further, the adversarial process ensures that information will be rigorously assessed before it takes the status of "fact.". . .

Influence accompanies access in legal proceedings because judges must respond to legal arguments and provide reasons for their opinions. Unlike in other institutions, arguments cannot be ignored or dismissed without discussion. Judges, in contrast to elected or other appointed officials, cannot easily duck the tough issues. Further, judges are limited by the Constitution, statutes, and precedent in the kind of responses they can make. A judge's dislike or disapproval of actions provides insufficient grounds to support a legal decision. This means, of course, that the positions of unpopular and politically weak groups, denied access to and influence with administrative, executive, and legislative branches, must be taken seriously by the courts.

To sum up, proponents of the Dynamic Court view assert that courts have the ability to act when other institutions won't, because judges are electorally unaccountable and serve with life tenure. Unencumbered by electoral commitments and political deal-making, and protected from recrimination, they can act to fulfill the constitutional mandate. Thus, as [Owen] Fiss puts it, courts can produce significant social reform because the judicial office is "structured by both ideological and institutional factors that enable and perhaps even force the judge to be objective—not to express his preferences or personal beliefs, or those of the citizenry, as to what is right or just, but constantly to strive for the true meaning of the constitutional value." Courts, then, can provide an escape from the pathologies of rigid bureaucracies, ossified institutions, and a reluctant or biased citizenry.

Courts as Catalysts—Indirect Effects of the Dynamic Court

In striving for the "true meaning of the constitutional value," courts base decisions on principle. Unlike legislatures or executives, courts do not act out of calculations of partisan preference. This means, proponents of the Dynamic Court view suggest, that courts can point the way to doing what is "right." They can remind Americans of our highest aspirations and chide us for our failings. Courts, [Alexander] Bickel suggests, have the "ca-

pacity to appeal to men's better natures, to call forth their aspirations, which may have been forgotten in the moment's hue and cry." For [Eugene] Rostow, the "Supreme Court is, among other things, an educational body, and the Justices are inevitably teachers in a vital national seminar." Bickel agrees, viewing courts as "a great and highly effective educational institution." In the Dynamic Court view, the courts have important indirect effects, educating Americans and heightening their understanding of their constitutional duty.

Court decisions also have indirect effects, proponents of the Dynamic Court view suggest, through dramatizing issues and spurring action. Courts can provide publicity for issues and serve as a "catalyst" for change. Where the public is ignorant of certain conditions, and political elites do not want to deal with them, court decisions can "politicize issues that otherwise might have remained unattended." This may put public pressure on elites to act. Indeed, litigation may "often" be "the best method of attracting public attention to institutional conditions and of publicly documenting abuses." By bringing conditions to light, and showing how far from constitutional or statutory aspirations practice has fallen, court cases can provide a "cheap method of pricking powerful consciences." Thus, litigation "serves as a catalyst, not a usurper, of the legislative process." This ability to dramatize may be particularly effective with custodial institutions such as hospitals, prisons, and mental institutions where court cases have brought inhumane conditions to light.

In addition, court action may invigorate and encourage groups to mobilize and take political action. In both civil rights and women's rights, for example, the federal courts are often seen as having served this role.

Thus, proponents of the Dynamic Court view assert that judicial decisions have important extra-judicial effects. . . .

Evolving Procedures

Much of the Constrained Court view's plausibility comes from Constraint III, the courts' supposed lack of implementation powers. Contrary to this view, however, proponents of the Dynamic Court view assert that not only are courts in a unique position to act, but they also have the "demonstrated ability to evolve new mechanisms and procedures" to cope with the complexities of significant social reform litigation. . . .

Other changes, it is suggested, that have allowed courts to overcome the obstacles suggested by the Constrained Court view include the court's retention of jurisdiction, the creation of monitoring commissions, and the active engagement of the judge. These steps are designed to allow the court to closely follow the implementation process. If court decrees are not being implemented, or if unforeseen circumstances render parts of decrees inappropriate, these mechanisms allow for speedy correction. For example, if judges retain jurisdiction, then any of the parties can immediately return to court if the decree is not being implemented or if changing circumstances require its modification. Similarly, monitoring commissions can inform the judge of implementation progress and alert the court to the need for further action. And, of course, the mere availability of these tools can influence the behavior of the parties. With these kind of tools

readily at hand, possibly recalcitrant parties may think twice before violating remedial decrees. Even with the uncertainties of institutional reform litigation, courts can create effective tools. . . .

The Dynamic Court view provides a powerful alternative to the view of courts as the "least dangerous branch." Pointing to pathologies in the other branches, it places courts in a unique position to act. Acknowledging, perhaps, that the Constrained Court view was accurate at the Founding and for part of American history, it maintains that great change has occurred over the last few decades and that courts now have the tools to effectively produce significant social reform. Unlike the Constrained Court view, it is congruent with judicial activism and the modern use of the courts to produce significant social reform. While courts cannot solve all problems, the Dynamic Court view does see them as powerful and effective, unconstrained by the concentrations of power and bureaucratic inertia that stymie self-initiated change in the other branches. . . .

A View from the Inside

11.5 Benched: The Pros and Cons of Having Judges Make the Law (2000)

Peter H. Schuck

Impact litigation—lawsuits that seek to use the courts to effect widespread social changes—enjoys a very good press. Impact litigation is a weapon brandished primarily by groups on the political left, as in the cases against Big Tobacco and the gun manufacturers. But even conservatives applaud it when their groups are doing the suing, as in challenges to affirmative action programs or environmental regulations.

Reprinted by permission. The full version was published in the *Washington Monthly,* and was updated in Peter H. Schuck, *Meditations of a Militant Moderate: Cool Views on Hot Topics* (Rowman and Littlefield, 2005).

We need to understand why impact litigation has come to play so central a role in our public life, and also why Americans of all ideological stripes should be wary of it. Reformers, I believe, expect too much from impact litigation, and even its critics often aim at the wrong target. Like war, impact litigation is a continuation of politics by other means, and like war it sometimes accomplishes good things. In the end, however, two practical and closely related concerns provide the strongest grounds for skepticism. First, judges' tools and capacities are not equal to the task, and, second, their well-intentioned rulings tend to aggravate the problems they seek to solve and often create new ones.

Two icons of impact litigation are *Brown v. Board of Education,* the 1954 school desegregation decision, and *Roe v. Wade,* the controversial abortion rights decision. Both were carefully designed by advocacy groups to bring an important constitutional issue before the courts that the groups felt the politicians were ignoring or mishandling. Sometimes impact cases are brought as class actions (as in *Brown*), sometimes as individual claims with broad social ramifications (as in *Roe*). Most impact cases seek a judicial order mandating that the defendant do, or refrain from doing, certain things . . . and rely on the U.S. Constitution. Many, however, seek money damages and invoke state law—for example, challenges to exclusionary zoning and property-tax-based school finance systems.

What Is Impact Litigation's Appeal?

The mother of all impact litigation, of course, was *Brown.* The NAACP lawyers, led by Thurgood Marshall, launched a long, carefully orchestrated campaign to gain a court order invalidating segregation in the public schools. The ruling's logic encompassed all forms of state-supported discrimination against racial minorities, not just schools. Subsequent decisions enforced this ruling in many ways—by limiting freedom-of-choice plans, by requiring busing, by equalizing expenditures, and so forth—and the political branches and the states fell into line. Many post-*Brown* impact cases—for example, those asserting the rights of women, gays, illegitimates, prisoners, the disabled, the mentally ill and retarded, and undocumented immigrant children—have been squarely based on it. Today, almost 50 years later, only a few hard-line conservatives are willing to say that *Brown* was wrongly decided. The decision is widely hailed as the Warren Court's greatest, most unexceptionable legacy to American social justice, and many aspiring causes have sought to wrap themselves in *Brown*'s mantle.

The appeal of impact litigation, however, goes well beyond *Brown*'s reflected glory. The often stirring social drama it presents lies not simply in the clash of lofty ideals, competing interests, warring parties, and jousting lawyers. Impact cases also enact cherished American myths that ordinary politics often seems to mock: the little guy against the big system, the right to a day in court, principle's triumph over expediency, the taming of corporate power, the disciplining of rogue or heartless bureaucracies, and the possibility of fundamental and structural social change.

Courts, law firms, the American Bar Association, law schools, and the rest of the legal establishment tend to boost impact litigation. It not only generates more high-profile activity and fees for lawyers but also projects an idealized and idealistic image of the profession. Most people view representing the rights of minorities, the downtrodden, and the voiceless (if they are not criminal defendants) as more admirable than the more mundane, common activities of trolling for paying clients and litigating commercial disputes. Lawyers see impact litigation in much the same way athletes see the Olympics—a vivid showcase for their talents and proof of both their social importance and their selfless endeavors. . . .

. . . Indeed, impact litigation can achieve some goals even when the legal merits are weak. Consider the flurry of governmental lawsuits against gun manufacturers. To most legal experts these cases are non-starters; most judges will not even submit them to a jury because, among other things, the governmental plaintiffs, unlike shooting victims, have not suffered the kind of direct harm that courts require. These cases, however, are better understood less as solid legal claims than as political ploys—intended to spotlight issues and to embarrass and pressure the industry into adopting safer designs and marketing practices that the government either cannot or will not mandate itself. . . .

[Lawsuits] against tobacco [companies] show two things: Legal rules can hobble a case even when the facts seem compelling, and lawsuits need not prevail in order to be politically effective. Consider the tobacco litigation. Even though smoking can cause cancer and even though the industry may have misled regulators and smokers, those facts alone would not suffice to win the case. A government would also have to prove that, like smokers, it was a direct victim of this deception and suffered direct financial harm as a result—a particularly daunting task given that governments may actually have gained a net financial benefit from smoking due to their vast tax revenues from the sale of tobacco products and their reduced pension liabilities from premature smoking-related deaths. The legal claims of individual smoker-plaintiffs, who do not face these problems, are not much stronger. For decades, smokers lost all suits against the tobacco industry because juries penalized them for their choices to smoke, while the courts found the mandated cigarette warnings legally sufficient to put the onus back on the plaintiffs. These "free-will" defenses will probably grow stronger over time unless juries accept smokers' claims that the companies addicted them as minors. Smokers did manage to overcome these defenses in two recent cases in Florida and California, a rare event. These victories, however, may not stand up on appeal—especially in Florida where the smokers brought a class action, which most courts reject in such cases.

Even so, tobacco litigation documents have already succeeded in demonizing the industry, affecting its stock prices and future prospects, and transforming the political landscape. The gun litigation, targeting a much weaker industry, may ultimately do the same. Much of the public, not to mention public-health agencies, favors these outcomes, and it seems beside the point, even churlish, to note how weak the plaintiffs' legal positions are. Impact litigation of this kind seems to vindicate the ironist's axiom that nothing succeeds like failure.

So What's the Problem?

If even legally weak impact litigation helps to make powerful social actors more accountable, reinforces the rule and prestige of law, and produces both educational and entertainment value, what is the problem? Where one stands on this question depends to some extent on where one sits politically. The left tends to favor suits against cigarettes, guns, prison systems, and welfare agencies while the right rallies behind legal challenges to environmental regulation, mandatory school busing, and restrictions on school prayer and abortion. Sometimes even those who claim to oppose impact litigation on principle buy into it, as when conservatives support a balanced-budget amendment to the Constitution that would move the most technical, highly-politicized fiscal issues into the courts. . . .

. . . [C]ritiques often heard in law school classrooms, courtrooms, and legislative chambers go to the legitimacy and institutional competence of judges to decide institutional reform cases. The legitimacy critique notes that the United States is organized constitutionally around separation of powers and majority rule. In such a polity lawmaking power must be lodged in representative and democratically accountable institutions. Thus the courts, being neither, may not legitimately exercise such lawmaking power and will erode their stock of legitimacy if they seek to do so. By contrast, the institutional competence critique argues that quite apart from any illegitimacy, the courts are poorly equipped to make law because of their training, access to information, the constraints of the adversary process, the limited efficacy of judicial remedies, and other inherent institutional attributes.

Judicial Legitimacy

Although the legitimacy critique lends itself to rhetorical flourish, it is far from clear what judicial legitimacy means. I define it as a sense that one is morally obliged to obey a judicial decision because it is law even if one strongly opposes it. A decision that fails to elicit this kind of moral response—or worse, elicits moral revulsion or rebellion—is illegitimate. One may treat a decision as legitimate out of ignorance, indifference, or habitual deference to authority, not just out of a considered moral duty. By the same token, viewing a decision as illegitimate does not necessarily spur one to any particular kind of action.

Consider *Roe v. Wade,* a notorious impact case that many thoughtful Americans denounce as illegitimate and a small number even confront with violence. Even so, the vast majority, including many who oppose it as wrongly decided or bad public policy, still treat it as law and obey it accordingly. Is *Roe* an illegitimate decision? The answer seems to depend on how many people view it not merely as bad law but as usurpation (a distinction not made in public opinion surveys) and how willing they are to act on that conviction.

The legitimacy critique also oversimplifies the nature of our law and politics. As every law student knows, the distinction between interpreting law and making it is a fuzzy one, especially when (as in much impact litigation) the judge must interpret open-ended phrases like "equal protection" and "due process of law." American politics is a remarkably fluid mixture of principle, discretion, pragmatism, competition, and raw power. Legislators who wish to curb "runaway judges" have many levers that, for sound political or other reasons, they often decline to use. By the same token, judges who decide "political" questions (as they often cannot avoid doing in our system) must expect harsh criticism or even reprisals (within constitutional bounds) intended to hold them politically accountable.

The legitimacy critique is also replete with interesting but unintended ironies. First, public esteem for the courts has been remarkably stable (and relative to other government institutions, remarkably high) over a long period during which impact litigation came of age and judicial activism (another ill-defined but rhetorically robust notion) both waxed and waned. Changes in the kinds of cases that the courts hear and how they decide them seem to have little effect on perceived legitimacy.

A second irony is even more striking. The Supreme Court's most controversial decisions rested on constitutional arguments that many commentators rejected at the time, *Brown* included. In each case, friendly critics strongly warned the Court not to enter what Justice Felix Frankfurter (in one of these cases) called a "political thicket." He was referring to social reform issues disguised as lawsuits, and he thought that courts could not adjudicate such policy disputes and still preserve their legitimacy. Yet these very reform projects— school desegregation, control of police misconduct, legislative reapportionment, limitations of presidential prerogatives, abolition of school prayer, and regulation of abortion, to name just a few—have in fact burnished the Court's public prestige. For different reasons, these cases have helped the Court to prevail at the "bar of politics" (in the phrase of the great constitutional scholar Alexander Bickel), and its political success has buoyed the prestige of lower courts as well.

A final irony: the Court's secure stock of legitimacy from these earlier battles has encouraged attacks on it. Now that we possess the advantages of living in a society in which Jim Crow is dead, legislatures must reapportion themselves, police must warn suspects of their rights, religious groups cannot directly receive government subsidies, and abortions are widely available to women who do

not wish to bear children, it is seductively easy to complain that the Court should have left these issues to the politicians, that it went too far, or that (as political scientist Gerald Rosenberg has argued) these important social gains would have occurred anyway had the courts not entered the fray. With these gains firmly entrenched—thanks in part to the Court—we can criticize it now for what it did then without any risk of losing the gains if we err in our counterfactual judgments. Because we can never know if we erred, we can never be refuted.

Institutional Competence

If the legitimacy critique is overblown, the institutional competence critique is insufficiently appreciated. Impact litigation maximizes the gap between a court's functional disabilities and the demands placed on its capacities. Although these disabilities are numerous, many of the most important can be reduced to three—information, incentives, and rights—which have bedeviled impact cases initially considered stunning victories for reform.

In our adversary system, a judge must base her decision almost exclusively on admissible evidence proffered by the lawyers and measured against the law. Her task is to resolve specific disputes, not solve social problems. The information she needs is usually quite limited in scope, historical in nature, of a familiar kind, and accessible through conventional evidence. Yet, most institutional reform cases seek to change social structures, practices, and values, that are created by a vast number of individuals interacting in intricate, opaque ways with incomplete information. Reforming an urban police department or school system is an exceedingly complex kind of problem in which a change in one relationship or factor will trigger hard-to-predict ripple effects elsewhere in the system, effects that judges cannot anticipate and usually lack authority to control. This is especially true where powerful contrary incentives motivate and constrain the institutions and individuals the court seeks to reform. Impact litigation to mandate low-income housing, for example, has foundered on market interests (not to mention bureaucratic and political ones) that neutralize and distort the courts' rulings and sometimes make shortages even worse.

A conscientious judge, working alone with only a generalist's training, must analyze problems like these in all of their technical detail, diagnose them, and fashion solutions that will be effective—not only here and now but over time, and in contexts quite different from the often atypical ones that the lawyers select for their test cases. The judge receives her information from partisan advocates and their hired experts. Within broad ethical limits, each side works to provide incomplete and one-sided (if not misleading) information, depicting both problems and solutions as far simpler than they really are. Unlike a legislature, a judge has very few tools for shaping the behavior of the numerous actors who must be induced to comply with her solution.

Indeed, a judge wields only two tools, both of them coercive: She can issue an injunction and then punish violators, and she can order wrongdoers to pay money. These tools, although ostensibly strong, are in reality pathetically weak; they affect only a narrow band on the broad spectrum of human motivation—and only the litigants at that. In contrast, legislatures and agencies can coerce everyone in society. More important, they can gain compliance through a variety of more flexible and positive inducements such as subsidies, bargaining, coalition building, information, public education, insurance, bureaucracies, and many more. The *Brown* decision alone produced little school desegregation until more than a decade later when Congress passed a statute providing federal agencies with a variety of fiscal and administrative sanctions to implement it. (Whether the desegregation that was ultimately achieved actually improved black children's education is a complex question that is hotly debated everywhere, including in black communities.)

Impact litigation seeks a judicial declaration of new legal rights. But although rights are among the most precious of human endowments, they are crude instruments for accomplishing most of what a complex society attempts to do collectively. A right is binary; one either has it or one doesn't. In contrast, sound social policy is a matter of finding the right point along a continuum; it is a matter of degree, of more or less, and of striking a nuanced balance. Once rights are recognized, they are diffi-

cult to change, whereas effective policy demands constant flexible adjustment in light of changing conditions. Rights are costly to define, defend, and challenge, yet policy needs to minimize the social costs of getting things done. Rights magnify the role of judges and lawyers but successful policy largely depends on non-legal institutions and competencies.

Under these conditions, one would expect judicial solutions to the kinds of problems that impact litigation takes on to be misconceived, impractical, or even perverse—and they often are. Consider *Brown*, the paradigm of successful impact litigation. Although desegregation has helped to achieve a more balanced racial mix in some school districts, in many communities, public schools—especially those in the largest cities outside the South—remain at least as racially segregated as they were before *Brown*, though no longer by force of law. . . .

Occasionally Good News

The story of impact litigation, of course, is by no means a uniformly bleak one. The civil rights revolution, a precondition for social justice, would not have occurred when it did without some judicial prodding and protection. School busing has worked better in smaller communities than in large metropolitan areas. The courts forced some prison and community mental health systems to be far more humane and eliminated their worst abuses. By most accounts (though not all), court-driven reapportionment has been a valuable and enduring reform. . . .

Even when impact litigation fails to gain its explicit ends through the courts, moreover, it can ease gridlock and invigorate social processes that produce desirable changes. Litigation against the tobacco industry, although unsuccessful in legal terms, unearthed documents that have galvanized anti-smoking efforts. Similarly, gun litigation has improved the prospects for sensible regulatory controls and new technological fixes. Death penalty litigation has focused public attention on previously obscure patterns of enforcement that profoundly trouble even capital punishment advocates; as a result, the public debate is taking a new turn. . . .

History Lessons

The history of impact litigation suggests some recurrent features. First, these and other examples suggest that impact litigation is likely to be most effective in seizing media and public attention at least momentarily, moving certain issues higher on the policy agenda, turning up evidence of abuses that policymakers have not pursued, and casting a lurid but revealing spotlight on corners of social life that the rest of us might otherwise ignore. Whether such litigation can frame workable, flexible, and politically sustainable remedies to complex problems, however, is far more doubtful.

Second, it is difficult to trace the actual effect of a case beyond the court decision (or settlement) itself. After all, the same forces that propel a case onto a court's docket also operate in other social domains where those forces might have produced the change anyway. (One can always say this, of course, but that does not mean it is necessarily wrong.) For impact litigation enthusiasts, it is enough that the case seemed to achieve its goal or even that one cannot prove the contrary, while skeptics can point to other possible causes and to unanticipated effects. In the case of *Brown,* for example, political scientist Gerald Rosenberg argues that evolving public attitudes, civil rights protests, economic growth, and other causal factors were already in motion, and that *Brown* in itself contributed little to the changes that ensued a decade later.

Indeed, impact litigation may undermine its successes by strengthening the hands of its opponents—another recurrent feature. Although *Roe v. Wade*'s survival seems secure for the time being, the decision clearly galvanized a conservative movement that ever since has stymied liberal reforms in many policy areas far beyond abortion. Even Justice Ruth Bader Ginsburg, perhaps the leading women's rights litigator at the time of *Roe,* now believes that *Roe* derailed the movement to liberalize abortion. By generating an immediate and powerful political backlash, *Roe* prompted more restrictive state laws, reversing a strong pre-*Roe* trend toward more liberal access to abortion. Congress responded to the judicial supervision of prison systems with a law limiting the continuing court supervision of those systems.

Although we cannot clearly delineate all the impacts of a complex litigation, numerous case studies establish that a decision's consequences will almost always differ both from what the plaintiffs originally sought and from what the court envisioned. The social and educational effects of *Brown* and its progeny are warning enough that impact litigation often produces unexpected and perverse results. This is especially likely in the institutional reform line of impact cases where a court's order is directed at, and must be implemented by, large bureaucracies such as school systems and police departments whose incentives and behaviors are opaque and whose operating routines are shaped by realities on the ground that are hard to grasp, much less change. An endemic feature of such cases is that a legal success here simply creates or aggravates problems over there, much as pushing against a pillow at one point causes it to puff out elsewhere. . . .

More generally, impact litigation's fragmented first-come-first-served approach to resource allocation and policy effectively empowers unelected advocates and judges to set the public priorities that the citizenry elected officials to determine, and then to deflect criticism by saying that a disembodied law required this. In our political system, accountability is already elusive precisely because responsibility is so hard to locate. Impact litigation makes it that much easier for everyone—legislators, bureaucrats, judges, lawyers, and litigants—to disclaim it. The buck stops nowhere; impact litigation keeps it moving.

Finally, experience with impact litigation confirms the limited effectiveness of top-down legal rules in regulating complex social behavior. Much top-down law, of course, is unavoidable—criminal and tax law, for example. But reformers could often achieve their goals more effectively by relying more on other techniques such as decentralized rules (as in allocating scarce organs), rights trading (as in environmental protection), auctions (as in allocating valuable broadcast spectrum), moving public funds from providers to citizens (as with vouchers), self-regulation (as in Internet policy), and improved information (as with hospital malpractice).

These alternative forms, however, can only succeed if reformers repose less confidence in the problem-solving capacity of judges and more in that of elected politicians, bureaucrats, and the private sector—a confidence that many reformers think has not yet been earned. So long as impact litigation remains a valuable political resource—one that moves issues onto and up the public agenda, intimidates and even coopts opponents, unearths documents that gain media attention, and does all of this in the still-prestigious name of law—it will be part of the reformer's arsenal. For better and for worse, impact litigation has become an entrenched part of our rights-oriented, individualistic, legal-political culture.

11.6 *Goodridge v. Department of Public Health*
440 Mass. 309 (2003)

MARSHALL, C.J. Marriage is a vital social institution. The exclusive commitment of two individuals to each other nurtures love and mutual support; it brings stability to our society. For those who choose to marry, and for their children, marriage provides an abundance of legal, financial, and social benefits. In return it imposes weighty legal, financial, and social obligations. The question before us is whether, consistent with the Massachusetts Constitution, the Commonwealth may deny the protections, benefits, and obligations conferred by civil marriage to two individuals of the same sex who wish to marry. We conclude that it may not. The Massachusetts Constitution affirms the dignity and equality of all individuals. It forbids the creation of second-class citizens. In reaching our conclusion we have given full deference to the arguments made by the Commonwealth. But it has failed to identify any constitutionally adequate reason for denying civil marriage to same-sex couples.

We are mindful that our decision marks a change in the history of our marriage law. Many people hold deep-seated religious, moral, and ethical convictions that marriage should be limited to the union of one man and one woman, and that homosexual conduct is immoral. Many hold equally strong religious, moral, and ethical convictions that same-sex couples are entitled to be married, and that homosexual persons should be treated no differently than their heterosexual neighbors. Neither view answers the question before us. Our concern is with the Massachusetts Constitution as a charter of governance for every person properly within its reach. . . .

Barred access to the protections, benefits, and obligations of civil marriage, a person who enters into an intimate, exclusive union with another of the same sex is arbitrarily deprived of membership in one of our community's most rewarding and cherished institutions. That exclusion is incompatible with the constitutional principles of respect for individual autonomy and equality under law. . . .

The larger question is whether, as the department claims, government action that bars same-sex couples from civil marriage constitutes a legitimate exercise of the State's authority to regulate conduct, or whether, as the plaintiffs claim, this categorical marriage exclusion violates the Massachusetts Constitution. We have recognized the long-standing statutory understanding, derived from the common law, that "marriage" means the lawful union of a woman and a man.

But that history cannot and does not foreclose the constitutional question. The plaintiffs' claim that the marriage restriction violates the Massachusetts Constitution can be analyzed in two ways. Does it offend the Constitution's guarantees of equality before the law? Or do the liberty and due process provisions of the Massachusetts Constitution secure the plaintiffs' right to marry their chosen partner? In matters implicating marriage, family life, and the upbringing of children, the two constitutional concepts frequently overlap, as they do here. . . . Much of what we say concerning one standard applies to the other.

We begin by considering the nature of civil marriage itself. Simply put, the government creates civil marriage. In Massachusetts, civil marriage is, and since pre-Colonial days has been, precisely what its name implies: a wholly secular institution. . . . No religious ceremony has ever been required to validate a Massachusetts marriage.

In a real sense, there are three partners to every civil marriage: two willing spouses and an approving State. While only the parties can mutually assent to marriage, the terms of the marriage—who may marry and what obligations, benefits, and liabilities attach to civil marriage—are set by the Commonwealth. Conversely, while only the parties can agree to end the marriage (absent the death of one of them or a marriage void ab initio), the Commonwealth defines the exit terms. . . .

Civil marriage anchors an ordered society by encouraging stable relationships over transient ones. It is central to the way the Commonwealth identifies individuals, provides for the orderly distribution of property, ensures that children and adults are cared for and supported whenever possible from private rather than public funds, and tracks important epidemiological and demographic data.

Marriage also bestows enormous private and social advantages on those who choose to marry. Civil marriage is at once a deeply personal commitment to another human being and a highly public celebration of the ideals of mutuality, companionship, intimacy, fidelity, and family. . . . Because it fulfils yearnings for security, safe haven, and connection that express our common humanity, civil marriage is an esteemed institution, and the decision whether and whom to marry is among life's momentous acts of self-definition.

Tangible as well as intangible benefits flow from marriage. . . .

The benefits accessible only by way of a marriage license are enormous, touching nearly every aspect of life and death. The department states that "hundreds of statutes" are related to marriage and to marital benefits. . . .

It is undoubtedly for these concrete reasons, as well as for its intimately personal significance, that civil marriage has long been termed a "civil right." The United States Supreme Court has described the right to marry as "of fundamental importance for all individuals" and as "part of the fundamental 'right of privacy' implicit in the fourteenth Amendment's Due Process Clause."

Without the right to marry—or more properly, the right to choose to marry—one is excluded from the full range of human experience and denied full protection of the laws for one's "avowed commitment to an intimate and lasting human relationship." Because civil marriage is central to the lives of individuals and the welfare of the community, our laws assiduously protect the individual's right to marry against undue government incursion. Laws may not "interfere directly and substantially with the right to marry."

Unquestionably, the regulatory power of the Commonwealth over civil marriage is broad, as is the Commonwealth's discretion to award public benefits. Individuals who have the choice to marry each other and nevertheless choose not to may properly be denied the legal benefits of marriage. But that same logic cannot hold for a qualified individual who would marry if she or he only could.

For decades, indeed centuries, in much of this country (including Massachusetts) no lawful marriage was possible between white and black Americans. That long history availed not when the Supreme Court of California held in 1948 that a legislative prohibition against interracial marriage violated the due process and equality guarantees of the Fourteenth Amendment, or when, nineteen years later, the United States Supreme Court also held that a statutory bar to interracial marriage violated the Fourteenth Amendment. . . . [T]he right to marry means little if it does not include the right to marry the person of one's choice, subject to appropriate government restrictions in the interests of public health, safety, and welfare. . . . See also *Loving v. Virginia* (1967). In this case . . . a statute deprives individuals of access to an institution of fundamental legal, personal, and social significance—the institution of marriage—because of a single trait: . . . sexual orientation. . . . [H]istory must yield to a more fully developed understanding of the invidious quality of the discrimination.

The Massachusetts Constitution protects matters of personal liberty against government incursion as zealously, and often more so, than does the Federal Constitution, even where both Constitutions employ essentially the same language. That the Massachusetts Constitution is in some instances more protective of individual liberty interests than is the Federal Constitution is not surprising. Fundamental to the vigor of our Federal system of government is that "state courts are absolutely free to interpret state constitutional provisions to accord greater protection to individual rights than do similar provisions of the United States Constitution."

The individual liberty and equality safeguards of the Massachusetts Constitution protect both "freedom from" unwarranted government intrusion into protected spheres of life and "freedom to" partake in benefits created by the State for the common good. Both freedoms are involved here. Whether and whom to marry, how to express sexual intimacy, and whether and how to establish a family—these are among the most basic of every individual's liberty and due process rights. And central to personal freedom and security is the assurance that the laws will apply equally to persons in similar situations. The liberty interest in choosing whether and whom to marry would be hollow if the Commonwealth could, without sufficient justification, foreclose an individual from freely choosing the person with whom to share an exclusive commitment in the unique institution of civil marriage. . . .

The plaintiffs challenge the marriage statute on both equal protection and due process grounds. With respect to each such claim, we must first determine the appropriate standard of review. Where a statute implicates a fundamental right or uses a suspect classification, we employ "strict judicial scrutiny." For all other statutes, we employ the "'rational basis' test." For due process claims, rational basis analysis requires that statutes "bear a real and substantial relation to the public health, safety, morals, or some other phase of the general welfare." For equal protection challenges, the rational basis test requires that "an impartial lawmaker could logically believe that the classification would serve a legitimate public purpose that transcends the harm to the members of the disadvantaged class."

The department [of public health] argues that no fundamental right or "suspect" class is at issue here, and rational basis is the appropriate standard of review. For the reasons we explain below, we conclude that the marriage ban does not meet the rational basis test for either due process or equal protection. Because the statute does not survive rational basis review, we do not consider the plaintiffs' arguments that this case merits strict judicial scrutiny.

The department posits three legislative rationales for prohibiting same-sex couples from marrying: (1) providing a "favorable setting for procreation"; (2) ensuring the optimal setting for child rearing, which the department defines as "a two-parent family with one parent of each sex"; and (3) preserving scarce State and private financial resources. We consider each in turn.

The judge in the Superior Court endorsed the first rationale, holding that "the state's interest in regulating marriage is based on the traditional concept that marriage's primary purpose is procre-

ation." This is incorrect. Our laws of civil marriage do not privilege procreative heterosexual intercourse between married people above every other form of adult intimacy and every other means of creating a family. [State law] contains no requirement that the applicants for a marriage license attest to their ability or intention to conceive children by coitus. Fertility is not a condition of marriage, nor is it grounds for divorce. . . .

The "marriage is procreation" argument singles out the one unbridgeable difference between same-sex and opposite-sex couples, and transforms that difference into the essence of legal marriage. Like "Amendment 2" to the Constitution of Colorado, which effectively denied homosexual persons equality under the law and full access to the political process, the marriage restriction impermissibly "identifies persons by a single trait and then denies them protection across the board." In so doing, the State's action confers an official stamp of approval on the destructive stereotype that same-sex relationships are inherently unstable and inferior to opposite-sex relationships and are not worthy of respect.

The department's first stated rationale, equating marriage with unassisted heterosexual procreation, shades imperceptibly into its second: that confining marriage to opposite-sex couples ensures that children are raised in the "optimal" setting. Protecting the welfare of children is a paramount State policy. Restricting marriage to opposite-sex couples, however, cannot plausibly further this policy. . . . Moreover, we have repudiated the common-law power of the State to provide varying levels of protection to children based on the circumstances of birth. The "best interests of the child" standard does not turn on a parent's sexual orientation or marital status.

The department has offered no evidence that forbidding marriage to people of the same sex will increase the number of couples choosing to enter into opposite-sex marriages in order to have and raise children. There is thus no rational relationship between the marriage statute and the Commonwealth's proffered goal of protecting the "optimal" child rearing unit. Moreover, the department readily concedes that people in same-sex couples may be "excellent" parents. . . . In this case, we are confronted with an entire, sizeable class of parents raising children who have absolutely no access to civil marriage and its protections because they are forbidden from procuring a marriage license. It cannot be rational under our laws, and indeed it is not permitted, to penalize children by depriving them of State benefits because the State disapproves of their parents' sexual orientation.

The third rationale advanced by the department is that limiting marriage to opposite-sex couples furthers the Legislature's interest in conserving scarce State and private financial resources. The marriage restriction is rational, it argues, because the General Court logically could assume that same-sex couples are more financially independent than married couples and thus less needy of public marital benefits, such as tax advantages, or private marital benefits, such as employer-financed health plans that include spouses in their coverage.

An absolute statutory ban on same-sex marriage bears no rational relationship to the goal of economy. First, the department's conclusory generalization—that same-sex couples are less financially dependent on each other than opposite-sex couples—ignores that many same-sex couples, such as many of the plaintiffs in this case, have children and other dependents (here, aged parents) in their care. The department does not contend, nor could it, that these dependents are less needy or deserving than the dependents of married couples. Second, Massachusetts marriage laws do not condition receipt of public and private financial benefits to married individuals on a demonstration of financial dependence on each other; the benefits are available to married couples regardless of whether they mingle their finances or actually depend on each other for support. . . .

It has been argued that, due to the State's strong interest in the institution of marriage as a stabilizing social structure, only the Legislature can control and define its boundaries. Accordingly, our elected representatives legitimately may choose to exclude same-sex couples from civil marriage in order to assure all citizens of the Commonwealth that (1) the benefits of our marriage laws are available explicitly to create and support a family setting that is, in the Legislature's view, optimal for child rearing, and (2) the State does not endorse gay and lesbian parenthood as the equivalent of being raised by one's married biological parents. These arguments miss the point. The Massachusetts Constitution requires that legislation meet certain

criteria and not extend beyond certain limits. It is the function of courts to determine whether these criteria are met and whether these limits are exceeded. In most instances, these limits are defined by whether a rational basis exists to conclude that legislation will bring about a rational result. The Legislature in the first instance, and the courts in the last instance, must ascertain whether such a rational basis exists. To label the court's role as usurping that of the Legislature is to misunderstand the nature and purpose of judicial review. We owe great deference to the Legislature to decide social and policy issues, but it is the traditional and settled role of courts to decide constitutional issues.

The history of constitutional law "is the story of the extension of constitutional rights and protections to people once ignored or excluded." This statement is as true in the area of civil marriage as in any other area of civil rights. As a public institution and a right of fundamental importance, civil marriage is an evolving paradigm. The common law was exceptionally harsh toward women who became wives: a woman's legal identity all but evaporated into that of her husband. Thus, one early Nineteenth Century jurist could observe matter-of-factly that, prior to the abolition of slavery in Massachusetts, "the condition of a slave resembled the connection of a wife with her husband, and of infant children with their father. He is obliged to maintain them, and they cannot be separated from him.". . . Alarms about the imminent erosion of the "natural" order of marriage were sounded over the demise of antimiscegenation laws, the expansion of the rights of married women, and the introduction of "no-fault" divorce.

Marriage has survived all of these transformations, and we have no doubt that marriage will continue to be a vibrant and revered institution. . . .

The marriage ban works a deep and scarring hardship on a very real segment of the community for no rational reason. The absence of any reasonable relationship between, on the one hand, an absolute disqualification of same-sex couples who wish to enter into civil marriage and, on the other, protection of public health, safety, or general welfare, suggests that the marriage restriction is rooted in persistent prejudices against persons who are (or who are believed to be) homosexual. Limiting the protections, benefits, and obligations of civil marriage to opposite-sex couples violates the basic premises of individual liberty and equality under law protected by the Massachusetts Constitution. . . .

Spina, J. (dissenting, with whom Sosman and Cordy, JJ., join). What is at stake in this case is not the unequal treatment of individuals or whether individual rights have been impermissibly burdened, but the power of the Legislature to effectuate social change without interference from the courts, pursuant to art. The power to regulate marriage lies with the Legislature, not with the judiciary. Today, the court has transformed its role as protector of individual rights into the role of creator of rights, and I respectfully dissent.

1. Equal protection. Although the court did not address the plaintiffs' gender discrimination claim, [state law] does not unconstitutionally discriminate on the basis of gender. A claim of gender discrimination will lie where it is shown that differential treatment disadvantages one sex over the other. [State law] enumerates certain qualifications for obtaining a marriage license. It creates no distinction between the sexes, but applies to men and women in precisely the same way. It does not create any disadvantage identified with gender as both men and women are similarly limited to marrying a person of the opposite sex.

   Similarly, the marriage statutes do not discriminate on the basis of sexual orientation. As the court correctly recognizes, constitutional protections are extended to individuals, not couples. The marriage statutes do not disqualify individuals on the basis of sexual orientation from entering into marriage. All individuals, with certain exceptions not relevant here, are free to marry. Whether an individual chooses not to marry because of sexual orientation or any other reason should be of no concern to the court.

   The court concludes, however, that [the law] unconstitutionally discriminates against the individual plaintiffs because it denies them the "right to marry the person of one's choice" where that person is of the same sex. To reach this result the court relies on *Loving v. Virginia* (1967), and transforms "choice" into the essential element of the institution of marriage. The *Loving* case did not use the word "choice" in this manner, and it did not point to the result

that the court reaches today. In *Loving,* the Supreme Court struck down as unconstitutional a statute that prohibited Caucasians from marrying non-Caucasians. It concluded that the statute was intended to preserve white supremacy and invidiously discriminated against non-Caucasians because of their race. The "choice" to which the Supreme Court referred was the "choice to marry," and it concluded that with respect to the institution of marriage, the State had no compelling interest in limiting the choice to marry along racial lines. The Supreme Court did not imply the existence of a right to marry a person of the same sex. . . .

Unlike the Loving . . . [case], the Massachusetts Legislature has erected no barrier to marriage that intentionally discriminates against anyone. Within the institution of marriage, anyone is free to marry, with certain exceptions that are not challenged. In the absence of any discriminatory purpose, the State's marriage statutes do not violate principles of equal protection. This court should not have invoked even the most deferential standard of review within equal protection analysis because no individual was denied access to the institution of marriage.

2. Due process. The marriage statutes do not impermissibly burden a right protected by our constitutional guarantee of due process implicit in art. 10 of our Declaration of Rights. There is no restriction on the right of any plaintiff to enter into marriage. Each is free to marry a willing person of the opposite sex. Substantive due process protects individual rights against unwarranted government intrusion. The court states, as we have said on many occasions, that the Massachusetts Declaration of Rights may protect a right in ways that exceed the protection afforded by the Federal Constitution. However, today the court does not fashion a remedy that affords greater protection of a right. Instead, using the rubric of due process it has redefined marriage. . . .

   Although this court did not state that same-sex marriage is a fundamental right worthy of strict scrutiny protection, it nonetheless deemed it a constitutionally protected right by applying rational basis review. Before applying any level of constitutional analysis there must be a recognized right at stake. Same-sex marriage, or the "right to marry the person of one's choice" as the court today defines that right, does not fall within the fundamental right to marry. Same-sex marriage is not "deeply rooted in this Nation's history," and the court does not suggest that it is. Except for the occasional isolated decision in recent years, same-sex marriage is not a right, fundamental or otherwise, recognized in this country. Just one example of the Legislature's refusal to recognize same-sex marriage can be found in a section of the legislation amending

[the law] to prohibit discrimination in the workplace on the basis of sexual orientation, which states: "Nothing in this act shall be construed so as to legitimize or validate a 'homosexual marriage'. . . ." In this Commonwealth and in this country, the roots of the institution of marriage are deeply set in history as a civil union between a single man and a single woman. There is no basis for the court to recognize same-sex marriage as a constitutionally protected right. . . .

A Comparative Perspective

11.7 From *The Rights Revolution: Lawyers, Activists and Supreme Courts in Comparative Perspective* (1998)

Charles R. Epp

Introduction

On October 29, 1958, at 5:45 in the morning, nine Chicago police officers acting without a warrant forced their way into James and Flossie Monroe's home, pulled the Monroes and their six children out of bed, and forced them to stand half-naked in the living room while they ransacked the home, dumped out the contents of drawers, tore clothes out of closets, and slit open mattresses. Officer Pape, the leader, beat James Monroe with his flashlight and called him "nigger" and "black boy"; another officer pushed Flossie Monroe; and several officers kicked and hit the children and pushed them to the floor. The officers eventually took Mr. Monroe to a station house, where he was forced to appear in a lineup and was questioned for ten hours about a recent murder. Throughout the ordeal, the officers refused to allow Monroe to call a lawyer or his family. In the end he was released— the victim of a story about a "Negro robber" concocted by the real murderers. The Monroe family sued the officers under a federal civil rights statute,

but the federal district court and the court of appeals rejected their right to sue in federal court. In 1961, to the surprise of many, the United States Supreme Court reversed and granted them this right.

A few years later a decision like *Monroe v. Pape* would seem routine. But in early 1961 the Court had yet to establish its reputation as a consistent defender of individual rights against official abuses of power. Only a few years earlier, for instance, in *Screws v. United States*, a criminal case brought against a Georgia sheriff who had brutally beaten a black man to death, the Supreme Court overturned the sheriff's conviction and created a difficult standard for convicting perpetrators of police brutality. The sheriff was acquitted on retrial under the new standard. The *Monroe* decision, by contrast, opened the door to civil lawsuits to redress official abuses of individual rights.

The decision, moreover, was part of a much larger transformation in which the Supreme Court, for the first time in its history, began deciding and supporting individual rights claims in a sustained way. As late as the mid-thirties, less than 10 percent of the Court's decisions involved individual rights other than property rights; the Court instead devoted its attention to business disputes and often supported property-rights claims brought by businesses and wealthy individuals. The Court's attention and support eventually shifted to modern individual rights. By the late sixties, almost 70 percent of its decisions involved individual rights, and the Court had, essentially, proclaimed itself the guardian of the individual rights of the ordinary citizen. In the process, the Court created or expanded a host of new constitutional rights, among them virtually all of the rights now regarded as essential to the Constitution: freedom of speech and the press, rights against discrimination on the basis of race or sex, and the right to due process in criminal and administrative procedures. Undoubtedly the depth of this transformation is limited in important ways: some rights have suffered erosion, and, as many Americans know, judicial declarations of individual rights often find only pale reflections in practice. But as I demonstrate in more detail shortly, the transformation has been real and it has had important effects. This transformation is commonly called the *rights revolution.*

Why did the rights revolution occur? What conditions encouraged the Supreme Court to regularly hear and support individual rights cases after largely ignoring or spurning them for 150 years? And why, after many years of hearing claims by powerful businesses, did the Court regularly turn its attention to the claims of "underdogs"? In sum, what were the sources and conditions for the rights revolution?

Sources and Conditions for the Rights Revolution

The U.S. rights revolution is usually attributed to one or more of the following: constitutional guarantees of individual rights and judicial independence, leadership from activist judges (particularly Supreme Court justices) who have been willing to use those constitutional provisions to transform society, and the rise of rights consciousness in popular culture. Conventional explanations tend to place particular emphasis on judicial leadership as the catalyst for the rights revolution. Constitutional guarantees, judicial leadership, and rights consciousness certainly contributed to the U.S. rights revolution. This [reading] shows, however, that sustained judicial attention and approval for individual rights grew primarily out of pressure from below, not leadership from above. This pressure consisted of deliberate, strategic organizing by rights advocates. And strategic rights advocacy became possible because of the development of what I call the support structure for legal mobilization, consisting of rights-advocacy organizations, rights-advocacy lawyers, and sources of financing, particularly government-supported financing.

This support structure has been essential in shaping the rights revolution. Because the judicial process is costly and slow and produces changes in the law only in small increments, litigants cannot hope to bring about meaningful change in the law unless they have access to significant resources. For this reason, constitutional litigation in the United States until recently was dominated by the claims of powerful businesses; they alone commanded the resources necessary to pursue claims with sufficient frequency, acumen, and perseverance to shape the development of constitutional law. And for this reason, too, constitutional law and the courts largely ignored the potential constitutional rights claims of ordinary individuals. The rights revolution grew out of the growing capacity of individual rights advocates to pursue the forms of constitutional litigation perfected by organized businesses, but for very different ends. The growth of the support structure, therefore, significantly democratized access to the Supreme Court.

Others have posited, of course, that political pressure and organized support for rights litigation influence judicial attention and approval for civil rights and liberties. My analysis builds on such research. But what is distinctive about my analysis is its emphasis on material resources, on the difficulty with which those resources are developed, and on the key role of those resources in providing the sources and conditions for sustained rights-advocacy litigation. Many discussions of the relationship between the Supreme Court and litigants assume that the resources necessary to support litigation are easily generated and that, as a result, litigants of all kinds have always stood ready to bring forward any kind of case that the Court might indicate a willingness to hear and decide. But that presumes a pluralism of litigating interests and an evenness of the litigation playing field that is wholly unjustified. Not every issue is now, nor has been in the past, the subject of extensive litigation in lower courts, due in part to limitations in the availability of resources for legal mobilization.

Implications of the Support-Structure Explanation

The support-structure explanation for the U.S. rights revolution is significant for two closely related debates in contemporary politics and constitutional law: (1) whether (or to what extent) democratic processes must be sacrificed in order to achieve protection for individual rights, and (2) how best to protect individual rights in modern society. Many people perceive a deep tension between rights and majoritarian democracy and believe that, if we wish to "guard the guardians" (the police and other public officials), we must turn unaccountable power over to judicial guardians. Some critics have claimed that the Supreme Court's decision in the *Monroe* case, for instance, amounts to a judicial usurpation of power because under the *Monroe* precedent, courts have constrained the discretion of public officials without regard to the wishes of democratic majorities.

The rights revolution, either implicitly or explicitly, is at the heart of the debate over the relationship between rights and democracy. For it was during the rights revolution, according to the advocates of contemporary individual rights, that courts finally began properly defending and protecting such rights. And according to the critics of the new rights, it was during the rights revolution that judicial power grew out of control and eroded the democratic process. Robert Bork, a leading critic of the new rights, has described the rights revolution as "the transportation into the Constitution of the principles of a liberal culture that cannot achieve those results democratically." Creating rights through judicial interpretation, he declares, is "heresy," and "it is crucial to recognize a heresy for what it is and to root it out." His use of the term "heresy" is deliberate, for the key problem, in Bork's view, is a heretical judicial interpretation of a foundational written text, the Constitution. In the judges' hands, Bork charges, the Constitution has been transformed from a mechanism for limiting

arbitrary governmental power into a source for arbitrary judicial power. As Bork observed, "the Constitution is the trump card in American politics, and judges decide what the Constitution means." This is a judge-centered analysis of the rights revolution, but it also asserts that judicial power depends on constitutional structure.

To a remarkable degree many defenders of contemporary rights accept the judge-centered interpretation of the rights revolution and of rights protection in general; they acknowledge that the rights revolution grew out of fundamentally undemocratic processes. But they defend many of the new rights on the ground that the results, in the end, strengthened democracy. In this view, for instance, the electoral reapportionment rulings of the early sixties deeply interfered with the democratic political process but did so in order to enhance the fairness of that process.

If my thesis is correct, however, the common emphasis on constitutional provisions and judges is exaggerated and the concern about undemocratic processes is ill founded. Of course it is unlikely that a majority of the population, if polled, would have supported each judicial decision in the rights revolution. But many legislative policies could not survive a popular referendum either. The meaning of "democracy" is thus complex and nuanced, and the critics recognize that fact by focusing mainly on the issue of process—claiming that the process of rights creation is judge-dominated and therefore is *intrinsically* less a result of broadly based action than is legislative policy making.

This [reading] is intended in part to refute that persistent claim by showing that the rights revolution depended on widespread support made possible by a democratization of access to the judiciary. Cooperative efforts among many rights advocates, relying on new resources for rights litigation—financing, organizational support, and willing and able lawyers—provided the raw material for the rights revolution. Many of those resources either were legislatively created or reflected a democratization and diversification of the legal profession and the interest-group system. Neither judges nor constitutional guarantees are irrelevant; judges ultimately decide whether to support rights claims, and constitutional guarantees may become rallying symbols for social movements and may provide footholds for lawyers' arguments and foundations for judicial decisions. But both the policy preferences of judges and the meaning of constitutional rights are partly constituted by the political economy of appellate litigation, particularly the distribution of resources necessary for sustained constitutional litigation. If the rights revolution developed out of the growth of a broad support structure in civil society, if rights litigation commonly reflects a significant degree of organized collective action, and if judicially declared rights remain dead letters unless they gain the backing of a broad support structure, then the rights revolution was not undemocratic or antidemocratic, even in the processes that created it. And if the evidence and analysis in support of that proposition is persuasive, then critics bear the burden of explaining why we should return to a time when only large businesses and the wealthy commanded the organizational strength, resources, and legal expertise to mobilize constitutional law in their favor.

The support-structure explanation is likewise pertinent to the other rights-related debate mentioned above—how best to protect individual rights in modern society. In the United States, great political battles are fought over judicial nominees. In other countries, some citizens wish for a John Marshall or an Earl Warren (great American Supreme Court Justices) to breathe life into their moribund constitutional law. And constitutional lawyers from the United States jet about the world engaging in "constitutional engineering," the process of creating new constitutions for other countries—on the assumption that new or revised constitutional structures and guarantees will re-form other societies.

Under the support-structure explanation proposed here, however, proponents of expanded judicial protection for rights should not place *all* hope in judges or constitutional reform but should provide support to rights-advocacy lawyers and organizations. If a nation—the United States or any other—wishes to protect individual rights, it would do well not to confine its efforts to encouraging or admonishing its judges, fine-tuning its constitution, or relying on the values of popular culture to affect rights by osmosis. Societies should also fund and support lawyers and rights-advocacy organizations—for they establish the conditions for sustained judicial attention to civil liberties and civil rights and for channeling judicial power toward egalitarian ends.

The Genesis of the Support-Structure Explanation

The standard emphases on judges, constitutional text, and popular culture reflect a nearly exclusive focus in past research on the U.S. case. In the United States, liberal judges, constitutional rights guarantees, and growing popular support for individual rights coincided at the time of the rights revolution, and so commentators attempting to interpret or explain the rights revolution commonly looked no further than those influences. But as I started to study the U.S. rights revolution I became aware of similar (or apparently similar) rights revolutions in other countries. In Britain, for instance, a country with a conservative judiciary and no constitutional bill of rights, individual rights nonetheless are gaining increasing judicial attention and support. Such developments encouraged me to look for other possible influences, and my focus here on resources for legal mobilization is the result. The four common-law countries selected for my comparative analysis—the United States, India, Britain, and Canada—have gained reputations as sites of rights revolutions (of varying strengths and focuses, to be sure) but differ in a number of dimensions, particularly in their constitutional structures, the reputations of their judges for creativity and activism, the presence of rights consciousness in popular culture, and the strength of their legal mobilization support structures.

In such a comparative investigation, clarity about what is being compared is essential. *Rights,* as I use the term here, consist of the new rights that emerged in judicial interpretation of U.S. constitutional law and statutes in this century. Constitutional rights in the past had been primarily the rights of property and contract. The new rights encompass, among other rights, freedom of speech and the press; free exercise of religion and prohibitions on official establishment of religion; prohibitions against invidious discrimination on the basis of race, sex, and a few other more or less immutable characteristics; the right of privacy; and the right to due process in law enforcement and administrative procedure. What precisely these new rights include and how they are to be applied in practice of course remain matters of some dispute.

I have focused, in particular, on women's rights and the rights of criminal defendants and prisoners. These two issues are especially useful lenses through which to analyze rights revolutions, for their status varies significantly from country to country and also over time. Criminal procedure is an issue within the traditional purview of common-law courts, yet until recently it received little attention in supreme courts. Criminal defendants form a diffuse, unorganized class; I examine how, in some countries and under some conditions, the rights claims of criminal defendants nonetheless came to form a major element of the rights revolution. The issue of women's rights, by contrast, is relatively new to judicial systems. Many countries' courts initially resisted the development of women's rights, yet those rights are now a significant part of the rights revolution in some of these countries. Moreover, the level of organized support for women's-rights litigation has varied significantly among countries and over time.

The *rights revolution,* as I use the term, was a sustained, developmental process that produced or expanded the new civil rights and liberties. That process has had three main components: judicial attention to the new rights, judicial support for the new rights, and implementation of the new rights. This [reading] examines each of the four countries in terms of these components. Judicial attention (or the "judicial agenda") is measured as the proportion of cases decided by a court per year focusing on particular issues, among them the new rights. Judicial support is gauged more informally, by examining the general direction of a court's policies with regard to rights. Implementation of judicial decisions is a complex and multifaceted matter and, with respect to implementation, this [reading] focuses on the extent to which courts have issued a continuing stream of judicial decisions that enforce or elaborate on earlier decisions.

Do Rights Matter in Practice?

It is important to emphasize that developments in the first two components—greater judicial attention to individual rights, and greater judicial support for them—may not lead to greater protection for those rights in practice. As Gerald Rosenberg has argued, the enforcement powers of courts acting on their own are relatively weak, and some of the key rights announced by the Supreme Court during the rights revolution were not implemented and had little of their intended effect.

Nonetheless, there is good reason to believe that an expansion of the support structure for legal mobilization may significantly enhance the implementation of judicially declared rights in practice. Rosenberg showed that the Supreme Court's decision in *Brown v. Board of Education* striking down racial segregation in public schools was implemented far more rapidly and substantially in the southern states that bordered the north than in the deep South because many officials in the border states favored desegregation and used the *Brown* decision to push for it. Similarly, Michael McCann found that union advocates of comparable worth policies used judicial rulings as leverage in private bargaining to gain favorable changes in work contracts. Those studies suggest that implementation of judicial decisions is greatly influenced by the acts and strategies of public officials and rights advocates. Yet the effectiveness of rights advocates in these endeavors is likely to be conditioned by their knowledge and resource capabilities. As Marc Galanter has written, "the messages disseminated by courts do not carry endowments or produce effects except as they are received, interpreted, and used by (potential) actors. Therefore, the meaning of judicial signals is dependent on the information, experience, skill, and resources that disputants bring to them." The presence and strength of a support structure for legal mobilization enhances the information, experience, skill, and resources of rights claimants and thus likely affects the implementation of judicial decisions on rights. The American Civil Liberties Union (ACLU), for instance, provides individuals with assistance in asserting and defending judicially declared rights in a wide variety of situations.

The dramatic expansion of the United States Supreme Court's attention to liberal rights, then, in conjunction with a vibrant support structure, provided a new assembly of bargaining tools and symbolic resources to a wide array of previously "right-less" individuals and groups. There are limits to the social changes produced by judicial rulings, and those rulings depend on support from government officials and on private parties having the capability to use them well. But judicial rulings may be used to great effect by rights organizers. The rights revolution in the United States did not merely result in judicial recognition of the existence of individual rights; it also gave rights advocates bargaining power and leverage that enabled them to expand protection for individual rights in practice.

An Illustration

The importance of the support structure for legal mobilization may be illustrated by the addition of a few details to the story of *Monroe v. Pape.* James and Flossie Monroe, it turns out, were not exactly lone individuals facing a hostile government on their own. The National Association for the Advancement of Colored People Legal Defense and Educational Fund (NAACP-LDF) for years had pushed a campaign of strategic litigation and political pressure against police brutality and racial discrimination in the criminal justice system, and it had gained the support of the Civil Rights Section of the United States Department of Justice. Then, in the late fifties, the Illinois chapter of the ACLU funded a large study of the problem of illegal detention and questioning by the Chicago police. In 1959, the organization published the study, titled *Secret Detention by the Chicago Police*, which documented, on the basis of a random sample of court cases, that more than half of all persons arrested in Chicago were held and questioned in police stations for more than seventeen hours without any formal charges being filed; 10 percent were held for more than forty-eight hours. The report showed that James Monroe's situation—at least from the time he reached the police station—was not unusual: the Illinois ACLU estimated that twenty thousand people in Chicago suffered similar illegal detention and questioning annually. Supreme Court Justices William O. Douglas and Tom Clark requested copies of the report, and Douglas soon cited it in a speech. Two years later, after the Monroes' appeal had wound its way up through the court system, Justice Douglas wrote the Supreme Court's majority opinion in the case. The NAACP-LDF and Justice Department work, and the Illinois ACLU study in particular, provided the background to the *Monroe* case.

And then there is the matter of how the Monroes managed to pursue their case up through the judicial hierarchy and present a persuasive legal argument, in an area of the law fraught with esoteric precedents and rules, before the Supreme Court. The main author of their brief before the Court, it turns out, was Morris Ernst, who had been one of the ACLU's leading lawyers since the twenties. The ACLU, then, provided direct support for the *Monroe* case.

The story of *Monroe v. Pape* gets even more complicated. Justice Douglas's opinion in favor of the Monroes was a classically incrementalist decision. By exposing the Chicago police officers to financial liability for their actions, the decision constituted a victory for individual rights advocates and a defeat for their opponents. But Douglas declined to take the additional step of exposing city *governments* to liability for the actions of their officers. And so civil rights advocates criticized the Court for not going far enough, for failing to give cities any incentive to properly train and discipline their officials. The NAACP-LDF, in particular, pursued a legal campaign to convince the courts to take that next step, which the Supreme Court eventually completed in 1978.

The right (really a remedy) won by James and Flossie Monroe thus rested on far more than judicial power and constitutional promises (although both were crucial), and the judicial decision that declared the right was not in any ordinary sense tyrannical. The new right grew out of the collective efforts of a large number of people who relied on organizational, legal, and financial resources that had been created by broad, collective efforts.

Conclusion: Constitutionalism, Judicial Power, and Rights

The basic lesson of this study is that rights are not gifts: they are won through concerted collective action arising from both a vibrant civil society and public subsidy. Rights revolutions originate in pressure from below in civil society, not leadership from above. But, as I have argued throughout this [reading], only certain kinds of pressure from below, particularly organized support for rights litigation, are likely to support sustained judicial attention to civil liberties and civil rights; and support from judicial elites is hardly irrelevant. In the end, the rights revolution developed and reached its greatest height and strength through an interaction between supportive judges and the support structure for rights-advocacy litigation.

That observation has important implications for theories of constitutionalism, judicial power, and rights. In standard understandings of constitutionalism, there is a deep tension between democracy and rights, and between the powers of democratic majorities and appointed judges. Participants in any constitutional democracy thus wrestle with a difficult dilemma. On the one hand, they seek to ensure that their constitution constrains arbitrary political power. This is not easily done, for recent history is littered with failed constitutions. On the other hand, they seek to ensure that their constitution does not rigidly shackle democratic majorities. But many commentators argue that the more effectively constitutional structures constrain political power, the less the system is democratic.

Although the constitutional dilemma is vexing with respect to any type of constitutional restriction, including the separation of powers, it is especially acute with respect to constitutional rights. Two major criticisms have been leveled at constitutional rights. Some skeptics argue that constitutional rights that are intended to protect individuals or minorities are merely parchment barriers, ineffective against political power. Other critics allege just the opposite, that constitutional rights too greatly constrain democratic majorities. Much of the writing on the proper role of judges in a constitutional democracy similarly assumes either, on the one hand, that judges lead by adapting the constitution to changing circumstances, or, on the other, that they follow by faithfully applying the "original intent" of the constitution's creators. In each of its forms, the dilemma of constitutional rights and judicial power is intractable because its poles seem to be so far apart.

One solution to this dilemma is that particular constitutional rights, even when created and enforced by unelected judges, serve democracy by improving the fairness of the democratic process. Yet that theory, and indeed most recent defenses of judicial power by constitutional theorists, accepts the assumption that judges exercise great power over democratic majorities; indeed, it is the belief

that judges exercise great power that motivates much constitutional theorizing about the proper limits of that power.

This [reading], by contrast, has addressed the dilemma by analyzing the political and social conditions for sustained judicial attention to rights. Undoubtedly, constitutional rights (and higher-law rights in general) are undemocratic *under some conditions* and are merely parchment barriers *under some conditions.* For instance, if only the wealthy, or only large private business corporations, have the organizational and financial capacity to mobilize constitutional law in their favor, then judicial policy making in the area of constitutional rights is likely to be undemocratic in the extreme. Only rights of interest to those select groups will be developed through judicial interpretation; for the rest of the population, rights will remain merely promises on paper. The conditions under which constitutional rights are developed and applied through judicial interpretation, therefore, are of great significance.

The central problem of most sweeping criticisms of constitutionalism and rights like those summarized briefly above, then, is that they are unconditional in nature. By claiming that rights are always merely parchment barriers, or are always set in stone, such unconditional analyses commonly miss the opportunity to explore the contingent conditions that shape the development of constitutional rights and judicial power in practice.

The most important implication of this study is that there is a third alternative to rights as "parchment" or "stone": rights are conditioned on the extent of a support structure for legal mobilization. Under conditions in which the support structure is deep and vibrant, judicial attention to rights may be sustained and vigorous; under conditions in which a support structure is shallow and weak, judicial attention to rights is likely to be intermittent and ineffective. Additionally, constitutional rights have proven to be remarkably variable over time. In those instances when constitutional rights have remained undeveloped through judicial interpretation, that is because rights advocates have had little capacity for pursuing their claims in the courts. But when rights have been developed through sustained litigation, the foundation for those limits is not judicial fiat but a broad support structure in civil society. Constitutional rights provisions, as *legal* guarantees, and judicial attention to rights are, therefore, constituted in cooperation with civil society.

Constitutional rights in general, and rights revolutions in particular, thus rest on a support structure that has a broad base in civil society. In the countries in this study, the leading pressure for building a rights revolution initially came from outside of the judiciary, principally from organized rights advocates. In the United States, most of the the key rights created during the rights revolution had been the subject of significant organizing pressure for some time before the Supreme Court took them up. In Canada, liberal supporters of expanded judicial protection for individual rights gained broad support and then pressed such issues on a hesitant Supreme Court, which eventually acquiesced and turned its attention to the new rights claims. Similarly, in Britain there had been growing concern about abuses of administrative discretion long before judges began to turn their attention to the issue. In India, the judicial rights agenda grew dramatically in the mid-seventies when, during the Emergency, the government imprisoned many members of the middle and upper classes. The experience brought home to these new victims an experience with arbitrary governmental power that had long been familiar to many members of the lower classes, and the new victims used their greater resources to mobilize a response. They subsidized rights-advocacy organizations, which proliferated and flourished, and they challenged their own preventive detention in court.

The continuation of nascent rights revolutions beyond their initial phases has also depended on broad support outside the judiciary. In each of the countries in this study, the judicial rights agenda has grown in a sustained way only to the extent that it has been supported by continued, organized efforts in civil society. And those efforts, centered in rights-advocacy organizations, government-provided legal aid, and the racial and sexual diversification of the legal profession, have been strong only to the extent that they have reflected either collective support or broad undercurrents of democratization. Thus the widespread growth of rights-advocacy organizations, government-provided legal aid, statutes authorizing the award of attorneys' fees to successful rights plaintiffs, and the racial and sexual diversification of the legal

profession, all reflect either collective support or democratizing trends. The crucial role of such resources in sustaining a rights revolution is evident in the countries in this study. Particularly in the United States and Canada, the support structure, once born, continued to grow, and that growth fueled the growing rights revolution in the two countries. The depth of the support structure has been more attenuated in Britain, and the judicial agenda has reflected that attenuation. In India, with the end of the Emergency in 1977, the middle and upper classes and opposition political parties withdrew their support from rights-advocacy organizations, many of which collapsed as a result. Although the Indian Supreme Court attempted through an unprecedented burst of judicial activism to lead a rights revolution, the effort fell short because it lacked a broad and deep support structure in civil society.

Although resources for legal mobilization thus play a crucial role, other forces are not irrelevant. Some structural characteristics of the judicial system greatly condition the potential for a rights revolution. The procedural hurdles placed in the path of criminal appeals in Britain have surely limited the development of significant judicial attention to criminal procedure in that country. Additionally, judicial control over the docket is clearly an important and perhaps even a necessary condition for a judicial rights revolution. If judges cannot eliminate routine economic disputes from their agenda, their attention is dominated by the many cases raising such issues. Thus, the Indian Supreme Court, which lacks control over its docket, focuses much of its attention on routine disputes; by contrast, after the U.S. and Canadian supreme courts gained significant control of their dockets (in 1925 and 1975, respectively), their attention shifted toward broader issues in public law, particularly individual rights.

Another important factor is judicial leadership, but its effects are complex and not dominant. In the early stages of the process, judicial support is neither necessary nor sufficient for development of a rights revolution. Thus, the earliest phases of the rights revolutions in the countries examined here all began in a context of judicial indifference or hostility. Organized support for rights cases may propel such cases onto the judicial agenda even in the absence of support from the judges. Litigants facing unsympathetic judges, moreover, often have held out hope that they may persuade the judges of the rightness of their cause and, as a variety of cases discussed throughout . . . have shown, sometimes they have achieved that goal. But ultimately, in order to sustain a rights revolution, judicial support is necessary—although it is not sufficient. As the experiences of both Canada and the United States indicate, the decisions of liberal judges encouraged further litigation by rights-advocacy lawyers and organizations. As the Indian experience again illustrates, this dynamic feedback between judicial decisions and external groups has occurred, however, only where the support structure is sufficiently strong to generate continued litigation. Obviously, the presence of a strong support structure cannot ensure that judges will ultimately support rights claims. But a strong support structure can reassure judges that if they do support rights claims, they will not be bereft of allies in the event of political attacks.

Bills of rights have contributed, too. Although it is common to argue that bills of rights empower judiciaries, that may be only a secondary effect of a much stronger relationship between popular movements and bills of rights. Judiciaries seem capable of deriving legitimacy from sources other than a bill of rights; and constituencies of support for judiciaries have not always been oriented toward a bill of rights. But in systems in which there exist broad constitutional rights guarantees, popular movements seem especially capable of using contradictions between political practice and constitutional promise as a means for organizing support for their causes. And when such movements have had access to resources for legal mobilization, they have turned to the courts, creating the conditions for a new range of judicial activity. Thus a bill of rights provides popular movements with a potential tool for tying judicial power to their purposes.

The variation among these four countries indicates that the growth of a support structure is not an inevitable outgrowth of other characteristics of society but is, instead, contingent on learning and political strategy. Certainly support structures have not emerged as an automatic consequence of industrialization or modernization. India's support structure undoubtedly is the weakest among the countries in this study. But Britain too, a country that industrialized and modernized long ago, until

very recently had a very limited support structure. Support structures thus appear to grow out of a wide range of complex factors. The development of rights consciousness surely is a necessary condition. Additionally, support structure development depends on a process of social learning regarding the techniques of organizational development and strategic litigation. The availability of resources for these efforts is crucial, and so patrons—typically private foundations and wealthy individuals—have played key roles in the start-up of rights-advocacy organizations. Political support for government-provided legal aid also has played a key role. Some of these factors clearly reflect the availability of disposable wealth in a society, and so industrialization arguably may condition their development. But industrialization is not sufficient, for much of the process depends on the efforts of rights advocates.

Nonetheless, the efforts of rights advocates may not bear fruit with equal ease in civil-law countries. Certainly, even in civil-law courts something like a support structure is likely to be essential for the mobilization of rights claims by individuals. Nonetheless, the influence of the support structure is likely to be greatest in common-law systems where rights-advocacy lawyers can cultivate precedents and build on them. Where judicial decision making relies little or not at all on precedent, as in civil-law systems, however, the growth dynamic arising out of the strategic cultivation of precedent is likely to be undercut.

Because learning, resources, and political strategy are so crucial to these processes (at least in common-law countries), it is clear that no single political ideology has an inevitable monopoly on support for litigation. Indeed, as support structures have developed to their fullest extent, as in the United States, they have developed diverse agendas. Just as civil liberties advocates in the twenties and thirties adopted many of the strategic litigation techniques used by the railroads and other corporations, by the late seventies political conservatives were adopting many of the techniques used by civil liberties advocates. Even among liberal rights advocates, differences have arisen. In recent controversies over pornography, proponents of freedom of speech sometimes clash with proponents of women's rights. Similarly, in controversies over procedures in trials involving violence against women, proponents of the rights of the accused sometimes differ with proponents of women's rights. Thus, as Paul Sniderman, Peter Russell, Joseph Fletcher, and Philip Tetlock have observed, the development of women's-rights claims has introduced new tensions into debates over rights. But these tensions exist mainly as a result of an increasingly diverse body of litigants.

The new constitutional rights thus have developed, in sum, out of a democratization of access to the judiciary. In 1915 the universe of litigants capable of pursuing sustained, strategic litigation consisted primarily of businesses. By the seventies that universe had expanded significantly in several countries and included not only businesses but criminal defendants, women, political dissenters, and members of minority religions and races, among others. That expansion in access transformed the field of strategic litigation.

The democratization of access to the judicial agenda, however, remains limited in important ways. In India, which is dominated by a state bureaucracy and plagued by great economic inequality, there remain great limits on access to the judicial agenda. Indian rights-advocacy groups and official legal aid, for instance, suffer from chronic underfunding. No support structure is static, however, and the continued efforts of rights-advocacy organizations, along with the growth of India's middle class, may generate the resources necessary for development of a broader support structure. In Canada and Britain too, although resource shortages are not as great as in India, rights-advocacy groups nonetheless still face significant financial limitations. Their legal professions and interest-group systems have developed the organizational structures capable of supporting sustained rights litigation, but resource limitations still limit the extent and frequency of litigation campaigns. By contrast, in the United States the political environment, the large population, and the size and diverse structure of the legal profession seem ideally suited for the growth of independent, nonparty organizations and other sources of support for sustained rights-based litigation.

Nonetheless, even in the United States there remain significant limits to the democratization of access to courts. One of the most important is the relative lack of support for strategic litigation by the truly poor; as a consequence, there is little litiga-tion aimed at improving the conditions of the least well-off. Rights litigation, as some critics have observed, benefits primarily the "haves," those groups possessing the resources necessary to pursue litigation. Thus, before the development of government-sponsored legal defense services, the rights of the accused generally failed to reach the appellate judicial agenda. Similarly, rights claims based on poverty or economic class still fail to reach the judicial agenda.

It may be objected that the failure of the courts to address issues related to economic deprivation results from the liberal-individualist bias of American society and law and not the lack of resources for litigation on such issues. But the Supreme Court, in fact, entertained a relatively large number of claims framed around the issue of economic deprivation *when those legal claims received the support of a government litigation-support program,* the Legal Services Program. The Court's attention to such claims declined rapidly when program funding was cut. The Supreme Court's opposition to rights based on indigence or class surely contributed to the failure of such issues to take a place on the judicial agenda, but the Court majority at one time opposed other extensions of rights only to reverse itself and support those rights after facing mounting litigation. Before the twenties, for instance, few Americans would have predicted that the United States Supreme Court would expand rights-based protections for freedom of speech, yet it did so; before the fifties, few would have predicted that the Court would intervene substantially in state criminal procedure, yet it did so; after the Court's decision in *Bowers v. Hardwick* in 1986, few observers would have predicted that the Court soon would accept an equal protection claim based on sexual preference, yet in *Romer v. Evans* (1996), during a litigation campaign by several rights-advocacy organizations, a far more conservative Court appeared to do just that;* before the eighties, British legal scholars generally denied that the House of Lords would interfere in the management of prisons or strike down a parliamentary statute, yet since then it has taken each step. To say, in retrospect, that the basic principles of American or English law allowed or even demanded those

---

*In *Lawrence v. Texas* (2003), the U.S. Supreme Court, by a 6–3 margin, overturned *Bowers* when it invalidated a Texas law forbidding consensual sodomy between same-sex couples.

developments, whereas the same principles now limit attention to issues related to poverty, is to fail to recognize the formidable legal barriers to the development of those earlier issues, and to fail to understand the nature of the forces that propelled exactly those previously neglected issues over the jurisprudential barricades and onto the agenda.

What are the prospects for the future? Opponents of the rights agenda have attacked the support structure for years, and their attacks are increasingly successful. Some sources of funding for rights litigation have recently been cut or are increasingly under threat. For instance, there have been deep cuts in legal aid in a number of western countries. In Canada, the government eliminated funding for the Court Challenges Program in 1992 (although it has since been reinstated) and, by the mid-nineties, some provinces were considering deep cuts in their legal aid programs. In Britain, in the late eighties the government radically changed the eligibility criteria for legal aid, producing sharp cuts in the number of people eligible for such assistance, and in 1997 the government began a drastic restructuring of the program. In the United States, by the mid-nineties the federal legal aid program faced the threat of deep cuts or outright elimination.

Whether the rights agenda will suffer as a result depends on the extent to which the support structure in each country rests primarily on government aid. For some rights claims, the support structure has multiple foundations but, for others, the structure appears to depend nearly entirely on government aid. In each of the countries in this study, appeals by criminal defendants and prisoners, for example, depend almost entirely on legal defender programs sponsored or aided by government. The capacity of nongovernmental resources to fill the gap left by the erosion of government aid varies greatly from country to country. In Britain, Canada, and India the few public-interest groups that have supported rights litigation remain relatively weak and lacking in resources. In the United States, the leading rights-advocacy organizations remain relatively well resourced and capable of supporting rights litigation at all levels of the judicial system. Those organizations fill a very different role than legal aid in the United States, however, and although some civil liberties and civil rights issues likely will continue to reach the highest courts, issues supported by legal aid likely will receive less and less judicial attention.

Rights, in sum, are not simply judicial gifts to isolated individual supplicants. Rights result from collective efforts and a support structure in civil society. But, for the same reason, rights are not magical solutions to any or all problems; they seem particularly incapable of addressing the growing problem of economic inequality in many advanced industrialized countries.

. . . Neither a written constitution, a rights-supportive culture, nor sympathetic judges is sufficient for sustained judicial attention to and support for rights. Protection of civil liberties and civil rights depend, in addition, on a support structure in civil society. Without a support structure, even the clearest constitutional rights guarantees are likely to become meaningless in the courts; but a vibrant support structure can extend and expand the feeblest of rights. Participants in constitutional democracy would do well to focus their efforts not only on framing or revising constitutional provisions, and not only on selecting the judges who interpret them, but also on shaping the support structure that defends and develops those rights in practice.

For Further Reading

Belasky, Martin. *The Rehnquist Court: A Retrospective.* New York: Oxford University Press, 2002.

Gillman, Howard. *The Votes That Counted: How the Supreme Court Decided the 2000 Presidential Election.* Chicago: University of Chicago Press, 2001.

Hertagh, Marc and Simon Halliday, eds. *Judicial Review and Bureaucratic Impact: International and Interdisciplinary Perspectives.* Cambridge: Cambridge University Press, 2004.

Volcansek, Mary. *Judicial Politics in Europe: An Impact Analysis.* New York: Lang, 1986.

Index